DISASTERS IN THE AIR

DISASTERS IN THE AIR

Mysterious Air Disasters Explained

Jan Bartelski

Airlife
England

First published in the UK in 2001
by Airlife Publishing Ltd

British Library Cataloguing-in-Publication Data
A catalogue record for this book
is available from the British Library

ISBN 1 84037 204 4

Typeset and designed by Celtic, Wrexham.

Printed in England by Butler & Tanner Ltd,
London and Frome

Airlife Publishing Ltd
101 Longden Road, Shrewsbury, SY3 9EB,
England
E-mail: airlife@airlifebooks.com
Website: www.airlifebooks.com

ACKNOWLEDGMENTS

Many individuals have contributed to various chapters but I would like to single out two people who have been particularly helpful in producing this book. My special appreciation is extended to Ron Penn, a former Fleet Air Arm pilot and captain with KLM, for editing the manuscript and assisting with the operational advice. I am equally grateful to my son, Stefan Bartelski, a computer expert, for producing computer programs that became an invaluable tool in analysing flight recorder read-outs of several disasters.

Regarding individual chapters, I would like to thank Doug Neale, a former WO/AG of 228 Squadron, for his so far unpublished reminiscences of the circumstances surrounding the Duke of Kent's crash in 1942. Also my brother, Lesław Bartelski, a member of the Polish Underground Army, later poet, writer and historian, for the little-known story about the Duke of Kent's visit to Poland in 1937.

I am indebted to the late Major Lubienski, for the historical background of the Gen. Sikorski accident at Gibraltar. To Arthur Smith, a wartime Liberator pilot with RAF Coastal Command and my colleague from KLM, for the help with the operational aspects of the Liberator. To Mr G.J. Hill, the founder member of the Aerospace Museum Society at RAF Cosford, for his trouble to make my inspection of the Museum's Liberator such a great success. To G/Capt. S. Wandzilak, Polish Air Force, a former Ministry of Defence accident investigator, for his assistance on the latest addition to the chapter on the Gibraltar crash.

I would like to mention the following for their assistance with the chapter on the Cairo disasters:
Airclaims Ltd, Heathrow Airport, for details of several accidents.
Lars Blomberg, a former KLM captain and IFALPA VP for the Middle East, for information about the PIA B720 accident investigation, and the so-far unpublished photographs of the crash site.
Aart van Wijk, a former KLM captain, for permission to quote parts of his book *Aircraft accident inquiry in the Netherlands*, relating to the KLM crashes at Cairo Airport.
Norman Barron, a former KLM captain, for his information on the DC6 and Electra II.

My particular gratitude goes to the late Bob Nelson, S/Ldr in the RAF, a former KLM captain, AAIB inspector and ICAO official, for the access to his documentation on the Hammarskjöld disaster which was deposited with the AAIB archives. Without his help such a detailed analysis of that event would not have been possible. Also to Arne Leibing, the former Chief Pilot of Transair, for his forthright opinion on the flying aptitude of the two pilots involved in the crash.

I am indebted to Prof. W. Leary, at the time of my research an aviation historian at the Georgia University, in Athens, USA, for the voluminous material on the Taipei crash. Also to Mark Kentwell, a captain with Ansett–ANA, for his invaluable advice on the operational aspects of the B727.

I would like to mention the following contributions that I have received on the Trident crash at Staines from:
Eric Pritchard, a former BEA Trident captain and member of BALPA and IFALPA Accident Investigation Study Group, on his first-hand account of the visit to the crash site.
W. Tench, CBE, FRAeS, the former Chief Inspector of Accidents, on the complex issue of the Public Inquiry versus an AAIB investigation.
Harry Hopkins, a former BEA Trident captain, member of BALPA Technical Committee and an aviation writer, on the results of simulator tests of the Trident stall problems.

In respect of Graham Hill's accident at Arkley Golf Course in 1975, I would like to express my thanks to:
Keith Smith, an actor, for his reminiscences of flying with Graham Hill.
Frank Pringle, a former KLM captain and AAIB inspector, for the background of the investigation, and for the so far unpublished photographs of the crash site. PC Geoff Rowe, retired Metropolitan Police PC, for the details of the police assistance during the investigation.
Finally, I must thank John Shanley, a former senior KLM captain and B747 instructor for the information on the KLM Training Department.

Sadly by the time this book went into print, Capt. A. Leibing, Capt. E. Pritchard and Bill Tench had passed away.

CONTENTS

1

1942 – The Missing Minutes:
the Royal tragedy over Scotland –
was it pilot error?

Just off the Caithness coast a forlorn stone memorial with a Celtic cross perches on the eastern side of a nine-hundred-foot hill known as Eagle Rock. Today, younger motorists passing the memorial by a mere two miles when driving on the A9 are probably not aware to whom it is dedicated. Only a poignant inscription on the stone face reflects a tragic event of the wartime past:

IN MEMORIAM OF
AIR CDRE H.R.H. THE DUKE OF KENT
K.G. K.T of C.C.M.G., G.C.V.O.
AND HIS COMPANIONS
WHO LOST THEIR LIVES ON ACTIVE
SERVICE
DURING A FLIGHT TO ICELAND ON A
SPECIAL MISSION
THE 25th OF AUGUST 1942.
'MAY THEY REST IN PEACE'

The inscription had led some researchers to believe that the Duke of Kent's visit was indeed some sort of a special mission that involved unusual risks. But the so-called special mission was intended as a routine inspection of local amenities for the British servicemen in Iceland. Due to wartime shipping difficulties, these amenities were austere and limited. As a result, a tour of duty never lasted longer than eighteen months.

But it was likely that the Duke had been asked by the Government to also call upon the Icelandic authorities, with which relations were very cool. They regarded the British and the Americans as 'unwanted guests'. The presence of the Allies in Iceland was due to an important strategic reason.

Before the war German 'tourists' visited the island in increasing numbers. They tried to be exceptionally friendly and sponsored several

Just off the Caithness coast a forlorn stone memorial with a Celtic cross perches on the eastern side of a nine-hundred-foot hill known as Eagle Rock.

communal projects, among them a large swimming pool. They also helped to build the only hard-surface road. The road was so straight that in emergencies it could be used as a landing strip. British Intelligence was fully aware of the German designs on Iceland. In the time of conflict, it could provide a deadly U-boat base to harass Atlantic convoys. After the war broke out, the only preventative step was to get in first. Without any ground, air or sea forces, the Icelandic government could not stop the invasion – except in showing resentment by ignoring the presence of the 'occupiers'. The attitude of the local population was equally cool. Perhaps the 'special mission' mentioned on the Caithness memorial was intended as a goodwill gesture to assure the Icelandic authorities that the Allied Forces would not stay longer than necessary.

The cause of the disaster is still shrouded in mystery. Wartime censorship had restricted the press to revealing only the bare details. Photographs of the wreckage were never published. The public had never been really told what lay behind the crash in the Caithness Hills. The Court of Inquiry, hastily convened after the accident, could not find a logical answer as to why the flying boat, expected to proceed over the sea at all times, struck a hill within the first half-hour of the planned seven-hour-long flight. The Assessors, senior RAF officers, blamed the captain for not following the designated track as instructed at the briefing. But it was a convenient way out. The dead captain could not answer back. It was another case of many similar one-sided verdicts referred to as pilot error that would invariably be repeated in aviation history.

The news of the Duke of Kent's death had soon spread around Europe with diverse comments. Based on wild rumours sweeping Lisbon, the German Ambassador to Portugal, Baron Oswald von Hoynigen-Huene, claimed in a secret telegram to his 'boss', the Foreign Minister Joachim von Ribbentrop, that the accident was due to sabotage. In his opinion, the Duke of Kent, like the Duke of Windsor, was sympathetic to the German cause and this was creating problems to the 'Government clique' and he had to be liquidated.

The crash has been a subject of several books and numerous articles, in particular by former RAF airmen. Unfortunately every research was hampered by the difficulty of piecing together the tragic event. For reasons known only to the close circle of officials, after the war the Air Ministry decided to destroy the original report of the Court of Inquiry and no copy had been lodged with the Public Record Office. It appears as if a chapter of history has been removed from the aviation annals. Tampering with documentation of an RAF Court of Inquiry, recognised as a legal proceeding under the King's Regulations and Air Council Instructions, seems a highly questionable

act. It is a standard practice that lawcourt records are preserved, in case new evidence emerges that may warrant a reassessment of the original verdict.

The captain of the ill-fated Sunderland was blamed for the crash without first ascertaining what had made him deviate from the track. He was condemned simply because he did not adhere to the instructions at the briefing.

Pilots do not take important decisions without a compelling reason, especially when they carry a VIP of royal rank. But in spite of attempts to sweep the Duke of Kent disaster under the carpet, evidence still exists that throws a different light on the circumstances surrounding the crash, and consequently, on its cause. The records of the weather situation on the day of the accident are still held in the archives of the National Meteorological Library at Bracknell and its Scottish equivalent in Edinburgh.

The actual wording of the verdict on the Caithness disaster as recorded in the documentation of the Ministry of Defence Air Historical Branch (RAF) is as follows: 'Responsibility for serious error rests with the captain who changed the flight plan for reasons unknown and descended through clouds without making sure he was over water and crashed.'

It sounds a totally irrational course of action by a relatively seasoned airman for the wartime circumstances. Naturally, in comparison with the present levels of experience in civil aviation, in terms of flying hours (with just over 1,000 hours of operational service on ocean patrols), he would have been regarded as a novice. Nowadays, an airline pilot is expected to amass at least several thousand hours before he is allowed to be in command of passenger-carrying aircraft.

But at the time, the twenty-five-year-old, Victoria-born Australian in the service of the RAF, Frank MacKenzie Goyen, appeared to be the right choice to fly a royal, taking into consideration his expertise on the Sunderlands and his sound airmanship. He was also known for his calculated cunning. On one of his patrols in the Mediterranean, he alighted on the sea in order to save fuel, so that he could shadow the Italian fleet all night and then bring valuable intelligence back to base.

Fatal misjudgements, such as flying into a hill, often seem baffling on the surface. In that respect, there is a similarity between the Sunderland disaster and that of the Air New Zealand DC10 in Antarctica. In both cases the pilots enjoyed an unblemished professional reputation. The captain of the DC10, Jim Collins, was the New Zealand Pilots' Association safety expert, evidently someone who took his airline job very seriously. Yet, according to the official report: '...the probable cause of this accident was the decision of the captain to continue the flight at low level towards an area of poor surface and horizon definition when the crew was not certain of their position and subsequent inability to detect the raising terrain which intercepted the aircraft's flight path.'

After the report was published, the press labelled Collins as unfit to have been in command of a plane carrying 250 passengers. Some journalists even implied that he could not have been quite sane at the time of the accident. Collins's wife received threatening letters from the angry public. It seemed incomprehensible that an aircraft equipped with the latest inertial navigation system could have been flown into the slopes of Mt Erebus.

Luckily for Jim Collins, one of his colleagues stood up in his defence. Gordon Vetty, former President of the New Zealand Air Line Pilots' Association, a senior DC10 captain and an instructor, did not concur with the verdict condemning someone he knew intimately from a professional point of view. Vetty had trained Collins as a pilot in the New Zealand Air Force and later in the airline, as a DC6, DC8 and DC10 captain, and regarded him as a first-class airman. Refusing to accept that Collins could commit such a foolhardy blunder, Vetty set out to examine every available piece of evidence in his free time between flights. In the end, he thought that he had found an answer to what had led to the aircraft striking the slopes of Mt Erebus. He argued that the land features Collins had observed a few

minutes before the impact looked to be what he would have been expected to see according to the track indication on his inertial navigational system. Unfortunately, without realising it, Collins was thirty miles to the left. The airline navigation section had altered the computer settings a day before the ill-fated flight but the pilots were never informed. What Collins believed to be an expanse of ice stretching ahead in McMurdo Sound, with a prominent glacier on his right, was in fact a similar scene of Lewis Bay just in front of Mt Erebus. But due to unusual weather conditions, the view of the extinct volcano was obliterated by whiteout. Pilots very rarely encounter such a freakish phenomenon and only those who regularly fly into the polar regions are aware of its deceptive effects. It was Collins's first trip to the realm of snow and ice. Continuing his low-level flight to show the passengers the beauty of Antarctica, he never expected he was heading for disaster.

At first the accident investigators blamed Collins for the senseless tragedy. But thanks to the indefatigable efforts by Gordon Vetty, Collins was vindicated after another governmental inquiry. In his book *Impact Erebus* published by Hodder & Stoughton (NZ), Vetty writes about visual illusions as follows:

'Although the range of our sensory receptors is immensely rich, perception of the world is not achieved by our sense organs alone. They provide the initial information, the data on which perceptual judgements are based, but these judgements depend upon additional information which is available from other senses and from the experience of the brain itself.'

In simple words – it is not what a pilot sees but what he believes he sees that counts. This is where the parallel enters the picture. Like his Air New Zealand counterpart many years later, the ill-fated Sunderland pilot had run into similar deceptive weather conditions. Both believed that the land features they observed at a certain moment denoted their correct position. Both were wrong. But in the case of the Caithness disaster, the final stroke that sent the flying boat to her doom was different.

Past theories about the Duke of Kent's crash vary from the ludicrous to those supported by plausible arguments. A conjecture such as the compass having been affected by iron deposits in the Scottish hills, or a radio beam 'bent' by the Germans, must be rejected out of hand. The Earth's magnetic field is continuously monitored

F/Lt Goyen at the controls of the Sunderland.
(228 Sq. Association)

A Mk III Sunderland. (Philip Jarrett)

by the Geological Institute. Had there been any noticeable change on the day of the crash, it would have been at once reported to the Court of Inquiry. The 'beam bending' theory is even more unrealistic. The Mk III Sunderlands, the version used on the Duke of Kent flight, were not fitted with radio navigational equipment capable of receiving beams. The only possibility was the reception of ground transponders with the help of the ASV Mk II, an early version of radar operating on 176 Mhz, used to detect German U-boats that had surfaced. As the transponder response was limited to the line of sight, it would have been impossible to generate out of Germany or out of Norway a signal that could distort the reception on the east coast of Scotland.

Other suppositions such as 'cutting a corner' over the Scottish Highlands in order to save fuel, or low flying to show the Duke of Kent the fascinating countryside, cannot be taken seriously.

Finally, certain vicious whispers about the crew

having been drunk, because someone noticed a crate of whisky being loaded onto the flying boat just before take-off, must be looked upon as the product of a sick mind. The crate of whisky had been most likely the Duke's present for the RAF Officers' Mess at Reykjavik, where he was going to stay during his visit to Iceland, and certainly not for consumption on board. In any case it would have taken longer than those few minutes in the air between the take-off and the crash for anyone to be seriously affected by alcohol.

Of various past theories only one is based on rational arguments. Roy Nesbit, a former RAF Coastal Command navigation instructor, advanced a probability of the output from the Distant Reading Compass (DRC) having been misused. This newly fitted device on the Sunderlands combined the advantage of steady gyro with 'not-so-steady' normal magnetic compass indications. With the introduction of the DRC, the crews were instructed to fly true

The crew of the ill-fated Sunderland. Sitting in the middle – F/Lt Goyen. On his left – P/O Saunders, the navigator. Second from the left, standing – F/Sgt Andy Jack. (228 Sq. Association)

headings, which were simpler to plot on the navigation chart. The navigator was supposed to apply magnetic variation by means of a corrector located at his table. It was believed that a misunderstanding had crept in through either the navigator forgetting to set the variation or the pilot misinterpreting his instructions. As a result, a heading with an error of thirteen degrees to port had been followed, which represented the difference between the true and the magnetic course. The course would have taken the flying boat over Eagle Rock. If, at that moment, Goyen decided to descend through clouds, presuming he was over the sea, so that his navigator could measure drift from wind lanes, this could have accounted for the accident.

A far-from-customary way of selecting the navigator for the Duke of Kent flight could have resulted in weakening the cooperation on the flight deck, adding weight to Roy Nesbit's theory. Goyen was at the time without a navigator and the squadron navigation officer was originally detailed for the flight. But, after a loud protest from other navigators, permission was given to draw lots for the honour. It was won by P/O Saunders. The unorthodox procedure was later strongly criticised by the RAF authorities.

Setting a wrong deviation when relying on true headings for navigation would not have been the only case in aviation history that had ended in disastrous consequences. In 1953 a BOAC Argonaut, on a night crossing over the Sahara, grossly deviated from the intended track. A young pilot, just trained to act as a navigator, set thirty degrees variation instead of three degrees. Confused by unexpected results from his astro shots, he refused to believe that he was drifting off so far away from his flight plan. By daylight the aircraft had to be crash-landed in a no-man's land, some nine hundred miles from its destination. Although everyone on board survived, unfortunately the co-pilot subsequently died from heat exhaustion.

Although misuse of the DRC, a relatively new instrument in 1942, offers a plausible explanation as to why the Sunderland had deviated from the track, this theory bears an important question mark. According to my calculations, the aircraft, if it followed a straight track, should have flown further than to Eagle Rock.

The theory about the misuse of the DRC has another weak point. It is known that for the first twenty-five minutes of the flight the crew could see the ground. According to the usual Coastal Command practices, the leg from Invergordon to abeam of Wick, a relatively short forty-minute coastal crawl for the seven-hour-long Atlantic crossing, would have been most likely taken care of by the pilots by simply following the coast visually. It should soon have been evident that they were not paralleling the shoreline as planned, but rapidly closing on it. In the poor visibility that prevailed during the flight, they were bound to keep their eyes wide open.

In my approach to assess the known facts about the crash, I tried to put myself in Frank Goyen's shoes as the captain in command of the ill-fated Sunderland, casting my mind back on my wartime experiences as a Coastal Command pilot with 304 Polish Squadron. Although I flew Wellingtons, the low-level over-water operations, whether in land planes or flying boats, hardly differed.

When establishing the cause of a disaster, a fundamental principle must be observed that all aircraft motions conform to certain physical laws, and this must be accounted for with the highest possible accuracy. The evidence on the Sunderland crash had been evaluated according to that rule.

The chain of events leading to the tragedy in the Scottish hills had already started at the take-off. Several sources claimed that the aircraft appeared to have made a relatively long run before becoming airborne. This was in spite of a ten knots headwind as recorded by the anemometer at RAF Invergordon, the point of departure of the Duke of Kent's aircraft. Equally, the ambient temperature could have had no effect on the take-off distance. At that moment the thermometer read 15°C, a borderline above which aircraft performance is expected to degrade. The reason for the flying boat's extra-long run can only be attributed to her being overloaded. In wartime, loadsheets were generally not relied upon to check the take-off weight except in Transport Command. With

the Sunderland in the normal operational trim, which included a full load of fuel and the usual consignment of depth charges as well as machine-gun ammunition plus standard crew of ten, the aircraft's weight should have been at its maximum of 58,000 lb. But the Sunderland, W4026, used for the Duke of Kent's flight, had special equipment. It had been fitted up as a VIP carrier. It was often used to fly high-ranking Royal Navy officers to various bases in the West of Scotland and Hebrides. W4026 even had curtains in the windows.

Moreover, on board were an additional crew member, W/Cdr Moseley, the CO of 228 Squadron to which the Sunderland belonged, and four passengers – the Duke of Kent, his private secretary Lt Lowther RNVR, his ADC P/O Strutt and his valet LAC Hales. Considering that the royal party needed a fair amount of luggage for the official visit, including the crate of whisky mentioned previously, the maximum take-off weight could have been easily exceeded by about 1,200 lb. The reason for bringing up this point will be evident later. There is little doubt that the Sunderland carried a full load of fuel, representing an endurance well in excess of twelve hours for a flight expected to last only seven hours. With the RAF wartime attitude, 'fill'er up', it looks certain that the tanks were topped up to the brim.

Every multi-engine aircraft conforms to two basic design criteria, either of which limits the maximum take-off weight – structural strength and take-off performance with a failed engine. The Sunderland was known to be a sturdy machine but was definitely underpowered. Therefore engine failure on take-off was of paramount significance. According to the Sunderland Mk III Pilot's Notes, the aircraft could only maintain level flight on three engines with maximum power at weak mixture if the weight was below 50,000 lb. On two engines it would have been only possible to continue at very light weights. Due to wartime demands, take-off weights in excess of the engine failure limitations had to be tolerated. As a result, the Sunderlands operated at maximum take-off weight were supposed to stay over water at all times. Only then would it have been possible to maintain a safe obstacle clearance with a failed engine, or to alight quickly if an emergency subsequently arose.

The first problem encountered in analysing the history of the flight was in establishing the length of time the Sunderland remained in the air. Official records are of no help. The take-off time, mentioned in the 228 Squadron Operational Record Book as 13.10 British Standard Time or 12.10 GMT, can be accepted to be exact to a minute. This information was likely to have been provided by the Tower operator at the base of departure, noted against a regularly checked clock, in those days a standard RAF practice. But the time of the crash, stated as approximately 14.00 hrs, is far too imprecise. The only information worthy of credence is the moment of impact determined from the hands on the Duke of Kent's watch. They were frozen at forty-two minutes past the hour. Unfortunately it is impossible to tell how accurately the watch had been set. Nevertheless, the Duke of Kent, a pilot himself, would have likely adjusted it frequently as most airmen do. Moreover, the platinum wristwatch was probably a fine piece of workmanship, expected to keep a precise time. Therefore its indication can be regarded as reasonably reliable. Of course, by modern investigating standards with the flight recorder data conforming to accuracy of a second or less, determining the length of the Sunderland flight may seem somewhat inexact. On the other hand, a variation even of one minute would have not appreciably affected my final conclusions.

According to the Sunderland Pilot's Notes, the aircraft's cruising speed was 120 knots. But an appendage states that at maximum take-off weight it may not be possible to maintain 120 knots even with full cruise power when weak mixture was set. As the flying boat was probably above 58,000 lb, a definite loss of speed could be expected. It is difficult to evaluate it precisely but it can be assumed to be about 2%, which is two knots, corresponding to the 2% weight excess. A further two knots must be subtracted for the position error of the pitot tube on the Sunderland, as stated in the Pilot's Notes, bringing the corrected cruising speed down to 116 knots.

It is known that on departure the Sunderland made an orbit over Cromarty Firth before setting course. This information comes from *The Times*, which reported on 27 August 1942: 'It was stated yesterday that the flying boat made a perfect take-off, climbing high into the sky and circling over the base before passing out of the sight of those on the ground.'

The manoeuvre would take no longer than three minutes. One minute would have been absorbed by the straight run after take-off to lifting the flaps and two minutes for a 360-degree rate-one turn with fifteen to twenty degrees of bank. That leaves twenty-nine minutes for the

en route flight. However, allowing one minute's tolerance for a possible error on the Duke of Kent's watch, to be on the conservative side only twenty-eight minutes were used in calculations. Using a computer program which determines the air distance while converting Corrected Airspeed (CAS) into True Airspeed (TAS), the calculations indicate that the twenty-eight minutes represent 54.5 nautical miles in still air. The actual difference between CAS and TAS is small at 1,000 feet, the average altitude the Sunderland had probably maintained *en route*, nevertheless every correction no matter how minute must be taken into consideration.

According to the weather chart of 13.00 GMT on 25 August 1942 (the nearest hour to the time of the accident) the wind at 1,000 feet was 140/20 knots. For that particular track, this represents a plus component of six knots, adding 2.8 nautical miles to the still air distance for the twenty-eight minutes of the flight, in total 57.3 nautical miles.

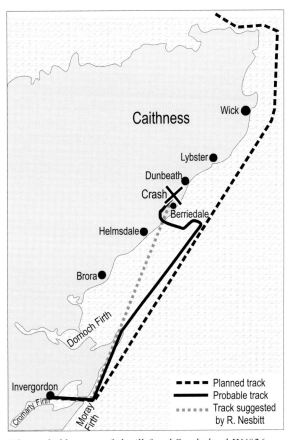

The probable route of the ill-fated Sunderland W4026 which crashed while carrying the Duke of Kent on 25 August 1942.

But the crash site lies only 38.9 nautical miles from the point where the Sunderland had set the course over Invergordon. Even if the flying boat was flown over the sea at all times, the short dog legs on departure would have added only 2.5 miles, 40.4 nautical miles in total. This is 16.9 miles less than the Sunderland would have covered while in the air. At a two nautical miles per minute cruising speed, it represents about eight minutes of flight. How can the eight 'missing' minutes be accounted for? The only explanation remains that the Sunderland did not follow a straight route.

There is no doubt that the weather conditions played a crucial role in the accident. Luckily, hourly weather reports from several stations in north-east Scotland could be still obtained from the Scottish Meteorological Office in Edinburgh. These reports show that Goyen must have been caught by surprise. But the lack of warning could have been due to a slow dissemination of met. information. At the time, high-speed teleprinters were not yet in general use. In some cases, such basic methods as the Post Office telegraph were still relied upon. Moreover, with the weather reconnaissance flights covering only the Western Approaches, chances of an inaccurate forecast were much greater when the air circulation was bringing adverse conditions from the east.

For several days before 25 August, the weather situation in the British Isles was influenced by a depression centred off Ireland, sending moist maritime air over England and Scotland. When Goyen ferried his Sunderland from Oban to Invergordon over Loch Linnhe and Loch Ness the day before the accident, the conditions were cloudy but the cloud base was relatively high, ranging between three to four thousand feet. Visibility was excellent, exceeding thirty miles.

But an overnight backing of the wind from SSE to SE brought extremely muggy conditions on the day of the accident. After traversing the North Sea for several days, the humid maritime air mass picked up even more moisture and began to affect the whole coastal stretch of eastern Scotland. A dull overcast day with low stratus and fog patches reigned, the actual situation varying according to the local circumstances and the topography of the land. Already early in the morning, stations to the east of Invergordon such as Aberdeen, Dyce, Peterhead, Kinloss and even Huntly, situated inland, were reporting drizzle or rain with cloud base at 500 feet. Only Invergordon enjoyed better conditions. The Grampians, lying in the way of the moist air mass,

must have helped to lift the stratus. Along the whole coast of Sutherland and Caithness the weather situation did not appear to be so critical at first. When Frank Goyen sat down to breakfast in the Officers' Mess at Invergordon before take-off, the local met. man estimated cloud base to be 2,000 feet and visibility 12.5 miles. Similar conditions prevailed at Tain and Wick, two stations close to the Sunderland's planned route.

But with every hour came a rapid deterioration. The weather observations around the time of departure present an illustration of the odds Frank Goyen had to face. Ten minutes before the take-off, Invergordon reported ten-tenths stratus at 1,000 feet, one-tenth at 200 feet, cloudy and misty, horizontal visibility both towards land and sea only 2,200 yards (two kilometres), relative humidity 94%, indicating a very humid air mass. Tain reported a total overcast with three-tenths of stratus and stratocumulus as low as 800 feet and patches at 300 feet but visibility somewhat better at two and a half miles (four kilometres). The worst conditions appeared to be at Wick on the north-east tip of Scotland, which the Sunderland was going to pass about five miles out to sea. The low stratus hung at 300 feet with visibility down to 2,200 yards.

One cannot help wondering what sort of a warning Goyen had been given just before his departure for Iceland. No particularly gloomy conditions were foreseen in the official Air Ministry forecast, valid for twenty-four hours starting from noon GMT 25 August 1942, which reads as follows: 'NW Scotland, Mid Scotland, NE Scotland, Orkneys and Shetlands – moderate to fresh easterly winds; cloudy, some occasional rain or drizzle spreading from the south; coast and hill fog at times in the east, rather close.'

The sole witness capable of throwing light on the weather conditions experienced in flight, was the twenty-four-year-old rear gunner, Flight Sergeant (later Flight Lieutenant) Andrew Simpson Wilson Jack, from Grangemouth in Scotland. He had miraculously survived the crash. Unfortunately he had been sworn to secrecy. His squadron room mate, also a wireless operator/air gunner, Doug Kneale, described the situation Andy found himself in as a result of the accident, in a letter to the author dated 11 December 1992.

'He remembered nothing until he came to in hospital two days later. His mother and sister had received a telegram reporting his death because it was at first thought that all on board had perished, quickly followed by a further telegram stating he was alive and in hospital. On the Saturday morning after the crash they visited him and although he was in pain and only half conscious he did refer to the crash. Later on they were asked to leave the room for a while and as they did so two "high-ranking" officers entered. They spent about twenty minutes or so with Andy during which time, with their assistance, he signed a document. From that point on he never again mentioned the tragedy to his mother or sister. One can only presume that he had been placed under the Official Secrets Act.'

A former WAAF gave a picture of the uneasy situation prevailing at RAF Station Oban, the 'home' of 228 Squadron at the time when Andy Jack was brought back for hospitalisation: 'How long it took to debrief him after his ordeal, I had no way of knowing. He was kept under security while hospitalised. I never saw him again. Things were never the same at Oban. A dark cloud seemed to cover everyone. NO TALKING was the order of the day'.

Yet many years later, F/Lt Jack must have been allowed to recount his experiences to Ralph Barker, himself a former wartime wireless operator/air gunner and later a journalist, writer and an official RAF historian. The recollections were recorded in Barker's book *Great Mysteries of the Air*, published in 1966 by Chatto & Windus.

From Andrew Jack's account it is known that, at the beginning of the flight, the Sunderland could keep just below the clouds cruising at about 1,000 feet. Although horizontal visibility was poor at Invergordon, slant visibility must have been better when they started the leg over Moray Firth because Andrew Jack observed that they passed over Tarbat Ness and he was able to discern Dunrobin Castle in the distance. But when the cloud base began to get lower, as evident from the 13.00 GMT weather observation at Tain, twelve miles NE of Invergordon, reported to be only 800 feet, Frank Goyen was forced to get down in order to keep below the stratus. Then with every minute of the flight, the weather must have become progressively worse. According to Andrew Jack they entered clouds about twenty-five minutes after take-off. It would have been somewhere abeam of Helmsdale. Wick, only thirteen minutes away, had already reported very bad conditions. It looked as if along the northern part of Caithness coast, the Grampians were by now no longer effective in blocking the banks of low clouds.

Without any data from a flight recorder, it is not easy to determine the Sunderland's actual route with any degree of certainty. However, according to Andrew Jack's account and other available information, it was possible to reconstruct the aircraft's likely movements. Taking as a yardstick the 57.4 nautical miles the Sunderland covered from leaving Invergordon, the 'eight missing minutes' were fitted into a coherent pattern according to the existing corroborative evidence. With the help of a computer, it was possible to work out how the flying boat had eventually found herself over Eagle Rock. The result is shown in the map. The confirmation that at a certain stage the Sunderland turned towards the land comes from two sources. One was Andrew Jack himself.

Even after fifty years, Doug Kneale was able to recount what his room mate had once confided to him in a 'one-off' disclosure:

'And then one evening Andy and I were sitting in the Mess partaking of a few beers. He was very quiet and from time to time he rubbed the backs of his hands, which had suffered from burns. He eventually suggested a change of scene so we popped along to a pub further down the sea front. A few beers later and continuing to rub his hands, he said, "I wish they'd stop irritating and reminding me." Appreciating what he was referring to I said "Cheer up Andy, you have a lot to be thankful for and time will prove a great healer." He gave me a rather strange look and then began to speak slowly and quietly, rather like thinking aloud than conversing.

Being a fellow rear gunner I could appreciate everything he said. It had been a normal take-off and after a little while they entered cloud so he centralised his turret and just sat back, as there was nothing to observe. He could hear snippets of conversation over the intercom but many remarks did not come over clearly, bearing in mind the size of the Sunderland cockpit and the mouth-to-mouth conversation that was possible. But he distinctly gained the impression that the Duke was on the flight deck if indeed occupying one of the pilot's seats. In fact this was a very strong feeling he had. After all, the Duke was a qualified pilot and not long before had co-piloted a Liberator across the Atlantic and back. And then came the words – "Let's go down and have a look" – followed shortly by a request that he keep a lookout for land. They gradually emerged from wispy clouds and to his surprise he noted that they were crossing the coastline whereas it should have been on his port side had they followed the prescribed track along the northern coast of Moray Firth to the Wick area before turning to port into the Pentland Firth then setting course for Iceland. The coastline disappeared in thickening cloud and within no time at all, oblivion.'

Another piece of evidence comes from an unexpected quarter. Although it could be looked upon as 'second-hand' and an expert accident investigator could view it with some degree of doubt, nevertheless its value cannot be underestimated. A few years back, a letter from a reader appeared in one of the aviation magazines in relation to the Duke of Kent crash. The reader claimed that during a holiday in Italy in 1953 he had met another Englishman who was a radar operator during the war, but in which arm he served was not disclosed. The radar operator happened to be watching the Duke's Sunderland flight on the screen. To his horror, the aircraft turned to port to take the short cut one valley too early. Unable to do anything about advising or helping the pilot, he was the very first person to realise the disastrous consequences once the blip on his screen had disappeared. Apparently many aircraft regularly took the short cut across the low part of Caithness, which would have saved forty-five minutes of flying, but he believed it to have been an unofficial practice.

In order to substantiate the story, the Public Record Office files were checked on radar installations. Unfortunately, with the secrecy surrounding this new invention during the war, there was only limited information. A document dated 1940 listed two sites on the north-east coast of Scotland – 'Chain Home' Station No. 48 at Cromarty and No. 49A at Thrumster just south of Wick. But with these two stations not having reported any periodical maintenance and calibration in 1942, it looks as if at the time of the accident they were no longer in operational use. Apparently their task had been taken over by a naval station at Invergordon, combining the sea and the air surveillance, as had been indicated by a letter from the Naval C-in-C at Rosyth to the RAF Units in eastern Scotland. The radar station at Invergordon would have amply covered the track followed by the ill-fated Sunderland, but most likely lacked a direct communication link with RAF aircraft or RAF stations. Moreover, the radar trace would have remained in the hands of the Navy and it

could have been the reason as to why it had not been presented at the Court of Inquiry. It is known that cooperation between the two services had at times not been the smoothest.

It looks doubtful that Frank Goyen intended to take a short cut as the radar operator claimed. Fuel saving would have been the last thing on his mind. There was nothing to worry about concerning weather conditions at the destination. Three meteorological stations in the south of Iceland reported almost clear skies with an excellent visibility. Above all, as an experienced Sunderland pilot, Goyen must have been aware of the dangers connected with an engine failure when traversing a stretch of land in an aircraft loaded to maximum.

But why did he find himself over the valley running out of Berriedale, a small village on the Caithness coast?

At a crucial moment, Goyen must have been faced with an important decision. Should he press on in the murky weather, paralleling the rocky coast only five to six miles away, relying entirely on his instruments and dead reckoning navigation, or should he turn towards the land, the outlines of which were still visible a few minutes earlier on. The clouds in that area could not have been thick. There were no fronts about, only a layer of moist air low down. Many craigs in the Scottish Highlands, which extended to over 2,000 feet, were bound to protrude above the cloud canopy.

First-hand evidence about breaks in low stratus had been provided by Captain Fresson, a Scottish Airways pioneer. On the day of the accident he was on a run from Inverness to the Orkney Islands in a DH89 Dragon Rapide. He recalled that flying on the outbound stretch at 4,000 feet, he encountered low clouds soon after his take-off from Inverness. The clouds persisted until Pentland Firth. A similar situation prevailed during his return flight in the afternoon. Although he departed from Kirkwall in sunny weather, at Thurso he was back over the same blanket of stratus. At that point he took up a southerly course and crossed the Caithness coast over Dunbeath only ten minutes ahead of the time at which the Duke of Kent's Sunderland crashed. From the fact that he had corrected his course for Inverness in that position, it looks certain that he must have recognised certain land features through the breaks in the clouds.

Keeping the land in sight rather than following it 'blind' in close proximity, does not appear to have been a foolhardy move on Frank Goyen's part. The ASV Mk II would not have been of much help to keep check on the distance from the coast. At such a close range, sea returns tended to 'drown' the echoes from the land.

It seems unlikely that the decision to make a detour around a patch of low stratus had been taken lightly or alone. Some ideas on the safest course of action must have been exchanged between Goyen and his second pilot, as well as his 'boss', W/Cdr Moseley, or even the Duke himself. Probably an additional factor in preferring to remain visual was Goyen's limited experience of flying on instruments. Most of his operational sorties were carried out in clear Mediterranean weather when he probably never lost sight of the sea or of the land. The Duke himself could have encouraged Goyen to get out of the murky stratus. Many years after the accident, a wing commander revealed that the Duke's dislike of flying in cloud was known in the RAF circles and he always asked to keep clear. The wing commander served with Prince George, as the Duke of Kent was known in his younger days, in the Fleet Air Arm, which before the war had been a part of the RAF.

The conversation on the flight deck, which Andy Jack overheard on the intercom, in my opinion supports the crew's intention to skirt around the patch of bad weather. But what had been said on the flight deck was not, 'Let's go down and have a look', but, 'Let's go down *there* and have a look' – meaning: to see if the coast was still visible. The word 'there' could have been easily missed by Andy Jack because wartime intercoms were far from hi-fi installations. Unfortunately the Court of Inquiry interpreted his testimony in a different way. From then on, it had been assumed that for some unknown reason Goyen planned to go down.

The detour accounts for the missing eight minutes. At first, Goyen must have turned back to get out of clouds. Once in the clear he headed for the coast, or what he believed to be its outline, intending to keep it in sight. But here the tragedy of the mistaken position had begun. It is known that the aircraft crossed the shoreline over 'The Needle', a spot five nautical miles north-east of Helmsdale, but Goyen was probably unaware of it. From Andy Jack's testimony it is evident that they must have been flying at that moment on a westerly course, for him to catch a glimpse of the land on the port side, or on his right from his rear-facing position. From the tail turret he could enjoy an unobstructed downward view, and probably through a break in clouds, he was able to spot a land feature. But for some unknown reason he had

failed to report it. On the other hand, the rest of the crew could have easily missed it, their view being obstructed by the flying boat's large nose and bulbous hull. From the fact that the Sunderland passed overhead the Duke of Portland's estate, situated inland about a mile west of Berriedale, it can be deduced that soon after crossing the coast, Goyen turned back onto his original course, intending to follow what he believed to be the shoreline. But it was the valley of Berriedale Water. From a glance at the topographical map, it is apparent that they are very similar in shape.

But what had made the valley look like a rocky coast? Like Collins's experience in Antarctica, another type of weather phenomenon must have led to Goyen's sensory illusion. Low stratus drifting from the sea would be initially lifted over the first range of hills with the help of a strong sea breeze, bringing foggy conditions with drizzle or even rain. But upon reaching the steep valley, the clouds would plunge down with an increase in

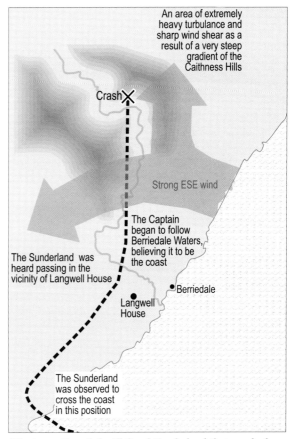

The last miles of the ill-fated Sunderland that crashed near Berriedale on 25 August 1942.

the air temperature at what the meteorologists call a dry adiabatic lapse rate, resulting in sudden dispersing through the 'foehn' effect. Consequently, the left side of the valley, and the higher of the two, would have likely remained clear leaving Goyen with an impression as if he were flying along the coastal cliffs and thus staying over the sea. Especially since, from an occasional downward scan, he could probably pick out the cascading stream resembling the waves striking the rocky coast.

From the airmanship point of view, remaining in visual contact with the ground made sense. At least Goyen had an idea of his whereabouts and like Jim Collins, he also thought he knew where he was.

Due to lack of information, it was not possible to determine at what altitude he was flying at that moment. But it can be presumed that he had climbed to somewhere between 1,200 to 1,500 feet. He would have to keep clear of the cloud canopy, which must have extended to at least 900 feet to cover the most prominent hill of 830 feet on the eastern side of the valley. If the hill had not been visible from the cockpit, Goyen must have been convinced he was over the sea.

Cruising only a few hundred feet above a layer of clouds might appear surprising for an airman of Goyen's calibre. But estimating the actual clearance in such circumstances can be very difficult. It is also possible that with a moist air mass, by the afternoon cumulus could have formed through orographic effect, producing a shower. In that case, the view from Goyen's cockpit windows could have been distorted once he was forced to cross an area of precipitation.

As a result of a KLM DC6 accident near Frankfurt Airport in 1952, when it was suspected that the pilot had misjudged his height during approach in rain and struck a small hill, Douglas Aircraft Corporation conducted a series of tests on the height distortion from the cockpit windows when covered by a film of water. It stems from a simple physical principle that light becomes refracted on passing from a thinner medium such as air to a denser medium such as water. This is why swimming pools always look shallower than they are. The tests were completed in 1973 and they showed the refraction to be in the order of 200 feet over the distance of one nautical mile. However, six years later, an alert member of the KLM Flight Technical Department spotted an error in the calculations and the figure had turned out to be double the amount – 400 feet over one

nautical mile. If Goyen happened to be passing through a shower, the cloud layer only a few hundred feet below could have looked as if it were miles away.

Although the crew in front of the aircraft could see something ahead that resembled land features, from his rear view position Andy Jack could have been given an impression of flying in clouds, in particular when passing through a shower. The lack of horizon definition due to poor visibility and flat light could have been further contributory factors.

Over a hilly land, the topography of the Scottish craigs and the weather elements would have created an ideal scenario for disaster. The meteorological chart for the time of the accident shows the geostrophic wind – that is flow of air unaffected by land features – to be at least twenty-five knots. The extra strength in that area was due to a sudden tightening of the isobars. The increase in the pressure gradient had been recorded over the past three hours by the barometers at Invergordon and Wick. Other factors such as a 'foehn' or a 'valley' effect, as well the usual upsurge of sea breeze during the day, could have whipped up the wind speed to a much higher figure. Andrew Jack could recollect that just before the crash the air was extremely turbulent. It could have only come from the local 'mistral'. Two farmers working on the nearby hill later claimed that as far as weather was concerned, it was a most miserable afternoon.

The isobaric wind direction was from the south-east. But the surface wind due to ground friction would tend to back by some thirty degrees, becoming easterly. The flow of air would be further affected in the Berriedale area by a barrier of hills rising steeply up to 2,000 feet only a mile from the coast. Like a river, the flow would split into two main streams. One part would be diverted in the south-westerly direction along the valley that parallels the coast. The other stream would break off to the north-west where no high ground stood in the way. Where the sharp split had occurred, a perfect stage was set for wind shear, one of the airman's deadliest enemies. (See map on page 19.)

For the benefit of those readers who may not be familiar with what havoc a sudden fluctuation of the wind speed or direction can play with aircraft performance, a brief explanation might prove helpful to understand the plight of the Sunderland's pilot. Whenever the wind environment changes faster than the aircraft mass can be accelerated or decelerated, such variations will be reflected by changes in the airspeed. In simple terms: if you fly into wind and it suddenly disappears, your airspeed will instantly drop by that amount. In such circumstances, loss of lift can be expected.

From the climb capability, quoted in the Sunderland Pilot's Notes to be only about 400 ft/min at maximum take-off weight, it is apparent that there was only very limited surplus power on the engines. Combined with drag from a large hull, some 25% higher than on a similar size land aircraft such as the Lancaster I, acceleration would have been very sluggish when loss of speed suddenly occurred.

Another problem over which Frank Goyen had no control could have contributed to his misfortune. The fact that the Sunderland was overloaded would have further weakened the response to the throttles. Unfortunately, by the time the flying boat came over Eagle Rock, not much weight would have been reduced by fuel consumption. For take-off and the half an hour in the air, she would have used about 125 gallons. Converted to weight, it represented only 890 lb. In addition, with the cruising speed of only 116 knots and the stalling speed of 87 knots, as worked out by interpolation from the figures in the Pilot's Notes – 85 knots at 56,000 lb – the margin amounted to only 29 knots. Such a narrow gap was bound to add to the handling problems. All these factors would have made the flying boat particularly vulnerable to the effects of wind shear.

When Goyen completed the turn to follow the valley of Berriedale Water, he must have run into headwind. But as soon as the Sunderland left the steep gorge behind, it would have come upon a split of the airflow with the wind direction veering abruptly from south-west to east. The sudden change of direction would have ensued in an appreciable drop of airspeed, leading to a catastrophic loss of height. Possibly further affected by a strong downdraught, the Sunderland went down like a stone through the layer of stratus, striking the eastern face of Eagle Rock in a nose-high attitude. A report in the *News of the World*, just after the accident, described the actual circumstances: 'The first impact is thought to have been a glancing blow which caused the flying boat to bounce into the air, turn over and crash with disintegrating force 100 yards away.'

Only in a nose-high attitude would it have been possible for the Sunderland to rebound back into the air. If a normal descent were being carried out,

the nose would have first hit the ground, resulting in an instant break-up.

It is interesting to note the *News of the World*'s comments just after the accident, recording the circumstances leading to the disaster: 'It is now deduced that after passing over a sharp eminence 900 feet high, the Sunderland dropped in an air pocket and struck the side of a rounded shoulder of the rim 800 feet above sea level.'

More circumstantial evidence points to the fact that Goyen was not trying to get below clouds for one reason or another. In October 1942, when Sir Archibald Sinclair, the Air Minister, gave a statement in the House of Commons about the accident, he revealed that the examination of the propellers showed the engines to be under power when the aircraft struck the ground.

Surely if Goyen did intend to go down, the power would have been substantially reduced. The nose-high attitude on impact signifies that he must have struggled to keep from losing altitude. Andrew Jack claimed that he had experienced a sinking feeling as the aircraft was going down. This denotes not a deliberate manoeuvre but a downward motion induced by some brute physical force. Even Captain Fresson supports this opinion in his 'log', an account of his views on the accident: 'I suspect that the throttles were at full power as the pilot desperately clawed for height.'

Wind shear and/or downdraught, the straw that broke the camel's back on the Sunderland's fatal passage over Berriedale Water, has been the cause of numerous crashes. This freak phenomenon can be encountered in the most unexpected locations, not necessarily in a mountainous terrain or near a thunderstorm. It is known to have precipitated accidents during approaches at night over desert, where strong inversions occur (see Chapter 4). In 1972 alone, four accidents, all to Boeing 727s, were due to rapid sinking from wind shear. For many years the 'sudden dropping out of the skies' baffled the investigators. As a result, this unpredictable freak of nature acquired in aviation circles the name of 'the silent killer'. Only recently, the crash of the DC10 from Dutch charter company Martinair has highlighted its catastrophic consequences.

The magnitude of downdraughts generated in the mountains by a standing wave is still not appreciated in the present day, in spite of many crashes by private aircraft in such circumstances. Even large jets are not immune to the effects of these freak weather phenomena. In March 1993, the crew of a Boeing 747 departing from

Anchorage in Alaska reported an area of extremely strong sink on the leeside of a 4,500 feet high mountain. The aircraft had been forced down at a descent rate of 1,000 ft/min despite application of climb power. At the same time, several momentary stall warnings sounded but these ceased as quickly as they came on.

It is quite apparent that flying in precarious wind conditions, of which Frank Goyen was probably not aware of at the time, caused the Duke of Kent accident. Moreover, with his limited experience of overland flights, he would not have known that in such a situation it was necessary to keep extra height above the ground. In civil aviation, 1,000 feet plus 10% of the altitude is prescribed as the normal terrain clearance. However in mountainous areas it is recommended to keep at least 4,000 feet above the highest peak. Many airline pilots would use an even higher figure once they observed a cloud formation ahead denoting a standing wave.

Could Goyen recover from the effect of wind shear and downdraught if he had realised in time what had hit him? Judging by the investigations of similar accidents, based on analysis of the flight recorder data, he had no hope. Simulator tests have shown that even if pilots did anticipate wind shear, most failed to arrest the sudden catastrophic sink. As a result of this lesson, the new generation of jets are fitted with a warning device triggered by the signals from the inertial navigation system.

A question is bound to arise. Why had Goyen not tried to climb above the clouds? Probably the main reason was Coastal Command habits. The crews had to rely on navigational information from the sea surface. Drift was measured from wind lanes as often as four times per hour and the pilots were asked to make two short doglegs at ninety degrees apart so that the wind could be calculated. Before the introduction of advanced radio aids, it was the prime method of finding the way over the sea in daytime. To get to the designated patrol area with any degree of accuracy, called for staying as much as possible below clouds.

When Goyen left Invergordon, it appeared from the local situation that he could remain within sight of the sea. The forecast did not indicate any unusual adverse weather ahead. Although some sources claim that he had been briefed to climb to 4,000 feet, there was no meteorological information on record to indicate that he would find himself above clouds. In that respect Captain Fresson, who took off from Inverness in the morning, was probably lucky. With the airport located further south, he could reach 4,000 feet before running into the patch of bad weather. But a heavy-laden Sunderland was no frisky Rapide.

Another factor, such as higher fuel consumption at 4,000 feet that adversely affected the flying boat's range, could have influenced Goyen's decision to stay low. According to the tests carried out by the Aircraft and Armament Experimental Establishment at Boscombe Down, the difference between starting at 1,000 feet or climbing to 6,000 feet, represented for the Liberator a loss of 300 miles in range. For the Sunderland with its poor climb performance, that figure would have been significantly higher.

Contrary to the verdict of the Court of Inquiry, which had squarely blamed Frank Goyen for the crash, there appear to be no basic flaws in his actions or in his airmanship. Although he was instructed to follow a designated track taking him at all times over the sea, such a directive was purely related to the Sunderland's poor performance on three engines at heavy weight. There can be no doubt that Goyen would not have ignored the consequence of an engine failure, but, as a captain, he was free to make a decision which he believed to be the safest under the circumstances. A detour around a patch of bad weather and staying within sight of the coast does not indicate any recklessness. Many colleagues from 228 Squadron remembered him as a level-headed captain. He could not foresee dangerous turbulence ahead because the flight over the sea was very smooth. Moreover his experience of flying over mountainous terrain, with its associated problems, was most likely extremely limited, as Coastal Command patrols were carried out 99% over the water. But in north Scotland, like in any area with 'cliff-like' hills, mountain waves can be very destructive, as Captain Fresson recollected in his book *The Road to the Isles*. He wrote that during a flight in a very strong wind his Rapide was thrown on its tail, totally out of control.

It was unfortunate for Frank Goyen that the opinion of the Court of Inquiry had been swayed by a snippet of conversation over the intercom – 'Let's go down and have a look'. From that moment it had been assumed that he intended to make a descent for some reason or another. No attempts had been made to interpret these words in any different way. But what the Assessors had presumed does not make sense. In the weather conditions prevailing on the Caithness coast at the time of the accident, no pilot would have dared to go down while closing in on high ground.

Andrew Jack owed his survival to two strokes of luck. One was occupying a rear-facing seat in his tail turret. According to the findings of many accident investigations, such a seating arrangement for passengers is highly recommended as a means of saving lives. His second stroke of luck lay in the tail breaking off upon impact while the rest of the aircraft flipped over and caught fire. Unfortunately after the tail had parted, a severed hydraulic line to the gun turret began to leak and the fluid became ignited. It was the reason why Andrew Jack had suffered burns on his face and hands. While the broken-off end section of the hull kept sliding on the moor, he was dragged along half-in and half-out of the turret until he fell out and sustained severe concussion. Although he could not recollect anything after striking the ground, the badly worn-out heels of his flying boots had suggested his horrifying ordeal. Doug Kneale described the surviving tail gunner's experiences after the crash:

'Eventually Andy came to feeling pain and realised his clothing was smouldering so he began to tear away and beat out the parts causing him discomfort. He then became aware of the burning wreckage and he passed out again. Eventually after regaining his senses, his first thought was that he must try to get help. He began to stagger down the mountainside and experienced further pain as his clothing chafed his injuries, so bit by bit he discarded it. When it came to his trousers he heard the sound of money in his pocket, he took it out, looked at it and thought "It's no bloody use up here" and scattered it. As darkness fell he came to a stream and knelt down to drink. The cold water reacted on his burns and he again passed out.

It was daylight when he came to and continued his descent and eventually reached a cottage. He attempted to open the gate and when a woman emerged, he passed out. While still in hospital he received a letter containing a postal order to the value of the money he had disposed of on the mountainside. A group of people assisting the recovery had traced his movements from the scattered clothing and near the trousers found the money, hence the postal order! He told me he would never spend it but would have it framed. Several years later when he met my brother, a Flight Lieutenant in the RAF, he still had it.'

Although Andrew Jack eventually recovered from physical injuries, his mental wound seems to have never healed. People who came in contact with him after his hospitalisation and his sick leave soon realised that he was a changed man. He turned into an introvert and did not mix freely as he used to do in the past. Apart from very rare remarks to his intimate friend Doug Kneale, he would never mention the crash even in conversation with his mother or sister. Only once did he show his feelings about the accident in the presence of his family. It was during a visit home when the results of the Court of Inquiry were announced in the House of Commons. Upon hearing about it, Andy hit the roof crying, 'They're wrong, they're wrong to blame Frank for this, he was the best skipper in the world.'

The verdict must have greatly distressed him. Unfortunately in the years to come, he was not given a chance to forget his nightmare. One example was his introduction as an instructor when he was sent back to Invergordon. The course officer presented him to the trainees with the following words: 'Your instructor will be F/Sgt Andrew Jack who was the sole survivor in the Duke of Kent crash.' No wonder, the haunting memories had made him brood through his life, leaving him with a house-size chip on his shoulder. He died in 1978, some sources claim as an alcoholic.

But Andrew Jack's traumatic aftermath was not a single case in aviation history. Such tormenting experiences often leave a bad psychological scar on airmen's minds. A KLM pilot involved in the 1961 Cairo crash emerged a different man in all appearances – physically due to face injuries and mentally due to a complete change of personality. It was to such an extent that even his close colleagues were not able to recognise him (see Chapter 4). Jim Thain, the captain of the ill-fated Airspeed Ambassador in which the Manchester United football team had been decimated, died at the early age of fifty-three. His friends claim it was due to becoming a broken man as a result of having been made the scapegoat for the accident. Recently, a BA captain, W. Stewart, committed suicide after the court found him guilty of a dangerous approach at London Airport in a Boeing 747.

For Pilot Officer the Hon. Michael Strutt, the Duke of Kent's newly appointed personal assistant and only twenty-eight years old, it was a sad fate. Strutt, the son of Lord Belper and brother of the Duchess of Norfolk, had just survived an operational tour as an air gunner on Wellingtons in Bomber Command. It was at the time when the losses on that type of aircraft were at their highest.

The original photo of the graves of F/Lt Goyen, the captain of the ill-fated Sunderland and W/Cdr Moseley, the C.O. of 228 Squadron. (228 Sq. Association)

For his post-operational rest he was going to be sent as a gunnery instructor to a station in the north-west of England. It was a job for which he felt temperamentally unsuited. As Strutt happened to know the Duke of Kent well, he asked his step-father Lord Rosebery to put in a good word for him with Downing Street and the Duke of Kent's office, to be appointed an ADC to replace S/Ldr Ferguson who was ill at the time. The flight to Iceland was going to be Strutt's first function in his new post.

The account of the accident cannot be closed without highlighting what a great loss the Duke of Kent's death had been to the RAF. In this day and age, when it is fashionable to cast aspersions on the Royal Family, it might be appropriate to remind those who were too young for active service in World War II, what a valuable contribution to the welfare of many servicemen, he had rendered.

Naturally, one can foresee a shrug of shoulders by the anti-royalists, dismissing it with: 'The Duke

of Kent was just an RAF Welfare Officer'. But to the thousands of airmen who had to endure a tour of duty on the 'off-the-beaten-track' RAF stations, even minor comforts helping to ease the daily drudgery were most welcome. Only those exposed to a dull monotonous routine could appreciate what the Duke had tried to achieve.

When war broke out, he gave up the offer of the post as Governor General of Australia. At his own request, he relinquished his honorary rank of Air Vice-Marshal, to serve first as a Group Captain, so that he could pursue a task in which he thought he could make himself useful to a nation in difficulties. He applied all his energies to see that those serving in the RAF did not feel forgotten men. He carried out his duties without any pomp or time-wasting ceremonies. He willingly under-took countless journeys in military aircraft with limited navigational aids. Such flights involved risk as well as discomfort. One day that risk caught up with him. This was the second time in the history of England that a king's son lost his life on active service. The last tragedy occurred over five hundred years ago. As the epitaph on the Eagle Rock memorial proclaims – 'may he rest in peace'.

During my research I came upon an interesting discovery. After noting the headlines in the *Scotsman* of 27 August 1942, 'Poland mourns a friend', I consulted a known Polish historian and writer Lesław Bartelski. His explanation revealed, and it is not a fairy tale but a historical fact, that during a visit in 1937 to a distinguished aristocrat, Count Alfred Potocki, at his Łańcut estate, now a museum, the Duke of Kent was approached by the Polish royalists to become the King of Poland. Apparently the British Royal Family had eventually granted approval. Nevertheless, Polish royalists did not exert much influence on the country's politics, run at the time by the military.

During World War II, General Sikorski renewed the suggestion that, once Hitler was defeated, the Duke of Kent should be crowned as king of the proposed Polish–Czech Federation. Foreign Office officials dismissed the idea as grossly romantic. But to Sikorski it was a very practical goal. He was well aware that after his unfortunate experiences with the French in 1939–40, Poland needed strong connections with a reliable country in the West.

In 1994 the present Duke of Kent and his wife visited Łańcut and were shown a short film about his father's visit to Poland in 1937.

2

1943 – IS THE GIBRALTAR DISASTER A REAL MYSTERY?

PART I

On the night of 4 July 1943, an RAF Transport Command Liberator departing from Gibraltar made what appeared to be a normal take-off. The aircraft was operated as a personnel, freight and mail carrier between England and the Middle East. Shortly after becoming airborne it began to lose height and crashed into the sea seven hundred yards from the shore. All eleven passengers, among them several VIPs, lost their lives, including General Sikorski, C-in-C of the Polish Forces and the Prime Minister of the Polish Government-in-exile.

The disaster, for which no obvious explanation could be found at the time, unleashed wild speculations that continued to echo for many years.

Aerial representation of Gibraltar Aerodrome showing the probable horizontal flight path of the Liberator, with the vertical path as observed by F/Lt Capes shown beneath.

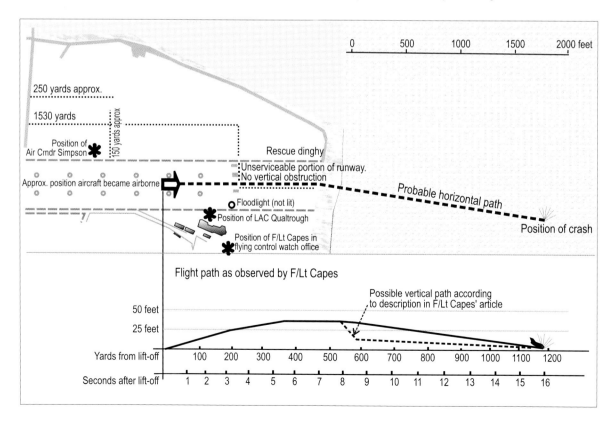

There is no doubt Sikorski's death struck a major blow to the cause of the Polish nation. Many Poles believe that it changed the course of the country's history.

The German propaganda machine immediately took advantage of the tragedy and began to broadcast allegations all over Europe that the British Secret Service had engineered the accident because Sikorski's controversial policy on relations with Russia had become too embarrassing to Churchill. No matter how despicable Goebbels's fabrications were to the Poles, soon disquieting ripples began to sweep through the Polish Forces in England.

In World War II Władysław Eugeniusz Sikorski was the strong man of the Polish Government-in-exile. An old hand in the fight for the country's independence, he had already started his activities in World War I. In 1920 he commanded an army that defeated the invading Soviet forces. In 1922 he served as the Prime Minister of re-born Poland. But after the *coup d'état* by Marshal Piłsudski in 1926, he was left on the sidelines and spent much of his time in France, writing books on military strategy.

When the Germans overran the country in 1939, Sikorski, who was at the time in Paris, was asked to form a government-in-exile in Paris. He was appointed as the Prime Minister as well as the C-in-C of the Polish Armed Forces. After France's collapse in 1940, he ordered evacuation of the Polish troops to England and continued to lead the government from British soil.

Following his political conviction that his country's independence had been for centuries more threatened by the Germans than by the Russians, as the head of the Government-in-exile he tried to reach an understanding with Stalin. It was despite bitter opposition from right wing circles. Many Poles had never forgiven the Soviet dictator for the treacherous stab in the back in occupying Eastern Poland in 1939.

After Hitler attacked Russia in 1941, Sikorski signed an agreement with the Soviet authorities. As a result, thousands of Poles were released from PoW camps, gulags or from remote parts of the USSR where many civilians from Eastern Poland had been deported. The next step was the formation of the Polish Army in Russia. Nevertheless, in spite of a new political accord, the Soviets refused to honour the pre-1939 Polish–Russian borders and with this issue unresolved, it had led to a split within the Polish Government. Three opposing ministers had resigned from the Cabinet.

From 1942 onwards the relations with the Soviets began to deteriorate. A bone of contention was the size and the deployment of the new Polish Army in Russia. Eventually in the summer of that year, Sikorski ordered evacuation of the already formed Polish units to the Middle East. This triggered off bitter deprecations from the Russian side. Upon the first signs of the Red Army's growing resistance to the German onslaught, Stalin already began to plan subjugation of all Eastern Europe to Communism. A strong Polish Army under British influence would have been a stumbling block in his pursuits and he used every means to bypass the pact he had signed with Sikorski. In the spring of 1943 another ominous shadow fell upon relations with the USSR. While Polish units were being formed in Russia the majority of the officers who were taken as PoWs in 1939 appeared to be missing. Stalin's explanation to Sikorski was that they must have fled to Manchuria. But soon a ghastly discovery signalled another probability. In *The Hinge of Fate* (published by Cassell), Churchill describes it:

'Early in April 1943 Sikorski came to luncheon at No.10. He told me that he had proofs that the Soviet Government had murdered the 15,000 officers and other prisoners in their hands, and they had been buried in vast graves in the forests, mainly around Katyn. He has a wealth of evidence. I said, "If they are dead nothing you can do to bring them back." He said he could not hold his people and they had already released all their news to the press.'

The information about the Katyn massacre had been provided by General Rowecki, the C-in-C of the Polish Underground Army in a radiogram 1 dz.1833/tjn/49 sent to London on 14 April 1943:

'The Germans discovered near Smolensk a mass grave of several thousands of our officers from the PoW camp at Kozielsk [a notorious PoW camp run by the Red Army] killed in March and April 1940. Several Polish representatives from Warsaw and Kraków took part in the inspection of the grave. Their revelations leave no doubt as to the authenticity of the mass murder. Public opinion is greatly disturbed, will report further details in a few days. Kalina [Kalina – Rowecki's code name].'

Although well aware of who had carried out the massacre, as the disclosures from the KGB archives have recently revealed, Stalin reacted violently to the Polish accusations. He claimed that SS units were responsible for the atrocities. But to all Poles exposed during two years of captivity to the most brutal treatment at the hands of the Russian secret police, NKVD, the forerunner of the KGB, it was clear who had committed the dastardly crime. The Polish PoWs from Russia sent to England to join the RAF, soon circulated their account as to why the 15,000 officers were liquidated. After the Red Army marched into eastern Poland in 1939 and several Polish divisions fell into its hands, Stalin decided to set up a Red Legion from the captured PoWs. As a first step, the NKVD was instructed to convert all officers to Communism. Nevertheless, every attempt to brainwash the incarcerated men had met with a wall of sarcasm. The infuriated NKVD agents reported widespread resistance to their chief Beria and when he brought up the matter with Stalin, the despot exploded. 'Get rid of them', he screamed and in a matter of weeks his spiteful order was mercilessly carried out.

The Katyn massacre had stirred revulsion in every Polish serviceman in England, but this was not the case with a large part of the British population. After three years of war, many people began to lean to the left and looked upon the Polish Government's accusations as a smear against the Soviets, who at that stage appeared to be bearing the brunt of the war. As a result of clever propaganda from the British Communist Party and their fellow travellers, public opinion swung against the Poles and there were frequent incidents of Polish servicemen being insulted on the streets. The left-wing sympathisers blindly believed in the Soviet assertions that SS units were responsible for the mass slaughter and regarded Polish allegations as an obstacle to the betterment of Anglo–Soviet relations. On the other hand, the deeply conservative section of the British public was not swayed. Stalin's bloody purges, including that of his own high-ranking officers, resulting in an evident weakness of the Russian Army at the start of war in 1941, were still fresh in many people's minds. The tenacity of the Polish pilots during the Battle of Britain had not been forgotten. By 1943 a bitter criticism began to be voiced about the treatment by the Soviet authorities of those members of HM Forces who came into contact with the Russians, such as the RAF fighter pilots stationed in the Ukraine or the sailors taking vital supplies to Murmansk under great risk.

The Katyn slaughter made a particularly dissenting impact on the Polish formations in the Middle East. As they consisted predominantly of men evacuated from Russia, unrest began to spread. With their first-hand knowledge of the Soviets' barbarity, the evidence collected by the Polish Underground Army was sufficiently convincing as to who was really responsible for liquidating the thousands of innocent officers. Moreover, the distressing news of the Soviet Union claiming eastern Poland as their territory had deepened the growing despair. To many Polish soldiers that part of the country was their homeland. There were talks of rebellion. Sikorski was well aware that only his personal appearance and a call to loyalty could restore the sinking morale. Especially when from his tour of the Polish units in the Middle East, the Chief of Staff Major-General Klimecki kept sending alarming warnings about the unrest coming to the boil.

Despite signs of a brewing storm, two Polish Cabinet ministers pleaded with Sikorski to give up his Middle East tour on the grounds of safety. During his service as Prime Minister, the General had flown many more miles in the bombers converted for carrying VIPs than any other Allied statesman. His wide travels included three visits to the USA and one to the USSR. Some of the journeys were not without risk. On his first return flight across the Atlantic, Sikorski encountered breathing difficulties and the pilot had to descend to a lower altitude. During his third mission for talks with President Roosevelt, after travelling to Montreal in a Liberator Sikorski was going to continue in a Hudson to Washington. But the flight had begun with a mishap. When during take-off the engines began to lose power, the pilot decided to make a wheels-up landing and overshot the runway. Luckily there were no casualties and only minor damage to the Hudson. Afterwards, there were rumours of sabotage. But engine problems after a start in very cold weather were not new on Hudsons. In 1941 Sir Frederic Banting, the co-discoverer of insulin, lost his life in an accident shortly after take-off from Gander in Newfoundland. The cause of both engine failures was most likely a problem with the oil cooler due to extremely low temperatures.

On another return flight across the Atlantic in a Liberator, Sikorski's oxygen mask froze up and he passed out.

The ministers were also concerned about an incident that took place during a flight in March 1942. A disgruntled senior Polish Air Force officer, travelling with Sikorski to the United States to take up the post of an assistant air attaché in Washington, hatched up a plot of 'psychological warfare'. According to his own subsequent admission, he smuggled a sabotage device on board, a firebomb, and pretended that he had found it in the aircraft and had defused it at the last moment. The plot was supposed to have been instigated by a dissident group of 'Young Turks' from the Polish Forces, who were dissatisfied with Sikorski's lenient policy towards the Soviet regime. The intention was to make Sikorski fear that he was a 'marked man'. They hoped that the attempt would discourage the General from continuing his political activities, in particular his visits to President Roosevelt. The existence of the plotter known as 'Łancuszek' (chain – in Polish) was only revealed after the war. Although a senior Polish Air Force officer was behind the 'bomb incident', Sikorski enjoyed the confidence of the Polish operational crews serving with the RAF. They saw their leader as being forced to walk a tightrope between the Allies' and the Soviets' pursuits.

At that stage of the war, apart from 'Łancuszek', Sikorski appeared to have been also a prey for retaliation from other quarters. To Hitler, the resistance movement in Poland (directed by Sikorski from London), began to feel like a thorn in the flesh. *Gestapo* headquarters in Warsaw kept sending frantic reports to Berlin about the threat from the Polish Underground Army that was expanding rapidly with the help of air supplies from England, dropped by Halifaxes flown by Polish crews. By 1943 it was not a 'paper tiger' but a highly disciplined force with several regional divisions, amounting to over 200,000 men.

After the Katyn affair came into the open, Sikorski became a target for attacks and threats, not only from the Soviets but also from the British Communists and left wing sympathisers.

Sikorski realised the risk in undertaking so many journeys by air. He had once confessed to his close friends: 'I am sure that sooner or later I shall die on one of these flights but I hope it won't happen before I complete my task and return to a free and independent Poland.'

PART II

Nevertheless, he did depart for the Middle East from RAF Station Lyneham on the evening of 24 May 1943. He was accompanied by his daughter Mrs Lesniowska; a Polish ATS officer, Col

Marecki; Chief of Operations Staff, naval ADC Lt Ponikiewski and Sikorski's faithful personal secretary Mr Kułakowski. In the party was also Lt-Col Victor Cazalet, who acted as the British liaison officer. He accompanied Sikorski on many journeys and became a close personal friend. Mrs Lesniowska was General Sikorski's only daughter. Her husband, a Polish Army officer, was captured by the Germans in 1939, and was a PoW in an *Oflag*.

Shortly after departure came the first twist of the subsequent drama in the form of a sick joke. Several members of the Polish Government received a phone call from an anonymous person who told them in Polish that Sikorski's aircraft had crashed at Gibraltar and all occupants were killed. But as two days before Sikorski's arrival a landing accident to a Liberator had taken place, it was possible that, with the usual communication delays, someone could have misinterpreted the message from Gibraltar.

North Front, as the airfield at Gibraltar was called, was hardly suitable for large aircraft. Although the runway was 1,800 yards long, in practice only 1,530 yards were usable, the rest being unserviceable. In October 1942, a Liberator crashed on landing. Fourteen passengers were killed and many others injured. (Among the injured was a Canadian ace, 'Screwball' Beurling, a fighter pilot who in June 1942 shot down twenty-seven enemy planes in fourteen days. After his operational tour in Malta he was returning to the UK on that Liberator.) A few weeks later an Albemarle had hit the sea shortly after take-off and the crew lost their lives.

In the Operational Record Book of 511 Squadron, which was carrying out flights to the Middle East through Gibraltar, it had already been noted in November 1942:

'It is hoped that the earliest opportunity will be taken to discontinue the use of this present dangerous and unsuitable aerodrome of North Front, little more than appropriate to a landing ground, in favour of the Algerian airports which have been for twenty years the principal bases for the French Air Force in North Africa and commercial airlines.'

For carrying VIPs, 511 Squadron, formed on 10 October 1941 from No.1425 Flight, relied on its most experienced pilots. One of them was newly promoted F/Lt Prchal, a Czech in the service of the RAF. Prchal was assigned to fly Sikorski and he had undoubtedly been selected due to his considerable flying experience for wartime circumstances as well as his reputation as a first-rate pilot. He was particularly known for his exceptional instrument flying abilities. One night he put a Hudson down in fog at Gibraltar without blind approach facilities.

After an overnight stop at Gibraltar for passenger and crew rest, the Liberator carrying Sikorski landed at Cairo West airfield on 26 May where the Polish C-in-C was met by R.G. Casey, Overseas Minister for the Middle East. For the next four weeks, Sikorski toured Polish units.

Appearing in person helped enormously to restore the troops' morale. To them, he was their saviour who had so indefatigably fought for their release from Soviet hands and brought them out of Russia. But heat and constant travelling had eventually taken their toll on Sikorski's stamina. Upon completing his Middle East mission, he intended to take a few days' rest in Egypt. Unfortunately, a telegram from Churchill implying that Sikorski's presence in London was a matter of urgency changed his plans and he decided to return at the first opportunity.

On the homebound stretch, Sikorski requested to be flown again by F/Lt Prchal. It was not only for his skills as a pilot and professional approach to his duties, but also because Sikorski felt strongly about the Polish–Czechoslovakian political cooperation, despite a centuries-long enmity between the two nations. He was the only Polish politician who maintained close relations with Czech counterparts and his dream was a Polish–Czech federation once Hitler was defeated.

To comply with Sikorski's request, Prchal had to be rushed back to operational duty just three days after returning from his last Middle East trip. Moreover, in order to take Sikorski out of Egypt on 3 July, he had to make the flight all the way from Lyneham to Cairo without a customary crew rest at Gibraltar. It had amounted to eighteen and a half hours in the air, at least twenty-one hours on duty. In appreciation for such a sacrifice, when they were leaving Cairo Sikorski gave the Czech pilot an inscribed silver cigarette case.

However, after the accident the Polish Air Force headquarters expressed grave concern about F/Lt Prchal's selection despite him being the only member of 511 Squadron with airline experience. Also the replacement of Prchal's regular second pilot F/O Rathgate by S/Ldr Herring, who unfortunately was rather new to the Liberators, was later criticised by the Polish authorities. This does not seem to have been justified in view of a mainly

relief role played by the second pilot in wartime.

On the return journey, in addition to the Polish party of seven which now also included Major-General Klimecki, the Chief of Staff, three additional passengers had boarded the Liberator at Cairo with Sikorski's permission. They were Brigadier J.P. Whiteley, an MP, and two civilians, Walter Heathcote Lock and H. Pinter. Nevertheless, information provided by the Ministry of Defence Air Historical Branch (RAF), classified Pinter as a Warrant Telegraphist in the Royal Navy. (A letter dated 16 July 1992.)

According to certain sources, the two 'civilian' passengers were believed to be important figures in the British Secret Service. The Air Historical Branch stated that they could neither confirm nor deny this information.

The rumours about a VIP of the British Secret Service expected to travel with Sikorski, could have perhaps started from an indication that Brigadier Fitzroy Maclean, later Sir Fitzroy Maclean, known for his connections with the intelligence circles, was going to board the plane. However, at the last moment, his departure from Cairo had been delayed.

PART III

After leaving Cairo at night on 2 July, the Liberator landed at Gibraltar on the afternoon of 3 July and Sikorski was met on the tarmac by Lt-General Mason-MacFarlane, his AOC Air Com. Simpson and Admiral Sir Frederick Collins. Luckily many details of Sikorski's stay in Gibraltar were recorded by Lt Łubienski. (Count Major Łubienski died in London on 8 February 1996, leaving three daughters, one of them the well-known actress Rula Lenska.) Chief of the Polish Mission (later a major and the adjutant to General Anders), he was more of a diplomat than a soldier and appeared to be on good terms with all British officials on the Rock. Before the war, he served as secretary to Col Beck, the controversial Polish Foreign Minister. Łubienski had been sent to Gibraltar to help with releasing Polish servicemen from the notorious Spanish detention centre at Miranda de Ebro. While fleeing France following her collapse after the disastrous campaign in 1940, many soldiers were arrested by the Spanish police and subsequently detained in appalling conditions, resembling those of German concentration camps.

Sikorski looked forward to meeting Mason-

MacFarlane again. He and the Governor of Gibraltar were old friends, perhaps because they were able to converse in French, as Sikorski's English was somewhat limited. One source claimed that it was also because they were both Freemasons.

Their friendship dated back to 1940 when Mason-MacFarlane was the Director of the British Military Intelligence in France. Their paths crossed again in Moscow. When Sikorski came to Moscow in 1941 for talks with Stalin, Mason-MacFarlane at that time headed the British Military Mission in Russia.

The visit to Gibraltar began with a touchy situation through a blunder committed by the Foreign Office. Major Łubienski in his recollections – *The Last Days of General Sikorski: An Eyewitness Account*, published by Orbis Books (London) Ltd, edited by Dr K. Sword – describes it:

'In the meantime in Gibraltar the Governor's military assistant Major Anthony Quayle [later a well known actor] phoned me, asking me to call at the Governor's office at once. As I entered the Governor said, "Łubienski, I am in a spot. I have just heard from Cairo that General Sikorski is on his way and will be arriving here this afternoon. He has asked if he can stay overnight before flying on to London tomorrow evening."

The difficulty, said General Mason-MacFarlane, was that Whitehall had, as usual, committed a *faux pas*; although the Soviets had broken off relations with the Polish Government, the Foreign Office had cabled him that the Soviet Ambassador, Mr Ivan Maisky, would also be arriving in Gibraltar on his way to Moscow in a Soviet plane during the afternoon and he and his party would like to spend the night in Government House. Mason-MacFarlane could hardly play host to both the Polish and the Soviet parties; indeed if they should meet under his roof it would produce a most embarrassing scene. The British Governor had no difficulty in choosing which of the two prospective guests he preferred. To those that he disapproved of, he could be very uncompromising. But he had a genuine and warm regard for Sikorski, while his feelings towards the USSR had been chilled during his stay in Moscow as head of the British Military Mission, and he had a particular dislike for Ivan Maisky.

Mason-MacFarlane therefore informed me that he intended to cable London that he could not put up the Soviet Ambassador after all, as the Governor's residence was full. He would suggest that Maisky's arrival should be postponed until breakfast time on the following morning, Sunday 4 July. Maisky could then fly straight on to Cairo, a few hours after arrival. A certain amount of subterfuge was obviously necessary, and arrangements were made with the Air Force Commanding Officer that Maisky's aircraft should leave for Cairo at 11 a.m. on the grounds that bad weather was anticipated later in the day. And so it happened. Maisky arrived at about 7 a.m. on Sunday morning, was met at the airfield and installed in the Governor's private rooms to have some rest. The Governor had breakfast with him and, as arranged, the Soviet Ambassador took off from Gibraltar at 11 a.m.'

After Maisky had left, that afternoon was devoted to a military parade for Sikorski during which he invested General Mason-MacFarlane and Admiral Sir Frederick Collins with the highest Polish decorations. Later Sikorski toured the Rock defences in the company of Sir James Grigg, the War Minister who had just arrived from the Middle East.

When next evening F/Lt Prchal phoned the Governor's residence, where Mason-MacFarlane was entertaining Sikorski and his entourage for dinner, to inform them that the take-off was set for 11 p.m., the whole party immediately left for the airfield. An additional passenger was going to travel on the plane. He was Jan Kazimierz Gralewski, a thirty-one-year-old courier from the Polish Underground Army, who operated under the name of Pancracy or Pankowski.

Gralewski reached Gibraltar on 23 June after he had clandestinely travelled from Warsaw since February. His journey took him first across Germany to Paris. After an unsuccessful attempt to get to Vichy, at the time the seat of unoccupied France's government, he had been directed to travel with a group of French smugglers to Pau, then across the Pyrenees to Spain. When he eventually arrived in a small Spanish port waiting for a boat to England or Africa, he was arrested, kept for a while in a local prison and then transferred to the internment camp in Miranda de Ebro. Released on the intervention of the British authorities, he continued via Madrid to Portugal, where he boarded a small steamer at Vila Franca in the Tagus estuary that was bound for Gibraltar.

Although in all British official documents he is listed as a colonel, it appears that he was only a simple soldier with the rank of a private (*Strzelec* – in Polish). According to the explanation provided by Major Łubienski during an interview in November 1992, to justify Gralewski's travel with the group of VIPs, the Polish authorities had upgraded him 'on paper' only.

In his private life Gralewski was a philosopher. After graduating from Warsaw University, he continued his studies in Paris and returned to Poland just two weeks before the outbreak of the war. He had a flair for speaking languages without an accent and his natural ability to get along with people made him an ideal courier. Although Gralewski's mission was under the control of the Polish Underground Army (*Armja Krajowa*), he worked in the Department of Foreign Affairs of the Polish Underground Government.

Gralewski was carrying an important report from General Rowecki, in a special code that could only be deciphered in London. It contained some very encouraging news for the Government-in-exile. Rowecki reported several spectacular attacks on prisons and convoys by the resistance units, and a particularly successful effort at Pinsk in eastern Poland. The action helped to release several hundred captured members of the

underground army and political detainees, without any casualties to their own ranks. Rowecki personally ordered the attack on the prison at Pinsk. Sadly he never got to know if his written report had reached his Chief. Five days before the Gibraltar accident, he was arrested by the *Gestapo*, taken to Sachsenhausen concentration camp and then executed in 1944.

Sikorski regarded Gralewski's immediate presence in London so important that he decided to take him along in his Liberator. Originally it was planned to bring Major Łubienski to England, as his mission in Gibraltar appeared to have been completed. Major Łubienski often remarked that this decision saved his life. For Gralewski it was a great surprise and an honour to be allowed to join Sikorski's party. In his diary, which was found on him when his body was washed ashore after the accident, Gralewski commented that he expected to be reprimanded by 'the older gentleman', meaning Sikorski, for having taken so long to reach Gibraltar (about five months).

Due to the lack of any central Underground Army archives in Poland, it was not possible to ascertain Gralewski's position in the Polish Army. Even his wife Alicja Iwanska, a writer, who had recently died in London, was not able to shed any light. A strict rule for all members of the

Royal Navy searching for the crash survivors of the Liberator.

resistance movement was not to discuss personal activities even with closest relatives, in order to prevent any details being dragged out by the *Gestapo* when captured. Gralewski was posthumously awarded the Polish Cross of Valour and the certificate dated 1947 bears the rank of lieutenant, most probably a posthumous promotion as well.

While Mason-MacFarlane and his staff took Sikorski's party directly to the aircraft, the two mysterious 'civilians' Mr Lock and W/T Pinter, who during their stay at Gibraltar were personally looked after by the head of the local Military Intelligence unit Lt-Col J.A. Codrington, were the only passengers to pass through the Air Despatch and Reception Unit. (Despite my appeal to the Defence Secretary of the past Conservative Government, information about their status in MI6 was refused, although it was announced at the time that access to wartime secrets had been made easier.) The duties of such units were not only to check arriving and departing aircraft for unauthorised passengers as well as the cargo for contraband, but also to provide a briefing on the use of parachutes, inflatable vests and other safety procedures. The lack of such instructions for the remaining passengers was later strongly criticised by the Court of Inquiry.

After a cordial farewell from the Governor of Gibraltar, Sikorski was the last person to board the Liberator through the rear hatch. The engines were started and the aircraft taxied to the west end of the runway for an engine run-up. Quite a large group of people watched it take off, climb in their opinion to about 100 feet and then, to everyone's horror, descend until the aircraft hit the sea. When everyone rushed in the direction of the crash, a Polish Air Force officer transiting through Gibraltar, screamed out in pain, 'Poland is lost'.

Fortunately a member of the rescue dinghy team, LAC Qualtrough, whose normal duties were that of a wireless mechanic, happened to arrive on the airfield. While waiting to cross the runway at the east end, he watched the Liberator take off and then sink down. He rushed to a dinghy that stood by on the beach, not far away. Five other servicemen soon joined him and another man operating the winch rapidly launched the dinghy. When about five minutes later they arrived at the scene of the crash, someone in the water hailed them. They pulled out a survivor wearing an inflated Mae West. He appeared to be conscious but he was unable to speak due to face injuries. Later it was established that the survivor was F/Lt Prchal.

As the searchlights installed on the top of the Rock began to illuminate the area where the Liberator ditched, the rescue crew continued to scout the sea and eventually they picked up a body in-between bits of wreckage. The person although not wearing a Mae West was floating, but unfortunately with the head under water. Soon the dinghy was joined by a small naval vessel and an RAF high-speed launch that was usually standing by at night outside the harbour at Commercial Anchorage. Within fifteen minutes, two more launches, both moored at the seaplane base on the western side of the peninsula, had joined the rescue party.

In the meantime, General Mason-MacFarlane rushed to the Control Tower to get in touch with the rescue launches by radio. When he was told that two survivors, one still conscious but the other hardly breathing, and two dead bodies were already lifted out of the water, he ordered the launch to proceed at once to the harbour. At the dockside, the identification soon revealed that the two dead men were General Sikorski and General Klimecki, while the person in the critical state, who died shortly after being picked out, was Brig. Whiteley. According to Major Łubienski, Sikorski was only partly dressed, his uniform jacket entangled in his feet and one of his shoes was off. On his head was a wound which appeared to have been inflicted by a sharp object. (From a letter from Major Łubienski dated 6 September 1992.)

F/Lt Prchal, the only survivor, was rushed immediately to the hospital. The two remaining launches continued to search the crash area until 4.20 a.m. and did eventually manage to recover the bodies of Col Cazalet still strapped to his seat and that of W/T Pinter, as well as thirty mailbags, some diplomatic papers and about 700 one-pound notes scattered among the debris.

The search was started again in the morning and was continued for four days. On 6 July the bodies of two crew members – W/O Zalberg, the navigator and Sgt Kelly, the flight engineer – were eventually reclaimed by divers from the submerged fuselage. On 7 July the remains of F/Sgt Gerrie, the WOP/AG, were retrieved from the bottom of the sea and on 8 July that of Polish officer, Col Marecki, partly eaten by fish. In the meantime, the Naval Dockyard began to salvage the crashed aircraft and many parts were brought ashore. Among the naval divers participating in the salvage operations was Lt 'Buster' Crabb. Many years later his death hit the headlines. His body was found floating in Portsmouth harbour after an attempt to spy on the steering gear of the Russian cruiser which brought Bulganin and Khrushchev for an official visit to England in 1955.

Unfortunately all salvage activities were stopped on 9 July when bad weather made the conditions at sea too treacherous.

Two crew members, S/Ldr Herring, 2nd pilot, and F/Sgt Hunter, WOP/AG, as well as three passengers – Mrs Lesniowska, General Sikorski's daughter, his secretary Kułakowski and the mysterious secret agent Mr Lock – were swallowed by the sea without a trace. In spite of great efforts by the Spanish divers, instructed by Mason-MacFarlane to find Mrs Lesniowka's body at all costs, it was never recovered. Stories circulated around Gibraltar that the divers, believing in a curse attached to touching a drowned woman's hair, had let her body slip away.

As soon as it was established that Sikorski was dead, General Mason-MacFarlane despatched a telegram to the British and to the Polish Government. The news was brought to Churchill by Sir Frank Roberts, at the time the Head of the Foreign Office Central Department. According to the recent revelation by Sir Frank, Churchill was deeply moved and wept over what he felt was a great personal loss. The Prime Minister would have been the last person wishing Sikorski dead. He held the General in great esteem and was well aware that with his departure, he had lost not only the strong man of Polish politics who could keep the nation united but also the sole Polish statesman capable of effectively dealing with Stalin.

On 6 July, *The Times* published Sikorski's obituary under the title *A Polish Patriot*. One paragraph was particularly touching:

'He was also a soldier of shining courage and great ability, proved on many fields which afterwards he developed in his books. Above all, he was man of honour. Since 1939 the tragedy of Poland has been written in Sikorski's face, lined with a sadness which never left him. His manner was friendly, reflective, and he had the strength of an equanimity which never surrendered to events. His mind was founded on faith in Polish recovery.'

PART IV

Three days after the accident, on 7 July, a Court of

Inquiry was convened at the Gibraltar Air Headquarters, to determine the cause of the crash. The Court was composed of the Presiding Officer G/Capt J.C. Elton from RAF Station Turnberry, and two members – W/Cdr A.W. Kay from HQ Coastal Command and S/Ldr D.M. Wellings from AHQ Gibraltar. Two additional members were acting as observers; one of them was W/Cdr S. Dudzinski from the Polish Air Force Inspectorate General who held a degree in engineering, the other, W/Cdr N.M.S. Russel, represented the Transport Command Headquarters.

The first person interviewed as a witness was thirty-one-year-old F/Lt Edward Maximilian Prchal. He was the captain of Mk II Liberator No. AL523. It was his fourth flight between the UK and Egypt. For wartime standards he was a highly experienced pilot with 3,500 hours to his credit, of which 360 were on Liberators. Trained as a pilot in the Czech Air Force as far back as 1929, upon leaving it in 1936 he flew for a Czech airline – Bata Company – on international services until 1939. When the Germans occupied Czechoslovakia, he escaped and first served with the French Air Force. In June 1940 he joined the RAF as a sergeant pilot. During the Battle of Britain, he destroyed a Dornier 17 and the same day, was himself shot down and was slightly wounded. In 1941 Prchal received his commission and after a spell in a night-fighter unit, was posted to 511 Squadron.

In his testimony to the Court of Inquiry which was given from his hospital bed, F/Lt Prchal described the events leading to the accident as follows (this quotation as well as all subsequent quotations come from the Public Record Office documentation A2/9234 – Proceedings of Court of Inquiry or Investigation – RAF Form 412):

'I received the "green" signal at 23.10 hrs and commenced to take off. At about 130 mph I was airborne. When I was about 150 feet I eased the control column forward to gather speed. My speed built up to 165 mph. I wanted to climb again so I attempted to pull back the control column but I could not do so. The control column was definitely locked. I told my second pilot over the inter-communication to check over the controls quickly. At this time the under-carriage was fully up and the flaps half-down, that is, normal take-off position. When I found I was unable to move the control column I put on trim in an endeavour to gain height but nothing happened. All this time I was pulling back on the control column but I could not move it backwards. I got no reply from the second pilot over the inter-communication and the aircraft was rapidly approaching the water. I then shouted out "crash landing" to the crew and closed the throttles. The aircraft immediately hit the water and I remember no more.'

Questioned by the investigating officers whether he was satisfied that the rudders, ailerons and elevators were functioning correctly once the aircraft became airborne, Prchal replied, 'Yes, definitely'.

During his testimony on 10 July, the Flying Control Officer at North Front, F/Lt Renalt Capes, a former Battle of Britain pilot with 7,000 flying hours to his credit, later a S/Ldr and in the post-war days a writer and a poet, described the Liberator's flight path at take-off:

'The aircraft became airborne at about No.12 flare which gave the pilot a take-off run of about 1,150 yards. The aircraft appeared to climb normally and had reached a height of about 30 feet when 100 yards past the Watch Tower. The aircraft then appeared to level off, flew for a short distance straight and level and then lost height steadily until it hit the sea. In my opinion all four engines were under full power until the aircraft crashed and there was no suggestion of a stall.'

On being questioned as to how he could follow the path of the aircraft so clearly on a moonless night, Capes replied, 'By the navigation lights'.

Other witnesses, such as Air Com. Simpson and AC1 Qualtrough stated that they had observed the aircraft reaching about 100 feet before it began to sink.

The first day of the proceedings was mainly devoted to interviewing various witnesses about the security arrangements at North Front Airfield. All arrangements appeared to be satisfactory and nothing was left to chance. But of particular interest were special precautions undertaken by the fitter in charge of the 511 Squadron maintenance unit stationed in Gibraltar, Sergeant Norman Moore. He was a specialist on Liberators as he had attended a technical course run by Consolidated Aircraft Corporation in California. Moore took extra steps to ensure the maximum possible security for Sikorski's plane. When the aircraft arrived, he instructed his second-in-command Corporal Davis to mount at once a guard from the 511 Squadron maintenance unit until

that airman was relieved by an Army sentry. Moore also insisted that one of his men would sleep at night in the aircraft near the rear entrance. Moreover, he provided a list of fitters who were permitted to enter the Liberator for servicing. Such strict security arrangements were unusual for the typical RAF practices at the time.

When late that evening Lt Łubienski, accompanied by Sikorski's secretary, wanted to collect from the Liberator the General's briefcase with medals which were going to be awarded next day, they found two Army sentries barring their way. After explaining the purpose of their visit, they were escorted to the rear hatch, which was opened by an RAF NCO. But the experience of LAC Titterington was different. Titterington, an equipment assistant from 27 ADRU, came to collect diplomatic bags in order to transfer them to a BOAC plane. During his two visits, the first one on the afternoon of 3 July at 5.50 p.m. and the second next morning at 7 a.m., he neither saw nor was challenged by a guard. The airman sleeping inside let him in because he knew who he was and what his duties were.

What had prompted Sgt Moore to such stringent arrangements will always remain an intriguing question. Łubienski, who was very familiar with the circumstances on the Rock, spoke very highly of Moore's security precautions. Was Moore concerned that someone with Communist sympathies within the RAF contingent in Gibraltar might try to sabotage Sikorski's plane? The fact that he had restricted the technical inspection to a small group of fitters whom he evidently trusted, suggests such a possibility.

The testimony by W/Cdr A.M. Stevens, the RAF North Front Chief Technical Officer, who conducted the examination of the salvaged aircraft parts as soon as they were recovered, revealed that there was no evidence of the control cable having been jammed inside the fuselage due to a loose piece of luggage or a mailbag. He had also carried out tests to see if pushing a rag hard against the Liberator's control cables would impede their travel. The test proved that it would have no effect. The rudder and the elevator locks were removed from the tail plane unit and despatched to the Royal Aircraft Establishment at Farnborough for a check by experts.

Stevens had further testified that the examination of the throttle pedestal showed the throttle levers to be in the nearly closed position. Both main ignition switches were found off. The flaps were comparatively undamaged and were approximately three-eighths down (normal position one-half or 50%). From the examination of the undercarriage it appears that it was fairly well up at the time of the impact with the water, as the locks, both up and down, were undamaged as well as the tyres and wheel fairings.

The only unexplained mystery was a mailbag originally stowed in the bomb bay. It was found by an Army sentry, lying close to the runway, about 400 yards from the take-off position.

Through which access hatch in the fuselage the bag had fallen out, was never determined by the Court of Inquiry. When recalled three days later for a further questioning, F/Lt Prchal told the Assessors that after he had finished engine run-up prior to take-off, he sent his flight engineer to inspect 'the inside door' (Prchal's expression) and the bomb door to see if they were properly closed. The 'inside door' was the entry point for the crew in the wooden floor on the bottom of the bomb bay on which freight was stowed. He could clearly recollect the flight engineer reporting everything in order. When questioned whether he had ever heard of a mailbag or any other article falling out while taxiing or in flight, he replied that he had not but a possibility always existed for an article that was not safely secured to drop out through the nose wheel aperture.

The Czech pilot was renowned for his strict adherence to procedures. His flight commander S/Ldr Sach maintained at the Inquiry:

'I have known him [Prchal] since he was posted to the squadron [511] in November 1942. His flying ability has been always outstanding and exceptional and he was never known to leave anything, no matter how slight, to chance. He exercises good discipline with his crew and his general bearing has at all times been of a high order.'

Sixteen days after the Court of Inquiry had been convened, the following conclusions were reached:

'The cause of the accident was, in the opinion of the Court, due to the aircraft becoming uncontrollable for reasons which cannot be established. The pilot, having eased the control column forward to build up speed after take-off, found that he was unable to move it at all, the elevator controls being virtually jammed somewhere in the system. It is impossible, from the evidence available and the examination of the wreckage, to offer any concrete reason as to why the elevator should have been jammed.'

Under 'Recommendations', the Report further stated:

'It is recommended that the provisions of K.R. & A.C.I. [King's Regulations and Air Council Instructions], para 703 'Securing of loose articles', should be strictly enforced. The mailbag, which was found on the runway after Liberator AL523 had taken off, had been stowed in the port forward bomb bay according to the information received from H.Q. M.E. In view of the evidence of 1st witness [F/Lt Prchal], however, the wooden door in the false floor to the bomb bay compartment must be presumed to have been closed, and, furthermore, had the bomb door itself been open, this would have been immediately apparent owing to the resulting draught. It is not possible, therefore, from the available evidence to explain how this bag came to be on the runway.'

However, Air Marshal Slessor, the C-in-C of Coastal Command, within whose sphere of authority the crash had taken place, RAF North Front being a Coastal Command Station, was not fully satisfied with the findings of the Court of Inquiry. Under pressure from Churchill, he ordered another hearing to be convened at Coastal Command Headquarters, starting on 3 August 1943.

At the proceedings, F/Lt Prchal, now having fully recovered from the shock and lacerations, was able to remember many more details of the cockpit drill prior to take-off, but he still could not throw any further light on why the elevator could have become stuck.

F/Lt Buck, from the Air Ministry Accident Investigation Branch, gave evidence on the final inspection of the wreckage:

'An examination of the pilot's flying controls was made. All sprockets and chains were subjected to a detailed examination. This examination showed no damage to the teeth or wells of the sprockets. An examination of the chains showed them to be in good condition, there being no signs of overriding or jamming on any of the links. Both chains were broken at the connecting link, but this was due to the impact of the crash. A complete examination of the control system showed no signs of any jamming previous to the crash.

An examination of the control locking mechanism showed that all locking pins were disengaged. There was no evidence to show that locks had been engaged at the moment of impact.'

During the proceedings, the Court of Inquiry visited RAF Station Lyneham where a test was conducted to explore the possibility of the flying controls becoming affected by raising the nose wheel. When the repeated tests indicated no connection whatsoever, the Court confirmed its original conclusions about being unable to explain the cause of the elevator jamming. By now the mystery of the crash was deeper than ever.

Air Marshal Slessor had finally accepted the finding of the Court but with a comment:

'I agree that there seems no reason for suspecting foul play of any sort, and the security arrangements at Gibraltar seem adequate. The fact remains, however, that the special sentry failed to notice an airman enter the aircraft and remove a mailbag, an omission which I consider should be the subject of disciplinary action. These guard duties on aircraft tend to become a mere form – I have myself frequently observed a sentry standing smartly at ease with his back to the aircraft he is supposed to be guarding.'

The inability of the Court of Inquiry to determine the cause of the crash and to explain how a mailbag which undoubtedly came from the crashed aircraft, could find its way onto the runway, had created great unease within the Air Ministry. Many arguments followed on how to announce the inconclusive report, whether by a press communiqué or by a statement in the House of Commons.

The proposed wording had been a subject of discussion between the Foreign Office and the Polish authorities who wished to drop any reference to the jammed controls. They argued that such an occurrence was unknown to the Liberators and that German propaganda might exploit it to its advantage. Nevertheless the first Liberator II to be delivered to the RAF, serial number AL503, only twenty production numbers earlier than the ill-fated Sikorski plane, crashed into San Diego Bay during the acceptance flight as a result of the elevator becoming jammed by a loose bolt. All on board were killed, including Consolidated Chief Test Pilot W. Wheatley.

Eventually under pressure from the Foreign Office, the Polish authorities dropped their objections and a statement was made in the House of

Liberator II AL504 which Churchill used on a trip to Moscow. This aircraft was missing on a flight from the Azores to Ottawa in March 1945.

Commons on 23 September 1942. In reply to Mr I. Thomas's question about the cause of the crash which had resulted in the death of General Sikorski and two members of the House, Captain Balfour, the Secretary for Air, stated:

'The findings of the Court of Inquiry and the observations of the officers whose duty is to review and comment on them reveal that this most regrettable accident was due to jamming of the elevator controls shortly after take-off, with the result that the aircraft became uncontrollable. After careful examination of all the available evidence, including that of the pilot, it has not been possible to determine how the jamming occurred, but it has been established that there was no sabotage. It is also clear that the captain of the aircraft, who is a pilot of great experience and exceptional ability, was in no way to blame. An officer of the Polish Air Force attended throughout the proceedings.'

To the House of Commons the death of the two MPs on active duty was a tragic loss. But to the Polish cause the departure of Lt-Col Victor Cazalet was a particularly crushing blow. A Conservative MP for Chippenham since 1924, Cazalet, at the time of the accident only forty-seven, was a keen sportsman. Educated at Eton and Oxford, he took part in World War I and won an MC. He travelled widely and his knowledge of Central Europe was unequalled among other MPs. This had led to him being offered the position of liaison officer with Sikorski in 1940. In 1941 he accompanied the General on a visit to the USSR. His book *I was with Sikorski in Russia*, published in 1942, is a first-hand account of the privation and degradation the Poles had suffered after they were deported to the outlandish parts of the Soviet Union following the Red Army occupation of eastern Poland in 1939. Cazalet was the chairman of the Parliamentary group known as the Friends of the Poles.

Brigadier J.P. Whiteley, the Conservative MP for Buckingham since 1937, also served in World War I and was severely wounded. At the outbreak of the last war, he had resumed active service and went through hellfire at Dunkirk.

As far as the British Government was concerned, the statement in the House of Commons appeared to have closed the case. Just prior to the parliamentary announcement, a copy of the Court of Inquiry Report had been forwarded by the Foreign Office to the Polish Ambassador at St James's Court, Count Edward Raczynski.

(Raczynski died in 1993 in England at the ripe age of 100.) It was the only copy ever received by the Polish authorities in London. The Report was accompanied by a letter from the Foreign Secretary, but signed on his behalf by Sir Frank Roberts. The letter stressed one point in particular, as quoted below:

'I have the honour to request that you will be so good as to communicate this document to the Polish Government for their confidential informations. I should be grateful if in doing so you would draw their particular attention to the fact that it is a secret document, that it should be only communicated to those officers whose duty it is to deal with such matters, and that its contents should not be disclosed by them either to other members of their Forces who have no duty in relation thereto, or to members of the public.'

The emphasis on such secrecy did not help to quell rumours still sweeping the Polish Armed Forces. Many believed that some clever means were used to engineer the accident without leaving any evidence of sabotage. The Polish authorities were far from satisfied with the results of the investigation and many internal discussions continued until the end of the war. At first the Court of Inquiry Report was studied by five senior officers from the Polish Air Force. In 1944 it was given to three lawyers from the Polish Ministry of Justice for a further analysis. Considering that the report, dealing to a large extent with the Liberator operating procedures, required intimate knowledge of such procedures and any new assessment also depended on a know-how of accident investigation, one must question such a course of action on the part of the Polish authorities. As expected the lawyers could not come to any conclusions as to whether the accident had been caused by sabotage. But it would have been like asking an accountant to diagnose a rare tropical disease. Surprisingly, no Polish Liberator pilot was ever consulted and, by then, quite a few had already amassed a considerable number of flying hours on that type of aircraft.

In February 1946, the Polish Air Force Headquarters in London tried to obtain a copy of the Court of Inquiry Report for the Historical and Archives Office of the Polish Army but the request was refused by the Air Ministry.

All official documents relating to the Sikorski crash were retained by the Air Ministry and later by the Ministry of Defence. The file was closed to the public for fifty years under the secrecy clause. It was eventually transferred to the Public Record Office on 15 December 1971 and was opened to general inspection on 2 January 1972, together with many restricted wartime files as a result of a change of rules at the time.

In 1958, the subject of securing the Court of Inquiry Report was again raised, this time by the Communist Government in Poland. The Air Ministry's reaction, one of a very few handwritten documents in the Public Record Office file on the Sikorski crash, is a 'Note of Action' by the Director Flight Safety, an Air Commodore. The Note reads:

'1. Between July and October 1958, there was considerable discussion by the Polish Government authorities, about this accident. To cut a long story short, there was a desire to see the actual proceedings of the Board of Inquiry, to settle for all time whether there could have been any sabotage, causing the Liberator to crash.

2. Because of Privilege & Precedent, this was obviously impossible. Finally, all questions were agreed as settled because Polish Officers, serving in the Royal Air Force, had both attended the Board of Inquiry, and others had subsequently seen the papers, they had been satisfied, and there could therefore be no reason to suppose that any vital or awkward information was being suppressed. There the matter was dropped.

3. This information was given by the then DFS for the record. It was deemed to be advisable in case the matter is again raised, following publication of an allegedly authentic book on espionage (*Spy Mysteries Unveiled* by Hinchley). The story there set out, talking about this crash, contains a mass of inaccuracies, and specifies sabotage.'

The Air Ministry official was right about the inaccuracies. In his book, Hinchley writes that he based his version of events on claims from General Lahousen, the chief of the sabotage section of the *Abwehr*, the German Military Secret Service. An *Abwehr* saboteur was supposed to sneak into North Front airfield and put sugar into the fuel tanks of the Sikorski Liberator, causing the engines to cut out just after take-off.

Although access to the Sikorski accident file had been emphatically refused by the Air Ministry to the Polish authorities or historical bodies on

the grounds of the fifty years secrecy clause, passages from the Court of Inquiry Report on the Gibraltar disaster were widely quoted, and in many cases verbatim, in the book *The Death of General Sikorski – Accident* by David Irving, published in 1967.

Finally the subject of the accident was raised again at an international symposium held by the London University School of Slavonic and East European Studies in September 1983, to commemorate the fortieth anniversary of Sikorski's death. The essay presented at the Symposium by Major Łubienski, ends with a following note: 'The mystery remains until today. Let us hope that one day we, or maybe our children, will be told what really happened in Gibraltar.'

PART V

But is the cause of the crash such an unsolvable mystery? The analysis of all available material on the Gibraltar disaster reveals certain weaknesses in the assessment of the facts by the Court of Inquiry. During the war investigations were generally short and mostly ad hoc proceedings. The Air Ministry Accident Investigation Branch (AIB) was not composed of highly experienced experts as is the case with the present Ministry of Transport Air Accident Investigation Branch. Officers serving on the Courts of Inquiry as Assessors were not specialists, but mostly senior men, often out of touch with the operating procedures of the latest wartime RAF aircraft. Moreover, in comparison with the present-day practices, the Gibraltar accident report was produced in a relatively short time – just a few weeks. In the past forty years, the AIB has usually taken between nine to eighteen months to finalise its findings. On the other hand, it must be appreciated that with the approaching invasion of North Africa, RAF manpower had to be directed to the most essential requirements.

After the crash various theories were propounded as to why the Liberator lost height and struck the sea. They must be carefully examined for their validity.

I   PILOT ERROR COMMITTED BY
     THE CAPTAIN

After the accident such a suggestion had been voiced by G/Capt G.A. Bolland, CBE, Station Commander of RAF North Front. Recently he has reiterated his view in a letter to the magazine

Aeroplane Monthly. Surprisingly, this theory was also supported by the Flight Commander of 511 Squadron, S/Ldr J.F. Sach. G/Capt Bolland claimed that while carrying out a take-off on a very dark night over the sea without a chance of seeing a horizon, F/Lt Prchal lifted his eyes off the instruments in an attempt to find a horizon, and finding none, cast his eyes down to the instrument panel, and at the same time, inadvertently eased off the control column forward so that the aircraft plunged into the sea.

Nevertheless at the Court of Inquiry, F/Lt Prchal stated that the conditions at take-off were perfect, visibility fifteen to twenty miles, and he was able to see the horizon clearly. He also stated that when he moved the control column forward he observed the nose going only slightly down.

Furthermore G/Capt Bolland's suggestion is contradicted by the fact that during the slow but steady descent – as clearly observed by F/Lt Capes – F/Lt Prchal called out 'crash landing', which was overheard on the Control Tower frequency. Moreover, just before the impact he shut the throttles and their actual position was later confirmed by a technical examination. F/Lt Prchal's actions indicate that he was fully aware it was impossible to arrest the sink. Had he inadvertently pushed the stick forward, he would have gone into the sea without calling on the radio or closing the throttles.

Unlike some wartime 'rogue' aircraft such as the B26 Marauder, P38 Lightning or P47 Thunderbolt, the Liberator was a very forgiving plane. It is unlikely that its handling characteristics could have contributed to the accident. My former colleague from KLM Royal Dutch Airlines Arthur Smith, a retired captain with 25,000 hours to his credit and a Coastal Command Liberator pilot, described the response of the controls:

'It is many years back and there were so many aircraft following the Liberator, however since I flew the Libs for more than two years, 1,250 hours, of which 300 hours were as an instructor, some impressions have remained. First, let me say the Lib was not a difficult aircraft, and had no markedly bad or even peculiar characteristics, so that once I ferried one, between two airfields, entirely solo. It handled very positively, of course more heavily than aircraft of today. As we always operated from fields without marginal runways, lift-off was smooth although with a heavy feel and the subsequent acceleration was slow. There was a standard trim setting for the elevator, with a

note in the engineer's book as to whether or not this setting should be adjusted. Once the gear was up, acceleration was positive and while I'm sure a small forward movement of the elevator control would have been necessary, I cannot remember the need for any large deflections. In the take-off stages, the elevator, although requiring more movement than a modern aircraft, was neither too sensitive, nor did it require more than a strong pull. I do not think it would be possible to overcorrect the aircraft easily. It was very stable.'

According to the take-off procedure as laid down in the Consolidated B24 Manual, there appears to be no discrepancy from the technique as used by F/Lt Prchal on the fateful night. The Manual states:

'The take-off speed increases up to 130 mph for a plane with full load. After leaving the ground the nose of the plane should be held down and the take-off course maintained until indicated airspeed reaches 135 mph. At this speed full control is available in the event of an outboard engine failure under average conditions.'

However the recommended take-off speed in the RAF Liberator Pilot's Notes was stipulated as 120 mph.

At the second hearing of the Court of Inquiry, F/Lt Prchal again insisted that he felt a distinct blocking of the elevator. When questioned why he let the speed exceed the usual figure, he explained: 'Normally I would allow my speed to build up to 155 mph but in this instance, as I could not pull the control column back, my speed built up to 165 mph before crashing.'

Trying to reach 155 mph, the recommended climb speed, soon after becoming airborne, must have been dictated by F/Lt Prchal's past experiences at Gibraltar. Due to the proximity of the Rock, wind shears and downdraughts could be frequently encountered and this called for an ample margin above the stall during the initial climb.

At the second sitting of the Court of Inquiry, S/Ldr Falk, Chief Test Pilot from the RAE at Farnborough, was called to give evidence. He had carried out take-off tests at various loads, including the maximum all-up weight. He stated that it would be possible for the Liberator to leave the ground with the controls locked but only if a speed of about 180 mph was reached. In his opinion, this would be unlikely to happen on the 1,530-yard-long runway at Gibraltar.

2 PILOT ERROR ON THE PART OF THE SECOND PILOT S/LDR HERRING

Many sources had pointed the finger at S/Ldr Herring because he was new to Liberators. He had only fifty hours on that type of aircraft and it was his first flight with F/Lt Prchal. On the other hand, he was a quite experienced and gifted pilot with 1,300 total hours and two 'exceptional' and one 'above average' flying assessments.

The technical staff from Consolidated Company in California believed that, due to Herring's lack of familiarity with the Liberator cockpit, instead of pulling the undercarriage handle up, he moved the autopilot lever to the 'on' position, thus making the controls feel very stiff. Nevertheless F/Lt Prchal testified that he himself lifted the undercarriage. Technical examination indicated the wheels to be almost fully retracted upon impact. As far as the autopilot making the controls feel very stiff, it must be stressed that all autopilots of that era were designed to be overcome with a moderate force. The Consolidated Flight Manual clearly states on page twenty-six under 'Special Instructions': 'Do not forget that the Automatic Pilot can be overpowered'. Another claim was that the flaps were prematurely lifted by S/Ldr Herring, causing the aircraft to sink. Herring, a pilot with a considerable experience on Spitfires, was supposed to have lifted the flaps instead of the undercarriage because the flap lever on the Spitfire was in the same position as the undercarriage lever on the Liberator.

3 LOSS OF TAKE-OFF PERFORMANCE DUE TO OVERLOADING

After the accident rumours began to sweep through Gibraltar that the Liberator had carried excessive baggage. Surprisingly there is no record of any attempt by the Court of Inquiry to cross-check the figures on the loadsheet submitted by the Middle East Transport Command Headquarters. Both ADCs to General Mason-MacFarlane, Major Quayle and F/Lt Perry, claimed after paying a visit to AL523 that they had never seen any Transport Command aircraft swamped with so many pieces of luggage and freight. David Irving in his book *Death of General Sikorski – Accident* produced quite voluminous second-order evidence of possible overloading.

Unfortunately as no information on the tare weight of Mk II Liberators operated by 511 Squadron was available, the loadsheet could not be analysed. Nevertheless, from the tests conducted by the Aircraft & Armament Experimental Establishment (A&AEE) at Boscombe Down between April and July 1942, it was possible to calculate the expected take-off run for the weight in question. Thus if the actual run was longer than calculated, it would be an evident indication that the aircraft was in fact overloaded. The A&AEE Report had been traced by the head of the Library and Information Service in the Defence Research Agency (formerly RAE and now DERA) at Farnborough. Although the A&AEE tests were carried out on the B24D, RAF designation Liberator Mk III, as far as aerodynamics and take-off power, the Liberator II was identical. The data from the A&AEE report were corrected for such factors as density, wind and runway surface relying on the take-off graphs from the Consolidated B24 Manual.

According to the loadsheet the all-up weight of AL523 was 54,600 lb. For that weight the A&AEE tests showed that the aircraft required 852 yards to become airborne in standard conditions (sea level, temp. + 15°C). However the tests were carried out using 110 mph take-off speed while F/Lt Prchal lifted the aircraft off the ground at 130 mph. Assuming a linear acceleration at that stage of his run, the extra distance amounted to 287 yards. Using the ambient temperature on the conservative side for a July night at Gibraltar at 25°C, the density correction increases the distance by sixty-seven yards and the asphalt surface by another nine yards, while the wind correction for 5 mph headwind reduces it by forty-nine yards. The final figure of the calculated take-off distance of 1,166 yards is very close to the actual distance of 1,150 yards as observed by two witnesses, Air Com. Simpson and F/Lt Capes. As they were standing only some 200 yards away from where the aircraft became airborne, they should have been able to judge the take-off distance reasonably accurately in relation to the runway lights. So there is no question of AL523 having been overloaded. In any case, later Liberator versions were permitted to take off with the weight as high as 65,000 lb and in some cases even up to 71,000 lb while relying on the same engine power.

What F/Lt Capes had observed about the aircraft's flight path is of special significance. His statement to the Court of Inquiry had been later reiterated on much the same lines in his article published on 20 April 1946 in the *Polish Daily*, a London-based newspaper. Capes recounted how he watched the take-off with great interest through the Control Tower window because it was a VIP flight. AL523's ground run looked no longer than one performed by any other heavily-laden Liberator. The initial climb appeared to be according to the usual practice, with a slight flattening out to accelerate shortly after the wheels had cleared the ground. He estimated that the aircraft went by at thirty feet when 100 yards past the Control Tower and then instead of continuing to climb, it suddenly levelled out. Capes intended to move away from the window but was stopped in his tracks after he noticed that the Liberator began to lose height. It seemed surprising because all engines sounded at full power and there was no backfiring. The descent was very slow but distinct. By now he became very apprehensive that the aircraft was heading for disaster. When it became apparent that the Liberator came down to only a foot or so above the water at some fifty yards after crossing the shore, Capes's hand went for the emergency button to alert the fire services. The alarm siren went off at the same time as the aircraft hit the sea.

Calculations from the take-off graphs show that at 100 yards past the Control Tower the Liberator should have reached thirty-seven feet. But as F/Lt Prchal eased the nose down to pick up speed, it would have accounted for a slightly lower altitude. It appears that up to this point the aircraft's progress was normal, denoting an unimpaired control response. It is very doubtful that the Liberator did eventually get to 150 feet as F/Lt Prchal claimed. The A&AEE tests indicate that at such an all-up weight six seconds were required to reach fifty feet, representing a rate of climb of 500 ft/min. It would therefore take eighteen seconds to gain 150 feet and the total flight lasted just over sixteen seconds.

It seems as if the 150 feet had been just a rough estimate on F/Lt Prchal's part rather than a clear-cut read-out from his altimeter. Pressure altimeters are known to show erroneous indications at lift-off. This is due to a rapid change of the angle of incidence that temporarily upsets the static system and the associated altitude fluctuations can often be seen on the flight recorder readings. In any case, F/Lt Prchal's attention at that stage was most likely tunnelled on the airspeed indicator rather than on the altimeter, the usual pilots' habit.

On the other hand, standing in the Control Tower about thirty feet high, F/Lt Capes was in a position to gauge the Liberator's height with reasonable accuracy as the aircraft passed him at his eye level. Furthermore he was a very experienced pilot as well as an air traffic controller, and witnessed many take-offs of Liberators at full load, as he mentioned in his article.

Whether the ill-fated AL523 had dropped down to only a foot or so above the sea shortly after crossing the shore as F/Lt Capes described in his article, looks questionable considering that the Liberator impacted 600 yards further on. But from the position where F/Lt Capes kept an eye on the descent, it would have been difficult to judge accurately at night. On the other hand, it was possible that the Liberator had initially come down close to the water level and the ground effect under the wings at 165 mph could have helped to keep it off the sea surface for a few seconds longer. Ground effect usually becomes noticeable at a height equal to half of the wingspan. In the case of the Liberator this would be about seventy feet.

Allowing six seconds for the climb and two seconds for the level stretch out of sixteen seconds of the ill-fated flight, leaves eight seconds for losing the thirty feet gained after the aircraft became airborne. It would represent a rate of descent of 225 ft/min and a glide path of about one degree. The very flat descent angle but much higher speed than at which normal ditching was performed, would have accounted for the extensive damage to the bottom of the fuselage.

In that respect, F/Lt Prchal's testimony about the angle of striking the sea seems surprising. He stated to the Court of Inquiry that it was between fifteen to twenty degrees. It was most likely only an impression from the aircraft violently pitching forward, after it hit the water.

The Liberator had ended up in three pieces on the bottom of the five to six fathom (nine to eleven metres) deep sea. The first portion to be lifted out of the water was the tail unit complete with the elevator, fins and rudders. It had sheared just forward of the tailplane's leading edge. The powerful wake generated by the fuselage on impact, could have helped in ripping the tail off as a complete unit. The next large piece recovered from the seabed was a section of the body forward of the bomb bays with the mainplane, the engines, and the nose section, with the underside completely demolished. Finally the fuselage shell from the rear bomb bay to the tail was retrieved from the seabed.

4   OUT-OF-LIMITS BALANCE AS A CONTRIBUTORY FACTOR TO THE CRASH

During the second hearing of the Court of Inquiry at Coastal Command Headquarters, F/Lt Prchal was extensively questioned about his take-off procedure. Nothing in his testimony indicated any special difficulties with the load distribution that could have upset the aircraft's centre of gravity. He claimed that it was the same as from Cairo with the exception of one additional passenger who had been placed near the centre of gravity. Moreover, during taxiing the plane felt well balanced on the wheels. On the other hand, S/Ldr Sach, Prchal's flight commander, testified that the analysis of the aircraft's loading indicated it to be on the tail-heavy side and if half flaps were used during take-off, this would account for the necessity to push the control column fairly well forward after take-off.

5   SABOTAGE

Several books cited sabotage as the reason for the crash. One previously mentioned, Hinchley's *Spy Mysteries Unveiled*, claimed that sugar had been deposited in the Liberator tanks by one of the German *Abwehr* V-men. This is supposed to have caused failure of all four engines. But in view of evidence produced at the Court of Inquiry, such a claim cannot be substantiated. The engines were deliberately closed by F/Lt Prchal once he could see that the crash was inevitable. Technical examination of the carburettors did not reveal any contamination by a foreign substance.

An even more complicated story can be found in *Canaris* by C.Whiting, a US Army colonel who had served with the OSS during World War II. He pointed a finger at Kim Philby, at the time of the accident the head of MI6 in Spain, for organising the sabotage but without explaining how it had been done.

The controversy over whether the accident could have been caused by foul play exploded in 1967 when a German playwright, Rolf Hochhut, tried to interest the English National Theatre in producing his play entitled *The Soldiers*. Relying more on rumours than substance and aware of the fact that English law did not allow suits for defamation of a dead person's character, Hochhut set out to crucify Churchill. The play alleged that the Prime Minister on the instigation of Lord Cherwell ordered Sikorski's liquidation and F/Lt

Prchal was involved in the plot. Originally the play was accepted by Kenneth Tynan, the Theatre's literary adviser, and rehearsals began. However as a result of many protests, Sir Laurence Olivier refused to produce the play and widespread polemics broke out within various sections of the public on the subject of artistic freedom. Eventually the allegations about the accident having been engineered by the British Secret Service were hotly disputed during a London Weekend Television programme *That Was The Week That Was* on 19 and 20 December 1968, hosted by David Frost.

The programme was produced on Winston Churchill's initiative, grandson of the wartime Prime Minister. He wished to expose the mischievous falsehood of Messrs Hochhut and Irving and the programme attracted considerable interest from the viewing public. Edward Prchal, especially flown from the United States for the occasion, Rolf Hochhut, David Irving, Carlos Thompson and Kenneth Tynan as well as Winston Churchill were amongst the participants. It was the only show during which the usually cool Sir David lost his temper when, after trying to pin down Hochhut about his 'unshakeable' evidence of Churchill's guilt, the German refused to substantiate his claim. Hochhut maintained that the evidence had been deposited for safekeeping in a Swiss bank and would only be revealed fifty years after the accident. It was supposed to have been a statement from a British Secret Service agent claiming to have taken part in the ill-fated Liberator's sabotage and to being able to produce proof to that effect. The fifty years have already passed and no such evidence has been made public.

The controversy over the play *The Soldiers* had triggered two books, published between 1967 and 1968. One was by David Irving, *Death of General Sikorski – Accident* and the other by an Argentine born actor/writer Carlos Thompson, entitled *The Assassination of Winston Churchill*. Both books contain a considerable amount of valuable material but are marred by the lack of scientific analysis and too many chair-borne inferences on the flying aspects of the crash. It seems regrettable that the authors did not seek advice from someone with flying or crash inquiry experience, such as for example the British Air Accident Investigation Branch, which by that time was recognised as one of the world's finest ensembles of experts.

Relying on the statement to the Court of Inquiry by Air Com. Simpson, that it took seventeen minutes from leaving the ramp to becoming airborne, which in his opinion was 'unusually long', some researchers claimed it had been done on purpose. It was to give someone a chance of sneaking on board and sabotaging the controls. Nevertheless the breakdown of the seventeen minutes indicates a normal time for piston engine operations. AL523 was standing 1,500 yards from the take-off position and taxiing alone would have consumed about half of that time. The run up of four engines, testing propellers as well as flaps and reading checklists could have easily accounted for the remaining time. The seventeen minutes represented an average departure time during my days of flying piston engine aircraft.

With the knives out for Sikorski from various quarters it seemed very probable that sabotage could have been the reason for AL523 striking the sea so shortly after take-off. However from the painstaking technical inspection of the wreckage it was evident that the flying controls had not been tampered with. In an interview with the *Sunday Express* in 1953, Prchal himself insisted that no way of sabotaging the aircraft, no matter how clever, could have led to the Liberator behaving in such a manner as that on take-off. The Czech pilot claimed: 'One might use explosives, timing or magnetic devices but trying to jam the elevator is out of the question.'

6   F/LT PRCHAL WAS INVOLVED IN A PLOT TO LIQUIDATE GENERAL SIKORSKI

A ludicrous myth still circulating about F/Lt Prchal having been involved in a plot to dispose of Sikorski must be exploded. How was it possible for F/Lt Prchal to come out alive from a sinking wreck while all other occupants lost their lives? This question still lingers on even fifty years after the accident. Unfortunately, it has led to speculations about his possible involvement in an underhanded game.

It cannot be said with any degree of certainty, but, in my opinion, F/Lt Prchal had escaped only with shock and minor injuries through having worn a full harness during take-off. He must have been the only person to do so in the Liberator. It is known from numerous accident investigations that pilots have often withstood crash impacts as high as 30 g without fatal injuries when protected by a full harness and in particular with the shoulder straps properly fastened.

According to the RAE Report Aero 1770 dated August 1942 on the tests carried out with models simulating the Liberator ditching characteristics, the aircraft would have been exposed to 6 to 8 g at a touch-down speed of 80 mph. Considering that AL523 had struck the water twice as fast, it can be expected for the deceleration to be more than double. Lap straps on the mounted sideways seats in the VIP compartment would have offered insufficient protection. The five passengers sitting on the floor in the bomb bay would have stood no chance whatsoever. They would have been thrown violently forward, resulting in instantaneous death.

As much as wearing a full harness had protected F/Lt Prchal from bad injuries, his knowledge of the evacuation procedures by heart had helped him save his life. In order for F/Lt Prchal to leave the cockpit of the sinking wreck, the entire wing and the nose section must have remained afloat for some time. Although the cockpit was found to be badly damaged, it could have happened while that section of the aircraft fell on the seabed or during the salvage operation. Such an opinion was expressed by the technical experts at the Court of Inquiry.

LAC Howes, an electrician from RAF Station North Front, reported his observations about the time it took the aircraft to sink:

'I was coming out of my billet, which is situated at the extreme of the Frontier Road about 100 yards from the eastern end of the runway, when I saw a Liberator taking off from west to east. I turned to go to the lavatory and as I did so I heard the engines cut. A second or two later I heard a loud crash and immediately started to run to the beach to see what had happened. I could see the aircraft floating in the water and immediately ran to the rescue dinghy, which I helped to launch. As we were rowing towards the aircraft I saw it sink. I estimate that about six to eight minutes elapsed between the time I heard the crash and the aircraft sank.'

Whether the Liberator had actually floated as long as LAC Howes claimed is open to discussion. Another member of the rescue team testified that they had reached the wreck in about five minutes. In any case, even two or three minutes would have been enough for F/Lt Prchal to perform certain actions dictated by the instinct of self-preservation. In that short time, he must have undone his harness and jumped across the cockpit to the second pilot position in order to cut off the master electrical switch. This would have been a normal pilot's reaction when he began to smell petrol fumes but he would have only been able to get at that specific panel on the cockpit starboard side if his second pilot was not in the way. Then F/Lt Prchal must have grabbed his Mae West and made for the escape hatch located in the roof behind the two pilots' seats. He would have had to pull a handle down and force the hatch inwards, requiring quite an effort on his part considering his injuries. Then he would have had to heave himself up on to the top of the wing. Once outside he would have had to put his Mae West on and fasten it as well as inflate it, all performed in the dark. To be sure of not being sucked in by a whirl from the sinking wreck, he must have decided to make for the wingtip.

That last action did not escape unobserved. It was reported by Douglas Martin, a radio operator from the Special Operations Executive, a secret organisation set up during the war to help various underground movements in occupied Europe. Martin recounted that on the night of the accident he was on duty on an observation post on the Rock. At a certain moment he could hear the roar of the engines and a plane came in sight flying out to sea. He said: 'It was a rather large plane and it hadn't really any great height. Then in a matter of seconds it started to drop down and within a few moments it landed on its belly. It looked more like an emergency landing at high speed.'

He wanted to inform the airport authorities at once and he rushed to his radio set. But then he realised that he could not describe exactly where the crash had taken place. As he clambered back to his little plateau close to the top of the Rock, he saw that the plane had nearly sunk and that on one wing there was something that looked like a man. Martin could not work out how the man got there or how he came out of the floating wreck. Then the man walked along the wing to the tip. He seemed sure of himself, holding himself quite upright.

A similar observation had been made from the Spanish side by the Italian Air Attaché. However, in his last version as presented in a recent Polish television programme, he insisted that he had seen several people leaving the sinking aircraft, claiming them to be British commandos who had perpetrated an act of sabotage.

Unfortunately F/Lt Prchal's testimony about certain of his actions during the crash appears to differ from facts. When questioned by the Assessors as to whether he wore a Mae West during take-off, he explained: 'No. I had my Mae West behind my back where I normally carry it.'

When Major Łubienski visited F/Lt Prchal in hospital a few days after the accident and asked him about having been found in the water with his Mae West inflated, F/Lt Prchal insisted that he had never put it on. Yet Major Łubienski clearly recollects that in the presence of General Mason-MacFarlane, he had himself undone all the fasteners of F/Lt Prchal's Mae West when the Czech pilot was brought ashore. (From a letter from Major Łubienski dated 23 September 1992.)

It must have been the same with the aircraft's master switch on the co-pilot's Auxiliary Switch Panel. By pulling down the master switch bar protected by a plastic cover and located just above the magneto switches, it was possible to short the primaries of all magnetos and, at the same time, break the battery circuit of the main electrical system preventing a short circuit or spark. But F/Lt Prchal insisted that he could not have done it because he was not in a position to reach the master switch.

When further questioned as to whether he thought that the second pilot could have taken such safety action, perhaps a fraction of a second before impact, F/Lt Prchal was unable to comment. But he was sure that the engines were running perfectly until he closed the throttles. It is unlikely that in the last moments before impact, S/Ldr Herring could have easily put his fingers on the master switch in a dark cockpit because he was new to the Liberators.

According to the pathologist's opinion, S/Ldr Herring had been most likely flung forward upon impact through the windscreen, instantly losing consciousness. As a result, his lungs would not absorb water and by floating on the surface, the strong southerly current would have quickly swept him away and he finally drowned. It is why his body and the other victims suffering from a similar fate have never been found. The likely reason for S/Ldr Herring having been catapulted out of the cockpit was that he had not fastened his harness and in particular, the shoulder straps. According to F/Lt Prchal's testimony, Herring got out of his seat just before the engine run-up to let the flight engineer watch the instruments and test the magnetos. Upon returning, he was asked to read the checklist and probably did not have time or did not bother to put his harness on fully or even partly. It appears as if the rest of the crew were also not properly strapped in, hence nobody had survived. During the war, wearing a harness for take-off or landing was not as widespread a practice as it is in civil aviation today.

Unfortunately F/Lt Prchal's successful escape from the sinking wreck had led to speculations that he was prepared for ditching as a result of his involvement in a plot to kill Sikorski. Such insinuations, as they were advanced in the play *The Soldiers* and echoed by some researchers, are ridiculous. No pilot is ready to commit suicide. Especially when it comes to putting down an aircraft on the sea with little chance of coming out alive. Arthur Smith commented about it: 'I can't verify the "floating ability" of a Liberator but I know that few of us had any confidence of surviving it more than a few minutes, if it did not break up in two on impact with the water.'

Ditching tests carried out with disastrous results by Consolidated at Langley in 1944, had clearly confirmed the pilots' fears.

The fact that F/Lt Prchal had performed ditching actions by the book, yet could not recollect any of them, may appear to be odd. But it is known that shock inducing temporary post-concussive retrograde amnesia does not necessarily affect one's mental faculties. In fact, it often enhances them.

The best illustration comes from an incident that took place in the world of sports. During a ski race at Megève in 1975, Konrad Bartelski, for many years Britain's No. 1 downhiller, badly crashed and was taken to hospital in a helicopter. Until today, he cannot remember anything of the race or of the flight. But in his book *The Autobiography Of A Skier*, published by Collins, he writes about brain reaction in such circumstances:

'One of the most peculiar aspects of the crash was that, although I was unconscious until about six o'clock [the accident took place at about one o'clock], I spent the time before that translating for Dieter [Austrian trainer who accompanied Konrad to the hospital] and the medical staff. Dieter spoke no French and they no English, so I, with my mind not registering on the conscious level at all, apparently served as an interpreter!'

Surprisingly, from the several languages Konrad spoke fluently, French happened to be his weakest. Yet in his oblivious condition he found no difficulty in conducting conversation in two languages. F/Lt Prchal's actions show a similar trend, the shock shifting his brain into a higher gear in order to save his life, even if he was not able to recollect anything later. One of the indications of his state of mind at the time was his

mumbling to his rescuers in Czech when he was brought on board the dinghy. After the crash he spent not several hours but three days lying semiconscious in hospital as a result of the shock.

Medical examination of the bodies recovered from the sea revealed that death occurred from injuries rather than from drowning. S/Ldr Canning, a senior medical officer at RAF Station North Front, reported that all the bodies showed head injuries and multiple injuries, the degree of violence in his opinion suggesting that the time of the death approximated the time of the accident.

It is known that from the passengers sitting in the VIP compartment, Lt-Col Cazalet was the only one to adhere to the safety instructions. While travelling to the airport on the night of the accident with the ADC to General Mason-MacFarlane, F/Lt Perry, Lt-Col Cazalet lamented how shocked he was by the careless attitude of the crew and his fellow passengers who never bothered to put the seat belts on. When found on the seabed, he was still strapped to his seat, with the parachute harness on and wearing a Mae West, which was not inflated.

There are definite indications that all passengers, in spite of not having passed through the ADRU, were issued with inflatable vests. F/Lt Postgate from RAF New Camp at Gibraltar, who was supervising the salvage operation, reported that he had picked up three to four Mae Wests in good condition, floating among the wreckage. But the regulations did not stipulate that the crew or passengers had to put on a Mae West for take-off and there was a good reason for keeping them off. With a scorching temperature inside the aircraft after standing for over twenty-four hours on a hot tarmac, wearing a piece of rubberised cloth would have been most uncomfortable.

7   CONTROL LOCKS PROBLEMS

An examination of the elevator and rudder locking assembly carried out by scientific experts from the Royal Aircraft Establishment at Farnborough had clearly discounted any possibility of the locks having 'snapped back' in the air while the controls happened to come momentarily into a neutral position. A fifty-year-old report traced in the RAE archives by the Registrar of the Defence Research Agency, is an indication of the considerable efforts on the part of the British authorities to ascertain the cause of the crash. It is contrary to the accusations by many researchers or wartime Polish Government officials.

PART VI

If the accident had not been precipitated by pilot error or sabotage, only an object that had somehow lodged itself in the controls could have caused the symptoms of the Liberator's peculiar behaviour after lift-off. It would not have been the only accident due to the same cause in the history of aviation.

On 8 September 1970, a DC8-63F from Trans International Airlines crashed at J.F. Kennedy Airport with a loss of eleven lives, only a few seconds after leaving the ground. An eyewitness observed that the aircraft looked out of control the moment it became airborne. The cause was eventually traced to a piece of tar, which got stuck between the elevator and the horizontal stabiliser jamming the controls in an up deflection. The piece of tar had been probably thrown up by the wash from a wide-body jet or when the pilot put on power for take-off.

The Gibraltar Court of Inquiry took into consideration only two openings in the fuselage through which an object could have dropped out – the rear hatch, used for boarding passengers and the port bomb bay, through which crew entered the aircraft. F/Lt Prchal added a third possibility – the nose wheel aperture.

But the chances of the rear hatch not having been properly shut were extremely remote. The task of ensuring that it was firmly locked lay with the ground mechanics once all VIPs had boarded the Liberator. The mechanics would have to first retract a small ladder before closing the hatch. G/Capt Bolland, Station Commander of

The sliding bomb doors on the Liberator, used as an entry point for the crew. On the Transport Command version with a wooden floor for stowing freight, 'the inside door' was installed to allow the crew to get in.

North Field, who was present when the aircraft left the parking ramp for the take-off position, when questioned by the Court of Inquiry as to whether he saw if the rear hatch was shut, replied: 'No, but I am convinced I should have noticed if it had not been.'

There was even less possibility of the roller-type blinds enclosing the four bomb bays having been left partly open. The blinds, which followed the curvature of the fuselage along special guide rails, were driven on Mk II Liberators, by an electric motor. Later models used hydraulics. On the 511 Squadron aircraft that were employed purely for transport duties, certain changes had been made. To prevent inadvertent operation, the electrical system was disconnected from the starboard bomb bays. While the mechanical linkage had been made inoperative on the rear port bay, the front port bomb door could be still electrically lifted, to allow the crew to get in. The roller blinds were of light construction, and as a result, wooden floors were fitted in all bomb bays. In the front port bay, a door was added as an entry point. Freight and mail were carried in the front bays while the rear bays were used for passengers who sat on a mattress without any seat belts. On the Liberators employed for ferry services or for transporting VIPs, a platform was constructed just behind the cockpit bulkhead to hold six passenger seats with seat belts. Take-off drill included a check by the flight engineer to ensure that the bomb bay blinds or the door in the floor were properly shut. On the night of 4 July 1943, it was unlikely that this procedure had not been strictly adhered to. F/Lt Prchal, a meticulous pilot, realising that there were several VIPs on board, had made doubly sure by insisting that the flight engineer reported to him a visual inspection of the bomb bay blinds and the entry door. He confirmed this at the second hearing of the Court of Inquiry: 'I then sent my flight engineer to the bomb bay to switch the hydraulic booster pump on, check the petrol cocks to ensure they were fully open, and to ensure that the bomb doors were closed. The flight engineer reported that all was in order.'

It would have been easy to notice if the doors were not properly shut because the light in the bomb bay compartment was always left on. It also does not look likely that during take-off a mailbag could have dropped out through an aperture in the nose wheel bay. Loose objects are inclined to drift backwards while aircraft accelerate and at the same time, the airflow around the nose wheel

The nose wheel aperture of the Liberator. On later models it was used as an entry point for the navigator.

The side-hatch lock is of a simple mechanical construction. It can be seen from the photograph that it could be left not properly locked without anyone noticing it. (Howard Levy)

The side-hatch open and locked in the up position. In the top centre of the hatch is the latch used to lock the hatch either in an up or a down position. (Howard Levy)

would tend to push any object in, rather than suck it out.

If a mailbag had not fallen out through either of the two entry points or the nose wheel opening, could there have been another way? In my opinion, it was the one that, surprisingly, the Court of Inquiry had never taken into consideration – the side-hatches. Their purpose was the operation of beam machine-guns. With the hatches in a closed position, the machine-guns were usually stowed to the side in the direction of the nose. But on the 511 Squadron aircraft, in order to improve the load-carrying capability, no beam guns were fitted. With the flights between the UK and Gibraltar operated outside the range of the German fighters, the only armament retained were four light machine-guns in the rear turret. As a result, the area around the side-hatches was unobstructed.

Photo of the wartime mail bag from which the size of the bag was estimated. (Post Office Archives)

In order to assess the feasibility of my theory on the elevator jamming, I paid a visit to the Aerospace Museum at RAF Cosford near Wolverhampton. The staff were most cooperative and I was provided with a technical guide on the Liberators, Mr G.J. Hill, a founder member of the Aerospace Museum Society, who spent part of his life working on that rare exhibit.

Mr Hill explained that the Liberator on display in the Aerospace Museum was a later version, built in 1944 and differed in minor details from the aircraft involved in the Gibraltar crash. On the Museum model, the metal side-hatches were replaced by transparent plastic panels, to allow the public to look inside.

As a result of my visit, a probable chain of events leading to the Gibraltar tragedy emerged. This started with two visits of an airman from the 27 ADRU who was instructed to transfer diplomatic mail to a BOAC plane. Evidently after searching the front left bomb bay, he did not

secure all bags properly. As some were only partly filled, perhaps he thought it was safe to just leave them lying on the top of the pile. At the same time, there are grounds to believe that the side-hatches were used for ventilation during the ground stop at Gibraltar.

The hatches were hinged at the top and could be lifted upwards and locked in the open position.

With the high temperatures prevailing in July at Gibraltar, the fitters working inside the Liberator, or perhaps the airman who stayed the night on guard duty could have opened the hatches for cooling. With the rear entry and the bomb bay door closed for security reasons, it would have been the only way to get some fresh air in.

The side-hatch lock is of a simple mechanical construction (see photograph at top right of page 48). It could have been left either undone or not properly fastened, when the hatches were brought down. The passengers, boarding the aircraft

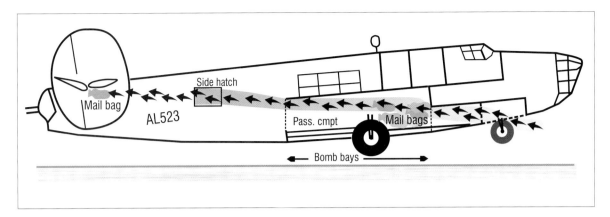

Diagram showing strong airflow through the fuselage with a side-hatch open at lift-off.

through the rear, would have been unlikely to notice any problem with the hatch, especially in the darkness. The flight engineer's inspection did not include the area past the bomb bay. Normally, an unfastened hatch would not have presented any danger, only a temporary nuisance.

The hatch, because of its heavy construction, could have been easily sent swinging up and down on the hinges through inertia, when the aircraft began to 'ride' the runway bumps. Arthur Smith recounts his experience of the Liberator's behaviour in such circumstances: 'When the runway was

Unfortunately in the path of the flying bag lay the horizontal control surfaces

Rearward view from the side-hatch. Horizontal fin is only three metres (or 11 feet) away.

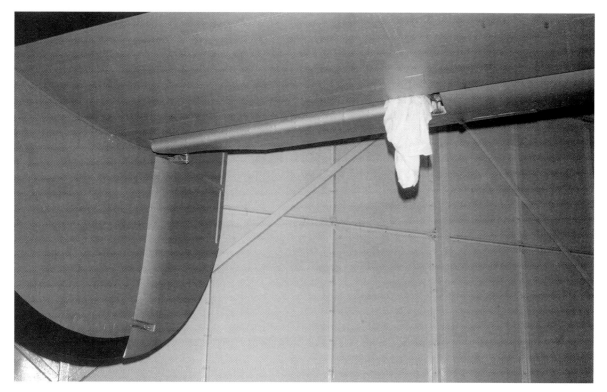

An old shirt was used as a substitute for a wartime mail bag during the visit to the Aerospace Museum at Cosford. The photograph shows how easily a mail bag could have slipped into the opening between the elevator and the horizontal stabiliser. The size of the opening between the elevator and the stabiliser on the photograph represents the actual situation at the ill-fated lift-off.

bad, one could feel the oleo legs thump.'

It is known that the surface at Gibraltar was in a poor state, due to the high frequency of traffic not allowing time for repairs.

The first mailbag that was found near the runway, not far away from the take-off position, must have dropped out early during the take-off run when the airspeed was still low. Then, as a result of a clockwise wash from the propellers, it was blown to the left side of the runway. At the Court of Inquiry, Gunner Miller from the 3rd Light Anti-Aircraft Regiment, Royal Artillery stated:

'I was on duty at my gun post which is sited on the north side of the runway about 400 yards from the west end, when at about 01.40B hours on July 5th I saw an object lying on the runway close by. On investigation, I found it to be a mailbag weighing about fifteen pounds. As soon as my duty was finished at 02.00B hours I took the bag to Flying Control and handed it to the officer on duty.'

A check on a bundle of letters weighing fifteen pounds indicated that it would only fill a wartime mailbag to about a quarter of its capacity. The size of the bag, approximately two by four feet, was determined from the photographs provided by the Post Office Archives (see page 49). Such an under-loaded, yet quite large bag could have been easily whipped up and blown out by the surge of air, when the hatch went momentarily up through a jolt from the runway bumps.

The second bag must have fallen out just as F/Lt Prchal lifted the aircraft off the ground. Normally when operating from a large airfield, no excessive rotation was required. However, the short runway at Gibraltar called for a positive stick deflection once red lights marking the end denoted that there was only a few hundred yards to go. It was a procedure F/Lt Prchal must have followed on many previous occasions. At the second hearing of the Court of Inquiry on 3 August, he made it evident to the assessors:

A closer view of the gap between the horizontal stabiliser and the elevator.

'First of all I had to pull the aircraft off the runway by a considerable movement of the control column backwards.'

Such a forcible manoeuvre could have easily sent an unfastened side-hatch upwards and it could have stayed momentarily open. As the door of the nose wheel bay would have remained open during lift-off, and it was not screened from the rest of the aircraft, as there were no tight dividing bulkheads, the resultant rush of air could have been extremely strong. Even without open hatches, wartime planes were draughty, in particular, the Liberator. The navigators complained about having to pin all their papers down otherwise they were blown into the bomb bay. When side-hatches were open in the air for action, waist gunners always felt exposed to a swoosh of cold air.

With the airspeed reaching 130 mph just after lift-off, a 'gale' would have swept through the fuselage. Especially with the high nose-up attitude at that moment, air would have been scooped into the nose wheel bay. The 'whirlwind' across the aircraft could have been further accentuated by venturi effect when passing between the platform on which the passenger seats were affixed and the bomb bays where the mailbags were stowed. This could have ejected the second bag through the momentarily open side-hatch. Although the Court of Inquiry claimed that F/Lt Prchal should have felt a draught if any access hatches were open, it would have been of a short duration and anyway, he was shielded by the cockpit floor.

Unfortunately, in the path of the flying bag lay the horizontal control surfaces, only three metres (eleven feet) away from the side-hatch. At lift-off, the elevator would have been deflected upwards leaving a gap between the stabiliser and the elevator's leading edge, which was large enough for a loose end of the mailbag to wedge in.

During my visit to the Aerospace Museum it was not possible to procure a proper wartime mailbag. Instead an old shirt used for cleaning the Liberator came in handy as a substitute. The photograph clearly indicates how easily a bag could have slipped into the opening between stabiliser and the elevator. The size of the opening on the photograph represents the actual situation during the ill-fated lift-off. The deflection of the elevator was performed by 'the Liberator expert', Captain Smith.

Once F/Lt Prchal had pushed the nose down in order to pick up speed, the edge of the bag would

General Sikorski's jacket and one shoe recovered from the wreckage. Due to high temperature inside the aircraft, it is likely that the General removed his coat and the shoes after entering it.

have got clamped, deadlocking the elevator. But a second or so later the bag must have unfolded and begun to flap in the airstream. As a result, flutter was transmitted to the control column via the cables. Ten years later when Prchal was able to recollect more details of the crash, he stated in an interview with the *Polish Daily* that he could feel strong shudder the moment the elevator became jammed.

With easing the control column only slightly forward, the Liberator should have continued to climb even if marginally. But it began to sink. It must have been a result of the flapping bag acting as a downward deflected elevator and the associated drag would have sent the aircraft into shallow descent. Moreover, the disturbed airflow over the elevator would have rendered the trim tab ineffective. No wonder Prchal could not feel any response, although in such circumstances it should have been quite pronounced. At the same time the resultant drag must have pulled the aircraft to one side, causing the Liberator to veer from the centre line of the runway as much as eight degrees to the right before crashing. This points to a probability of the bag having been flung out through the starboard hatch and having got stuck near the vertical fin.

What the best-placed eyewitness, F/Lt Capes, had observed appears to concur with the suggested chain of events. When the aircraft levelled out on passing the Control Tower, this must have been a result of the bag deadlocking the elevator. The

subsequent descent, a second or so later, had been caused by the bag unleashing its full muscle when it had fully unfolded, sending the Liberator to its doom. In spite of F/Lt Prchal's desperate effort to pull the deadlocked control column back, the aircraft continued to lose height, and as F/Lt Capes kept watching it with apprehension, his hand had gone for the alarm button.

Unfortunately, the Court of Inquiry had been misled by F/Lt Buck's testimony that the controls were not fouled in any way. He attended the hearing on 5 August at Coastal Command Headquarters, on behalf of the Air Ministry Accident Investigation Branch by special arrangement with the AIB Chief Inspector Air Com. Vernon Brown. F/Lt Buck stated at the time: 'The elevator and rudder control surfaces and hinge lines were particularly examined for jamming by some external body. There was no evidence of this having occurred.'

This is contrary to the statement made by W/Cdr Stevens from the Gibraltar Air Headquarters, who in the past had participated in numerous accident investigations as a technical expert. During the first hearing he reported as follows:

'I am the Chief Technical Officer at Gibraltar and I was present during the salvage operations of Liberator AL523. The first portion of the aeroplane to be lifted out of the water was the tail unit complete with elevators, fins and rudders. This had broken off just forward of the leading edge of the tail plane. I first inspected the elevator trimming tabs, which I

The ceremonial procession at Gibraltar. The coffin of General Sikorski is taken to the Polish destroyer Orkan, *in which it was brought to England for burial at the Polish Air Force Cemetery in Nottingham. The Catholic Bishop of Gibraltar, the Rt Rev. R. J. Fitzgerald, walks in front of the gun-carriage bearing the coffin.*

found to be almost in the neutral position. The elevators were free to move except for some damage on one end to the skin which prevented total movement up and down.'

Such damage would have been unlikely to be caused directly by impact. Most probably it had been inflicted when the mailbag was wrenched out of its clamped position upon striking the sea, or by F/Lt Prchal trying to force the elevator with the wedged-in bag. As the elevator's construction was only a metal frame covered by fabric, it was far from sturdy.

Nevertheless, some journalists persist in claiming that the 'real secret' about the cause of the crash will soon be revealed when certain papers kept in custody in a Swiss bank are released in the near future. I doubt that any new revelations could appreciably change the picture of events on that fateful night. The report of the Court of Inquiry contains sufficient evidence to support the theory of a mailbag having jammed the elevator. This appears to be the only feasible explanation for that particular flight path of sixteen seconds duration from lift-off to impact. A point to bear in mind is that if one mailbag had been found to have fallen overboard, another bag could have easily followed. According to the evidence gathered at the two sittings of the Court of Inquiry, neither sabotage nor pilot error could have accounted for such a pattern of the aircraft's behaviour.

An unfortunate chain of minor omissions, which had started with sorting out the mailbags without securing them back safely, then opening the side-hatch without making sure that the lock was fastened before take-off, may appear insufficiently convincing to have precipitated a tragedy of such historical magnitude as the Gibraltar crash. But a similar minor contributory factor – an improperly shut cargo door on a Turkish Airlines DC10 – later precipitated a disaster of equal significance but with a much higher toll of lives.

One cannot help wondering what sort of letters the mailbag contained, to bring such wrath on General Sikorski. This will remain a secret for ever. The fatal bag, like the bodies of several unfortunate victims, had been irretrievably swallowed by the sea.

Has the crash changed the course of political developments as far as Poland is concerned? Historians vary in their opinions. But one point is clear. The removal of a strong hand at the helm during the most critical stage of the war for the Polish nation eventually led to catastrophic consequences.

The Polish Underground Army, after preparing several years for uprising, stormed out on to the streets of Warsaw to fight the Germans once the Red Army began to close on the other side of the River Vistula that cuts the city in two. But at the end of the day it had proved a disastrous action. Without Sikorski, the Polish Government was incapable of averting Warsaw's final destruction. The Soviets, after encouraging the Resistance Movement over the radio to strike against the Germans, stood by and watched the inhabitants of the beleaguered city being bled to death. At no time did the Soviets try to help the Poles. The Allied leaders could not persuade Stalin to lift his hand. He regarded the Warsaw Rising as a 'misadventure' of right wing elements.

But it was not the end of the Soviet despot's sly game. The aircraft bringing air supplies from the West to Warsaw were not allowed to land on Russian soil for refuelling, considerably reducing their load-carrying capacity. Prof. R. Service in his article *Unlocking Moscow's War Secrets* which appeared in the *Daily Mail* on 8 July 1992, called this game one of the most cynical and shameful pieces of manipulation in the whole war.

It is no secret that Sikorski's successor Mikołajczyk did not measure up to the General's statesmanship or political foresight. But could Sikorski have stood up better to Stalin's perfidious and hypocritical designs once the Red Army rapidly began to gain ground in eastern Europe? It is a difficult question to answer, but at least Sikorski had more experience in dealing with the Russian despot.

The account of the Gibraltar tragedy cannot be closed without mentioning F/Lt Prchal's subsequent fate. Once he had recovered from injuries, he continued his duties with 511 Squadron, flying VIPs. After the war, he returned to Czechoslovakia and in 1946, he joined the national airline as a senior captain. But finding the post-war political climate in his country unpalatable, he escaped with his family to England in a stolen Dakota and landed at RAF Manston. He asked for political asylum and it was granted. Unfortunately, at the time, flying jobs in England were scarce. A year later he emigrated to the USA and taught Czech at a US Army Language School. When he died in 1984, his wish was to be buried in England where he spent several happy years. One part of his ashes was scattered over the Channel, the scene of his many dogfights during the Battle of Britain, another was buried at Brookwood Military Cemetery.

PART VII

Although more than five decades have already passed since the Gibraltar tragedy, new theories about the cause of the crash still continue to emerge.

After this chapter had been completed, a sensational revelation appeared in the memoirs of Col K. Iranek-Osmecki, published in Poland in 1998. The book was written many years earlier but but it was only recently edited for publication by Col Osmecki's son, Jerzy. The memoirs describe the Colonel's wartime experiences during his two visits as an emissary of the Polish Government-in-exile in London to the underground army in Poland.

In the postscript to the book written by the son, a new version of events is presented of how the Liberator of Gen. Sikorski was supposed to have been sabotaged during the ground stop in Cairo, prior to flying the General back to England via Gibraltar. This was arranged or was carried out by an intelligence agent, Lt Szarkiewicz, formerly Szapiro, a Pole of Jewish descent.

Apparently Szarkiewicz, who stayed in England after the war, and owned a cinema in Kilburn, confessed on his deathbed to Col Osmecki (at the time the director of the Polish National Treasury in London) that he was responsible for Gen. Sikorski's accident.

From the description in the postscript, Szarkiewicz appears to have been a personality of contrasts, a James Bond-type individual capable of committing a dastardly act.

During the Spanish civil conflict he was an arms dealer on behalf of the Polish Government, and made enough money to buy a cinema in England after the war. Following the collapse of Poland in 1939 when many army units were evacuated to Romania, he joined a Polish intelligence post in Bucharest. At the time, he was regarded as a first-class agent. He continued the same duties with the Polish Army in the Middle East. He came into prominence with the 'Mikicinski' affair. Samson Mikicinski, although of Jewish descent, was a double agent working for the German Intelligence Service – *Abwehr*. He was allowed to bring into Poland a considerable amount of money on behalf of the Polish Government-in-exile in France destined for the underground movement, in exchange for the information about its activities.

Mikicinski, who wormed himself into the confidence of the Chilean consul in Poland, and was given a position as his secretary, was able to use a Chilean diplomatic passport for his undercover activities.

When the Chilean consulate in Warsaw was closed because the Germans claimed that Poland no longer existed, Mikicinski moved with the consul to Turkey, from where he continued his work for the *Abwehr*. Turkish authorities found his activities troublesome, and reported his presence to the Allies.

In 1941, when it was clearly established that Mikicinski had close contacts with the *Abwehr*, Lt. Szarkiewicz and a team of helpers were sent from Palestine to abduct Mikicinski in Istanbul. After Szarkiewicz arranged to meet him, he overpowered him and drugged him with an injection. The renegade was brought to Palestine on board a small aircraft. When interrogated, he admitted working for the *Abwehr*. As there were no Polish courts in the Middle East and Mikicinski was a civilian, he could not be tried by the military. Szarkiewicz found another solution to dispose of Mikicinski. He arranged a change of prison, and while escorting Mikicinski, allowed him to escape. But this was for a few steps only. When he caught up with him, he shot him in the head, killing him instantly.

Polish Government officials held widely diverse opinions about Szarkiewicz and his activities. He had many protectors within army circles but, as a result of his obnoxious behaviour, also many enemies. He was strongly supported by Gen. Modelski, vice-minister of defence. After Mikicinski 's execution, Modelski brought Szarkiewicz to London to work in the headquarters of the Polish military intelligence service (known as the Second Section of the General Staff), and assigned him to the investigation of the earlier mentioned 'bomb-on-board' affair during Sikorski's flight to America in 1942. The investigation brought Szarkiewicz in close contact with Duff-Cooper, the Home Office Secretary and with Gen. Sir David Petrie, the head of MI5, who both, on Churchill's orders, were intimately involved in the proceedings.

However when Gen. Sikorski learnt about the underhand 'liquidation' of Mikicinski, he personally ordered Szarkiewicz's removal from the Polish intelligence service and his detention in the Polish penal camp at Rothesay on the island of

Bute in Scotland. The camp was known for extremely harsh conditions and questions were raised in the Parliament about Polish authorities allowing inhuman treatment of the inmates.

At his own request, Szarkiewicz was eventually discharged from the Polish Army and in 1943 joined the British Secret Service.

According to his account, he was posted to Cairo shortly before Sikorski's arrival in the Middle East. In his confession Szarkiewicz claimed that as a British intelligence agent, he had access to the Liberator and was able to sever the elevator cables in such a manner that they had eventually failed during take-off from Gibraltar. In the postscript it had been alleged that he could have used acid for that purpose, because of his good knowledge of chemistry.

Jerzy Osmecki admits that the source of the claim is secondhand. Szarkiewicz confessed his 'crime' to Col Iranek-Osmecki, who shortly before his death in 1984, in turn passed all the details to his son. Although the 'elevator control tampering' theory is based on unsubstantiated disclosures, and sounds far-fetched to anyone with a deeper knowledge of the Gibraltar crash, its implication has been far-reaching. With Col Iranek-Osmecki's memoirs having been extremely well received in Poland, many Poles believe that his son's account is very credible.

In the postscript, Jerzy Osmecki goes deeply into Szarkiewicz's background, in order to show that he had a motive, capability and unscrupulousness, as well as a possibility of help from the British Secret Service, to stage a sabotage. One person mentioned was supposed to have been James Klugman, a Special Operations Executive officer in Cairo, known for his strong left-wing sympathies. He was later branded, together with Maclean, Burgess and Philby, as a Soviet agent. To Stalin, disposing of Gen. Sikorski meant removing an obstacle in his plans to set up Soviet rule in Eastern Europe.

The account of Szarkiewicz's confession has echoed even as far as the Polish community in England. On the 53rd anniversary of Gen. Sikorski's death, *Tydzien Polski,* a highly respected Polish weekly published in London, carried an article by a former underground courier J. Nowak-Jezioranski. The article, based more on hearsays than facts, also contains an open letter from Nowak to the Foreign Secretary Robin Cook, which was going to be handed to him during his official visit to Warsaw in July 2000.

Nowak pleads with the Foreign Secretary that all British secret service records relating to the Gibraltar tragedy should be made available to the Polish historians in order to determine whether there was any involvement of Soviet spies such as Philby, Klugman or any other agent, in a possible sabotage action. Nowak claims that he had carefully studied the Court of Inquiry Report on the Gibraltar accident, and came to the conclusion that in view of wartime circumstances requiring strict secrecy, certain findings could not be disclosed at the time.

Sadly the obsession of suspecting that Sikorski's aircraft was sabotaged is not new within Polish circles. Such a rumour had begun shortly after the crash and persisted for decades. It is similar to the allegations that the DC6B carrying the UN Secretary Dag Hammarskjöld could have been brought down by a single bullet. Both are contrary to certain clearly established facts. The investigators at Gibraltar had found no evidence of sabotage.

The Liberator's elevator operating mechanism is a sturdy system consisting of two control columns, two separate sets of cables, two bell cranks and push-pull tubes attached to the elevator surfaces. Cables are shrouded for most of the length of the fuselage. To disable the system it would require severing both sets of cables or both duplicated sections of the mechanism.

As most parts of the crashed aircraft were salvaged from the sea bed, W/Cdr Stevens and F/Lt Buck had the opportunity to inspect the system in detail. F/Lt Buck stated:

'The entire operating mechanism of the control surfaces were examined and no defect was found which could not be attributed to the crash or salvage. The cables had parted under severe tension.'

Had the cables been severed for any reason other than the force of the impact, this would have been evident to the investigators. The cables were made of strands of high tensile wire and were several millimetres thick. Equally sturdy were four turnbuckles used to tension the cables. To weaken the cables or turnbuckles with the help of acid looks hardly possible as it would have required a considerable amount of fluid.

Sgt Moore, in charge of Sikorski's Liberator maintenance, stated to the inquiry that, after checking the Form F.700 (daily Inspection record), despite an inspection having been already carried out by his fitters, he himself checked the whole aircraft just before departure, and was absolutely convinced it was fully serviceable. Any experienced mechanic was bound to notice signs of tampering with the elevator control system.

If the cables broke at the moment of lift-off, this would manifest in an extremely light force to operate the control column. But F/Lt Prchal reported the opposite. Airflow over the elevator surfaces would have kept them on an even keel, and the aircraft would have continued to climb. The only effect on the elevator control could have come from the trim tab. Prchal claimed it was ineffective.

Equally puzzling is how Lt Szarkiewicz could

have entered an aircraft which was going to carry a VIP. In such circumstances, it would have been guarded and all visits strictly controlled. Moreover, it would have required quite a long time to remain inside in order to tamper with the controls, and this would have been noticed by the guard.

In my opinion the Air Minister, Capt. Balfour, was fully justified in stating in the House of Commons in 1943 that it has been established that there was no question of sabotage. The Court of Inquiry Report mentions only one mystery – how could a mail bag from the aircraft have found its way onto the runway?

3

1944 – THE WARWICK SAGA

PART I

In view of a great number of highly realistic aviation documentaries having been shown in recent years, it is disappointing that in January 1997 the BBC presented a 'tabloid' version of a wartime drama about the crash of a Transport Command aircraft, under the title – *The Gold Plane*.

It was claimed that the programme was based on sixteen-year-long research by Derek Fawkes, a retired police superintendent. Fawkes tried to solve the mystery of a disaster which had taken place on the early morning of 17 April 1944, just off the Cornish coast. A Vickers Warwick exploded in the air shortly after take-off and crashed into Newquay Bay. Twelve service passengers and four crew members lost their lives.

But the focal point of what was supposed to have been a documentary was not the tragic event itself. With local rumours flying around at the time that the Warwick carried gold and was destroyed by a bomb, *The Gold Plane* programme had been 'spiced' by allegations that the British Secret Intelligence Service (SIS) had planted an explosive device on board the ill-fated aircraft.

It seemed as if, in the eyes of the programme producers, the story of the crash was too dull without some element of sensation. Otherwise it might have depicted just another RAF accident, one of the many that were occurring almost daily throughout the war years. The possibility of a more likely factor that could have caused the disaster, such as a mechanical failure or handling difficulties, was not even seriously considered.

Many former wartime airmen have found the BBC's account as to what lay behind the Warwick crash, to be completely detached from reality. *Aeroplane Monthly*, a well-known aviation publication, described it as 'a farrago of nonsense'.

The history of the Warwick's ups and downs would have made a far more interesting documentary, for the largest British twin-engine plane of that era was one of the most costly failures of wartime aircraft production. Throughout the long years of its development, the Warwick had been bedevilled not only by numerous mechanical flaws, but also by a string of handling weaknesses. In operational service it had acquired a reputation as one of the most troublesome aircraft in RAF history. This had been a result of a series of accidents and dangerous incidents, of which a large proportion had occurred during flight testing or training.

PART II

Fawkes must be highly praised for the part he played in establishing the identity of one of the airmen who perished in the crash. Only fourteen bodies out of sixteen victims were recovered from the submerged wreck. The divers who searched Newquay Bay with the help of an RAF rescue launch, were not able to find the last two, despite thoroughly combing the seabed. Only much later were the bodies washed ashore. By that time, one was so badly decomposed that identification had proved to be difficult. As a result, the unlucky victim was buried in a local cemetery as an 'unknown seaman'.

In spite of strong opposition from the Ministry of Defence, Fawkes arranged to have the remains of the 'unknown seaman' exhumed and examined by a pathologist. It was established that the body was that of the captain of the ill-starred Warwick, Flying Officer Gavel, a Canadian. He was later re-buried with military honours in the presence of his brother, who came over from Canada especially for the occasion.

The retired police superintendent must be given special credit for his humanitarian achievement. Through his efforts, at last a wartime blunder of failing to conduct a proper identification has been put right.

Nevertheless when it came to determining the cause of the crash, the available evidence was far from expertly assessed and the programme began to sound like a 'Hollywood' version of a wartime event. The principal theme became sabotage and elimination of a secret agent. The Warwick's appalling safety record was not even mentioned.

Fawkes claimed that he had consulted former pilots from the Warwick squadrons and was told that the aircraft could fly on one engine. But there were two different models. An earlier version fitted with American engines was known to have been grossly underpowered. It was incapable of maintaining height on one engine unless all-up weight was drastically reduced.

On the other hand, the later variant, fitted with stronger engines, could even climb at maximum take-off weight if an engine failed. Naturally the views of the pilots who flew the later models would not reflect the difficulties experienced with the earlier models that were suffering from poor single-engine performance and the ill-fated Warwick belonged to that group.

But after so many intervening years, finding airmen who could throw light on the Warwick's numerous deficiencies would have been like looking for a needle in a haystack, particularly in the case of those who had served in the RAF squadrons equipped with the underpowered models.

Out of 846 Warwicks built by Vickers at Weybridge in Surrey, 389 were fitted with the less powerful engine although only 239 finally reached various RAF operational units. With a ratio at the time of about two crews to one aircraft, the Warwick pilots represented an extremely small percentage of the total RAF flying corps. Moreover, with the numerous crashes some had not survived to tell the tale. Then, with the passing years, age had also taken its toll, so the number of former Warwick pilots still alive was bound to have dwindled to next to nothing.

It must be stressed that the Warwick's single-engine performance was not its only shortcoming. Right from the earliest test flight of the prototype, various mechanical weaknesses and handling flaws began to plague the ill-conceived project.

Surprisingly, none of the pilots interviewed by Fawkes condemned the Warwick as a flying coffin.

Nor had they tried to make it apparent that, in view of its poor safety record, the Cornish disaster had been more likely caused by some mechanical failure rather than by foul play.

Out of the twelve years of the Warwick's service in the RAF, there had not been one year without a new problem surfacing. Some deficiencies were not even fully rectified when the aircraft was phased out in 1952. Many handling shortcomings stemmed from an outdated elevator and rudder. At an Air Ministry meeting as far back as 1942, it was already claimed that: 'Flying controls were designed a long time ago and the standard is not up to present day requirements.'

The perpetual crises during the development of the Warwick would have made an interesting story. There were not many wartime aircraft blemished with so many flaws that were responsible for the loss of lives of so many test pilots.

PART III

A general impression prevails that the Warwick was a development of the Wellington, but this was not the case. Both projects came into existence at the same time, the Warwick simply being the bigger brother of the two.

The birth of 'the twins' goes back to 1932 when Germany walked out of the Geneva Disarmament Conference and decided to build larger bombers than so far agreed. As a result, the British Government was forced to follow suit and the Air Ministry issued a tender for a general purpose and torpedo bomber to replace the outdated biplanes, such as the Overstrand or the Heyford. Together with many other competing companies, Vickers Armstrong, one of the oldest aircraft manufacturers, submitted two proposals – one for a biplane along more conventional lines and another for an advanced monoplane. It was planned to base both projects on a unique lightweight basket-like construction termed geodetic. This new method had been developed by Barnes Wallis – later the inventor of the Möhne Dam bomb – from his experiences of working on airships. But in the case of the proposed biplane, Vickers planned to only use 'lattice' sections covered by fabric for constructing the fuselage, whilst the entire monoplane was going to be made from 'lattice' frames, including the wings and the tail structure.

At first the Air Ministry opted for the biplane. However, under pressure from the Vickers management, Air Vice-Marshal Sir Hugh (later Lord) Dowding, had been persuaded to accept the monoplane on the grounds that it was a far more advanced concept. Dowding's decision ended the era of the bomber biplanes in the RAF, and gave Vickers a chance to prove the numerous advantages of the geodetic construction. Thus a novel idea of aircraft design was born that served England extremely well during World War II.

The Air Ministry ordered 176 of the new monoplanes. The Wellesley, the name that was later adopted by the RAF, turned out to be a very successful design, and in 1938 it had beaten the world record in long distance flying.

Encouraged by this success, Vickers began to work on two new geodetic projects: a twin-engine mid-wing medium bomber which became the Wellington and a very similar design, but a larger version designated as a heavy bomber, which was later known as the Warwick. By working side by side on two related projects the company believed that the development would benefit from a joint design study.

The Air Ministry placed a contract for the Wellington prototype at the end of 1935. The first test flight was made by Mutt Summers, Vickers' chief test pilot, in June 1936 from Brooklands airfield in Surrey.

Unfortunately, when subsequently undergoing evaluation trials by the Aircraft & Armament Experimental Establishment, then based at Martlesham Heath, the aircraft crashed as a result of the tail breaking off during a high-speed dive. The cause was soon discovered to be an overbalanced elevator. When the Air Ministry ordered a replacement prototype, Vickers decided to incorporate many design features from the Warwick, which was already in an advanced stage of construction. In fact, the new Wellington was going to be a scaled down version of its bigger brother, retaining the shape of the Warwick's tail and outer wing. This had made both aircraft very similar in appearance, only the Wellington's fuselage had been shortened by deleting several centre sections and the wingspan was also reduced. As much as 60% of common parts were used in the construction.

Flight tests of the second Wellington prototype had shown that it was a successful design and no serious snags had been experienced. With the Bristol Pegasus engines available in sufficient quantities, production was started as early as 1938. On the other hand, the Warwick's progress was hampered by the lack of an adequately powerful engine.

Eventually, the first prototype of the Warwick, which was fitted with two Rolls-Royce Vulture engines (a twenty-four cylinder, 2,000 hp version of two 'X' configured Kestrels) was completed in 1939. It was four years after the order was placed on the Vickers books and by now the price tag came to a staggering sum of £41,700 (the present day value of about £5 million), while a Spitfire cost only £6,000. Flight tests had revealed considerable deficiencies. The aircraft was slow, its single-engine performance inadequate and handling characteristics poor. Moreover, the Vulture, which was anyway intended for the Avro Manchester, had to be scrapped due to incurable teething problems. As a result, the production of the Warwicks had to be delayed until a suitable engine substitute became available. This also resulted in the demise of the Manchester and the most fortunate development of the Lancaster.

The second Warwick prototype was fitted with two early Bristol Centaurus engines, an eighteen-cylinder version of the fourteen-cylinder Hercules, but it did not take to the air until 1940. Contrary to previous experiences, flight tests had shown that it was capable of a promising performance. In fact, the prototype was even faster at certain heights than the Hurricane. Nevertheless, the Centaurus engines were still not being made in sufficiently large quantities to warrant starting a production line of the Warwick. By that time, the Wellingtons were coming out of the Vickers factories in great numbers and soon became the mainstay of the RAF bomber force.

In an attempt to find a replacement for the Centaurus engine on the second Warwick prototype, the Ministry of Aircraft Production allocated Vickers two Pratt & Whitney Double Wasp R2800s, for a trial installation. The Double Wasps became available as a result of the French Government's cancellation of a contract after the collapse of France. Unfortunately, the P&W R2800s could only be brought over from the USA by sea and with hold-ups on the way the conversion of the second prototype was considerably delayed.

From the flight tests of the Double Wasp-powered prototype, it was immediately evident that the single-engine performance had markedly deteriorated as a result of the R2800 producing some 580 hp less than the Centaurus at climb power, the rating which was normally used during an engine-out operation.

The tests had also revealed that both the

rudder and the rudder trim were not sufficiently effective to provide satisfactory control under asymmetric conditions. Consequently the tailplane had to be re-designed. This, combined with tooling difficulties, had further delayed the start of the production line.

The first production line bomber version of the Warwick, destined for the RAF, was not completed until April 1942. Even then, it never entered operational service. It crashed while undergoing acceptance tests by the Aircraft & Armament Experimental Establishment, now based at Boscombe Down. During a high-speed run, fabric on the upper wing surface became detached and the aircraft was sent into an uncontrollable dive. The crew of four lost their lives, among them S/Ldr Carr, a very experienced test pilot.

The second production Warwick also came to grief. After undergoing further evaluation trials by the A&AEE, it was then sent to the Royal Aircraft Establishment at Farnborough for a check because of the difficulties of starting the engines. During one of the attempts, an engine caught fire and the aircraft was completely burnt out.

As a result of continuous problems, only six Double Wasp-powered Warwicks were completed at Weybridge in 1942, in spite of 150 having been ordered.

By that time, the aircraft as a bomber became outclassed by the Lancaster and the Halifax. A new role had to be found for the troublesome project and the Air Ministry decided to adapt the bomber version to three new specifications – an Air-Sea Rescue (ASR), a general reconnaissance and a transport variant.

In spite of the fact that the directional control deficiency was still not properly cured, 168 ASR Mk I Warwicks were built in 1943 and towards the end of the year, two RAF squadrons received the first batch of aircraft from the production line.

On the Air-Sea Rescue variant the bomb bay was modified to carry either a lifeboat or containers with life-saving equipment such as inflatable Lindholme dinghies. The lifeboat was slung under the fuselage, suspended on lugs fitted to the bomb bay. An early version of the lifeboat was twenty-three feet long, weighed 1,700 lb and was powered by a small two-stroke engine. It could be dropped onto the sea with the help of six small parachutes. The later model – Mk II – which only came into service at the end of the war, was seven feet longer and equipped with a bigger engine. It weighed 3,600 lb and used two large parachutes. Both models were built by the renowned yacht designer Uffa Fox.

At the beginning of 1944 two more squadrons were equipped with the ASR Warwicks. Despite the unsolved directional control deficiency, over 3,000 ASR sorties were successfully flown in the last eighteen months of the war, saving the lives of several thousand aircrew who were forced to ditch. A lifeboat dropped close to the scene of a ditching could provide badly needed shelter, particularly in cold weather, until the unfortunate airmen were finally picked up by a rescue vessel. In many cases the crews were able to reach the shore with the help of the motor that was fitted to the lifeboat.

In view of the Warwick's spacious fuselage, in 1942 the Air Ministry decided to convert fourteen redundant Double Wasp-powered bombers to a civil version. This was to meet BOAC requirements for a mail, freight and passenger carrier in that order of priority. Designated as C Mk I, the Warwicks had all armament removed and the openings for gun turrets covered by a fabric fairing. They were fitted with cabin windows, passenger seats, freight floor and even carpets. For night flying, flame dampers were installed, which extended the exhaust pipes five feet further back. The conversion of the BOAC fleet was completed in 1943.

After several months of unsatisfactory operations in North Africa and on the Mediterranean routes, the Warwicks were withdrawn from service by BOAC. This was due to all-up weight limitations, the consequence of a poor single-engine performance in hot weather. In such circumstances no useful payload could be carried.

The Warwicks were transferred to RAF Transport Command and later allocated to 525 Squadron. One of these aircraft was BV 247, formerly G-AGFB (No. 4 aircraft from the production line of the civil versions), which crashed off the Cornish coast.

A military variant of the C Mk I was developed in 1944, designated as C Mk III, intended as a freight and troop carrier. The main difference from the BOAC configuration was that a wooden pannier was fitted under the fuselage to carry freight and no passenger seats were installed. The engines were a later version of the R2800 Double Wasp, which produced slightly more horsepower on take-off. Eighty-seven C Mk IIIs were built in 1944 and thirteen in 1945.

For the Warwick, 1945 was an ill-fated year. As a result of several accidents, which were suspected to have been caused by the still uncured directional instability, urgent tests to find the root of the problem were undertaken by Vickers at Brooklands. At the time, the only Warwicks available were the GR Mk II development versions fitted with the Centaurus engines.

The first pilot who survived to report a vicious rudder weakness and its grave consequences was Vickers test pilot Mutt Summers. While checking the effect of progressively increased rudder deflection at low speeds, all of a sudden the rudder locked in a full deflection and it could not be centralised. Despite applying maximum power on one engine and banking steeply, Summers was not able to keep the Warwick straight and the aircraft side-slipped from 3,000 feet to the ground. Luckily the impact was cushioned by a row of trees with dense foliage. Although the aircraft was completely destroyed, Summers and his flight observer miraculously escaped without serious injuries.

Next day, an identical problem was encountered by S/Ldr Longbottom during the same type of test on another GR Mk II Warwick. Unfortunately on that occasion, the aircraft went into a spin while approaching Brooklands airfield and Longbottom, the only one on board, was killed. A month later, W/Cdr Maurice Summers, the brother of Mutt, had again run into the same difficulties while testing variable rudder travel and the Warwick crashed in an uncontrollable dive. While bailing out, the pilot and the technical observer were badly hurt. As a result, all Warwicks were grounded.

By now Vickers had thrown in the towel and asked the RAE for assistance. After an extensive aerodynamic research, it was suggested to reduce the rudder travel and to fit a dorsal fin. Although this had cured the problem with rudder locking at large side-slip angles, the tests subsequently conducted by the A&AEE revealed that the single-engine handling characteristics of the Centaurus-equipped Warwicks were badly affected by the new modifications and that minimum speed with a failed engine was above the best climbing speed. Nevertheless, the suggested changes were incorporated in all production aircraft, except that some Transport Command C Mk III Warwicks were not fitted with the dorsal fin.

The troublesome bigger brother of the successful Wellington, of which 11,461 were built, continued to suffer further setbacks. Three GR versions of the Warwick I crashed within two months when a dinghy, which was stored in a roof compartment close to the tail, had inflated for an unexplained reason and wrapped itself around the rudder.

Moreover it was discovered during the A&AEE flight tests of the static system that the position error on the Warwick was much higher than on most aircraft. There was a twelve-knot difference in the airspeed indication, and a 100-foot variation in the altimeter reading when the altimeter was set to QFE for landing.

Although 1,178 Warwicks were originally ordered, only 846 were built. Out of the fourteen ex-BOAC Mk Is and 100 C Mk IIIs completed in 1944–45, only eighty-four had reached Transport Command squadrons in England. Seventeen were sent to the Far East but were hardly used as a result of problems with the covering fabric in hot and humid weather.

The first RAF unit to receive the transport version was 525 Squadron, for the operation of long-range flights to North Africa via Gibraltar.

After the liberation of France, 167 Squadron was the second RAF unit to be assigned the transport version of the Warwick C Mk III, and had the largest number, thirty-eight. They were going to be used on the runs to the Continent to repatriate 8th Army soldiers and to bring back Allied PoWs released from the camps in Italy. During the first flight of 167 Squadron to Naples in December 1944, piloted by the Squadron Commander, W/Cdr Collins, an engine failed and an emergency landing had to be carried out at Toulouse. The Warwicks did not stay with 167 Squadron long. Within eight months they were replaced by Dakotas and Ansons.

At the end of the war, 301 (Polish) Squadron which was re-formed from the original Special Duty 1586 Flight, received ten C Mk IIIs. The reason for allocating such a small number was the shortage of aircrew in the squadron, as a result of heavy losses when carrying supplies to the Warsaw Rising in 1944. The squadron commenced freight operations to France, Italy, Greece and Norway in October 1945.

Another Polish RAF unit, 304 Squadron, formerly operating Wellingtons on Coastal Command patrols, received twenty-six Warwicks towards the end of 1945. Both Polish squadrons were stationed at RAF Chedburgh in Suffolk.

Cynics claimed that there was a sinister motive behind equipping the two Polish squadrons with an aircraft with such a poor safety record. When, as a result of the Yalta Agreement Poland fell under Communist domination, many Polish airmen refused to return to their country once the war had ended and the Air Ministry was forced to resettle them in England. One way to reduce 'the unwanted baggage' was to supply Polish squadrons with the Warwicks. But this cynical claim was no exaggeration. The two units suffered ten crashes within six months. Fortunately the casualty rate was low and only five crew members lost their lives.

Most accidents had occurred during training. In one case, an instructor was killed while demonstrating a single-engine landing. But operational flights also took a share of casualties. A Warwick from 301 Squadron had spun-in while flying through a thunderstorm and crashed twenty miles south of Lyon. All four crew members were killed.

But there were also lucky escapes. When bad weather one day suddenly closed all airfields in Norway and Germany, a Warwick from 301 Squadron had to be ditched off the Danish coast. Fortunately the crew were quickly rescued. Another similar 'close shave' was a crash landing due to the failure of both engines.

Adding 'insult to injury', the first assignment for the Polish squadrons was to deliver a dangerous cargo to Italy. *Aeroplane*, the oldest English aviation magazine, reported on 21 December 1945:

'Four Vickers-Armstrong Warwick C Mk IIIs of RAF Transport Command left an East Anglian airfield recently, carrying consignments of bomb safety fuses to Udine, in Northern Italy. The fuses will be employed to detonate the explosives used in Austrian brown coal mines near the Austro–Italian frontier. Two more Warwicks left England at a later date with a further consignment.'

An entry in my logbook shows that I flew one of the Warwicks in the second group.

But as 304 Squadron operated Wellingtons for the longest period of all RAF units (from November 1940 until October 1945), it must be said in fairness that it was logical to re-equip the squadron with a type of aircraft that was closely related to the Wellington.

PART IV

Although flight tests have shown that the Warwick was blemished by a directional control weakness which was suspected to have been the prime cause of several accidents, the day-to-day operations in Transport Command had soon revealed that the Achilles' heel was not the hazardous handling trait but a minor fault with the P&W Double Wasps, which had led to a very high number of single-engine landings.

How grave the problem was can be seen from the figures of engine failures in the two Polish squadrons. During nine months of operating the Warwicks, 301 Squadron suffered thirty failures and 304 Squadron sixteen.

Considering that during the two years that 304 Squadron was flying the Mk XIV Wellingtons on anti-submarine patrols, there was not even a single case of the sleeve-valve Hercules XVII showing signs of malfunctioning, the experiences with the P&W R2800 was a shock to both the pilots and the fitters.

Mechanically the R2800 was a sturdy engine. It was an eighteen-cylinder version of the well-proven fourteen-cylinder P&W R1830 engine, with a swept volume of 2,803 cubic inches. Over 100,000 R1830s were built during the war. They powered the Liberators, Dakotas, Catalinas and Sunderlands. They were known to be one of the most reliable radial engines in the world.

Many Double Wasp components, such as cylinders, pistons, connecting rods and crankshaft, were identical to those used on the Twin Wasp.

In the long run, the Double Wasp had also given sterling service. A later improved version was fitted, among others, to the Thunderbolts, Marauders, Corsairs, Bearcats and Avengers. The only other aircraft apart from the Warwick that was using the early series of the R2800 was the Lockheed Ventura I. In the post-war years all the DC6s and DC6Bs relied on a highly developed C version.

The problem with the early R2800s was the ignition system. Unlike the R1830 engine, which had two separate magnetos, the series A and B of the R2800 were fitted with a newly developed Bendix Scintilla Type DF18 dual magneto. Its distinctive feature was the provision of true double ignition from a single unit, but two distributors were still used. High-speed pivotless contact point breakers were actuated by two separate cams. (See diagram on next page.)

A magneto is basically no different from a car ignition, except that the primary current is generated by rotating magnets and stationary coils, and thus the system need not be connected to the main electric circuit.

It was not the basic principle of double ignition from a single unit that was causing all the troubles, but a fault in a minor component costing probably only a few pennies to manufacture.

The entries in the RAF Form 540 – Operations Record Book – of 301 and 304 Squadron show that as much as 80% of engine malfunctioning occurred as a result of faulty ignition. The first symptoms were an intermittent cutting out of the engine, then the coughs would progressively increase, often accompanied by strong backfiring, until finally all power would be lost. In most cases, the remedy on the ground was either to reset or to replace contact breakers.

The ordeals to which the two Polish squadrons were exposed in connection with the ignition problems on the P&W R2800s are best described by the following entry in the 301 Squadron OR Book:

'During this period [of operating the Warwicks] there had been only one fatal accident to a squadron crew. Operation of the Warwick CIII has not been without its headaches and worries. Mechanical failures in the air have been frequent, and good luck as well as good management has contributed to the freedom from fatality in other instances. Yes, there were few, if any pangs among the aircrews at parting company with an aircraft which had proved itself so unreliable.'

With so many magneto breakdowns on the Warwicks, it was only a matter of time before the inevitable would happen; something all pilots from 301 and 304 Squadron dreaded – a double engine failure. The spine-chilling event took place during the inaugural flight of 301 Squadron to Athens in September 1945, with a load of Greek banknotes on board. The captain of the aircraft was the squadron commander himself and all other crew members were senior squadron officers.

The accident is described in the 301 Squadron OR Book:

'While crossing the Channel on the way to Naples, port engine cut out but only for short time. At Naples magneto contact breakers changed. Over Adria port engine cuts out again. Due to rain, descent to 3,500'. Port engine working very badly till approx. 30 miles from Corinth channel. Then ceased altogether. Starboard engine starts to cough and works very badly. It is impossible to keep altitude which is 1,300'. Decided to make crash landing. W/C Pożyczka slightly injured.'

The Warwick had been put down on a stretch of sandy beach, which helped to minimise the damage, and this had also accounted for only one minor casualty at the time. During landing, the underbelly

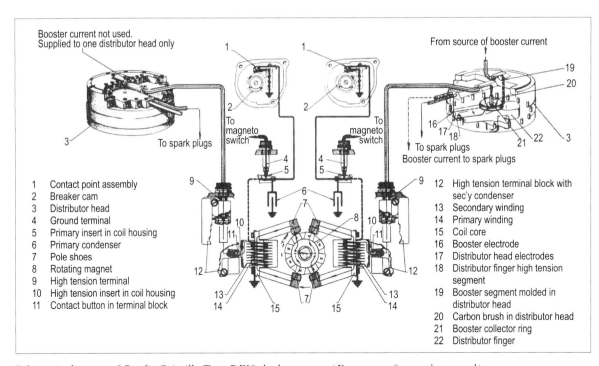

1   Contact point assembly
2   Breaker cam
3   Distributor head
4   Ground terminal
5   Primary insert in coil housing
6   Primary condenser
7   Pole shoes
8   Rotating magnet
9   High tension terminal
10   High tension insert in coil housing
11   Contact button in terminal block

12   High tension terminal block with
     sec'y condenser
13   Secondary winding
14   Primary winding
15   Coil core
16   Booster electrode
17   Distributor head electrodes
18   Distributor finger high tension
     segment
19   Booster segment molded in
     distributor head
20   Carbon brush in distributor head
21   Booster collector ring
22   Distributor finger

Schematic diagram of Bendix Scintilla Type DF18 dual magneto. (From manufacturer's manual)

wooden pannier broke off and crates with drachmas were ripped open, spilling thousands of notes on the beach. It took several days for a battalion of the Greek Army to collect all the money.

Unfortunately, W/Cdr Pożyczka's so-called slight injuries proved fatal in the long run. He died nine months later from a complication resulting from the damage to his spine.

From all 304 Squadron pilots and out of sixteen cases, it was my bad luck to have suffered the highest number of engine failures requiring a single-engine landing – seven in total. One more failure occurred during a joint training flight with another crew but I was not at the controls. Considering that I have only 110 hours on Warwicks, the rate of failures per hours flown must be one of the highest on record.

The story of the joint training flight did not have a happy ending. I was assigned for the first part of the instrument flying exercise and when the other crew took over, an engine began to misfire and the propeller had to be feathered. Upon our return to base, a single-engine landing was attempted. Unfortunately the captain misjudged the approach and crashed in a field adjoining the airfield. (See photograph on page 67.) No one was hurt but we did kill a cow.

Out of the eight engine failures in the days of my flying the Warwicks, six were due to a faulty ignition system, two due to an oil leak.

According to information I was given by the fitters who serviced the R2800 magnetos, the majority of the troubles with the ignition were caused by premature wear of the fibre base on the cam follower that triggered the contact breakers. It was due to having been manufactured from an insufficiently hard material. In some cases the base would deteriorate even faster for no apparent reason. But it was suspected that this was caused by excessive vibration on some of the engines.

In general, contact breakers fitted to the later 'B' series of P&W 2800s which powered the Warwick C Mk IIIs, were inferior to those on the earlier 'A' series engines, which the ex-BOAC aircraft were using.

It was known that the double magneto unit was difficult to service. Setting the contact points was a far from simple procedure, as it is outlined in the Maintenance Manual: 'IMPORTANT: Do not adjust contact points for a fixed clearance. Never use a feeler gauge between the points.'

Adjustments could only be made with the help of a timing light and this required time as well as patience.

The cams that operated the contact points' breakers had to be regularly oiled by depressing a plunger mounted on the housing. The amount of oil pumped on to a wick had to be carefully controlled. Too little oil could accelerate wear of the cam follower, while too much could foul the contact points.

A further complication was the synchronisation of the two contact breaker assemblies. It was not possible to do it by adjusting the points, and once synchronisation was found to be outside tolerances the magneto had to be replaced.

Uneven wear of the cam followers would affect synchronisation of the magneto and this could lead to a slow deterioration of the ignition system. I never experienced, nor had anyone in my squadron, a rapid engine failure on a Warwick.

My experiences during a flight to Greece had taught me that the warnings in the Maintenance Manual about the difficulties in adjusting the contact points were fully justified.

When I was approaching Athens Airport, then known as Hassani, the engine began to cut out and as it became worse, the propeller had to be feathered, requiring a single engine landing. Once the fault was diagnosed as excessive wear of one of the contact breakers and this had been rectified, I took the aircraft up for an air test. But even before reaching circuit height, the engine began to cough again and I had no option but to feather the propeller. After several hours of repair work on the magneto, the same problem recurred on the subsequent air test.

It was known that the R2800 was prone to catching fire during starting. The most likely cause was a weak or intermittent spark due to premature wear of the contact breaker base, leading to the flooding of the carburettors with petrol. Seven cases of engine fire on the ground were recorded.

PART V

In 1942 the first production Mk I bomber, BV 214, was sent to A&AEE at Boscombe Down for evaluation trials. It was the same aircraft that later crashed when fabric on the wings became detached.

The A&AEE tests had not only corroborated the unsatisfactory single-engine performance reported by the Vickers test pilots, but had also revealed that during asymmetric flight the rudder control was very marginal. This especially applied

Magneto fitted to the R2800 Pratt & Whitney engine which was used on the Warwick. The photograph was taken at Brooklands Museum.

to the rudder trim. At lower speeds it was not possible to fly the aircraft with 'hands off'. A&AEE recommended that both the rudder and the rudder trim should be re-designed.

A further concern to the A&AEE test pilots was the Warwick's inability to maintain height on one engine when the propeller was allowed to windmill. Although with a feathered propeller it was just possible to stay level if the weight was 37,000 lb or less, with a windmilling propeller, the aircraft would lose height at a rate of 325 ft/min when the minimum comfortable speed of 120 mph was maintained. But the rate would become even higher with a slight increase of the airspeed.

The A&AEE report underlined the consequences of weight reduction from the maximum structural limit of 45,000 lb (46,000 lb for the GR version):

'The weight quoted [37,000 lb] does not represent any practical load that can be reached in Service, since the only jettisonable load is fuel and, even if all the fuel were jettisoned (an impracticable case), the maximum weight after take-off at 45,000 lb would only be reduced to about 38,000 lb.'

Moreover the A&AEE tests had shown that during a single-engine flight, cylinder-head temperatures had to be carefully monitored. Closing cooling gills improved performance but would result in dangerously high temperatures, particularly in hot weather.

Further evaluation trials were conducted in 1943 on Warwick BV 243, a civil transport version allocated to BOAC under the registration G-AGEX. This aircraft was identical to the ill-fated BV 247 (or G-AGFB).

On BV 243 modifications to the rudder were already incorporated. The cord and the range of the rudder trim tab were greatly increased. Moreover, a mass and a small horn balance had been added.

Nevertheless it soon became evident from the flight tests that these modifications were not satisfactory. Simulated engine failures on take-off were also tried. The results indicated that even at a relatively low all-up weight of 37,000 lb it was not possible to keep the Warwick straight until at least 40 mph above the lift-off speed had been attained.

Even if the minimum safety speed on one engine was reached, the climb capability was very marginal. At 35,000 lb the rate of climb was only 120 ft/min with the propeller feathered, but if the dead engine were kept windmilling, this would result in a loss of 130 ft/min.

A circuit on one engine could be made at a speed as low as 115 mph, but fifteen degrees of bank was required to relieve the foot load on the rudder. The minimum airspeed for 'zero' foot load was 125 mph, but even as small a decrease as 5 mph made the foot load quite noticeable.

Moreover, at such low speeds the aircraft was tricky to control longitudinally. This was due to a great deal of 'elevator hunting', an irritating feature, which made accurate flying difficult especially under asymmetric conditions. The AA&E test pilots stated in their report: 'In bumpy air conditions the horn balance elevators cause considerable fore and aft movements of the control column and the rudder has tendency to "tramp" so that the aeroplane is unpleasant to fly.'

It must be pointed out that the A&AEE tests were conducted in relatively good flying conditions. In poor weather or at night, and above all in turbulence, a Service pilot would have probably found that maintaining height on one engine was far more critical. This meant that it was advisable to reduce weight even below the recommended figure, in particular when an emergency arose close to the ground.

The 'engine-out' procedure was outlined in the *Pilot's Notes – AP 2068A (for the ASR Warwick Mk I fitted with two P & W Double Wasps)* – under 'Emergencies', as follows:

'Engine failure during take-off
A circuit and landing should be attempted only if the AUW [All Up Weight] does not exceed 37,000 lb and the safety speed 110 mph (95 kt) has been reached.
Engine failure during flight
To maintain height in temperate conditions, weight must be reduced to 37,000 lb by jettisoning the lifeboat (if carried) and containers, and, if necessary, some fuel load.'

It must be mentioned that directional control during an engine-out operation was a weak point not only of the Warwick but of the Wellington as

A sad end for Vickers Warwick 233A of 304 (Polish) Squadron. There were no injuries to crew members but a cow was killed when the aircraft overshot while making a single-engine landing, and ended up in a field. The feathered propeller can be clearly seen on the starboard engine.

well, which had a very high single-engine speed on take-off of 130 mph.

In view of the Warwick's poor performance on one engine at high weights, jettisoning of fuel was a matter of great urgency, in particular on the passenger version where no parachutes were carried.

Fuel could be discharged from the wing tanks by two chutes fitted under each wing. The inboard chute was located only two feet away from the engine nacelle. This differed from the arrangement on the Wellington where only one chute was provided and it was much further away from the engine.

The procedure was as follows: 'The complete contents of the wing fuel tanks may be jettisoned by operating the valve control on the right-hand side of the cockpit. The valves must be kept open for three minutes; 800 gallons will be discharged in the first minute. The amount of air pressure used is small.'

PART VI

After painting a rather black picture of the Warwick's handling characteristics and the problems with the P&W R2800 ignition system, the reader might expect that I would not have a good word for the 'flying coffin'. Nevertheless it may sound surprising, but I liked flying the Warwicks. Perhaps like with many pilots, it was a case of developing attachment, and only the good side of the controls' responses remained imprinted in one's mind.

Contrary to the test pilots' criticism, I did not find the engine-out operation particularly difficult. In fact, it was no more difficult than on the DC3, on which I have made two single-engine landings in my flying career.

But perhaps I was lucky that the variant of the Warwick that I was flying at the time had the benefit of three modifications to the rudder and several more to the rudder trim. On the other hand, our Warwicks were not fitted with the mandatory dorsal fin. Moreover, all my engine failures occurred whilst the aircraft was relatively light and consequently I was never faced with the critical situation of uncontrollably losing height. This was due to the fact that when the war ended, urgent supplies were no longer the top priority and the take-off weight of Transport Command Warwicks was restricted to comply with their single-engine capability. The payload was limited to

about 3,000 lb. and the up-lift of fuel to 500 gallons, which meant that only two wing tanks were used out of four. These restrictions brought the all-up weight for take-off to about 37,000 lb. The consequence was frequent intermediate landings for refuelling. For example during flights to Italy, stops had to be made either at Toulouse or Istres, near Marseille.

As far as the sensitivity of the controls was concerned, the elevator, the rudder and the ailerons were in my opinion, light and responsive within the normal operating range. Landing was not particularly tricky, but the aircraft would not easily tolerate a heavy bounce on touchdown. Perhaps it had something to do with the flexible wings, which were inclined to accentuate any 'kangaroo hop'.

According to the Pilot's Notes, the controls became sluggish below 104 mph (90 kt) and correcting the aircraft after a bounce could present a problem. The outcome was quite a few 'bent' Warwicks on landing, in particular by pilots with limited experience on that type of aircraft.

In the spring of 1945, I was an eyewitness to such an unfortunate event. Watching a GR Warwick Mk II, which was being delivered by an Air Transport Auxiliary pilot, coming in to land at RAF St Eval, I saw that the aircraft touched down hard. Then, after a leap back in the air, it went out of control and side-slipped on to the wingtip. A split-second later, the brand-new Warwick was just a heap of crumpled metal and torn fabric. As it immediately burst into flames, the pilot could be seen running away from the wreckage like an Olympic sprinter. He continued at the same speed all the way to the Control Tower, not so much to get away from the fire, but to present a delivery form that he wanted quickly signed so that he could catch the next train home.

A similar accident, unfortunately with a loss of five crew members, took place at the end of 1945 at Leuchars airfield in Fife. With Press censorship having just been lifted, a picture of an air crash appeared in a newspaper for the first time in years.

Apart from the engine weaknesses, there were other mechanical snags with the Warwick. The undercarriage was not one of its stronger parts. Whether the tendency for excessive bouncing came from misjudged landings or a design fault it resulted in three collapsed undercarriages within two months in 304 Squadron. A fracture of the jack retaining plate on the oleo leg was found to be the cause. All three cases happened during training on the same dual control Mk I Warwick and to the same instructor.

In the book *All-Weather Mac*, published by Macdonald in 1963, W/Cdr McIntosh, the squadron commander of 280 ASR Squadron, recounts similar problems during his introductory period: 'As the Warwicks began to arrive, there were inevitably snags to be ironed out, undercarriage fouling, fabric fraying on control surfaces and that sort of minor thing.'

Nevertheless, like myself, he appears to have been fond of the renowned RAF dud: 'The Warwick was really a first-class aircraft for ASR work.'

Finally it must be mentioned that geodetic construction was responsible for one of the Warwick's unusual characteristics – extensive wing flexing in turbulence. Faint-hearted pilots were recommended not to watch the wingtips as flapping could look quite alarming. On the other hand, this helped to 'ride out the bumps', making the Warwick one the most comfortable aircraft in rough weather.

Flexing was even more spectacular on the Windsor, a four-engine version of the Warwick, powered by Rolls-Royce Merlins. It had a twenty-foot-longer wingspan to accommodate the outboard engines. Moreover, the fuselage was increased by four feet and an unusual four-legged undercarriage was fitted which retracted into the engine nacelles. Only two prototypes were built.

As in the case of the Warwick, the Windsor did not live up to the designers' expectations. The first prototype broke its back on landing after only thirty-five hours of flight testing. The second prototype showed too many further weaknesses to be considered suitable for operational use.

Captain Eric Brown, in his book *Wings of the Weird & Wonderful*, Airlife 1985, vividly describes his impressions of the Windsor's aeroelastic distorsions: 'This phenomenon consisted of flexing of the wing up and down through a six-foot arc, which looked very frightening from my line of sight. The sweep of the arc decreased somewhat in the cruise, but still gave the impression of a giant bird flapping its way through the air.'

It would have been interesting to see what the Windsor's wing flexing looked like in heavy turbulence.

PART VII

In the spring of 1944 the battle in Italy was progressing slower than expected. Urgent troop reinforcements and supplies had to be rushed to the North African airfields, from where they were transferred to the front line. In order to speed up the deliveries, Transport Command stepped up flights via Gibraltar. Due to the acute shortage of transport aircraft, the discarded BOAC Warwicks were put back into service and allotted to 525 Squadron, which was specially formed in September 1943 at RAF Weston Zoyland, to operate the additional North African flights.

The first Warwick delivered to 525 Squadron was the ill-fated BV 247. The squadron's fleet was eventually made up of mainly ex-BOAC Warwicks and only towards the end of the operations did the squadron receive a few C Mk IIIs, the true military version.

During the planning stages of the North African operation, it became evident from the fuel consumption tests carried out by A&AEE in July 1943 on the ex-BOAC BV 255, that the Warwick's range for the stretch from England to Gibraltar would be very critical.

With the standard contents of 1,010 gallons in the wing tanks, the practical range based on 80% of the still air distance (that is with 20% of contingency reserve), was calculated to be 1,165 nm, while the actual distance was 1,150 nm. This did not allow much for a strong headwind.

Some P&W R2800-powered Warwicks were equipped with extra fuel tanks, but only the ASR models were in this group and the last few of the ex-BOAC aircraft. The auxiliary tanks held 280 gallons, bringing the total capacity to 1,390 gallons. The additional amount would have hardly allowed for a direct flight from England to North Africa.

Despite the considerable experience gained by Transport Command from operations between England and Gibraltar on the Liberators, Halifaxes and Albermarles of 511 Squadron, the impending flights by 525 Squadron were approached with caution in view of the Warwick's critical range. Consequently, an experimental flight with ten servicemen on board, planned for October 1943, was delayed due to unfavourable winds.

Eventually the inaugural flight departed on 2 November 1943 from RAF Station Portreath in the south-western corner of Cornwall. Portreath was selected as it was the closest airfield to Gibraltar. Later flights were transferred to RAF St Mawgan, a Transport Command Station, which had a much longer runway and was located only twenty miles further to the north.

Throughout the winter months, 525 Squadron

flew transport services at regular intervals and without any mishaps. By February 1944, some 50,000 lb of freight and 119 service passengers were carried to and from North Africa. During that period, F/O Gavel made several trips.

It appeared that, in spite of the Warwick's tarnished reputation, pessimism was not justified. The aircraft flew with reasonably high payloads, often as much as 5,000 to 6,000 lb. But it was only a matter of time before good luck ran out.

PART VIII

The allegation by Fawkes that BV 247 was sabotaged by a bomb must be closely examined During the war, it would not have been particularly difficult to smuggle a small explosive device on board. Due to shortage of manpower, security checks were generally sketchy. The Air Dispatch and Reception Units, whose duties were to supervise movements of Transport Command aircraft, were not staffed to search passengers or to inspect every consignment of freight and this would only have been done in exceptional circumstances.

Fawkes claimed that the bomb was about sixteen inches long and contained about a pound of explosives. The trigger was supposed to have been an electric circuit run on a dry-cell battery and activated by bellows, which would expand through the drop in air pressure when climbing.

The description of the bomb resembles a device that was used by Arab terrorists to destroy a Swissair Convair 990 in 1970.

A point must be stressed about relying on changes of air pressure to activate a trigger. Only a relatively large drop of pressure could expand the bellows sufficiently to close the electric circuit. A few hundred feet of altitude variation just after take-off most certainly would have no appreciable effect.

It was suggested in the programme that the explosive device was probably placed under the pilot's seat. This sounds most unlikely, as the seat would have to be adjusted to suit individual pilots and any object under the seat would have been easily detected.

Fawkes believed that the bomb was intended to liquidate an undesirable person. In order to substantiate his theory, he checked the passenger and the crew list. But the crew were not a likely target, so it had to be someone from the service personnel. He investigated their backgrounds and out of the twelve occupants on board, he narrowed down his suspicion to two men. Both

were French. One was Commandant Roger Baudouin and the other Lieutenant Maurice Schwob.

Baudouin was a crypto-analyst at the Government Code and Cypher School at Bletchley Park. Judging by his position, he was probably someone not particularly controversial and there appears to be no reason as to why the British or some other secret service would want him out of the way.

This could not be said of Schwob who was supposed to have been given a list of Cagoulards, the members of a secret Fascist organisation active in France before the war were called. To some Frenchmen in Algeria, who at the time were beginning to cooperate with the Allies, revelations of their unsavoury past could spell danger and they may have wished to have Schwob silenced.

At that particular stage of the war, travel permits were strictly controlled. Anyone who was allowed to leave England would have enjoyed the explicit trust of Government officials and would have been strictly screened. With D-Day approaching, security arrangements were considerably tightened as newspapers reported on 17 April 1944 (the day of the Warwick crash):

'Under pressure from the military commanders for the "Overlord" invasion of Europe, the British war cabinet has clamped on diplomatic privileges, held up diplomatic bags and put all foreign embassies under surveillance.

Even friendly embassies have been included, since it was reckoned that they would not be completely secure against spies, dupes or chumps. There has been only one protest about the restrictions from officials of General de Gaulle's Free French.'

But why should the British Secret Service have gone to all the trouble of destroying an aircraft with fifteen innocent people on board, in order to eliminate one person who was anyway expected to travel with the approval of the highest authority, passes all comprehension.

Gervase Cowell, a former Special Operations Executive adviser on French affairs interviewed on the *The Gold Plane* programme by Fawkes, was of the same opinion. To Cowell, evidently a highly rational individual, the suggestion that the crash was caused by an act of foul play sounded like nonsense. His actual words reflected the commonsense of his argument: 'As a policeman, you will surely realise that on the evidence you've got, you would not get conviction for riding without a rear light?'

Fawkes's reply did not produce a satisfactory counter argument: 'Not in a criminal court but in a civil court which would consider balance of probabilities.'

But such a balance of probabilities in favour of a bomb would be very much in question, considering the very poor safety record of the Warwicks. Wild theories may have made the programme sound like a great thriller, but in life the naked truth is often undramatic and mostly not so involved.

PART IX

The particulars of the Warwick's single-engine performance as well as a résumé of the fuel jettisoning procedure, together with an account of the P&W R2800 ignition problems, should provide the reader with a comprehensive background to my reasoning as to what caused the explosion of the Warwick BV 247. It had nothing to do with the possibility of a bomb having been planted on board.

After more than fifty years, it was not easy to reconstruct with any degree of certainty the events on the night of the crash from the scanty evidence that is still available. Therefore, a detailed analysis of every possible contributory factor was necessary, in order to substantiate that shortly after take-off F/O Gavel found himself in an extremely critical situation from which there was no easy way out. The Pilot's Notes did not cater for the combination of adverse odds with which even a superhuman could not cope.

The most important contributory factor to the BV 247 accident was the all-up weight on departure from St Mawgan. The more load that was carried above 37,000 lb, the more difficult it would have been for the pilot to keep the aircraft from sinking to the ground if an engine happened to fail. It was therefore important to establish the take-off weight as accurately as possible. But this seemed at first an insurmountable task.

Fortunately an A&AEE report from 1943 could be traced and it contained the Warwick C Mk I loading instructions. Relying also on an old RAF loadsheet made out for one of my flights on the Warwick C Mk III, the actual take-off weight of BV 247 on the night of the accident could be calculated to the nearest 100 lb.

During the evaluation trials at Boscombe Down, BV 243 (the sister ship of the ill-fated

BV 247) was weighed and its tare weight was established to be 26,722 lb, including engine oil. The report also specified the weight of service equipment as 656 lb. For overwater flights special life-saving equipment – a large inflatable rubber dinghy – was expected to be carried on board and this would have added 360 lb. The total came to 27,234 lb.

According to the 525 Squadron OR Book, the payload consisted of twelve service passengers, and 1,680 lb of freight. Together with four crew members it came to 5,520 lb. From my old RAF loadsheet, I obtained the average weight per passenger or per crew member as 240 lb, and this included luggage and a personal dinghy.

The next problem was to determine the exact amount of fuel BV 247 was expected to carry for the stretch to Gibraltar. As the aircraft was not fitted with auxiliary tanks, most probably the main tanks were used to their full capacity of 1,100 imperial gallons. This converted to weight represented 7,272 lb, based on an average specific gravity.

It is unlikely that less fuel had been put in the tanks. The entries in the 525 Squadron OR Book indicate that most flights between St Mawgan and Gibraltar were of about seven hours duration, which required a minimum of 1,100 gallons, including the contingency reserve.

The final figure of the take-off weight, including fuel, came to 41,020 lb. This was about 4,000 lb above the Warwick's capability to maintain height on one engine and about 6,000 lb above if it had been necessary to make a climb in order to complete a landing circuit.

The fateful flight, for which F/O Gavel was rostered as the captain, had been scheduled to depart St Mawgan on 17 April 1944 for Maison Blanche airfield in Algeria, with an intermediate landing at Gibraltar. Other crew members were: second pilot F/Sgt Rowe, navigator F/O Gardiner and radio operator F/O Austen, another Canadian.

The consignment of freight contained one item of a particular importance – £45,000 in one-pound notes, pay for the British forces in North Africa. It represented over five million pounds sterling at today's value.

The 525 Squadron OR Book described the circumstances surrounding the accident:

'17.4.1944. Warwick BV 247 on leaving RAF St Mawgan in the early hours of the morning, *en route* to Gibraltar with 12 passengers, exploded and crashed into Newquay Bay, approximately 5 minutes after take-off. The

AIRCRAFT LOADSHEET.
No 216 GROUP TRANSPORT COMMAND
R.A.F.

Date 2/2/46. FLIGHT No SN62. FROM: NAPLES. TO: ATHENS.
AIRCRAFT TYPE & No NAR. 335 Sqdn. No 244 NAME OF OWNER RAF.

WEIGHT COMPUTATION
Payload Computation

				Take-off	
WT.OF A/C PREPARED		E.	Authorised maximum all-up weight......	45000	43000
A. FOR SERVICE ...... 2.9.5.0.		F.	LESS:'Weight less Fuel & Payload' (Total at D.)	30350	30350
CREW		G.	Available for Fuel & Payload (E-F)	14650	12650
(1. N. KROTELSKI	12.0.0.				
(2. 2. CHEN			FUEL LOAD US/IMP GALLONS		
(3.		H.	Total in tanks .... gals.		
B. (4.		J.	Estimated for run up... gals.		
(5.		K.	" on take off. 500 gals. 3600		
(6.		L.	" for flight.. 400 gals.		
(7.		M.	" on landing... 100 gals.		
EXTRA EQUIPMENT					720
(1.		N.	Available for Payload(Col.1=G-K.Col2=G-M)	11050	11930
C. (2.		O.	Actual Payload(Must not exceed lower figure in N.Cols.1 & 2)	2782	2782
(3.		P.	ADD.Estimated weight of Fuel(Totals at K and M)	3600	720
(4.		Q.	ADD:'WT.less Fuel & Payload'(Total at D)	30350	30350
D. WT. LESS FUEL AND PAYLOAD (A+B+C)		R.	ACTUAL ALL-UP WEIGHT (O+P+Q)	36732	33852
30350					

LOAD SUMMARY

Qty.	Item	Destination	Manifest No.	Weight	Wt Next Stop	Recei
13	FREI	ATHENS	—	2782	2782	

PAYLOAD 2782 2782
TOTAL WEIGHT FOR NEXT STOP 2782
THROUGH PAYLOAD

E.TD.
LOADSHEET PREPARED BY CAPTAIN'S SIGNATURE

An original RAF Transport Command loadsheet for the Warwick C Mk III used to estimate the take-off weight of the Warwick which crashed near Newquay in 1944.

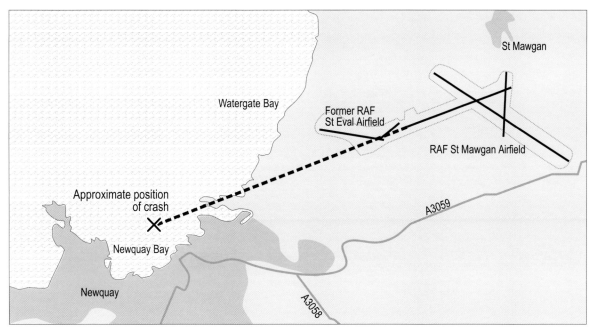

Estimated flight path of Warwick I BV 247 of 525 Squadron, which crashed on 17 April 1944.

bodies of two of the crew (F/O H.C. Austen – WAG, and F/O A.G.T. Gardiner – Nav) and twelve passengers were recovered.

The bodies of the Captain, F/O A.G. Gavel and the second pilot, F/Sgt M.K. Rowe were not recovered.'

The official record of the inquiry by the Air Ministry Accident Investigation Branch stated (this information was provided by the RAF Museum at Hendon): 'Pilot probably lost control while endeavouring to maintain height after engine failure in fog patch. Engine failure after take-off – reason unknown.'

But running into a fog patch just after becoming airborne, would have been unlikely to have created any stability problem for F/O Gavel. All Transport Command pilots frequently practised instrument flying under a hood. Moreover, he had received an unusually extensive course on the Link Trainer for wartime circumstances, which amounted to 136 hours. Consequently, the lack of visual horizon should not have affected his ability to continue climbing safely.

Moreover, any fog was probably thin. I often experienced this when flying Coastal Command patrols out of RAF St Eval, an airfield less than half a mile away from St Mawgan. Due to the fact

that both airfields were located on top of 300-foot-high cliffs and not far off the coast, a sea breeze would bring moist air and during the night it was usual for wisps of fog to form.

F/O Gavel would have quickly crossed a fog patch and continued climbing in clear air. The 6,500-foot-long runway at St Mawgan would have helped him to maintain a steady course after leaving the ground. At the time, it was an exceptionally long runway. The majority of other RAF airfields were equipped with only 4,000-foot-long runways.

With the long history of the Warwick's rudder deficiencies, the investigators must have presumed that an inability to keep the aircraft straight was the most likely explanation for the crash. Nevertheless, it looks doubtful that this had been the cause of diving into the sea.

Although the Pilot's Notes contains a warning about an excessive use of the rudder, it does not appear to have been unduly critical when correcting for engine failure, as it is stated in the Notes:

'On aircraft not fitted with a dorsal fin it is possible, at low speeds, to use the rudder so as to produce excessive skid or side-slip; if this is done rudder overbalance may be experienced. Harsh use of the rudder in this manner should, therefore, be avoided. This does not restrict the use of the rudder necessary to check swing in the case of engine failure.'

Even if BV 247 was not fitted with a dorsal fin, this should not have presented an undue problem to F/O Gavel. He was a relatively experienced pilot with a total of 800 hours. By the time of

the accident, he had completed 140 hours on the Warwicks, out of which seventy were at night. He previously carried out several take-offs at higher weights than on the night of the accident. One entry in 525 Squadron OR Book shows a weight of 42,500 lb when departing from Portreath for Gibraltar on 3 March.

RAF Report on the crash of Warwick I BV 247.

The fatal take-off was made in the west-south-westerly direction towards Trevelgue Head. Due to a lack of accurate information on the Warwick's flight path, the actual position of the accident could be only roughly estimated. It is known that the aircraft fell down into Newquay Bay, which is in line with the runway. The bay is just over one nautical mile wide and its middle point lies only three nautical miles from the airfield. At the usual climb speed of 115 knots, it would have taken one and a half minutes to arrive overhead the bay. Therefore the statement in the OR Book that the crash occurred five minutes after take-off cannot be correct.

If both engines operated normally, in one and a half minutes the aircraft should have reached about 1,000 feet, according to the performance figures from the A&AEE report. But with a probable loss of power on one engine shortly after becoming airborne, BV 247 would have struggled to maintain barely a few hundred feet above the ground. Over the sea the clearance would have increased by 300 feet.

When the engine began to cut out, the only way to stop the aircraft from sinking to the ground would have been to keep the ailing engine running even if it was delivering only partial power. This could minimise the loss of height while the weight was being reduced by jettisoning fuel. It would require at least thirty seconds to bring the weight down to 37,000 lb, and in those crucial moments staying in the air by any means regardless of the risks involved, was the only solution.

Only after the all-up weight was sufficiently reduced to maintain safe height, and if the power on the ailing engine was eventually completely lost, would it have then been advisable to feather the propeller and shut the engine down.

A search through the 525 Squadron OR Book has not revealed any entries about previous problems with the ignition system on the R2800s. Consequently, F/O Gavel may not have been aware that they were prone to backfiring once the magneto began to malfunction.

Initiating fuel jettisoning while the engine was backfiring would have created an extremely dangerous situation. This was due to the fact that when fuel was discharged from the wing tanks with the help of air pressure, it would have formed a plume of fine spray. With the flaps at that moment still extended for take-off, the spray would have been very likely drawn under the wing.

But what F/O Gavel may not have realised was

that the outlet of the exhaust pipe, which had been lengthened by the installation of flame dampers, was as close as ten feet (three metres) from the inboard fuel-dumping chute. This was a grave design oversight. If the ailing engine backfired into the plume of fuel spray, it could be expected that the consequence would have been catastrophic.

We must be grateful to former superintendent Fawkes for his indefatigable efforts to collect every shred of evidence. With a typical police officer's thoroughness in his inquiries, he managed to trace an eyewitness of the last moments of the ill-fated Warwick. A former Home Guard sergeant reported seeing flashes in the sky, followed by an explosion. The flashes were clearly from a backfiring engine, which could have eventually ignited fuel while it was being discharged from the chutes.

The fact that the aircraft debris was not spread over a large area is an indication that the explosion did not take place inside the fuselage. This contradicts any suggested theory of a bomb having been planted on board.

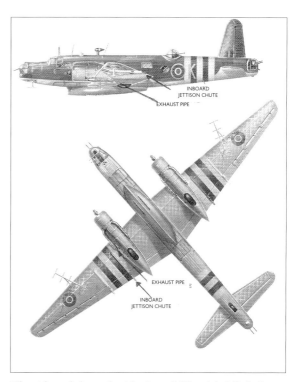

The side and the underside view of Warwick Mk I, the Air Sea Rescue version, showing the proximity of exhaust pipes and inboard fuel jettison chutes. The aircraft is very similar to the Warwick C Mk I, used by 525 Squadron.

A powerful blast that probably occurred just aft of the wing trailing edge, where fuel was being jettisoned through the dumping chutes, must have ripped the tail unit off, sending the aircraft nose-diving into the sea. This is why the divers were able to find fourteen bodies as well as the case with £45,000 inside the submerged wreck. The fate of F/O Gavel and his co-pilot appears to have been different. It looks as if they had been thrown out of the cockpit through the front windows when the Warwick struck the water and their bodies were swept away by sea currents.

The report of the Accident Investigating Branch criticised the Flying Control Office at St Mawgan for not initiating a prompt search. It was believed that this could have saved the lives of some crew members. However, considering the circumstances of the crash, it was most unlikely that there were any survivors after the Warwick struck the sea.

No evidence has surfaced that foul play had anything to do with the demise of BV 247. It must have been a tragic combination of two factors, a design flaw in positioning the inboard jettison chute too close to the exhaust pipe, and a manufacturing weakness of the magneto contact breakers, a frequent cause of backfiring engines, which was the most likely reason for the explosion. On their own, the two innocuous factors would have been harmless, but together they turned the ill-starred Warwick into a flying bomb.

The BV 247 accident made such a strong impact on HQ 44 Group Transport Command that ten days later all 525 Squadron flights were suspended and the Warwicks were forthwith withdrawn from service. At the same time, the squadron received notification that it would shortly be re-equipped with Dakotas.

In June 1944, the last 525 Squadron Warwick, which was undergoing repairs at Gibraltar after a landing accident, had been finally brought back to base but without any payload. A month later, transport operations were started on the Dakotas.

4

1951–65 – THE CURSE OF THE PHARAOHS

PART I

Cairo's connections with flying activities go as far back as World War I. When Turkey joined the Austro–German side, the British Government stationed two Royal Flying Corps squadrons on a small landing field at Heliopolis on the north-eastern outskirts of the city, in order to protect the Suez Canal from attacks by the forces of the Ottoman Empire. Although Egypt gained independence in 1923, the British kept the defence of the Suez Canal in their hands, and Heliopolis was turned into a permanent RAF base. Between the two wars it also served as Cairo's main airport for commercial traffic.

But with the arrival of high-performance aircraft requiring longer take-off and landing runs, Heliopolis eventually outlived its usefulness. Surrounded by a built-up area, it could no longer be expanded. In World War II, Heliopolis was only used for communication services by light aircraft, which catered for the needs of staff officers from various military headquarters in Cairo. Another nearby airfield, Almaza, although built much later, was also suffering from the same drawback and its operational role during the war was equally limited. It mainly served as a personnel transit centre and housed a small detachment of Halifaxes and Dakotas from Transport Command.

During the North African campaign in 1941–43, a number of landing grounds sprang up around Cairo. One of them was LG 219 (Kilo 8), otherwise known as Mataryah, situated only eight kilometres from the city. In the early days it was only used as a transit station for RAF squadrons during their formation or while waiting to be transferred to an advanced airfield.

Towards the end of the war, the American Air Force took over LG 219 and built two long runways. Planned as a staging post for ferrying aircraft between the USA and the Pacific combat zone, it was renamed Payne Field. From the operational point of view, the location was far from ideal. The approach from the south-easterly direction passed over high sand dunes, which rose to 1,500 feet as close as ten miles from the airfield. There were no lights on the barren stretch of desert and a landing at night could prove to be a tricky procedure. But with the Cairo–Suez railway line running along the airport's northern boundary, it was not possible to move runway 16/34 further to the north, where the land was flat.

As a result of being the only large airfield close to the city, and at the time equipped with relatively modern radio aids for the early post-war years, Payne Field eventually became the main commercial airport for Cairo. At first it was known as Farouk Airport, named after the king who then ruled the country. Almaza was taken over by the Egyptian Air Force and Heliopolis, used only by the local gliding club, was in the end swallowed up by building developments.

After World War II, Cairo Airport became a busy destination for many airlines and also a transit-refuelling stop for services to East Africa and to the Middle and Far East. Despite these growing requirements from the international side of air transport, passenger facilities and landing aids had not been modernised since Payne Field was taken over by the Egyptians. Most of the radio aids inherited from the American Air Force, were becoming out of date and no new facilities were installed. As a result of poor maintenance, there were frequent breakdowns.

The invasion by the combined forces of Britain, France and Israel in 1956, left Egypt impoverished. Nasser refused to clear scuttled ships from the Suez Canal until Israel gave up the conquered territories and soon the loss of revenue from toll charges was deeply felt. Moreover, rebuilding the army and the air force became a top priority, and as a result, government funds or aid from Russia were predominantly funnelled into defence. The financial allocations to the Civil Aviation Department were greatly curtailed and this brought a gradual deterioration of the aeronautical services and airport facilities.

By the end of the fifties the situation at Cairo Airport became very critical. Complaints from pilots about numerous deficiencies kept reaching the headquarters of the International Federation of Air Line Pilots' Associations in London. Many cases were reported of radio beacons frequently going off the air, erratic radio communication, out-of-date or incorrect weather observations, weak runway lights, and approach lights that were switched on only after a specific request. Moreover, the lack of alertness and poor discipline displayed by air traffic controllers, as well as by ground radio operators and meteorological observers, often created a potentially hazardous situation. Although the ICAO Technical Assistance Mission provided expert help, the training of the local staff was not up to international standards.

As a result, Cairo Airport, as one of the first in Africa, was put on the IFALPA black list. Although in that region there were many more badly equipped airfields, in view of the much higher density of traffic at Cairo Airport, the chances of an accident were much greater.

At the 1959 IFALPA Annual Conference in Helsinki, a report was compiled on the numerous deficiencies at Cairo Airport. Having just been appointed as the IFALPA Regional Vice-President for the Middle and Far East, it fell upon my shoulders to present the report to the Egyptian authorities. An opportunity arose during a stopover in Cairo on my way to the Far East.

When I called at the Department of Civil Aviation and asked to see the Director General in order to discuss the problems with the airport facilities, at first I was not given civil treatment. I was kept waiting for an hour and then advised that I would not be received by the Director but by his deputy, E.A.M. Bahgat.

After I was shown into Bahgat's office, I was not invited to sit down. Consequently I got straight to the point and after a brief introductory explanation, I placed the IFALPA report on the Cairo Airport deficiencies on Bahgat's desk. He began to read it, without uttering a word.

Watching his face showing signs of annoyance, I could foresee a heated discussion looming ahead. But it turned out to be a bad-tempered outburst on his part, complaining that the report was an attempt by IFALPA, which had Israeli and other 'imperialistic' pilots' associations in its ranks, to smear Egypt's good name.

This was my first exposure to dealing with the aviation authorities in the Middle East and a shock as to how pilots' constructive criticism could be misinterpreted. I pointed out that Cairo had not been singled out as the only below-standard airport. The top of the list was headed by New York Idlewild Airport, as it was then called.

Through a stroke of luck I had brought with me the Conference document on the deficiencies at Idlewild and showed it to Bahgat. The report was very critical of the inadequate landing aids and the airport was condemned as a disgrace to the world's richest country. As the only point of entry from Europe to the USA for all foreign airlines, and considering the volume of traffic, it was expected that the best available facilities should have been installed. Instead, there was only a bare minimum of radio aids provided.

After reading the Idlewild report, Baghat's attitude at once changed. I was finally asked to sit down and we began to discuss IFALPA's complaints as two equal partners. I outlined the problems with the night landing facilities and our priorities for the most pressing improvements. This called for minor but urgent rectifications, such as cleaning the runway lights, reducing waiting time for a reply from ATC and more realistic weather reports. As a longer-range project, IFALPA was suggesting that, even ahead of an ILS for which airlines were pressing after it had been withdrawn from service due to a total breakdown, visual approach aids should be installed on all runways at the earliest opportunity. In view of fine weather generally prevailing in Egypt, costly electronic equipment was less urgent than the everyday requirements for safe night landings, such as approach lights or a VASI.

From the subsequent discussion it became apparent that Bahgat appreciated the order of priorities suggested by IFALPA, and he could understand our anxiety about rectifying the shortcomings that mattered most in day-to-day operations. He then asked me for my personal impression of the situation at the airport on my arrival a day earlier.

I enumerated all the problems that I had encountered. They included several calls over a period of five minutes before the Approach Controller replied. I had to ask for the weather report and it was not correct. From looking out of the cockpit windows it was evident that visibility varied in different sectors of the airfield, but only one figure for general visibility had been provided. Finally, the green threshold lights were not switched on. Bahgat kept making notes and then asked me if I could see him again during my stopover on the way back from the Far East. But what came as a surprise was that he insisted on giving me a lift in his car back to my hotel. In the days of the country's dire petrol shortage, this was a generous gesture. It seemed that in spite of a frosty start, IFALPA's constructive efforts to bring the attention of the authorities to the hazardous deficiencies had, in the end, been recognised.

Upon my return from the Far East, changes were already apparent. When I called Approach, the controller promptly replied and passed on a weather report without me even having to ask for it. Runway lights shone brightly and the controller wanted to know if I would prefer to have them dimmed.

I soon learnt from KLM Flight Operations what lay behind this sudden turnaround in the practices of the airport personnel. It was a result of Bahgat's lightning visit to the airport in the middle of the night, shortly after my departure for the Far East. Apparently quite a few heads had rolled when some members of the staff on duty were caught sleeping.

Unfortunately, as it often happens in that part of the world, the sweep of a new broom did not last long. My subsequent flights through Cairo revealed that the aeronautical services were gradually returning to their old lax ways and the radio facilities were suffering from failures just as frequently as in the past.

Further visits to the Directorate of Civil Aviation produced only a few minor changes for the better. In the long run there had been a series of ups and downs, but in the end the overall improvement was marginal. One of my attempts to provide help was to give a lecture, at Bahgat's request, to the Egyptian air traffic controllers on the cardinal points of cooperation between pilots and ATC.

There was no doubt that to make Cairo Airport safe required a major renewal of the outdated landing aids and a drastic re-training of the personnel. In the opinion of IFALPA, plugging holes could not cure the perennial shortcomings.

Unfortunately, after having been transferred to the KLM North Atlantic routes, I had to give up my function of the IFALPA Regional Vice-President of the Middle and Far East. My successor continued the uphill struggle with the same degree of limited success.

IFALPA's concern about potential hazards during night operations had been born out by a number of tragic disasters. Between 1951 and 1965 six civil and one military aircraft crashed near Cairo Airport with a high toll of lives, all in similar circumstances. Three of these accidents took place within two miles of each other. Furthermore, two undershooting incidents were known to have occurred, resulting in heavy damage. In most cases, the finger had been pointed at the pilots for committing airmanship blunders.

PART II

The horrendous disaster at Cairo Airport in 1965, the sixth in a spate of puzzling accidents, attracted wider than usual attention from the press. The media strived to find a mystical explanation as to why this aircraft and several others earlier on, had literally dropped out of the skies during night approaches.

In a programme by one of the major British radio stations, a parallel has been drawn between the fate of the archaeologists who had the audacity to 'disturb' the sanctuaries of the divine Egyptian rulers and that of the pilots who dared to overfly them. The cause of the Cairo crashes was supposed to have been akin to the case of the famous British Egyptologist, George Herbert, 5th Earl of Carnarvon, who died soon after entering the Tutankhamun burial chamber.

Carnarvon's assistant, Howard Carter, after exploring many sites in the Valley of the Kings, discovered towards the end of 1922 an entrance to a tomb. However, only in the spring of 1923 did he and Carnarvon manage to break in and they came across a magnificent collection of Egyptian art. But the find seemed to have a curse attached to it. Within six weeks, Carnavon was dead, and in the following years seven members of the excavating team met with the same tragic fate. Carter did not live to a ripe old age either. He died at fifty-eight.

The sudden illness to which Lord Carnarvon had so rapidly succumbed in Egypt, supposedly blood poisoning from a mosquito bite, had been the subject of sensational speculation in newspapers all around the world. The drama was heightened by the mysterious death of his favourite dog on the same day and a quarter of Cairo plunging into darkness from a power failure. Although the latter may have appeared like some omnipotent omen, to the airline crews who made frequent stopovers in Cairo, electricity cuts were known to be the order of the day.

Listeners of the sensational radio programme were left with an impression that like the demise of Lord Carnarvon and the members of his entourage, the Cairo crashes were brought about by a Pharaoh's curse. Some mysterious hand had tried to avenge the disrespect the pilots had displayed by overflying the sacrosanct burial sites.

PART III

The first officially recorded accident at Cairo Airport took place on 19 November 1951. A DC3 of Devlet Hava Yollari, the national Turkish airline, crashed on final approach after a scheduled flight from Ankara. The aircraft struck a sand dune, broke in two and was totally destroyed. Out of seven occupants on board, four crew members and one passenger lost their lives. The approach was at night and in relatively good weather. A pattern seemed to have been set for future accidents of the same nature. Although a limited record of the Turkish Airlines crash had been preserved, it is certain that it happened while the aircraft was on finals to runway 34, as it is the only area around the airport where there are high sand dunes.

Eight months later, on 23 June 1952, a SAS DC6, registration SE-BDD, crash-landed at the airport, after striking a sand dune during approach to runway 34. The aircraft lost its undercarriage and landed on its belly. The crash was not classified as an accident because there were no casualties, but the DC6 sustained heavy, although repairable, damage.

Five years later, another disaster took place in similar circumstances but a few miles further away. On 20 February 1956, a DC6B, registration F-BGOD, from a private French company, Transport Aérien Intercontinentaux (TAI), struck a hill in the desert during an approach at night.

The aircraft was on a scheduled flight from Saigon to Paris with refuelling stops at Karachi and Cairo. It was under the command of Captain Charles Billet, a DC6B check pilot who was giving route instructions to another captain.

At 02.24 hrs GMT the aircraft reported over Suez (sixty nautical miles east of Cairo) and gave the estimated time of arrival over Cairo Airport as 02.37 hrs. After Suez, descent was initiated from the last assigned cruising altitude of 8,500 feet and when passing 4,500 feet, the captain thought that they were too high for the approach and, in order to expedite the descent, he called for the landing gear to be lowered and the flaps extended to twenty degrees.

Although it was a clear night, he told the pilot under training, who was flying the aircraft from the left-hand seat, to execute an ILS approach purely on instruments, while he would keep a visual look-out. In order to save time, a direct approach without a procedure turn was planned. This meant proceeding slightly to the north-east of the outer marker, in order to intercept the localiser beam and subsequently the glide slope. For the trainee captain it would have been his first experience of using ILS.

The laid-down procedure at Cairo Airport called for crossing the outer marker outbound at 2,000 feet, then upon turning inbound, descending to and maintaining 1,700 feet until intercepting the $2\frac{1}{2}°$ glide slope. This procedure would have taken three minutes longer than a direct approach.

However the aircraft did not arrive over the airfield at the expected time, probably due to the airspeed having been prematurely reduced for the approach. At 02.37 hrs, the captain reported fifteen miles out and the Cairo Airport lights in sight. But as it was subsequently established, the aircraft was at that moment, actually twenty miles away. The captain later stated that the airport lights were to the right but it was difficult to be sure because they were not isolated from the local illumination.

He was subsequently cleared for a visual approach and was told to change over to the Approach frequency. After issuing landing instructions, the controller asked the pilots to call 'downwind'. But the message was never acknowledged and there was no further contact with the aircraft, in spite of endless attempts to get in touch on every available frequency. Two hours later, the wreckage was sighted eighteen miles to the south-east of the airport. Out of sixty-four occupants, only six passengers and six crew members survived, among them both pilots.

During the interrogation, the trainee captain stated that, when he first saw the ILS localiser needle deflected to the right, he continued on a heading of 280°, waiting to intercept the 229° localiser beam. Once the needle began to centre, he turned onto 230°, while maintaining 2,000 feet by applying thirty-one inches of boost (this should have been ample on a DC6B for a level flight). He then expected the outer marker to come up shortly.

Just as the turn onto 230° was completed, the captain noticed the red warning flag on the ILS indicator come into view. But it was too late to warn the co-pilot and the aircraft struck the ground at 1,360 feet amsl, on a heading of 240°. It was totally destroyed by fire.

The examination of the crash site revealed that the first mark on the sandy soil was a six-metre-long imprint made by the nosewheel. This pointed to a nose-down attitude on impact. But the trainee captain insisted that the aircraft hit the ground in a level flight. The investigators argued that if this was the case, the aircraft could have not cleared a hill that was forty feet higher than the initial point of impact and located 250 metres further back. To miss the hill, the aircraft must have been descending at a rate of about 500 ft/min, which was the same as required to follow a 2½° glide path.

At first, a wrong setting on the altimeter had been suspected but the QFE, set on the left-hand instrument panel, was found to be correct. A remote possibility of the static system having been blocked was also considered. This would have resulted in the altimeter showing higher altitude than in reality. But the investigators claimed that any error of that nature would have also been reflected in a wrong ASI indication. Nevertheless, such errors would not have been of the same magnitude (see chapter 5).

Judging by the rate of descent of 500 ft/min just before the crash, the investigators concluded that the trainee captain must have followed the localiser and glide slope needles, which just happened to centre but most likely as a result of the breakdown of the ILS signal. Lacking experience of ILS procedures, he failed to notice that the warning flag came on. It was known that the glide slope transmitter was out of service but it was possible that the localiser signal could also have gone off the air momentarily. The investigators were of the opinion that, as a result of relying on an inoperative ILS, the trainee captain initiated a premature descent over high terrain, eighteen miles from the airfield, in a belief that he was safely on final. They estimated that the aircraft struck the ground fifteen seconds after commencing the turn to intercept the localiser.

In respect of the probable cause, the report by the Egyptian Civil Aviation Department of the Ministry of Communication, stated that: 'The accident was due to the failure of the pilot-in-command to monitor the co-pilot during a direct approach procedure and the reliance of the latter exclusively to fix his position relative to the runway at an altitude below the minimum safe altitude. The factor of crew members' fatigue cannot be ruled out.'

Indeed the crew had been on duty for twenty-one and a half hours from the time of leaving Saigon. Weather conditions could not have contributed to the accident. Visibility was good and only 4/8 clouds were reported over the airport at a height of 1,200 to 3,000 metres.

Analysing the conclusions reached by the Egyptian investigators reveals certain shortfalls in their reconstruction of the events just prior to impact. They claimed that the aircraft had lost 640 feet (from 2,000 feet to impact at 1,360 feet) during the 50° turn (from 280° to 230°), which at 'rate one' of 3° per second, would have taken seventeen seconds to complete.

But with the rate of descent at 500 ft/min, as presumed by the investigators, only 140 feet would have been lost in seventeen seconds. A corresponding time for 640 feet would have been seventy-six seconds. This means that the aircraft could not have been flown into the ground as if in a controlled descent following a 2½° glide slope. But due to an undetermined factor, a rapid sinking of 2,200 ft/min had been experienced which caught the pilots by surprise. Such a high rate of descent would have been exceptional for a DC6B. It could only have been attained by a steep dive and this would have been shown by different ground marks on impact. The only probability was an unusual meteorological phenomenon.

The French judicial authorities regarded the TAI DC6B crash as a case of manslaughter. In respect of air disasters, French criminal code was at the time very Draconian. Even during the pioneering days of aviation activities in France, 'astronauts' whose balloons had been forced to land in a field, could face criminal proceedings.

One of the first post-war cases was the TAI accident. Captain Billet was found guilty of 'involuntary homicide' and was sentenced to pay a fine of 5,000 francs. At the time, this sum probably represented a month's salary. Nevertheless, the court had taken due notice of the fact that the crew were most likely extremely tired after a flight of twenty-one-and-a-half hours duration and had an insufficient prior rest of only twenty-two hours instead of thirty-seven hours.

PART IV

The next disaster that took place at Cairo Airport, two years later almost to the day on 19 February 1958, involved a DC6B, registration PH-DFK, from KLM Royal Dutch Airlines. Flight 543 was a Middle East service from Amsterdam to Cairo, with intermediate stops at Prague, Vienna, Athens and Beirut. The cockpit crew consisted of three pilots, Captain John Musselman, a Canadian in service with KLM, a regular first officer and a trainee second officer as well as a flight engineer and a radio operator.

Captain Musselman was a route instructor with a total of 10,500 flying hours, out of which 3,880 were on the DC6Bs. The second officer was undergoing route familiarisation, in order to be upgraded as a first officer.

During base training, the second officer received fifteen hours dual on the DC6B, and up to the time of the accident, he had made five trips to the Middle East. His total was 2,000 hours and 530 were on the DC6B. He had already carried out one landing at Cairo Airport two weeks earlier, on runway 05.

Upon arriving over the airfield, weather conditions were good; wind was reported as 110/14 kt, visibility twelve kilometres and the sky was clear. The trainee second officer occupied the left-hand seat. This was at the time a standard KLM practice when the co-pilot had been assigned to make the landing.

In view of a reported light east-south-easterly wind, the trainee planned to land on either runway 16 or 05, but Tower instructed him to use runway 34. In the conditions of a negligible wind, assigning runway 34 for landing was a matter of convenience for the air traffic controllers. Upon completing their ground run, aircraft ended up close to the terminal, and this simplified taxi instructions, thus reducing the controllers' workload.

However, at night the pilots were faced with serious safety handicaps. High sand dunes on final without any obstruction lights, no radio beacons or approach lights to align with the runway and a lack of illumination on the ground to help in orientation, could turn the approach into a highly hazardous undertaking. A mandatory right-hand circuit, which prevented the pilot in the

left-hand seat from keeping the runway in sight until shortly before final, was a further undesirable complication.

At 01.10 hrs GMT Flight KL 543 advised that it was fifteen miles out, the airfield in sight and requested visual approach. Tower cleared it to land. Three minutes later the aircraft reported 'downwind' and was asked to call on final. Hardly a minute elapsed when it was heard reporting that it had hit something. At first, the controller failed to acknowledge the message. Then after a long pause, he just cleared the aircraft to land. The pilot immediately requested an emergency landing, but in reply, the controller only repeated his last instruction. In spite of another request, there was no response from Tower.

Shortly afterwards the DC6B touched down on runway 34 seriously damaged. Then after running on hard surface for about 1,400 metres, it veered off sharply to the right onto soft sand and came to rest.

The only casualty was the first officer. He was thrown forward into the running propeller of No. 1 engine, when he climbed out on the wing through the emergency exit just before the aircraft came to a standstill. He was fatally injured. Luckily fire did not break out and all other occupants safely evacuated the wreck.

During the preliminary inquiry, the Egyptian investigators claimed that, had runway 16 or 23/05 been requested, permission to use it would most likely have been granted. However, no inquiries were conducted to find out as to why, on this occasion, the tower controller had assigned runway 34 for landing. In view of adverse factors such as a hazardous approach over high grounds and a tail wind component on a not particularly long runway (2,000 metres only) which had a very steep down-slope gradient (1.65%), it was a rather careless selection and a grossly unsafe practice.

According to his testimony, the second officer joined the downwind leg after leaving the Radio Range on a heading of 135° (27° to the runway heading). This heading was maintained for about a minute while speed was reduced from 190 knots to 168 knots, the limit for the flap extension, at which flaps were lowered to twenty degrees. At that moment he realised that he was too close to the runway and picked up a heading of 120° for about thirty seconds, before turning onto base leg. During that time, he continued to decelerate to the approach speed of 125 knots. On base leg he called for the undercarriage to be lowered and engine power to be set by the flight engineer to

28 in boost with 2,400 RPM, recommended power for a rate of descent of 500 ft/min. Shortly afterwards the captain performed the final checklist with the assistance of the flight engineer, and this could have momentarily prevented him

from monitoring the instruments.

The second officer continued to turn towards final but he could not see the runway because of the right-hand circuit. The last figure he remembered noticing on the altimeter was 900 feet (if a

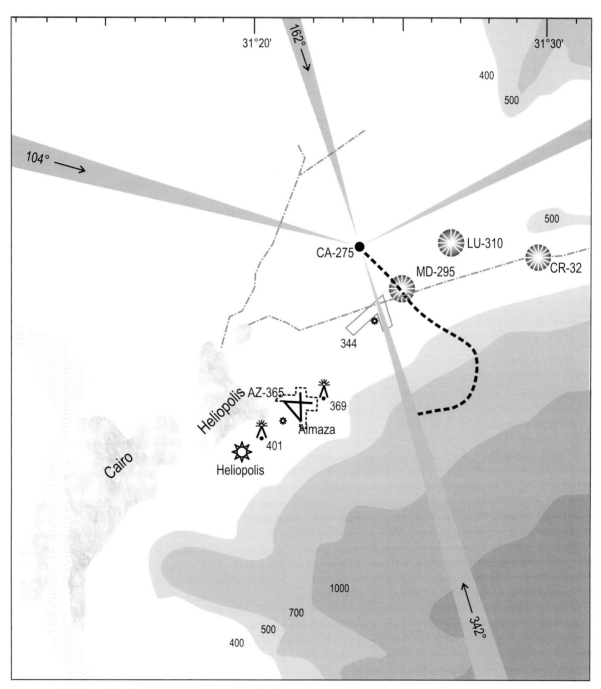

Horizontal flight path of KLM DC6B PH-DFK which crashed at Cairo Airport on 19 February 1958. For vertical flight path see page 84.

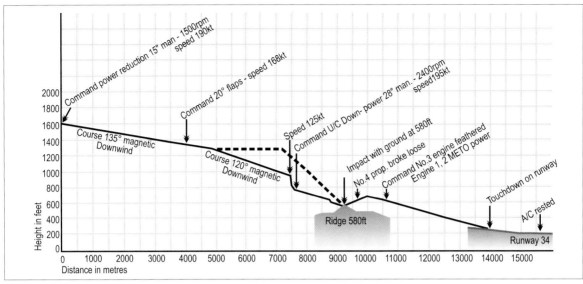

Vertical flight path of KLM DC6B PH-DFK.

2½° glide path was followed, it should have read 970 feet). While banked to the right, the aircraft scraped a ridge of a sand dune at a height of 580 feet. As a result, the propeller of the No. 4 engine came off and the No. 3 engine began to vibrate so heavily that it had to be feathered at once. Also, about one-third of the right elevator and the right horizontal stabiliser were torn off when the tail struck the ground.

The captain immediately took over and called for METO power (Maximum Except for Take-off) on the two operating engines. He managed to get the aircraft under control and eventually, put it down on the runway. Although the right leg of the landing gear was sheared off during the initial impact, with great skill he brought the battered DC6B to rest without any further extensive damage.

In their conclusions, the Egyptian investigators claimed that the premature contact with the ground was a result of the second officer failing to maintain proper height due to disorientation through a lack of visual contact. The actual wording of the probable cause was as follows: 'The captain did not check the aircraft's altitude from time to time during a night landing by visual means. A contributory factor was the appreciable drift of the aircraft from a normal circuit over hazardous terrain which resulted in the aircraft hitting the ground and partially disintegrating before crash landing.'

As the DC6B was not fitted with a Flight Data

Recorder, only a 'presumed' flight path was reconstructed by the investigators. This was supposed to have been prepared in accordance with the testimonies of both the pilots at the controls. However, due to a difference in their statements on actual altitudes during approach, the investigators decided that the figures provided by the second officer were more consistent and they were used for plotting the descent profile. This was a surprising decision as he was not only the least experienced crew member in the cockpit but the captain, by virtue of not flying the aircraft himself, had had a better opportunity to monitor flight instruments.

After examining the altitudes and the rates of descent as shown on the investigators' graph, it became apparent that they considerably differ from the usual practices of a visual circuit on piston-engine aircraft.

The standard altitude maintained until turning for base leg was 1,000 feet above the airfield level. Then the undercarriage was lowered and this would cause the aircraft to descend at approximately 500 ft/min. However, it would take about fifteen seconds for the resultant drag to become effective. At the same time, on command from the pilot handling the aircraft, engine power was adjusted (in KLM by the flight engineer) to maintain the required rate of descent (usually 500 ft/min). When establish on final, full flaps would be extended.

But according to the investigators, after leaving

the Radio Range at 1,600 feet the aircraft began to descend at 320 ft/min with the throttles fully retarded (1,500 RPM and 15 in boost), while airspeed was reduced from 190 to 168 knots. This appears to be so far, a normal routine. However on passing 1,300 feet, the descent is shown to have increased to 655 ft/min. Such a high rate could have not been achieved while, at the same time, the aircraft continued to decelerate from 168 to 125 knots. Moreover, instead of levelling out at 1,300 feet, which was the circuit altitude at Cairo Airport with a field elevation of 300 feet, the descent was continued downwind and base leg down to 800 feet (500 feet above the airport level). Only then, according to the investigators, did the second officer call for the landing gear to be lowered, which was rather late. At such a low altitude full flaps should have been already extended.

It is further shown on the graph that in a matter of a few seconds, the airspeed suddenly rose to 195 knots, which was twenty-seven knots above the limit for the flaps in the approach position. Such high speed could have been only attained by a prolonged and excessive nose-down attitude and this could not have gone unnoticed by the captain and by the flight engineer. On the DC6B the flight engineer occupied a forward-facing seat, situated between the two pilot stations.

But if the standard circuit altitude of 1,300 feet had been maintained until descent was initiated during a turn for base leg, the loss of height from that position until impact would have occurred at a rate of about 1,100 ft/min. It appears to be another case of a rapidly sinking aircraft, very similar to that of the TAI DC6B. (See the diagram on page 84.)

Considering that in both instances this happened with a fair amount of power on the engines and before full flaps were extended, which would have increased drag to maximum, most likely another factor rather than a faulty pilot technique must have contributed to the excessive rate of descent. The DC6B was known for its high stability in the approach configuration and first-class handling characteristics.

Captain Norman Barron, a retired KLM pilot with 23,000 hours to his credit, who served during the war with Fighter and Coastal Command, was one of the most experienced in KLM on the DC6 series. He had 6,000 hours and ten years on that type of aircraft, and regarded the DC6B controls as very effective. As an example, he recounted one of his incidents: 'After extending the flaps, half of my starboard flap broke and retracted, yet I was able to keep the wings level.'

Only unusual circumstances over which the pilots had no control could have led to a catastrophic deviation from the planned glide path.

Nevertheless, the Dutch Aviation Board, under whose authority the pilots involved in the Cairo crash were licensed to fly aircraft registered in the Netherlands, arrived at different conclusions from the Egyptian investigators. The official version from the Board's verdict reads as follows:

'The Board is of the opinion that a careless preparation of the landing, insufficient monitoring of the flight by the second officer, insufficient supervision by the captain and insufficient attention of both pilots to the indication of the altimeters and insufficient caution for the elevation of the terrain in the approach zone of runway 34, caused the loss of altitude, which led to the collision of the aircraft with the elevated terrain south of the aerodrome.

The Board expresses its special appreciation of the very competent manner in which the captain has controlled the heavily damaged aircraft after collision, by which action the extent of the accident was greatly reduced.

Furthermore the Board has considered the question as to whether the second officer can be blamed for the error committed by him. The fact that the person concerned, although legally licensed as a first officer, performed his duties under the supervision of the captain does not release him entirely of responsibility for the errors committed by him

Consequently, the Board punishes the captain by suspending his privileges to act as the pilot-in-command on aircraft registered in the Netherlands, for a period of two weeks. At the same time, the Board punishes the second officer by a reprimand.'

PART V

The third crash, which took place at Cairo Airport on 11 June 1961, involved a KLM Lockheed L-188C Electra II, registration PH-LLM. The aircraft left Amsterdam for an intercontinental service KL 823 to Kuala Lumpur in Malaysia with intermediate stops at Munich, Rome, Cairo and Karachi. KLM began to use Electras at the end of 1959 and PH-LLM, the last one to enter service, was only six months old.

From Rome, Flight KL 823 was dispatched to Cairo with twenty-four adults, three children and two babies. In command of the aircraft was thirty-nine-year-old Captain Kenneth Reynolds, a British pilot. On approaching Cairo, he received a weather report, which stated that the actual conditions were: cloud cover 4/8 at 3,000 feet and a light north-westerly wind. This meant that landing would have to be made on runway 34, as 23/05, the main instrument runway, was closed for extensive repairs.

According to a statement at the inquiry, Reynolds claimed that he had prepared for the approach by studying the Visual Manoeuvring Chart. This called for a right-hand circuit, performed partly on instruments. He was fully aware of high ground on base leg and final. The crash-landing of the DC6B PH-DFK was still fresh in the minds of all KLM pilots.

The requirement for a mandatory right-hand circuit was later defended by the Egyptian authorities. A left-hand circuit would have involved overflying Almaza, a military base for troop carrying squadrons, located two nautical miles south-west of Cairo International. But at night the right-hand pattern was purely a 'desk' rule. In many years of flying through Cairo, I have never seen Almaza used during the hours of darkness. In any case, being so closely located to the international airport, regardless of which circuit had been designated, only close cooperation between the two Tower controllers could assure effective separation.

By 1961, still no obstruction lights had been placed on the numerous high sand dunes in the area of the approach to runway 34. Only a single, red flashing marker, hardly visible from an aircraft, was installed after the KLM DC6B crash. Due to work in progress on extending the runway to the south-east, there were no proper threshold lights. Instead, a 500-metre-long row of goose-necks had been positioned on each side of the runway.

Although this was Reynolds's first flight as a captain on the Electra, he was an experienced pilot with a total of 11,500 hours, of which 5,000 were in command. Moreover, he was used to operating into poorly equipped airfields, having flown for several years in Indonesia, on secondment from KLM to Garuda. He was also familiar with Cairo Airport through his earlier flights as a co-pilot.

During his conversion to the Electras,

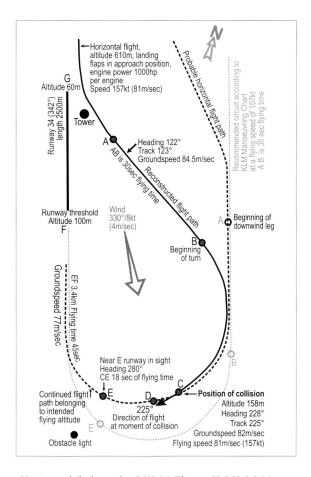

Horizontal flight path of KLM Electra II PH-LLM which crashed at Cairo Airport on 11 June 1961. For a vertical flight path see page 87.

Reynolds received six hours base training and eighty-seven hours route training, during which he acted as a co-pilot. His first officer, one of the most senior Electra co-pilots, was also an experienced airman. He had close to 4,000 hours, of which 750 were on the Electras.

At 01.22 hrs GMT, Flight KL 823 was told to proceed to the Cairo Radio Range and instructed to descend to 2,000 feet. The landing information was: wind 360/6 kt and runway in use 34.

After reporting over the Range station, the aircraft was cleared for a standard beacon approach to runway 34. As no such procedure had been previously promulgated, when later queried, the controller insisted that his actual words were 'visual right-hand contact approach'. But this could not be verified by the tape recording of the ATC messages, as a vital part of the tape was 'conveniently' erased. However, the radio operator's log had confirmed the original version of the controller's instruction. This sudden 'evaporation' of evidence was one more case of ATC tampering with a tape recording after an accident (see chapter 11).

In his testimony Reynolds stated that, when he left the Radio Range at 2,000 feet on QNH, he made a 45° turn to the left in order to establish on the downwind leg. He decided to maintain 2,000 feet in spite of the Manoeuvring Chart calling for only 1,200 feet. He reckoned that with the Electra capable of achieving a 2,000 ft/min descent when power was fully reduced, he should have no difficulty in making a landing once he was on final and had the runway in sight. He told the co-pilot to watch the runway lights and advise when it was time to start a right turn for base leg. The Manoeuvring Chart stipulated that a downwind heading should be continued for thirty seconds after passing abeam the threshold of runway 34.

Shortly after leaving the Radio Range station at 2,000 feet, the aircraft reported, 'downwind, runway in sight', and was cleared for approach and told to change over to the Tower frequency. When the pilots repeated their downwind position to Tower, the controller informed them that surface wind was 330/8 kt and asked them to call on final. A minute later, he observed a flash of fire in the south-easterly direction.

The Electra struck a 518-foot-high sand dune, while descending in a right turn with the undercarriage down and the flaps extended for approach. The position of the crash was exactly on the flight path that Reynolds intended to follow and only a mile away from the spot where the KLM DC6B touched the ground three years earlier.

At first, the propellers of No. 3 and No. 4 engine scraped the crest of a sand dune and then, after a further contact with the ground at an estimated speed of 160 knots, the aircraft caught fire. The Electra continued to plough across the desert in flames for another 400 metres and hit two more crests, shedding numerous pieces. On coming to a standstill, the fuselage broke into three parts – nose section, forward cabin and main cabin with the tail unit.

Out of twenty-nine passengers, seventeen lost their lives and twelve were badly hurt. Three crew members were killed, the co-pilot, the purser and a steward. The flight engineer, radio operator/navigator and stewardess sustained severe injuries. Reynolds's face was badly smashed from hitting the instrument panel and one of his legs heavily crushed when the cockpit collapsed after the Electra came to an abrupt stop with a force of over 30 g.

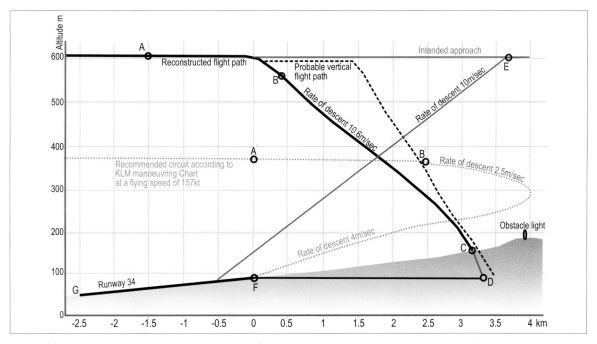

Vertical flight path of KLM Electra II PH-LLM which crashed at Cairo Airport on 11 June 1961.

At the time of the accident the flight recorder was inoperative and, as a result, the Investigating Committee could only construct what they called – 'a probable flight path'. This was based on speculative presumptions, one of which was the time of commencing the descent. It was not easy to establish when the aircraft left 2,000 feet. Reynolds could not remember any details. The only information that could throw any light came from the flight engineer. He recounted that, as soon as the turn for base leg was initiated, Reynolds called for the landing gear to be put down and at the same time he reduced power. The flight engineer could distinctly remember the circumstances because he began to watch engine instruments in the turn, to make sure that the throttles were not retarded too far which could have resulted in negative power.

Eleven days after the accident, KLM brought an Electra to Cairo for a flight test. It was carried out in conditions similar to those on the night of the crash. The members of the Egyptian and the Dutch Investigating Committees joined the test as observers. Various manoeuvres were performed and the difficulties attached to the right-hand circuit at night were demonstrated to the Egyptians. But they claimed that, had a left-hand circuit been requested in good time, permission would have been granted but the aircraft would have had to wait five to ten minutes.

However in practice, this would not have been so prompt. The pilots knew that after the Suez war, the Egyptian military authorities were very reluctant to authorise any deviations from the laid-down routes or approach procedures for civil traffic. It could often take quite a long time for a request to be approved, even in the cases when it

was necessary to quickly avoid hazardous weather conditions, such as a thunderstorm. Moreover, the military often treated the pilots harshly for their inadvertent mistakes. Overflying a military base or a prohibited zone could result in strong disciplinary measures.

The tests with the Electra showed that, with the undercarriage down and the flaps extended for approach, when engine power was fully reduced, the rate of descent amounted to 2,000 ft/min and with 15° of bank, to 2,200 ft/min.

From these figures, the Investigating Committee reconstructed a sequence of events prior to impact, based on an attempt to correlate the loss of altitude with a specific period of time. (See the approach diagram on page 86.)

For their 'probable' flight path, the investigators assumed that it took fifty seconds from the moment when the aircraft reported downwind at 2,000 feet (at 01:10.05 hrs) to striking a sand dune at 518 feet (at 01:10.55 hrs). Both these times were based on the testimony of the tower controller. But as they were recorded to the nearest minute, for the purpose of an accident inquiry, this is not sufficiently accurate.

The investigators claimed that the resultant loss of 1,482 feet, which in their opinion must have begun shortly after the aircraft last reported maintaining 2,000 feet, was supposed to have taken forty-three seconds. This represented a descent rate of 2,067 ft/min, very close to the performance figures obtained from the test.

The Committee were of the opinion that the captain reduced power while still proceeding on the downwind leg and this was contrary to his original plan. They considered that, although it was very difficult to determine the exact moment of initiating the descent, forty-three seconds between closing the throttles at 2,000 feet and impact, seemed 'highly acceptable'.

In their preliminary report, the investigators tried to account for the premature power reduction along the following arguments.

Sensory impressions: Factors relating to night flying (such as those mentioned in *Approach: The Safety Review of the US Navy – July 1961*):

> 'When there is nothing to be seen which can give a horizon reference, a pilot is likely to get a false impression of aircraft attitude. Darkness or reduced visibility may contribute to causing a false sensory impression which can completely obscure the fact of descent or climb, may have played a role in the reduction of power and commencement of the descent.'

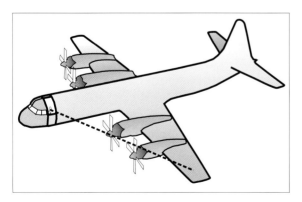

Drawing shows the restricted rearward view from the cockpit windows of the Electra II.

However, this safety bulletin was intended for relatively inexperienced US Navy pilots. Reynolds, with many landings on airfields where the only means of getting on the ground at night were the runway lights, would have been less likely to be affected by a lack of visual cues.

The Investigating Committee claimed that the accident could be attributed to the following cause:

'The Captain, who carried out the landing manoeuvre from the left-hand seat, maintained insufficient height above the hilly ground south of Runway 34 for unexplained reasons, with the result that the aircraft struck the ground and crashed during the descent.

Additional factors:

The extent to which Captain Reynolds and Co-pilot Heuts obtained an erroneous impression of the height above the ground due to atmospheric conditions, which may cause a sort of optical illusion, is difficult to determine (*fata Morgana*). A special point to be mentioned is that during and after the war most air accidents have occurred in comparable weather conditions at Cairo in the area south of Runway 34. This phenomenon is not imaginary, as some accidents have occurred at Bahrain under the same circumstances.

Attention was likewise drawn to the foregoing in the report concerning the accident to the PH-DFK on 19 February 1958

Since the accident in 1958, a red obstruction light has been placed on the hilltop 636 feet high in line with and 4 km from the beginning of Runway 34; this light, however, is in practice only visible when one is flying directly over it. No other lighting or radio aids have been installed yet

For a captain piloting the aircraft from the left-hand cockpit seat it is impossible to keep the runway in view during a right-hand circuit and to estimate the correct distance on the downwind leg. For initiating his right-hand procedure turn he must rely on the directions of his co-pilot. In this case where he was flying into a Stygian darkness (no moon) without a single reference point except practically invisible flashing light (fed by gas cylinders), this procedure with a modern high-performance aircraft is a difficult task, especially as he has to commence a turn on the advice of his co-pilot to get into the correct approach position.'

The analysis of the Electra's 'probable' flight

path as reconstructed by the investigators, revealed that some of their presumptions about the circuit pattern that was supposed to have been followed were unrealistic. But this seems rather surprising because KLM safety experts were included in the investigating team.

Reynolds stated that his plan for approach was to leave the Radio Range station in the direction of the runway and, once he had it in sight, to turn diagonally on to the runway heading (about 120° M), in order to join the downwind leg. But the actual execution appears to have been different. The Tower controller observed that the Electra had not passed overhead the Range station but about a mile to the east. This would have made it easier for the co-pilot to watch the runway and there was no need to get any closer as visibility was sufficiently good. But the investigators' graph shows that the aircraft came almost overhead the runway and this would have made it difficult to keep it in sight.

The graph further shows that the aircraft followed a heading of 122° until just abeam of the runway threshold. From that position and at the aircraft's angle of 138° in relation to the runway, the co-pilot would not have been able to see the lights. With the Electra's wings placed well forward and large engines, the arc of view to the rear was rather limited.

Captain Norman Barron, who flew 3,000 hours on Electras with KLM, describes what a pilot could see from the cockpit windows and what were the aircraft's flying characteristics:

'The large, forward-protruding engines restricted somewhat the view from the cockpit to about 30° aft of abeam, so that, when performing a right-hand circuit, day or night, flying the runway reciprocal on the downwind leg was essential until about half a minute after passing abeam the end of the runway, by which time approach flaps had been extended. A safe obstacle clearance height should have been maintained until the runway threshold was in view, which would be when the aircraft was well into the base leg turn.

Apart from the rather restricted horizontal angle of view from the cockpit, the windscreen panels themselves were large, giving an excellent view forward, considerably better that those of the DC6 series

The aircraft itself was a delight to handle, with good manoeuvrability, and excellent response from the Allison engines with their large, electrically-operated four-blade propellers. Landing circuit was similar to that of the DC6B, only slightly wider.'

Captain Barron's view confirms that the downwind leg just prior to the crash, must have been flown on a course parallel to the runway, so that the co-pilot could warn Reynolds when to start the turn for base leg. As a result, the circuit pattern must have been different from that shown on the investigators' graph and more along the lines of the observations by the tower controller.

The turn for base leg is shown on the investigators' graphs as having been initiated abeam the threshold of runway 34. But this would have been contrary to the usual procedure and, as an experienced Electra co-pilot, the first officer would have been unlikely to have chosen that position. It would have been too early and by extending the downwind leg for at least twenty seconds (the Manoeuvring Chart recommended thirty seconds), this would have put the aircraft in a correct position for final.

It is important to establish as accurately as possible when the aircraft began to turn for base leg, as this determines the moment of initiating the fatal descent. Unfortunately, without the Flight Recorder data it can only be 'guesstimated' from the limited evidence. However, the investigators' claim that it took forty-three seconds from leaving 2,000 feet until striking the ground appears to have been based on an incorrect reasoning.

Taking into consideration the flight engineer's statement that power had been reduced when the turn for base leg was initiated, which was most likely twenty seconds past abeam the threshold of runway 34, then it would have taken thirty seconds at the Electra's usual circuit speed of 160 knots to cover the distance from the start of the turn to impact. The loss of 1,482 feet in that period of time represents a descent rate of about 3,000 ft/min. Even if this looks high for a turbo-prop aircraft, it must be borne in mind that with power off and 15° of bank, the Electra was capable of 2,200 ft/min.

Again the similarity of circumstances to the cases of the two DC6Bs suggests that pilot error could not have precipitated the aircraft's uncontrolled sinking to the ground.

The aftermath of the Electra disaster was very disquieting. While hospitalised in Cairo, Reynolds was kept under armed guard. The official explanation was that he was detained for further questioning in connection with manslaughter charges pursued by the Heliopolis District Court.

When a freight hold of the ill-fated Electra broke upon impact and several cases with bullion were scattered in the desert, the authorities regarded this as bringing taxable goods into the country without a customs check, a criminal offence under Egyptian law. As a result, KLM was heavily fined for 'illegal' import.

During his stay in hospital Reynolds suffered badly from hot weather. His room was not air-conditioned, and this was not helping in his recovery. Under pressure from the Dutch Embassy, he was eventually allowed to leave Egypt for a further operation on his face in Holland.

But even after he had recovered his ordeal continued. As a result of a separate assessment of his case by the Dutch investigators, Reynolds had to face proceedings of the Dutch Aviation Board.

The conclusions of the DAB were as follows:
'The accident was caused by the pilot-in-command's inattention to his instruments, so that he did not notice (or anyhow did not realise) that the aircraft lost height rapidly as a consequence of the reduction of the engine power, so that it contacted the ground and crashed. The pilot-in-command deviated without known reason from his intended approach procedure, which included a steep descent, which should have commenced about a minute later than the moment at which it was actually commenced. His intended approach procedure meant that a rate of descent of more than 10 metres/sec [about 2,000 ft/min] had to be applied, which rate is considerably higher than the usual one under normal circumstances and the rate of descent recommended on the KLM Manoeuvring Chart for Cairo Airport. The Board finds no cause to pronounce that a right-hand circuit carried out by a pilot seated in the left-hand pilot's seat should be dangerous. The Board considers that the accident was not caused by this circumstance.

The pilot-in-command sustained such injuries in the accident that it must be assumed that he shall not be able to act as a commercial pilot again. The seriousness of the mistake which was made and the grave consequences thereof, have the inevitable result that the pilot-in-command has to be punished.

Consequently, having regard to Article 37 of the Aircraft Disaster Law, the Board punishes Captain Reynolds by withdrawing the licence which entitles him to act as the pilot-in-command on Dutch registered aircraft, for a period of three months.'

The verdict was rather harsh considering that it had not been established with any degree of certainty when Reynolds initiated the fatal final descent. No FDR data were available that could confirm or disclaim his alleged error of judgement. In any case, the testimony of the flight engineer throws doubt on the investigator's claims as to when the power had been actually reduced.

It was also inappropriate for the Dutch Aviation Board to assume that as a result of the accident, Reynolds became physically unfit to fly an aircraft. The judgement was not in their hands but lay with the examiners of the Dutch Medical Aerospace and Aviation Institute at Soesterberg, where KLM pilots undergo their six-monthly checks.

Nevertheless, in the end Reynolds's licence was permanently withdrawn. The DMAAI examiners claimed that one of his legs was so badly injured in the crash that he was no longer capable of operating the rudder with the required force. As it later transpired, they were more concerned about the state of his mind but could not find an appropriate rule to invalidate his licence on those grounds.

The accident had a devastating effect on Reynolds from both a mental and a physical point of view. He appeared to have become a different person. Not only had his facial features altered as a result of several operations but also he seemed to have lost the will to live. Although before the accident he was a quiet and unassuming person, after the accident he became totally withdrawn and even his friends found it difficult to hold a conversation with him.

But Reynolds's crucifixion was not yet at an end. Two and a half years after the crash, he was summoned to appear before the District Court at Heliopolis – *Tribunal Correctionnel d'Heliopolis*. By that time he had left KLM and emigrated to the USA. As a result, the trial took place in absentia and he was sentenced to one year in prison. But the Court declared that if Reynolds were not apprehended within three years of passing the sentence, the charges would be dropped.

PART VI

Pakistan International Airlines Flight 705 on 20 May 1965, operated by Boeing 720B AP-AMH, was an official inaugural service from Karachi to London, with intermediate stops at Dhahran and Cairo. This was the second service on that route, as a proving flight had already been made five days earlier.

Several high-ranking PIA officials, as well as a party of Pakistani journalists under the leadership of Major-General Hayauddin, were invited to participate in the opening of the new service. In total, there were 114 passengers on board.

At Cairo special European guests were expected to join Flight 705, including the correspondent from an aviation magazine, *Aeroplane*.

The cockpit crew consisted of two pilots, a navigator and a flight engineer. The pilot-in-command was Akhtar Aly Khan, one of the most senior captains in PIA. This was his first flight on a Boeing to Cairo, although in the past he made several trips on piston-engine aircraft. During his flying career, thirty-seven-year-old Captain Khan had amassed over 13,000 hours, 10,000 in command with 2,200 on the Boeing 707 or 720. The two-years-younger first officer had close to 7,000 hours, 4,000 in command and 2,800 as a co-pilot on the Boeing 707 and 720. He took part in the proving flight, so it was his second trip to Cairo in five days.

On approaching the airport, Flight 705 was cleared to the VOR station and to descend to 12,500 feet. The weather for 23.30 GMT was reported as: 'Wind 020/4 kt, visibility 10 km, no clouds, temp. 18°.'

The main instrument runway 23/05 was again closed for repairs and only runway 16 or 34 was available for landing. But even with a light surface wind prevailing, the tower controller assigned the runway with a dangerous approach over high grounds. It appeared as if past careless ATC practices still continued.

In view of other traffic ahead, Flight 705 was initially cleared to 6,500 feet and was told to hold on the north leg of the Radio Range. But as the preceding traffic had landed by the time Flight 705 had completed a procedure turn, Tower cleared it for a left-hand circuit approach. Further descent was carried out at a rate between 1,000 and 1,200 ft/min. When abeam 'CM' radio beacon a steady left turn was initiated and the aircraft suddenly began to lose height at an alarming rate of 2,500 ft/min and hit a sand dune at 780 feet above sea level. At first, No. 1 and No. 2 engine struck the ground, followed by the left wingtip. Thereafter the aircraft began to disintegrate and was soon consumed by fire.

The position of the crash was 2.1 nm south-west

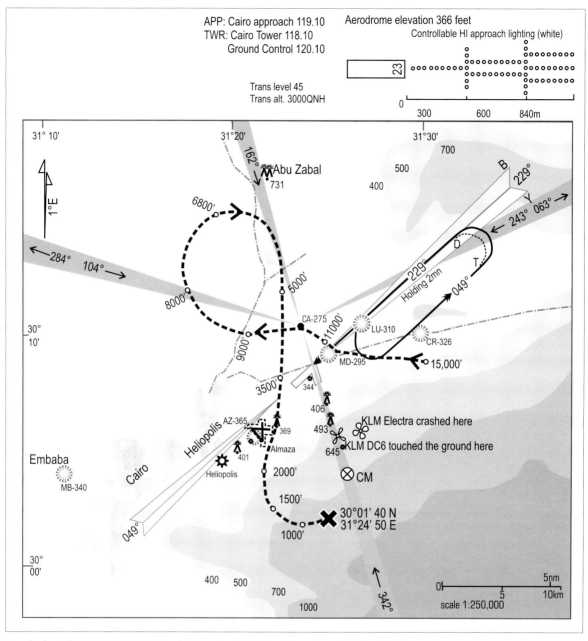

APP: Cairo approach 119.10
TWR: Cairo Tower 118.10
Ground Control 120.10

Aerodrome elevation 366 feet
Controllable HI approach lighting (white)

Trans level 45
Trans alt. 3000QNH

Crash chart for PIA Boeing 720B which crashed at Cairo Airport on 20 May 1965.

of 'CM' beacon, or 3.8 nm due south of the threshold of runway 34. The wreckage was spread over an area of 1,250 metres, by far larger than all previous disasters. At the time of the crash, landing gear was in the up position and flaps were extended to 20°. All engines appeared to have been operating normally. The Flight Recorder and one

altimeter, which was found to have been correctly set, were recovered from the wreck.

About a minute before the crash, a Swedish captain of a departing aircraft, while taxiing to the take-off position, observed traffic proceeding in the south-easterly direction. He presumed it was PIA 705, which had just called that it would

Photo of the PIA Boeing 720B that crashed 6 miles form Cairo Airport. It shows how the wreckage was spread over a large area. The photo was taken by Capt. L. Blomberg, a KLM pilot and IFALPA Regional Vice-President for the Middle East, when he attended the crash enquiry.

be shortly turning final. He then heard a brief rattle on the Tower frequency, which sounded as if a weak VHF transmission had broken through from an aircraft that was either too low or too far out. At the same time he observed an orange ball of fire bursting out in the distance. Two more explosions quickly followed, giving an impression of a wall of flames sweeping across the horizon from right to left. When he heard Tower asking PIA 705

for the latest position, he advised the controller (the actual transcript of the ATC tape recording): 'We saw a big flame on the final for 34... you better check if this is the 705 you missing.'

At first the controller went silent. Then after a long pause, he could only say: 'Stand by.'

Out of 114 passengers on board, 108 were instantly killed and six severely injured. All thirteen crew members perished in the crash. But

The remains of the PIA Boeing 720B. (L. Blomberg)

through a miraculous stroke of luck, six monkeys had got out a freight compartment unscathed and were later found in the desert.

One of the most tragic aspects of this disaster was the inadequate rescue services. Although the crash site was located only six miles away from the airport, the search party and the fire brigade could not reach the wreck. A dark moonless night and the lack of suitable vehicles to traverse the sandy stretch of desert hindered all rescue efforts.

The earliest help to arrive on the scene, four hours after the Boeing 720 crashed, was a military helicopter. In spite of similar problems experienced during the Electra accident in 1961, the authorities had taken no steps to remedy the past grave deficiencies of the rescue services.

The Egyptian investigating team was composed of the officials from the Civil Aviation Department, under the chairmanship of deputy DCA, E.A.M. Bahgat. They were assisted by two Air Force officers, three professors and a pilot from United Arab Airlines, Captain Shams, Director of Flight Operations.

In accordance with ICAO recommendations, the Pakistan Department of Civil Aviation, as the country where the aircraft was registered, were invited to join the proceeding as accredited representatives, as well as several advisers from the airline PIA. In attendance were also observers from Boeing and Pratt & Whitney, the aircraft and engine manufacturers respectively, and experts from CAB and FAA.

On request from the Pakistan Pilots Association, IFALPA representative Captain Lars Blomberg, Regional Vice-President for the Middle East, was included in the Pakistan delegation. Captain Blomberg had previous experience in accident investigations.

In parallel with the civil aviation proceedings, an inquiry was also conducted by the local judiciaries (the Heliopolis District Court).

In his report to IFALPA, Captain Blomberg was rather critical of the way fieldwork had been performed:

'The Egyptian Department of Civil Aviation was responsible for conducting the investigation. Judging from several days of my participation, I consider that the way the Egyptian officials carried out the proceedings was most hurried and inefficient. For example, there were no attempts to rope off the wreckage area, to prevent looting and more possible evidence disappearing every day, or to mark the position of the aircraft parts or crew bodies upon their removal. No examination of crew remains had been carried out. The result was that a proper investigation was almost impossible.

Although the Egyptian authorities made no restriction for a large group of technical experts from abroad to take part in the proceedings, the fact that these experts were hardly consulted, was most discouraging. Any voluntary advice or assistance was often taken as criticism.

Moreover, I found the manner by which the Pakistan officials at times delayed or withheld much needed information, very hindering.

To summarise, it appeared that the investigation was more influenced by political and national consideration than a joint effort by all concerned to find the real cause and it was not possible to learn from this accident enough to prevent a possible reoccurrence.'

In the accident investigation report by the Egyptian Board of Inquiry it was stated about the events just prior to impact:

'Down to 1,500 feet the pilot was following a normal approach procedure for landing on runway 34 and nothing abnormal was reported. During a left-hand turn, the bright lights surrounding Cairo Airport gave an adequate reference to the attitude of the aircraft, even at very low altitude at night. Therefore any abnormal nose down attitude should have been detected and an immediate correction taken.

Thereafter, the aircraft inexplicably descended at an abnormal high rate with the engines nearly idle, landing gear retracted and flaps 20°, until it struck the ground. The reason for the increased rate of descent could not be established.'

This was a complete reversal of the original view expressed by the Egyptian civil aviation officials. At first they claimed that the pilot, upon turning onto base leg, believed that he was too high and tried to dive towards the runway in order to avoid an overshoot. Immediately after the press release of that statement, IFALPA refuted the allegation, pointing out that no pilot would attempt a landing without the undercarriage having been lowered and the flaps fully extended.

The final conclusion by the Egyptian Board of Inquiry in respect of the probable cause of the accident was as follows: 'The aircraft did not maintain the adequate height for the circuit and continued to descend until it contacted the ground. The reason for the abnormal continuation of descent is unknown.'

From the FDR it was possible to obtain a clear picture of circumstances surrounding the crash. (See the chart of the B720 approach on page 92.) The read-out revealed that, after the B720 was cleared for approach, it made a turn to join a left-hand downwind leg, while descending from 6,500 to 1,500 feet at a rate of between 1,000 to 1,200 ft/min. This was a normal rate with the flaps extended to 20° and the throttles fully retarded. In fact, Captain Khan followed a procedure which he had practised on the simulator only a few days earlier. He would have known what altitude should have been reached at various points of the approach. From the plot of the horizontal flight path it is evident that he aimed for the 'CM' beacon located 3.2 nm to the south and in line with runway 34, in order to position on final. If a 3° glide path was to be maintained from 'CM' to the threshold of runway 34, the altitude to cross the beacon should have been 1,350 feet.

But after passing 1,500 feet, the rate of descent suddenly escalated to 2,500 ft/min, and then between 1,000 feet and 800 feet (the last readable altitude on the FDR) eased off a little to 2,000 ft/min. At the same time, the airspeed rose slightly from 175 to 190 knots. But what appears to be significant was the increase in the positive g from 1.0 to 1.15 during the last eighteen seconds before impact.

From the FDR read-out it is evident that the sudden loss of altitude on final had nothing to do with a faulty flight technique and the increase in the rate of descent can be only attributed to some unusual downdraught. At the time little was known about the existence of such weather phenomena.

Considering that the pattern of all five previous crashes was very much the same, the allegations by the Egyptian investigators about paying insufficient attention to flight instruments or disorientation being the primary cause in all of these cases can no longer be regarded as reflecting a true picture of events.

It is surprising that in spite of the availability of several flight parameters from the FDR, the Egyptian investigators were unable to find an answer as to why the PIA B720 had sunk to the ground so rapidly on final.

PART VII

The similarity of circumstances in which all these accidents had occurred could have easily swayed even the most rational mind to believe that they were a result of some supernatural force. Especially after an interesting aspect of one of the earlier crashes became known, the scriptwriter of the radio programme on the desert tragedies cannot really be blamed for insinuating that the curse of the Pharaohs could have been the cause of the Cairo disasters. It had been learnt that the TAI DC6B struck the ground close to a quarry

from which, according to the Egyptologists, came the limestone that was used to bedeck the walls of the pyramids in ancient times.

Nevertheless, after examining weather conditions at the time of these accidents, a common denominator became apparent. They all occurred on a clear night during a season of the year when the sun is still strong but the hours of darkness bring a rapid cooling of the layer of air close to the ground. In daytime, the dunes, in particular the slopes directly facing the sun, can reach extremely high temperatures. Powerful thermal currents often develop and 'dust devils' can be observed. On the other hand, as soon as the sun disappears below the horizon, ground temperature as a result of an extremely low humidity, can drop as much as 50°C within a very short time. This can lead to the development of strong inversions only a few hundred feet above the desert.

At the time of the Cairo accidents, little was known about the effects of large temperature variations on air pressure pattern in specific local circumstances. Meteorologists generally associated inversions with stable conditions, which as a result of slack movement of air masses would give rise to a fine and windless weather. But it was eventually established that shallow desert inversions often produce extremely strong but short-lived bursts of wind.

The earliest information about these peculiar weather phenomena came from the US Air Force. Pilots flying over Mojave Desert at night reported encountering winds as strong as 100 mph in areas where a marked temperature variation was observed. Nocturnal low-level jet streams, as they were named, turned out to be very freak occurrences, and without any data from the FDRs, which at the time were not fitted, pilots' reports were of little scientific value. But a research study, undertaken by the American Weather Bureau, eventually confirmed that these strong winds were not just a product of pilots' imaginations.

Depending on the circumstances, aircraft performance can be drastically degraded by a low-level jet stream. Crossing it at right angles may not present much danger but an abrupt variation of wind speed or direction along the path of an aircraft taking-off or landing, can result in catastrophic consequences, particularly when there is not enough engine power to compensate for the sudden loss of airspeed (see chapter 1).

It was eventually discovered that low-level jet streams were not confined to the Mojave Desert. They have been encountered in other parts of the world where a dry but an extremely hot climate prevails, but unfortunately their occurrences were seldom reported.

In the early days of piston-engine operations pilots never realised that aircraft performance could be dangerously affected by certain weather conditions other than turbulence. When loss of speed was experienced that could not be easily accounted for, the pilots were generally reluctant to report the incident for the fear of making a mountain out of a molehill.

In my case, a 'peculiar behaviour' of the L749 Constellation, for which I could not find an immediate explanation, occurred during an ILS approach at Delhi Airport in India, executed at daybreak on a very hot pre-monsoon morning. The weather forecast indicated that settled but slightly hazy conditions were to be expected. Although Tower reported the surface wind as calm, as soon as I commenced my approach I had to use climb power to keep the aircraft on the glide path. This continued all the way from the outer marker to 100 feet above the ground. Immediately after the landing, I looked at the windsock but it hung listlessly. An inspection of the aircraft revealed no loose panels that could have accounted for such a high power requirement. For many years the cause of this incident remained a puzzle, until I came across the US Air Force reports on low-level jet streams.

However, in all the cases at Cairo Airport, rapid sinking had been experienced but with little or no change in airspeed. Was it possible that this had been caused by an air current, created by large temperature differences between two adjacent layers of air, similar to the case of low-level jet stream but in a vertical plane?

The first hint that these 'mysterious' premature descents on final could have been due to some unknown weather phenomenon came from two accidents at Bahrain Airport in 1951. Two DC4s from Air France crashed into the Persian Gulf while coming in to land. This happened within two days and a mile from each other. The investigators suspected that the coincidence may have been connected with some unusual circumstances and a reference to that effect was later made in the Egyptian DCA report on the KLM DC6B disaster at Cairo Airport.

The first DC4 accident took place on 12 June and the second on 14 June. Both aircraft were executing a timed approach procedure from overhead the airfield and, for no apparent reason, began to lose height on final and subsequently struck the sea.

The co-pilot of the first DC4 stated that, after a procedure turn had been carried out at 1,000 feet, more power was required to maintain altitude. But when the flaps were extended to 30° the aircraft climbed slightly. Then shortly after he reported to Tower passing 800 feet on final the DC4 hit the water.

Although the weather on the first night was hazy, two days later visibility was good. The co-pilot of the second DC4, the only one who survived the accident, was able to recollect that during the timed procedure, the captain complained about difficulty in keeping the airspeed steady. When the co-pilot glanced at the altimeter on final it read 500 feet. A few seconds later the altitude was down to 300 feet. Then, within the next three to four seconds, they crashed into the sea. The loss of 500 feet in such a short time would have represented at least double the rate of a normal descent.

Even if there were no high sand dunes around Bahrain Airport that could generate 'vertical' wind, the island is situated close to the desert and in some circumstances strong temperature differences can exist between an extremely hot landmass and relatively cool sea.

The investigators of the two DC4 accidents could not establish what exactly had led to the rapid sinking on the approach but they believed that one of the contributory factors was a lack of visual reference.

As the years went by, the list of crashes from a sudden loss of altitude was getting longer and longer (see chapter 7). In August 1958, a Vickers Viscount 700 undershot the runway at Benina Airport in Libya with a toll of thirty-six lives. The investigators believed that the cause of the accident was misinterpretation of the altimeter reading by the captain. Nevertheless, the circumstances were similar to that at Cairo Airport, and it was possible that a downdraught on the approach over the desert could have suddenly escalated the aircraft's rate of descent with fatal consequences.

In 1960, an Air France L-049 Constellation plummeted into the sea in circumstances similar to those at Bahrain Airport. The accident took place just off the coast of Africa while the aircraft was making an approach to Yoff Airport, at Dakar in Senegal. It was established from the available evidence that the loss of altitude on final had been most likely caused by a powerful downdraught of about 1,800 ft/min.

On the night of 30 June 1966, a Trident IE of Kuwait Airways, registration 9K-ACG, crash-landed while making a beacon approach to Kuwait Airport. Between outer and middle locator the aircraft suddenly lost 800 feet and flew into the ground. Luckily not one out of eighty-three people on board was hurt. Pilot error was cited as the cause and the captain was sacked.

But downdraughts were not the sole contributory factors in all these accidents. Although bad visibility seldom entered into it, all the fatal approaches were conducted at night and with limited or no radio aids at all. While in daylight inadvertent descent could have been speedily observed and arrested, on a dark night, in particular without any lights on the ground, the chances of averting a disaster were very much slimmer. Flight instruments alone could not warn the pilots quickly enough that the aircraft had begun to sink so rapidly that drastic remedial action was required.

In addition, fatigue could have played a significant role by slowing down reactions of the pilots and reducing their awareness of a dangerous situation. Nevertheless, some accidents have occurred after a relatively short flight.

PART VIII

In spite of widespread opinion that the Cairo accidents were primarily caused by airmanship errors, as a result of the incident that I experienced at Delhi Airport, I began to have doubts whether the pilots could be really blamed.

But after another 'mysterious' degradation of the L749 performance, which occurred while I was making a letdown at Cairo Airport to runway 16, my doubts grew.

When I started the approach, the skies were clear but visibility on the ground was somewhat limited. However, lower down I ran into a thin layer of stratus that was not mentioned in the local weather report. When upon reaching my landing limits there was no break in the clouds, I quickly initiated an overshoot, bearing in mind the high hills ahead. At first the climb was normal, but at 800 feet above the airport level, and in spite of maintaining the same attitude, the aircraft suddenly refused to climb any higher. Even applying METO power on all four engines, made no difference and although I was able to keep the airspeed steady, the aircraft still refused to climb.

Although I was aware that I was heading towards a sector where safety height was 2,600 feet, I dared not initiate a turn, for the fear of adversely affecting the airspeed when I applied the bank. The 'enforced' level flight seemed to take ages, but in fact, lasted no longer than about a minute and a half. Then, as I broke clouds, the aircraft suddenly resumed a normal climb without any action on my part.

At first, I dismissed the incident as having no special significance. However, after reading the reports on the investigations of Cairo crashes, it has crossed my mind that there could be a connection between the loss of climb performance that I experienced during the overshoot and the rapid sinking of the ill-fated aircraft on final approach. The only difference in the circumstances was that I was able to apply all available power on the engines and there was no extra drag from the landing gear. This must have effectively counteracted a strong, downward air current.

After checking with the approach chart, it was apparent that my Constellation stopped its climb in the same area that all crashes took place, close to the high sand dunes south-east of Cairo Airport.

The enigma as to how such strong downdraughts could develop without any large convection clouds in the vicinity remained unsolved. At the time, neither meteorological books nor aviation safety publications could throw any light on the process of the desert air currents' formation. It was hard to believe that so far scientists had found no explanation.

However, upon coming across evidence of another probable hazardous downdraught at Cairo Airport, I became convinced that there was a definite link between the forces of nature and the past crashes.

A week after the PIA disaster, I happened to be passing through Cairo and I contacted Don Knutson, Boeing Chief Test Pilot, a member of the investigating committee into the PIA accident. He brought me up to date on the progress of the investigation and showed me the Flight Data Recorder read-out. It revealed a catastrophic increase in the descent rate just before impact.

Finally my long-standing opinion was reaffirmed that night landings on runway 34 were highly critical. The inadequate approach aids and incompetent air traffic control were not the only contributory factors, but there was also a so-far-unknown weather phenomenon which could greatly escalate the chances of an accident. Consequently, I suggested to the other IFALPA

Principal Officers (in a letter dated 11 June 1965) that a ban on using runway 34 at night should be considered.

Nevertheless, a decision of such importance required consulting individual members' associations. Pilots could run into difficulties when observing the ban, as it may have been contrary to directives issued by some airlines. As only runway 16/34 was available at Cairo Airport, the pilots were told that they could only consider diversion to another airfield if the weather for an approach to runway 34 was below the company limits and, at the same time, the tailwind component on runway 16 was too high for a downwind landing.

Although a large number of the IFALPA member associations did express their support for the ban, some were taking time with their replies. One pilot association strongly condemned the indifferent attitude to safety shown by the Egyptian civil aviation officials. Whilst the shortcomings of the landing aids remained unresolved, considerable sums of money had been recently spent on a new 'palatial' terminal building.

But soon another tragedy brought a further pressure on the IFALPA Principal Officers and the decision on the ban could not be delayed until support from the majority of the membership has been secured. The investigation of the PIA accident was still in progress, when on 7 July an Antonov An-12 of the Egyptian Air Force crashed into the sand dunes ten miles east of Cairo with the loss of twenty-one lives.

This was a turning point for IFALPA and the following notification, dated 9 July 1965, was sent to all members:

'The Principal Officers recommend that, due to the inadequate safety standards associated with Cairo Airport, no operation should take place on runway 34 during the hours of darkness.

Note: With runway 23/05 closed for major reconstruction and with runway 16 of little value due to problems associated with overshoot towards high ground, the above may well amount, as far as the operation of large jets is concerned, to the closure of the airport for night operations.

This information is currently being released to the press and at the same time we are initiating correspondence with the Egyptian Civil Aviation Authorities and the ICAO Regional Office.'

IFALPA's action received wide publicity from the media and reports highlighting our reasons for the ban appeared in many newspapers around the world. The reaction of the Egyptian authorities was as it could have been be expected. Their position was given in a press communiqué on 13 July:

'War Minister Abdel Wahab el Bistry today said that traffic at Cairo Airport had not been affected by the banning of jet night landings on one of the runways by airline pilots. Sixty-two aircraft took off and landed at the airport last night.

The Minister said that the main runway would be operational in two days after being equipped with all facilities.'

There was no record kept by IFALPA to show how many pilots failed to comply with the ban. It had been left up to the conscience of the individual members to observe the recommended safety precaution. The reaction of the airlines varied from company to company. Some airlines even 'instructed' their pilot not to use runway 34 at night.

One important aspect of the ban was that it had at last brought the disgraceful state of Cairo Airport to the attention of high-ranking officials in the government. For Egypt, as one of the leaders of the Arab world, the lack of up-to-date landing facilities was a disgrace to that nation.

However, improvements were only slowly introduced. After the country had recovered from the Yom Kippur War, another much longer runway was constructed, parallel to 23/05, and better radio aids were installed.

The most interesting outcome of the IFALPA action was the eventual fate of runway 34. After my election as IFALPA President in 1967, I paid a courtesy visit to the new Egyptian Deputy Director of Civil Aviation. Contrary to my expectation, I was cordially received. Past differences seemed to have been forgotten and IFALPA's ban was recognised to have been made for the benefit of safety.

During our talks, I learnt some significant news about runway 34. The Deputy DCA informed me that night landings on that runway had been recently stopped on the order of the Civil Aviation Department. This was the result of a survey by ICAO specialists to site a proposed VASI. The experts had established that, even with the highest acceptable glide-slope angle of 3°, the terrain clearance would have been outside safety tolerances and it was decided to discontinue to use runway 34 except during daylight and in clear weather conditions.

It seemed a Pyrrhic victory for IFALPA to have been right in imposing the ban. But the delay before the Egyptian authorities realised that using runway 34 at night was unsafe caused a needless loss of many lives.

PART IX

Accidents from a sudden loss of height on take-off or landing continued in the jet age (see chapter 7). Twenty-seven cases attributed to the catastrophic effects of low-level wind-shear or unexpected downdraught were recorded in the USA between 1964 and 1982. Most of the crashes were associated with flying in the vicinity of or passing underneath a thunderstorm.

But there were also cases of unaccountable rapid sinking in clear air in seemingly settled weather. One of the most mysterious was that of an All Nippon Airways Boeing 727-81 in Tokyo

Bay. On 4 February 1966, the aircraft was making a visual approach at night. With a relatively good visibility, only broken clouds at 3,000 feet and a full moon, these conditions should not have presented any difficulties to the pilot.

However, while joining base leg for runway 33R at Haneda Airport, the aircraft suddenly plummeted down from 2,000 feet and crashed into sea. This happened only a few seconds after the last radio message. The crash claimed the lives of 126 passengers and seven crew members. Ninety per cent of the wreckage was recovered from the bay and it was possible to examine all parts for possible failure. The altimeters were in order and were set correctly. No malfunctioning of the engines, controls or flight instruments was discovered. The FDR and CVR did not indicate anything unusual prior to the sudden loss of height.

The circumstances of the crash were reminiscent of the Cairo disasters, but the climatic conditions were entirely different. It is known that, in the winter months, cold air often descends from the nearby mountains towards relatively warm

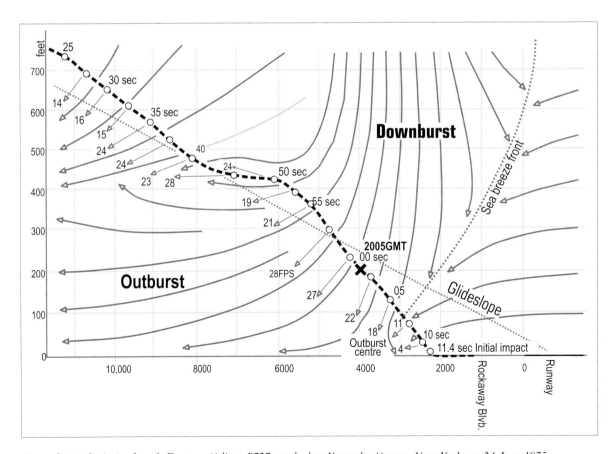

An analysis of a 'microburst'. Eastern Airlines B727 crashed at Kennedy Airport, New York, on 24 June 1975.

Tokyo Bay. However, the investigators were unable to explain how such a strong downward air current, causing an uncontrollable descent, could develop in these circumstances.

As a result of several more accidents of a similar nature, the International Civil Aviation Organisation initiated a study to establish what specific weather conditions could lead to a dangerous degradation of aircraft performance. The summary of the findings was as follows:

'The majority of strong wind-shears occur in stable atmospheric conditions, usually associated with a night-time inversion. In these cases maximum wind speeds and shears may occur at heights well above 200 ft.

The next highest number of strong wind shears, as observed by aircraft and on meteorological towers, occur in unstable flows with strong gusty winds. These, while rapidly fluctuating, can be sometimes four to five times larger in magnitude than the steady-type shears in stable conditions

Horizontal wind shears are thought to be caused mainly by difference in terrain, for example by a flow around a hill or around buildings or by moving from a smooth water surface onto rough land area [an example – Bahrain DC4 crashes].'

It emerged from a detailed study of three particular cases, that the most severe loss of aircraft performance were caused by a 'microburst', a powerful downdraught relatively small in size, often as little as 4,000 to 5,000 feet in diameter with a duration of no more than from two to five minutes. Microbursts usually appeared in the vicinity of high-level convection clouds or during a passage of a thunderstorm.

For years the scientists strived to develop devices capable of detecting dangerous air currents. At first, such methods as balloon sonde or laser beam were tried but without success. Eventually the National Center for Atmospheric Research in Colorado, designed a novel radar equipment based on the Doppler principle, which became known as Terminal Doppler Weather Radar, and which proved to be the answer to locating areas of violent weather lying in the aircraft's flight path.

TDWRs were installed at six airports in the USA. A colour-coded display was used and close proximity of two patches of contrasting colours, spelled the possibility of a treacherous wind shear.

A similar method was used to detect dangerous downdraughts or 'vertical winds', which were known to descend at a speed as high as 65 to 85 mph.

Several months' surveillance of weather conditions at Denver's Stapleton Airport in Colorado, with the help of TDWR, had revealed that microbursts were much more common than was originally believed. They were observed at least once a day, often in clusters and not necessarily in association with a thunderstorm. Hot and dry weather was particularly conducive to their formation.

Extensive research was also undertaken prior to opening the new Hong Kong Airport, Chek Lap Kok, to determine if its location in the shadow of a large mountain could be a source of hazardous downdraughts in certain weather conditions. The results were very revealing and the most advanced Doppler weather radar was installed at Chek Lap Kok.

The lesson from the studies at Stapleton Airport strongly suggests that treacherous air currents of an even higher frequency and strength can be expected to occur over the African desert, where extremely large diurnal temperature changes take place.

In parallel with the development of ground equipment for detecting sudden wind changes, progress has also been made with airborne installations. In establishing the criteria for measuring hazardous wind shears or downdraughts, calculations have shown that a downward vertical current that imposes one-twentieth of a g on an aircraft would increase the angle of its glide path by one-twentieth of a radian. Translating it into pilots' language, this means by approximately 3°.

Using this formula, the FDR read-out of the B720 fatal descent at Cairo Airport, was analysed. It can be seen from the upsurge of positive g during the last eighteen seconds before impact that the aircraft's glide-path angle would have increased between two and a half and three degrees. At an airspeed of 190 knots, this represents an escalation of the descent rate by about 1,000 ft/min. Together with the correct descent rate of 1,200 ft/min, it would have amounted in total to 2,200 ft/min, which is close to what the FDR had registered in the last moments before impact. An interesting point is the slight increase in the airspeed. It is an indication of running into an outflow of air that had been bounced off the ground. Similar occurrences were noted in other crashes due to microbursts.

With the help of scientific findings it was possible to ascertain that a sudden outbreak of 'vertical' wind had been the most likely cause of sending the B720 to its doom. As the six other disasters at Cairo Airport occurred in similar circumstances, neither disorientation nor negligence in monitoring flight instruments, as the investigators claimed, appears to have been the prime factor in losing height, but the most probable cause was a microburst, at that time a completely unknown weather phenomenon.

Nevertheless, the aviation authorities blamed the pilots for the accidents and took an unprece-dented step in punishing some of them for a 'crime' they did not really commit. Despite new scientific proofs on the existence of dangerous downdraughts, the conclusions on the cause of the Cairo crashes were never revised. As a result, three airmen – Charles Billet, John Musselman and Ken Reynolds – still bear a stigma attached to their names.

This is one more example, among hundreds of others, underlining a popular misconception that flying is a glamorous occupation. The public seem to forget that it can be at times a most cruel profession (see chapter 12).

5

1961 – COULD A SINGLE BULLET BRING AN AIRLINER DOWN?

PART I

AN AUSPICIOUS LETTER TO THE EDITOR

The following letter to the editor appeared under sensational headlines in the well-known English newspaper, *The Guardian*, on 11 September 1992:

'HAMMARSKJÖLD PLANE CRASH "NO ACCIDENT"

'Yet again United Nations personnel are being killed in peacekeeping and humanitarian missions. Year after year it happens on the many scraps of earth on which they have been obliged to serve.

Now the Italian crew on a mercy mission to Bosnia have been shot down we feel it is time that we should say that we are convinced that UN Secretary-General Dag Hammarskjöld was killed in the same way in 1961 when his aircraft crashed over Ndola, Northern Rhodesia. He was flying to settle the Congo crisis, in many ways as complex as that in the skeleton of Yugoslavia.

We are the representatives of the UN at Katanga, centre of that storm, immediately before (O'Brien) and after (Ivan Smith) Hammarskjöld was killed.

Vividly we were made aware of the brutal work of mercenaries, hired guns employed by European industrialists to prevent the UN from resolving a crisis at the heart of Africa which, at that time threatened to spark a cold war into a hot one, but from their selfish interests threatened their profits. We saw and felt the bare fangs of commercial interests cornered on a patch of gold.

Ivan Smith was beaten by their agents in a failed attempt to kidnap him in 1961. The masters sought to prevent a settlement (as in Bosnia now). They tried to prevent Hammarskjöld from meeting Tshombe, their black stooge, before they could tell the UN Secretary-General in person that European interests were paramount and he must not "sell out to the blacks".

Soon after the crash Ivan Smith interrogated the man who had been on duty in the control tower at Ndola airport at the time of the crash. It took an hour. When he understood it was an inquest by a personal and not part of an official inquiry he revealed. "You are right to enquire. It was not a normal accident."

Our subsequent enquiries over many years prove that the European industrialists who controlled Katanga had sent two aircraft to intercept Hammarskjöld before he met Tshombe so that they could persuade him to cooperate. They never meant to kill him. O'Brien believes that they also smuggled an agent into Hammarskjöld's plane as added persuasion and thinks the body count after the crash is in doubt. Both of us met Sir Roy Welensky on different occasions after the event and he was honest enough to be enigmatic about the whole affair in which his country was deeply involved.

Ivan Smith has gathered startling evidence that the industrialists gave their two rogue pilots permission to send a warning shot across the UN plane if it refused to divert to Kamina for consultations. The warning shot must have hit a wire and caused the plane to veer out of control so that it could not complete landing. On the record is the second man shouting: "Christ, you've hit it". It looked like a flying accident. Two official inquiries were complete and found no evidence to the contrary. Why should they if only a wire was hit?

Reluctantly we open this case in the interests of peace and peoples who work for it. Bosnia is subject to raw race and religious prejudice causing brigands to commit the same type of insane acts from which we suffered in the Congo. In the name of peace should not its agents of the UN be protected?

George Ivan Smith. Stroud, Glos.
Connor Cruise O'Brien. Dublin.'

Nevertheless a question still remains. Was it possible for a single bullet to bring a large airliner down?

PART II

THE BACKGROUND OF THE
NDOLA DISASTER

The volatile political situation after Belgium abandoned the Congo was closely connected with the tragedy that had struck the United Nations Secretary-General Dag Hammarskjöld.

In the mid-fifties and early sixties Africa was swept by a cry for independence. But withdrawal of colonial rule left many parts of the Dark Continent in deep turmoil, often evolving into a total breakdown of law and order. In the ensuing vacuum the opposing world powers tried to manipulate the newly born African States into adopting their political systems. On the one hand, the Western World with its vested interests in mineral deposits, sought to retain its past footholds by offers of financial aid, while the Soviet Union and its satellites contrived to get a foot in the door by popular appeal to the masses.

In learning how to stand on its own feet, the former Belgian Congo became a country bitterly torn by an internal conflict. As soon as independence had been granted in June 1960, the old colonial administration was disbanded. But the Belgians had not prepared the Congolese to run their country. Power was too hastily transferred into the hands of local politicians who had no experience of handling administrative matters.

Even before the reins were handed over, feelings ran high among the indigenous population against their colonial masters. After the declaration of independence, the quest for revenge got out of hand and riots erupted. Many Belgians were savagely attacked and some were killed.

Lacking an effective police force, the newly formed central government was not able to prevent lawlessness. The Congo National Army, the only power in the country that could have restored order, mutinied against Belgian officers who were helping with the transition. Without a strong hand from their former superiors, the troops went on the rampage and began to terrorise the white population. Looting, rape and murder became widespread. Tales of bloodshed soon spread, putting fear into all European settlers in Africa about their future.

When the Congo's independence was proclaimed, the Province of Katanga (now Shaba) broke away from the Federal Republic and declared that it would form its own government.

The Congo, producing mainly palm oil and cotton, was as a whole not a rich country, with the exception of Katanga where the biggest copper ore deposits in the world are located. Fifty per cent of the national income came from the Katangan mines.

The multi-million-dollar industry was in the hands of three powerful conglomerates, with the Belgians, the French and the British as major shareholders. Cheap native labour made mining very profitable.

One of the conglomerates, Union Miniére du Haut-Katanga, was the mainstay of Katanga's economy. It was the largest copper producer in the world, supplying 8% of the total demand. It was also the sole producer of cobalt as well as other rare metals, such as germanium – essential for making transistors – and uranium. The uranium that was used in manufacturing the atom bombs dropped on Hiroshima and Nagasaki, came from Shinkolobwe mine, near Jadotville (now Likasi), seventy-five miles north-west of Katanga's capital Elisabethville (now Lubumbashi). This relatively small area of immense mineral riches was of special strategic importance to the West.

Although Katanga lies close to the equator, its climate is relatively cool – similar to other parts of Africa located on high elevated plains, such as Kenya or Zimbabwe. The 'eternal spring' conditions attracted many white settlers and in 1960, 40,000 foreigners of various nationalities resided in Elisabethville. With generous salaries provided by the mining industry, they could enjoy a luxurious life style.

The principal force in the drive for Katanga's independence was a local African politician, Moise Tshombe. In June 1961 he was elected as the Katangan President and during his rule the administration was run under the watchful eyes of foreign specialists, mainly Belgians, Swiss and French.

Fearing nationalisation of the mining industry by the authorities in Leopoldville (now Kinshasa), the UMHK provided as much as four-fifths of the $100 million required to establish the Province's own administration and army.

After Katanga's secession was announced, the Federal Government appealed to the United Nations for help to restore law and order in the Congo, as well as to bring the breakaway province under federal rule. Paralysed by the mutineering soldiers and rioting population, weakened more-over by feuding political parties, the Leopoldville regime could not mount a military action.

The United Nations responded by sending a 20,000-man-strong peacekeeping force to monitor all parts of the country, including Katanga. The UN units came from seventeen different 'neutral' countries, but mainly from Ireland, India and Sweden. A large fleet of aircraft had been flown in to cope with transportation problems due to an inadequate road and rail infrastructure.

At first Tshombe would not allow the UN troops to enter Katanga. But in August 1960 Hammarskjöld flew to Elisabethville, bringing with him the first UN contingent, five plane-loads of Swedish soldiers.

Throughout the thirteen months of dealing with the Congo upheavals, the UN Secretary-General was faced with a tough but thankless task. Born in Jönköping in 1905, Dag Hjalmar Agne Hammarskjöld came from a family of high-ranking civil servants. An economist by education, at first he served as the Under-Secretary in the Ministry of Finance, then in the Foreign Office, and finally as an expert non-party member in the Swedish Cabinet, in charge of foreign economic relations. In the post-war years, he represented his country at the UN and at the European organ of the Marshall plan, the Organisation for European Economic Cooperation.

His activities brought him to the attention of the French and the British Governments, who were seeking a politician of 'neutral' status to break the long deadlock with the Soviet Union over the replacement of the previous UN Secretary-General, Norwegian Trygve Lie.

During his eight and a half years as the UN chief, the indefatigable Swede helped to settle many conflicts around the world. But the Congo crisis was his crucial test. He was constantly sub-jected to a three-pronged attack. Britain, France and Belgium were accusing him of undermining their commercial interests in Katanga. The non-aligned nations felt he was not doing enough to eradicate neo-colonialism. The Soviet Union wanted to get rid of him for trying to bring peace to the troubled Congo, which would have been an obstacle in their efforts of spreading Communism in Africa.

The resolution passed by the Security Council in July 1960, which had authorised the UN peace-keeping force, also called on the Belgian Government to withdraw all their officers and political advisers from Katanga. Although in principle the authorities in Brussels were against separatism, they took no practical steps to imple-ment the UN resolution.

In February 1961, the Security Council passed another resolution, calling for the removal of all remaining Belgian Army officers, foreign advisers and mercenaries from Katanga. Connor Cruise O'Brien, an Irish diplomat, formerly with the UN Secretariat in New York, was sent to Elisabethville as the chief UN representative, to implement the Security Council resolution. His first action 'Rumpunch' had met with success and quite a number of 'undesirable' Belgians and mercenaries were soon expelled. But 'Rumpunch' escalated the anti-UN feelings especially among white settlers and hired mercenaries. From then on, every UN official was considered to be an enemy, and even Hammarskjöld became a target of vicious attacks from the Katangan Press.

But Tshombe continued to oppose all anti-secession moves and refused to dispense with the services of foreign advisers in his administration or with the former Belgian officers and mercenar-ies in his army. The old campaign of hatred against the UN was stepped up and their officials were often harassed by the Katangan authorities.

Frustrated by the unsatisfactory progress of his mission, O'Brien arranged another roundup of the remaining 'undesirables', codenamed 'Morthor', in the hope that this would weaken their influence on the Katanga regime, finally leading to its aban-doning the secession.

The action was planned to coincide with Hammarskjöld's visit to the Congo. Armed with a warrant from the Federal Government, O'Brien sent Indian troops to arrest Tshombe and three cabinet ministers. He also instructed the UN force to take over Radio Katanga in order to proclaim integration of the province with the rest of the Congo. Unfortunately, the action misfired and fighting broke out in Elisabethville between the UN troops and Katangan soldiers led by the mercenaries. O'Brien was later blamed for mis-handling 'Morthor'.

Tshombe had managed to evade arrest and, after at first hiding in the residence of the British Consul, fled Elisabethville for Northern Rhodesia. On his orders, the Katangan Army attacked the UN units, which took up key positions in the centre of the city. Fighting also broke out in other parts of the Province. One of the fiercest skirmishes flared up at Jadotville. It was soon apparent that the UN peacekeeping force was no match for the 7,000-man-strong Katangan Army, equipped with modern weapons and reinforced by some 700 mercenaries.

Moreover, mercenary pilots in the service of the rebellious province, strafed the UN troops causing heavy losses, with one of the three Potez Fouga Magisters which the Katangan air force had clandestinely acquired. Bombs were also dropped on Elisabethville Airport as well as on the residence of the UN chief representative, and an attack was carried out on Kamina, a former Belgian NATO base, and at the time a UN stronghold.

The French-built Fougas, which were smuggled out of France early in 1961 and were flown to Katanga on board a large transport aircraft by an American charter company, were originally designed as twin-engine jet trainers but were subsequently developed into strike fighters, armed with two machine-guns and equipped with a bomb rack. Although by the standards at the time they were outdated, the UN in the Congo had no military aircraft at its disposal to repel air attacks.

The situation for the UN troops considerably worsened when the Irish units at Jadotville were overwhelmed by the Katangan Army and had to surrender.

Upon arrival in Leopoldville for talks with the Congolese government about the UN aid, Hammarskjöld was faced with a hard-pressed situation. The UN units were brought to the Congo to preserve peace and, in his opinion, should have never been used to settle internal dispute by force.

To stop unnecessary bloodshed, Hammarskjöld was determined to negotiate an immediate cease-fire with Tshombe and he postponed his return to New York. But a meeting would have to take place on a neutral territory. Ndola in Northern Rhodesia's Copper Belt was selected, mainly because its airport had a sufficiently long runway to accept large aircraft.

The British Government, responsible for foreign policy of the Dominion of the Federation of Rhodesia and Nyasaland, feared that the outbreak of hostilities in neighbouring Katanga could soon spread to other parts of Africa and decided that immediate steps should be taken to defuse such an explosive situation.

Lord Lansdowne, the Permanent Under-Secretary of State for Foreign Affairs, was sent to the Congo to discuss the issue with the Leopoldville Government and with Hammarskjöld. If Tshombe was prepared to enter into negotiations, Lansdowne offered to help with the arrangements. On the Rhodesian side, Lord Alport, a former Parliamentary Under-Secretary for Colonial Affairs, and at the time, the British High Commissioner in Salisbury (now Harare), acted as an intermediary with Tshombe. A UN aircraft was put at Hammarskjöld's disposal to take him to Ndola.

The stage was set for a disaster that had its roots in the conflict over Katanga's riches. In his book *To Katanga and Back* published by Hutchins, Connor Cruise O'Brien, comments on his part in the blame for the Ndola tragedy:

'I knew that my pressing for renewed action in Elisabethville – following up Rumpunch – my emphasis on urgency, leading to the timing of action for the morning of his [Hammarskjöld's] arrival in Congo, and my failure to avert certain errors in its execution, were among the links in the chain that had led to his death.'

PART III
HISTORY OF THE FLIGHT

On that fateful Sunday, 17 September 1961, two aircraft took off for Ndola from Ndjili, the main Leopoldville airport. A DC4, registration OO-RIC, carrying Lord Lansdowne, departed at 15.04 hrs GMT (16.04 hrs local time). The second aircraft, a DC6B, despatched under UN Air Command Flight Order 673, followed forty-seven minutes later. It was taking Hammarskjöld on his truce mission with Tshombe.

The DC6B, registration SE-BDY, known as 'UN One' and nicknamed by its crew 'Albertina', was the personal transport of General Sean McKeown, Irish commander of the UN forces in the Congo. It was hired from a Swedish charter company Transair Sweden, AB, based at Malmö. The aircraft was purchased two months earlier from the American Arabian Oil Company, especially for the UN operations in the Congo. It was previously used on the run between Dhahran and Amsterdam.

Three pilots, two of whom were captain rank,

were rostered for the flight. Thirty-five-year-old Per-Eric Hallonquist was the pilot-in-command, with twenty-eight-year-old Lars Litton as his co-pilot. The flight engineer was twenty-seven-year-old Nils-Goran Wilhelmsson. The third pilot, a reserve captain, was thirty-two-year-old Nils-Eric Aarheus.

Two more men were regarded as crew – a cabin attendant and a radio operator from the Swedish contingent of the UN troops. The radio operator was not a member of the flight crew but was sent in case Hammarskjöld needed to communicate with the UN headquarters in Leopoldville via long-range radio. As the messages were going to be transmitted in Morse and in Swedish, this required a specialist telegraphist.

Originally Hammarskjöld was going to travel with Lord Lansdowne in the DC4 and they planned to leave at 11 a.m. local time. However, the DC6B became available when it had been flown back to Leopoldville early in the morning, after it took General McKeown to Elisabethville for an inspection of the military situation there. The DC6B was faster, more comfortable and it was pressurised, so it could operate at higher altitudes to avoid turbulence.

While taking off on the return flight from Elisabethville, 'Albertina' was slightly damaged by machine-gun fire from the Katangan troops who occupied one side of the airport. A bullet had gone through the cowling on No. 2 engine and had pierced the exhaust pipe. However, this was quickly repaired after the aircraft landed at Ndjili.

Lord Lansdowne, who was on his way to Salisbury, only intended to stop at Ndola long enough to check if the preparations for the meeting between the Secretary-General and Tshombe had been satisfactorily carried out. For political reasons, Lansdowne could not remain while negotiations were taking place. The non-aligned nations believed that Great Britain had a vested interest in the outcome of the Katanga settlement and his presence could have been interpreted as a sign of undue influence.

The DC4 took an almost direct route of 960 nm, overhead Villa Henrique de Carvalho (now Saurimo), in Angola, which lay about halfway. The route at first crossed the Congo, then Angola and finally Northern Rhodesia. The aircraft proceeded in accordance with the flight plan filed with ATC at Ndjili and was sending position reports at the required intervals. It landed safely at Ndola at 20.35 hrs (GMT).

However, the flight with the UN Secretary-General on board was a cloak and dagger operation. The UN Commander at Leopoldville was informed about it only forty-five minutes before take-off.

The instructions for the flight came from UN Air Operations at Ndjili Airport. The two DC6B captains discussed their proposed course of action with Major Ljungkvist, the duty officer, who later testified before the UN Investigation Commission (the actual wording from the report):

'...when I was with Captain Hallonquist and First Officer Aarheus, we discussed the route of this flight, and at that time the last beacon to be used on the way down was Luluabourg. After that, he told me, "There is no radio navigation for me, so I have to go Luluabourg, and after that I do not know if I am going to follow the Angolan border or whether I am going to take another way." He told me, "I am going to prepare the rest of the flight plan during flight, depending upon special conditions."

Captain Hallonquist was going to be the navigator. He was a navigation specialist with the company and a teacher. He told me he will do the navigating himself.'

Hallonquist was advised to keep as far away as possible from the area where the Fougas' activities could be expected. The security side of the flight was discussed with Hammarskjöld and he endorsed all the precautions, including total secrecy about the route.

Nevertheless, the flight preparations appeared to have been made without due care. It was subsequently learnt that Hallonquist received no briefing on weather or other information for the flight. The actual route was only known to the crew. In order to keep it as secret as possible, the captain did not intend to file a flight plan with ATC at Ndjili. But at the last minute he was persuaded by the air traffic controller to fill out the required form, naming his destination as Luluabourg (now Kananga) and Leopoldville as an alternative. The endurance was stated as thirteen hours and twenty-five minutes.

Whether these precautions, which in some respects degraded safety, were justified, it is difficult to judge. There is no doubt that the attacks by the Fouga aircraft caught the UN command by surprise. Perhaps this accounted for Captain Hallonquist insisting on unorthodox safeguards. Evidently, the fighting power of the Katangan Army, supported by the mercenaries, was initially grossly underestimated.

Due to the great secrecy that surrounded the flight, only limited particulars about various check points on the way to Ndola, eventually came to light. According to the investigators, the aircraft was supposed to have proceeded at first due east to a position at 04° 35'S, 29° 25'E (20 nm north-west of Kigoma in the former Tanganyika, now Tanzania). It was further presumed that it turned to the south-south-east and followed Lake Tanganyika until 137 nm south-east of Albertville (now Kalemie). Then the course was again changed to the south-south-west, towards the Katangan border, to a position of 13° 00'S, 30° 19'E, (94 nm east of Ndola). From there the aircraft took up a westerly heading to Ndola Airport. (see the map on page 123.)

After clearing the Ndjili Tower frequency, the aircraft maintained radio silence for the first four hours. No in-flight reports were sent to Nairobi Flight Information Region, even upon entering its area.

The first message was transmitted at 20.02 hrs (GMT) to Salisbury Flight Information Centre (FIC) on H/F frequency 5521 Kc/s, although 'Albertina' was still outside Rhodesia. (The transcripts were made from the tape recordings at Salisbury Airport.) The SE-BDY pilots asked for the estimated time of arrival of the DC4 OO-RIC at Ndola. But before replying, Salisbury enquired about their destination and the type of aircraft. This was given as Ndola and DC6B. Messages often had to be repeated several times due to poor propagation conditions. Salisbury came back again with a request for their ETA at Ndola. The pilots replied 'stand by' and eventually gave it as approximately 22.35 hrs. After acknowledging the message, the ground station informed SE-BDY that OO-RIC was due at 20.17 hrs.

At 20.32 hrs 'Albertina' asked for the actual arrival time of the DC4 at Ndola but was told to stand by.

At 20.40 hrs Salisbury received the first position report from SE-BDY (the actual wording from the transcript): 'Checks 432B at 20.35 Flight level 175... Flying on advisory route 432 to avoid Congolese territory.'

View looking back at approach path showing swath cut by the crashing DC6B and the initial shallow approach angle.

At 20.49 hrs, the requested arrival time of the DC4 at Ndola was passed to the DC6B, as 20.35 hrs.

According to testimony by Lord Lansdowne, the captain of the DC4 tried several times to contact 'Albertina' in the air but without success. But contact on H/F would have been hardly possible, as pilots never keep a listening watch on that frequency band due to strong background noise.

At 21.11 hrs SE-BDY passed its second position report: 'Abeam Kasama at 21.06, estimating abeam Ndola 21.47. Request descent to F/L 160.'

Salisbury FIC replied that there was nil traffic at that level.

Radio communication was still marginal, as was evident from a number of messages that had to be repeated through occasional misunderstanding.

Nine minutes later the pilot was queried: 'What are your intentions on arrival at Ndola?'

He replied: 'We are keeping outside Congolese territory proceeding around the border to Ndola to land at Ndola.'

But this was not what the ground operator meant to ask and he re-phrased his original question.

'On arrival Ndola are you night-stopping or proceeding elsewhere?'
'I'm taking off almost immediately ... (unreadable).'
It was not the end of queries from Salisbury FIC.
'Are you returning to Leopoldville tonight?'
'Negative.'

When asked what was the destination upon leaving Ndola, the pilot cut his reply short: 'Unable to say at present.'

At 21.32 hrs, after checking with the aircraft whether it had reached FL 160, Salisbury FIC advised SE-BDY to call Ndola Approach on frequency 119.1 Mc/s. Radio contact was established at 21.35 hrs and the pilot informed the ground that they were estimating abeam Ndola at 21.47 and ND beacon at 22.20.

The controller queried the ETA (as there was no recording equipment at Ndola Tower, the transcripts were prepared from flight progress strips and from the controller's memory).

'Confirm ETA ND in two-zero minutes or at 22.20.'
'22.20.'

View of the final path of the DC6B SE-BDY.

A close-up of the badly damaged engine.

'Roger. Ndola weather. Wind 120/7 kt, visibility five to ten miles with slight smoke haze. Control QNH 1021, QFE 877. Duty runway one-zero. What time do you wish to make your descent?'

'Roger on your weather, request descent clearance at five-seven.'

'No traffic in area, at five-seven clear to descend to 6000 feet on QNH, report top of descent.'

'Roger.'

It may be a point of interest that about that time 'Albertina' was passing close to a memorial dedicated to another historical figure equally deeply involved in the African affairs as the UN Secretary-General, namely, Scottish missionary David Livingstone.

At 21.42 hrs Ndola Approach called SE-DBY.

'Are you proceeding Salisbury after landing Ndola?'

'Negative.'

'Roger, are you night-stopping Ndola?'

'Negative.'

'Due to parking difficulties would like your intentions?'

The pilot seemed evasive.

'Will give them on the ground.'

'Roger.'

At 21.47 hrs the DC6B passed a position report: 'Now abeam Ndola.'

The controller was able to observe on his VHF Automatic Direction Finding equipment that the bearing from the aircraft was 279° (M), which was exactly due east of Ndola – 270° (T). He replied: 'Roger, report top of descent.'

But the pilot never advised ATC about leaving FL 160.

Six minutes later the controller came up with another query.

'Will you require refuelling at Ndola?'

'Stand by.'

It took a minute before the pilot replied: 'May require a little.'

For the next sixteen minutes there was no further R/T conversation.

At 22.10 hrs the pilot reported: 'Your lights in sight, overhead Ndola, descending, confirm QNH.'

The controller replied: 'Roger, QNH 1021 millibars, report reaching 6,000 feet.'

After passing over the airport, 'Albertina' soon disappeared out of sight and no further messages were received in spite of continuous calls from the ground.

Later, the Rhodesian Investigation Commission was able to establish that upon completing the procedure turn for final approach, the DC6B, while still in a slight left turn, at first began to brush the tops of trees that were about twelve metres high. The actual altitude, as subsequently measured by the land surveyors, was 4,357 feet. (Ndola Airport elevation was 4,160 feet.) According to the investigators, the aircraft was descending normally. A trail of slashed foliage had been left behind when the propellers began to mow the branches. Bits of propeller rubber de-icing boots were later found on the ground. Once the ill-fated DC6B began to cut deeper into the young but dense tropical forest, the angle had increased to about 5°. This could be accurately measured from the marks on the trees.

Lower down, the tree trunks ripped away the left wingtip, and subsequently, further sections of the wing. About 250 metres after the first encounter with the trees, the left wing caught a nine-foot-high anthill and upon striking the ground it came off, together with No. 1 engine and the nose. Four crew members on the flight deck – three pilots and the radio operator – were thrown out onto the ground. The flight engineer must have been trapped in the wreck. The aircraft then slewed around about 200°.

Fuel in the ruptured wing tanks had most likely exploded instantly and the whole area as far back as 100 metres became engulfed in flames. Ammunition carried by two Swedish soldiers began to blow up. In time the fire became so intense that some parts of the fuselage were completely melted down.

The aircraft impacted the ground 8.05 nm from the airfield Control Tower, on a bearing of 279° (T), at an altitude of 4,290 feet. The area is known as Dola Hill. The crash site laid only 4.7 nm away from the nearest Congo border.

Out of sixteen people on board, fifteen died instantly or very shortly after impact. One person survived, but five days later he eventually succumbed to burns and injuries.

Among those who lost their lives were:

Dag Hammarskjöld, the UN Secretary-General

Heinrich Wieschhof, American, Secretary-General's senior adviser on African affairs

William Ranallo, American, personal aide to Hammarskjöld

Vladimir Fabry, American, legal adviser to

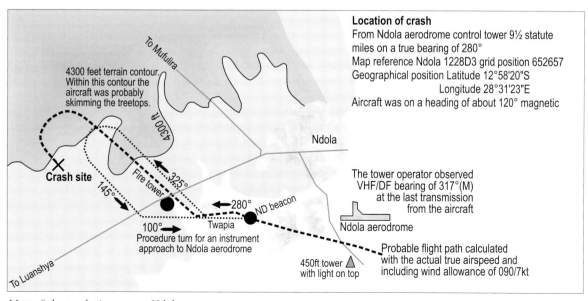

Map of the crash site area at Ndola.

the UN operations in the Congo

Miss Alice Lalande, Canadian, secretary to Dr Linner, chief UN representative at Leopoldville

Sergeant Serge Barrau, French, UN Security Officer

Sergeant Francis Eivers, Irish, UN Security Officer

Warrant Officer Hjelte, Swedish, Hammarskjöld's personal guard

Private Persson, Swedish, also a personal guard

The flight crew were all Swedish:

Captain Per-Eric Hallonquist, pilot-in-command

First Officer Lars Litton, acting as co-pilot

Captain Nils-Eric Aarheus, reserve captain

Flight Engineer Nils-Goran Wilhelmsson

The two others that were regarded as crew members were also Swedish:

Assistant Purser Harald Nook

Sub-Lieutenant Karl Eric Rosen, the radio operator.

The survivor who had later died in the local hospital from uraemia caused by burns, was Sergeant Harold Julien (in Rhodesian documents his name is given as Julian), American, the UN chief security officer at Leopoldville.

The bodies of most victims were badly charred; three were beyond recognition. There were two exceptions, Julien, who received only partial but heavy burns, and Hammarskjöld, who had not been at all affected by the fire. His death was due to internal injuries.

The Secretary-General occupied a seat in the rear cabin, in what was known as a private VIP compartment. While the crashing aircraft cartwheeled, the tail must have caught a thick tree trunk and broke off, taking the rear part of the fuselage with it. From the position in which Hammarskjöld's body had been found, it looked as if he was thrown out upon impact through a break in the fuselage into an area surprisingly free of flames. He could be easily identified by a disk worn on his wrist with his name on it, which had been given to him as a Christmas present by his aide Ranallo. His watch had stopped at twenty-five minutes past ten. He wore no jacket and one of his shoes was missing. He sustained severe fracture of the spine, crushed ribs and breastbones, heavy internal haemorrhage in numerous places

and a broken thigh bone.

The only survivor, Sergeant Julien, was able to recollect during his short lucid moments in hospital that he opened the emergency exit, jumped out and ran away, whilst he saw that the others were trapped in the wreckage. Apart from his burns, he had a compound fracture of the ankle. This meant that he could have tried to run at first but eventually he must have crawled across the fire and, as a result, was badly burnt.

Later, controversy broke out as to whether Hammarskjöld was still alive after the crash. The forensic pathologist from the Rhodesian Government, Dr Ross, believed the Secretary-General died on impact: 'After sustaining such injuries, it is inconceivable that survival could be more than momentary. It would be a merciful assumption that he was killed instantaneously.'

But the ambulance orderly, who took Hammarskjöld's body away, was of the opinion that the Secretary-General could have been alive for a short while. The orderly noticed that Hammarskjöld's hand was clutching dead leaves and dried grass. From his experiences of dealing with victims of many accidents, he thought that the position of the Secretary-General's body indicated his having made some attempts to move away from the blazing inferno.

The Chief Fire Officer of Ndola, one of the first rescuers to reach the crash site, backed the view of the ambulance orderly: 'I was struck by the way he was lying. I thought he had been thrown from the plane but had got away from the wreckage and lain down.'

Two Swedish pathologists, who examined the Rhodesian medical report, also shared the same view. They thought the results of the post mortem indicated that Hammarskjöld lived for a certain period after the crash. Their opinion was summarised in the UN Commission report:

'Severe congestion was found in head and neck. This gives some support to the assumption that suffocation as a result of breathing difficulties (severely crushed chest, high spinal fracture and crushing of the lungs from haemorrhage) are significant as the ultimate cause of death. It is not possible to estimate with certainty how long he may have lived after the crash. The haemorrhages which took place as a result of the wounds could have developed in a shorter time than a few hours. We agree with the pathologists' opinion that Hammarskjöld's wounds would have been fatal in any case.'

But how the UN Secretary-General had actually died on that fateful night will remain forever a matter of conjecture.

PART IV

THE SEARCH AND RESCUE

When, after passing overhead the airport, the DC6B did not report reaching 6,000 feet or being on final, the Air Traffic Controller on duty, Campbell Martin, tried several times to contact the aircraft. But he was not unduly concerned about the lack of a reply or the DC6B not coming in to land. At the time he thought that the aircraft was probably circling near the airport while the Secretary-General was receiving a message on the UN channel.

In any case, Martin was following the instructions from the Airport Manager, J.H. Williams, who had been briefed on the arrangements for Hammarskjöld's arrival by Lord Alport, the British High Commissioner in Rhodesia. He was told it was not certain that Hammarskjöld would be landing at Ndola and could possibly proceed to another destination.

But one person on the airport became very perturbed about the loss of contact with 'Albertina' – the DC4 pilot, Captain Deppe. He was waiting at the beginning of runway 10, for take-off clearance to Salisbury. Deppe, a very experienced pilot, seconded from SABENA to the UN operations, was familiar with the local circumstances, having spent some time in the Congo.

The DC4 landed at Ndola one hour and thirty-five minutes before the DC6B passed overhead the airport. This gave Lord Lansdowne a chance to have a talk with Lord Alport and other waiting officials. Although Lansdowne was reluctant to have any direct contact with the Katangan leader, he was forced to see him and his Foreign Minister Kimba and Finance Minister Kibwe. Tshombe, after waiting several hours at the airport, became very agitated. He wanted reassurance that the UN Secretary-General was on his way. But the meeting lasted only a few minutes.

As soon as Lord Lansdowne was told that Hammarskjöld's aircraft was approaching Ndola, he boarded the DC4. His mission was completed and his further presence could only complicate the delicate situation.

When for several minutes there was no reply from 'Albertina' to the controllers' calls, Captain

Deppe, sensing that something could have gone wrong, asked Tower if he could contact the DC6B himself. But his attempts also remained unanswered.

When twenty-five minutes later he took off and was told to keep below 6,000 feet, which indicated that ATC expected 'Albertina' to be still in the area, he tried to contact 'Albertina' again. As a pilot he was aware that in the air the VHF range would be considerably extended and even if the DC6B had been on its way for some time to another destination, it should still have been possible to establish contact. Especially as the 'Albertina' pilots would have most likely remained on the Approach frequency as there was no other VHF station for miles around. As a result of several unsuccessful attempts on VHF as well as on the H/F channel, he became so alarmed that he passed a warning message to Lord Lansdowne in the cabin.

It is no wonder that when they landed at Salisbury three hours later, the first thing Lord Lansdowne did was to question his deputy D.A. Scott, who met him at the airport, about the news of Hammarskjöld's aircraft.

Lansdowne became deeply concerned once he was told that nothing had been heard of the DC6B. From his talks with Hammarskjöld at Leopoldville earlier in the day, Lansdowne was certain that the Secretary-General was determined to get to Ndola and had no reason to proceed to another destination.

Although the lack of anxiety on the part of the air traffic controller on duty about the 'disappearance' of the DC6B may have looked like a sign of incompetence and dereliction of duty, there were certain extenuating circumstances for him not being unduly alarmed at the time.

By not disclosing their intention as to the type of approach they were going to perform, the pilots must have given the impression that they were not going to land immediately.

But in spite of the extenuating circumstances, the controller committed a grave error of judgement. He failed to apply the appropriate emergency procedures once no further messages on flight progress had been received from the DC6B. When Captain Deppe asked if he could try to contact 'Albertina' and made several unsuccessful attempts both on the ground and in the air, this must have indicated a probability of some dire emergency or even a catastrophe. But the controller ignored all warning signs.

Based on the ICAO Annex 12 – *Standards and Recommended Practices for Air Navigation*

Services – Search and Rescue, and ICAO Document 4446-SAR/501 – 'Procedures for Air Navigation Services – Search and Rescue', three distinct actions that had to be taken, were laid down by the Federal Civil Aviation Department of Rhodesia: 'Uncertainty', 'Alert' and 'Distress' Phases, bearing the code names INCERFA, ALERFA and DETERFA respectively.

'Uncertainty Phase' was considered to exist when after thirty minutes a routine position report had not been received, or when an aircraft failed to land thirty minutes after its expected time of arrival.

'Alert Phase' should follow the INCERFA situation once subsequent communication checks failed to established radio contact, or when an aircraft was cleared to land but had not landed within five minutes, or when information was received that it was experiencing a dire problem and a forced landing was likely, or when it was highly probable that an aircraft was about to make an emergency landing.

'Distress Phase' was considered to exist when extensive communication checks, following the alert phase, revealed that the aircraft could have crashed or was in severe difficulties.

In practice, the dividing line between these instructions was not that clear-cut and it was left up to the air traffic controller or the airport authorities, to decide on the most appropriate actions under the circumstances.

Once INCERFA was declared, a Civil Air Search Officer should have been immediately appointed. DETERFA called for the Search and Rescue Services to be at once notified and a search, from the air as well as on the ground, to be initiated as soon as practicable. In the case of an aircraft overdue over Rhodesia, Tanganyika or Nyasaland, a search would have been conducted by the Royal Rhodesian Air Force (RRAF).

But the Ndola controller waited fifty-two minutes before declaring the 'Uncertainty Phase', the least urgent of the three. The report of the Rhodesian Investigating Commission tried to account for his reasons:

'He [the controller] was at all material times in contact with and under the instructions of the Airport Manager, Mr J.H. Williams. Mr Martin's personal impression at the time, that the aircraft had refrained from reporting termination of its authorised descent, because it was purposely holding off to enable the Secretary-General to complete radio communication with a base outside Rhodesia, was genuinely

held, and sufficiently explains why he found no reason to question the prevailing belief expressed to him by Mr Williams that the aircraft was holding off or had proceeded to some other destination.'

However it was Lord Alport, as he later admitted, who was convinced that 'Albertina' was flying around in the vicinity of the airport or had most likely 'pushed off' elsewhere. He thought that either Hammarskjöld wished to land after Lansdowne departed or he no longer wanted to hold cease-fire talks with Tshombe because of some breach of the agreed conditions.

Once Lord Lansdowne boarded his DC4, Lord Alport, a somewhat overbearing personality, was the highest British official at the airport and his opinion must have weighed heavily with the Airport Manager. This must have influenced the decision not to initiate the overdue action as soon as there was no reply from 'Albertina'.

During the subsequent inquiries, Lord Alport explained his reason:

'I thought it possible that something had occurred in Elisabethville or that Mr Hammarskjöld had received a message from Leopoldville, or New York, which made him decide to postpone his meeting with Tshombe and to go elsewhere.

It did not strike me as strange that Mr Hammarskjöld should not notify Ndola of his intentions, partly because of the circumspect attitude of the aircraft in its contact with Ndola Control, and partly because I thought that he would wish, if indeed he changed his mind, to have a proper opportunity of dealing with the publicity which would ensue.

At 1.15 a.m. local time [an hour and five minutes after "Albertina" passed overhead the airport] Mr Williams asked me whether I thought that he should put into operation the normal overdue procedures which I understand were due to operate sixty minutes after contact had been lost. I said to him that he should institute whatever procedures were proper in the circumstances and as far as I was aware this was immediately done.'

At the least, the 'Uncertainty Phase' should have been declared at the earliest. But there were many signs that the situation was far more serious. The aircraft was cleared to an altitude from which either a visual landing or an instrument approach was expected to be initiated. When the DC6B reported descending to that altitude and had not landed within five minutes or failed to reply to the calls from Tower, alarm bells should have been rung and an air as well as a ground search in the vicinity of the airport should have been immediately organised.

But what happened on the fateful night of 17–18 September 1961, was a string of misjudgements due to lack of diligence and initiative, as the record of the events indicate.

Only at 1.02 hrs local time, fifty-two minutes after the last call from 'Albertina' was received, was the 'Uncertainty Phase' declared. At 01.15 hrs Williams sent a signal to Salisbury Flight Information Centre, asking if they had any message from the DC6B. The Salisbury Airport Manager immediately informed the Director of Civil Aviation, Lt-Col Barber, that Hammarskjöld's aircraft had been observed passing overhead the airport but it did not land. He said it was presumed at Ndola that it had gone to another destination, but no message to that effect was received from the DC6B.

After Lord Alport went to his private plane to catch some sleep, Williams checked with Salisbury on the latest news, and in spite of having been informed that nothing was heard of or from the aircraft, he asked if the airport could be closed. He left for a local hotel at 3.10 a.m., where he was staying after returning from a holiday in England as his house was not yet ready for immediate use. Before leaving, he notified the local police that 'Albertina' was overdue. Also, the air traffic controller went home and the airport was closed. The only person left in charge was the communicator, whose normal duty was to handle ATC messages. He was instructed to contact the Airport Manager if anything important was reported.

Under the circumstances, 'shutting shop' appears to have been a sign of irresponsibility. Especially when information soon began to drift in to the Ndola police station about flashes or a glow having been observed in the distance shortly after 'Albertina' passed over the airport.

One report came from a police officer, Assistant Inspector van Wyk. He was on a night patrol when he noticed a sudden flash of light on the horizon at about fifteen minutes past midnight local time (22.15 hrs GMT): 'The light was of a deep red glow' – he later described it – 'and it spread upwards from the ground; it stretched over an arc of forty-five degrees north-westwards of the place where I was standing.'

But because a glow of light was not an uncommon sight with bush fires and lightning flashes frequently occurring at that time of the year, van Wyk had only reported his observation to the officer in charge, Inspector Begg, when he returned to the Ndola police station, which was almost two hours after he saw the glow.

Begg immediately put two and two together about a possible connection between the flash and the disappearance of the DC6B, and he and van Wyk went straight away to the airport. Unfortunately the only person on duty in the Tower was the communicator, who tried to raise Williams on the phone, but in vain. The two police officers drove to the hotel and the Airport Manager was dragged out of bed. He insisted that he could do nothing until daylight. Nevertheless, Begg decided to check up on van Wyk's observation. He sent several Land Rovers in the direction of the flash but nothing was found.

The report of the UN Investigating Commission was very critical of Williams's half-hearted attitude to a probable emergency situation:

'It is, we think, a matter of comment that Mr Williams' implied intention to initiate action at first light was not carried into practice. Though Mr Williams did not suggest that it affected his action, we have taken into account the fact that his official return from leave did not require his attendance at the airport until his normal duty time on that morning, but his part in the arrangements on the previous day and his acceptance of the police report as properly made to him, imposed upon him, as we see the matter now, an obligation to accept as from the time of his actual return, the responsibility normally borne by the Airport Manager during his duty times.'

In the circumstances of an important flight, Williams's lack of initiative seems surprising. He was an old hand in aviation, having joined the RAF in 1936. During the war, one of his duties was to organise VIP flights, including that of the Prime Minister, Winston Churchill. He retired with the rank of wing commander. After the war, he went to Rhodesia and took up the position of Airport Manager at Ndola. Later the Zambian authorities put him in charge of developing a new airport at Lusaka.

Although first light came at 05.38 hrs local time and the sun rose twenty minutes later, Williams showed up on the airport at 09.00 hrs, only to learn that two hours and fifty minutes earlier, Salisbury FIC had already originated a DEFERTA signal. It was after air traffic controller Budrewicz came on duty at 05.50 hrs (the official hour of opening the airport for traffic was 06.00 hrs) and learnt about the police report on the observed flash. At 06.45 hrs he sent the following message to Salisbury: 'Person reported to the police here seen great flash in the sky at airport, 23.00 hrs in direction of Mufulira.'

Eight minutes later 'Distress Phase' was declared by Salisbury.

As it was subsequently revealed at the accident investigation, six other people had witnessed a similar flash during that fateful night. A further observation by another policeman on patrol duty, which was reported to the local police station during the night, should have raised the alarm that it was another ominous sign of a possible tragedy to the DC6B.

Assistant Inspector Vaughan was driving on the road leading from the north into Mufulira, a mining town thirty-five miles to the north-west of Ndola. It was about an hour after the crash when he saw a flicker of bright light and then a shining object falling down. From the road, although thirty-five miles away from the crash site but located 300 feet higher, he would have had a reasonably good view. The bright light was most likely an explosion, which must have thrown a burning object upwards. This could have been an oxygen bottle that was eventually ignited by the raging fire.

But only after Vaughan was told by the Mufulira police that the DC6B was overdue did he recount what he had witnessed. Two cars were at once dispatched in the direction of the observed light but nothing was spotted. Next morning another patrol extensively searched the area but there was no sign of the missing aircraft.

Although an air search should have been started at daybreak, the initiation was delayed for several reasons. Due to radio communication difficulties with the Congo, only at 7.44 a.m. (local Ndola time) did Leopoldville ATC advise Salisbury FIC that the DC6B had not landed at Ndjili Airport. It took a long time for the message to arrive because it had to be relayed by two stations, Johannesburg and Luluabourg. Earlier messages from Lusaka and Elisabethville also indicated that there was no sign of 'Albertina' anywhere.

But instructions to commence an air search were not issued by Salisbury Rescue Coordination Centre until 09.42 hrs local time. The appointment of a Civil Air Search Officer by the Director of Civil Aviation, who was initially in charge, was not made until 2.10 p.m. Williams was selected to conduct the search.

Although airlines flying in the vicinity of Ndola and a military Canberra on a routine patrol were asked to look out for the missing DC6B, and even with quite a number of RRAF aircraft available at Ndola, only one Provost was sent up at 10.02 hrs. The pilot, Flying Officer Gerald Craxford, initially searched the area to the north and to the south of the airport. But after it had been worked out from the two police reports that the flashes were observed to the north-west, the Provost was instructed to proceed in that direction.

About the same time, African charcoal burner Mazibisa came to the Forest Commission Office and reported that he had seen the crash. F/O Craxford was advised to inspect the area and twenty-five minutes later he spotted the wreckage. The first police patrol arrived on the scene shortly after 3 p.m. and the ambulance an hour later. Within ten minutes Hammarskjöld's body had been located and he was identified by Col Ben Matlick, American air attaché at Leopoldville, who arrived at Ndola earlier on that morning in one of three US DC3s brought in to help with the air search at the request of the UN command at Leopoldville.

The only survivor, Sgt Julien, was straight away taken to the local hospital. He was conscious but in a very critical state. He sustained burns on 55% of his body and, having been exposed to the hot sun for several hours, his condition had badly deteriorated.

The UN Commission, one of whose tasks was to investigate the reasons for the delay of the air search, was very critical of the apathetic efforts by the Rhodesian authorities. In the report it was stated:

'It is true that the Director of Civil Aviation testified that it was only at 07.00 (9 a.m. local time) that he had been informed of the signal [about the observation of a flash by the Ndola police]. This, however, in the Commission's view cannot absolve the Federal Department of Civil Aviation of the responsibility for the delay in the initiation of an air search.

Although SE-BDY crashed nine and a half miles [statute] from an airfield on which eighteen military aircraft capable of carrying out an air search were stationed, the wreckage was located by the Rhodesian authorities only fifteen hours after the crash and more than nine hours after first light on 18 September, 1961.

The Commission is fully aware of the difficulty of conducting an air search over an area covered by bush and forest. It believes, nevertheless, that in the present case the delay in commencing search and rescue operation was increased by shortcomings in liaison and cooperation between the aviation officials concerned, by lack of initiative and diligence on their part and by delay in applying the prescribed procedures.

Undue weight appeared to be attached to the groundless impression that the Secretary-General had changed his mind after flying over Ndola and decided to land at another airport without informing the Ndola tower. Had that degree of diligence been shown which might have been expected in the circumstances, it is possible that the crash would have been discovered at an earlier hour and Sgt Julien's chances of survival materially improved. Had he survived, not only would one life have been saved but also a possible source of direct knowledge of the conditions and circumstances surrounding the tragedy.'

Disturbing revelations were later brought to light by the Press about the lack of cooperation between RRAF and American officials in the Congo, who offered to help with the air search after they were asked by the UN in Leopoldville. The Americans immediately dispatched three DC3s to Ndola but were not allowed to participate in the rescue operation by the local RRAF officer in charge, Squadron Leader Mussel.

The 'resentment' of the RRAF towards 'American intervention' was revealed in his testimony to the UN Commission. Mussel stated that: 'Underhand things were going on with strange aircraft arriving without prior notification and American Dakotas were sitting on the airfield with their engines running, in my opinion, so they could transmit messages.'

It appears that right from the start, mistrust began to develop between the Rhodesian authorities and the other interested parties over the Ndola disaster.

PART V
THE ACCIDENT INVESTIGATION

The Hammarskjöld crash was, at the time, one of the most extensively investigated cases in aviation history. Not only in terms of time and efforts but also in the number of parallel proceedings. Apart from the two inquiries, one conducted by the Rhodesian authorities and the other by the United Nations Commission, judicial public hearings were held at Ndola and Salisbury, and there was also research undertaken into various aspects of the Ndola accident by a Swiss expert, Dr Frei-Sulzer.

When the crashed aircraft was located, in view of the importance of the accident, the Rhodesian Federal Government set up the Investigating Board of Inquiry under the chairmanship of the Director of the Civil Aviation Department, Lt-Col Maurice Barber. The members were: G/Capt Blanchard-Sims, DCA Senior Operations Officer, Mr Madders, DCA Chief Inspector of Aircraft and W/Cdr Evans, an RAF officer, Air Adviser to British High Commissioner in Rhodesia. The Board members had either no previous or limited experience in accident investigation. In the post-war years there were only two major crashes on Rhodesian soil.

In accordance with customary procedure, the State of aircraft's registry, Sweden, was invited to participate in the proceedings as well as the operator Transair Sweden AB.

The Swedish accredited representative was Mr E.A. Landin, Inspector of the Royal Civil Aviation Board. The RCAB was an equivalent of the British CAA or the US FAA. These two agencies are seldom directly involved in accident investigation as opposed to the AAIB and the NTSB, which are independent departments. The choice of the technical advisers looked equally surprising. According to the official list, only two were aircraft inspectors, temporarily attached to the Swedish RCAB. The four remaining were: Dr Bratt, Minister for Sweden to the Republic of South Africa, Mr Nylen, legal adviser to the Swedish RCAB, Mr Landin, Assistant Director of the Swedish National Institute of Technical Police and Mr Danielsson, Superintendent, Criminal State Police.

Transair was represented by Captain Pearsson, Director of Flight Operations, Mr Virving, Chief Engineer and Mr Hellberg, Chief Flight Engineer.

For the first time in the history of accident inquiries, international organisations were invited to participate. At the suggestion of ICAO, the UN headquarters in New York appointed Mr J.P. Fournier, head of the ICAO Technical Mission to the Congo, as their accredited representative, assisted by T.R. Nelson, deputy head of the ICAO Technical Assistance Branch. Captain A. McAfee, a Viscount pilot from Central African Airways at Salisbury, represented the International Federation of Air Line Pilots' Associations.

Fournier, a former Canadian Navy helicopter pilot, was an experienced inspector of accidents from his service with the Quebec Department of Transport. He took part in several major aircraft disaster inquiries. Later he was appointed as head of the Department.

Nelson, a former Squadron Leader in the RAF and a captain with KLM, attended numerous accident investigations, among them all four Comet I crashes, on behalf of the AAIB. Later he joined ICAO, where one of his tasks was to re-write the ICAO Manual on Accident Investigation.

Contrary to accepted procedure, no delegation had been invited from the country of the aircraft and engine manufacturers. Only a Pratt & Whitney specialist was allowed to inspect the engines once they were brought to a hangar at Ndola Airport. The altimeters were sent to Kollsman, the US instrument maker, for scientific tests.

The examination of the wreckage, collecting other associated evidence, and interviewing witnesses lasted from 19 September until 2 November 1961. Every piece of the crashed aircraft, even the most minute, was identified, listed and marked on the wreckage plan. An area of about two by one and a half miles behind the crash site was searched by 180 policemen for any parts that could have fallen off before the aircraft brushed the trees. Nothing was found.

When in the last week of September all parts of the wreckage were removed to Ndola, soil on the crash site was raked and put through a quarter-inch sieve. Numerous nuts, bolts and bits of mechanism were recovered, but no items were found that did not belong to the crashed DC6B or its occupants.

All parts were again examined after they were stored in a hangar at Ndola Airport. Large melted sections of the fuselage were broken down into small pieces by a steam hammer, in order to check if they held any bullets.

On the night of 9 October, five flight tests were carried out with a Transair DC6, especially brought for that purpose from Sweden. As the only DC6B of Transair was lost in the crash, a DC6 was used, but there was no difference in flight characteristics between the two variants. The captain was the same pilot who, in 1951, had been involved in a DC6 accident at Cairo Airport (see chapter 4), when he served as a co-pilot with SAS. Several different approaches were tried, including a simulated instrument procedure.

The investigators then began to look into the probable cause of the accident under four main headings: Sabotage or internal interference; Attack or external interference; Material failure; Human failure.

Although an unlikely possibility, sabotage had been carefully looked into, as opportunities did exist for planting a bomb. When the DC6B returned from Elisabethville early in the morning on the day of the accident, it had undergone a thorough inspection. Upon completing it, the ground engineers closed all doors and went for lunch. 'Albertina' was left unguarded for four hours. During that time, it would have been possible for a terrorist to sneak in unobserved and place an explosive device in a compartment with an external access door, such as hydraulic or heating, or in the nosewheel bay or in the main gear well.

But with the hour of the DC6B take-off unknown and the flight plan not even completed before the departure, it would not have been possible to set a time fuse. A barometric trigger would have only worked on reaching a preset altitude during climb. But the accident occurred at the end of descent.

Planting a bomb in the cabin was out of question, even if someone from the local staff, such as a cleaner, was prepared to take the risk. Security was far too tight. The guard had extensively searched the aircraft before the passengers came on board.

The fact that the DC6B was still undamaged when it began to brush the trees and no signs of a bomb explosion were found during scientific examination of the salvaged parts of the fuselage precluded a possibility of a mid-air break-up.

Wild speculations had flared up when a Danish newspaper reported that 'Albertina' carried not sixteen but seventeen occupants and the extra person could have been a hijacker. This information came from one of the Tshombe agents in Europe. The terrorist was supposed to force the captain to fly to Kolwezi, the base of the Katangan Air Force, but in the struggle before landing at Ndola, the aircraft went out of control and crashed.

To disprove such a claim, all the officials who saw off Hammarskjöld at Ndjili Airport were interviewed. It was confirmed that every person who had boarded the aircraft was known. The pathologists were certain that there were only sixteen bodies recovered from the crash site. Police checked the whole area nearby for a possibility of someone having walked away into the forest. Nothing evident was traced. These unlikely and highly speculative rumours were, in the end, discounted.

Perhaps the most controversial of all theories was the possibility of the aircraft having been shot down by Katangan fighters or by a ground machine-gun attack. The political situation in the Congo at the time of the accident warranted that such a criminal act should seriously be taken into consideration.

Nevertheless, the investigators concluded that, to make an aircraft of the DC6B size crash, the controls would have to be extensively damaged. No bullets were found, except those carried for security reasons. Although some had been found in two bodies of the Hammarskjöld security guard, ballistic tests proved that the bullets had not travelled through a barrel. A suspicious hole near the co-pilot window was checked under a microscope and a metallurgical test was conducted. The hole was found to be too small to have been made by a machine-gun bullet and moreover, it did not contain any residual metal that could come from a bullet. The Katangan Air Force commander was interviewed and he assured the investigators that all Fougas were on the ground at Kolwezi airfield on the night of the accident. Potez, the Fouga manufacturer, had calculated that the range of the aircraft was insufficient to complete a sortie to Ndola and back to Kolwezi.

Even if 70% of the DC6B was destroyed by fire, it was possible to determine that there were no signs of any mechanical fault with the aircraft. All four engines were operating normally prior to impact. The power was set as expected for the approach conditions. The landing gear was down and locked. From the way in which the flap control quadrant was wrapped around the lever, it was evident that the flaps were extended to 30⁰. The landing lights were still retracted. Normally they were not switched on until about 500 feet above the runway.

Judging by the relatively flat rate of descent at the time of brushing the trees, the investigators concluded that the flight controls must have been in order.

All three altimeters, two on the instrument panel and one at the navigation station, showed the correct QNH setting as provided by the Ndola Tower air traffic controller. They were tested in the USA by the manufacturer, Kollsman, in the presence of CAB inspectors. No faults were found that could have resulted in wrong indications.

It was established that the repairs on the pierced exhaust pipe from the bullets during take-off at Elisabethville were carried out in accordance with the approved maintenance instructions and that the damage could have in no way contributed to the accident.

When all other possibilities failed to provide a rational explanation as to why the aircraft prematurely struck the ground, the investigators began to concentrate on the possibility of pilot error.

Several theories were put forth. The one advanced by W/Cdr Evans was that, as a result of fatigue, the pilot had misread 4,600 feet for 6,400 feet, confusing the relative position of the two pointers, the same in both circumstances. However, on examination this theory did not appear to have been based on rational arguments. It would have been unlikely that with the co-pilot monitoring the instruments as well as the flight engineer, who occupied the centre position on the DC6B and was able to see both panels, an altitude other than 6,000 feet, as laid down in the approach procedure, could have been maintained all the way from overhead the airport until the descent on final.

In the opinion of the investigators, there could have been no question of fatigue. Hallonquist had had twenty-four hours' rest before starting the flight, which, in any case, was not unduly long.

Another possibility was put forward by Lt-Col Barber. He believed that Hallonquist had mixed up the approach charts. Instead of using a Ndola chart, he selected one for Ndolo, an airfield at Leopoldville, which was seldom used after Ndjili had been built. Ndolo's elevation was 951 feet while Ndola's was 4,160 feet. This could have accounted for descending below the safety altitude on base leg to runway 10 at Ndola. But the instrument approach at Ndolo had to be carried out from the east as opposed to the west at Ndola Airport.

According to Transair, their pilots were issued with Jeppesen, a widely used route manual with approach charts in a loose-leaf binder. For secondary airfields in the Congo, they sometimes relied on the US Air Force 'Flight Information Publication – Terminal', which was freely distributed at Leopoldville to UN personnel. In the USAF manual, the charts for N'Djili (the actual spelling of the main Leopoldville Airport) and Ndolo followed each other. With most flights of the UN operations originating at Leopoldville, the pilots should have been familiar with the names on the pages that were so close to each other.

Transair checked all Jeppesens issued to their pilots and three could not be accounted for. These must have been in the hands of the 'Albertina' crew. Only one Jeppesen was recovered from the crash, but with the Ndola chart missing. The remaining two manuals must have perished in the fire. The investigators presumed that Captain Hallonquist had most likely pulled out the Ndola approach chart from the loose-leaf-binder, so that he could clip it onto a small panel on the control column, which was provided for that purpose. This was a standard practice in many airlines.

Four different verdicts as to the cause of the Ndola disaster were eventually announced. The findings of the Rhodesian Investigating Board, with one exception, were endorsed by the Federal Government Court of Inquiry under the chairmanship of the Chief Justice, Sir John Clayden. Two assessors were: Sir George Lloyd-Jacob, a Chancery Division judge from England and Jack Newton, Chief ICAO Air Navigation Bureau and a former group captain in the RAF.

Two judicial hearings were held, one at Ndola and the other in Salisbury. The technical report by the Board of Investigation was examined and 120 witnesses were heard. In the end, the Court of Inquiry came to a slightly different conclusion from the Investigating Board. While the Board maintained that the aircraft was carrying out an instrument approach procedure ending up with a loss of height which could not be accounted for, the Commission expressed the view that the cause of the accident was probably pilot error. Hallonquist was supposed to have been making a visual circuit and when turning on base leg, he lost height while trying to look for the runway. The report offered the following arguments:

'In support of the view that the Ndola instrument procedure was not carried out are the facts that the aircraft did not pass over the airport exactly on the course it should have taken as it proceeded to the non-directional radio beacon and for thirty seconds thereafter.

It flew over a house three-quarters of a mile to the north and slightly to the west of the beacon. At that stage, to make the amount of noise that one witness heard, it must have been below 6,000 ft, the correct altitude in an instrument approach. It then approached a house seven miles to the north-west of the airport. The procedure turn would not have taken it so

far out, nor would the aircraft have appeared to be so low.

The altitude of the aircraft as it crossed over the airport was considered by the Commission to be about 6,000 feet asl (above sea level), based on the evidence of eyewitnesses.

The absence of a report from the aircraft, as requested on reaching 6,000 ft, may well have been because the aircraft had already reached that altitude when the request was made. It is certain that the aircraft started its descent soon after it passed over the airport.

In the country west of Ndola there is bush. After the lights of Ndola were flown over, and as the descending turn was made to the right, there would be blackness ahead. If, in the course of the turn, the aircraft came far too low, the slight rise in the ground between the place of the crash and the airport would obscure the lights of the runway and of Ndola as the aircraft came back to a course on which those lights might otherwise have been seen to port.

Failure to recognise the dangerous altitude of the aircraft in relation to the airport elevation, and the slightly higher elevation of some of the country to the west, is unexplained in view of the apparent correct setting of the three altimeters, which, as far as can be determined, were functioning properly.'

The Commission's conclusions were summarised in a short paragraph under the title:

'Probable Cause

It was strongly urged that the Commission should not conclude that the accident was due to pilot error. Reasons have been given for saying that other suggested causes were not really possible. Reasons have also been given for concluding that the approach was made by a visual descent procedure in which the aircraft was brought too low. It could not be said whether that came about as a result of inattention to the altimeters or misreading of them. The Commission felt it must conclude that the aircraft was allowed, by the pilots, to descend too low.'

Parallel to the Rhodesian inquiries, the UN set up its own investigating body under the chairmanship of Rishikesh Sahda, a delegate to the UN from Nepal, to look not only into the probable cause but also into other aspects of the Ndola crash. Throughout the proceedings a close cooperation was maintained between the two working groups.

The UN Commission had the benefit of a technical report prepared by Nelson and Fournier. In addition, Nelson was personally debriefed by the UN officials in their New York headquarters. The Commission began its work in December 1961 and continued until March 1962. Eighty-eight witnesses were interviewed and, out of those, twenty-four had not given evidence to the Rhodesian Commission. Nevertheless, none could materially contribute to solving the mystery of the crash.

In order to assist the members of the Commission, the United Nations appointed Dr Frei-Sulzer, Chief of the Scientific Department of the Zurich Police and Professor of Science Criminology at the University of Zurich, to perform scientific tests of the wreckage. In his report, he emphasised the cooperation and help he had received from the Rhodesian authorities and an engineering company at Ndola in melting down large parts of the fused fuselage to ascertain that they did not hold bullets. Originally, the Rhodesian authorities were reluctant to do it themselves, for fear of being accused of destroying evidence. It was an extremely critical metallurgical process, requiring accurate temperature control, and this allowed Dr Frei-Sulzer to make sure that there were no lodged bullets in the 4,000 lb of fused aluminium.

He also inspected suspected holes in all metal sections that were still stored in the hangar at Ndola. In his opinion, 'none of the holes in the remaining identifiable parts of aircraft were caused by shooting'. He also confirmed that there was no trace of explosion prior to impact. Examination of the aircraft control cables indicated that there were breaks only with typical signs of overstrain from impact. The sharp cuts came from cutting the cables for transportation from the crash site to Ndola, as an inspection by a magnifying glass had revealed.

Upon completing his scientific tests, Dr Frei-Sulzer offered the following conclusions:

'The re-examination of the wreckage in the hangar and melting down of the fused parts of the wreckage allow us to exclude the possibility of hostile actions from the air and from the ground and leave no room for the suggestion of sabotage.

As no evidence of technical failure could be found and considering that the aircraft obviously made a perfectly normal approaching procedure turn and was normally trimmed at the moment of the first impact with the trees, the only abnormal fact was the dangerous low altitude of the aircraft in relation to the airport elevation, probably due to human failure.'

Considering that Dr Frei-Sulzer was no aviation expert, his last statement appears to be presumptuous.

The opinion of the UN Commission on the involvement of human factors in the crash varied from that of their Rhodesian counterpart and Dr Frei-Sulzer. They did not accept the view that Hallonquist was making a visual landing as the Rhodesian Commission had suggested, because the Transair instructions clearly stipulated that at an unfamiliar airport an instrument approach was mandatory at night. As a result, the UN Commission brought an open verdict in which none of four possible principal causes, air and ground attack, sabotage, mechanical failure or pilot error, were singled out as the prime probability.

Many countries took their own view as to the cause of the crash. As soon as it had been revealed from the forensic examinations that bullets were found in the bodies of two Swedish soldiers – Hammarskjöld's personal guard – speculations about a probable retaliatory action by mercenaries began to fill the front pages of every newspaper in the world.

The most violent accusations of a likelihood of foul play appeared in the Swedish press, insinuating that 'Albertina' had been a victim of hired assassins. Transair added fuel to the fire by claiming on Swedish television and radio immediately after the crash that the aircraft had most likely been brought down by 'enemy' fire, probably a rocket. Even the Western and US media took up that line, hinting that this could be the answer to the cause of the disaster.

The Swedish Foreign Minister condemned the 'Katangan soldiers of fortune' in the strongest words for a possible involvement in the dastardly act, pointing out that: 'The mercenaries systematically sought to sabotage the UN work for peace in the Congo.'

The Congolese authorities in Leopoldville shared the same conviction. When the Central Government proclaimed 19 September 1961 as a day of national mourning, Prime Minister Aduala declared that: 'It was a tribute to a great man who had fallen victim to the shameless intrigues of the great financial powers of the West.'

The African and the Indian press accepted foul play as a fact. They pointed a finger at the Rhodesian authorities, 'which were inspired by the British Government and the African traitor Moise Tshombe', for engineering the destruction of Hammarskjöld's aircraft with the help of the mercenaries.

PART VI
WAS HAMMARSKJÖLD SHOT DOWN?

In 1992 the Ndola disaster came back into prominence through the letter to the Editor of *The Guardian* by two UN officials in the Congo at the time of the crisis. Next day the whole Western Press echoed the sinister news. Canadian newspapers claimed in their headlines 'HAMMARSKJÖLD WAS SHOT DOWN'.

But in their letter, Ivan Smith and O'Brien had only repeated an old story that in the past had already proved to be without foundation. It was a tale of a Belgian mercenary pilot, Beukels, who was supposed to have 'confessed' on tape in 1967 to a French diplomat, Ambassador Claude de Kemoularia, the head of the UN Information Office in Geneva, that Beukels was responsible for shooting down Hammarskjöld's aircraft. At the time, de Kemoularia had never made it official and only privately informed the UN officials and Swedish diplomats. The taped 'confession', which was reproduced in a programme by the BBC in 1992, was not a recording of the mercenary's voice but de Kemoularia translating his notes about the 'confession' into English.

Although one person in England was intimately familiar with the intricacies of the Ndola accident inquiry, he had been denied an opportunity to put the allegations by the two former UN servants in a correct perspective. This was T.R. Nelson, the UN representative at the investigation and a former member of the AAIB. His letter to the Editor, explaining the view of the Rhodesian Board of Inquiry that the disaster had been not been caused by external interference, was turned down by *The Guardian*. Even pressure from Nelson's local MP was of no help.

Eventually in March 1993 *The Guardian* published a letter from Mr Bengt Rosio of the Ministry of Foreign Affairs in Sweden. Rosio strongly refuted the allegations outlined in the letter by the two former UN officials. In respect of

the tale by the Belgian mercenary pilot, he wrote: 'Although the story told to M. de Kemoularia is a fabrication, it is regrettable that he did not take it to the police instead of keeping it to himself for twenty-five years, until his sources can no longer be traced.'

Perhaps the strongest argument that it was most unlikely for SE-BDY to have crashed due to severed cables was that, on the DC6B like on all aircraft of that era, the elevator was connected to the captain's and co-pilot's control columns by two separate cables – an upper and lower one (four in total – see the diagram on page 127). It would have to be a miraculously lucky shot to have cut all four cables by a single bullet. Moreover Dr Frei-Sulzer clearly established that there were no sharp cuts in the cables, only breaks from stress on impact.

But the world was made to believe that the allegation by Ivan Smith and O'Brien were the real cause of the Ndola disaster.

PART VII
ANALYSIS OF THE INVESTIGATORS' CONCLUSIONS

In spite of the staggering sums of money that were spent on the various inquiries into the Ndola disaster, my research indicated that the conclusions as to the cause of the crash were flawed by incorrect interpretations of vital facts. Moreover, certain early formed but faulty presumptions were repeated throughout all the reports without having been checked to see if they were valid. The origin of such erroneous surmises can only be attributed to inadequate pilot input into the inquiries, in particular in respect of the DC6B operating procedures and the aircraft systems.

In a way, this is not surprising. Out of the seventeen members of the investigating team who were involved in the preliminary work, only Captain Pearsson of Transair was familiar with the DC6B. Moreover, only two other participants had an intimate knowledge of airline operations: Alan McAfee, the CAA Viscount captain, and Bob Nelson, a former KLM pilot.

The lack of experience in accident investigations among some of the members of the Board of Inquiry certainly did not help in assessing the complex operational factors. Only Nelson and Fournier had previously served as accident inspectors with their national agencies. The rest of the so-called 'flying experts' were mainly 'desk pilots' whose know-how of flying procedures could have

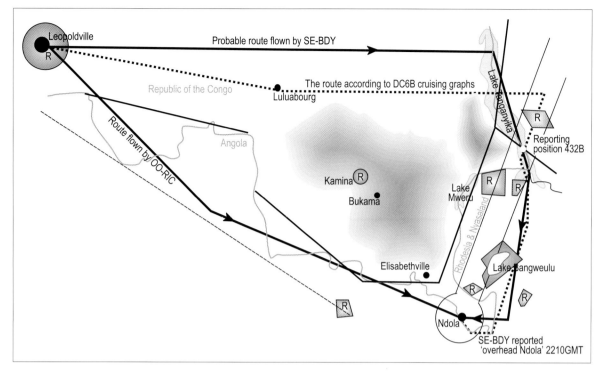

Probable route of DC6B SE-BDY from Leopoldville to Ndola on 17 September 1961.

been out of date. On the other hand, among the technical specialists there were several highly qualified experts.

Equally, the lack of knowledge about aircraft operations was wide-ranging among the advisers serving on the Swedish delegation. The IFALPA representative, Captain McAfee wrote at the time that: 'The counsel for the Rhodesian side was very experienced in aviation matters, while the counsel for Sweden and other observers were not.'

The first example as to how some evidence was misinterpreted can be seen in the investigators' reconstruction of the probable route of the ill-fated SE-BDY. (See the map above). Although this has no direct bearing on the conclusions as to the cause of the crash, it is an illustration of how certain facts were incorrectly assessed.

It is known that, on the insistence of the air traffic controller at Leopoldville Airport, Hallonquist filed a flight plan specifying that his first stretch of the flight would be to Luluabourg at FL 135 (13,500 feet). It is most unlikely that he would have risked violating ATC rules while carrying a VIP of Hammarskjöld's status.

FL 135 was probably selected because it was the highest altitude at which minimum 'comfortable airspeed' could be maintained with a take-off weight of 90,544 lb using a 'constant 1,100 BHP' cruise system. This would have resulted in a lower TAS than the alternative system of '190 knots constant IAS'. Hallonquist evidently did not want to catch up on Lord Lansdowne's DC4 and his concern in that respect is indicated by making his first radio contact with Salisbury FIC to check on the ETA of OO-RIC at Ndola.

Surprisingly, the investigators claimed that just because FL 175 was reported over Lake Tanganyika, it was maintained all the way after take-off.

Other stretches of the investigators' 'probable route' also do not agree with the facts. Hallonquist reported flying on Advisory Route 432, but this is not reflected on their map. The time of 20.35 hrs when SE-BDY called over the reporting point 432B is, in my opinion, most likely correct. If, as it was claimed, the aircraft was at that moment 34 nm further to the south, the ground speed on that leg (290 knots) would have been too excessive.

Hallonquist must have been aware that, without filing a flight plan for the later stretches of the route, adhering to a correct quadrantal altitude separation was an important safety factor. Maintaining FL 175, the stipulated altitude for the second quadrant (odd + 500 feet), as he reported to Salisbury, indicates that he must have followed a south-south-easterly heading (and not south-south-westerly as the investigators presumed) from 432B to abeam Kasama as that heading would have taken him away from the Congo border. It would have been logical in view of trying to keep as far away as possible from the Fougas' air base at Kolwezi and would have accounted for a more realistic ground speed resulting from the longer distance.

Hallonquist's request at abeam Kasama to change altitude to FL 160 confirms that he strictly observed the separation rules and must have only then changed his heading to south-south-westerly (even quadrant).

Finally the investigators made another erroneous assumption. In spite of Hallonquist informing Salisbury FIC that he intended to fly around the Katanga pedicle, in order 'to avoid Congolese territory' as he reported, they had shown on their map that he cut across directly to Ndola. This cannot be correct because the air traffic controller saw on his automatic VHF/DF indicator that the aircraft was approaching the airport on a bearing of 317° (M).

The more likely route that was followed from Leopoldville to Ndola, with various check points that agree with the times reported by the crew, is marked as a dotted line on the investigators' map.

Among hundreds and hundreds of pages of documentation on the Ndola crash, the most important misinterpretation of evidence was a short paragraph in the report by the Rhodesian Investigation Board. Appendix 1.8, under 17. INSTRUMENTS, reads:

'Altimeter Unit "A"

In position on captain's instrument panel. Glass unbroken, case undamaged, static line found disconnected.'

Surprisingly, the entire instrument panel, which was found close to where Hallonquist's body lay, had sustained relatively little damage. Four more altimeters were recovered from the cockpit area of the wreckage. One instrument came from the co-pilot's panel and one from the navigator's station. Two were spare altimeters. This was possible to determine from a wire that held an identification tag in place, which had most likely perished in the

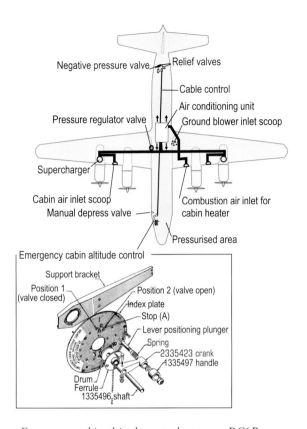

Emergency cabin altitude control system – DC6B.

fire. All four altimeters were far more damaged by impact or by fire than the instrument on the captain's panel.

But the significance of a disconnected static line was dismissed as irrelevant to the cause of the crash. The Rhodesian Board of Investigation stated in the report:

'It was noted that the aircraft captain's altimeter, which was in comparatively good condition, was found disconnected from the static supply. However, had there been a break in the static line as a result of disconnection during flight, the effect would have been immediately apparent as the captain's VSI (Vertical Speed Indicator) would have remained stationary, and the airspeed indicator and altimeter would under-read, i.e. the indicated height would have been lower that the actual height. In other words it would have erred on the safe side. The Board cannot see how this can have any significance as a causal factor in the accident. Additionally, as the co-pilot's and

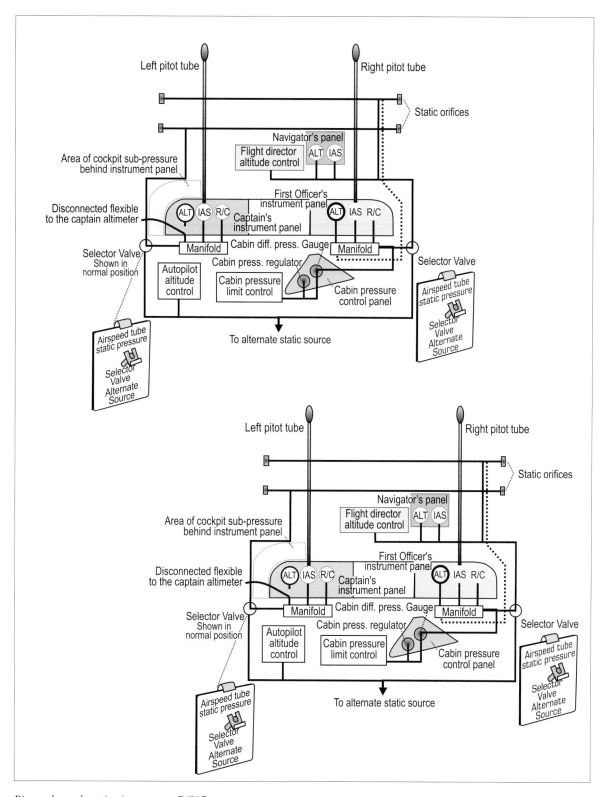

Pitot tube and static air system – DC6B

navigator's static instruments were connected to a separate supply any discrepancy in the readings should have been obvious. The simple misreading of an altimeter cannot be ruled out as a possibility.'

Such a presumption would have been correct only if the cabin was pressurised. But the investigators committed a CAPITAL ERROR. The DC6B (DC6 and DC6A as well) was the only piston-engine aircraft requiring residual cabin pressure to be dumped before landing. Although I have over 4,000 flying hours to my credit on the DC6s and I can still recollect the drill to be taken during approach, I sought confirmation of this particular procedure from Captain N. Barron, one of the most experienced DC6 pilots in KLM with 6,000 hours and ten years on that type of aircraft. He recounted when such action was to be performed: 'It was at about 2,000 feet above ground level on approaching the airport and was included in the preliminary landing check.'

The reason for this procedure was an unreliable automatic depressurisation system which was supposed to have been activated when the undercarriage oleo legs were compressed upon touchdown. As result of an unfortunate incident of a cabin crew member having been blown out of the aircraft while opening the door after the automatic system failed, Douglas recommended releasing residual cabin pressure before landing by opening the manual emergency relief valve. The handle to operate the valve was located on the right-hand side of the co-pilot's seat.

What circumstances could have caused the lead to the static system to be disconnected in flight, as well as at what stage of the flight this could have occurred with dangerous effects on altimeter readings, will be carefully analysed.

In order to understand the implication involved, a brief description of the static system in general and that of the DC6B as well as its various connections, is necessary.

The static system supplies the airspeed indicator, the altimeter and vertical speed indicator with an undisturbed source of outside air pressure. For that purpose five orifices are provided, two flush-mounted on each side of the aircraft's nose and one aft of the pressure bulkhead in the unpressurised tail cone of the fuselage.

The captain's and the co-pilot's instruments receive a separate static air supply from one port and one starboard orifice via distribution manifolds mounted on the back of each instrument

panel. The manifolds are connected to the respective instruments by flexible lines, allowing the panels to be swung downwards for easy access. Flexible lines are attached to the instruments by a 'quick disconnect' screw-on coupling with a rubber pressurisation seal inside it.

On the DC6B, the co-pilot's side, apart from its own instruments, also supplies static air to the navigator's airspeed indicator and altimeter, as well as to the cabin pressurisation controls and 'Altitude Hold' mode of the Flight Director.

Both the captain's and the co-pilot's side can be connected to an alternate system by a changeover switch. (See the diagram on page 125.) The switch is located within easy reach just to the left of the captain's control column and to the right of the co-pilot's column.

In view of the lack of first-hand evidence, such as the Cockpit Voice Recorder, certain presumptions regarding the crew's actions have been made in my analysis on the balance of probabilities and various clues fitting into the chain of events.

On the surface, it does not look physically possible for the flexible line coupling to become detached in flight. That is, unless the altimeter has been recently changed by an inexperienced instrument fitter and not by a qualified specialist. The presence of two spare altimeters in the cockpit of SE-BDY points to a possibility of a replacement having been carried out after the aircraft's arrival in the Congo, and the discarded instruments having been left in the cockpit for safe storage.

Re-connecting the hose fitting should not have presented much problem to an expert. But it could be tricky to someone who has not done this work before. This is because the thread on the altimeter connection was rather short (only one-quarter inch or 6.5 millimetres) and the rubber pressurisation seal had to be correctly compressed. Supply of static air would still be satisfactory as long as the seal remained compressed, even if the coupling was not securely screwed on.

In view of the safety aspects involved, the recommended procedure for changing an altimeter was for a qualified fitter to replace the unit and for an inspector to check if the connections were secure, and then affix a seal. In major airlines this was often complemented by accuracy tests with specialised equipment.

But the experts from Kollsman, the altimeter manufacturer, and from the CAB, made the following observations (Report of UN Commission, Annex IX):
'The captain's altimeter

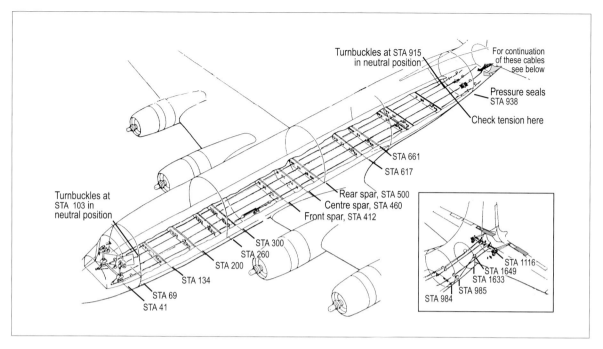

Diagram shows elevator control cables in the DC6B. (Douglas Maintenance Manual)

There was light impact damage to the case of this unit but no evidence of exposure to excessive heat. The hose fitting was still intact and the rubber pressurisation seal was still in place. The inspector's lead seal was not present.

The co-pilot's altimeter

The case of this instrument had a slight indentation near the center. The dial, pointers and setting markers were fire damaged. The glass cover and hose fitting were missing. The pressurisation seal was in position. There was no inspector's seal.'

But why a need for changing altimeters? The most likely answer lies in the age of SE-BDY. It was built in 1952, one of the earlier DC6Bs to be rolled out of the factory hangars. Altimeters fitted at the time had only a limited scale for setting barometric pressure, generally from 28.0 to 31.0 inches (respectively 1,000 feet down to 1,750 feet up). For the Congo operation, the range was inadequate to set QFE at the airports located on high elevated plains, such as Elisabethville (4,035 feet), Kamina (3,855 feet) or Kolwezi (4,733 feet).

After SE-BDY was brought from the United States to the Congo, the need for a wide-range type of altimeter must have become apparent and replacement instruments must have been sent from

Sweden, to be changed on the spot.

The circumstances that led to the flexible line having become detached in flight, were most likely created not only by faulty workmanship but also by the fact that the aircraft arrived overhead Ndola earlier than planned.

On the DC6B, descent from higher altitudes, particularly in the tropics, had to be carefully planned. For passenger comfort, cabin altitude had to be reduced at 300 ft/min or less, dictating a relatively slow descent. Moreover, some power on the engines had to retained in order to prevent overcooling and the engines being 'run' by the propellers, which could impose negative loads on the connecting rods. With a maximum airspeed limit of 245 knots, in practice the rate of descent was restricted for a long period to about 500 ft/min, with a maximum of 700 ft/min.

On the other hand, due to the difficulties of keeping the cabin cool during an approach in high temperatures, it was advisable to delay leaving cruising altitude as long as possible and to make a relatively quick descent.

Proceeding around the Katanga pedicle would have been 27 nm longer than that shown on the investigators' map (125 nm instead of 98 nm). If the usual figure of 220 knots ground speed during descent was used for computing the ETA for

Ndola this would have been 22.20 hrs, and it is what the pilots had originally advised the air traffic controller.

But Hallonquist had probably not realised that the TAS during descent from 16,000 to 6,000 feet would have been much higher than from 10,000 to 0 feet, a descent that was normally performed on flights in Europe. Moreover, after spotting the Ndola lights in the distance, he must have cut the corner, which would have accounted for the 317° (M) bearing and not 340° if he had kept altogether clear of the Katanga border.

As a result, Hallonquist found himself over the airport ten minutes earlier than he planned. This would have brought a problem with the cabin altitude, as the rate of decrease was based on a descent lasting twenty minutes. But the release of residual cabin pressure, in particular when the differential was a bit high, could not often be smoothly performed when the emergency relief valve was manually operated. Long, flexing cables from the cockpit to the tail, the pressure of the spring keeping the valve in position, possibly the valve sticking due to tar accumulation from cigarette smoke (a frequent occurrence on the DC6s), moreover, the short arm of the handle used for depressurisation which did not allow much feel, all these factors often led to a rapid 'popping out' of the valve. To old hands on the DC6s, it was not an uncommon experience, invariably resulting in 'blocked' ears.

A sudden drastic change of pressure in the cabin could have had a catastrophic effect on a flexible line if it was not properly attached or was, for some reason, weakened. The latter had been my experience during take-off on the DC8, which was also fitted with flexible lines to the instrument panel. The rush of pressurised air from the compressors' bleed when the throttles were opened for take-off ruptured a weakened flexible line between the ASI and the pitot tube. As a result, the instrument began to over-read and I was forced to hand over the controls to my co-pilot.

There is an evident indication that the 'Albertina' pilots were experiencing problems with the altimeters on approaching the airport as their message reveals:

'Your lights in sight, overhead Ndola, descending, confirm QNH.'

'Roger, QNH 1021 millibars, report reaching 6,000 feet.'

'Roger, 1021.'

The pilots' message did not sound like the

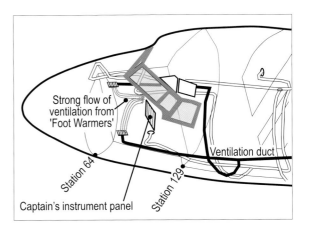

Strong flow of ventilation from 'Foot Warmers'

Ventilation duct

Station 64

Station 129

Captain's instrument panel

usual R/T patter. During descent it is customary to first specify the altitude followed by the word – 'descending'. Omitting the altitude could have only been the result of some confusion about its indications. Moreover, asking for QNH to be confirmed implies that the pilots were suspecting that there something not quite right with the altimeters. After flying in the Congo for two months, Hallonquist was bound to have known that ground pressure in the equatorial belt never changes more than two to three millibars. It is also significant that 1021 mb was acknowledged by the crew, as if they wanted to make sure that they had been given the right QNH.

Let us first look at the implication of a detached connection from the static system.

In comparison with the airspeed indicator or vertical speed indicator, the altimeter is an extremely sensitive instrument. This can be easily demonstrated by attaching a plastic tube to the static connection on the back of the instrument and giving it a slight suck. The indicator needle will immediately 'jump' as much as 1,000 feet up. At 5,000 feet only as little variation in pressure as 0.45 psi or 29.25 mm of a column of water is required to change the altitude by 1,000 feet.

On the other hand, an incorrect static pressure would have affected the airspeed indicator to a far lesser extent. At the usual DC6B approach speed of 130 to 140 knots, a pressure drop equivalent to 45.7 mm of a column of water between the pitot and the static source, would have caused only ten knots variation in the airspeed indication, while the same amount would have resulted in an altitude change of about 1,500 feet.

If the flexible line did become detached in flight through a sudden depressurisation, what would be the consequences?

It might appear at first sight that the altimeter should have read the cabin altitude, which would have been equalised with the outside conditions. However, with the emergency pressure relief valve fully open, the flow of air in the cabin would have been greatly increased because the compressors would be still operating. The ground blower, which on the DC6B (but not on the DC6) could be used in the air, was most likely switched on to help in ventilating the aircraft. Its effect would be quite significant.

The cockpit would also receive greatly augmented ventilation via the pilots' 'foot warmers', located under the rudder pedals. (The term used in the DC6 Flight Manual is not really appropriate, as foot warmers also served to cool the cockpit.) The stream of air would be then deflected by the curvature of the fuselage, creating an area of sub-pressure and, when passing behind the instrument panel, this could be increased by venturi effect. As little as a 0.7 psi drop in pressure would have made the altimeter over-read by 1,500 feet if the detached end of the flexible line was exposed to it. (See p. 128)

Contrary to the claim by the investigators that a fault in the static system would have been immediately evident to the pilots through considerable changes in the airspeed and the vertical speed indications, the loss of ten knots in the airspeed, corresponding to 1,500 feet in altitude variation, would be hardly noticeable and its effect on aircraft performance or handling characteristics minimal. Especially when the actual weight was 12,000 lb below maximum landing weight.

The vertical speed indicator would have most likely shown an unusual reading at first, but once the flow through the cockpit had stabilised, the VSI would have been working in a correct sense as long as the overall cabin pressure was 'catching up' with the outside air as it would have been expected to do.

The problem with the altitude indications must have started only when the aircraft was approaching the airport, otherwise the pilots would have asked earlier for the QNH to be confirmed. Judging by the fact that the DC6B struck the ground some 1,600 feet lower than the altitude it was supposed to have maintained, the captain's altimeter must have suddenly begun to indicate much higher than the co-pilot's instrument.

The crew's first reaction was probably to set the navigator's altimeter to QNH for a cross-check. This is indicated by the altimeter having been set to 30.17 inches (the nearest setting to 1021 mb). In normal circumstances, it was always left on 29.92 inches (or 1013 mb) to determine flight level during cruise. Being connected to the right-hand static source, it would then have shown the same altitude as the co-pilot's instrument. Nevertheless, this would have given no indication as to which altimeter was correct beyond the fact that there was something wrong with one of the static systems, but without any hint as to which side was at fault.

The next step would have been to select the alternate static source. The captain's instruments would not have registered any change, as the effect of sub-pressure would still govern the indication. If a detached flexible line had not been suspected, the same reading on the main and on the alternate static source could have convinced the pilots that the captain's altimeter was reliable and was showing correct altitude.

However, with the selector on the captain's side left in the 'Alternate' position (as it had been found in the wreckage), switching over the co-pilot's side would have resulted in interconnecting the right-hand static system with the venturi-affected source of air pressure. (See the diagram on page 125.) Now the captain's and co-pilot's altimeter would have indicated the same or near the same altitude, the exception being the navigator's instrument, which was in any case, outside the usual scanning range.

Although the alternate static system would be still supplied by air pressure from the tail cone, the small bore of the lines would have greatly restricted the flow and would have little effect on the overall indications, except perhaps for a very small discrepancy between the readings of the captain's and the co-pilot's altimeters.

The two altimeters showing the same or near the same altitude could have convinced the pilots that the problem had been solved and it was safe to proceed with the planned instrument approach procedure, which was stipulated by Transair regulations as compulsory for a night landing on an unfamiliar airport.

There are indications that Hallonquist tried to get some idea about his actual height above the airfield by visual means. Instead of aligning the aircraft for the instrument approach procedure by passing directly over the runway, which would have been a logical step under the circumstances, he proceeded slightly south, in my opinion in order to pass close to the 450-foot-high tower with a warning light on top. The tower is marked on the Jeppesen chart. Whether this could have given any indication, is difficult to assess.

In respect to the actual altitude that was probably maintained during the approach, the report of the Rhodesian Investigating Board stated as follows:

'An analysis of the results of these flights [test flights with the Transair DC6], together with discussion with the witnesses at the time, shows that the majority of witnesses were emphatic that the aircraft on test was never as low as SE-BDY on the night of the accident. As the lowest flight during these tests was 6,000 feet (1,840 feet above the ground) over the airport and 5,300 feet (934 feet above the treetops) over the crash site, it would seem to indicate that SE-BDY was low over the airport and very low during the turn to approach the airport. In fact, this points to SE-BDY being below 6,000 feet MER when overhead the airport and much lower than the obstacle clearance limit of 4,660 feet (500 feet above the airport) specified on the Ndola approach chart in the Jeppesen Route Manual, after passing over the airport and during the turn to approach.'

From the tests it looks as if, in the last two minutes before striking the trees, the altitude was about 1,600 feet too low. The position of the crash suggests that the pilots were following the prescribed instrument approach procedure. Although the point of impact differs by 0.8 nm from the horizontal path as drawn on the approach chart, the chart does not allow for the curvature of a 45° turn (from 280° to 325°) and the distances were computed using 150 knots TAS in still air conditions. The curvature together with the southeasterly wind component of seven knots (surface wind on the airport), would have accounted for the 0.8 nm discrepancy. (See the approach chart on page 111.)

It was known that the easiest way to spot the wreckage from the air was to follow the instrument approach procedure. It is interesting to note that the last heading of 120°, as indicated by the swath cut in the forest, would have taken the aircraft directly to Ndola beacon.

Surprisingly, the Rhodesian Commission (the judicial Court of Inquiry) believed that Hallonquist was making a visual approach. This was based on the arguments that the aircraft did not pass over the airport, flew over a house about a mile from the beacon and was heard heading to the north. The Commission, which did not have

any active pilots as advisers, appears to have drawn ill-considered conclusions.

The probable reason for flying south of the runway has already been explained. The position of the aircraft over a house at three-quarters of a mile from the beacon was judged by its occupant only by the amount of engine noise, not by a visual check of the overhead passage. At that point, Hallonquist could have applied power in order to maintain level flight and by virtue of making, at the same time, a 30° turn to the right to intercept the outbound leg from the beacon, the roar would have been directed towards the house located in a valley. This would tend to accentuate the noise level, making it sound as if the aircraft was passing overhead.

Regarding the claim of a woman witness, living on a farm seven miles to the north-west of the airport, it was again a case of having heard the aircraft rather than observed it, which could have left her with an impression that the DC6B was flying in her vicinity.

Vital information from the only surviving, but short-lived, witness, Sgt Julien, was looked upon as irrelevant. The opinion of the Investigating Board on his recollections was as follows:

'Medical evidence regarding this is that those statements made on the 18th September are unreliable because he was delirious at the time and that statement made during the last twenty-four hours of his life, with regard to sparks in the sky, may have also no significance as he was then uraemic and part of the picture of this disease is spots and flashes of light before the eyes.'

Nevertheless, the doctor claimed that, in spite of heavy sedation, Julien spoke coherently during his lucid moments and what he said appears to fit into the chain of events. The following conversation was recorded by Senior Inspector Allen of the Northern Rhodesia Police:

Allen: 'The last we heard from you, you were over Ndola runway. What happened?'
Julien: 'It blew up.'
Allen: 'Was it over the runway?'
Julien: 'Yes.'
Allen: 'What happened then?'
Julien: 'There was great speed. Great speed.'
Allen: 'What happened then?'
Julien: 'Then there was the crash.'
Allen: 'What happened then?'
Julien: 'There was a lot of little explosions all around.'

On the last evening, Sister McGrath heard Julien say: 'We were on the runway when Mr Hammarskjöld said, "Go back", then there was an explosion and I was the only one that got out ... all others were trapped.'

Sitting in the window seat behind the wing would have given Julien a chance of a good downward view, as is indicated by his several remarks about flying over the runway, something that must have got stuck in his mind. Helped by a slight shine of the setting moon, he was probably able to observe that the aircraft was skimming treetops and this could give him an impression of travelling fast. Little explosions after the crash were most likely the ammunition carried by two soldiers, which had been set off by the fire. Seeing sparks could be also accounted for. When passing very close to high trees, the propellers on the low-mounted inboard engines could have clipped the tops, sending a shower of leaves into hot exhaust gases, which were burnt in the process. From the cabin window, this could look like sparks.

Even Hammarskjöld's last words, 'Go back', just before the crash appear to make sense. The investigators claimed that it was meant to tell the pilots to return to the point of departure. But it is probable that when some people in the cabin noticed the aircraft flying dangerously low, they could have panicked and jumped out of their seats. The Secretary-General may have tried to stop them by shouting, 'Go back', meaning go back to their seats.

Although the investigators were of the opinion that, just prior to the crash, the aircraft was making a normal approach descent, the examination of the wreckage plan shows that between one of the earliest marks made by the propellers on the trees and the subsequent marks seventy metres further on, the loss of height was only four feet, representing a glide path angle of only 1°. This means that, for all practical purposes, the aircraft was flying level. Most probably the 'erroneous' altitude was maintained with the help of 'Altitude Hold' mode. The DC6B (but not the DC6) was equipped with a Flight Director, which greatly improved accuracy of instrument flying.

The fatal loss of height, probably just twenty to thirty feet in my opinion, was due to following the command of the FD pitch bar when the aircraft had 'ballooned' after flaps were extended to 30°, a known occurrence on the DC6s. With the bar centred in order to return to the pre-selected altitude, a very shallow descent would have been initiated, which would have resulted in momentarily overshooting the original altitude. This could have been enough to strike the treetops.

PART VIII
THE AFTERMATH

Although from a number of clues it looks very probable that the prime reason for the Ndola disaster was a disconnected static line to the altimeter, there may have been other, but perhaps less vital, contributory factors.

If the pilots were experiencing problems with the altimeters, a rush decision to proceed with an instrument approach over an area totally devoid of visual references would not have been a prudent move. Instead of taking time to cross-check altitude indications by all possible means, the pilots tried to land as soon as possible. The perspective of the approach lights from the cockpit when making a visual pass overhead would have made it immediately apparent that the aircraft was far below normal height.

Above all, an electronic aid, which could have been used to check true altitude, must have been disregarded by the crew. SE-BDY was equipped with radio altimeter Model AVQ9. This type was basically used for pressure pattern navigation on oceanic crossings. The indicator was mounted at the navigation station behind the captain's seat. It could be set to two positions – 0 to 800 feet, or 'Times Ten' 0 to 8,000 feet. During examination of the wreckage, the switch of the radio altimeter had been found in the 'off' position.

The UN Investigating Commission, in which Sweden was strongly represented, claimed that 'the crew was highly competent and experienced and Captain Hallonquist was considered to be a reliable and cautious pilot by all who testified'.

But this was not the opinion held by some Swedish pilots. In 1966 a book was written about the Ndola crash by B.A. Bengs, a SAS DC6 captain. He was not only critical of the way Transair had been operating in the Congo, but also of Hallonquist's execution of the letdown to Ndola. Bengs claimed that, by leaving his cruising altitude late, Hallonquist found himself under pressure to reduce speed and altitude for the approach. This affected his concentration and when he came out of the turn on base leg he failed to spot the approach lights in time, which resulted in a fatal loss of height.

The UN representatives from ICAO for the

Ndola investigation, expressed great concern that the flight had not been conducted according to accepted ICAO Air Navigation procedures. A particular criticism came from Bob Nelson, who believed that, by not advising the air traffic controller about an intended instrument approach procedure, the pilots committed a grave error of judgement. It could have given the controller an impression that they were not going to land immediately and consequently rescue action was delayed. Moreover, the pilots commenced the approach without a clearance from the Tower.

Having failed to file a flight plan for the entire route, it would have been extremely difficult to conduct a search had the aircraft happened to crash *en route*. Moreover, proceeding on an established advisory route without prior notification and giving no position reports to Nairobi Flight Information Region was exposing the aircraft to the possibility of a mid-air collision.

A further adverse opinion about the two Transair captains came from Captain Arne Leibing, the company's former Chief Pilot. Leibing, who during his aviation career also flew for Swissair and Finatlantic, was appointed as the Chief Flight Inspector and Pilot Examiner with the Swedish CAA upon giving up active flying in 1969. He is the author of several books on safety. In a letter dated 2 September 1997, he writes as follows:

'I was having my breakfast listening to the morning news when it was announced that Hammarskjöld had been killed during the approach to Ndola. My wife nearly got choked when I spontaneously said that either of those two captains must have been at controls.

The reason for my reaction was that, from the day they were hired, I didn't feel they were captain material. When I was in Swissair, I met them several times after they had crossed the Alps at 14,000 feet in their unpressurised C-46s, carrying seventy-five passengers on board. Talking to them, they just laughed it off.'

Another controversial point was that fatigue was not regarded by the UN Commission as a probable contributory factor to the accident. The report stated:

'It is noted that there was sleeping accommodation for the crew on the aircraft and that apparently Captain Aarheus and First Officer Litton alternated as co-pilot. First Officer Litton, according to the testimony of Major Lyungkvist, had announced his intentions of sleeping during the first part of the flight. In view of these facts, it is believed that there was no violation of international standards and recommended practices, nor of special regulations applicable in this respect.'

The UN report was not correct. At that time there were no international (ICAO) standards and recommended practices in force for flight time limitations. Each State had its own rules. Whether these rules were violated by Captain Aarheus, F/O Litton and F/E Wilhelmsson, it is not possible to tell. No details of the Swedish regulations were included in the report.

Nevertheless, from starting the flight to Elisabethville in the evening of the night before the accident, until when the crash occurred, out of twenty-nine intervening hours these three airmen would have been on duty twenty-one hours with seventeen hours in the air. Considering that night flying is very fatiguing and daytime sleep does not help a pilot to easily recuperate, on approaching Ndola most of the crew must have been at the end of their tether. Although Captain Hallonquist had had an adequate rest he was the only one, and an aircraft the size of a DC6 cannot be operated single-handed. In particular, the flight engineer could have been very tired as there was no one on board to relieve him.

Despite the claim by the UN Commission that there was no breach of national flight time regulations, the Swedish Airline Pilots' Association had brought to light a fact that during twenty days before the accident, F/O Litton had flown 158 hours, when the legal limit was 125 hours in thirty days.

The investigation of the Ndola disaster had put not only Transair but also the whole UN air operations in the Congo under scrutiny. Fournier and Nelson sent reports to the UN headquarters in New York about shortcomings in the maintenance of the UN fleet and frequent violations of air rules by the UN pilots. The flight with Hammarskjöld on board without ATC clearance and regular position reporting was only one example of numerous similar cases. In spite of ICAO being the specialised aviation agency of the UN, the large fleet of UN aircraft in the Congo often did not comply with the ICAO standards and recommended practices. UN pilots frequently crossed neighbouring countries without previous notice, presenting a hazard to international traffic.

IFALPA became very concerned about the potentially dangerous situation and the subject was discussed at the Stockholm Conference in 1962. As result, it was decided to bring the following recommendation to the attention of the UN Secretary-General for appropriate action:

'IFALPA strongly urges the United Nations, when operating their own means of air transportation in areas served by scheduled airline operators, to operate in accordance with ICAO rules, and/or the rules of the State overflown, which rules require specific and established operating procedures, separation criteria and discipline.'

PART IX
POLITICS BEHIND THE SCENES

An important question must be raised as to why so much emphasis was placed during the investigation on the possibility of foul play, even when it was evident from the early stages that not a shred of supporting evidence had been found. Unfortunately, this was done at the expense of insufficient attention being paid to the operational aspects of the crash such as the problem with the altimeters; especially in view of overwhelming evidence from the witnesses that in the last part of the approach the DC6B was flying dangerously low.

Transair, as the only party in the investigating team intimately familiar with the DC6B operating procedures and aircraft systems, was expected to provide expert advice. But as it can be seen from the data on the DC6B cruise systems, which were used to determine the probable route, their information was inexact and this had resulted in computing an unrealistic air distance for the flight.

During the examination of the wreckage, cooperation between the Swedish delegation and the rest of the team was at first satisfactory. Nevertheless, right from the start the Swedes were of the opinion that the most likely cause of the accident was an air or ground attack and concentrated on searching for supporting evidence. It was known that Transair Chief Engineer Bo Virving spent most of his time looking for marks that could have been made by a rocket or machine-gun bullets.

Certain aspects of the Ndola tragedy soon began to cloud relations. In spite of the Rhodesian authorities claiming extenuating circumstances for taking fifteen hours to find the wreckage, the Swedish delegation suspected that the delay was intentional. This was in order to give the Rhodesian Secret Service a chance to dispose of evidence that could point to the Rhodesian authorities having been in collusion with the Katangan rebels to down the aircraft.

As the investigation progressed, relations started to deteriorate. Although on the surface, it looked as if there was no rift, halfway through the proceedings, a 'silent' political battle broke out. According to recent information received from Bob Nelson, this coincided with the arrival of Dr H. Bratt, the Minister for Sweden to the Republic of South Africa (the equivalent of an ambassador), as an adviser to the Swedish accredited representative.

Bratt appeared on the scene when a difference of opinion arose as to the value of testimonies provided by the local African witnesses. This evidence had been brought to the attention of the Investigating Board by Sven Mattsson from the International Federation of Free Trade Unions. He was sent to Rhodesia in order to help with organising African trade unions in the Copper Belt. Through his connections, Mattsson produced several witnesses from local charcoal burners working for the Forestry Commission. According to one Swedish source he found his witnesses in the local beer halls. Some Africans testified that they had actually seen the DC6B crashing and some that they had only heard an explosion.

At first, three charcoal burners told the investigators that they were awakened during the night by loud bangs and saw a fire in the distance. But the police subsequently established that the charcoal burners visited the crash site at dawn but had never reported it to the authorities. They took away a UN code machine from the wreckage, believing it to be a typewriter. One of the charcoal burners tried to sell it on the local market. Later, all three were charged with theft and sentenced to two years of hard labour.

Further testimonies came from five more charcoal burners. One was Farie Mazibisa, President of the United African Charcoal Burners' Association. They all claimed they saw two aircraft flying close together before the crash, one of which was smaller than the other.

However, even the UN Commission, which would have been expected to be appreciative of the efforts from the local African population to produce evidence, expressed concern about the reason for Mazibisa's providing the testimony, as their report stated:

'Mr Mazibisa in his first statement to the Rhodesian Board of Investigation told only about discovering the wreckage and said nothing concerning the night of 17 September. It was only a week later, after he had talked to Mr Mattsson, a trade union organiser, who had urged him to tell everything he knew, that he made a second statement to the Board concerning events during the night [about observing two aircraft flying together].

Mr Mazibisa said he had not told what he saw to the authorities at first because he had been afraid and some people had said he might be accused of having caused the crash.'

To the Rhodesians, introducing evidence through Mattsson on the presence of another aircraft flying close to DC6B, could have appeared as politically motivated. Judging by the political climate in Sweden at the time, Mattsson was probably left-leaning. Facing a growing nationalism of their African population, the Rhodesians must have regarded him as a troublesome agitator, not only stirring unrest among local workers but also interfering with the crash inquiry. The Investigating Board had already interviewed fourteen other witnesses and none had observed a second aircraft at the time of the DC6B arrival at Ndola.

As a result of Mattsson's continuing to produce witnesses with further incredible stories, tension had developed between the Swedish delegation and the rest of the investigators. Mattsson's activities were questioned, as he was not a member of the investigating team. It is on record that the representative of ICAO, J.P. Fournier, asked Mattsson why he was so concerned with this matter and if he had any Communist sympathies.

Surprisingly it was the UN Commission that expressed doubts about the credibility of the testimonies from the charcoal burners:

'With respect to witnesses who displayed strong anti-federal feelings, it was suggested that they might have testified deliberately intending to embarrass the Rhodesian Government. It was also pointed out that some witnesses, particularly under cross-examination, claimed to distinguish details such as the wings, engines and retracted landing gear of the aircraft, which it was believed would be impossible to see at night.'

In the delicate balance of vested interests

The memorial to Secretary-General Dag Hammarskjöld erected at the crash site.

between the two States involved, Sweden and Rhodesia, it was only natural that the Swedish side tried to protect Transair. The company stood to lose its reputation by having been the incompetent operator of 'UN One' if it was established that the Ndola accident was due to a fault on Transair's part. Consequently, many factors, which right from the start appeared to have been too ridiculous to precipitate the crash, were given unprecedented attention.

On the other hand, as a result of inadequate operational input from Transair, the possibility of a disconnected altimeter causing the accident had been disregarded. It is incredible that none of the four inquiries into the Ndola disaster ever questioned what two spare altimeters were doing on board SE-BDY, or if the reason could have been that they were recently replaced. Moreover, if that were the case, had the change been carried out by a qualified engineer?

The endless allegations about foul play having been the cause of the disaster led the world to believe that Hammarskjöld was probably killed through some conspiracy of Western industrial interests. Political expediency and not the truth had won the battle of wits.

6

TAKE ME TO HAVANA

'The problems of the world would not be solved by diplomats or statesmen, they would instead be solved by aviators for aviators recognise no boundaries, artificial or natural, for they cross them all with equal ease; and they speak the same language.'

H.G. Wells, 1936

PART I

Although this book deals with air disasters, to many pilots the biggest disaster that has ever struck civil aviation since its inception, has been hijacking. Only the shocking figures that reflect the number of passengers, crews and even ground personnel involved in the offences committed on board an aircraft can underline the magnitude of this cancerous malady. Over the years, 15,000 innocent travellers, 1,500 pilots and cabin staff were bullied and terrorised into submission by ruthless thugs. Some passengers and crew members have paid with their lives. In comparison, only a few fatalities occurred amongst hijackers and a great proportion managed to get away without any punishment.

Should we not ask ourselves some pointed questions? How was it possible for civil air transportation, the world's most technologically advanced industry, to become a sitting duck for all sorts of terrorist activities? How did we arrive at such a despicable situation? How much was it connected with governments condoning air piracy to suit their own political ends? Why were international conventions to prevent crimes aloft and agreed upon by all states sidestepped by some states? Has any aviation organisation taken steps to stop the escalation of air piracy?

By now it is scarcely remembered that, true to

H.G. Wells's predictions, the international pilots' fraternity launched several actions with the gloves off, to force the authorities into recognising 'unlawful seizures of aircraft' as a hazard to air navigation and making it a punishable offence. But when some newly-emerged governments tried to exploit hijacking for political gains and turned a deaf ear to pilots' protests – a result of the pilots' patience having worn thin – the drastic countermeasures were regarded as infringement on a country's sovereignty. Even the travelling public, in whose interest the campaign was waged, were hardly appreciative or even conscious of the pilots' endeavours.

The rapid post-war expansion of air services undoubtedly opened a flood of possibilities to commandeer a plane, and all early cases bore a strictly political character. In fact, during the tensest years of the Cold War from 1947 to 1953, twenty-seven cases were noted of which only twelve did not succeed. Fugitives from behind the Iron Curtain enacted most of the effective attempts. The first post-war hijacking took place in July 1947 from Romania to Turkey. Unfortunately all the so-called 'bids for freedom' were, in the eyes of some misguided politicians, the only means of breaking out of tyranny. As a result, these were not regarded in the Western world as plain crimes and were often condoned for political reasons. In many instances, those who took over an aircraft by force were given asylum and were looked upon as heroes.

But air piracy was not a post-war syndrome. The first ever recorded case dates as far back as 1930. In that fateful year for civil aviation, Peruvian revolutionaries, desperate to flee the country after their coup had failed, hijacked a three-engine Ford 7-AT that was operating on a government mission. But what they did not reckon with was that the captain, Byron Richards, came from a macho breed of pilots, toughened by dicing with dangers in his barnstorming days. In spite of having a gun pressed against his back, Richards landed the aircraft at the nearest airfield and over-powered the armed hijacker. His bravado must have sprung from a premonition that many governments would in future turn a blind eye to the crime on board, and the only way to deal with terrorists was to take the law into one's own hands and teach them a lesson. The years to come have proved him right.

Would Captain Richards have ever dreamt that he could face another similar ordeal in his lifetime? It seemed more than a million-to-one probability. Yet thirty-one years later, when Richards was flying from Los Angeles to Houston in the most modern jet at the time, the Boeing 707, two gunmen, an ex-convict father and his adolescent son forced their way into the cockpit and demanded to be flown to Cuba. Richards calmly refused, claiming that he did not have enough fuel and would have to land at El Paso, his scheduled intermediate stop. But it was only to play for time. On the ground, Richards persuaded the hijackers to release all passengers but for four men who had to remain on board as hostages. In the end, the hijacking attempt was foiled when FBI marksmen shot at the plane's tyres during take-off and the B707 came to a grinding halt. The two culprits were disarmed and taken into custody. At the trial, the hijacker was given the harshest possible sentence of twenty years in prison and his son was committed to a reform school.

The taking over of a Peruvian plane in 1930 looked like a one-off case and the world did not seem to worry about the future consequences. But there was to be a rude awakening just one year later with the first ever recorded criminal sabotage to an airliner. For the first time since the birth of commercial aviation in 1919, infringements against the heavier-than-air machines began to rear their ugly head.

Fortunately, for the next sixteen years nothing noteworthy occurred. But the idea of comman-deering an aircraft was given prominence in the famous novel *Lost Horizon* by James Hilton, published in 1933. In the days when the aeroplane was still a daring mode of travel, the story in which the hero Hugh Conway was hijacked to an imaginary valley in the Himalayas seemed an extraordinary, yet on the other hand, visionary feat. But in one respect Hilton was out of tune with future events. In the book, a shady American character, Barnard, while being spirited away to Shangri-La

with Conway and his companions, remarks sarcastically, 'You Britishers make jokes about the hold-ups in Chicago and all that but I don't recollect any instance of a gunman running off with one of Uncle Sam's aeroplanes.' It took thirty years before Hilton would have to eat his words after 'take me to Havana' became a household slogan in America.

The period 1953 to 1958 was relatively quiet with only three recorded cases. It looked as if the menacing of civil air transport was slowly dying down. Unfortunately a blatant act of aggression against the freedom of navigation did remind the prospective terrorists how easy it was to hold an airliner to ransom. The story sounds like a thriller, but it actually took place in real life. On 22 October 1956, five leaders of the Algerian National Liberation Front, FNL, including Mohammed Ben Bela the commander of the Algerian Liberation Army, and Mohammed Khider the head of the political committee, were flying from Morocco to Tunis for talks with the Tunisian Prime Minister and the Sultan of Morocco on the progress of their fight for independence. At Rabat Airport the FNL leaders were first directed to the wrong aircraft. It was a French DC3 and it was later construed by reporters as a kidnapping attempt by the French secret service. Eventually the FNL leaders boarded the right aircraft, a DC3 lent by the Sultan of Morocco, flown by a French pilot. To avoid Algerian territory, at the time under French rule, the aircraft took a detour to the north over the Mediterranean and as a result a stop at Palma de Majorca for refuelling was necessary. After the DC3 left Palma, the French Air Force were watching it on radar and gave the pilot instruction on the radio to change course for Algiers. To alleviate the FNL leaders' suspicions that the aircraft was not proceeding to Tunis, the pilot was told to remain over the sea until the time of arrival at the intended destination. After landing at Algiers, the FNL leaders were overwhelmed and although they carried guns and travelled on false passports they offered no resistance. They were immediately handcuffed by the French police waiting on the airport and later transferred to France, to be charged before a military tribunal with inciting riots in Algeria.

The Tunisian authorities sent a vigorous protest to the French President. The outraged Sultan of Morocco broke off diplomatic relations. The rest of the Arab world was equally appalled. In the riots which broke out on the North African coast over thirty Europeans were killed. But a large section of the French population acclaimed an act which had made a mockery of freedom of navigation and, in practical terms, amounted to a legalised piracy. Capturing the ellusive FNL leaders meant a setback for the Algerian rebellion and deferring self-rule.

How could one of the world's leading governments justify snatching an unarmed airliner over the high seas? Using an aircraft as a pawn in a political game could have given France an initial success, but in the long run it certainly generated food for thought in the minds of many revenge-seeking Arab factions.

The early sixties were another relatively peaceful period with the exception of 1961 when four hijackings were recorded, one of which was the case of the unlucky Captain Richards. Unfortunately, dark clouds slowly began to appear on the American horizon, foreshadowing a fresh outbreak of the air-piracy plague. Although at first sporadic incidents occurred mainly from Cuba to the States, eventually the trend was reversed and with every month it grew alarmingly in numbers. Soon 'take me to Havana' began to look like an epidemic. In the hijacking game the Cuban authorities played their cards with great finesse. On the one hand they enjoyed twisting the tail of their powerful neighbour, but on the other they made sure of not provoking America into military intervention. Officially all hijackers were arrested, but were often quickly set free on arbitrary pretexts. The Cubans did not intend to discourage further attempts. All on board were treated with utmost consideration. Passengers were usually taken for a tour of Havana and its showpiece surroundings acclaimed to be the triumph of the Cuban Communist system. The commandeered planes could leave as soon as they were refuelled, but the passengers had to travel back on the Cuban airline. The authorities were not doing it out of the goodness of their hearts. For handling the hijacked aircraft, very high landing fees were imposed. Just the same, the US airlines did not quibble about paying the extraordinary charges, being glad to have their valuable planes back quickly. For the Castro regime, it was a source of badly needed dollars. Some aviation pundits claimed that this never-ending income was supposed to have helped in expanding Havana Airport.

American pilots regarded every act of piracy as a potential threat to safety. For years, the US Air Line Pilots' Association tried to bring to the attention of their government that unpunished cases abetted the escalation of hijacking and one day a relatively minor incident could end up in a tragic disaster. But with relations at daggers drawn between the United States and Cuba, neither side was willing to enter into an agreement to curtail the harassment of the airliners. Politics played the prime role in this aviation Cold War.

Whilst in the early sixties America suffered from a bad bout of 'unlawful seizures of aircraft', the situation on the other side of the Atlantic was relatively static. An exception was a KLM DC9 commandeered in 1962 by a mentally deranged individual. As the incident ended up without any serious consequences, it was quickly forgotten.

However, the year 1967 changed it all when a brazen act of apprehending a small jet woke Europe up to the fact that it was no longer immune to the spreading malady. At first, the incident appeared to be of no particular consequence to pilots-at-large but, as subsequently the hijacked crew were denied human rights, a storm of protests broke out.

On 30 June, a few hours after dictating a draft of a call-to-arms for the Congolese people, the ex-President Moise Tshombe was taken to Algiers by force while enjoying an aerial sightseeing tour of the Balearics. He was one of several guests on board a Hawker Siddeley 125 executive jet flown by two English pilots, David Taylor and Trevor Copleston. The aircraft belonged to a charter company, Gregory Air Services from Denham Airfield, which was run by Ken Gregory, a former manager of Grand Prix racing drivers Stirling Moss and Mike Hawthorn. Already established for five years, the company was also engaged in various other activities such as a flying school and sales, as well as management and maintenance of executive planes.

As it subsequently came to light, the hijacking was the upshot of an elaborate plot that took over a year to implement. Its web involved fake companies, misleading trails and invented identities. Surprisingly, it also involved, although not in a direct way, a top executive from one of France's respected finance houses. The main figure in the intrigue was a Frenchman, Francis Joseph Bodenan, a shadowy character with a criminal record. Nevertheless, Bodenan enjoyed mystifying links with the financier who happened to have known him since his childhood. The financier often helped Bodenan when the drifter was in trouble with the law. The last brush came in 1954 when, after a violent quarrel, Bodenan gunned down two of his business associates, allegedly intelligence service agents from the French Resistance during the war. Together they ran a scrap metal business and it appeared that the feud was over Bodenan misusing the firm's funds.

After giving himself up to the police, he denied any involvement in the shooting and claimed that the two men were liquidated for spying. But in 1956 Bodenan was convicted for murder and sentenced to twelve years hard labour. Although it came out during the trial that he had not committed the crime alone, he refused to name his accomplices. On the other hand, he remarked to the judge that he could make sensational disclosures but preferred to remain silent. Consequently, the real grounds for gunning down the two men were never established.

To anyone seeking a 'Jackal', Bodenan offered ideal qualifications. He was unscrupulous, ruthless with the gun and, above all, endowed with tight lips. His trial had likely attracted the attention of the *Service Documentation et Contre Espionage* (SDECE), the French 'dirty tricks' department, known for its brutal methods during the fight with the Algerian insurgents over independence. Later the SDECE had shown its muscle by two spectacular kidnappings, that of Algerian leader Ben Barka and a despised political opponent who had fled for safety to Germany.

Upon his release from prison, Bodenan headed for Belgium posing as a highly-polished businessman. He appeared to have been coached for his new role whilst still behind bars. In Brussels he made it widely known that he was a consultant, based in Geneva, for a very reputable French development concern called SEDEFI, in which his 'protector' was an important figure. To create a proper businessman's image, Bodenan set up a company on paper which was known as *Groupement International pour le Developpement Economique et Technique* (GIDET). Its scope was never clearly defined, but through a newspaper advertisement he managed to interest a Belgian in investing in this new venture. To convince the Belgian of his credibility, Bodenan had gone into an elaborate charade of staying in high-class hotels, being chauffeured around in expensive cars and claiming important finance connections in France. But a few days after he was handed a cheque for £15,000 as a share in the GIDET, then many times more than today's value, he claimed that he was robbed of the money by two gunmen when he was leaving the bank after he had cashed the cheque. But as he promised to refund the money, the case was never reported to the police.

This was no doubt a subterfuge to create a fund for starting his undercover activities without any inkling of the financial support coming from France.

The selection of Brussels as Bodenan's business site was made with an ulterior motive in mind. Here the former strong man of Katanga, Moise Tshombe, still had many friends and associates from the Belgian copper mining concern in the Congo Union Miniére du Haut Katanga (UMHK) (see chapter 5).

But Tshombe's enemies, particularly from the left-wing camp, greatly outnumbered his friends. He was never forgiven for sanctioning the execution of his political arch-rival Patrice Lumumba and for strong pro-western activities during his rule of Katanga. After he was ousted as Prime Minister of the Congo by President Kasavubu in 1965, Tshombe went to live in exile in Spain. His successor General Mobutu feared Tshombe's comeback with the support of mercenaries who remained very loyal to their former chief. Mobutu ordered Tshombe's trial *in absentia* and as a result, the past ruler of Katanga was sentenced to death. But so far, he had managed to stay out of reach of his adversary.

With a price on his head, Tshome was extremely careful whom he mixed or dealt with on business. Just the same, helped by the new image of a respectable businessman, Bodenan managed to worm his way into Tshombe's circles. At first he befriended a Brussels lawyer named Sigal and through him, he met Marcel Hamboursin, a former paratrooper with the British forces during World War II and Tshombe's close friend from the days at the Union Miniére. Bodenan began to peddle a grandiose but fake scheme for hotel and tourist development in Majorca where Tshombe spent most of his time. Being at that stage of his political and business career at a loose end, Tshombe had eventually taken the bait and the die was cast for his kidnapping.

Before the hijacking, Bodenan, using SEDEFI as a cover, had already chartered a HS125 executive jet from Gregory Air Services to tour Europe for six days. On that occasion the aircraft was flown by Captain Burns and Captain Ward. During those six days nothing particular occurred that could have aroused suspicions about any underhanded intentions. Now it is evident that the charter served a dual purpose. One was to create an impression that an executive jet was Bodenan's usual mode of getting about, and another was to check on the HS125 maximum range without making direct inquiries. It seemed an expensive way to do this but money appeared to have been no object. The extravagant plot to kidnap Tshombe was estimated to have cost around fifty thousand pounds, which at today's rate would be more like half a million pounds.

When the HS125 was chartered by Bodenan for the second time, the itinerary was going to include Geneva, Rome and Spain. Burns and Ward were requested to pilot the aircraft. But as they were not back from a flight, they were substituted at the last minute by Captain David Taylor and co-pilot Trevor Copleston. This later resulted in surprising repercussions.

Bodenan boarded the jet at Geneva and asked to be taken to Rome. He explained that he had to

Captain David Taylor, pilot of the plane in which Moise Tshombe was abducted, who was forced to land at Algiers on a flight over the Mediterranean island of Ibiza. (Associated Press, London)

attend to business in the centre of the city. Taylor found it surprising that the Frenchman was back at the airport in less than two hours. The journey to and from the city would have taken much longer. The reason for a call at Rome can only be speculated upon. It was probably the easiest place to pick up a gun without attracting police attention.

The next destination was Palma de Majorca where a nightstop was planned. Upon arrival, Bodenan announced that he would not need the aircraft the next day but he wanted it to be ready for another flight to Rome. He went straight to the Hotel del Mar, the most expensive hotel in town, where he and the crew were booked. Surprisingly, he left his suitcase behind on the plane. Taylor had the HS125 refuelled according to the Frenchman's instruction, and the two pilots followed. When they arrived in the hotel, Bodenan was in the foyer and he insisted on paying their taxi after he noticed that Taylor had to change English pounds. He invited the pilots for a drink and during conversation made it clear that all their nightstop expenses were taken care of. Taylor, who spoke passable French, tried to argue that it was their company's responsibility but Bodenan laughed it off, saying that he had arranged with the reception not to accept any money from his crew. So far he appeared to be very amiable and generous. He soon excused himself and joined another party. The pilots subsequently learnt that it was the Belgian lawyer Sigal, his wife and Hamboursin. Later that evening Bodenan called Taylor and told him that he had changed his mind and that the next day he wanted to be flown to Ibiza for lunch.

When the following day, a party of seven appeared on the airport, which included Sigal, his wife and Hamboursin, the pilots instantly recognised Moise Tshombe among the group of passengers. Bodenan asked Taylor if it was possible to make a sightseeing tour of Majorca before landing at Ibiza. To Taylor it was a godsend solution to the problem of the limit to the maximum landing weight as a result of refuelling for Rome, and he arranged clearance with air traffic control for a low-level flight over the island.

After lunching at Ibiza, the party returned to the airport at six in the evening. Again Bodenan asked Taylor to show the passengers the beauty of the Balearics and he specifically asked to take them over the southern tip of Formentera, the closest point on the island to the North African coast.

What should have been a joyride with an abundance of champagne, turned into a horrify-ing ordeal. All of a sudden, the usually amiable Bodenan pulled a gun and terrorised his guests into submission by firing two shots into the aircraft's floor. Then he focused his attention on the pilots and ordered Taylor to fly to Algiers.

On the surface, the reason for spiriting Tshombe away to this deeply socialist Arab republic looked obscure. Nothing politically significant appeared to have been gained and it was doubtful that the Algerian authorities were in collusion with Bodenan or even knew of the hijacking in advance. Insiders claimed that the kidnapping was connected with France's ambitions in Central Africa, in particular in the Congo, and with certain French intelligence agencies trying to prove their worth. Mobutu was well aware that, until Tshombe was 'neutralised', his rule was at stake. Playing into Mobutu's hands by delivering Tshombe to Kinshasa for imprisonment or even for an execution, France would likely have been rewarded by political and economic favours.

The reaction of the Algerian authorities to the hijacking was not only to lock up Tshombe but also the crew and the remaining passengers. Why the English pilots were not speedily released like Tshombe's bodyguards – two Spanish policemen – was never clearly explained. Instead, a string of accusations was hurled against Taylor and Copleston. At one point, the authorities announced that they would be charged with 'war crimes' for their service in the RAF. No doubt this was the result of the Arab world still smarting over the Suez Canal war. Some Arab states had still refused to establish full diplomatic relations with Great Britain.

But the service record of the two pilots was far from detrimental. Taylor was an ex-Cranwell cadet and towards the end of his RAF career flew with the 'V'-bomber force. Copleston had twenty years of service behind him and upon relinquishing his Commission, joined Ken Gregory's charter company. Neither of the pilots was engaged in any mercenary activities such as flights for Katanga rebels, nor did they take part in the Suez Canal war. They were both highly dedicated to flying and were known for impeccable integrity.

Soon the Algerian authorities came up with other unconvincing grounds for their incarceration. They insisted that, as Taylor and Copleston were substituted for another crew at the last minute, it looked suspicious and the reason had to be investigated before they would be set free. Later, the authorities accused the two pilots of putting up no resistance to the hijacker which could mean that they were his accomplices. Finally the fact that SEDEFI, the company Bodenan was using to charter the executive jet, was registered in Liechtenstein but conducted no business there, called for an inquiry into its background.

As England had no diplomatic relations with the Democratic and Popular Republic of Algeria, the Foreign Office was powerless to press directly for the release of the two pilots and had to rely on the Swiss Ambassador to Algeria for help. On the other hand, although the hijacking was committed on board a British-registered aircraft and the crew were British, the case ought to have been of considerable concern to the British Government. But no steps were undertaken to use any influence either with the French whose national was involved in an unlawful seizure of a British plane, or with the Spanish from whose territory the air piracy was perpetrated.

The chances of the two pilots being set free were further jeopardised by a vitriolic campaign waged by the English Press. The Algerian regime was compared to the lawless and brutal rulers on the Barbary Coast two hundred years ago. In an editorial, a leading London newspaper called for all Algerian nationals to be banned from entering England.

Although the incarceration without any specific charges was a gross violation of human rights as recognised by the Chicago Convention, surprisingly no loud voice of protest was heard from any organisation claiming to be the champions of such causes, such as Amnesty International.

But to the Principal Officers of the International Federation of Air Line Pilots' Associations (IFALPA), it was one more case of great concern in the recent spate of problems with African governments over ill-treatment of aircrews in transit (see chapter 7 – the note about brutal imprisonment of pilots in Liberia). Also Belgian crews in the Congo were forced to operate under constant interference from the trigger-happy military.

One of the fundamental principles of IFALPA was freedom of transit and the Federation were ready to take a strong stand. Pilots believed that, as the servants of the travelling public, they must not be impeded in the course of their duties, in particular when on a flight away from their own country.

The Federation was started in 1948 by thirteen founder associations. Its aim was to represent the airline pilots' views on safety at international forums, in particular at the International Civil Aviation Organisation, where safety standards are agreed upon. In time, the Federation's activities were expanded to include surveying deficiencies in navigational and landing aids and to pressing civil aviation authorities for speedy remedies (see chapter 4). Recently, another sphere that had begun to absorb IFALPA's attention was the abuse or ill treatment of aircrews.

When it became apparent that Taylor and Copleston were an innocent party to the hijacking in spite of the Algerians' allegations to the contrary, and that they were detained as hostages purely for political reasons, IFALPA took an interest in their plight. To the Federation this was paradoxical conduct by a government which was committed through its United Nations' membership to observe international conventions. As far back as 1963 an agreement had been reached, under the auspices of ICAO known as the Tokyo Convention, to deal with crimes on board an aircraft. Although the Republic of Algeria had not yet ratified the Convention, the authorities were expected to follow it in spirit. One of the provisions clearly stipulated a speedy release of the hijacked passengers, crew and plane.

With deadlock in the political relations between Algeria and England, the fate of Taylor and Copleston appeared to have been laid aside with no release in sight. Although the two pilots were not affiliated to IFALPA, in the eyes of the Federation they were flying colleagues who, through no fault of their own, were denied basic human rights. For this reason IFALPA felt that an action in their defence was necessary. Moreover, they were not the only pilots suffering from the Algerian authorities' eagerness to put airmen behind bars at the slightest pretext.

Two weeks after the Tshombe hijacking, a Swiss pilot, Marcel Juillard, was imprisoned in Algiers for no apparent reason. Juillard was chartered to fly two Swiss arms dealers to Biafra. He operated a one-man aviation company at Geneva Airport with a turbine-converted DH Dove – Riley 400. On the way back, while they stopped at Tamanrasset in Southern Algeria for refuelling Juillard was asked by the local chief of the police to drop off two young policemen at Hassi Messaoud. As the oilfield lay on their route and there was no other means of transport across the Sahara, Juillard agreed. But he was shabbily repaid for his gesture of goodwill. In flight, one of the Swiss arms dealers took a short 8 mm movie film of the desert scenery and after landing at

Hassi Messaoud, the policemen reported it to the authorities. The two passengers as well as Juillard were arrested, taken to the notorious El Harrach prison outside Algiers Airport and charged with spying. Later they were also accused of dealing in war weapons with Biafra and of illegal possession of firearms, after documents on the transactions and a gun were found in the luggage of one of the passengers. Unfortunately the documents revealed that their intermediary was a major in the Israeli Army stationed in West Africa, possibly a Mossad agent, and this probably accounted for the Draconian charges. Although Juillard had no business connections whatsoever with his passengers, he was also detained without a trial. He was, however, one of some three hundred Europeans locked up in Algeria for no explicit reason.

In spite of pleas from Juillard's wife and the editor of Swiss aviation magazine *Interavia*, IFALPA refused to support Juillard's case, when it was learnt that he was involved in selling two surplus DC7s to Biafra to be used as troop carriers.

Once the alarming news reached the Federation that Taylor and Copleston were kept in very primitive conditions and in isolation at El Harrach prison, and that rough methods were used during their interrogation, the Principal Officers decided to initiate an action in their defence. However, initially their hands were tied. In accordance with the usual procedure of consulting the member associations, the British Air Line Pilots' Association was contacted by telegram for their support. Eventually IFALPA received a much-delayed reply by letter (dated 26 July 1967) which stated that: 'As neither of the pilots in prison in Algeria are members of BALPA, we are not prepared to ask IFALPA to take up cudgels for them.'

When in the following weeks it became apparent that the approaches via the diplomatic channels or the Red Cross were so far in vain, IFALPA decided that intervention could no longer be postponed. Several pilots' associations expressed their support and eventually even BALPA changed its mind. The Federation's first step was an appeal to the President of the Algerian Republic, Col Boumedienne.

However, when no reply or even an acknowledgement had been received, more drastic measures were discussed at a pilots' meeting. For the first time in the nineteen years of IFALPA's existence, suspending air services to a country was proposed as a weapon against a government's obstinacy.

In the meantime, other avenues were pursued. As using a pilot of Arab nationality as an intermediary could smooth the way, Captain Salem Nasif from the Lebanese Pilots Association was contacted and asked to take up the Taylor and Copleston case with the Algerian Ambassador to Lebanon. At first this new avenue looked promising. The Ambassador assured Nasif that he would get in touch with Algiers about the latest situation, but he was under the impression that the pilots were already set free. However if this was not so, he would endeavour to arrange a visit for Captain Nasif to discuss their release with the Foreign Ministry officials in Algiers. Unfortunately, relying on diplomatic channels soon exposed weaknesses. During the Ambassador's absence for the African Unity Congress in Khartoum, Nasif was given evasive answers by the Embassy staff and was not able to report any progress. However, he learnt a point of great interest to IFALPA. There were to be no criminal charges against Taylor and Copleston.

Another avenue that failed was an appeal by IFALPA to the ICAO President. His reply stipulated that ICAO could not take up the release of the two pilots unless it was requested by a member state. Although the ICAO Council, the governing body, had the powers to deal with a dispute between states, at first it would have to be shown that the offending state acted against the spirit, if not the letter, of an international convention. In simple words, ICAO was reluctant to get mixed up in this case.

Even help from the Russian Pilots' Union, although not an IFALPA member but regularly attending Annual Conferences as observers, was sought when their delegation was visiting Stockholm at the invitation of Swedish pilots. Also the Cuban Pilots' Association, a long-standing participant in IFALPA activities, was requested to intervene with their authorities. It was hoped that these avenues could have some influence as both Cuba and the USSR enjoyed close political relations with the Republic of Algeria.

Finally, at the request of IFALPA Principal Officers, the French Pilots' Association – *Syndicat Nationale des Pilots de Ligne*, lodged one petition directly with the Minister of Transport in Algiers and another with the French Foreign Ministry pleading for them to intervene on behalf of Taylor and Copleston. The petitions included a paragraph which reflected the pilots' current ominous mood: 'The 30,000 pilot members of IFALPA are bound by international agreements, which provide, among other measures, for boycott action against any country which maltreats airline crew members.'

The response of the Algerian authorities was a vicious attack by the government-controlled press on IFALPA for interfering with the country's sovereign rights. Furthermore, the authorities declared that they would never bow to pressure from any international organisations. It was an expected reaction from a young regime, sensitive to a loss of face.

When the pilots' patience began to wear thin, the IFALPA Principal Officers were given further encouragements from their members to stop air services to Algiers. As a result of this, at a meeting on 21 August a decision was taken to commence the boycott on the 26th. However, the action was to be limited to three or four days only, mainly as a show of pilots' solidarity.

On 23 August, BBC News reported that Taylor and Copleston had appeared on Algerian television the night before and seemed fit and well. The same evening they were handed over to the Swiss Embassy in Algiers and they flew to London the next morning on an airline service.

What had finally led to the change of heart after eighty-six days of incarceration will remain a matter of conjecture. As the IFALPA President at the time, I would not claim that our endeavours alone succeeded in freeing Taylor and Copleston. On the other hand, the threat of a boycott was a sufficient embarrassment to the authorities to have made them look as if they had refused to observe human rights and even their own laws. But the release was greeted in the Western world as a triumph of various diplomatic efforts. IFALPA was given no credit and in the eyes of the media, the Federation played only a very minor role in securing the two pilots' freedom.

The Taylor and Copleston affair exposed weaknesses that opened a way for future terrorist actions against aircraft. The first weakness was that there was no provision in international agreements when more than two countries were involved in a hijacking case. The second weakness was that the western world had shown little interest in protecting their flight crew from abuse by foreign authorities, in particular by regimes with whom delicate political relations prevailed.

In respect of speculations as to why the two pilots were set free, various opinions were expressed on the conclusion of the affair. Upon his release David Taylor wrote to IFALPA:

'As Captain of the HS125 G-ASNU recently forced to land in Algeria, I am writing to thank all members of IFALPA for their efforts to effect our release. In particular I would like to thank those pilots who were willing to suspend flights into Algeria. There was, I am sure, considerable risk of unpleasantness or worse to them on resumption of their flights into Algeria and I am relieved that it never had to be put to test. I feel sure that the threatened pilot action had considerable influence on our release although it is difficult to tell at this stage how much since several separate efforts were all coming to a head at the same time. It is fairly safe to say that we were not released by normal diplomatic means.'

When expressing his appreciation to IFALPA on the phone immediately upon his arrival in England, Trevor Copleston revealed that he was aware of the Federation efforts through Mr Dawbarn, the British Consul General who was allowed to visit him on two occasions. Mr Dawbarn even told him the number of days the proposed boycott was planned for, and appeared to be strongly in favour of such an action. This was an interesting opinion from someone on spot.

One of the Foreign Office officials involved in the Taylor and Copleston affair, stated in a letter to IFALPA headquarters, as follows: 'We have no indication from the Algerians about what actually caused the pilots' release but I can't help feeling personally that IFALPA's action probably played quite a part in it. You certainly brought tactful pressure to bear from all angles.'

Although it is unlikely that comments could ever be obtained from the Algerian officials, of particular interest is the view from someone familiar with the Arab mentality. Captain Nasif recounted his impressions in a short resumé. (The extract from his letter is quoted in its original form. However, I have added my own explanations for the 'Anglicised' French words used by Nasif whose mother tongue was French and was on a par with his Arabic.):

'a: The Algerian authorities must have been convinced of the innocence of both pilots during the first week of investigation. However, the hasty and rather discourteous attitude of the British press (before IFALPA stepped in) – plus the then anti-British sentiment, especially after the ME events [the Suez Canal War] rather complicated matters.

b: IFALPA intended action and campaign inadvertently reached the public. Considered immixation [interference] and chantage [black-mail]. A be damned all attitude set in – (This is a congenital characteristic of my blood brothers when faced with such circumstances. I believe there is a very adequate colloquial English term for it.) On the other hand a glimmer of light: IFALPA cable to Cuban Pilots' Association, considered, quote: "Correct manner of dealing not threats."

c: Algerian authorities were aware of IFALPA inter "pourparlers" [informal discussions] and difficulties encountered; awkward situation of pilots in Algiers; reluctance of SNPL [the French Air Line Pilots' Association] to go all out.

In view of all this and the consequent (unexplained) release of Copleston and Taylor, I think I would be, perhaps correct in assuming that this was due, mainly to the good offices of the French (authorities) through SNPL; the Cubans and of those of the Algerian Ambassador to the Lebanon.'

Without the slightest indication about the motive behind the release, it would be difficult to make a judgement as to what extent Captain Nasif was correct in his assessment. The Cuban Pilots' Association's intervention does not appear to have exerted any influence. Nothing of any importance was reported to IFALPA by them. The Algerian Ambassador could not have been effective as he was busy at the African Unity Congress at Khartoum. Equally the French authorities would have been unlikely to involve themselves in a matter that could antagonise the Arab world whilst they were trying to court it for economic reasons.

Nevertheless, the support by the French Pilots' Association had undoubtedly made an impact on the Algerian officials, in particular on those with close connections to civil aviation. The fate of Taylor and Copleston was in the hands of the Revolutionary Council, a Politburo-style governing body. It was known that the President of the local airline, Air Algerie, a young politician educated in Russia and formerly the Chief of Air Staff, had close links with the Council. Air Algerie was operated entirely by French pilots and through the connections with their colleagues in France, they were kept informed of the SNPL feelings about Taylor's and Copleston's case. This would have been likely to have been made known to the Air Algerie President who would have passed it on to the Revolutionary Council. Even five years after gaining independence, Algerian politics were still strongly influenced by the French.

El Al Boeing 707 4T-ATA, which was hijacked to Algiers on 23 July 1968. After the aircraft was broken up on completion of its airline service, the nose was preserved and is now exhibited in the Cradle of Aviation Museum on New York's Long Island.

PART II

In numerical terms, 1968 was one of the blackest years in the aviation history of the USA. That year alone, the FAA summary on various hijacking incidents was three pages long. But despite all the cases in America of armed men commandeering aircraft to Cuba with a regular monotony, none led to a political confrontation. On the other hand, an outbreak of air piracy on this side of the Atlantic revealed a new aspect of the horrifying malady. This was the taking over of an aircraft as a demonstration of political grievances.

Just after midnight on 23 July 1968, an Israeli Airlines Boeing 707-420, registration 4T-ATA, took off from Rome for Tel Aviv with ten crew members and thirty-eight passengers on board. The captain was forty-one-year-old Oded Abarbanell, a former President of the Israeli Pilots' Association who had represented his union at several IFALPA Annual Conferences. His First Officer was Maoz Poraz, thirty-four, with a service record in the Six-Day War.

At the top of climb when the seat belt sign was switched off, three men jumped out of their seats and began to terrorise the passengers and the cabin staff with their guns. They were Palestinians, who, as it was subsequently established, had booked in a day earlier at a hotel close to Fiumicino Airport under the names of Shimiyu, Fazal and Jacoob. One of the hijackers admitted later that he followed an El Al stewardess on a layover in Rome.

One of the hijackers brandishing a gun forced his way into the cockpit. At that moment, Poraz was in the observer's seat, having given up his front seat to a trainee third pilot Avner Slapik. Upon noticing a strange person entering the cockpit, Poraz jumped up. The reaction of the hijacker was to fire a shot and then hit Poraz hard with the gun, cutting a deep wound on his head. He then brutally pushed the co-pilot out of the cockpit. Later the Israelis claimed that that it was a vicious premeditated attack to frighten the crew into submission. But Poraz himself told me that he thought it was a nervous reaction on the part of the Palestinian in presuming that Poraz was going to put up a fight. As a result of the scuffle, an extremely tense atmosphere prevailed for the rest of the flight and a feeling of terror swept through the cabin. A passenger, Father d'Allesandro from Collodi in Italy, reported that, when Poraz's blood began to drip onto the plate of the passenger sitting next to him, the hijacker dipped his finger in the blood and after putting it to his mouth remarked: 'It doesn't taste bad for an Israeli'.

The terrorist who took over control in the cockpit ordered the captain to inform Rome Air Traffic Control Centre that they were going to divert according to company instructions. As an act of defiance could have led to a more explosive situation, Abarbanell resignedly complied with the hijacker's order. But the air traffic controller could not grasp the meaning of the message and queried it. The Palestinian grabbed the microphone and in an excited voice started to jabber that it was no longer El Al Flight 426 but Al Jiddah 707. His strongly accented English combined with a poor microphone technique only further confused the air traffic controller. A request to repeat the message resulted in a similar jabbering but one sentence stood out loud and clear – 'We are diverting to Algiers'. When by now the totally perplexed air traffic controller questioned the reason, an American aircraft butted in advising him that it was evidently a hijacking.

Once the hassle on the radio was over, the terrorist handed the pilots a slip of paper with a magnetic course to steer. When after half an hour Abarbanell caught sight of the Tunisian coast, he could see that the course had been worked out from Rome directly to Algiers while his Boeing 707 was hijacked over Sorrento, one hundred and fifty miles to the south-east. As a result, they were heading for the heart of the Sahara. Abarbanell admitted later that, although he felt butterflies in his stomach, he had to remain calm, as, judged by his badly shaking hands, the terrorist appeared to be far more on edge. In order not to provoke him into a catastrophic outburst of temper, Abarbanell had to use all his composure and patience to persuade the Palestinian that a change of course was necessary. An hour later, which was two hours after leaving Rome, the aircraft touched down safely at Algiers Dal-El Beida Airport. At least a forced landing in the Sahara had been averted.

International aviation organisations such as ICAO and IATA were at once informed by El Al of the alarming development. On the other hand, IFALPA headquarters in London was advised by the Israeli Pilots' Association only the next morning. When on the following day the media reported that the hijacked aircraft was still on the ground, IFALPA sent a telegram to the Algerian Minister of Transport requesting information on the wellbeing of the crew and passengers and bringing to the Minister's attention the provisions of the Tokyo Convention relating to their speedy release. Unfortunately, the situation was complicated by the fact that a state of war still existed between the Arab countries and Israel. Nevertheless, all non-Israeli passengers were flown out to Paris on the first available airline service. Later Israeli women and the stewardesses were also released.

When the next few days brought no indications as to what the Algerian authorities intended to do with the crew and the male Israeli passengers, IFALPA decided to send their representatives to discuss the situation on spot. This became particularly urgent after the press reported that an appeal by IATA, which was relayed by the Air France President to the management of Air Algerie, brought no response.

Although as IFALPA President I was expected to head our mission, I was unfortunately away on a long flight to West Africa. Consequently Captain Forsberg, the Deputy President and a Finnair pilot, and Captain O'Grady, a Principal Officer, an Irishman flying for Air Lingus, were asked to represent the Federation. On arrival they were treated by the Algerian authorities in an offhand manner. It took two days before they were allowed to see the hijacked crew and have lunch with them. Poraz's wound still had not healed but otherwise the rest of men were well.

A meeting with the officials from the civil aviation department did not produce any results, nor did a visit to the Ministry of Justice. Unfortunately international politics began to play an important role in the crisis. The Palestinians pressed the Algerian Government to hold the crew and the male passengers captive until Israel agreed to release 100 political prisoners for every crew member or passenger. The Algerians suggested that IFALPA use their good offices as an intermediary. This was strongly refused. Not only would horse-trading have been against our principles but using pilots in a barter would have encouraged further hijacking attempts, and they could spread like wildfire.

When Forsberg and O'Grady returned from Algiers on 2 August, we met in Amsterdam together with Captain Jackson, the IFALPA Executive Secretary and Captain Zeyfert, the chairman of the Dutch Airline Pilots' Association. It was a gloomy meeting. Our pleas to free the El Al crew on humanitarian grounds came to nothing. Now it looked as if IFALPA would have to resort to stern measures. Nevertheless before making anything official, we decided to wait until

the next session of the Algerian Revolutionary Council, scheduled for 8 August, when new directives could be taken. If no fresh development was apparent, the boycott was going to be set for 18 August.

Two days after the meeting, the Algerian *Chargé d'Affaires* in London advised IFALPA headquarters that the EL Al crew were not under arrest but only under a judicial detention pending investigation, similar to proceedings used in the case of an air accident. Although it did not alter their situation, it was an indication that the Algerian officials had begun to take notice of IFALPA intentions. At the same time, the Algerian Press Agency, the authorities' mouthpiece, announced that the government was now prepared to receive an IFALPA delegation.

Unfortunately the announcement came as I was departing for another long intercontinental flight. As Captain Forsberg and Captain O'Grady were flying European routes, they were available at short notice and they were asked to proceed to Algiers again. When the news of the proposed visit reached the Israeli Pilots' Association, they warned the Federation that, according to information received from a very reliable source, the Algerian authorities had no intention of discussing the fate of the incarcerated crew but were playing for time. Indeed, the warning was correct. Forsberg and O'Grady were given no opportunity to meet any high-level government officials and according to my strict instruction, returned as soon as it was evident that there was no chance of any fruitful talks.

Now no other course of action appeared to be left but to announce the boycott. An official notification was scheduled for the day of my return to Holland, which was 13 August. The boycott was to start at 00.00 hrs Central European Time on Sunday 18 August. The only dissenting voice among pilots' associations came from the Lebanese, but under pressure from Arab public opinion, they could not do anything else.

Our announcement was extensively reported by all European press and TV. *The Times* and the *Express* gave our proposed measure front-page coverage. During a press and TV conference in Holland, I stressed IFALPA's great concern over safety hazards connected with hijackings and over the lack of urgent steps by many governments to curtail escalating air piracy. Using the El Al crew to bargain for concessions from the Israeli authorities would only encourage further attempts.

It must be appreciated that with a small paid staff at the IFALPA London headquarters already stretched to the limits, a considerable burden was placed on the shoulders of the five elected Principal Officers as a result of the proposed action. They had to perform their IFALPA activities in free time between flights.

With Captain Forsberg and Captain O'Grady involved in two visits to Algiers, I undertook much of the preparations for the boycott during my time off after my last intercontinental flight. My agenda was full of diverse commitments. It began with a call at the Italian Embassy in The Hague. As the hijacking originated on Italian territory, their authorities offered to act as an intermediary. At the request of the Israeli Pilots' Association, I pressed the Ambassador to arrange for medical checks of the detained crew by an Italian doctor during the boycott, so as to be sure that they were not ill-treated.

Another of my duties was a visit to Paris, to call upon the Air France General Manager Pierre Cot. The French pilots requested IFALPA to put pressure on their airline management not to interfere with the proposed stoppages of services to Algiers. A briefing on Cot's background was not necessary. He was a widely-known figure in France from his legendary flying feats and from serving as a pre-war air minister. Expecting understanding from another pilot, I was not disappointed. When I outlined the purpose of my visit, Cot immediately assured me that he would comply with his pilots' wishes. However he feared that a boycott by the Air France pilots alone might not be effective, as Air Algerie was bound to step up its services to France. The interview was over in a matter of minutes without wasting any time on empty talk. I left Paris feeling a bit more hopeful. Indeed Cot's assurances were soon put into practice. Air France announced that it would not guarantee bookings on flights to Algiers after 18 August.

There were also other sources of support. One came from Maurice Serf, the chairman of the French Air Traffic Controllers' Union and President of the International Controllers' Federation – IFATCA. He was also the Chief of the Paris ATC. Maurice pledged that his men would try their best either to stop, or at least delay, Air Algerie flights from landing in France. In view of the strongly pro-Arab and anti-boycott attitude of the De Gaulle Government, this would have been an act of defiance, probably inviting repercussions. Just the same, the French air traffic controllers' action could help to paralyse all

services to and from Algiers. Additional support came from most unexpected quarters. Although only limited assistance was expected from the French ground personnel, whose main union, CGT, was Communist orientated and sympathetic to the Arab cause, a morale-boosting offer came from a senior employee in the Air France booking office. He saw no difficulty in 'sabotaging' Air Algerie bookings which Air France handled.

Upon my return to Holland, I was contacted by the United Nations representative in Europe, Mr George Ivan Smith (see chapter 5). He wanted a briefing on the progress of our actions. He also asked me to see the UN Secretary General in New York. Expecting a response from the Algerians, I decided to remain in Holland and it was arranged for Captain O'Grady to visit U Thant.

My call on the Dutch Foreign Minister in The Hague was less satisfactory. Unfortunately Mr Luns was away on a state visit to Israel and I was received by the Head of the Middle East Department. He advised me that, although the Dutch authorities were very sympathetic to the plight of the El Al crew, their relations with both the French and the Algerian governments were at a low ebb and consequently the Ministry could do little to help. However, a side benefit of my visit was a comprehensive briefing on the various personalities in the Algerian government who were dealing with the hijacking and into whom I could run during our negotiations.

The last but the least agreeable function fell upon my shoulders at the time of announcing the boycott. The KLM management asked me to meet an El Al representative who came to Holland on a special mission to seek the support of KLM and IFALPA. I was very reluctant to have any direct contact with the Israeli side, except for their pilots' association, but I could not refuse a request from the KLM directors who gave considerable support to my IFALPA commitments. I accepted it only on the assurance that the meeting would take place in strict secrecy. At the agreed hour, I waited in the most secluded part of the Amsterdam Hilton and I was approached by 'the man from El Al' in a manner of a spy meeting his controller. I wasted no time in expressing my annoyance at his attempt to exploit El Al's influence on IFALPA. I pointed out that our interests differed. While his airline sought the release of the aircraft as well, we were concerned only with the crew and the remaining passengers. I told him in undiplomatic terms that I strongly objected to this meeting, which, if reported by the Press, could harm the IFALPA cause.

It took years before I eventually learnt the identity of the mysterious El Al envoy. Only after reading a book on Mossad, the Israeli Intelligence Service, did it became evident that he was the El Al President himself, Mordecai Ben-Ari, a well known personality in Israel, and that his mission had been instigated by Mossad.

My most trying duty after announcing the boycott was to answer the never-ending phone calls from reporters, pressing for tip-offs on the next course of action should the boycott fail. As the subject had been already discussed within IFALPA, I could not avoid stating, nevertheless with some reluctance, that we would probably instruct our members not to accept Algerian nationals as the Algerian authorities showed no respect for air safety. For this statement, the Algerian press labelled me a violator of the United Nations Charter. It seemed a hypocritical outlook from a country that refused to observe international conventions.

Two days after announcing the boycott, a new development seemed to signal a turnaround in the attitude of the Algerian government. I received an official invitation to Algiers via their *Chargé d'Affaires* in London, to meet the government officials. Luckily I still had several days of flight leave left, so at last I was able to represent IFALPA. I was going to be assisted by another Principal Officer, Captain Nicolaieff, and the SNPL Secretary General, Captain Landrigin. The inclusion of Nicolaieff and Landrigin – both Air France pilots – was a great help. Their colleagues were staunch supporters of the boycott and, as Air France operated thirty services per week to Algiers, they were expected to take the brunt of the IFALPA action. Moreover, with French being an official language in the Algerian governmental offices, Nicolaieff and Landrigin could act as interpreters.

Despite expressing a willingness to meet IFALPA representatives, the Algerian government issued a statement that the El Al crew would not be released until a judicial investigation was completed. At the same time, the statement criticised the pilots for their action and warned them of falling into a trap of a 'Zionist plot against the Arab world'. The government also tried to mobilise all Arab trade unions to counteract any measures that could be taken by the French ground personnel in refusing to handle Air Algerie services.

Upon my arrival in Algiers, I faced the first of many pinpricks to come. I was asked by the Immigration Officer to fill in an entry form which I flatly refused to do, and I showed him my letter of invitation from the Algerian Government. But it made no difference. As it was a matter of principle, I began to arrange a booking for the return flight to Paris. However, a distressed senior Air Algerie employee showed up in time showering apologies, and I was escorted to a taxi without any further immigration or customs formalities.

But it was not the end of our minor tribulations. As soon as we checked in at the hotel, Nicolaieff phoned the Foreign Ministry to advise them of our arrival. There was no response for several hours although a day earlier IFALPA headquarters had notified the Foreign Ministry of our plans. In the end, I asked Nicolaieff to call the Ministry once more and make it clear, in his most forceful French, that as working pilots we had no time to waste.

The reaction was immediate and we were requested to come as soon as possible. However the Foreign Minister Abdelaziz Bouteflika (then only thirty-five years old and now recently elected as the new President of the Algerian Republic), who personally handled the El Al case, was busy and we were received by Layachi Yaker, the Director of Economic Developments and number two at the Foreign Ministry (who, in the years to come, served as the Trade Minister). As soon as we were shown to his room, Yaker, who spoke excellent English, wasted no time in expressing his annoyance over IFALPA's action and attacked our 'noisy propaganda' in connection with the boycott that sounded to him like an ultimatum to a sovereign state. Moreover, he deprecated the abrupt departure of Captains Forsberg and O'Grady on their second visit, which as a result gave the government officials no chance to discuss the Boeing 707 affair with them. Hardly able to hold my temper, my reply was equally caustic. So far IFALPA was very patient, but the Algerian Government had disregarded all our pleas for the release of the crew. I stressed that we could never accept trading the pilots for the Palestinian commandos that were held in Israeli jails. Such barter could only lead to the escalation of hijackings and in order to put an end to it we had no option but to apply the strongest possible measures and announce the boycott.

Air piracy was, to pilots, not a political but a safety issue. Consequently, our members pressed for action. They were gravely concerned about Algeria refusing to observe the provisions of the Tokyo Convention and allowing their airport to become a second Havana. As far as cutting their visit short, I pointed out that Captains Forsberg and O'Grady were not paid officials. They were using their free time in between flights to put things right for the good of the whole air transport industry. They could not waste their precious time off unless the government officials intended to hold fruitful talks.

Surprisingly, the frank exchange of accusation and counter-accusation appeared to have cleared the air. Yaker could see that IFALPA was not prepared to be kicked around. As a result, his attitude changed and he insisted that whilst Bouteflika was busy Nicolaieff and I straightaway visit the detained El Al crew. Yaker wanted us to convey to Abarbanell, quoting his exact words as recorded in my notes, that 'the solution to the problem with the crew and passengers will be found and they must not assume that the Algerian Government intend to extend their detention unnecessarily'.

Transport was immediately arranged and we left for a destination that was at the time the most guarded secret in Algeria. We were accompanied by Mr Boudjaki, a very senior Foreign Ministry official who looked no more than in his mid-twenties. His English was immaculate, acquired as I was told from attending a university in the USA. Boudjaki explained that the Ministry was anxious to show me that, despite the tension between Israel and the Arab countries, they were doing their best as a gesture to IFALPA to provide acceptable conditions for the crew. Nevertheless some restrictions were unavoidable and due to security reasons, a periodic change of quarters was necessary.

Soon it was evident that we were heading for the airport. Shortly before we reached the entrance, a gruesome building where the hijackers were kept was pointed out to me. Boudjaki suggested a brief visit, if I wished, to show me that that the Al Fatah hijackers were actually locked up as common criminals and were not treated by the authorities as heroes of the Arab cause. I had no intention of seeing the notorious El Harrach prison and I politely declined. 'Mr Tshombe is also there,' my 'guide' added, 'and I am sure, Captain Bartelski, you are very familiar with that case.'

The El Al crew were kept on the military side of the airport in the Algerian Air Force barracks. A whole block was reserved for them and was guarded by soldiers with guns. I was assured it was not intended to treat them as prisoners but was for security reasons. All possible efforts were made to ensure that the sympathisers of the Palestinian cause were not able to get close to the compound, which could only be entered after visitors were identified by the chief of the guard. At the time of our arrival, he was nowhere to be found. As the guard knew Boudjaki well, they were prepared to let us through, but I insisted on waiting as such an important rule could not be bent for anyone.

After a while the chief appeared and I was shown to the crew's quarters. All the doors were fully open. When Abarbanell saw me, he greeted me by my first name and introduced me to the rest of the detainees. I never hid the fact that I knew him personally from various IFALPA meetings and I had already made this clear to Yaker earlier on. The quarters looked somewhat Spartan but were roomy and clean. Comfortable chairs, tables to write on, books and radio were provided. The crew and the passengers were allowed to send letters to their families. One of the sensible precautions was to issue all the detainees with Algerian Air Force khaki uniforms, so that they could not be easily distinguished.

On enquiring about living conditions, Abarbanell replied and I am quoting his exact words from my notes: 'We're treated fine but when the hell do we get out of here?' There were, however, minor grumbles. They had to keep the place clean by themselves and make their own beds. But as the chief of the guard explained, it was to limit as much as possible the access of their own people in case a devout Moslem tried to avenge his blood brothers. Food was reasonable but typically military. The midday and evening meals were served with wine. The crew had the use of the nearby swimming pool for an hour a day. This time restriction was imposed due to the special precaution of clearing everyone from the immediate vicinity. Even religious beliefs were respected. One of the young passengers told me that for those who wished to visit the local synagogue on Saturday special arrangements were made to take them to the service.

Soon Abarbanell started to complain that, according to what he was told by Forsberg and O'Grady, he had expected to be released much earlier. I had to point out the gravity of the political situation in connection with the state of war existing between Israel and the Arab countries. Finally I passed on Yaker's message about the government's intentions not to detain the crew indefinitely. Then Boudjaki and the chief of the guard retreated to a far corner, so I could talk freely to Abarbanell. Unfortunately I had nothing more to add to comfort him.

When we returned to the Foreign Ministry, it was already dark. Again I was kept waiting in the reception room. Finally at about nine o'clock, Bouteflika appeared together with Jacques Landrigin and two Frenchmen from the International Transport Workers Federation who came with us from Paris.

Bouteflika apologised for not being able to see me earlier but the discussion with SNPL took longer than he expected. As he only spoke French and mine was rusty, Yaker acted as an interpreter. Bouteflika advised me that if I wished, he was at my disposal for an immediate meeting despite the late hour. He suggested however, that it might be more convenient for me to postpone the meeting until the next day in order to have a talk with Landrigin on the outcome of their discussions. He indicated that some misunderstanding between the Algerian Government and SNPL had already been cleared. With a hard day behind me, I felt that it would be better to have a good night's rest before a strenuous wrangle to come, so I agreed to a meeting on the following day. The Foreign Minister insisted on personally seeing me off to the car provided by the Ministry, which was going to take me back to my hotel. His courtesy seemed overwhelming.

But the meeting next morning started with a vitriolic attack by Bouteflika on the IFALPA boycott. He regarded it as an ultimatum to a sovereign state. By adopting such an uncompromising measure, IFALPA was interfering with the friendly relations that were recently established between France and the Arab countries. Moreover, our action would most likely further aggravate the already strained relations with the Western world. In his opinion, we did not represent unbiased pilots' views as we had in our ranks members such as South Africans, Portuguese and Rhodesians, known for their imperialistic attitude towards Africans.

To be sure of understanding Bouteflika's arguments correctly, I insisted on an English translation. As it turned out, Yaker proved to be an excellent interpreter. I found it a great advantage to be provided with an official version rather than waiting for Nicolaieff to put the proceedings into English.

I was getting slowly weary of the political slant being constantly brought into discussions and I made it evident in my reply. To IFALPA, the release of the crew was a matter of humanitarian principles. I strongly repudiated the allegations of any political bias in our ranks. The Federation was a voluntary body and every association, regardless of their nationality, colour or creed could join in, provided they obeyed the constitution. Politics were of no interest to pilots. In trying to put an end to hijackings, safety was our prime consideration.

Nevertheless, it looked as if the initial attack which Bouteflika had launched on IFALPA was the usual practice at all high-level political discussions. The icy atmosphere of the meeting soon changed when he outlined the Algerian Government's tricky position. They had neither wished nor asked for the hijacked aircraft to be brought to their country. In fact, it was an embarrassment and they were concerned that it could provoke a deeper conflict with Israel. They had already given proof of goodwill by releasing all Israeli women. But as the leader of the Arab world, it was their duty to help the oppressed Arabs. Algeria was willing to do everything in her power to solve the problem to the satisfaction of the friendly and the hostile parties. They shared IFALPA's concern over hijacking in general. The FNL leaders had suffered from a seizure of an Air Maroc airliner. Moreover, not long ago Israel had forced down two Arab aircraft and these were regarded as acts of dangerous aggression. The Government wished it to be known that all future cases would be dealt with according to the ICAO Tokyo Convention and its ratification by the Algerian Republic would be speeded up. The El Al crew were required as witnesses in an investigation into the circumstances surrounding the Boeing 707 affair. Therefore detaining them did not contravene the Chicago Convention on human rights. Finally Bouteflika made an explicit statement that was of great importance to IFALPA. He gave an assurance that the crew would not be part of any bargain with the Israeli Government and the Algerian authorities would not wait for any reciprocal gesture from the Israeli side. However, for a solution to the problem, time was required to cool off the present tense atmosphere in Algeria.

Without mincing words, I pointed out that holding the crew just because they were Israelis was an encouragement for further hijacking attempts, and brandishing guns on board an aircraft was an invitation to disaster. The pilots were very concerned as to what effect tolerating such actions would have on safety. Moreover, if one government was not prepared to observe international conventions and held a crew as hostages, perhaps the other involved government could try to retaliate and commandeer the offending country's aircraft in return. This could ensue in a hijacking war in which a certain country would likely prove to be more effective. Even without spelling out the country, my argument seemed to have got home and an ominous silence reigned for several long seconds.

What followed took some time to sink into my head, perhaps at first as a result of Bouteflika's using guarded language. But in the end, he made the position of his government clear by stating (in his exact words as translated into English), that 'a solution to the problem with the El Al crew will be found as soon as the investigation is completed, provided IFALPA is prepared to advise their members that the boycott was no longer necessary'.

Now the end of an international conflict was in my hands. Nevertheless, the timing of the release was still a worrying factor. On the other hand, an important point had been gained for IFALPA, which was that the crew would be set free without preconditions. Trying to decide on the spur of the moment whether I could trust the Algerian authorities after so many let-downs, made me come out in a cold sweat in spite of the stifling atmosphere in the conference room. But as our prime objective appeared to have been achieved, I consented to the Algerian proposal. I stressed however, that I took my decision believing in the honour of the Arab people and their respect for law and order. I knew that they were high-principled about such matters.

Once the agreement had been reached, Bouteflika excused himself and left the room. From now on it was up to his assistants and myself to prepare a joint press communiqué. Soon the meeting lost the air of stiff formality. Before we began to draft the statement, the Algerian officials outlined their difficulties of putting 'the solution' into practice. The main problem was public opinion. After weeks of press attacks on IFALPA, time was needed to avoid stirring up mass protests from the population. The PLO had to be appeased and it was being arranged.

I fully agreed with Bouteflika's assistants that our communiqué should be in general terms and indirectly worded. This was reflected in the last paragraph of the joint statement:

'IFALPA, not wishing to interfere with the conduct of affairs by a sovereign state, decided to withdraw the recommendation previously issued to member associations, in order to permit the government of Algeria to reach a solution to this problem. We received

assurances that it will be completed as soon as possible, and the conclusions, as far as the crew is concerned, might be communicated to IFALPA.'

Two words never featured in the statement – release or boycott. But the roundabout wording was in IFALPA's interest. Any direct hint of setting the crew free without reciprocal concessions was bound to arouse protests from some faction of the Arab world and pressure could again mount to use the crew in bargaining for the Palestinian commandos. We also agreed that both sides should refrain from any further comments to the Press.

The date for completing 'the investigation of the Boeing 707 affair' was set for 26 August, the Algerian Foreign Ministry's diplomatic description of the time period required to cool off the country's inflamed atmosphere. The 'solution' to the problem (the crew's release) was going to take place shortly after that date.

While waiting for Bouteflika's corrections to the draft, the informal atmosphere that continued to reign encouraged a conversation of personal nature. The Algerian officials freely admitted that they were amazed by the intensity of IFALPA's campaign. This made them check up to see if I had any Jewish ancestors. What in their eyes gave credence to our impartiality was the multinational background of the Principal Officers. They knew that I was a Polish-born British-naturalised subject flying for the Dutch Airline and that Forsberg was Finnish but of Swedish descent. They were also aware that Nicolaieff although born in France came from a White Russian family. When he mentioned to Yaker and the President of Air Algerie that he still spoke to his mother in her native tongue, they began to converse with him in Russian. They had both attended a university in Moscow. From a further conversation it transpired that, no matter how embarrassing the boycott threat had been to the Government, deep inside the officials respected IFALPA for its high moral values and integrity. I was assured that when a batch of recently trained pilots of Algerian origin started to work for the local airline, they would be encouraged to form an union and join IFALPA.

Drafting the statement proved more involved than I anticipated and it took over three hours. Two versions were being prepared, one in French for the Foreign Ministry and one in English for IFALPA. This called for an accurate synchronisation of the wording. Moreover Bouteflika kept insisting on constant changes. I was determined to catch the last plane to Paris, so I could get home that night. The next day I was scheduled for a flight to Sydney and, frankly, I was looking forward to getting away from politics and pressure. But as the final draft was only ready when the Paris service was due to depart, the Air Algerie Caravelle was kept waiting for forty-five minutes with all passengers on board until Nicolaieff and I arrived at the airport.

Nevertheless, once Algeria was left behind, I was consumed with doubts as to whether the officials would honour their word about releasing the crew. I had never bothered to ask for the actual date. The less that people knew, the better. A slip of the tongue and protests from the hijackers' sympathisers could mount again. I was promised that the 'solution' was going to be so arranged that it would catch everyone by surprise. However, during the flight back to Paris, Jacques Landrigin, who was also returning on the same plane, told me the exact date given to him by an obliging official. It was set for 31 August.

The mission to Algiers had opened my eyes to the extreme differences in mentality between an Arab politician and an airline pilot. It was like two incompatible worlds, one full of tunnel-vision concepts, long toes and roundabout approaches, the other perhaps too direct and down-to-earth for those who held power. For the pilots, with their ultra-pragmatic outlook and being generally quick to speak their mind, it was difficult to find a platform for discussions with the politicians. The disparity of the mentalities could not be described in a few words. Perhaps the best illustration would be a reply that I had from one of my colleagues when I told him about Bouteflika calling some pilots imperialists. He laughed it off with: 'Of course the guy was right, wives claim all pilots are imperialists at home.'

At first, my flight to the Far East felt a relief from the turmoil of the last few days. But it was only temporary. I was reminded of my involvement with international politics upon landing at Beirut for a two-day stopover. Beirut was at the time a PLO stronghold and it did not help that my photograph had appeared in every local newspaper and my name was frequently mentioned on TV and radio. No wonder the immigration officer seemed surprised to see me. Just the same, he greeted me with a loud 'welcome to Lebanon' salutation. An equally cordial reception was extended by the staff in the Riviera Hotel, where Terry Waite had stayed just before he was abducted.

During the two days of my stopover in Beirut, the KLM Station Manager, on instruction from the Lebanese Security officials, kept frequently checking up with me as to whether the PLO tried to bother me.

As the date of the El Al crew release drew nearer and I found myself on the home stretch from the Far East, I began to feel very apprehensive about the promise by the Algerian Government. This was not helped by the fact that one of my colleagues, whom I met en route, showed me a Dutch weekly magazine with an article which had appeared after my departure from Holland. It accused me of 'conveniently' disappearing on a flight to the Far East and leaving IFALPA affairs unattended.

The night before 31 August, I was back in Beirut and could not sleep from anxiety. However, the next day I heard the welcome news on the Lebanese radio. The El Al crew were already on their way to Paris and the hijacked Boeing 707 was going to be flown out of Algiers the following day by Nicolaieff himself. I immediately sent a telegram of appreciation to Bouteflika.

Upon my return to Amsterdam, I expected the newspapers to acclaim an IFALPA victory. But it had turned out like the Taylor and Copleston case. Only the Italian Government were given credit for their diplomatic efforts in securing the release of the crew in exchange for a small number of Palestinian commandos held in Israel. The Algerian authorities were recognised for their 'sensible' solution and the Israelis for their patience and forbearance.

IFALPA was nowhere mentioned. It was the price we were paying for complying with the agreement not to comment to the media before the crew was set free. Now everybody else claimed their achievements.

Sadly, the Israeli authorities ignored the impact of the planned IFALPA boycott. Upon the release of the crew and the passengers, Prime Minister Eshkol stated on the Jerusalem Domestic Radio Service that the success of ending the hijacking drama was due to political actions of all international, governmental and public bodies and thanked them for their actions to secure the release.

The Foreign Minister Abba Eban claimed that: '...there was no deal with Algeria. The government undertook in principle to make a gesture of a humanitarian nature and it will fulfil its undertaking. The plane, its crew and passengers [surprisingly in that order] have been returned without our doing anything in return and no Fatah men will be released.'

Nevertheless, the Israeli pilots believed that the successful outcome of the Boeing 707 affair was due to an entirely different source. On 2 September, the *Jerusalem Post* reported:

'El Al Air Crew Union leaders criticised the Foreign Ministry for taking what they alleged, too much credit for the release of the hijacked El Al plane and its crew and passengers. Captain David Gutman declared that the IFALPA boycott threat had greater influence than any deal, such as the one reportedly reached between the Foreign Ministry and the Italian Government. He said that IFALPA officers had told him in London that Algerians had promised the release between 26th and 31st August in return for the removal of the boycott. He said they accordingly recommended that the boycott threat be removed and the Algerians kept their promise.'

Of the greatest significance was the statement by the Algerian authorities, which was broadcast by the Cairo MENA service in Arabic on 31 August. It most accurately reflects the Algerians' attitude to the Boeing 707 affair:

'An Algerian political source told a MENA correspondent today that the decision to release the crew and passengers of the Israeli plane was made on humanitarian basis. He added that the Israeli plane, captured by the Palestinian fedayeen, will be detained in Algeria pending the results of negotiations with U Thant, Rome and the Red Cross on the release of about thirty Palestinian fedayeen held by Israel.'

Another big disappointment to IFALPA, and in particular to myself, was a press statement, repeated by all media in Europe, which Abarbanell made upon his return to Israel. He claimed that he and his crew were ill-treated during the detention. Living conditions were appalling and they had to fend for themselves, including cleaning their own toilets. I reacted by sending Abarbanell a strongly-worded telegram, reminding him what he told me when I saw him in Algiers.

At the same time, I refused an invitation from the Israeli Pilots' Association for my wife and myself to go to Tel Aviv for a week's visit at their expense. This would have been against the principle of being impartial. Federation policy was not to stand up for the Israeli pilots but to fight air piracy on safety grounds. In the same spirit, two months later I turned down an invitation for a cocktail party given by the Algerian *Chargé d'Affaires* in London on the anniversary of the country gaining its independence.

Looking back, I am certain that the planned IFALPA boycott was the prime factor in the Algerian Government's decision to release the crew. But their initial obstinacy seems surprising as only a year earlier they were confronted with a similar action over the incarceration of Taylor and Copleston. There is no doubt that the Algerian Government was under strong pressure from the Palestinians. A week after the hijacking a joint delegation had arrived in Algiers composed of the PLO, Al Fatah and the Popular Front for the Liberation of Palestine, for the first time displaying a united front. They pressed the authorities for arrangements through the International Red Cross, to exchange 1,000 Arab guerrillas held in Israel for the El Al crew and the Israeli passengers. As a result, IFALPA's initial protests were treated with indifference and the two visits by Forsberg and O'Grady had not produced any results.

It was known that within the Algerian Revolutionary Council there were two opposing factions. One was headed by Col Boumedienne, who favoured a hard line, while Bouteflika and his followers insisted on adhering to the international agreements. Despite the initial obstinacy, the penny dropped when it became evident that IFALPA really meant to stop all air services to Algeria. A boycott could have played havoc with the tourist traffic at a busy time of the year and could affect national income through the loss of French visitors. Above all, it was an embarrassment for the authorities that they were not taking any steps to discourage air piracy.

At a later stage, they could see that keeping the El Al crew as hostages was a bad mistake. IFALPA's accusations of condoning the El Al hijacking and not treating it as a safety matter did a lot of harm to Algeria's image, as at the time they were seeking a seat on the ICAO Council. As a result, the endeavours were dropped.

Nevertheless, Bouteflika and his supporters must be given credit in one respect. Before boarding the Caravelle for Paris, I was assured that in future all air piracy cases would be dealt according to the Tokyo Convention, even if the Convention was not yet ratified by the Government. Moreover, strong steps would be taken to stop Algiers from becoming a second Havana. The years to come have proved that the authorities have stuck to their word.

Another factor behind releasing the El Al crew earlier than the officials perhaps might have wished was the impending ICAO General Assembly scheduled for the beginning of September in Buenos Aires. Such meetings, a gathering of all heads of civil aviation departments, are held every five years.

For the first time IFALPA had been invited as observers and it would have been embarrassing for the Algerian civil aviation officials to participate in the Assembly's proceedings side by side with the Federation if the El Al crew were still detained in Algiers. It could have led to an awkward situation as we intended to voice strong objections to the delays in ratifying the Tokyo Convention by a number of states. Surprisingly, one of them was the United States.

During the first week in September 1968, I attended the Assembly on behalf of IFALPA. It was a frustrating experience. Soon after my arrival, it became evident that reaching a unanimous agreement to stamp out hijacking looked far from certain. The delegations were divided into two camps. One side was ready to adopt Draconian measures and the other was reluctant to take any further steps in case some 'doubtful' political advantages could be lost. In the latter camp were predominantly the Arab countries and Cuba. Although IFALPA was in the centre of all delegates' attention as a result of our strong stand on the Algerian issue, to certain government officials the 'pilots' voice' appeared to carry little weight.

The main battle over various proposals took place at the Legal Subcommittee on hijacking. The Arab camp was represented by a Lebanese lawyer who evidently knew nothing about the operational side of civil aviation. Due to the time period of my attendance at the Assembly being limited by my flying duties, I was allowed to present our statement as soon as the discussions on crime on board an aircraft were opened. Nevertheless, I had to wait the whole morning while the delegates first discussed procedural matters. It seemed as if bureaucracy was far more important than the grim reality of the plague of hijacking.

Our statement emphasised safety hazards in connection with commandeering an aircraft, such as the loss of aircraft control from a struggle in the cockpit, possible catastrophic damages due to use of weapons in flight, interference with air traffic control which could end in a mid-air collision, the hijackers' ignorance of operational limitations and fuel reserves, and forcing pilots to land at an destination unknown to them.

The most important point of the statement was IFALPA's 'suggestion' for the governments to adopt forthwith, even before accepting the entire Tokyo Convention, the provisions dealing with a speedy release of the crew, the passengers and the aircraft after hijacking. In spite of clearly underlining the word 'suggestion' in our statement, as a result of a briefing on procedures by a 'friendly' delegate, the Lebanese lawyer attacked IFALPA's proposal as being out of order, claiming that observers were not allowed to table a motion. This had put my back up and in forceful language I told him that he evidently was not paying enough attention to my statement, which only included an important point for consideration but not a definite proposal. It appeared as if certain government officials from the Middle East were determined to play down the pilots' influence on curtailing crimes committed on board an aircraft. Nevertheless, it would be only fair to mention that 'IFALPA's suggestion' was in the end adopted by the Assembly as a resolution.

My last link with fighting air piracy was to chair the IFALPA Annual Conference convened at Amsterdam in March 1969, at which our policy on the anti-hijacking measures was going to be significantly strengthened, particularly in the cases where states refused to observe the Tokyo Convention. Then, after fifteen years of serving the Federation, I intended to stand down. I expected it would be the end of my involvement with hijacking but fate decided otherwise.

Just over a year later on 'Black Sunday', 6 September 1970, five aircraft took off at about the same time from several different airports in Europe, all bound for New York. Out of the five, only one reached America. A TWA Boeing 707 was commandeered over Frankfurt and a Swissair DC8 over Zurich. Both had ended up on an abandoned wartime landing ground, known as Dawson's Field, located near Zarqa in Jordan, twenty miles north of Amman. Two more aircraft which departed from Amsterdam, a PanAm Boeing 747 and an El Al Boeing 707, met with the same fate but the final outcome was different. By a strange coincidence they were both parked on a distant apron side by side, together with a KLM DC8 also leaving for New York at the same time.

The fate of the PanAm jumbo jet was very tragic. At first, in order to refuel, the pilot was forced to make a perilous night landing at Beirut after the airport authorities switched off all runway lights. Eventually the aircraft ended up in Cairo and it was destroyed on the ground by the terrorists.

But this was not the last case in the series of brutal hijackings. Two days later, a BOAC VC10 was also forced to land at Dawson's Field. In the end, all the aircraft that were brought there were destroyed by the terrorists. The mass air piracy act, perpetrated by the members of the Popular Front for the Liberation of Palestine, was the blackest day in aviation history. The intention was to hit the travelling public below the belt when traffic across the Atlantic was at its highest due to the start of a school term.

Out of the four hijackings on 6 September the only fatalities occurred on board the El Al Boeing 707.

The El Al departed Schiphol Airport three minutes ahead of a KLM DC8 and both aircraft followed the same route initially overhead London before commencing their North Atlantic crossing. As the captain of the KLM DC8, I became an innocent bystander to one of the most dramatic hijacking events. Moreover, I was the only lucky one to reach New York that day.

After London Radar took over control, the El Al Boeing was assigned Flight Level 280, while I trailed only a few miles behind and at 2,000 feet below. With the cockpit temperature like in a sauna, a result of an unusually hot day, a full load of passengers and a shortage of ground air conditioning units at Schiphol, the co-pilot and I slumped in our seats, panting for breath.

Suddenly we were awoken from our lethargic state by a piercing voice emanating from the overhead cockpit speakers, screaming: 'I am hijacked, I am hijacked'.

London Radar immediately pinpointed the aircraft that had transmitted the spine-chilling message, and in an impassive tone of voice as if nothing unusual had occurred, the radar controller advised the pilot: 'El Al 219, then maintain Flight Level 280'.

A few moments later the same agitated voice could be heard shouting frantically: 'I am going down, I am going down'. Then without waiting for radar guidance, the El Al Boeing began to dive through my altitude. In those few seconds, I had no time to check as to how close the aircraft was to my position. But much to my relief, I was soon assured by London Radar that there were a few miles to spare. Nevertheless a risk of collision did

exist as long as the emergency descent was not controlled by radar.

Shortly afterwards the El Al aircraft was assigned an alternate VHF channel and I also tuned in, leaving the co-pilot to listen out on the ATC frequency. After several minutes of dead silence, all of a sudden the El Al pilot asked for an emergency straight-in approach to Heathrow Airport. He warned the air traffic controller that he was going to land close to maximum take-off weight as he had no time to jettison fuel. He also asked for the ambulances and fire trucks to be standing by. The reason for such a hasty landing, as I learned later, was that one of the crew members had been seriously wounded and was bleeding to death.

Nevertheless, on short final the captain changed his mind and insisted on making a circuit over the airport. Radar controller advised him that under IFR rules he must immediately climb to 2,500 feet, the minimum safety height for the area. An argument followed and eventually the pilot was allowed to proceed visually but with the help of advisory radar vectors. When queried why he had abandoned the straight-in landing, he just blurted out: 'I had to call my airline on the company frequency'.

Eventually the pilot came down without any problem, in spite of the aircraft having been grossly over the maximum landing weight. Even before the end of ground run, he was heard screaming: 'Where the hell are the ambulances and the fire trucks?' The Tower controller pointed out that they were following behind the Boeing on the grass verges and advised the pilot to change over to the Fire Control frequency. The exchange of messages on the new channel was quite revealing. One fire truck informed Control that they had just removed a dead body, one badly-wounded crew member and three unexploded grenades from the El Al Boeing. It was the last message that came over on that channel.

I continued on my way to New York, thanking my lucky stars for having been spared a mid-air collision. Upon landing at Kennedy Airport, to my surprise I was met by a much larger than usual contingent of KLM staff, all displaying signs of excitement. Only then I learned that out of the five aircraft that left Europe for New York about the same time I was the only one to make the other side of the Atlantic. The American media were already broadcasting special news about the mass air piracy.

As the circumstances surrounding the El Al

hijacking were of a particular interest to me, I took the trouble to find out more about its background. The two air pirates were members of the Popular Front for the Liberation of Palestine (PFLP). They boarded the Boeing at Amsterdam, El Al's scheduled intermediate stop between Tel Aviv and New York.

One of the hijackers was twenty-four-year-old Leila Khaled, a Palestinian born in Haifa living in Lebanon, and travelling on a false Honduras passport. Her companion was twenty-seven-year-old Patric Arguello, an American known to the FBI and the CIA for his Communist sympathies. Although born in Los Angeles, Arguello carried a

Leila Khaled, hijacker of El Al Boeing 707.

Nicaraguan passport. How Khaled managed to pass a strict El Al security check at Schiphol Airport seemed puzzling. Her photograph was displayed in the El Al office with a warning to look out for her. Arguello was able to smuggle his weapons on board because they were made from non-ferrous materials and they did not show on the screening equipment that was in use at the time.

I was particularly interested as to why the El Al captain made a frantic emergency descent in spite of being aware that another aircraft in close vicinity was below him. A few weeks later, I was put in the picture by a contact in the Israeli Pilots' Association after news leaked out that the captain of the hijacked Boeing had been suspended from duty for two months.

To appreciate what had forced the captain to make a sudden dive requires a description of the security arrangements on the El Al aircraft, which virtually turned them into flying fortresses. The partition between the flight deck and the cabin had been made bulletproof and a special lock was fitted to the door. Two security guards constantly travelled on board. One occupied the front aisle seat in the first class while the other remained at the back of the aircraft. The guards were issued with special guns, which could fire low velocity bullets that would not penetrate the aircraft skin. Nevertheless, the bullets could disable a terrorist when fired at a close range. With such an arrangement, an attempt to commandeer an El Al plane looked to be hardly feasible.

But Captain Uri Bar-Lev committed a breach of security rules. He allowed the security guard who sat in front to stay on the flight deck during departure from Schiphol Airport and the subsequent climb. The guard pleaded that after six months of service, he had never seen a take-off from the cockpit and the chances of hijacking on the Amsterdam–New York stretch were practically nil. Unfortunately, he chose the wrong occasion.

The problem arose when Arguello and Khaled rushed to the front, terrorising the cabin staff with guns and demanding that they tell the captain to open the cockpit door. At that moment, the security guard was behind the bulletproof partition and unable to make use of his special gun. During a scuffle Arguello hit the steward, Shlomo Vider, on the head with his pistol and when Vider tried to retaliate the American shot him in the leg. After Bar-Lev was informed by the stewardess on the intercom of the grave development, he realised that only drastic action could remedy his earlier blunder. In order to throw the hijacker off

balance, he put the aircraft into a steep descent without asking ATC for clearance.

When during the dive Arguello was pushed down to the floor, Vider tried to grab him but he was shot in the chest and stomach. Leila Khaled also fell down and dropped her grenades on the floor. Luckily they did not explode. The Press later remarked that it was due to cheap grenades that came from Czechoslovakia. But the truth was that although Leila Khaled claimed she had removed the pins an investigation by the British police revealed it was not the case.

Several passengers jumped on the Palestinian girl and pinned her down. When the second security guard managed to reach the front, he pumped bullets into Arguello. The American was not killed outright but died later while on the way to hospital after landing.

Doctors, who happened to be travelling on board, examined the badly-wounded steward and advised the captain that an immediate blood transfusion was necessary to save his life. But before landing at Heathrow, Bar-Lev tried to contact his company on a long-range radio for specific instructions, as the orders were to bring hijackers to Israel at any cost – hence his request for another circuit. The so-called perfect security arrangements on board the El Al airliners had led to a bloody battle with one hijacker dead and one crew member badly wounded. Later Captain Bar-Lev was blamed for not adhering to the company's rules.

Once on British soil, Leila Khaled was under the jurisdiction of British law and she was detained by the police pending a trial on hijacking charges. But the PFLP were quick to retaliate by commandeering a BOAC VC10 two days later and forcing it to land at Dawson's Field. Khaled was eventually exchanged for the British passengers. Nine days later she gave a press interview in Beirut and had the insolence to claim that the shoot-out on board was the fault of the El Al crew because they refused to comply with her orders. Like many hijackers from the Middle East, she got away with her hijacking crime, scot-free.

The continuous lack of effective measures by governments to eradicate crime on board aircraft brought a new outbreak of terror, which also included several attacks on aircraft or passengers on the ground. The pilots' pleas or protests seemed to have been totally in vain. In 1972, driven to desperation, IFALPA made a final bid to bring the lack of ratification of the Tokyo Convention by numerous states to the world's attention. Captain Forsberg, the IFALPA

President at the time, called for a twenty-four-hour worldwide strike by all Federation members. Unfortunately not all were allowed to participate. Some governments threw the book at the pilots and threatened legal action if they joined the strike. Several airlines obtained a court injunction to prevent their crews from showing solidarity with their colleagues, among them most of the American carriers. This was a great surprise as one would have expected that they would welcome a worldwide action on hijacking. As IFALPA's protest was intended for the good of the air transport industry in general and every air traveller in particular, one could not help wondering who was one's worst enemy.

In my case as the initial architect of the worldwide pilots' action, it was a day to celebrate. Even if it meant arriving home a day later by being delayed in Rome. Unfortunately, I was soon shown how unsympathetic some members of the travelling public could be to the pilots' efforts in trying to stop air piracy. When the strike was over, I was walking across Fiumicino Airport to my aircraft when one of my passengers accosted me and began to give me a piece of his mind about our 'worthless' action, which had delayed his business for twenty-four hours.

Did the world short-change itself by playing down the pilots' efforts to stop crime on board? Could we have stopped the terrorists by showing more strength and by having been given proper support from the authorities and from the public? Those are difficult questions to answer. Many people in the air transport industry doubted the effectiveness of pilots as a pressure group. Just the same, in many cases even the terrorists recognised the pilots' moral power. An interesting example was that the members of the Lebanese Pilots' Association were the only negotiators allowed to enter the disused airfield at Zarqa and talk to the hijackers.

As a result of some irresponsible governments for years applying only half-hearted measures to stamp out the plague of hijacking, in the end all the airports had to be turned into fortresses and fortunes had to be spent on security. This has taken the lion's share of the funds badly needed for improvements of navigational and landing aids – something that was bound to have lowered safety standards.

But did turning the airports into fortresses stop the terrorists? It does not seem likely. With millions of passengers passing through the airports daily, it is easy to be one step ahead of the security arrangements. No fortress can be made impregnable, as two hideous disasters have proved, that of the French airline UTA DC10 and the PanAm 747 at Lockerbie.

As for solutions, are there any? One step is that no country should be allowed to offer terrorists a safe haven or give any support for actions against civil airliners. A government that does not comply with the letter or even with the spirit of international conventions to eradicate crime on board should be denied interstate air transportation.

But it took more than two decades before the United Nations decided to follow IFALPA's example of banning air services to an offending country as a means of pressure when all flights to Libya were suspended. Unfortunately, this decision was taken only after numerous lives were unnecessarily lost.

7

1968 – The Taipei Drama

PART I
THE BACKGROUND

On the evening of 16 February 1968 Captain Hicks reported at the Hong Kong Flight Operations of Civil Air Transport to take a flight back to Taipei. CAT was Taiwan's flagship airline, but was supported by American finance. Although Hicks was not designated as the pilot-in-command, he checked the weather forecast and other dispatch forms, as he was going to fly the CAT Boeing 727 that was shortly due in.

As airline practices go, this was a somewhat unusual arrangement. On paper, the company's Chief Pilot, Stuart Dew, had been assigned as the captain. But Hicks, as the Assistant Director of the Flying Division, was Dew's superior and had the authority to add his name to the crew list. This gave him a chance to keep his hand in flying. Neither of the two pilots considered it abnormal that Dew, even as the pilot-in-command, would occupy the observer's position while Hicks flew the aircraft from the left-hand seat.

Hicks came to Hong Kong with his wife two days earlier on company business combined with a short holiday. He had already flown the Boeing 727 on the way out with Dew as the captain, so the present routine was not new.

After the visit to Operations, Hicks called at the Air Traffic Control Office to fill out an ATC clearance form and then rejoined his wife in the airport lounge, waiting for the Boeing 727 to land. When the aircraft came to the assigned parking position, he went out to meet Dew, who, expecting the same arrangement as two days earlier, greeted him with, 'Go ahead and get the aircraft ready.'

A Chinese first officer, occupying the right-hand seat, was going to be Hicks's co-pilot. The flight engineer was also a Chinese. The three pilots were mature men with considerable flying experience but new to the Boeing 727, a recent acquisition to replace the ageing Convair 880.

Flight CAT 12 departed slightly late, but for the rest it was a normal routine. With the weather conditions on arrival expected to be overcast with light rain, an instrument letdown looked to be on the cards.

In poor weather, Taipei Airport was not one of the easiest places to come into. Although situated on a flat stretch of land almost at sea level, there were several high hills on the approach. Moreover, mountain ranges in close proximity extended to over 8,000 feet.

During the initial descent Hicks followed the route as designated on his flight plan until he converged on the ILS. Once established on the localiser, he came down to 2,000 feet, waiting to intercept the glide slope. When the Flight Director and the blue light of the Outer Marker indicated that it was time to commence a three-minute-long final approach, he lowered the aircraft's nose without realising how close he was to disaster. Sixty seconds later the Boeing 727 crashed and was completely burnt out.

From that fateful moment, both Hicks and Dew faced an ordeal that lasted a year. After a hasty accident investigation, the two American pilots were charged with manslaughter and put on trial.

THE PRINCIPAL CHARACTERS

Hicks, age fifty-one, the more experienced pilot of the two, began his aviation career before World War II. In his long years as an airman he amassed 22,000 hours. During the final stages of war he served as a flying instructor and upon leaving the service, he was offered a job with China National

Aviation Corporation. At first he flew 'The Hump Airlift' across the Himalayas. Then, as the struggle for power broke out in China, he took part in the CNAC operations launched to support the Nationalists against the Mao Tse-tung forces. He helped to evacuate wounded soldiers and dropped supplies to the cut-off units.

After the fall of Canton, the entire CNAC fleet was transferred to Hong Kong and Hicks flew out one of the aircraft. There he met Gloria Pritchard, a British-born Shanghai-raised girl. They were married in 1950. Throughout his married life he was known as a very devoted family man.

After a spell of training pilots for the Indonesian Air Force, in 1952 Hicks joined Civil Air Transport in Japan. In 1953 he was transferred to Taipei, which remained his home for sixteen years. During the Vietcong uprising against the French in Vietnam, he flew clandestine missions for the CIA. Such risky flights were undertaken only on a voluntary basis. Hicks believed it was his duty to help his country. When dropping supplies to the French units during the siege of Dien Bien Phu, his aircraft was badly damaged by enemy flak.

After the Geneva Armistice, he returned to the commercial operations in Taipei. In 1963 he was appointed as Assistant Director of the Flying Division, a job which involved more paper work than flying. Nevertheless, when arrangements were made to replace the Convair 880, he was the first CAT pilot to be trained on the B727 by Boeing in Seattle. He received an extended flying course of twenty-eight flying hours. Such a long course was only given to the management pilots. Before the B727 was introduced on the CAT international services, he flew for several months with Southern Air Transport, the CAT sister company, which operated charter flights for the US Army. During that period he flew 140 hours on the B727.

Hicks was regarded by his colleagues as a first-rate pilot and was known as 'Mr Precision' for his highly accurate instrument flying.

The captain officially assigned for the ill-fated flight, was Stuart E. Dew, aged forty-six. Upon completing his training with the Army Air Corps, he received his pilot's wings in September 1944 and was given a conversion to the C47 and the C46. He was then posted to a Troop Carrier squadron, operating out of Shanghai and Peiping. In the summer of 1946 he was selected to fly General Marshall when he came to China for the futile mediation between the Nationalists and the Communists. After leaving the service at the

end of that year, Dew joined CAT and after several years of flying the line, was eventually appointed as Chief Pilot. During his aviation career, he logged 20,000 flying hours, 5,000 hours on jets. Dew also had a reputation of a competent and a precise pilot. By the time of the accident, he had completed 104 hours on the Boeing 727.

Forty-five-year-old First Officer Pak-Him Wong (or Pak-Him Huang as he was referred to in various Chinese documents), a former medical student known within the company as Jimmy Wong, was a Chilean-born Chinese. He received his pilot training with China National Aviation Corporation in 1944 in Calcutta. He joined CAT in 1950 and by 1968 had amassed 17,000 hours. Although quite senior in the company and recognised as a reliable airman, he was shy and many captains regarded him as insufficiently assertive in his co-pilot's duties. His total of flying hours on the 727 was 108.

THE AIRLINE

Civil Air Transport was formed in 1946 as an American private venture in China. It was a brainchild of General Chennault, founder of Flying Tigers, and Whiting Willauer, a former US Government official who worked for the American aid to China during World War II.

CAT had a long history of ups and downs. The company was originally formed to carry supplies to the Chinese hinterland for the United Nations Relief and Rehabilitation Administration – UNRRA. This was in the early post-war days, when both road and rail transport could not cope with the backlog of American aid piling up in the seaports.

After fighting broke out between the Nationalists and the Communists, CAT, along with the Chinese Air Force, assisted Chiang Kai-shek's army in the civil war. When the Communists started to sweep southwards, CAT helped to evacuate 200,000 fleeing Nationalists to what was then known as Formosa.

After total collapse of resistance on the Chinese mainland, the new Communist rulers began to claim the ownership of the country's two principal air carriers, China National Aviation Corporation and Central Air Transport Corporation. At the time both airlines were based in Hong Kong. Just before the West recognised the new Chinese Government in Beijing, Chennault and Willauer persuaded Chiang Kai-shek to allow

CAT to take over the two airlines on behalf of the newly formed Taiwanese Government. The two Americans feared that if a fleet of one hundred transport aircraft fell into the Communist hands, it could be used for a paratroop invasion of Formosa. With the island lacking organised defence, this would mean the end of the Nationalists' resistance.

Nevertheless, as a result of a prolonged political and legal wrangle, the CNAC and CATC fleets remained impounded in Hong Kong and were left unattended for three years. The aircraft were eventually awarded to CAT but by that time many had deteriorated beyond repair.

In 1949 CAT began to operate passenger services out of Taipei with its own aircraft. When, due to poor loads, the airline's prospects looked bleak, the CIA stepped in and began to support CAT financially in order to preserve the US airlifting capacity in the Far East. But with the economic difficulties continuing to mount, a year later the CIA was forced to take over the airline fully. During Taiwan's crucial years as a newly established country, it suited the authorities to allow an American-backed airline to operate international services for Taiwan, in particular when most pilots were not of Chinese origin. The government constantly feared their own airmen deserting to the Communists and taking away valuable aircraft. A painful lesson had been taught when in 1949 the CNAC general manager defected to the mainland with twelve planes.

The outbreak of the Korean War brought a lucky break. General MacArthur accepted Chennault's offer to transport troops to Korea by CAT, and, as a result, some of the company's operations were transferred to Japan. When fighting with Vietcong intensified, the airline operated clandestine flights for the CIA to drop agents and supplies. With the expanding military involvement of the US in Vietnam, CAT became a part of an aviation conglomerate known as Pacific Corporation, whose various subsidiaries such as Air America, Air Asia or Southern Air Transport, were either fully or partly owned, but directly controlled, by the CIA in Washington. The president of Pacific Corporation was General Doole, a former PanAm Vice President, who upon retiring received the CIA's highest award.

After the Americans had withdrawn from Vietnam, CAT returned to purely commercial operations. Although through its widely advertised 'Mandarin Jet' services the airline was known as one of the most prominent air carriers in the Far East, it operated only a single jet on its international services, at first a Convair 880 and later the ill-fated Boeing 727.

In accordance with Taiwanese law, 60% of the CAT shares were supposed to have been held by Chinese interests and only 40% officially belonged to Air America. But it was on paper only. With the complex financial arrangements for financing the purchase of the B727 from SAT, it would not have been easy to determine the actual balance of the ownership.

THE AIRCRAFT

The ill-fated Boeing 727-92C was rolled out of the manufacturer's hangar in August 1966. After sixteen months of service with SAT, the aircraft was transferred to CAT and re-registered in Taiwan as B-1018 in January 1968.

In comparison with the demanding Convair 880, which the CAT pilots had been flying for seven years, the Boeing 727 was a docile aircraft to handle and more stable during instrument approaches. It had already been in service with many airlines for over four years and most of the initial problems had been ironed out. The main remaining criticism was slow spooling up of the engine turbines, which required seven to nine seconds from idle to full thrust. In combination with the high-lift devices which considerably increased drag in approach configuration, the Boeing 727 was prone to fast sinking if power was not quickly applied. To minimise the chances of an accident, the FAA recommended that full flaps were not to be used during instrument approaches.

The CAT B727 was fitted with the most advanced flight director at the time, the Collins F-108. It was also equipped with an autopilot capable of performing coupled approaches, which allowed Category II instrument landings.

TAIPEI SUNGSHAN AIRPORT

Taipei Airport had a bad reputation among pilots. Being located close to high ground and suffering from frequent poor weather in winter months called for reliable approach aids. Unfortunately most of the facilities were substandard. By the time of the accident, the ILS was twenty years old. It was an early military version, known as SCS-51. It was originally installed on an US Air Force base and later dismantled and transferred to Taipei.

By 1968 the ILS began to show signs of wear and tear. When in 1962 a typhoon hit Taiwan and the airport was flooded by ten feet of water, the entire installation was submerged for several days. After it was cleaned of mud and then dried, it was put back into service without any examination by the manufacturer, as it could operate within the prescribed tolerances. Until 1966 the US Air Force regularly flight-tested the ILS. When the inspections were taken over later on by the Taiwan Civil Aviation Administration, complaints from pilots kept trickling in that both the localiser and the glide slope signals often suffered from marked deviations.

Taiwan air traffic control was regarded by the pilots as inefficient. Near misses were the order of the day. But even if confronted with incriminating evidence, the controllers refused to admit their mistakes. Their knowledge of English was poor and they could only understand standard R/T phraseology. More complex queries from pilots were ignored.

THE ACCIDENT

The Boeing 727 took off from Hong Kong at 21.18 hrs local time. It crashed fifty-eight minutes later. At first, the aircraft touched down on a rice field at 740 feet above sea level, at a relatively flat angle of 2°. The position was 9.1 nautical miles west of the airport, exactly on the centre line of the runway. According to one survivor, the touchdown did not seem any different from a routine landing except for strong vibrations.

After rolling on a muddy field for 200 metres, the aircraft came off the ground. Unfortunately it struck first some trees and then a brick farmhouse on a small tea plantation, and fell back to the ground. After cartwheeling, it broke into several parts and caught fire.

One occupant of the farmhouse was killed. Three crew members lost their lives and eight were hurt. There were eighteen fatalities among fifty-two passengers; the rest sustained light to heavy injuries.

In his testimony, Dew described the tragic event:

'There was this moment of complete astonishment and then my thought was – "Well, we've hit the ground, this is it." Evidently we bounced back in the air. Hicks applied full power. I don't know whether it was instantaneous or in response to what I told him about

levelling off but I did know that he jammed the power on and then we started ripping through whatever it was and I thought we were finished. But I was completely astonished that we finally came to a halt and were all alive.

I hollered at Hugh to open the side window. He reached it and gave it a tug. It slid open and he heaved himself out. As I recall I thought I had completely lost my arm. I looked down and I tried to stick it out and only the very upper portion just below my shoulder was all I could see, the rest was just dangling. I reached over, grabbed with my other arm and hung on to it as I flung myself out of the window. There were flames all about and we just got away. I realised I was going to pass out and a couple of crew members made me sit down in the mud. It did not seem long before some sort of help came. They put me with some of the others into the back of a Chinese military weapon carrier and brought us to the County Hospital.'

The most tragic aspect of the crash was the death of Hicks's wife, to whom he was so deeply devoted. She perished in the fire. The trauma nearly broke him. He lost the will to live. According to his friends, were it not for the young children needing his care, he would have probably committed suicide.

THE ACCIDENT INVESTIGATION

The CAA appointed the Director of Flight Safety Section and the Technical Chief, as well as a controller from Taiwan ATC Centre, as the members of the investigating team. None had any training or experience in accident inquiries.

The CAA team arrived on the scene of the crash twelve hours after the event at ten o'clock next morning, although the site was easily accessible by road. They were joined by Doug Dreyfus, the CAT Flight Safety Supervisor and a former CAB accident inspector. According to Dreyfus, the CAA people had no idea what to do and had to be guided by him. Although they evidently lacked know-how, they were careful not to appear ignorant.

Contrary to the practices followed in many countries when the investigators assume control of the crash site, police took charge and nothing could be done without their permission. When the Flight Data Recorder and the Cockpit Voice

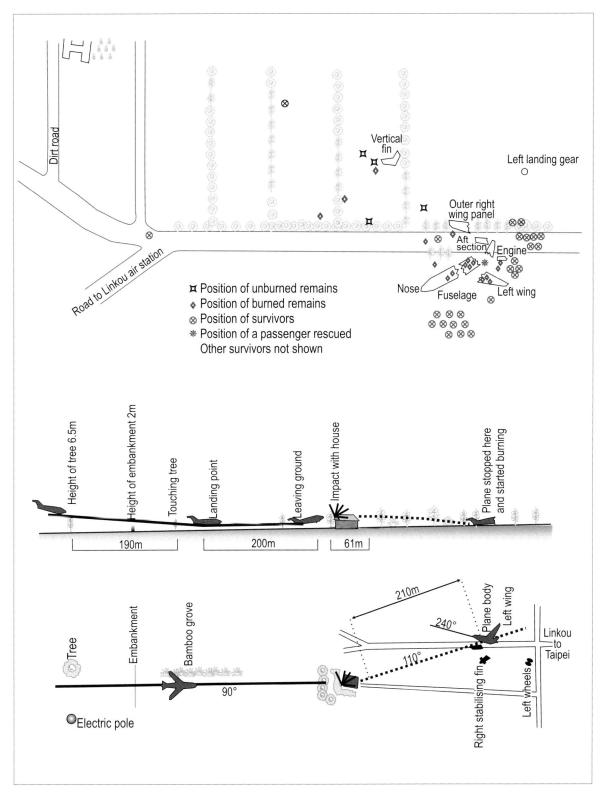

Diagram of the CAT B727 crash at Linkou, Taiwan.

Recorder were recovered from the wreck, the police impounded both units. They were released to the investigators only on a temporary basis for compiling FDR read-outs and transcribing CVR tape.

Four days after the accident the CAA team produced a preliminary report and the findings were finalised shortly afterwards during three meetings held on 21, 22 and 23 February. These meetings were also attended by officials from the Ministry of Communication and Transportation, CAA high-ranking personnel and representatives from CAT as well as from Boeing. At the final meeting, the conclusions of the investigating team were presented by the presiding chairman, the Director of the CAA, which were as follows. (As is customary in all accident reports, the language of the investigating authority, in this case Mandarin, was used in the official documents. The text quoted is the original unedited translation of the minutes prepared by a CAT employee. This was done for the benefit of the non-Chinese representatives from the airline and from Boeing.)

'Co-pilot Huang saw the warning light [Minimum Decision Altitude light on the radio altimeter] and notified Mr Hicks, according to the talk between Dew and Hicks recorded on the voice recorder. Judging from the information we have gathered, the accident was caused by the altitude of the aircraft which was too low. Any objections ? (No)

Then we shall conclude the following:
Mr Hicks has grown unfamiliar with piloting Boeing 727 and was careless, too. Between GM and LK [two beacons on the approach] he failed to maintain altitude, was too low to intercept the glide landing path (map included).

There is no doubt that the accident was caused by the mistake on the part of the pilot.'

It is evident from the minutes of the meetings that only the CAA personnel took part in the discussions because they were conducted in Chinese.

In part III of the CAA report under 'Analysis and Conclusions' the cause of the crash was assessed as follows:

'The pilot, Hugh Hicks, who was actually at the controls, failed to maintain proper altitude while approaching the Linkou outer marker and the aircraft was far below the required altitude; consequently the aircraft would not intercept the glide path. When the radio altimeter warning light came on, the pilot failed to take corrective action in time. The wheels touched the ground for about 200 metres. The aircraft was then pulled up in the air but it hit trees and a farmhouse and subsequently crashed. It was concluded that the accident was caused by careless operation in piloting the aircraft.'

The unwarranted haste and a lack of investigating expertise had resulted in a questionable assessment of the evidence. Although the report followed established practices, its general standard, and in particular, the graphic presentation of the FDR data, left very much to be desired.

Moreover, failing to flight-test radio aids after the accident, was not in accordance with the recommendation of the ICAO Manual on Accident Investigation. The CAA investigators claimed that no malfunctioning of radio aids had been reported: 'Six other aircraft had smoothly approached and landed at Taipei International Airport using the Instrument Landing System within a period of two hours before and after the accident. The accident was not due to any deficiency of the Instrument Landing System.'

To analyse the available evidence in eight days and to issue a report immediately afterwards, would have been considered in the Western world, as an extremely poor practice. Above all, obtaining a statement from Dew while in hospital still under sedation following an operation on his broken arm was against basic human rights. This raised an outcry from many CAT pilots.

But the CAA proceedings were not the only action that had been undertaken by the authorities. On the instructions of the Legislative Assembly (usually called the Executive Yuan, the highest policy making body in Taiwan, an equivalent of a Parliament in other countries) the judicial officials began to conduct their own inquiries.

The first person to be questioned by the Taipei Police Criminal Investigation Department was the co-pilot P.H. Wong. Unfortunately the record of the interrogation was poorly translated into English and, moreover, Wong was probably still suffering from shock, therefore his testimony bore many inconsistencies. Nevertheless, one statement was of particular significance. During the interrogation Wong was asked: 'You warned the captain at 1,900 metres and again at 1,600 metres. Since the aircraft characteristics permit pulling up in a second or two provided throttle is in open position, how was it that the plane which developed no mechanical malfunction couldn't be pulled up at 1,900–1,600 metres? [metres should have been feet]'

Wong replied: 'There wasn't enough time because of fast sinking.'

It was an important point that Wong never repeated in the course of the CAA investigation or at the trial.

During a press conference on 4 March 1968, presided by the Deputy Minister of Communication and Transport, the relevant parts of the final report were read out to the attending reporters. It was also announced that the licences of both pilots had been revoked and a copy of the report was forwarded to the Taipei District Court for further action. The CAA conclusions on the cause of the accident became a basis for manslaughter charges instituted by the Court against the two American pilots.

After a CID interrogation on 26 February, Hicks was told to limit himself to his residence. From that moment a policeman stayed permanently in his house. In practice this amounted to having been placed under house arrest. One source claimed that had it not been for the president of CAT, Hugh Grundy, who had close connections with many high ranking officials and who had pledged that Hicks would not leave the country before the trial was completed, Hicks would have been remanded in prison.

THE TRIAL

On 5 March 1968, Dew and Hicks were indicted on manslaughter charges arising from negligence that had resulted in the deaths of twenty-two people. The charges carried a sentence of two years in prison for Hicks and five years for Dew as being responsible for the disaster in his capacity as the captain. In addition, they could be heavily fined. Both were forbidden to leave the country.

To many people in Taiwan, the indictment came as a surprise. The unusual haste, only twenty-four hours after the CAA report had been made public, and the fact that criminal prosecution for involvement in an aircraft accident was the first case in Taiwan's legal history, initially drew comments of concern from the Press. Moreover, it seemed odd that the co-pilot had not been blamed in any way although from the CVR transcript it appeared that his warnings about not

China Post, June 1968

PAGE 2

China Post 英 文 中 國 郵 報

Publisher: NANCY YU-HUANG Tel. 543042-543043
Address: 8, Fu Shun Street, Taipei, Taiwan, China.
Cable Address: CHINA POST P.O. Box 2018.
Subscription rate: One month NT$50.00

社址：臺北市撫順街八號 電話：五四三○四二，五四三○四三
郵政撥劃八八○○

Be Calm

Jan Bartelski, president of the International Federation of the Airline Pilots Associations, reportedly said a few days ago that its members might boycott Taipei if Captains Hugh H. Hicks and Stuart E. Dew of the Civil Air Transport (CAT) were convicted by the Taipei District Court. Both American pilots were at the controls of the ill-fated Boeing 727 jetliner which crashlanded near Linkou on last February 16. Twenty-one of the 63 persons aboard the plane were killed.

As a matter of fact, the threat was made prematurely. The District Court has decided to hold another debate on the air crash case. It was originally scheduled to announce its verdict on last Monday. Besides, even if both American pilots were convicted, they would be able to appeal to a higher court against their conviction.

We know full well that some foreign pilots might be scared away if Captains Hicks and Dew were convicted. According to many legal experts here, if a pilot has committed an error which led to an air crash, the civil aviation law instead of the criminal law should be applied. The severest possible punishment stipulated in the civil aviation law is the revocation of a pilot's license.

The fact is that Bartelski's threat may be considered as interference with the Republic of China's internal affairs and as an infringement on its judicial independence. The reason is that the threat was made before the conclusion of the case. The Republic of China is an independent country and has its own laws. The two American pilots have been indicted and tried under the Chinese law because the accident occurred on the territory of the Republic of China. Whether that law does or does not conform to international practice is another question.

Furthermore, any such open threat made before the conclusion of any legal suit is tantamount to infringing upon judicial independence. It is true that no airline pilots have been held criminally responsible for their personal errors which led to air accidents. However, Bartelski cannot defend himself if he is accused of infringing upon the Republic of China's judicial independence for the simple reason that he made the threat before the conclusion of the case.

We hope the Federation will not carry out its threat even if the two American pilots were convicted because it is crystal clear that its members are not going to benefit from the threatened boycott.

having passed the outer marker were far from effective.

When Dew and Hicks were charged, the CIA, although reluctant at first, eventually agreed to provide legal assistance. Phillip Bostwick, a former US Navy pilot who specialised in air accident litigation and was a senior partner in a Washington law firm, was appointed as one of the defence counsel. As the court proceedings were to be conducted in Chinese, Dr Twamoh, Taiwan's most prominent barrister, was also engaged.

After a visit to Taipei, Bostwick became convinced that a fault in the ILS had most likely contributed to the crash. As earlier on he was in contact with the International Federation of Air Line Pilots' Associations over the PIA B720 accident at Cairo Airport (see chapter 4), he brought the possibility of an ILS deficiency to the Federation's attention. Especially since immediately after the ILS was flight-tested by an FAA inspection aircraft from Manila, it was declared 'out of service'.

It was no secret in Taipei that the decision by the District Court to prosecute Dew and Hicks had been approved by the highest judicial authorities, including the Minister of Justice and the Chief Judge.

The first hearing on 25 March was conducted in an agitated atmosphere. This was a result of a Press campaign which had aroused public opinion to a high pitch against Dew and Hicks. The two pilots were stoned and spat upon when they were entering the court. During the hearing, they were jeered by the spectators in the public gallery.

The prosecutor was given a free hand in his accusations. By mainly presenting the gory aspects of the crash, instead of pure facts, he intended to emotionally influence the three judges rather than to convince them of negligence allegedly committed by the defendants. One example was a continuous display of large photographs with the burnt bodies of the crash victims.

Although Dew and Hicks pleaded not guilty, they were not allowed to sit down during the entire court session, even though Dew was still not fully fit after an operation on his arm.

Two weeks later, the CAA ordered CAT to discontinue all international services. *Time* magazine alleged that behind the measure lay an ulterior motive to pave the way for the expansion of the government-backed China Airlines. The airline was only recently established by a group of retired high-ranking air force officers, who held influential posts in the Government. After the Malaysian authorities suspended China Airlines services to Singapore and Kuala Lumpur for under-cutting air fares, the officials began to look for an excuse to take over the CAT routes.

Although at the press conference the Minister of Communication denied any underhand moves, it was generally known that the Legislative Yuan had set up a special committee to look into the implications of the CAT B727 disaster. In the Yuan's opinion, the crash was due to poor management and consequently, the country's reputation had suffered badly. Moreover, many cases of discrimination were reported by the Taiwanese employees.

The anti-CAT feelings within the Government circles did not originate overnight. Already, after the first accident of a CAT C46 in 1964, when sixty-nine lives were lost, undercurrents began to run high against the American-backed air carrier. Many Kuomintang politicians (Kuomintang, National People's Party in Mandarin, was the ruling party headed at the time by Chiang Kai-shek) believed that in view of recent economic expansion and political stability, it was time for Taiwan to have its own flagship airline operated by local personnel.

In April and May, three more court sessions were held, again with the crowds jeering in the public gallery. The defence pleas over a possible deficiency of the ILS installation were ignored by the judge, who appeared to have been totally unfamiliar with aviation matters. The presentation of technical evidence was hampered by the court interpreter's poor knowledge of scientific expressions.

One of the American CAT pilots who was asked to testify on behalf of the defendants was appalled by the Chinese court procedures. It was impossible to convey to the judges anything of a flying or electronic nature. According to the pilot: 'It all looked like a scene from the film *The Naked Ape.*' The prosecutor treated Dew and Hicks like common criminals. During the last hearing on 20 May, the judge declared that the verdict would be announced on 27 May.

The progress on the case was regularly reported to IFALPA by its members who visited Taipei for the court hearings. Pressure began to mount on the Principal Officers to take a strong stand. During my flight to the Far East I was met in my capacity as the IFALPA President by several representatives from the regional pilots' associations and we discussed the possibility of boycotting Taipei Airport.

A decision in that respect was not easy. The two American captains were not members of any professional fraternity. They were not line but executive pilots in the service of CAT management.

Nevertheless other aspects dictated adopting firm defensive measures on behalf of Hicks and Dew. The accident might have been precipitated by deficient landing aids and experts were not allowed to examine them. The Court did not observe basic human rights. Moreover, with the moves behind the scenes to replace CAT by China Airlines, the two pilots appeared to have become pawns in a political game.

Above all, the impact of the trial on civil aviation authorities in other developing countries would have to be considered. IFALPA feared that the institution of criminal proceedings by unscrupulous governments against pilots involved in a accident, in order to cover up for their deficient aeronautical services, could escalate and quite a few pilots could find themselves behind bars.

The first hint that IFALPA contemplated a boycott of Taipei Airport appeared as early as 19 April 1968 in a Hong Kong publication, the *Asia Letter*. The news was probably leaked out 'on purpose' by the President of the Hong Kong Pilots Association. It was widely known that he felt strongly about defending the two American pilots at all costs. During his visits to Taipei, he did a sterling job in morally supporting Hicks, whose grief over the loss of his wife seemed to be endless.

IFALPA attached great importance to the court session scheduled for 27 May, during which the verdict was to be finally announced, and the Deputy President Captain O. Forsberg, a Finnish pilot, was sent to represent IFALPA. In addition, several members from the regional pilots' associations came to Taipei for that important day.

During his visit to Taiwan, Captain Forsberg met the Director of Civil Aviation and the Minister of Communications and Transport. Forsberg expressed IFALPA's deep concern over the superficial accident investigation and the conduct of the court officials.

The day of 27 May turned out to be of startling development. During the court session, without Dew and Hicks present but packed with 200 spectators, among them many foreign reporters, the presiding judge announced that 'the discussions on the case will be reopened'. This meant that no verdict would be passed now. When later questioned by reporters, the judge denied that some outside factors had influenced the Court's decision.

The following day, one of the three judges had been replaced due to his appointment to a post in Kaohsiung City Council, and as a result the trial was going to be started anew. Such a change of winds indicated how much the so-called independent judicial system in Taiwan was under the thumb of the ruling party.

'The 'outside factor' happened to be the IFALPA threat of boycott. Two days before the verdict was going to be announced, I was asked by the Dutch Press Agency if rumours about the boycott were true. My reply is best reflected in the Agency's press release which was printed in the Kuomintang organ the *Central Daily News* on 1 June:

'The Hague, Netherlands, May 25 (CNA-UPI): The President of the International Federation of Airline Pilots Associations (IFALPA) threatened today to "boycott" Taipei if two Civil Air Transport (CAT) pilots were convicted on criminal charges arising from a CAT crash on Feb.16.

They were the first airline pilots in history to be tried on criminal charges arising from a crash. The verdict is scheduled to be handed down on Monday in Taipei.

Jan Bartelski, president of IFALPA, said today his organisation plans to petition President Chiang Kai-shek of the Republic of China, to suspend court proceedings and reopen the investigation by civil aviation authorities.

He said that, "the investigation has not covered all possible grounds and was too short as it lasted only two weeks."

"Many points," he said, "were not looked into. Besides it was not proved the crash was the pilots' fault."

If Chinese authorities should not meet IFALPA's position and the two pilots were convicted, airline pilots "of course would obviously be afraid to fly into Taipei," Bartelski said, "and very likely they will boycott the place."'

On the same day a vitriolic reply to the threat by IFALPA was unleashed by the militant faction of Taiwan's Press in an article by the *China Post*, a newspaper published in English, under the title 'Be calm'. An extract is quoted:

'The fact is that Bartelski's threat may be considered as interference with the Republic of China's internal affairs and as an infringement

The China News

Independent   報 日 國 中 文 英   Objective

An Enlightened Public is The Best Security of A Nation

ol. 18, No. 328   Taipei, Sunday, May 26, 1968   8 Pages Today

Court Trial Of Air Crash Case Said Unprecedented

By prosecuting two Civil Air Transport pilots for the air crash last Feb. 16, the Republic of China has shattered all international precedents, a ranking civil aviation official said. He refused to be identified.

The common international practice is to revoke the license of a pilot if he is responsible for a plane crash, he said.

The Chinese prosecution has indicted Capt. Stuart E. Dew, 46, of Hamburg, Arkansas, and Capt. Hugh H. Hicks, 51, of Hannibal, Ohio, for manslaughter by professional negligence, which resulted in the death of 21 and injuries on 42 others on board Boeing 727 over Linkou, near Taipei last Feb. 16.

The two pilots have pleaded not guilty and blamed the Instrument Landing System, operated by the Taipei International Airport. The Civil Aeronautics administration defended tha the ILS functioning perfectly on the day.

As the Taipei Disctrit Court set to pronounce its sentence on the two defendants tomorrow, Jan Bartelski, president of the International Federation of the Airline Pilots Associations, issued a statement in The Hague threating to boycott Taipei if the two CAT pilots are convicted.

Bartelski said his organization plans to petition President Chiang Kai-shek of the Republic of China to suspend court proceedings and reopen investigation by civil aviation authorities.

He added that if Chinese authorities should not meet IALPA's petition and the pilots are convicted, airline pilots "of course would obviously be afraid to fly into Taipei and very likely they will boycott the place."

James Wei, director of the Government Information Office refused to comment further beyond saying that the position of the Chinese government is to leave the case entirely in the hands of the Chinese court.

on its judicial independence. The reason is that the threat was made before the conclusion of the case. The Republic of China is an independent country and it has its own laws. The two American pilots have been indicted and tried under the Chinese law because the accident occurred on the territory of the Republic of China. Whether that law conforms to international practice is another question.'

Surprisingly a week later, the *Central Daily News* came out with a conciliatory editorial, probably as a result of certain Kuomintang factions opposing the criminal proceedings and fearing possible economic consequences of a boycott (a translation from Chinese):

'An influential aviation expert pointed out that while a state has an independent jurisdiction over legal proceedings, there was yet no precedent, worldwide, of criminal prosecution of surviving pilots on the ground of pilot error. An IFALPA boycott, according to the expert, was once enforced against Liberia and lifted only after an open apology to the pilot censured for contempt of the Liberian President.

The same source indicated that air accident reports for the past fifteen years as compiled by the International Civil Aviation Organisation have attributed 40% of all major air tragedies, averaging twenty to forty a year, to pilot error. However, no surviving pilot was ever prosecuted, the most severe administrative action taken being licence revocation.

As to possible consequences of an IFALPA boycott, concerned airlines have revealed that there is little they can do if the pilots refuse assignments on safety grounds. IFALPA members have hinted that they would abide by the organisation's decision should boycott be declared.'

The reference to Liberia was not correct. No boycott was ever enforced against that country. Only a request to that effect came from the Rhodesian Pilots Association. The background of this incident is as follows: Captain Piet Tideman, a KLM pilot on a stopover in Monrovia, had been brutally treated by the State Security Police for allegedly insulting the Liberian President or his wife. But Tideman could not have been involved in any scene. A witness observed that the KLM pilot was not close enough to the President's party leaving the hotel where he was staying. Just the same, the authorities were reluctant to offer an apology

but instead, after protracted pressure, Tideman was given 5,000 US dollars in compensation.

In the following months, the wheels of Chinese justice kept rolling on but only very slowly. It took six weeks before the trial was reopened. It was conducted in a different atmosphere and without the hostile prosecutor. Dew and Hicks were no longer treated like reprobates. They were allowed to sit down and present their testimonies without interruption. Moreover, the court had agreed to the defence's request for an affidavit to be submitted by W. Ruh, an electronics expert from the US manufacturer of the ILS installation at Taipei Airport.

Eventually the court proceedings appeared to have come to a halt and, although the two pilots were still expected to remain in Taipei, the policeman had been removed from Hicks's house. Just the same, it looked as if 'the game of chess' between the Taiwan authorities and IFALPA still continued. The delay in the court proceedings lasted until the end of September.

Then disturbing news reached the Federation. The CAA would not allow Ruh to inspect the ILS installation, and some of the maintenance records were missing. On the other hand, Ruh had been given a chance to present his testimony in court and he stated that, from the evidence he was able to acquire so far, it appeared that the ILS was defective and could have contributed to the accident.

With no acquittal in sight, IFALPA decided to send Captain Forsberg again for the court hearing scheduled for 5 October. However, nothing of any particular importance had transpired during that session except that, side by side with the criminal proceedings, a civil action was heard which arose from a compensation claim by the family of a cabin attendant killed in the crash. If the two American pilots were found to have been negligent, the family was asking for a sum above that stipulated by law.

During his visit to Taipei, Captain Forsberg was interviewed by Chinese journalists with the militant reporter from the *China Post* present. Forsberg denied that IFALPA threatened a boycott and said that my statement earlier on to the Dutch Press Agency was only an indication of the pilots' mood in general. But in the editorial of the *China Post* on 12 October Forsberg's denial had not been mentioned. Instead, an article under the title 'Truth, Truth, nothing but the Truth', stressed that, regardless of the consequences for the CAA, the real facts about the ILS deficiency must be brought to light. This seemed a turnabout in the *China Post*'s militant attitude and an acceptance of the fact that IFALPA was justified in contemplating drastic action in the defence of the two American pilots.

Nevertheless, upon return from Taiwan, Forsberg stated in a report to the Principal Officers: 'I said time and again it was extremely unfortunate we were not able to handle this case without the threat of boycott coming out in the newspapers.'

In the following months Bostwick kept IFALPA up to date on the progress of the case, either by telegrams or by transatlantic phone calls. Two obstacles appeared to be in the way of Dew and Hicks' acquittal. One was the final settlement of civil claims and the second, finding a face-saving formula for the authorities. The CAA was concerned that, if the court did accept the ILS deficiency as a contributory factor to the accident, the Agency may have to face claims for compensation.

However, another tragic event had led to speeding up of the proceedings. On 2 January 1969 a DC3 of China Airlines, the ongoing 'darling' of the Taiwan authorities, crashed in the southern part of the country. All twenty-four on board were killed. The following day IFALPA received notification from the defence lawyers that the Taipei District Court had passed all records of the case to the Chinese Air Force (in all Government documents Taiwan was always referred to as China) for their opinion on the probable cause of the CAT accident.

The Court's action drew strong protest from the Federation in a letter to the Vice-Minister of Communication and Transport. IFALPA argued that in most countries an assessment from the military would not be acceptable to the civil aviation authorities. Moreover, if an outside agency was going to be involved in further proceedings, the Federation insisted on their own expert, a pilot with a degree in electronics, to be allowed to attend any new inquiry.

But even before IFALPA received a reply from Taipei, the Chinese Air Force presented their findings to the court convened on 17 January. The conclusions were compiled by Colonel Ying-lung Chow, a graduate of the aeronautical safety seminar at the University of Southern California. Chow studied in particular, 'visual illusions during instrument flying'.

The Chinese staff working for the defence counsel prepared the translation and it is quoted in its original form:

'...during complete darkness of night in cloudy and raining weather in the course of true weather instrument flying, Captain Hicks possibly developed some sudden visual illusions and unknowingly misread the instrument indications, thinking that he had flown past LK [Linkou beacon in the Outer Marker position] where in fact he had not, and should descend for a landing. Because of darkness and rain, he could not clearly see conditions outside and did not discover his error until after touchdown, when it was too late for correction and the accident ensued.

According to aviation physiology and aviation psychology, it is possible for pilots to develop illusions during true weather instrument flying. It is difficult for any experienced flyer having developed such an illusion to correct his error, thus giving rise to accident. This has occurred in military and civil aviation, in China and abroad. The illusion is a sudden physiological reaction. As the illusion is developed, even if the flyer has paid all possible heed, he could not help it.

Hicks said time and again that he lowered altitude on the misindication of an instrument light. This ties with the development of visual illusion, which caused him to mistakenly think of having reached the outer marker. He thus developed illusion impromptu, a sudden physiological reaction which nobody could help, and therefore cannot be held to have paid such heed as he could have.'

This was a masterpiece of a way out by which the 'wise' Chinese seemed to have appeased everyone, including IFALPA. On 20 January, during the last court session, the two American pilots were acquitted. Echoing the CAF report, the court declared that, as human errors were unavoidable in flying, Hicks should not be held responsible for his mistake. As far as Dew was concerned, he was not guilty of negligence because he gave Hicks a proper warning.

Finally the two men could go back home. Hicks had been through an agonising ordeal in losing his wife and being forced to look after three young children by himself. Adding insult to injury, during the early days of the trial his son was stoned by a local mob and bore a scar on his lip for ever.

On the conclusion of the trial, both Hicks and Dew expressed their deep gratitude in touching letters to IFALPA for the uncompromising stand. Hicks was particularly indebted to Captain Forsberg for the moral support he had received during the two visits. Similar efforts by many members from various pilots' associations in the Far East, who frequently attended the court hearings, were equally appreciated.

An unpublicised incident in the Taipei drama depicted the frustration experienced by some of the pilots connected with that case. When the acquittal of Dew and Hicks began to drag on, a Hong Kong based pilot, who shall remain nameless, but nevertheless whose identity was well known to the local pilots' circles, came to Taipei with a Convair 880. Just before taking off on the way back, he stopped in front of a small wooden hut, turned his aircraft round and with a mighty blast of his engines at full power, blew the hut to smithereens. Unfortunately the Airport authorities took a dim view of his outburst of temper and he was banned from flying to Taipei. As a result he was fired by his airline.

After the accident a book was published based on the ordeal of the two American pilots. It was a bestseller called *Band of Brothers*, written by Ernest Gann, a former airline pilot himself. He was invited to Taipei by his friend and old flying colleague Tom Boyd, at the time the CAT Director of Flight Operations. Gann was a well-known author of several aviation novels, some of which found their way into films such as *The High and the Mighty*.

Boyd believed that Gann's visit could generate favourable publicity for Dew and Hicks. He provided his friend with confidential documents on the accident but, once 'certain quarters' learned about it, a CIA agent raided Gann's hotel room and confiscated his papers. The outcome was that Boyd resigned from his managerial post in CAT.

Gann did not seem to have much luck with a factual account of the disaster and his manuscript was rejected by the publisher. In the end he was forced to produce a fantasised version, although some chapters did reflect the actual happenings.

Many years after the accident, an interesting account of moves behind the scenes to manipulate the trial came to light from a reliable Chinese source with close contacts to the Executive Yuan.

The Yuan's debates had clearly influenced the course of the court proceedings. Shortly after the accident, the Minister of Communication and Transport, Sun, who later became the Prime Minister, assured the members of the Yuan that 'a firm but a fair hand will be used to show the

foreigners that this time Taiwan would not let shortcomings in an important industry such as civil air transport, get by.' As a result, the Press, which was controlled by the Government, was allowed to crucify Hicks and Dew. But this had soon got out of hand.

The debates were invariably attended by two key figures. One was Chiang Kai-shek himself. Although he 'sat on the fence' over Hicks and Dew's case, in private he was against the prosecution. As a father figure, he always tried to assume the role of an impartial Speaker during discussions. The other dominant personality was his son Chiang Ching-kuo, a devout conservative. He advocated taking strong measures to protect the Chinese public from unsafe airline operations, regardless of the world's opinion.

At first, the threat of boycott had made an adverse impact on the debates, stirring Chinese pride and helping to unify the pro-conviction factions. It had also aroused anti-foreign feelings at all levels of the Government. But in time the shock that the worldwide pilots' organisation contemplated a refusal to land at Taipei Airport if the two American pilots were sent jail gave the 'sensible elements' within the Yuan a chance to argue, and with a progressive success, that IFALPA action could harm the booming tourist trade. Furthermore, it was not an international practice to indict pilots on criminal charges as a result of an accident.

In the end, commonsense did gain the upper hand and during the last debate before the court verdict was to be announced, an unequivocal decision was taken to acquit the two Americans. However politics dictated that it could not be done overnight. Time was needed to cool down public opinion. In addition, the delaying tactics by CAT to settle the compensation for the families of the deceased kept deferring the conclusion of the case. It appeared as if the CAT management in Taipei had little to say in such matters and all decisions were taken somewhere else. No doubt it was by the Pacific Corporation whose sole interest was to get out of commercial flying in Taiwan without undue losses. Once compensations were settled, only finding a face-saving formula remained. It looks certain that the China Airlines disaster had accelerated the 'way out' and in a matter of days, the court verdict was announced.

It is difficult to judge the trial proceedings by Western standards. Some evidence, such as the CVR transcripts, would have been considered inadmissible on the grounds of self-incrimination.

In Chinese courts the defendant is guilty until proven innocent. The two American pilots faced an unenviable plight. They were constantly harassed by a hostile prosecutor who later admitted to one of the defence counsels that he was convinced of their negligence. In his opinion this was the prime cause of the disaster and, as Chinese lives were lost, it was his patriotic duty to convict the two Americans.

The indictment of Dew and Hicks, which was based on the provisions of a criminal code principally instituted for cases of reckless driving, seems a Draconian way of administering justice. Although the Taiwan Press claimed that the CAT accident was the first ever case of initiating criminal proceedings against pilots as a result of 'negligence', the sad plight of Charles Billet, John Musselman and Ken Reynolds, seemed to have been forgotten (see chapter 4).

The attitude of the authorities as to how far an airman can be held responsible for the fatalities in a crash varies from country to country. But it had been eventually accepted in the Western world that in view of the complexity of aircraft operations, it would be difficult to demarcate the line between negligence and below-par performance.

Nevertheless, the Taipei drama seemed to be repeated six years later in Greece and it again aroused an outcry from the pilots' fraternities.

After a Swissair DC8 crashed at Athens on 7 October 1979 with the loss of fourteen lives, Captain F. Schmutz and his co-pilot M. Deuringer were sentenced in 1983 to five years, two months and sixteen days in prison (this appears to be a peculiarity of Greek law). Nevertheless, they were released on bail pending an appeal. Eighteen months later, their sentences were reduced to heavy fines.

The accident took place at night and in heavy rain. The aircraft touched down 700 metres beyond the threshold of runway 16. As it was very slippery at the time, the DC8 overran the runway and crashed into a ditch that had not been filled in.

In marginal weather, using runway 16 could prove tricky. In spite of complaints from IFALPA for many years, landing aids were inadequate and it was not possible to execute an instrument approach. Due to restrictions on overflying the city, the mandatory visual right-hand circuit had to be cut short. The only help to establish on final was a M/F locator and a VASI.

The fatalities during the DC8 crash were a result of the aircraft breaking up when it ran into the ditch. Yet the Greek civil aviation authorities chose to find scapegoats for the despicable standards of one of the busiest airports in Europe.

PART II

Even if the Taipei drama did satisfactorily end for the two American pilots, a question remained unanswered. What did really happen on that fateful night of 16 January 1968? Was it Hicks's fault or had an ILS malfunctioning caused the disaster?

With time on my hands after retiring from flying, at last an opportunity arose to look into the intriguing question. I soon learnt that not one but two more reports were compiled on the Boeing 727 crash. The two were prepared by Doug Dreyfus, the CAT safety inspector, and were intended for the company's internal use. One of the reports was eventually forwarded to the FAA in Washington.

Like the Taiwanese CAA investigators, Dreyfus blamed Hicks for the crash. In his report he claimed: 'The probable cause of this accident was the failure of the crew to properly monitor all instruments and follow prescribed procedures during an ILS director approach.'

Many years later he confirmed his opinion in an interview: 'It was a pilot problem, not an ILS failure. Hicks failed to establish passage of the outer marker. He then became hypnotised by a single instrument, the newly installed Flight Director and failed to scan his instruments.'

Although the Taiwanese investigators and Dreyfus may have regarded the Taipei accident as a case of an airmanship blunder compounded by the lack of Hicks's recent flying practice, from my research I arrived at different conclusions from those presented in the official reports.

My analysis had shown that some evidence about the crash had not been properly evaluated. Although this could have been expected from the inexperienced Taiwanese investigators, it comes as a surprise in the case of Dreyfus. He claimed to have attended 130 inquiries during his service with the NTSB as an air accident inspector.

The most surprising errors were found in the investigators' graphs of the ill-fated Boeing 727 flight path, which were prepared by Taiwan CAA personnel evidently lacking the necessary expertise.

A short explanation may be appropriate as to how a flight-path graph is constructed. Air positions are determined by the aircraft's headings and indicated airspeed, both obtained from the FDR read-out. IAS has to be converted to TAS according to altitude and temperature. Air positions are plotted backwards from the point of impact, generally at either five or ten-second intervals. In the absence of ground fixes, wind allowance must be applied to air positions in order to establish the actual flight path.

An examination of the investigators' graph revealed that it was just a plot of air positions based on indicated airspeed and not on true airspeed, as it should have been. For a letdown that was started at 5,000 feet, this represented a difference of one nautical mile, a significant amount for accident investigating purposes. But the most important fault in the plot was the lack of wind allowance.

A new graph was constructed with the help of a computer program (see Graph 1), using TAS for

determining air positions. Ground positions were based on the pilots' messages to ATC, recorded on the CVR, when passing radio beacons during the instrument approach. It may be argued that these positions may not have been accurately reported because the aircraft could have passed some distance away from the beacons. Nevertheless, evidence does exist that the Boeing 727 flew either directly overhead or very close to all navigational facilities.

The new graph, with plots of both a 'still air' flight path and an actual ground track, revealed a considerable divergence between the air and the ground positions in the last five minutes of the flight. This could have only been due to a sudden outbreak of strong wind. But such a possibility was ignored by the CAA investigators and by Dreyfus.

Further discrepancies in reconstructing the

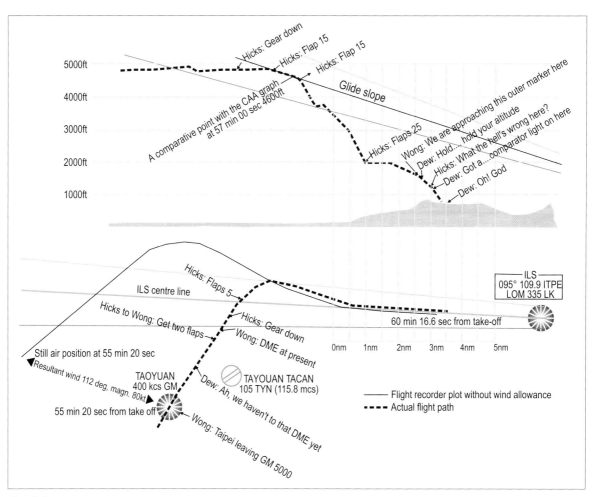

Graph 1.

events prior to impact came from an incorrect synchronisation of the FDR and the CVR time-bases by the Taiwanese investigators. According to Fairchild, the manufacturer of the recording equipment that was fitted to the ill-fated B727, these time-bases cannot easily be aligned in some circumstances.

On the Boeing 727 the two recording units were not connected to the same radio bus and, if during the crash electrical power to various buses was not interrupted simultaneously, the FDR and the CVR could have stopped operating at different times. As a result, the end of the recording could not be relied upon for matching the two time-bases. The only effective way was to define a datum, a 'key point', by which a certain action by the crew, reflected by their remarks recorded on the CVR, could be correlated with a significant change of the FDR parameters.

After numerous attempts to find a logical 'key point', eventually Hicks's call for 25° of flaps was selected. According to the ILS procedure for Taipei Airport, the call was expected to have been made upon leaving 2,000 feet when the aircraft intercepted the glide slope.

But an incorrect alignment of the time-bases did not appear to have been the only problem. My repeated tests indicated that the exchange of crew messages during the last twenty seconds of the CVR transcript, took longer than twenty seconds. That part of the recording appeared to have been, for some reason, compressed.

The accuracy of the CVR time-base can be verified with specialised equipment. A check can be performed by extracting traces of the 110 V/ 400 cycles current generated by the aircraft's inverter. The traces are invariably planted on the tape through leaks in the electric cables, which are never perfectly shielded. When the traces are compared with a laboratory-produced signal, it can be established whether the speed of a CVR tape during replay is correct. It seems surprising that the CVR recording of the ill-fated Boeing 727 cockpit conversation had not been sent to agencies capable of a scientific examination such as the US NTSB or the British AAIB.

Without a chance to have the CVR tape checked by experts, it was not possible to determine what could have caused the tape to shrink. The intense fire, to which the ill-fated Boeing 727 had been subjected, could have been one possibility. Although a special shield is supposed to effectively protect the CVR unit for thirty minutes from a fire at 1,000°C, the wreckage was burning

for much longer. With the loop tape used in CVRs, it can be expected that the section close to the recording head could have shrunk as a result of metal being a good heat conductor.

My analysis indicated that, due to an incorrect synchronisation of the FDR and the CVR, and the shrinkage of a small but vital section of the tape, the difference between my 'key point' and that of the investigators, amounted to twenty-one seconds.

When the twenty-one seconds difference was applied to the whole transcript of the cockpit conversation, at last certain crew actions or remarks began to concur with the aircraft's actual flight progress.

The examples were as follows:

During an ILS approach to Taipei Airport flaps extension to 25° was expected to take place at 2,000 feet on QNH and I used it as my 'key point', but the investigators marked it on their graph at 1,660 ft.

Wong testified that he warned Hicks at 1,600 feet about approaching the outer marker. The investigators' graph shows it at 1,380 feet. The twenty-one seconds correction puts it back to 1,630 feet.

Advice about levelling off, which Dew claimed to have given Hicks at 1,500 feet, is marked on the graphs at 1,100 feet. The corrected timing puts it back to 1,515 feet.

Hicks stated that he asked for the gear to be lowered on intercepting the one-half 'up' dot of the ILS glide slope signal and this is supported by the 'amended' correlation of the FDR and the CVR. But according to the investigators, the aircraft was never close to the glide slope.

Another error, which was hard to believe could have found its way into an 'official document', had been discovered in the investigators' graph of the vertical flight path. The angle of the ILS glide slope had been drawn at 3½° as opposed to 3° in reality. It is not surprising that the Boeing 727 descent profile, as shown on the graph, came nowhere near a correct flight path. Even if Hicks had performed a perfect ILS approach, this would have never been reflected on the graph.

Yet these 'official documents', containing many inaccuracies and errors, formed a basis for manslaughter charges against Dew and Hicks.

It is difficult to determine why the investigators had never made any allowance for wind. One possible reason was that they relied on information provided by the Taipei meteorologists, who claimed the wind to be light on final approach.

An account of the weather situation, especially prepared by the Taipei Weather Bureau for the investigation, gave the following picture on the night of the accident:

'1. The surface meteorological map at 2000 hours, 16th Feb shows: high atmospheric pressure at Siberia and Outer Mongolia extended towards South west; low atmospheric pressure was on the sea east of Japan; cold front extended southwest from this low pressure and formed a stationary front across the Bashi Strait to South China sea.

2. The 2100 hours Taipei International Airport weather report was: cloudy with light rain, ceiling 2500 ft, horizontal visibility 4 miles, surface wind, easterly/13 kt; temperature 12°C; dew point 10°C; QNH 30.17 in Hg; rainfall 0.2 mm.

3. The upper wind analysis in the Taipei area based on the 2000 hours en route cross section was: from surface to 500 ft, easterly/10–15 kt; above 10000 ft, south-westerly wind/15–20 kt; only above 18000 ft did the wind speed increase to 60 knots.

4. The 2000 hours high altitude temperature and humidity report at Taipei made by the Taiwan Weather Bureau was: from surface to 5000 ft, cold polar air mass; above 5000 ft, warm advection.

5. Turbulence analysis: On the afternoon of 16th Feb 1968, there was neither thunderstorm nor cold front passing. With respect to air mass analysis, the cold air ran under warm air, and no significant instability was observed. The air current was advection. The lower level wind speed was well below 25 knots, unlikely to cause any turbulence.

According to the above analysis, weather factor was irrelevant to the 727 accident.'

As the so-called analysis appeared to have been just a repetition of a routine assessment of the weather situation on the night of the accident, a check was made on the wind pattern in the last thirty minutes of the flight with the help of the FDR data. This showed that the Boeing 727 had run into a 166-knot north-westerly jet stream over the Taiwan Straits, just before it had left cruising altitude. The existence of such a strong wind was not mentioned in the analysis by the Taipei Weather Bureau.

The check had further shown that, during initial descent, the wind was close to what had been claimed in the official analysis. But the most significant discovery, which could have accounted for the large divergence in the air and the ground positions, was that after leaving 5,000 feet the aircraft encountered – for the next five minutes – an eighty-knot-strong, low-level jet stream from the direction of 112° (M). This was confirmed by the fact that it took much longer to decelerate to the recommended approach speed due to running into such a strong wind (see chapter 1).

According to the information received from Boeing, in level flight at 5,000 feet with power off in clean configuration, the Boeing 727's airspeed was expected to decay at a rate of 1.24 knots per second. The resultant decrease during the fifty seconds attempt to slow down should have amounted to sixty-two knots. According to the FDR readout it was only twenty-seven knots (from 265 to 238 knots). There could be no question of the throttles not having been fully closed. Hicks, Dew and Wong had confirmed it in various statements.

Two factors most likely contributed to the formation of the low-level jet stream. One was a sharp temperature difference at 5,000 feet between cold air under-runnings a warm sector. The second was the katabatic effect from a valley that was situated between two ranges of mountains with the peaks extending to over 8,000 feet. It is significant that the direction of the low-level jet stream was the same as that of the valley.

Two years before the Taipei disaster, an article in *The Daily Telegraph* under the title 'Boeing 727s not to be grounded by US', highlighted a probability of strong winds having contributed to several unexplained accidents. The relevant extract is quoted:

'Investigators looking into the causes of the crashes [from baffling rapid descents] have been considering a meteorological phenomenon known as "low-altitude night jet stream". This is caused by cold air from nearby mountaintops descending to ground level some ten to perhaps hundred miles on the leeward side of the mountains.

Meteorologists say that these streams reach velocities from 30 to 60 mph and have been known to touch 100 mph. Sometimes, it is said, the streams are only a few yards wide.'

My research indicated that the low-level jet stream near Taipei was about five nautical miles wide, stretching from the GM beacon to the crash site.

The actual weather on the ground also appears to have differed from the information provided by the Taipei meteorologists. According to a witness, at the 750-foot-high plateau where the accident took place and only nine miles away from the airport, the ceiling was only fifty feet and visibility virtually nil.

Graph 1 (page 174), based on a computer analysis, shows an entirely different picture of the aircraft's horizontal and vertical flight path from that presented by the CAA investigators. It reveals that Hicks followed the ILS procedure correctly, although the investigators regarded it as inconsistent.

The FDR data reveal that, after leaving 11,000 feet, Hicks had to descend fast in order to cross the GM beacon at 5,000 feet as cleared. Consequently he came over the beacon at 295 knots. This was rather high at that stage of the approach. After taking up a heading of 50° (M) from the GM beacon to intercept the 95° (M) ILS beam at an angle of 45° Hicks kept the throttles fully closed in order to decelerate as quickly as possible for the final approach. At first, speed reduction conformed to the expected rate, but upon encountering the low-level jet stream, the rate markedly decreased. At the same time, the Boeing 727 had been slightly blown off the intended track. The heading of 50° (M) should have taken it directly over a TACAN station at Taoyuan Air Base.

Although TACAN was a navigational aid for exclusive use by US and Western Air Forces, as it shared frequencies with the civil DME installations it was possible to obtain a distance read-out on the VOR/ DME receiver that was fitted to the Boeing 727.

The CAT pilots were quick to learn that Taoyuan TACAN could be used as an indication that the ILS localiser would be shortly intercepted. But at the same time, they were aware that some TACAN stations were not co-located with other navigation facilities such as M/F beacons, as was the case of the GM beacon and Taoyuan TACAN. This was revealed by the CVR transcript of the cockpit conversation:

'Hicks: 'You never know whether to trust these damn ADFs or not.'
Hicks, shortly later: 'Notice you guys sort of lean on your DMEs.'
Dew: 'We're learning to, Hugh, and they're new toys with us. They are not co-located.'

It is further evident from the CVR transcript that the crew kept an eye on the DME indications from Taoyuan TACAN. Nevertheless, as a result of a sudden outbreak of strong wind, the overhead passage must have been somewhat delayed and Dew warned Hicks: 'Ah, we haven't quite got to that DME yet.'

However, the CAA investigators ignored the implication of the warning, as if unaware of the existence of a TACAN station at Taoyuan. Nevertheless, it is shown on the area navigational chart valid for the period that covered the accident. Dew's warning is a confirmation that the Boeing 727 was passing close to the TACAN station and not several miles to the north-west as was shown on the investigators' graph.

The unexpected slow deceleration after passing the GM beacon must have put Hicks under pressure. To reduce the speed as quickly as possible, he asked for the initial flap extension of 2° nine knots above the stipulated limit of 230 knots.

Shortly afterwards, Wong advised Hicks, 'DME at present time', and then, in a matter of seconds, the aircraft converged not only on the localiser but at the same time on the glide slope. This prompted Hicks to ask for the landing gear to be lowered. In the CAT report, he gave an account of his action: 'We got the raw data [the ILS localiser and glide slope indications] to show ahead and above and I asked Jimmy for gear down.'

But in his report, Dreyfus criticised Hicks's action as out of sequence. According to the laid down procedure, flaps should have been extended starting with 2°, 5°, 15° and then upon the glide slope interception the gear should have been lowered, followed by 25° of flaps. Nevertheless, Mark Kentwell, a Boeing 727 Ansett–ANA captain, was of a different opinion:

'We often used the gear out of sequence for faster deceleration (max. ext. speed 270 knots) if we allowed ourselves to be tight on ILS by approaching the descent point too fast. The B727 2 deg. and 5 deg. maximum extension speeds – 230 and 215 knots – are relatively low for circuits and these flap setting give little drag. As on many smaller airports we had no 10,000 feet/250 knots speed limitations and quite often held 300 knots plus to within 15 miles, for a straight-in approach on the ILS.'

Despite the claims by the Taiwan CAA investigators to the contrary, Hicks actually intercepted the glide slope at 5,000 feet and followed it for about a minute. (See Graph 1 on page 174.)

The chain of his predicaments began upon completing the turn to intercept the ILS localiser, when the pitch command of the Flight Director suddenly displayed a signal to go down. The out-of-line indication could only be attributed to an abnormal precession of the attitude gyro. This had been probably aggravated by a long procedure turn, and by a 'ballooning' when 15° flaps were extended. (The latter was recorded on the FDR.)

The resultant discrepancy between the indications of the captain's and the co-pilot's horizon must have been more than 4° for a warning light to appear on the Comparator Panel. This had eventually attracted Dew's attention. But he did not regard the fault to be serious as he later recounted in the CAT report:

'...we proceeded normally, descending and reducing speed and started the flaps down, gear down and I knew we were getting close to the outer marker. At about that time, I did notice the Comparator light. This was the Comparator light on the vertical gyro pitch on both the co-pilot's and captain's sides, and I started scrutinising these instruments very closely to see how much deviation there was. I didn't say anything and I didn't hear Hugh or the co-pilot Jimmy mentioning these things, but I was watching them very closely and I wasn't going to bother any of the pilots if it was still in the ball park, which it was. I could see a little variation, I don't remember which

one was up a little more. It didn't appear to me to be more than two to three degrees pitch spread in these instruments. I didn't feel like it was worth bothering them about it.'

According to Mark Kentwell, malfunctioning of the attitude gyro could lead to difficulties when using the Flight Director during an instrument approach: 'A 4° pitch error would have a considerable effect on a Boeing 727. For example, at 6° up body-angle with 15° of flaps, the aircraft can fly level at 150 knots. At 2° body-angle, with same weight and configuration, the aircraft can only fly level at 190 knots.'

The fault in the attitude gyro had been previously reported to the CAT technical staff. But this information only came to light *ten years* after the accident, when Ward Reiner recounted it in a letter:

'I was the Chief of Maintenance [of CAT] at the time of the crash... There was one item on the logbook when Doug [Captain D. Smith] had come in from Tokyo [Captain Smith flew the ill-fated Boeing 727 to and from Tokyo on the afternoon of the accident and then the aircraft was taken over by Dew on the way to Hong Kong] that the gyro horizon was precessing – nothing dangerous, so we held it

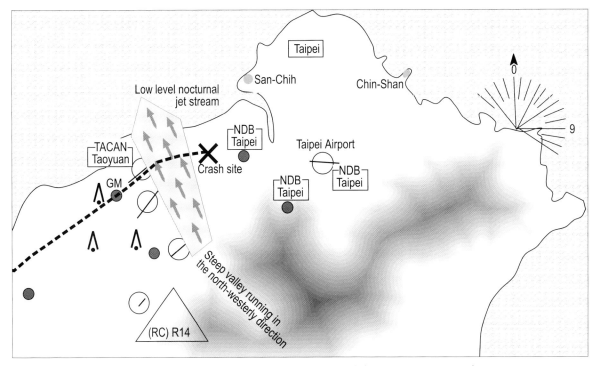

Diagram of the probable nocturnal low-level jet stream in the vicinity of the Taipei International Airport.

to the "overnight service" due on the HKG-TPE return trip (it crashed).'

Unfortunately an incorrect FD signal resulting from a fault in the attitude gyro had triggered off adverse consequences. It can be seen from the FDR read-out that to comply with the FD 'fly-down' command, Hicks responded by pushing the control column hard forward, which was reflected in a reading of 1.2 negative g. Then upon reaching the lower edge of the glide slope, he levelled out for twenty seconds. This would have been consistent with the program in the FD computer which instantly sends a strong overriding input, in order to stop the aircraft from further dropping below the glide slope. (See Graph 1 on page 174.)

What had followed is a matter of conjecture. The badly precessing gyro could have again upset pitch signals, forcing Hicks to continue descending. On the other hand it is also possible that after several erratic FD commands, he decided to come down to 2,000 feet and wait to intercept the glide slope. This would have been in accordance with the laid-down ILS procedure.

When, upon levelling out at 2,000 feet, Hicks maintained that altitude for twenty seconds without any variation, it looks certain that he was relying on the Altitude Hold mode. The Flight Director must have been set earlier on to the Glide Slope Auto mode, as it is evident from his statement in the CAT report: '...turned the mode select to glide slope auto, descended to 2000 feet and kicked on the hold.'

But Dreyfus claimed that Hicks did not use the Glide Slope Auto mode or Altitude Hold at all, and started his descent from 2,000 feet purely on the FD pitch command, believing that it contained the glide slope signal. With a lack of such input, Dreyfus argued, Hicks descended too steeply and struck the ground. This was based on the presumption that the aircraft had never intercepted the glide slope. Nevertheless my analysis had shown it to be to the contrary.

What had followed from 2,000 feet down, is best described by Hicks's own words:

'I remember changing power to hold altitude and we got the blue light. [The outer marker signal] When we got the blue light, we had a deflection on our flight director (yellow bird as we call it) and I didn't like the looks of it, so I didn't want to follow it. I was hedging on it, fearing that there might be something wrong, it might not be positive enough and I was letting it drift gradually.'

When Hicks left 2,000 feet under the impression that the blue light and intercepting the glide slope beam had denoted passing the outer marker, in fact he had still six miles to go. Equally, Wong appeared to have been under the same impression and in his testimony he stated that, after noticing the ILS glide slope pointer moving towards the centre, when he was asked by Hicks to extend the flaps to 25° he did it without hesitation.

Although what the crew had observed on the ILS indicator may look questionable, an incident that took place three weeks after the crash adds credibility to their testimony.

Captain Botthof, a PAA pilot, flying a Boeing 707 to Taipei on a clear day, decided to make a practice ILS approach. According to his affidavit presented to the Taipei District Court, he put the aircraft on autopilot and coupled it for an automatic approach. After descending to 2,000 feet, he switched on the Altitude Hold mode, waiting for the glide slope signal to come in view. But when the pointer began to centre, it was evident from the landmarks below that he was nowhere near the outer marker. Moreover, the Automatic Direction Finder needles were still 'hunting' and did not point straight ahead. On the other hand, the glide slope signal was steady and no ILS warning flag appeared. But what had followed did not seem the usual routine. Although the Flight Director gave a 'fly-down' command, to Botthof's surprise, the autopilot did not respond to the glide slope interception and did not initiate a descent. As during his previous approaches on that day everything had functioned satisfactorily, the abnormal indication on the FD could only have been attributed to a fault in the ILS transmission.

Had the approach been executed without any visual reference, the abnormal glide slope signal would have been, in Botthof's opinion, a serious safety hazard. As a result, he reported the incident to the CAA in writing after landing at Taipei Airport. He also filed a report with the PAA Chief Pilot and instructed the maintenance staff to check the airborne equipment. But it was found to be in order.

Why the investigators or Dreyfus had never taken the possibility of a false glide slope, which could have misled the Boeing 727 crew, into consideration is a mystery. For it is widely known that early versions of glide slope transmitters could produce 'ghost' signals.

According to the information received from the Royal Aircraft Establishment at Bedford, the home of the Blind Landing Experimental

Unit, spurious glide slope signals at high angles were invariably present in the 'null-reference' type of ILS installations, common in the post-war years. In the case of a 3° glide slope, a 'ghost' signal would sometimes show at 6°, but they would mostly occur at 9°. In respect of abnormal signals below the glide slope, the RAE offered the following comments:

'With certain glidepath installations which have more antenna elements than the conventional null-reference type (e.g. the so called M-array), it is possible to produce a false glidepath below 3° if the ground in front of the glidepath is not sufficiently flat. By special adjustments during setting of these installations, any low spurious glidepath can be usually suppressed.'

With a 3° glide slope, such 'ghost' signals can be expected to show halfway, that is at around 1.5°. From Graph 1 on page 174, it can be seen that the ill-fated Boeing 727 had probably picked up a false glide slope at 1.6°. Two possible factors could have contributed to its occurrence – an 830-foot-high hill on the approach or a barbed-wire fence on the perimeter of the airport. After the accident the fence was quickly replaced by wooden railings.

It is interesting to note that the CAT Boeing 727 and the PAA Boeing 707 were both equipped with ILS receivers for Category II operations. The six aircraft that had landed around the time of the crash relied on much older and less sensitive sets.

Hicks's claim that he had observed a blue light on the outer marker indicator may look on the surface like a product of his imagination. Nevertheless, a CAT pilot testified that he had also seen the same signal when he was passing over two different sites west of Taipei, one of which was at Linkou where the ill-fated aircraft crashed. Four other pilots claimed that their outer marker indicator flashed-on every time they flew over what looked like 'an antenna farm' near the PO beacon at Hin-shu.

The electronics experts were in agreement that such spurious signals could have been generated by ground radar. The ILS specialist Ruh explained how it was possible for an airborne receiver to be activated:

'Although marker receivers do operate at one frequency of 75 M/Cs using 400 cycles modulation and have rejection filters to increase the selectivity, strong harmonics from high power radars modulated at 400 cycles could cause false indications if an aircraft were low enough

and in the general proximity of the beam.'

At the time Taiwan bristled with numerous 'early warning' stations, particularly in the north-western approaches facing the mainland of China. Some of these stations assisted U2 spy flights by the Taiwanese Air Force out of Taoyuan Air Base. A powerful radar was known to operate in the Linkou area.

When, thirty-five seconds before the crash, the aircraft was passing 1,600 feet, the co-pilot, Jimmy Wong, suddenly exclaimed, 'We are approaching this outer marker here.'

When queried about his remark, he told the investigators he tried to bring Hicks's attention to the fact that they had not yet passed the outer marker. It seems to have been a confusing way, considering that in his last two radio messages, first to the Approach Control and then to the Tower, he repeated, '2,000...we are approaching outer marker'.

What had motivated Wong to give Hicks a half-hearted warning is not easy to determine. His version, as he told the investigators, was as follows:

'During this period I knew that we had not reached LK [the outer marker M/F locator] because looking at my watch I knew that insufficient time had passed since we left the GM beacon. For that reason I warned Captain Hicks twice to maintain his altitude.'

Nevertheless, his claim about the time factor could not be substantiated. Calculations indicated that it would take just as long from the GM beacon to the outer marker at the groundspeed experienced during a normal approach (about 140 knots), as on that particular occasion from GM to impact over a much shorter distance (about 6 nm) but at a much lower ground speed of 90 knots.

In my opinion, the reason was different. Wong must have noticed all of a sudden that the ADF needles no longer hunted but were pointing directly ahead. Frequent problems with the erratic reception of the M/F beacon at the outer marker position stemmed from the limited distance at which it could be effectively received. In the Taiwan Air Information Publication the beacon was listed as a low power facility with only 5 nm nominal range. Bad atmospheric conditions and the mains voltage being affected by heavy domestic consumption on a cold winter night could have easily reduced that range. Wong had uttered his warning when they were about four miles from the beacon.

It must have been difficult for him at that moment to determine which of the indications was correct. In the space of one minute, he was confronted with two conflicting clues about their position. At first, intercepting the glide slope had pointed to having passed the outer marker. But shortly afterwards the ADF had contradicted it. Perhaps still confused, he muttered out as if to himself, 'We are approaching this outer marker here'. But in his affidavit to the court, he claimed that he had warned Hicks twice – the first time at 1,900 feet and the second time at 1,600 feet. There is no evidence on the CVR of any warning at 1,900 feet.

Eleven seconds after the so-called warning from Wong while the aircraft was passing 1,500 feet, Dew was the first person in the cockpit to observe that the ILS G/S indicator was showing the aircraft to be below the glide slope. But being under the impression that they had passed the outer marker, Dew was not alarmed. He knew that, after leaving the 630-foot-high hill behind, on which the outer marker transmitter was located, they had ample clearance from the ground below.

As the CVR revealed, in a voice devoid of any anxiety he said to Hicks: 'Hugh.'

Hicks: 'Yeah.'
Dew: 'Hold... hold your altitude.'
Hicks: 'I think we're low, aren't we.'
Dew: 'Yeah.'

Although the investigators, as well as many people in Taipei, believed that the rapid loss of height on final was due to Hicks's misuse of the Flight Director and his lack of recent practice on the Boeing 727, my computer analysis indicated that the most likely factor that had caused the Boeing 727 to prematurely strike the ground was wind shear, perhaps in combination with a powerful downdraught generated by the low-level jet stream.

The conditions for this dangerous weather phenomenon were evident. The average wind from GM to impact was calculated to have been 112/80 knots, but it was probably stronger away from ground friction. With a light wind reported at Taipei Airport, it can be expected that a shear – as much as forty knots – could have occurred between 1,500 feet and the point of impact at 734 feet. This would have presented a death trap for a Boeing 727 in approach configuration.

During the first twenty seconds after leaving 2,000 feet, the rate of descent was about 700 ft/min. This was as to be expected on a 3° glide path. But in the next forty seconds the sink became catastrophic. After passing 1,500 feet, the rate dramatically increased to about 1,400 ft/min and the Boeing 727 was rapidly closing on a 750-foot-high hill. At 1,350 feet the sink reached the highest rate of 2,300 ft/min over five seconds, more than three times the normal rate. On the other hand, all the way from 1,800 feet the airspeed remained constant at 150 knots. Only ten seconds before the impact it dropped down by five knots but in the next five seconds, it rose to 157 knots, possibly due to the 'outflow effect' of the vertical current. This appeared to have been a repetition of the circumstances surrounding the B720 accident at Cairo Airport.

In his testimony, Wong described the final moments before the impact:

'I don't recall seeing a comparator light come on in the cockpit before the crash. I do recall seeing the minimum altitude (MDA) light [during the approach check list the Radio Altimeter was set to 350 feet]. I did not say anything to Captain Hicks when I saw the MDA light because he had already applied full power to all three engines before the light came on.'

Had the circumstances been normal, there should have been no difficulty in arresting the sink, in particular after Hicks pushed the throttles fully forward. According to Boeing, with a 25° flap-setting, only half of the power increment was necessary to stay level compared to that in the case of 40° of flaps.

When the Comparator lights suddenly came on shortly before impact, Hicks queried the surprising development in an agitated tone of voice: 'What the hell's wrong here?'

At the same time, he pulled the aircraft's nose abruptly up, with a force of 1.07 g. Dew came back with a swift explanation: 'Got a... Comparator light here'

Whether or not a Comparator light did come on, had never been established during the investigation. This was another example of how superficial the proceedings had been. When I contacted Dew and Hicks on that matter in 1979 neither of them was able to throw any light. Both claimed that too much time had passed for clear recollections.

But from putting oneself in the shoes of the CAT crew, one possibility is evident. The only red lights on the Comparator Panel that could have alarmed the pilots was the ILS failure indicator.

Although at that moment, the aircraft was passing 1,100 feet, it could have already descended below the line of sight from the glide slope transmitter. This could have been due to a hill that lay directly ahead, blanketing the reception.

Although in the last few feet above the ground the angle of descent was far less steep, the frantic application of power came too late and the wheels touched a rice field, situated 3.8 nm from the outer marker.

The last words on the CVR – 'Oh God!' – were spoken by Dew when he suddenly realised what had happened. As he explained in a letter many years later, it was his reaction to accepting that meeting his Maker was inevitable.

From the available evidence it was not possible to determine whether, apart from the 'ghost' signal not having been properly suppressed, the glide slope was otherwise unsafe. After the trial Ruh claimed that the ILS installation was not a 'killer' but it was 'sick'. It was like an old decrepit radio set which could still play but with strong distortions.

William Henning, from the FAA flight testing unit stationed in Manila, who periodically came to Taipei to help the Taiwan CAA personnel with the calibrations of the ILS, often found the localiser or the glide slope transmitter out of tolerance and would instruct the local staff how to rectify it. However, during a test, which was carried out on the request of the FAA in Washington a month after the accident, he could no longer adjust the glide slope. As a result, the usually friendly CAA people at the airport gave him, this time, the 'cold shoulder' treatment.

The purpose of such a detailed description of the last vital five minutes of the tragic event is to convince the reader that pilot error, which was claimed to have been the cause of the accident and

was the reason for manslaughter charges, was a conjecture without any clearly substantiated grounds.

A pilot is expected to cope with one malfunction or one emergency at a time, but with three in a row, that is a badly precessing horizon gyro, a false glide slope indication and wind shear, the odds were too high even for 'Mr Precision', as Hicks was known within CAT. In spite of the insinuation that he was 'rusty' in flying the Boeing 727, according to Mark Kentwell who was familiar with the high standards of flight checks by Australian Department of Transport, the accuracy of Hicks's instrument flying on the night of the accident appeared to have been well within the Australian D of T limits.

On the other hand, many pilots I discussed this case with, were of the opinion that Dew, as a captain, was at fault for allowing another pilot to handle the aircraft without himself occupying the co-pilot's seat, which would have given him instant access to the controls. But to indict the two Americans on criminal charges as a result of an incompetent investigation was criminal in itself.

When interviewed many years after the accident, Dew claimed that he could have possibly averted striking the ground had he been flying the aircraft himself. But he was not aware that the cause of the catastrophic sink was most likely wind shear or unusual downdraught.

Finally, credit must be given to the Taiwan authorities in one respect. A few years after the tragedy at Linkou, the old Sungshan Airport was replaced by a modern super-airport, equipped with the most up-to-date radio aids, including a Class III ILS. The new airport was built on the coast, away from the city and the hilly surroundings. It was named after *Generalissimo* Chiang Kai-shek.

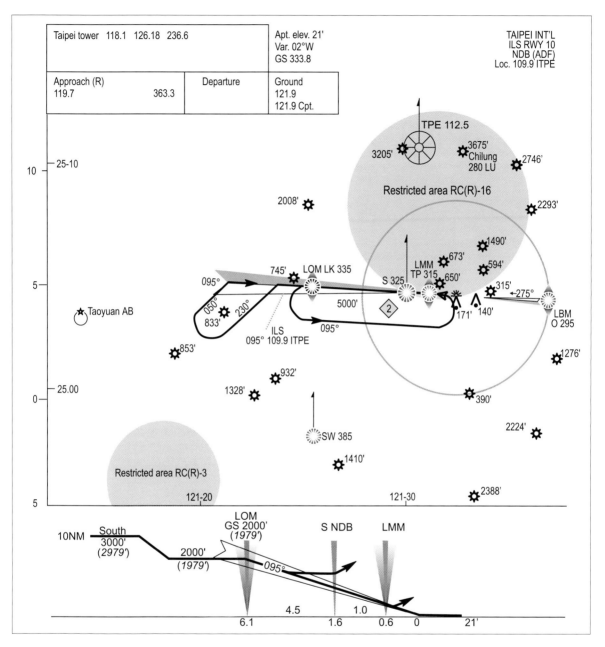

Approach chart for Taipei International Airport valid for the period in which the CAT B727 crash took place.

8

1972 – The Trident Disaster at Staines

PART I

During mid afternoon on Sunday 18 June 1972, a larger than usual crowd of pilots had gathered in the BEA crew room at London Airport's Queen's Building. Some were rostered for stand-by duties in case of a service delay or a crew member suddenly falling sick, but the majority came to learn news of their particular concern.

Two topics were on everyone's lips. One was the twenty-four-hour worldwide stoppage of air services announced for the next day by the International Federation of Air Line Pilots' Associations. Driven to desperation, IFALPA intended to put pressure on the governments for a speedy implementation of the Tokyo Convention on hijacking (see chapter 6). As no BEA aircraft had ever been commandeered and its pilots had not been exposed to the dangers of crimes on board, and despite recent horrifying cases of air piracy in Europe, they were lukewarm to what appeared to them as a distant cause. After the British Air Line Pilots' Association (BALPA) was assured by the Government that everything was being done to stamp out hijacking worldwide, officially BALPA did not support the IFALPA action. Nevertheless, it agreed to individual members' decisions only on the understanding that BEA undertook not to discipline any pilots who, as a matter of conscience, decided to participate in the show of IFALPA solidarity.

The second topic, which was of a much wider interest, was the eagerly awaited result of a ballot arranged by BALPA on the proposed strike by the BEA pilots. An incident, which took place that afternoon in connection with the brewing industrial clash, was later construed as having had a fateful bearing on the cause of a BEA Trident accident. The aircraft, registration G-ARPI, on a

service to Brussels, crashed one and a half hours later near Staines with a heavy toll of lives. In the disaster all 112 passengers, six regular crew members and three deadheading pilots were killed.

The unrest within the BEA pilot workforce was not purely over pay as the newspapers were claiming. For a group of co-pilots the main grievance was job satisfaction. Selected to supervise training of new entrants, they were stuck for months on end in the Trident observer's seat, teaching their younger colleagues the ropes of line operation. An urgent demand for a large contingent of new pilots to be converted to the Tridents had led to this frustrating practice. When the terms of the 'airborne desk job' were indefinitely extended, deep discontent began to spread. Although the supervisory co-pilots were paid a special allowance for the assignment, they felt that, by being denied the opportunity to practise take-offs and landings, their flying careers were adversely affected. It was only to be expected that the pressure for the strike came mainly from the disgruntled co-pilots. Older captains believed that every means of reaching an agreement with the management should first have been exhausted before embarking on such a drastic step.

Between 1957 and 1967 there were thirty-three major pilots' strikes worldwide, ranging from twenty-four hours to thirty-eight days. It is interesting to note that the bitterest clashes took place in airlines which were under direct governmental control. IFALPA studies had revealed that the lack of communication between management and pilots, mainly lay behind strained relations, rather than pure grievances over pay. BEA was no exception.

In 1967 IFALPA suggested holding an international symposium to discuss ways of improving understanding between the top brass and the rank and file, based on the experiences of those airlines which had successfully solved the communication problems. The world carriers were equally divided between those supporting and those against holding a symposium. BEA was opposed. In February 1968 IFALPA received a letter from the BEA Chairman advising them that they did not wish to attend any labour-related forums. It is not surprising that industrial friction in BEA came to a head shortly afterwards.

In the group of pilots rostered for stand-by duties at Heathrow Airport was Captain Stanley Key. Being fifty-one, with only four more years before his retirement, had probably influenced his attitude to rocking the boat. His opposition to the strike was widely known and he was recognised as the leader of a move within the BALPA BEA Council to soft-pedal drastic measures. With the support for the strike coming mainly from the younger pilots, there was a chance of 'hot-headed' action being voted in, as the first and second officers outnumbered the captains by two to one. Key, like many senior men, felt that the supervisory co-pilots should fight their own battle and should not drag others into an action that was of less interest to the rest of the pilot corps. On the other hand, the co-pilots believed that they had exhausted all possible avenues. Although withholding their supervisory services had halted the training programme of new entrants, it did not exert the expected pressure on the management and they felt that they were at the end of their tether.

For his outspoken views against the strike, Key, and a few other senior captains, became a target of numerous offensive inscriptions that began to appear in the Trident cockpits, in particular on the table at the third pilot's station. Similar uncomplimentary notes were also directed at the BEA management. Many pilots regarded the scribbling, which was often noticed by ground engineers and traffic staff, as unprofessional and to be deplored.

With a tense atmosphere in the crew room on that fateful Sunday, it was easy for friction to develop. A row broke out between Captain Key and First Officer Flavell, two men with very opposing views on the proposed industrial action. According to witnesses, Flavell confronted Key with a query as to how his effort of enlisting anti-strike support among his fellow captains was progressing. Key appeared to have lost his temper and gave Flavell a piece of his mind in an abusive manner. Although at first he looked very angry, he soon offered a gesture of conciliation by taking the impetuous first officer by his arm and apologising to him. The incident was later highlighted at the accident inquiry. Medical experts maintained that the outburst of temper could have started a heart attack that eventually led to Key's incapacitation on board the ill-fated Trident.

Half an hour after the incident, Key was called out to take a flight to Brussels. The scheduled crew were delayed *en route* and, as a full load of passengers had already checked in, a replacement team had to be quickly arranged. With the news of IFALPA's twenty-four-hour stoppage of air services on the front page of every newspaper, businessmen tried to grab every available seat before Monday and consequently all planes were full.

Due to a shortage of experienced co-pilots, Key ended up with two second officers, the lowest BEA pilot rank. It meant that they both were very junior in the company.

On most of the first generation of jets, the crew complement consisted, especially in the USA, of a captain, a co-pilot and a flight engineer, sometimes known as a system engineer. Generally the flight engineer was a holder of a commercial pilot's licence, who, after a spell at the flight engineer's panel, would eventually graduate as a full-fledged co-pilot. This step-by-step progress ensured that a young entrant would receive a relatively long exposure to line flying before being upgraded to a more responsible position as the second-in-command of a public transport aircraft.

As a result of BEA policy to dispense with flight engineers, the Trident crew complement differed from other airlines. The cockpit was laid out so as to allow airframe and engine anti-icing to be operated from all three forward-facing positions. The flight engineer's panel would be alternately manned by the two co-pilots, who carried equal qualifications. On a line flight with several sectors they could swap places to get a share of take-offs and landings from the right-hand seat. Only in cruise would the pilot handling the systems sit facing the flight engineer panel; otherwise he would adjust his seat in the forward direction to monitor flight instruments during departure and arrival procedures.

However, on the flight to Brussels, Second Officer Jeremy Keighley, the more junior of the two co-pilots, was officially not permitted by his lack of qualification to man the flight engineer's panel and therefore could occupy only the right-hand seat. After the withdrawal of training services by the supervisory first officers, he was unable to complete his full conversion to Tridents

These are the crew members of the British European Airways Trident jet liner which crashed at Staines, Middlesex, England in June 1972, killing all 118 persons aboard in Britain's worst ever air disaster. They are, left to right, Stanley Key, pilot, Simon Ticehurst, Second Officer and Jeremy Keighley, Second Officer. (Associated Press, London)

which included operating aircraft's systems from the middle seat.

Consequently, as if defying logic and common-sense, Keighley, though adequately trained except for handling the flight engineer's panel, but very new to line flying, was allowed to act as the second-in-command. On the other hand, vastly more experienced Second Officer Ticehurst was reduced to a purely monitoring role without immediate access to the flying controls. With quite a few entrants not having completed their training, such practices were common in BEA. Forty-four senior captains became so concerned about the potentially hazardous situation that they sent a letter of protest to the Chairman of the Civil Aviation Authority. Some captains would disregard the company's directive and would put the more experienced co-pilot in the right-hand seat. When other captains, unhappy with having been assigned a crew member who was not fully qualified, requested to be given an adequately trained replacement, they were flatly refused. At the Public Inquiry on the Staines crash, the reason was explained as follows: 'It is plain the Assistant Flight Manager took the view, understandably but wrongly, that this was simply another move in the industrial dispute.'

However, to the pilots it was a matter of safety. Their professional pride would not allow them to use unprofessional tactics in order to gain some doubtful industrial advantage.

Teamwork is essential to the safe operation of a modern jet, and if one crew member falls ill in the air it is regarded as an emergency. Such loss of a pair of eyes and hands can be particularly critical during an approach in a busy terminal area or during a landing in fog. By bureaucratically applying the CAA rules in respect of the qualifications required to occupy the right-hand seat, BEA management appeared to have closed their eyes to the possibility of the captain suddenly becoming indisposed while handling the aircraft.

It had been borne out by quite a number of past accidents and serious incidents that an extreme difference in age and experience between the captain and the other crew members can adversely affect the cooperation in the cockpit. A senior captain teamed up with a very junior co-pilot might be inclined to operate the aircraft single-handed in the fear that 'the greenhorn's' assistance would lead to trouble. On the other hand, a young pilot could feel intimidated by the captain's age and experience and it could preclude him from pointing out any error committed by a

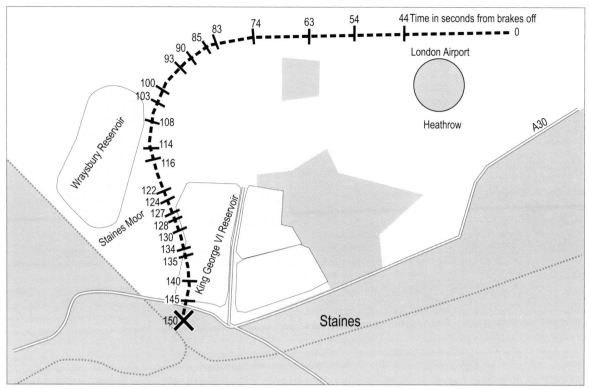

Horizontal flight path of the ill-fated Trident I PI.

man of much more senior status. Teamwork on board could be further degraded if an ill-matched crew had never previously flown together.

Monitoring the crew member who is handling the aircraft is a vital aspect of cockpit duties. Although it might appear to the uninitiated to be just a matter of keeping an eye on what the other person is doing, in fact, it is a skill that cannot be acquired overnight. The ability to assess quickly that the pilot at the controls has not only deviated from the laid-down procedure but is unaware of having done so, can only be learnt through long exposure to line flying. No amount of training or directives can completely bestow the degree of confidence necessary to issue a warning or to take over the controls in such a manner as to not create confusion, which could lead to an even more dangerous situation.

The differences in flying experience and in ages could not have been greater on the ill-fated Flight 548. In his long aviation career, Key, a former wartime pilot, had amassed 15,000 hours with 4,000 hours on the Tridents. He was also a Route Check Pilot and was known for his strict adherence to the laid-down procedures.

Twenty-four-year-old Simon Ticehurst, the more experienced of the two second officers, had a total of 1,400 hours to his credit, 750 on Tridents. On the other hand, Jeremy Keighley, twenty-two, fresh out of the College of Air Training at Hamble, had only 250 hours in total. He was very new to the Tridents, with only twenty-nine hours on line flights. A further case of bad luck was that the three crew members had never flown together before.

In effect, an oversight in the BEA training scheme had further jeopardised the taking over of the controls by the more experienced of the two co-pilots if Key happened to become incapacitated in flight. Ticehurst was never given any instructions on what to do in such an emergency or how to assume command.

PART II

Flight 548 was due to depart at 4.45 p.m. British Standard Time. But it had been delayed for fifteen minutes to take on board a supernumerary crew who were going to bring back a Vanguard freighter from Brussels. Captain Collins, a former senior first officer on the Tridents, was accommodated in the cockpit on the observer's seat, while the two co-pilots were allocated a spare cabin attendant's seat and a passenger seat that was originally reserved for an infant. It was later claimed that Collins's presence could have distracted Key. This appears to be a wrong conclusion. Many captains would have more likely welcomed the presence of a former senior co-pilot on the flight deck, in particular someone familiar with the Trident and capable of keeping an eye on the less experienced in the crew.

Accommodating the three deadheading pilots necessitated removing a small load of freight and eventually Trident PI left the ramp at two minutes past five o'clock. The weather looked dismal. An approaching cold front brought in patches of low clouds at 600 feet and a solid overcast at 1,000 feet. It was raining heavily and a strong gusty wind blew across the runway, aggravating handling problems.

Soon after leaving the ground, strong turbulence began to buffet the Trident. Nevertheless, Flight 548 proceeded as cleared and, at the ILS Middle Marker of runway 28R, left turn was initiated in accordance with the DOVER ONE Departure Procedure. Next the flaps were lifted and engine thrust was reduced to comply with the noise abatement regulations. So far, the progress looked routine except that the speed was ten to fifteen knots lower than recommended. Occasionally it fell by as much as twenty knots. Twenty-one seconds after flaps were lifted, the 'droop' was selected to the up position.

The droop was a complementary high-lift device, utilising the wing's leading edge. Like flaps, it was only used for take-off and landing, as it lowered stalling speed appreciably. Now the droop appeared to have been operated out of turn. The standard procedure would have been to continue climbing to 3,000 feet, then apply full climb power until a speed of 225 knots was reached, and finally select the droop up.

But on that fateful afternoon it was lifted up at only 1,780 feet and at 162 knots. This was fifteen knots below the stalling speed in that configuration and as a result, in a matter of seconds the aircraft had plummeted to the ground like a stone.

PART III

Weekend traffic streaming back to London was as heavy as could be expected from a summer Sunday afternoon, even though the fateful 18 June 1972 was a rather miserable day. With lashing rain and strong wind, driving conditions were unenviable. Perhaps that was the reason why so few motorists had noticed that an aircraft suddenly dropped out of low clouds and belly-flopped on a meadow close to the A30 road at Staines. An alert eye would have been required to spot the lightning plunge during the five seconds that it was possible to observe it. Furthermore, the area of impact was shielded from the road by a row of tall trees.

Surprisingly, the first rescue steps were not initiated by the aviation authorities as would have been expected, but through the great presence of mind displayed by a thirteen-year-old boy, Trevor Burke. He was walking near the scene of the crash with his younger brother and, to his horror, he noticed an aircraft crashing on a nearby field. Later he recounted to the press:

'We were out with the dog and I looked up and saw the plane. It was just coming out of the mist when the engines stalled and it seemed it glided down. It was just like a dream. The plane just fell out of the sky. We just about saw it hit the ground because it was right in a clump of trees. When it did hit the ground, the front hit first and the back bit was just blown away.'

Recognising the gravity of the situation, Trevor ran a quarter of a mile back home for help. He also called on a Mrs Castledine to tell her about the crash. He was sure that, as a former nursing sister, she would know what to do in such circumstances. Mrs Castledine, no newcomer to all sorts of accidents, rushed out to the wreck, trying to take care of the victims. She made desperate efforts to comfort those whom she was able to get close to, and who appeared to show any signs of life. Later she was commended for her brave conduct.

An ambulance driver who happened to be passing by, stopped to give Mrs Castledine a hand. The driver alerted his control by radio and more ambulances were soon on the way. A vigilant motorist who witnessed the accident from the road, called at the nearest private house to phone the airport authorities. From then on, a rapid build-up of rescue services had begun. In no time at all, thirty ambulances and twenty-five fire trucks appeared on the scene. With three police divisions bordering the area, there was no

Officials examining part of the wreckage of the British European Airways Trident airliner in a field near Staines minutes after taking off from London's Heathrow airport on a flight to Brussels. All 118 passengers and crew aboard were killed.

shortage of officers to cope with all sorts of problems.

Through a stroke of luck, the first pilot on the scene of the crash was someone very familiar with the Trident. Moreover, Captain Eric Pritchard of BEA was a member of the BALPA Technical Committee and the chairman of both IFALPA and BALPA Accident Investigation Study Groups. On that fateful day, he took to London Airport an old friend and an IFALPA associate, Captain Bassett from PanAm, who was staying with the Pritchards during his stopover in England. At the same time, Eric arranged to meet Stan Key, on stand-by duty at the airport. Both shared the same view about the strike. When Eric went looking for Key, he was told that Key had been just called out for a flight to Brussels but there was disturbing news about its fate. Recently Eric recounted the events on that day:

'On being told by the BEA duty Operations Officer of their concern over the Brussels flight, I went to the CAA Unit in Terminal 1, identified myself by my BEA and BALPA identity card and asked what information they had on Flight 458. As I recall, the CAA personnel had very little knowledge so far or they were not prepared at this stage to divulge any information, but did eventually admit that London Airport was closed to larger aircraft such as the B747 due to reduced fire cover. After some time it had transpired or was just discovered that Trident PI was down in a field near the "Crooked Billet" public house at Staines. BEA immediately made arrangements for me to go to the crash with a police escort. This was necessary because of the traffic congestion brought about by sightseers. The journey from the Central Area to the site took the best part of an hour and can be only described as unbelievable.

I introduced myself to the Police Officer in charge by producing my ID cards and I was given access to the wreck. I was the first pilot on the scene, even ahead of the AAIB inspectors. By then, all the bodies had been removed from the wreck. My inspection of the crash site revealed the following:

1. The aircraft had impacted in a high nose up attitude. The No. 2 engine had dug a considerable crater. The tail section was almost if not completely separated from the rest of the airframe.

2. There was little evidence of any forward movement, in fact, the complete aircraft apart from the tail unit looked intact though distorted and broken, mainly the fuselage. Both wings suffered not much visible damage. I noticed that the droop and flaps were retracted.

3. At a certain moment, a small fire broke out which was quickly extinguished but luckily did not spread any further. The ground in the vicinity of the wings was heavily contaminated with kerosene and the fire hazard was extremely great. In my opinion, an early outbreak had been prevented by the fact that there was no significant forward movement on impact.

4. All visual clues pointed to a high rate of descent consistent with a deep stall. The actual field was quite small and the aircraft had missed both the trees and high voltage electric power lines which lay between the field boundary fence and the A30 trunk road. I checked the flight deck and recorded the readings of the aircraft instruments together with the position of controls, the frequencies on the radio sets, the trim setting, the position of power levers, flaps and droop, as well as the gear selector. The engineer panel was difficult to examine in detail due to deformation. It was about two-thirds of its normal height. The Stick Pusher dolls eyes [indicators on the circuit breakers] showed an activation. It looked that the Stick Pusher Dump lever had been operated but apart from recording this, it was not possible to draw any immediate conclusions as it may have been as a result of the impact.

5. I saw a radio head-set laying on the flight deck floor between the co-pilot's right rudder pedal and the fuselage wall and I recorded this

in my notes. This set undoubtedly belonged to Captain Collins.

6. I did not record or indeed remember the odd comments [graffiti] about Stan Key on the flight deck desktops. I thought at the time of the Public Inquiry and I still do now, that they were totally irrelevant to the accident.

In summary, there was nothing untoward in the flight deck "look and record" that was out of place except the droop selector and its attendant controls as well as Collins's head-set.'

Hardly an hour after the Trident crashed, the story was already being reported by several radio and television stations on their six o'clock news. As soon as the exact location of the accident was revealed, the whole area around Staines was invaded by the public, desperately trying to have a look at the scene of the tragedy. Despite continuous warnings on the traffic information services, that the section of the A30 road between Crooked Billet and Wraysbury roundabouts was closed, the sensation seekers would not give up.

Later in the evening, a BBC Radio air correspondent described the 'rescue nightmare':

'There's been a particularly ghoulish slant to this whole accident. From the time of the crash, thousands of sightseers have been pouring into this area. All roads were completely blocked, the police were unable to clear them in spite of repeated appeals made over loudspeakers, and the ambulances were taking up to an hour to travel the last two miles to the scene. The police are now having to patrol the woods around here because, more than four hours after the crash, people – some of them with children – are still trying to get through the woods to have a look at the scene. The Minister of Aerospace himself took two hours to get here and he's just described the sightseers as "Ghouls, unfortunate ghouls".'

Although the authorities subsequently denied that the jammed roads had affected the rescue operation in any way, two recently broadcasted television programmes confirmed the traffic chaos as originally described by the BBC air correspondent. A film of the totally congested A30 in the vicinity of the crash site, taken two hours after the accident, clearly shows mile-long lines of cars at a standstill. As a result, lifting cranes urgently required to extract trapped victims from the wreck were delayed for a considerable time. If the victims had had to be evacuated rapidly and in great numbers, the transfer to the hospitals would have been badly hindered. But as it had turned out, only one passenger was pulled from the wreck alive; unfortunately he died a few hours later in the nearby hospital. The media's irresponsible reporting of the exact location of the Trident crash could have played havoc with the rescue efforts.

Another black mark in the Staines disaster was that the London Airport authorities were completely unaware of an aircraft crashing only two miles from the airport boundary. Contrary to the later assurances by the CAA that Air Traffic Control did function efficiently at the time of the accident, the official statement contradicts the known fact that the controller on duty failed to notice the Trident disappearing from his radar surveillance screen. Consequently no alert phase was initiated. The airport authorities had learnt about the accident from an outside source.

As a result of the Trident striking the ground in a high angle of attack with a little forward motion and then pitching forward onto its nose, most of the passengers were thrown forward. Although the fuselage cracked in several places on impact, leaving wide gaps, unfortunately many occupants of the front cabin were jammed inside by the luggage and freight that broke through the aircraft's floor. Appalling weather conditions did not help with the enormous difficulty of extracting the bodies from the crashed aircraft. Some victims could only be accessed with the help of lifting cranes. The rescue workers persevered in their search for over an hour and half until it looked certain that the whole wreck was cleared of the human remains.

Shortly after the accident, the Minister of Aerospace, Michael Heseltine, announced that a Public Inquiry would be convened to look into the Staines disaster.

PART IV

When it was evident in the late fifties that the BEA fleet of turbo-prop Viscounts was showing signs of obsolescence, the management decided to order pure jets as a replacement. With no short-haul aircraft on the market to meet BEA requirements, several British manufacturers were approached to submit proposals for an entirely new model. Finally, a tender from de Havilland Aircraft Company was accepted and the idea of the DH121 was born. As BEA's services were hardly

affected by the performance limitations of short runways, high-altitude airports or hot weather conditions, the company wanted a relatively low-powered aircraft for reasons of fuel economy and fitted with simple flaps to cut down maintenance costs. On the other hand, the airline specified that the new project should include automatic landing capabilities.

About the same time Boeing began to work on a similar project, but based on far more flexible specifications to suit the requirements of customers from all over the world. As a result, the new American short-haul jet, the Boeing 727, was going to be fitted with more powerful engines as well as with sophisticated lift devices such as double slats and triple-slotted flaps to improve take-off and landing performance.

The DH121 and Boeing 727 were similar in two respects. Both aircraft were fitted with three engines in the rear and the stabiliser assembly was placed on the top of the vertical fin – the so-called 'T-tail' configuration. In spite of the T-tail offering performance advantages, its basic weakness lay in a tendency to deep stall, from which recovery was very critical. The problems had already been known from experiences with military planes of similar design. Nevertheless, the airworthiness authorities did not recognise the hazardous shortcomings until the tragic crash of a BAC 111, another T-tail project. As a result, only then did they begin to insist on effective remedies before such types of aircraft were allowed to enter airline service.

Two solutions were possible to prevent uncontrollable deep stall: one was to improve the aircraft's aerodynamic characteristics; the other to fit 'corrective devices', such as a stall-recovery system. Based on extensive wind tunnel tests, Boeing opted for the first solution by placing the wings as far back as possible, and the elevator well away from the turbulent airflow during a stall. This idea proved to be effective and the Boeing 727 passed stall tests with flying colours. Vertical controls on another T-tail project, the DC9, then under construction by Douglas, had to be extensively re-designed at a cost of ten million dollars.

However, with the development of the DH121 already in an advanced stage, radical aerodynamic changes could not be contemplated, and it was decided to only fit corrective devices. Due to financial difficulties facing de Havilland Aircraft Company, Hawker Siddeley Group took over de Havilland. The DH121 project was then re-named Trident. When it became apparent that the

Trident's flaps were inefficient, complementary means of improving lift for take-off and landing had to be considered.

A basic re-design of the wing was out of the question on the grounds of expense, because the Hawker Siddeley Group were also short of funds. A novel solution was sought and for the first time in the history of British aircraft manufacturing, the wing leading edge was utilised to improve lift. The leading edge was swung downwards through 26° by means of reversible screwjacks powered by a hydraulic motor, and at the wing root a short Kruger flap was used. The device, which acquired the name of the 'droop', was capable of reducing stalling speed between twenty to thirty knots, depending on the aircraft's weight.

Unfortunately, flight tests revealed that the Trident's stalling characteristics were adversely affected when the droop was lowered. No typical symptoms were experienced which normally preceded a stall, such as buffeting. The Trident appeared to be suffering from a bigger share of stall problems than similar designs. Once the loss of lift had occurred, the nose would pitch up from the gravity effect of the rear mounted engines and if this tendency remained unchecked, the aircraft could reach such a high incidence angle that the turbulent wash from the stalled wing surfaces would render the elevator totally ineffective. The wash could affect the flow of air to the engines as well, resulting in the loss of power and thus further reducing the chances of recovery. The consequence would be a catastrophic, near-vertical sink in a flat attitude at an extremely high rate of descent.

The first warning as to how dangerously the Trident's stall could develop came in 1962. It happened to two de Havilland test pilots, Peter Bugge and Ron Clear, while making test stalls by progressively applying higher attitude. After a critical angle of attack was reached, the Trident began to sink tail-down in a deep stall. There was no response from the elevator and a crash looked inevitable. What had saved the two pilots from falling to the ground was that at a certain moment the wing dropped and, when corrected by the opposite rudder, the other wing followed in the same way. While still rapidly losing altitude, the aircraft continued to gyrate left and right until the roll became so deep that the nose dropped down. At last the controls responded and a recovery was eventually attained. From this incident it was evident that, apart from the possibility of getting out of control, the unpredictable dropping of a wing was another undesirable characteristic of the Trident's stall.

These hazardous traits called for two separate corrective devices to be incorporated. One, a warning system to alert the pilot that a potentially dangerous situation was imminent, and the other, a means of counteracting the pitch-up tendency once the loss of lift had occurred.

The stall warning system worked on a simple principle. When an electro-mechanical probe sensed a critical speed, an electric motor would be activated to vibrate the control column. Hence the name 'Stick Shaker', soon widely adopted in aviation circles. Unfortunately, sensing probes proved unreliable in operational service and the pilots were reporting more spurious cases of Stick Shaker activation than genuine warnings.

The corrective device intended to counteract the pitch-up tendency was a pneumatically operated ram that would literally kick the control column forward out of the pilot's hands once imminent deep stall conditions were detected. The concept of 'Stick Pusher', as it was popularly named, was so novel at the time and the pilots so cautious of something that 'took over the stall', that the then UK chief certification test pilot came to BALPA to give a presentation of its working and the reason why it was needed.

Stick Pusher was triggered in flight by sensing-probes measuring angle of attack. The probes, in the form of rotating cones with slits, were not exactly of a sturdy construction and rotated on equally light bearings. As a result, they had to be carefully protected and maintained. They were plagued by unreliability and in the eight years of service prior to the crash of Trident PI, out of ten known incidents of Stick Pusher activation only four were originated by genuine circumstances. All other cases were a result of spurious signals. With an alarming proportion of false operations, pilots became wary of the 'corrective gadgets'. The lack of confidence was further undermined by a tragic accident to a Trident in 1966, during stalling tests before its delivery to BEA. The Stick Pusher failed to prevent the aircraft from entering deep stall and in the resulting tragedy the crew of six were killed.

Although the Trident's aerodynamic development may have lagged behind the competition, the flight guidance system was based on a very advanced concept, a forerunner of the systems to come. Among many novel features, the system offered fail-safe automatic landing capability in low visibility. One of the basic changes from the earlier instrumentation designs was that the sensing sources, such as pitot probe and static vents, did not feed information directly to the respective flight instruments but via a sophisticated electronic management system. In spite of relying on untried components, the flight guidance and the associated autopilot proved effective and the first-ever automatic landing on a passenger service was carried out at London Airport on 10 June 1965.

Even if aerodynamic improvements were incorporated on some later versions of the Trident by replacing the droop with slats and more powerful engines were fitted, the stained reputation had made sales slump catastrophically. Apart from BEA, Tridents were delivered to only five overseas customers: China, Iraq, Kuwait, Ceylon and Pakistan. In total only 117 were built. In contrast, the Boeing 727, which entered airline service about the same time, reached an astounding production figure of 1,832 aircraft.

PART V

As a result of frequent misadventures to the 'heavier-than-air' machines during their early pioneering days in England, in 1912 the Royal Aero Club and the Royal Aeronautical Society appointed a Special Committee to collect information on all known crashes with the intention of analysing the causes and recommending ways to avoid similar occurrences. The first investigation was carried out as early as May 1912 and the report served as the basis for a lecture at the Society's meeting.

World War I deferred the creation of governmental machinery to deal with civil air crashes and the Accident Investigating Branch was eventually set up in 1920. The inspector-in-charge was made directly responsible to the Air Minister for the technical work in order that, quoting the official wording, 'the Minister would be able to speak without fear or favour in respect of the disaster'.

But it was soon apparent that the investigating activities would have to be given a legal status, empowering the inspectors with certain rights, such as access to private property, retaining the wreck as evidence or summoning witnesses for interviews.

The Air Navigation Act passed by Parliament in 1920, conferred powers on the Minister of Civil Aviation to issue the Air Navigation (Investigation of Accidents) Regulations. The Regulations, which became statutory in 1922, provided for two different forms of action: one informal, otherwise known as 'private', which could be pursued by the Chief Inspector of Accidents, and formal or 'public' proceedings under the guidance of a Court of Inquiry with its members appointed by the Minister.

The British 'Public Inquiry' in place of an investigation by experts, became a unique institution within worldwide air accident investigating methods, and in the course of many years there were only minor changes to its original status. Although only three Public Inquiries were conducted before World War II, with the greatly increased number of air accidents in the post-war years such actions became more frequent.

On paper the Court of Inquiry seemed an ideal forum for 'washing the dirty linen in public' in respect of any consequences that could have arisen out of an aircraft accident. But once civil air transportation became a highly complex technological industry, the reverse appeared to be true. Looking back at the results, none of the Public Inquiries ever produced what could not have been better achieved, and at a lower cost, by an investigating team of trained experts. An inherent handicap of judicial proceedings was the way in which evidence was assessed. Instead of being examined and evaluated without haste and pressure in the undisturbed atmosphere of an accident inspector's office, it invariably became an object of a nitpicking battle on the courtroom floor by the opposing counsel. Witnesses called to testify at a Public Inquiry on complex aeronautical matters were often exposed to ridicule when cross-examined by the sharp-tongued barristers. Particularly bitter feelings were aroused during the Public Inquiry on the Vanguard crash at Heathrow Airport in October 1965. As a result, several senior airline captains vowed never to give testimony at a Public Inquiry again.

Another drawback was the pace dictated by the Court's timetable, which often required the inspectors involved in fieldwork or preliminary technical examinations to complete their findings by a certain date.

Two contrasting views were held about the decision to convene a Public Inquiry on the Staines accident. The legal circles felt that, by making the investigation 'open', the public would benefit from better access to information on the puzzling aspects of the Trident disaster. On the other hand, the pilots justifiably feared that the Government responsible for operating aviation services such as air traffic control, communications and navigation facilities, could influence the course of the proceedings. As the Attorney General was going to present the case, he was in a position to tone down any adverse criticism. In the pilots' opinion, the Public Inquiry could turn into political machinery to whitewash shortcomings of the aviation services, and at the same time, become an opportunity to seek scapegoats. To them, it looked to be an unproductive exercise at the taxpayer's expense and a paradise for lawyers to collect exorbitant fees.

The aviation press received the Minister's announcement on holding formal proceedings with bitter criticism. It was best illustrated by what *Flight*, the leading UK aviation magazine, had to say at the time:

'Do Public Inquiries serve the cause of air safety? The old question arises again with the decision by Mr Heseltine, Britain's Minister for Aerospace, to order a Public Inquiry into the recent tragedy near Heathrow. Public Inquiries are the exception rather than the rule.

Not all Public Inquiries have measured up to the standards expected. Counsels representing the dead or bereaved have sometimes grossly harried honest and conscientious men in public, tripping them with clever words which are reported, sometimes with relish and out of context, in the next day's papers.'

Another subject of concern to many pilots about the Minister's decision was the role the Air Accident Investigation Branch was going to play in determining the cause of the Trident disaster. According to the Civil Aviation (Investigation of Accident) Regulations 1969, it is stated under the heading 'Public Inquiries': 'In any such case (i.e. where the Secretary of State has directed that a Public Inquiry is to be held into the accident) any inspector's investigation shall be discontinued.'

The findings so far compiled by the inspector-in-charge of that particular crash inquiry were no longer an internal matter of the Air Accidents Investigation Branch, but were expected to be forwarded to the Attorney General for his perusal at the Court's sessions.

But the interest of the AAIB, independent by tradition and bound by its own ethics of not publicising any controversial aspect of a disaster until the preliminary investigation was fully completed, lay only in establishing the cause and in suggesting ways of preventing further failures of either a human or mechanical nature. Arriving at conclusions and subsequently issuing AAIB safety recommendations for the benefit of the travelling public could be best achieved through a patient assessment of every contributory factor and often with the help of experts from a particular field of aviation. In view of the high level of technology present in constructing a modern jet, scientific research is sometimes required to determine the origin of a complex problem. It was unlikely that an answer to that problem could be formulated at a Public Inquiry by a wrangle of lawyers without any aviation background and only acquainted with the facts through a brief.

It may appear to those outside aviation circles that, as a result of the statutory definitions, the AAIB activities are informal or 'private'; nevertheless, their findings are never classified as confidential and they are regularly circulated to all sectors of the aviation industry in the interest of safety. Furthermore, far more comprehensive and detailed reports have been produced by the accident inspectors than by the legal profession when summarising the outcome of a Public Inquiry.

Another concern to the flying fraternity was the unrestricted access during the Court's proceedings, by counsel representing various interests, to the records of periodical medical examinations of a pilot involved in an accident, or to the assessments of his flying performance contained in his personal file. Yet in normal court cases, if such information were obtained without the consent of the individual concerned, it would have to be tested first if it was to be admissible evidence. In many sectors of life, personal particulars are looked upon as sacred.

According to the government legal experts, the conclusions of an accident report, whether reached by an inspector's investigation or a Public Inquiry, would not be indiscriminately accepted by the courts in evidence. Nevertheless, the law cannot stop an unscrupulous lawyer from exploiting personal data obtained at a Public Inquiry to augment the arguments which he may use during a civil litigation for compensation claims above the limit laid down by the Warsaw Convention.

At the preliminary hearing in September 1972, members of the Court of Inquiry were announced, selected by the Lord Chancellor at the suggestion of the Chief Inspector of Accidents. Evidently the authorities attached great importance to the outcome of the Court proceedings, as a High Court judge, the Honourable Justice Lane was appointed as the Commissioner. He was a former wartime pilot who was awarded an AFC. Later he became Lord Chief Justice.

The Press came up with adverse comments about the appointment of the two so-called

Pieces of the BEA Trident which crashed shortly after take-off from London Airport in June 1972, killing all 118 persons aboard, held at the Royal Aircraft Establishment at Farnborough. (Associated Press, London)

'independent experts' who were selected as assessors, because they were both either directly or indirectly on the Government payroll. Sir Morien Morgan, C.B., was a director of the Royal Aircraft Establishment. Captain Jessop was the deputy managing director of the 70% BEA-owned subsidiary Northeast Airlines and was an active member of the BEA Safety Committee. Finding an assessor with a suitable flying background presented a problem, for the only other UK Trident operator was Northeast Airlines. Captain Jessop, respected as fair-minded and informed, was finally appointed despite his BEA connections after the mutual agreement of the main interested parties was reached.

PART VI

The Trident Public Inquiry, which was held in London at the Piccadilly Hotel, began at the end

of November 1972 and continued to the end of January 1973. The Commissioner and the Assessors had the benefit of a visit to the BEA Training Centre at Heston, where they were given a demonstration of a Trident I simulator. Later they were shown a rig at the Hawker Siddeley factory at Hatfield, on which Tridents were constructed, as well as what was left of the ill-fated PI, re-assembled in a hangar at Farnborough.

A basic simulation rig, with rudimentary visual perspective lines on a monitor display, was also assembled at Hatfield. It was programmed to simulate the flight path and aircraft behaviour derived from the ill-fated Trident's flight recorder trace. A small group of selected pilots was invited to 'fly' it and a record was made of their stall recoveries, but bearing in mind that all participants were aware in advance of the problem to come.

Just before the Christmas recess, Captain Evans, the BEA Trident Flight Manager, took Justice Lane and Morgan up for three take-offs and landings at Heathrow Airport, to familiarise them with the flight procedures.

It seemed as if, to make any progress in the proceedings, the Court members had to be first acquainted with basic knowledge of the Trident operation. Such costly steps would not have been necessary if the investigation had been conducted by AAIB inspectors. Through their regular training, the inspectors would have not been newcomers to procedures and flight techniques of a particular type of aircraft.

The various governmental departments were represented by no fewer than seven Queen's Counsel or top-ranking barristers.

On the opening day of the Court of Inquiry, the Attorney General outlined in his address five possible factors that his department was putting forward as contributory factors to the crash. They were:

1. The captain was not fully fit due to considerable pain from a heart attack.
2. 'The droop' was prematurely selected up, sixty-three knots below the recommended speed.
3. There were no attempts to re-select the droop to the 'down' position.
4. No action was taken to get out of the stall.
5. The 'Stick Pusher' override lever was operated to the off position.

There are two points worth noting in connection with the accident. The Trident design was unique in having separate and independently-operated levers for flaps and droop selection, one alongside the other. The second point was that it was probably the first accident positively identified as being caused by a 'configuration stall' – i.e. the aircraft went rapidly into a stalled condition at constant airspeed by retracting a lift-producing device. Stalls were always traditionally taken from the viewpoint of a critical loss of airspeed in a fixed configuration, which generally occurs more slowly.

From the address by the Attorney General it was evident that the trend of the Public Inquiry would be in favour of a theory that Key's cardiac problems had led to an irrational action on his part. There was no mention of any possibility of a mechanical fault in the droop selecting mechanism, although troubles had been reported in the past. Unfortunately, the inspector responsible for the technical investigation of the droop committed suicide four days before the Public Inquiry. According to what his wife had revealed to the Press, the pressure of work to get his report ready

in time had affected his mind. It was an unfortunate upshot of the Trident investigation for which no one accepted responsibility.

The cross-examination of the first witness, the inspector-in-charge of the AAIB preliminary investigation, was an example – of which there were many more to come – of the way the counsel representing various parties put questions to the witnesses. Often such questions were not directly related to the cause of the accident, but the lawyers were trying to obtain answers that could later be used in their own civil litigations.

What the pilots feared about the outcome of the Trident Inquiry became far worse in reality. The battle of words was particularly unproductive when it came to assessing whether Second Officer Keighley was sufficiently qualified and experienced to occupy the right-hand seat on a line flight. Days were spent arguing as to whether twenty-nine hours of line flying was far too little to take over the command of public transport aircraft should the captain become incapacitated – something that was implicit to any airline pilot.

As a result of the legal wrangles, the Inquiry, originally planned for two weeks, had to be continuously extended as it went along and ended up with thirty-three working days.

The proceedings had also shown an ugly side. A New York lawyer, representing the families of four US citizens killed in the crash, used tactics which may have been common in American courts, but which, in other parts of the world, would leave a nasty taste in one's mouth. His aim was to find 'the skeletons in the cupboard' which could be later used in litigations for compensation above the limit stipulated by law. His address to the Court was summarised next day in a newspaper column:

'The American lawyer representing some of the relatives who died in the BEA crash in June, yesterday called Captain Stanley Key a "sad figure" who was physically sick and had emotional problems.

He told the inquiry into the disaster that he believed the crash was caused by Captain Key's medical and emotional background, the inexperience of the second pilot, and because the plane was not capable of meeting a demonstrable need.

Inside the cockpit there was "such tension that there could have been no communication but silent bitterness on the part of the young crew towards Captain Key".

It was a pity that no one could have

interpreted the indication that Captain Key was not well and told him to take two weeks off for a thorough medical examination.

It is inconceivable that the graffiti in the cockpit did not have an effect on Captain Key. One sentence had read: "Who will be God's next representative in BEA when Captain Key dies?" If it did nothing more it showed the extent to which Captain Key was the target of derision. The fact that the BEA management did not know of the graffiti was abdication of management responsibility.

It was shocking that a man with ten hours on the Trident could be in the right front seat.

There had been a failure to anticipate an obvious danger in premature droop retraction, and a failure in the airline not providing adequate training and information to crew members on this.'

But what the newspaper had not reported was that the American lawyer took on the case for a contingency fee. It meant that only if he won the claim for higher compensation would he be able to charge a percentage of the proceeds from the insurers. In some aircraft accidents such 'rake-offs' have turned out to be as high as fifty per cent, in particular when the costs of the lawyer's own inquiry into the accident were added to the bill.

To many people the ethics of taking a cut from 'blood money' must appear to be highly questionable. Legal circles in the United States became concerned about the profession's image resulting from such dubious practices. In May 1987, an editorial on this subject appeared in a Georgia newspaper, Atlanta Constitution:

'A Washington-based legal reform group has produced an information kit for families of aviation disaster victims to help to cope with the "tug of war" between lawyers and airlines' insurers that follows the crash.

Lawyers in the past have swarmed to crash sites, to tap into the litigation gold mine that follows most crashes.

"The competition is really a multimillion-dollar tug of war played out between disaster lawyers on one end of the rope and disaster insurers on the other," said Glenn Nishimura, the executive director of Halt, a non-profit citizen advocacy organisation. "Using tactics bordering on the unethical, they harass, intimidate and pressure people at most vulnerable moments.""

To pilots the concern about such practices went

even deeper. It was due to a loophole at the time in the Warsaw Convention on the limits of compensation, which allowed 'the agent' of an airline, in this case a pilot, to be sued if a slightest doubt existed that he had not followed procedures to the letter or if his performance was less than perfect. As a result of trying to find a possible culprit for this so called 'negligence', many pilots involved in an accident invariably became the target for derogatory attacks from American counsel during court sessions.

The Public Inquiry summarised the causes of Staines disaster as follows:

1. Captain Key failed to maintain recommended climb speed after power was reduced for the noise abatement procedure.
2. The droop was retracted sixty knots below the recommended speed.
3. The crew failed to monitor speed errors and observe the movement of the droop lever.
4. The crew failed to recognise the reasons for the Stick Shaker and the Stick Pusher operation.
5. The crew had unnecessarily overridden the operation of the Stick Pusher.

The lack of concentration and impaired judgement due to discomfort from a heart attack were considered to be the cause of Captain Key's poor speed control, and his lifting the droop up having mistaken the flap and droop lever, or his ordering to be lifted up.

According to the opinion of the Court of Inquiry, the presence of Captain Collins on the flight deck occupying a seat just behind the third pilot's position could have contributed to distracting Second Officer Ticehurst's attention from monitoring the flight progress properly. Other factors listed which could have influenced a lack of remedial actions, were:

1. The airline had not provided any training in case of incapacitation of one of the crew members.
2. Second Officer Keighley was insufficiently experienced.
3. The crew had probably not been aware that the stall was due to lifting the droop up.
4. The simultaneous operation of the Stick Shaker and the Stick Pusher, which meant that the aircraft had already stalled, could not have been understood by the crew.
5. There was no provision of a mechanism to prevent retraction of the droop at too low speeds.

In chapter IX of the Court of Inquiry report, answers were provided to certain questions of relative importance. One of the questions was: 'Did the Air Traffic Control operate efficiently during the ill-fated flight?'

It was followed by the briefest answer in the whole chapter, amounting to one word: 'YES'. Similar assurances were given in the earlier part of the report that the police were able to control the crowds near the crash and the reports that traffic congestion on the close-by roads had impeded rescue operations were not borne out by the facts.

How the 'YES' answer to the first question could have ignored the fact that the radar operator had failed to notice the ill-fated Trident disappearing from his surveillance screen, and consequently no alert was immediately initiated, is one of many examples of the Court doctoring its findings to the satisfaction of the respective authorities. This also applies to the opinion that the crowd control was satisfactory in spite of the evidence to the contrary. Although these two points may not have been of much importance as far as the cause of the accident, as a result the credibility of the Court's conclusions on the operational and technical aspects of the Staines disaster could be questioned.

To the same extent, the following statement in the report of the Court of Inquiry is far from convincing in view of the poor Trident sales: 'Both Hawker Siddeley and BEA are justly proud of the Trident and the record it has earned. We heard nothing but praise of the aircraft from all quarters. It is a reputation which is well deserved and nothing we have heard in this Inquiry has done anything to tarnish it.'

After the publication of the report, many people in England were led to believe that Key's lack of alertness due to a heart attack, had been the prime cause of one of the worst disasters at the time.

PART VII

Whether the findings of the Public Inquiry had realistically accounted for what had precipitated the Staines accident is highly debatable. Certain of the Court's ideas appear to have led to foregone conclusions. The weakness of the proceedings lay in the fact that the assessment of the evidence collected by the inspectors during their fieldwork and preliminary technical examination, had been taken entirely out of their hands. Instead of relying on expert opinion, relative laymen were entrusted with determining the cause of a complex accident from the flight technique point of view. Considering that the principal aim of any inquiry is to prevent future accidents, it is questionable whether the Court of Inquiry had fulfilled the role for which it had been intended.

Some evidence contained in the report needs to be re-assessed as to whether it had a crucial bearing on the cause of the Staines disaster. This in particular applies to the incident between Captain Key and First Officer Flavell. Medical experts did claim that the upsurge of blood pressure as a result of Key's out-burst of anger could have triggered off a heart attack. But is it correct to presume that the crew room incident was of such gravity that it had culminated in fatal consequences?

The Court of Inquiry report stated that, although Key lost his temper, the outburst had subsided as quickly as it had flared up. Since he was known among his colleagues as a difficult and argumentative individual, he must have been used to sniping remarks. Taking this into consideration, the incident does not appear to have been sufficiently serious to have resulted in life-threatening stress. None of the witnesses who came in contact with Key during flight preparations an hour before take-off had observed any signs of physical weakness or incoherent manner that could be associated with a grave cardiac development. In such circumstances, certain symptoms such as excessive sweating or difficulty in breathing or walking should have already been apparent.

J. Coleman, the gate supervisor at the time of the departure and the last person to visit the cockpit, was in a position to notice if Key displayed any signs of losing his faculties. In that respect, the Court of Inquiry report stated as follows: 'Mr Coleman came on board to discuss the load, and he observed nothing untoward about the Captain or crew.'

From the heated discussion that took place about the correct loading of the aircraft, it looks as if Key was displaying his usual vigour about adhering to the proper procedures. Apparently he insisted in strong words that the loadsheet could not be 'adjusted' and some freight had to be removed, even if it involved a delay.

The conversation with the ground engineer during engine starting again gives no hint that Key was in any way unwell. The same applies to his tone of voice during the subsequent exchange of radio messages with Ground Control, Tower and

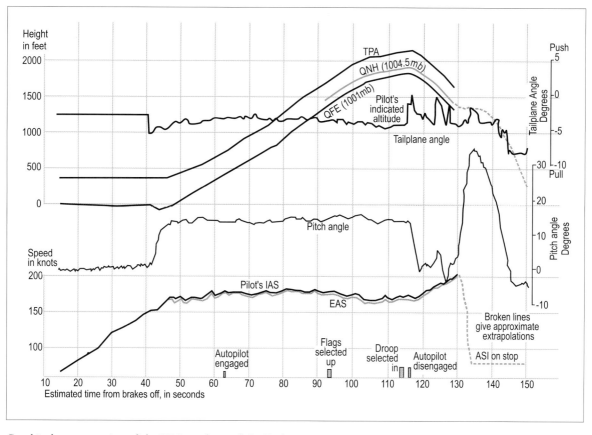

Graphical representation of the FDR read-out of the Trident I PI.

Approach Control.

If his lack of ability to think clearly was not evident twenty minutes before the crash, it would be unlikely that shortly afterwards he committed a fatal mistake which, as it was alleged by the Court of Inquiry, was a result of his brain having been clouded by a heart attack.

On the other hand, the check on a minor technical problem, which was performed while the aircraft was already lined up on the runway, and delayed the take-off for about a minute, could have an important bearing on Key's vital actions in flight. According to the Court of Inquiry report, it was probably the amber 'low pressure warning light' on the Stall Recovery System, that came on. After the crash, the pressure control valve was found in a partly-open position, a result of a maintenance oversight. The likely cause of the warning light illuminating was that, while waiting for take-off clearance with power at idle, the engine compressors were unable to maintain air pressure in the Stall Recovery System due to a slight leak and, as a result, the warning light was triggered. As it was not a 'nuisance warning' precipitated by a spurious signal, by which some aircraft systems are occasionally afflicted, Key could have been left with impression that the Stick Pusher on PI was not fully serviceable and had to be treated with caution.

According to the FDR read-out, the first sign of a disparity between the recommended and the actual climb speed became apparent shortly after becoming airborne. The Speed Lock of the autopilot was switched on twelve knots below the laid-down safe climb speed of 177 knots. This seems surprising considering the aircraft was already heavily buffeted by turbulence. During the entire two minutes of climb this disparity persisted and the laid-down safe climb speed of 177 knots was never reached.

The Court of Inquiry report stated that FDR recordings of several flights which Key made shortly before the accident had shown that, apart from a tendency to engage the autopilot at a speed and height lower than average, his speed control was as good as that of the other captains.

An analysis of Trident PI's initial climb performance, based on every flight in the sixteen days prior to the crash, revealed that the effect of power reduction for noise abatement purposes was no different from the rest of the Trident fleet.

According to the laws of physics governing flight, an aircraft can lose speed if it encounters either a downdraught or a wind shear. Downdraughts are mainly experienced when flying over mountainous regions, in or near a thunderstorm or when crossing a vigorous weather front.

Speed loss from wind shear becomes marked when an aircraft runs head-on into an abrupt reduction of wind strength or a change of wind direction. This can be particularly dangerous at low altitudes during climb or descent (see chapters 1 and 4).

A similar effect can be expected in a turn when there is a strong headwind component present. As soon as the aircraft moves away from that direction, the airspeed will start to decay and if engine power remains constant, it may be insufficient to compensate for the loss of momentum.

In the case of PI's climb on the afternoon of the crash, the change in the wind speed and direction with altitude had undoubtedly played a critical role. The surface wind was 210/17 knots, but it was reported that by 1,000 feet the strength had gone up to twenty-eight knots and by 2,000 feet to thirty-five knots. At the same time, the direction of the wind would have veered to the west by about 30°, when clear of ground friction.

The Flight Recorder read-out showed that during the climb to 900 feet on the runway heading, the airspeed had increased by six knots. This would have been expected from the increase of wind strength with altitude. But when the Trident started a turn on passing 900 feet, it would have moved away from the headwind – its component estimated to have been at that stage about thirty knots from direction of 240° (M) – and, as a result, the speed began to decay rapidly, as shown on the FDR. The airspeed drop could not have been due to noise abatement power reduction alone, in particular in that lifting the flaps at the same time, thus improving acceleration through reduced drag, should have counteracted it.

At the Public Inquiry, suggestions were advanced that this could have been due to the autopilot acting sluggishly during the rapid airspeed changes due to turbulence. However, after the Court was provided with the performance data

by the manufacturer and with similar studies by the CAA, it was accepted that: 'The automatic flight control systems were functioning properly according to their design object.'

This is contrary to what the FDR parameters of the tail-plane incident angle had shown, in that there was a marked movement of the tail plane, most likely to compensate for the speed loss. Whether this was within the envelope of the autopilot capability could have only been established by an experienced investigator in view of two adverse factors, that is turbulence and wind shear. But at the Court of Inquiry this matter was played down by counsel representing the autopilot manufacturer.

Of particular significance is the paragraph in the Court of Inquiry report entitled 'SPEED', which stated: 'One of the most important facts disclosed by the FDR was the consistent failure by the handling pilot to achieve the appropriate speed for the relevant stages of the flight'.

In the Court's opinion, the error, which was introduced shortly after the aircraft became airborne, had subsequently contributed to the critically low speed once the flaps were retracted and power was reduced for noise abatement.

This conclusion must be closely examined. On the Trident the FDR read-out does not necessarily reflect the information which could have been displayed on the captain's instruments. In simple words: what the FDR records is not necessarily the same as what the captain sees on his panel.

However, the Court of Inquiry believed that Key's poor speed-keeping was due to a different reason: 'It is probable that there was some connection between the grossly abnormal speed error and Captain Key's physical conditions on one hand and the movement of the droop lever on the other.'

Why Key had failed to maintain safe climb speed in adverse weather conditions and very strong turbulence, when every pilot would be expected to stay on the high side, becomes a crucial question.

It was assumed that Key was already suffering from considerable discomfort which affected his judgement. Indeed, the autopsy indicated that his cardiac condition was abnormal and he was afflicted by advanced arteriosclerosis. The ailment, which must have started at an early age, probably between twenty and thirty, had not been detected during six-monthly medical examinations for his pilot's licence. It is surprising that Key had not shown any signs of high blood pressure, usually associated with arteriosclerosis, but to many people, including his GP, he appeared to be a picture of robust health.

It was discovered during the autopsy that Key's arteries were constricted by as much as 50% and that there were two signs of damage on the wall of his left coronary. One, an old tear which had healed up and which at the time probably did not bring on any symptoms of a heart attack, and a new bleeding that occurred, as quoted in the exact words of the report: 'not more than two hours before the death and no less than about a minute'.

The pathologists believed that the last haemorrhage, judging by the colour and the composition of the congealed blood, had not been caused by impact and only a physical or emotional stress could have started it. They thought that a string of minor irritations, such as the row in the crew room or noticing the disparaging graffiti upon entering the cockpit, could have raised Key's blood pressure to such an extent that it caused a rupture in the wall of the coronary.

'The process [the initial rise in blood pressure which resulted in the rupture of small blood vessels] thereafter would be gradual but dynamic, culminating in the separation of the intima, at a time which medically at least, can be only the subject of surmise, but may have been in the last thirty seconds of life.'

Using the graffiti as grounds for Key's agitation seems illogical, as it was stated at one session of the Public Inquiry that he had seen several such uncomplimentary inscriptions earlier on and was not at all bothered by them. A similar argument can be put forward about the effect of his row in the BEA crew room.

But could Key's incapacitation have been the only reason for his 'irrational' actions? If it was not the case, what else could have accounted for maintaining low airspeed and retracting the droop prematurely?

Quite a number of factors point to a possibility of the captain's ASI having displayed a higher speed than the actual speed that was registered on the FDR.

The first hint that the instrument may have been over-reading comes from the fact that the Speed Lock was switched on twelve knots too low. At that stage of take-off, Key would have his eyes glued on the airspeed indication. The Court of Inquiry report stressed this: 'The experience borne out of the tests conducted by the accident inspectors on the simulator, have indicated that pilots' attention during climb would be tunnelled on the airspeed and the attitude indicator in an endeavour to fly what they considered to be a safe speed.'

It would have been unlikely for Key, known for the accuracy of his speed-keeping, to switch on the airspeed lock twelve knots lower than required, particularly in turbulent weather. In such circumstances he would have most likely elected to maintain airspeed on the high side rather than on the low side. As he was not flying the aircraft manually, he had an opportunity to keep an eye constantly on the prime flight instruments. Had he noticed any speed drop, it would have been easy to correct it with the autopilot pitch trim wheel and then re-engage the Speed Lock.

Yet after flaps retraction and power reduction for noise abatement, the speed was allowed to fall by as much as twenty knots below the safe figure. This seems surprising, considering the aircraft was at that moment not only affected by heavy turbulence but was also in a turn.

With his background knowledge as a check pilot, Key must have been aware of bank effect on stalling speed, in particular that BEA had recently issued a safety circular on the subject. Although the 23° bank that had been maintained during the turn would have increased stalling speed by only eight knots, a similar amount could have been expected from heavy gusts. The combination of the two adverse factors called for extra caution, which Key must have been well aware of. But he took no corrective action. It can only be presumed that looking at his airspeed indicator, he was satisfied with the speed.

PART VIII

Erroneous indications on the flight instruments are exceptionally rare. If pilots were asked what they considered to be the most dependable instrument on their panel, they would invariably point at the airspeed indicator. In the days of direct driven instruments, the cases of failures could have been counted on one's fingers. Reliability is also high with electronic systems though there is much more to go wrong. In view of the pilots' unshakable confidence in the ASI, a faulty reading was bound to catch out even an experienced and cautious captain as Key. It could have led to total confusion if other warnings contradicted the ASI reading.

It can be argued that a discrepancy in the speed indication that lasted as long as a minute should have been spotted by the two other crew members. Over the years, BEA developed a highly effective 'monitored approach system', used for letdowns, approaches and landings. However, as far as other critical phases of flight such as initial climb were concerned, the company directives were less specific. Therefore, noticing at that stage a difference in readings between two corresponding flight instruments would depend on many factors such as cockpit workload, crew alertness, time available and, above all, distractions. The time factor to determine which instrument indicated correctly

would have played a crucial role in avoiding the Staines disaster.

Assuming that the captain's ASI was overreading, a question could also be raised as to why Key did not notice the difference on the stand-by ASI. If there happened to be no warning flag on the primary ASI – and such a possibility will be dealt with later – he would have no reason to suspect that his speed was wrong as a result of an instrument fault. He most likely presumed that his higher than required speed at that moment was due to a strong updraught and it did not strike him to check other indications. By being located at the bottom of the instrument panel, the stand-by

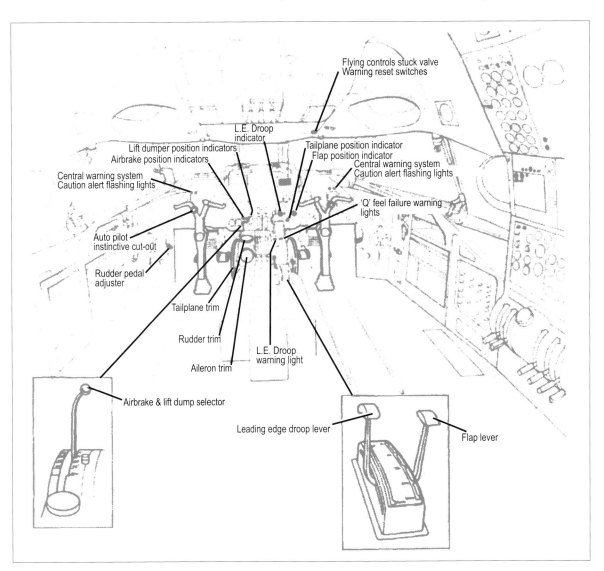

Flying controls stuck valve
Warning reset switches

L.E. Droop indicator

Lift dumper position indicators
Airbrake position indicators

Tailplane position indicator
Flap position indicator
Central warning system
Caution alert flashing lights

Central warning system
Caution alert flashing lights

'Q' feel failure warning lights

Auto pilot instinctive cut-out

Rudder pedal adjuster

Tailplane trim

Rudder trim

Aileron trim

L.E. Droop warning light

Airbrake & lift dump selector

Leading edge droop lever

Flap lever

Trident I cockpit layout.

ASI lay outside the usual scanning cycle and, moreover, the control column would have been in the way of a cursory check. With Key being short in stature, the position of his eyes in relation to the instrument panel would have been lower than most pilots, making a downward scan even more difficult.

The impression of encountering a powerful updraught after the flaps were retracted could have been accentuated by the fact that the gusts became less frequent but much stronger. According to the FDR read-out, at that stage they oscillated as much as 0.15 g up and down. Captain Bassett, a PanAm captain and IFALPA All Weather Landing expert, who took off that afternoon in a Boeing 747 for New York, reported that he experienced the worst turbulence for many a year.

If the ASI happened to be over-reading through a fault in the instrument system, the resultant increase above the 'target' climb speed as observed by Key would not have caused him much concern and would have probably been looked upon as an added safety factor. On the other hand, if the speed continued to increase, it could not be ignored. Once it began to approach the limit with the droop lowered, which was 250 knots, this called for action to prevent its damage.

Two immediate solutions were possible. One was to increase the attitude to hold the airspeed below 250 knots until 3,000 feet was reached, and then lift droop according to the procedure laid down in the Aircraft Operating Manual. But any upward change from the already quite high incidence angle of 15° would have resulted in an unusually steep attitude. On instruments and in turbulence it could prove to be a precarious manoeuvre that could have led to overcorrecting the aircraft and inducing instability.

The other possibility was to retract the droop even before reaching 3,000 feet. With the altimeter just coming up to 2,000 feet on QNH setting, Key may have reckoned that the clearance from the ground was adequate. As it was just a matter of leaning across and pulling up the droop handle, which was on the captain's side of the flap/droop levers assembly, it would have been quicker for him to do it by himself rather than giving a command or explaining the reason why the droop should be operated out of turn. In particular, if his ASI showed that the speed was rapidly approaching the 250 knots limit.

Once the droop started to come up, a number of warning lights, including the 'droop out of position' amber light, would have flashed, adding to the confusion and distracting Key's attention from the only instrument that could have warned him of a dangerous situation, the stand-by ASI. While several indications pointed to stall, the trustworthiest instrument on the panel, the main airspeed indicator, probably showed a contradictory picture. The unexpected outcome of lifting the droop, must have come to Key a like a bolt from the blue, in particular when the Stick Pusher and the Stick Shaker activated almost simultaneously. But the most alarming experience was probably the control column having been kicked hard forward by the Stick Pusher, disconnecting the autopilot.

Key's other reactions underline his belief that the speed was far from critical and that the problem lay with a malfunction of the Stall Recovery System. At the back of his mind could have been the low-pressure amber warning light before take-off.

It is evident from the FDR read-out that during eleven seconds of the Stick Pusher operation, he took off the bank and made three frantic attempts to bring the nose back to the original attitude. But this was far from simple. Captain Hopkins, a Trident pilot and a member of the BALPA Technical Committee at the time of the accident, explained the complications involved, as follows:

'In many recovery trials I found this oscillation between push and release to be most disconcerting and difficult to control. The essential thing is to be first bearing down on the control column as the pusher releases, and then to ease off the pressure on the control, otherwise very rapid rates of pitch can develop and secondary stall ensue even before the nose again reaches the horizon.

At the time of the accident there was no in-flight training and, to my recollection, the simulator algorithm was not valid for below-stall airspeeds under these conditions.'

The three 'kicks' which the Stick Pusher had applied to the control column were powerful enough to record on the FDR an increase of a half g. Key's endeavours to lift the nose back to the original attitude must have been equally forceful to register a similar amount. Had he been suffering from a terminal heart attack, it is unlikely that he would possess sufficient strength to exert such a hard pull. But the physical stress, combined with the shock of facing a catastrophic situation, could have at that very moment ruptured his coronary wall. This would be consistent with the pathologists' opinion that the haemorrhage could have started as close as one minute before Key's death from impact.

Another controversy, concerning the Court of Inquiry claim that Key's impaired judgement had made him retract the droop mistaking it for flaps, is his action, which most likely he had taken himself, to turn off the Stick Pusher or had ordered it to be turned off. Disabling it was a serious action, for it could only be re-connected on the ground.

The subject of which crew member could have lifted up the droop or could have disconnected the Stall Recovery System was extensively discussed at the Public Inquiry, but no clear answers were provided.

Taking into consideration the two co-pilots' limited flying experience, and the fact that their training on the Stall Recovery System was performed only on the simulator, it would appear that Key most probably disconnected the Stick Pusher himself. But to do so, he would have to turn round and bend down, in order to place his hand on the lever located on the rear wall of the centre pedestal, then move the lever to the 'off' position. For a 'dying' man, who was supposed to have been slumped in his seat, this would have been quite an effort.

More indications point to Key's conviction that his speed was far from catastrophically low. Had he realised that he was stalling, an instinctive reaction would have been to apply all available power and lower the droop. But the throttles were never touched. After impact they were found in the noise abatement setting.

Whether the two co-pilots were closely involved in the alarming events on board is difficult to assess without the help of the Voice Recorder. Unfortunately it was not fitted to the Tridents. Only general presumptions can be made as to the reasons why the co-pilots did not actively participate in the actions on the flight deck.

In the case of Ticehurst occupying the third pilot's seat, a probable explanation is that he could have failed to notice the speed discrepancy because at the critical time he was pre-occupied in writing down the clearance Key had just acknowledged. According to the Court of Inquiry report, an entry was found to that effect.

Once the aircraft began to stall, Ticehurst, like Key, when suddenly confronted with a catastrophic development was probably caught by surprise. Unless he kept cross-checking both instrument panels at regular intervals, his chances of spotting a speed discrepancy were very low. The view of the stand-by ASI on the captain's panel was even more obstructed from the third pilot's position.

As far as Keighley was concerned, the situation could have been different. It was probably his first take-off in very strong turbulence. Such experience could not have been exactly soothing for the nerves of a very young pilot and the psychological effect could have been very detrimental to his concentration. He may not even have been aware of why Key retracted the droop as his ASI would have displayed a different reading. It would have been too much to expect from a youngster with limited experience to work out in a flash what went wrong at that moment. A verbal warning that the right-hand ASI indicated a dangerously low speed would have had to be very rapid and explicit, as every fraction of second counted in order to get out of trouble.

It is surprising that during the Public Inquiry, there was no mention that Captain Collins could have tried to re-select the droop down. This is borne out by what Captain Pritchard had observed about the wreckage at Staines. He believed that is why the head-set was found in the right-hand corner of the cockpit, far away from the observer's seat. The Court of Inquiry report stated that the head-set was plugged in and set to 'intercom'. Other evidence points to the probability of Collins having made a frantic attempt to reach the droop. Captain Pritchard recounts his observation:

'I asked a fireman who removed the bodies from the flight deck where he found Collins's body. He was quite sure that it lay across the pedestal.

I do not think that Collins, being an experienced Trident pilot, would have sat for take-off without strapping in.'

From the observer's seat Collins would not have been able to see the captain's instruments, but he would have had a good view of the co-pilot's ASI. Although Keighley may have been overwhelmed by the events, Collins must have noticed that speed was low and after un-clipping his straps, leapt forward trying to re-select the droop. This could have accounted for his head-set finding its way into the right-hand side of the cockpit. Unfortunately, this remedial action could not prevent the disaster because the aircraft had already entered a deep stall.

In the Court of Inquiry report there was only

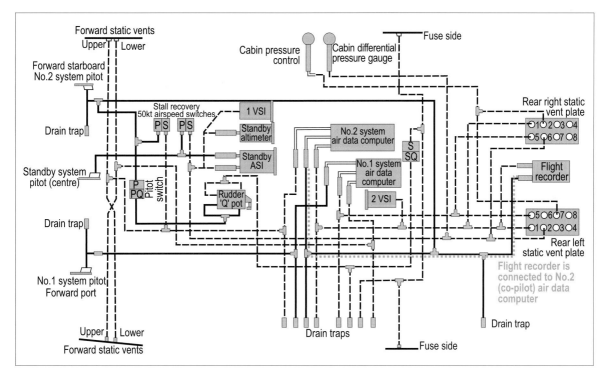

Diagram of Trident I Air Data Computers.

one reference to Collins: 'Captain Collins was found to be holding in his right hand a can of Aerosol Air Freshener. This type of can is standard issue to all freighter captains of whom Captain Collins was one.'

Such a remark should have never been included in the report. It was totally irrelevant to the events on board the ill-fated Trident.

PART IX

Any argument that Key had been misled by a faulty ASI must be corroborated by an analysis of whether it is technically feasible for the electronic instruments to display erroneous indications without a warning flag showing. Although normally highly reliable, as distant reading instruments depend on a chain of components, the effects of a component failure or a faulty interaction between two components have to be looked into.

A brief description of the Trident's instrument system might help to understand its basic mechanism. The above diagram shows that the aircraft was equipped with two separate Air Data systems, incorporating the following components:

analogue air data computer, altimeter, airspeed indicator and machmeter.

In each system, pitot head and static vent pressures are converted into electrical impulses by transducers in the Air Data Computer (ADC) and, after the required corrections are applied, these impulses are distributed to various instruments and the autopilot. From the diagram of the pitot and static system it can be seen that pressure from the starboard side is shared by No. 2 ADC and the FDR as well as certain other systems. *It is clearly evident that if a fault happened to develop in the port system, which exclusively serves the captain's instruments, such a fault would not be recorded on the FDR.*

The ASIs are provided with an amber and black warning flag. The flag is designed to come into view on both ASIs when there is a computer failure or when comparator circuits, incorporated in each air data system, detect more than ten knots discrepancy between the airspeed indicated in one system and the ADC output of the other. The flag is relatively small and its colour scheme does not help it to be readily noticed when it appears.

An electronic device called Control Synchro is

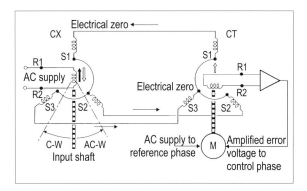

Diagram of the Control Synchro of the Air Data Computer.

used to pass signals from the ADCs to the respective instruments such as the airspeed indicator, machmeter and altimeter. The 'transmitter' sends the ADC output to the 'receiver', which in turn slews a rotor with the pointer attached to it. In the case of simple servos, the governing factors are the changes in the magnetic field, while on the airspeed indicators and altimeters used in conjunction with the air data systems, 'error voltages' are used to control the master/slave combination with the help of an amplifier. In theory, any discrepancy in the indication of the instruments should be detected by the comparator circuit.

When recently consulted, an authority on aircraft instruments was of the opinion that the most likely reason for malfunctioning of a servo system leading to an error in the ASI indication without triggering warning flag could have been an internal resistance in the circuit that had suddenly developed in the master/slave combination. The increase in resistance could have been caused by a weak solder joint that had eventually failed or by a loose connection brought about by the aircraft's vibrations in heavy turbulence.

But a fault in the circuit may not have been the only cause of incorrect speed indication. Although relatively little trouble was experienced with the Trident ADCs, a possibility of some other hardware component failure cannot be excluded. By present-day standards, the analogue ADCs of the early era were relatively crude devices. They relied on electro-mechanical transducers to convert data from pitot and static probes, and these transducers were not particularly strong.

Moreover, an ADC could have been adversely affected by excessive voltage 'spikes' when heavy wattage electrical appliances were switched on or off in the service galley. At the time of the ADCs' introduction into operational service, relatively little was known about the detrimental effect of extremely rapid voltage changes and a need for stringent filtering networks.

In general, one of the main weaknesses of analogue computers is their insufficient accuracy when comparing output or input data for errors and this could have also accounted for the lack of the warning flag when an error in the airspeed indication had developed. Therefore, when it was recognised in the aviation industry that they were incapable of producing the required standard of performance, McDonnell Douglas was the first aircraft manufacturer to fit digital air data computers on the DC10.

Although during the DC10 ground course I was assured that their fault detecting capability was foolproof, operational experience soon showed otherwise.

While executing an arrival procedure at Tokyo Airport at night, I was instructed to maintain 200 knots. On the DC10 it was a matter of dialling the required speed and the autothrottles would do the rest. However, the landing checklist was interrupted by air traffic control claiming that my speed was too high and that I was closing on the traffic ahead. An immediate check on both ASIs revealed a discrepancy of twenty knots, my side indicating a higher value. No red warning light illuminated at any time and this should have come on as soon as the difference had exceeded more than one knot. The erroneous indication was later traced to a faulty ADC, which also controlled the autothrottles. If the so-called 'foolproof' digital device had failed to warn about a speed discrepancy between two ASIs, such a probability would have been much greater with an analogue computer.

PART X

It may appear that some of my arguments on what had really caused the PI disaster are based on circumstantial evidence. But circumstantial evidence was used in the conclusions arrived at by the Court of Inquiry, in particular in respect of poor speed control and a premature droop retraction. There is no doubt that Key's degenerated arteries could have brought on a heart attack at some stage of his life. But no evidence has been found that Key was incapable of performing his functions effectively until the Trident struck the ground. His impaired judgement was only a presumption by the Court of Inquiry, based on the opinion of medical experts, who even then were contradicted by the following paragraph in the report:

'At second 108 [seconds from releasing the brakes on take-off] Captain Key is making his final R/T communication "Up to 60". It is true that the message was unduly terse. He should have given his aircraft prefix; he should have said "Up to flight level 60"; he should have acknowledged the instruction to squawk. Those omissions are not sufficient to indicate imminent collapse, particularly when his tone of voice appears to be normal.'

But Key's other transmissions were also brief. Although they technically contravened the standard R/T procedure, they were typical examples of how pilots are forced to observe economy of words in busy terminal control areas as a result of an endless exchange of messages. A more likely explanation as to why Key was so concise is that he might have begun to take notice of the rapidly escalating airspeed.

The paragraph in the report reads further: 'It does not seem reasonably possible that Captain Key collapsed during those eight vital seconds from 108 to 116. [At 116 the droop was retracted.] There is, in fact, ample evidence of pilot input from the FDR traces up to at least second 124 when the second stick-push took place.'

Several indications point to Key having been convinced that his airspeed was above the minimum safety speed. He fought the Stick Pusher, believing it to be a spurious activation as a result of the minor technical problem observed just before take-off. Consequently, he most likely de-activated the Stall Recovery System himself. He did not lower the droop again and did not apply full climb power, although there was still as much as 20% power available. As it was established that Key himself was handling the aircraft, it does not look likely that the co-pilots were involved in operating the control column.

There is no doubt that Keighley was far too inexperienced to occupy the right-hand seat in the cockpit. Moreover, heavy turbulence would have most probably affected his composure. Therefore it can be expected that Key was left to perform most, if not all, actions by himself.

As no Cockpit Voice Recorder was installed on the Tridents – which could have provided the only evidence capable of throwing light on the actual circumstances on board – it was wrong for the Court of Inquiry to assume that the accident had been caused by Key's impaired judgement brought on by a heart attack. It is regrettable that much of the Court's time was devoted to discussing industrial aspects in connection with the accident. In the opinion of many former BEA pilots, this had no bearing whatsoever on the Staines tragedy.

Quite a number of BEA pilots have advanced different theories as to what could have led to the premature retracting of the droop. But the only theories about mechanical problems with the selection mechanism that the Court took into consideration were those that the Trident manufacturer was able to disprove.

An open verdict would have been a correct answer to the tragedy of 119 lives: 118 occupants of the Trident PI who perished in the crash and a senior engineering AIIB inspector who took his own life as a result of the pressure of work in connection with the accident.

9

1973 – The Tragic Outing to Switzerland

PART I

At first it sounded like a dream idea when a bunch of enterprising housewives from several neighbouring villages in North Somerset decided to organise a one-day outing to Basle in a chartered aircraft. The excursion was intended to combine sightseeing with a shopping spree. Since they all lived close to Bristol Lulsgate Airport and the flight was expected to take an hour and forty minutes, the trip to Basle by air looked more expeditious and much more fun than going to London for shopping by train. Most of the housewives were members of the local women's clubs such as the Cheddar Mums' Night Out, the Axbridge Women's Guild or a skittle club from Congresbury, so they knew each other by sight.

Early in the morning on 10 April 1973, 139 passengers, predominantly women, some with their children, boarded a Vanguard from Invicta International Airways, a charter company with its headquarters at Ramsgate in Kent. Weather in England was relatively good but Europe was under a freak cold spell for mid-April. In fact, a fierce blizzard raged all night and many parts of Germany, France and Switzerland were covered by a foot of snow. Particularly affected was the Upper Rhine Valley where Basle lies. Nevertheless, slightly warmer conditions were expected on arrival, snow turning into rain. Despite a not very encouraging weather outlook, nothing was going to spoil the joyful prospect of setting foot for the first time in Switzerland for a flock of animated women.

The Vanguard, which was stationed at Luton, had to be positioned first to Bristol and Flight IM 435 departed for Basle at nineteen minutes past eight. Over England and France flying conditions were smooth, but once the aircraft entered clouds

during the descent, it became very rough. One woman passenger later recounted that, although she was never prone to airsickness, on this occasion she was badly affected. At times, turbulence was so severe that, as the aircraft went up and down like a big dipper, younger children could not help screaming with fright. In the end, they became so hysterical that the stewardesses had to restrain them.

The first approach misfired. When the Vanguard broke clouds, it was nowhere near the runway. In fact, it had just missed a hill at Basle, five miles away from the airport. The surviving passengers could recollect seeing streets and houses out of their windows. After circling around, the pilots made another attempt to land. But as it was later established, the aircraft commenced the instrument let-down on the wrong side of the airport, in the southern, instead of in the northern sector, and was rapidly closing in on a range of hills only a few miles ahead.

Then, all of a sudden, a rapid climb was initiated but it was too late. The ill-fated Vanguard brushed the treetops on a 2,000-foot-high steeply-rising hill. Unfortunately, it could not clear a slightly taller peak 100 metres further on and struck the slopes. The crash took place about half a kilometre away from Herrenmatt, a tiny hamlet in the parish of Hochwald in Canton Solothurn. The isolated settlement, situated high in the Jura hills, overlooks the valley of the river Birs, a tributary of the Rhine.

As the aircraft struck dense forest it began to scatter bits of the nose and the engines over an area of 1,000 square metres. After felling dozens of trees in the process it somersaulted and then broke into two parts, both of which came to rest upside down. The larger part, the middle section of the fuselage with the left wing up to the outboard engine, was badly crushed on impact. One hundred and eight passengers and four crew members were instantly killed. The right wing caught fire but the flames soon died down. Through a miraculous stroke of luck the rear section of the cabin and the tail assembly were hardly damaged and this accounted for the relatively large number of survivors. Two cabin attendants and thirty-six passengers came out of the crash alive but many were badly injured. The only person to escape completely unharmed was one of the stewardesses. Mrs Cole, who was sitting in the rear cabin, later recounted that, when they brushed the treetops, she thought the aircraft had touched the ground upon landing. The only thing she could recollect about the subsequent events, was that she found herself hanging upside down, held in place by her seat belt. She was only slightly injured but her daughter was killed.

It was a heartbreaking tragedy for the five small Somerset communities. Of the 108 people that perished in the crash, twenty-one women and children came from Cheddar, twenty-one from Axbridge, twenty from Congresbury, nine from Redhill and six from Wrington.

When repeated radio calls from Basle Tower to Invicta Flight IM 453 remained unanswered, the Swiss Federal Aviation Office's Search and Rescue Services and the Accident Investigation Bureau were notified by the French Air Traffic Control at Basle Airport that a British charter aircraft was overdue and had presumably crashed in the hills to the south of the city.

A raging blizzard and snowbound roads hampered efforts to trace the missing aircraft. The area where it was believed the Vanguard had gone down was only accessible by a secondary road to Hochwald, a small village in the local hills, and by a cart track further on. Just the same, a very early report, which could have speeded up locating the crash, was ignored.

When a boy from Herrenmatt heard an aircraft flying over the hills, followed by an explosion, he took his dog and began to scout the surroundings. Once he found the wreck – although he did not speak any English and could not understand what the bewildered survivors were trying to tell him – he realised that he must get help at once. He rushed back home and phoned the local police. But they took no notice of his call. Later the accident investigation report offered a doubtful extenuating excuse: 'A very early report about the location of the crash was not followed because of an unfortunate combination of circumstances.'

With only the clothes on that they wore in the aircraft, the survivors were at the mercy of wintry weather with a bitterly cold wind. At 2,000 feet, the temperature was well below freezing. Their plight seemed hard to believe since they were only six miles away from the centre of Basle, a bustling city with 220,000 inhabitants and only two miles from Aesch, a small town in the foothills.

Even when the rescue party were eventually able to trace the crashed aircraft, it took forty-five minutes for the survivors to receive medical attention. Seriously injured passengers had to wait another half an hour before they were transported to the local hospital. But in spite of enduring freezing conditions for over three hours, none of the survivors had suffered from exposure. Later in the day, the remains of the less fortunate passengers were brought to Dornach, another small town in the Birs valley. A gymnasium in the local school was turned into a mortuary where the bodies were temporarily laid to rest. In the days to come, the deceased were brought back to Bristol on an Invicta Vanguard freighter. Each coffin was bedecked with flowers and wreaths donated by the Swiss people, a moving sight for the freighter crew.

When the Solothurn Cantonal police arrived at the scene of the crash, they immediately cordoned off the whole area with two rings. An inner ring was set up to protect the wreckage from souvenir hunters, while an outer ring kept the access road closed, except for the officials. Once the snowstorm abated the investigating team began their preliminary field work. After fifteen days, all parts of the ill-fated aircraft were finally recovered and stored at Othmersingen. According to the Swiss accident report, the woodland and the crops on the hillside, were badly damaged by the crashing Vanguard.

PART II

As the disaster occurred on Swiss soil the Swiss Federal Commission of Inquiry was responsible for the investigation. The accredited representatives came from the British Air Accident Investigation Branch as the country of the aircraft's registration, Vickers, the airframe manufacturer, Rolls-Royce, the engine manufacturer, the operator Invicta International and the French aviation authorities. The latter were included because Basle Airport is situated just across the border on French territory, owned by a Swiss–French consortium, but financed mainly by the Swiss. All services, including Air Traffic Control, were operated at the time by French personnel.

Throughout the investigation there was an evident lack of cooperation between the Swiss and the French authorities. Unfortunately, this had resulted in a delay in arranging a flight check of the radio aids at Basle Airport at the earliest opportunity. Consequently, they were not tested until the day after the accident. A recommendation in the Manual of Aircraft Accident Investigation, compiled by the International Civil Aviation Organisation for guidance of the member states, clearly stipulates that: 'When there is any reason to suspect that a navigation aid may be involved in the causal area, the investigator should request, without delay, special ground and flight tests.'

Just before the crash, pilots had reported difficulties with the reception of radio beacons and, as it appeared that this could have something to do with a heavy snowfall, it was vital to check the navigation aids in the prevailing conditions. With a change of weather expected during the course of the day, no time should have been wasted on bureaucratic wrangles. Evidently national chauvinism stood in the way of arranging a flight test in the shortest possible time. The Swiss Federal Aviation Authorities had an aircraft equipped for testing radio aids standing by at Zurich Airport, less than fifteen minutes flying away. But the French had to bring their plane from the Paris area and this was going to take time.

Failing to arrange a flight test quickly or to take up the offer from the Swiss and, at the same time, allowing other traffic to use questionably reliable radio aids for instrument approaches, reflects badly on the French civil aviation authorities. Their disregard for a potentially dangerous situation, created by a suspected fault in their navigational facilities, could have led to another accident from the same cause.

There were other examples of an uncooperative attitude on the part of the French authorities. Not until eight months after the accident was the Swiss Federal Aviation Bureau given permission to make its own flight test of the instrument landing facilities at Basle Airport. Moreover, the Swiss Investigating Commission was provided with only very brief statements from the Basle air traffic controllers who were on duty at the time of the crash. The controllers were not allowed to appear at the Public Inquiry, which was scheduled to be held by the Swiss cantonal authorities at Solothurn in November 1974. Only two French officials were sent to Solothurn: the Basle Airport commandant and the French representative on the Swiss Investigating Commission. When Kurt Lier, the head of the Swiss Federal Aviation Bureau was informed of such limited French participation, heated arguments broke out, and as a result, one of the French delegates refused to attend the Inquiry.

It took fifteen months to compile the accident report, which was subsequently accepted by the British AAIB, then translated into English and published by the HMSO.

The Swiss Federal Commission of Inquiry came to the following conclusions on the cause of the accident:

'Loss of orientation during two ILS approaches carried out under IFR conditions.

The following factors contributed to the occurrence of the accident:

Inadequate navigation, above all imprecise initiation of final approach with regard to height and approach centre line, confusion of navigational aids and insufficient checking and comparison of navigational aids and instrument readings (cross and double check).

The poor reception of the medium frequency beacons and technical defects in the No. 1 ILS localiser and No. 2 glide slope receiver made the crew's navigational work more difficult.'

The Commission were of the opinion that the airworthiness of the radio navigation equipment on the Vanguard G-AXOP was questionable. The faults found in the ADF and ILS equipment were such that the safety of ILS approaches was likely to have been impaired. The Certificate of Airworthiness was renewed without the cause of the defects in the ILS or ADF, as reported by the crews, having been ascertained.

PART III

Before Flight Invicta IM 435 left for Bristol, there was a change in the crew. As the scheduled first officer was not able to make the flight and there were no co-pilots available, another captain stepped in. It was company policy, in such circumstances, for the command to be alternated with each segment of the route. On the first stretch from Luton to Bristol, the pilot-in-charge was the originally assigned captain, forty-seven-year-old Ivor Terry, a very experienced airman. He joined the RAF towards the end of the war and obtained his wings in 1947. During his service career, he flew a variety of aircraft such as Lancasters, Shackletons, Valettas and Neptunes. He came to Invicta in 1968 and when in March 1971 the charter company acquired five Vanguards, he was straight away checked out as captain on the new type. By the time of the accident, he had completed 9,172 hours, 1,256 on the Vanguards. According to the records of his proficiency checks, the Swiss Investigating Commission were of the opinion that Terry was a level-headed and conscientious pilot.

However, this could not be said about the other captain, Anthony Noel Dorman, a thirty-five-year-old Canadian. The two men were of an entirely different calibre. Dorman joined the Royal Canadian Air Force in 1963 but was soon discharged on the grounds of lacking aptitude for flying. Nevertheless, he was determined to carry on with his aviation career. At first he obtained a private pilot's licence, then, later on, a commercial licence. In 1969 Dorman got a job with Nigerian Airways. At the time, the airline was desperately short of pilots and both the airline and the local civil aviation authorities accepted his flying record without any query. As a result, he was issued with the equivalent Nigerian licences. However, when Dorman's flying logbook was checked by the British AAIB, numerous discrepancies were discovered and it looked doubtful whether the total of flying hours which he claimed was genuine. Furthermore, there was no record of him actually obtaining an instrument rating in Nigeria, a mandatory requirement for an airline pilot. After Dorman came to England in 1970, in order to qualify for the British Airline Transport Licence, he had to undergo an instrument-rating test on a light twin-engine trainer. Between 1970 and 1971, it took him nine attempts to pass the test, failing eight times, either due to unacceptable standard of flying or insufficient theoretical knowledge. On joining Invicta in 1971, he obtained a type rating for the BN2, DC3, DC4 and the Vanguard. In each case, he needed more than one go to pass the required test. He was promoted to captain on the Vanguards six months before the accident. In March 1973 he passed his last flight check with a satisfactory result.

Both pilots were familiar with Basle Airport. In his five years of service with Invicta, Terry carried out sixty-one landings, fourteen times on instruments. Dorman made thirty-three landings as captain with nine instrument approaches. They knew each other well from the professional side,

through Dorman having made seventeen trips as a co-pilot to Terry, twice to Basle.

The series 952 Vanguard G-AXOP, powered by four Rolls-Royce Tyne 512s, had initially started its service with Trans-Canada Airlines, which later became Air Canada. The Vanguards had not enjoyed the same degree of success as their world-wide-used forerunners, the Viscounts, and only forty-three were built. The prototype first flew in 1959 and the Vanguards started their operational service with BEA and Trans-Canada in 1961. However, they rapidly became out of date as a result of public demand for jet travel. By 1967, they were phased-out of passenger services and converted to freighters. Although this extended their utilisation for several years, by 1973 they were considered to be totally obsolete and only a very few remained in service.

The Vanguards were equipped with integrated flight instruments of an advanced design and they were certified for all-weather landings at lower limits than most aircraft of that era.

PART IV

With the shadow of doubt hanging over the pilots' standards of instrument flying during the two approaches to Basle Airport, the flight was checked for other possible navigation errors *en route*. Tracings from surveillance radars, provided by the UK Civil Aviation Authority and the French military radar, covered the entire stretch of airways over England and France until Héricourt beacon, 30 nm west of Basle Airport. It was established that the aircraft remained constantly on the centre line with the exception of a 10 nm deviation at Luxeuil VOR (position 50 nm from Basle). No probable reason had been put forth in the accident report for that error, but, judging from the weather situation in the Luxeuil area, it was possible that the pilots could have been trying to avoid a large cumulus that may have shown on the airborne radar. As at that position the aircraft was already descending, the only way to ensure passenger comfort was to go around turbulent clouds. Criticism was also levelled at the pilots for maintaining high speed during descent over quite a long period. Although this was above the limit stipulated for the BEA-operated Vanguards, G-AXOP was originally registered in Canada under slightly different airworthiness specifications, therefore the airspeed was not above the maximum laid down in the Invicta Aircraft Flight Manual, based on the Air

Canada version. The investigators had made no attempts to obtain in-flight weather reports in the Luxeuil area at the time of the Vanguard passing the VOR, nor did they check if the pilots could have been forced to maintain high speed during descent due to the late issuing of clearances. But these two points were brought up in the report, as further examples of other alleged non-compliances with the operating procedures.

Freak weather conditions no doubt played a crucial role in the accident. The meteorological situation was summarised in the accident report as follows:

'A strong cold air current was flowing from the North Sea into the Western Mediterranean area. In the upper Rhine Valley area this led to an intensive upward motion of the wedged-in warm air with cloud formations and considerable falls of snow even in the low lying areas. This meant that the met conditions were unfavourable for flight operations owing to severe icing and moderate turbulence in clouds. Strong northerly wind remained almost to ground level with low cloud base and poor visibility.'

The weather forecast for Basle Airport, for the period of 07.00 –16.00 hrs was: '020/15 kt, Visibility 2 km, moderate rain, 6/8 800 feet, 8/8 2,000 feet, temporarily 06.00–12.00 vis. 1500, heavy rain and snow 8/8 400 feet, intermittent 0600–1200 visibility 1200 m.'

The actual met observations were:
'08.45 [the nearest observation to the time of commencing the first approach] – Wind 360/9 kt, visibility 1 km, Runway Visual Range 1300m, light snowfall, 8/8 at 400 feet, trend: visibility improving to 1500 m.
09.15 [the nearest observation to the time of the accident] – Wind 340/10, Vis 1200 m, RVR 1700 m, light snowfall, 8/8 at 500 feet, trend – visibility 1500 m.'

Critical deterioration in the RVR down to 500 metres, which had occurred between 09.05 and 09.09 hrs, was not reported to the pilots.

PART V

After leaving Héricourt beacon at 8.49 GMT (all subsequent times are in GMT – the usual practice in all accident investigations), the Vanguard was cleared to the Basle outer locator BN at Flight Level 70 and advised to contact Basle Approach. According to the testimony of the controller on duty, he verified the position of the Vanguard on his radar as well as by the bearing from the radio transmission. He then passed the following landing information, which included the latest weather report: 'Wind 360/9 kt, Runway Visual Range at Alpha [position which covered first sector of the runway] 700 metres and at Bravo [position covering the second part] 1,300 metres. Snow. Ceiling 8 octas at 120 metres. Temperature zero degrees. Runway in use – 34. Contact Tower.'

The values of RVR – the electronically measured visibility – look questionable. In most cases the RVR is higher than the observed visibility, as is apparent from the Basle Airport Met Office report issued five minutes earlier, which gave visibility as one kilometre and RVR as 1,300 metres. In a light snowfall, a variation of 600 metres between two transmissometers situated only about one kilometre apart is very unlikely. There were no storm clouds over Basle, as was later verified by Zurich Radar, which could have accounted for such large differences along the 2,370-metre-long runway. The recording of the RVR measurements revealed that there was a continuous difference in the readings between two transmissometers, ranging from 500 to 900 metres. This points to a likelihood of the transmissometer lens at the Alpha position, having been obscured by a snow deposit. The controllers had made no attempts to check the accuracy of the RVR measurements even if was apparent that, in a light snowfall, visibility was expected to be uniform. Consequently, the pilots were given an inaccurate picture of the landing conditions along various sectors of the runway. Just the same, information with a lower RVR value than the actual would not have had a really serious bearing on the safety of flight.

The changeover from Approach to Tower at more than 20 nm from the airport, was not only against the rules but also against commonsense. Although the accident report quoted the following explanation from Basle ATC about the instructions issued to the controllers, it basically applied to VFR conditions: 'When traffic is light, aerodrome control may operate the approach control service after reaching agreement by the competent controller regarding the way the service should be operated.' As it transpired from further inquiries, much stricter rules were expected to be applied for IFR operations.

Basle Airport was equipped with surveillance radar but its coverage was limited to below ten thousand feet. It was primarily used for separation from military traffic, frequently operating in the nearby restricted zone R103A (Mulhouse).

Local beacons were not marked on the radar screen and consequently aircraft could not be positioned on final. Moreover, the radar suffered from the usual blind spot above the antenna and, as the antenna was located on the airport, it was not possible to monitor final approaches from about three nautical miles out to the touchdown point. On the other hand, the Approach frequency was equipped with a direction finding facility, which enabled the controller to see on his radar screen from where R/T transmissions came. The Tower frequency was not provided with the same facility and consequently, radar verification could not be quickly performed.

After changing over to the Tower frequency, the pilots queried if runway 34 was in use but they were advised that it was runway 16, normally designated for instrument landings. As Approach Control is an ultimate authority in such matters, such contradictory information issued by Tower indicates poor coordination between the two ATC units.

The instrument landing procedure for runway 16 stipulated proceeding first to the MN beacon, situated 5.2 nm NNE of BN (see the approach chart on the following page); this was to be followed by a left turn to intercept the localiser at 2,500 feet on QNH until closing on a rather flat, 2.44° glide slope at 1,930 feet.

According to the graph of the horizontal flight path constructed from the FDR data by the Swiss investigators, after passing BN the aircraft took up a north-westerly course instead of proceeding north-east to the MN beacon. Although, two minutes later, a report was received by Tower that the Vanguard passed over MN, in fact, it was nowhere near that beacon. Then, on completing the procedure turn, the aircraft took up a heading for BN, in order to commence final approach. However, just after passing the beacon, the pilots informed Tower that they would proceed outbound once more and would call again over MN.

This first attempt to intercept the ILS could have given the investigators an impression that the performance of the pilot flying the aircraft was far below standard. It can be seen from the graph of the vertical glide path that, upon levelling out at 2,500 feet, the aircraft porpoised several times about 200 feet up and down. Then, instead of proceeding to MN, a tight holding pattern was executed over the BN beacon while climbing

steeply and then following with an equally steep descent. Judging from the plot of the horizontal flight path, the turns were made at double the standard rate of turn (six degrees per second). As this would require maintaining 38° of bank for thirty seconds on instruments, such a manoeuvre does not appear to be safe when performed on a civil airliner. Nevertheless, without the detailed FDR data available for analysis, it is difficult to draw conclusions as to what exactly occurred at that moment.

As far as erratic height-keeping, the investigators were of the opinion that turbulence could not have been a contributory factor as g-forces, registered on the FDR, were only slight and the Vanguard was known to be a stable aircraft. The claim of insignificant turbulence seems surprising in view of the reports to the contrary by several surviving passengers.

From the graph of the vertical flight path on page 216 it is apparent that the altitude variations to the north of the airport were far more pronounced than on the southern side. What could have caused strong turbulence at the start of the first approach is difficult to determine without actual meteorological reports. Nothing in the topography of the terrain could have contributed to such heavy gusts, except for the fact that the Rhine Valley rapidly narrows where they were encountered.

Circumstantial evidence strongly supports a probability that Dorman was handling the aircraft during the first aborted approach. It had been established that he occupied the left-hand seat, from his blood particles found on the left control column. The company instruction stipulated that, under Instrument Flying Conditions, the crew member in that seat was expected to make the landing. Moreover, it was learnt from the tape-recording of R/T conversation that Terry made all transmissions on the airways over England and France and during the first approach. The voices of the two pilots were later identified by an Invicta Training Captain. The fact that Terry handled R/T communication indicates that, in accordance with the company's directives, he was the non-flying pilot.

After Terry reported commencing the first final approach, 'BN inbound', Tower cleared the aircraft to land. Nevertheless, the Vanguard was never seen breaking clouds over the runway and, according to the FDR data, fifty seconds later made an overshoot several miles away from the airport.

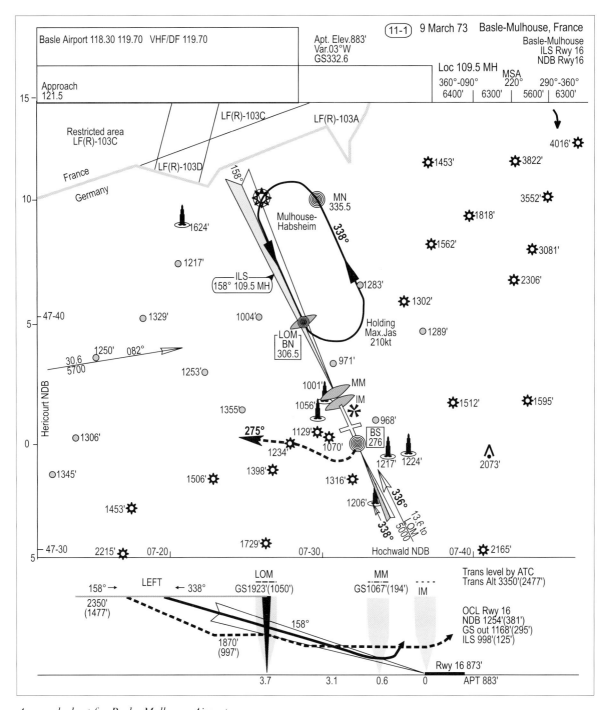

Approach chart for Basle–Mulhouse Airport.

Surprisingly, it took forty-four seconds before Dorman – not Terry – advised Tower that they had abandoned their approach. When queried what they intended to do, he replied: 'We'll try another approach'. From then on, he began to handle radio communication. This looks as if

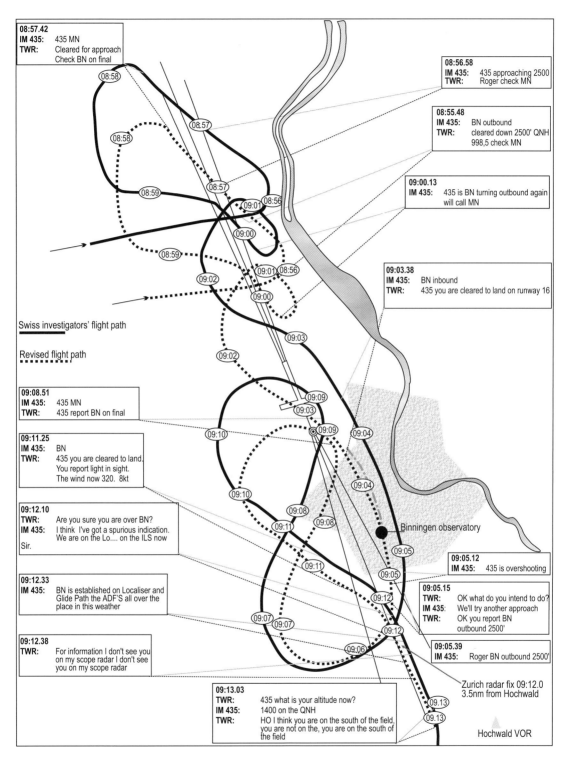

08:57.42
IM 435: 435 MN
TWR: Cleared for approach
Check BN on final

08:56.58
IM 435: 435 approaching 2500
TWR: Roger check MN

08:55.48
IM 435: BN outbound
TWR: cleared down 2500' QNH
998,5 check MN

09:00.13
IM 435: 435 is BN turning outbound again
will call MN

09:03.38
IM 435: BN inbound
TWR: 435 you are cleared to land on runway 16

Swiss investigators' flight path

Revised flight path

09:08.51
IM 435: 435 MN
TWR: 435 report BN on final

09:11.25
IM 435: BN
TWR: 435 you are cleared to land.
You report light in sight.
The wind now 320. 8kt

09:12.10
TWR: Are you sure you are over BN?
IM 435: I think I've got a spurious indication.
We are on the Lo.... on the ILS now
Sir.

09:12.33
IM 435: BN is established on Localiser and
Glide Path the ADF'S all over the
place in this weather

09:12.38
TWR: For information I don't see you
on my scope radar I don't see
you on my scope radar

09:13.03
TWR: 435 what is your altitude now?
IM 435: 1400 on the QNH
TWR: HO I think you are on the south of the field,
you are not on the, you are on the south of
the field

Binningen observatory

09:05.12
IM 435: 435 is overshooting

09:05.15
TWR: OK what do you intend to do?
IM 435: We'll try another approach
TWR: OK you report BN
outbound 2500'

09:05.39
IM 435: Roger BN outbound 2500'

Zurich radar fix 09:12.0
3.5nm from Hochwald

Hochwald VOR

Horizontal flight path of Invicta flight IM 435 as determined by the Swiss investigators (continuous line) and my own research (dotted line). Note that the flight path (running above Binningen observatory) which was observed by the witnesses on the ground, is marked in a long dash and a dotted line.

Terry had most likely taken over the controls.

The second approach was executed ten miles further to the south than the procedure called for. Instead of passing over MN and turning back to the outer marker, the Vanguard made a procedure turn close to the airport and then began to head in the direction of what the ADF must have indicated as the BN beacon. Upon receiving a position report 'over BN inbound', Tower again cleared the aircraft to land. The subsequent R/T conversation is the best illustration of the events that followed. At 09:12.10 hrs (that is one minute and fourteen seconds before the crash) the following exchange of messages took place:

Tower: 'Invicta 435...Basle.'

Dorman: '435.'

Tower: 'Are you sure you are over BN?'

Dorman: 'I think we got a spurious indication. We are on the Lo... on the ILS now, Sir.'

Tower: 'Ah!'

At 09:12.33, Terry: 'BN is established on Localiser and Glide Path... the ADFs are all over the place.'

(In my opinion, the first part of the message should be interpreted as: 'BN... [which was meant to be the position of the aircraft] established on Localiser and Glide Path.')

At 09:12.38 hrs, Tower: 'For information I don't see you on my scope radar... I don't see you on my scope radar.' (The actual wording of the official transcript.)

At 09:13.03 Tower: '435 what is your altitude now?'

Both pilots started to reply at once but Terry's message had got through clearer: 'One thousand four hundred on the QNH.'

Most likely, Dorman tried to report the altitude with reference to QFE – a setting to indicate read zero feet on landing – as his altimeter was found set to Basle QFE, but Terry corrected it firmly.

Tower: 'Ho, I think you are on the south side of the field... you are not on the... you are on the south of the field.'

At that moment, the crew initiated a panic overshoot. Surviving passengers later reported that it felt like an abrupt manoeuvre. Without any information from the Cockpit Voice Recorder, which could have thrown light on the reason for this frantic action, it is not possible to determine whether it was due only to the controller's warning. Judging by the height of the ceiling when the Vanguard broke clouds over Basle during the first approach (about 1,500 feet on QNH), it is possible that this time the pilots had also caught sight of the ground, just as Terry reported 1,400 feet (the actual figure as obtained from the FDR was 1,443 feet). At that moment, they would have been over Birs valley with a deadly, steep hill looming up on the left. This could have accounted for the urgency of pulling up fast and at the same time, making a 25° turn to the right. Unfortunately, despite a high rate of climb at about 1,700 ft/min, twenty-one seconds later the aircraft struck a hill which lay almost on the centre line of the ILS, ten nautical miles from the airport.

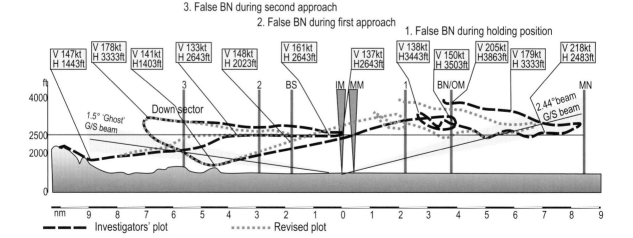

Probable vertical flight path of Invicta flight IM 435.

PART VI

The conclusions of the accident report implied that the pilots' incompetence, resulting in loss of orientation, was regarded by the investigators as basically the cause of the Basle disaster. The history of Dorman's marginal proficiency was an invitation to point the finger at the likely weak-link, because he was designated as the pilot-in-command on the stretch to Basle. But also present was another captain, regarded by the investigators as a highly reliable airman. Is it likely that he would be sitting in the cockpit inactive when he could see his colleague committing a string of blunders?

By assuming at an early stage that the accident was precipitated by pilot error, the investigators continued this line of inquiry without taking other probable causes into consideration. As a result, the most crucial question – 'What had made the pilots commence the fatal approach ten nautical miles away from the outer marker?' – had not been answered.

The Basle inquiry was not the only case where some unsatisfactory aspects of a pilot's career, or his performance at the time of the crash, or his unfamiliarity with the airport, immediately introduced a slant about human failure. The claims of disorientation must be closely examined as there are important factors that could have contributed to the pilots believing that they were over the positions as reported on the radio.

PART VII

By the time of the Vanguard crash, the subject of radiation from power lines, which could affect radio aids to navigation, was not new to the aviation experts. Already for some years, complaints had been drifting in from pilots about confusing signals in certain locations. When towards the end of 1966, particularly troublesome interference was experienced for several weeks at Watford, where a radio beacon was located which was frequently used for a holding pattern at London Airport, the Civil Aviation Authority contacted the Central Electricity Generating Board for a possible explanation. Checks had already been carried out to see if a nearby commercial radio transmitter could have affected the ADF reception, but the results were negative.

Jim Naylor, a senior technician with the Electricity Board, admitted that the problem could have stemmed from their side, as a result of a recently introduced, novel way of passing messages along the power lines. As a precaution, the Electricity Board at once discontinued using a certain band of medium wave frequencies on the power lines, which they had assigned for that purpose. Extensive tests followed, carried out in cooperation with the Post Office, the Home Office and the Board of Trade, to determine the extent of power line interference on ADF reception. But it took three years of air and ground tests, before it was clearly established that indeed, in certain conditions, the grid radiated signals that the aircraft's ADF could recognise as a beacon. The strength depended on several factors, one of which – and the most unpredictable – was the weather. The quantity of moisture in the air appeared to have a definite connection with the interference. Another critical factor was the frequency used for transmitting the power line messages. If it happened to be close to that of the beacon, and the aircraft's ADF was not very selective, the radiation could often override the signal from a nearby beacon, in particular if it happened to be a low-power installation.

This potentially dangerous situation, which could play havoc with air navigation, was created by the need of the electricity industry to pass information along the power lines while they were live. It was often the only way to find a fault in the grid. In the early days, the messages were sent in short bursts a few seconds at a time, but when the demand for passing information had increased, several European countries introduced continuous carrier transmissions. In the UK this method did not come in use until 1966. However, as soon as a new installation started operating at Watford and Luton, two places where important navigational facilities were located, reports from the pilots about erratic ADF reception began to flood in.

The most puzzling aspect of the problems with this type of interference was why the electricity authorities in the countries which introduced this new method had not ascertained first whether any radio beacons operating on a borderline frequency were located in the vicinity of the power lines used for transmitting messages.

When, as far back as four years before the Basle accident, conclusive proofs of hazardous effects were finally obtained, the UK Electricity Council issued strict guidelines on the limitations of using continuous carrier transmissions. In May the same year, Jim Naylor attended a meeting of an international electricity committee in Rome, in order to present the findings of the British Board and to alert other countries to the potential dangers of the power line interference. But none of the countries appeared to have taken heed of his warning.

The first suspicion that a 'ghost beacon' could have lured an aircraft into disaster came from an accident in October 1972, involving a Viscount from a French domestic airline, Air Inter, with a loss of sixty lives. The aircraft was supposed to be making an approach to Aulnat – Clermont-Ferrand Airport – but it crashed twenty-seven miles away, striking a hill at Noirétable in Loire. Weather at the time was stormy with heavy turbulence. The head of the French investigating team, General Forestier, blamed the pilot for navigation error. Nevertheless, Captain Leluc, a friend of the dead pilot and a former radio operator, had different ideas about the cause of the crash. He believed that the aircraft's ADF reception was affected by interference from the nearby power lines and, as a result, the pilot was given an indication of a wrong position. Just the same, it took Captain Leluc two years of campaigning to convince the French civil aviation authorities that he was not talking through his hat. Eventually, in June 1974, an aircraft fitted with multiple measuring equipment was sent out to flight test radio aids in the Belfort and Basle area where a massive electric grid spans the countryside. The results were an 'eye opener'. The 'flying laboratory' detected interference generated not only by power lines, but equally strong signals were observed from electrified railway tracks and badly shielded electrical equipment in local factories. Moreover, a harmonic frequency of spurious radiation could produce a signal that could be received on the aircraft's ADF primary frequency.

Shortly after the results of tests on the power line interference came into the hands of Electricité de France, the company discontinued using 306 kHz in the Basle area, the frequency of the BN beacon. Unfortunately, this was undertaken several months after the Vanguard crash.

In September 1974, three weeks before the Public Hearing was going to be held at Solothurn, the Swiss Investigating Commission were handed the findings obtained by Forestier's team. Nevertheless, the investigators were of the opinion that navigation errors were probably caused by a faulty ADF and ignored the results of the tests by the 'flying laboratory', as well as the reports from several pilots about their incidents with power line interference in the Basle area.

PART VIII

The most likely change of the handling pilot after the first aborted approach is not without significance. Although only a CVR recording of the conversation between the pilots could confirm that Terry took over the controls during the overshoot, nevertheless, the fact that Dorman began to make radio calls strongly suggests such a probability. The aircraft handling may have been exchanged for two different reasons.

One possibility is the consequence of a previously reported fault in the No. 1 ILS receiver, which provided information to the captain's instruments. The analysis of the horizontal flight path shows that, upon intercepting the ILS localiser during the first approach, the aircraft had not followed the centre line but, after drifting off to the left, began to parallel the beam. Only twelve hours earlier, a similar problem had been experienced on the same aircraft during an instrument approach at Luton Airport, when the co-pilot noticed that the captain's ILS instrument showed the aircraft to be on the localiser, while his instrument indicated a displacement to the left. Once visual contact was established, it was evident that the aircraft was to the left of the runway centre line. However, as after landing there were no further signs of discrepancy, the captain did not think that it was necessary to make an entry in the technical log. Just the same, he maintained that he had informed the ground engineer about the ILS malfunctioning in the air but the engineer could not recall having been told. Moreover, the captain asked the co-pilot, who was going to travel next morning to Bristol as a passenger on the same aircraft, to bring the problem of the ILS reception to the attention of the next crew. When later interviewed, the co-pilot insisted that, before departure from Luton, he briefed the crew accordingly.

After the Basle crash the incident with the faulty ILS indication was reported by both pilots to their superiors. For some reason the AAIB did not learn of this until about six months later and only when one of the pilots contacted the Branch directly.

Further inquiries revealed that, eleven months earlier, a similar malfunctioning had been observed during a landing at Luton and it was reported to the company's technical staff.

The origin of a fault in the navigational equipment that occurs only in the air is extremely difficult to pinpoint. It took a week of extensive flight and ground tests, as well as the advice of top electronics experts, to find the cause of paralleling the ILS beam by a KLM DC10. Only after checking every inch of the cables and replacing every component of the aircraft's ILS installation had the fault been eventually traced to the antenna coupler, a unit no bigger than a packet of cigarettes and located in an inaccessible section of the tail. A hairline crack in the circuit board was producing false signals but only in the air, when flexing of the fuselage imposed stress on the coupler's mountings, expanding the crack.

When the pilots broke cloud over a built-up area and not in front of the runway, they might have realised that this could have been due to the same fault in the ILS reception about which they were warned. As a result, Dorman might have suggested that Terry carry out the next approach, as the only dependable indications came from the co-pilot's instruments.

The other possible reason why Terry took over was that he became concerned about Dorman's erratic instrument flying. How much it was due to turbulence and how much due to his below standard proficiency is difficult to assess. Having had Dorman as a co-pilot on many occasions, Terry would have been aware of his weaknesses.

As far as obeying orders, when two captains are scheduled to alternate command on consecutive sectors of the route, this would largely depend on their personalities. But no matter what the company rules dictated, a pilot who was senior in every respect – that is in age, in experience and in years of service with the company, as was the case with Terry – would have been unlikely to have sat back and allowed his colleague to make serious mistakes without doing something about it. When it was evident that safety was in question, he may have even gone so far as to assume command.

What seems particularly significant in that respect, is that forty-four seconds elapsed from the moment the aircraft began to overshoot before Dorman, and not Terry, reported to Tower, '435 overshooting', and during that period the aircraft was climbing on a south-south-easterly course, instead of immediately turning to a heading of 275° as the approach chart stipulated. Moreover, the fact that Dorman, when questioned about their intentions, had a ready answer – 'We'll try another approach' – implies that a discussion must have previously taken place about their further actions.

With the role change of the handling pilot, who was known for his marginal proficiency, it could be expected that from then on the procedures should have been properly followed. Nevertheless, the second approach, which was most likely executed by Terry, was again not initiated over the outer marker but even further away than the first approach. It must be asked what could have caused a levelheaded and conscientious pilot, as Terry was regarded by the investigators, to commit such a basic error. This was never clearly answered by the Swiss inquiry.

PART IX

When radar vectoring service or a VOR is not available, as was the case with Basle Airport, an M/F outer locator becomes a key facility for positioning the aircraft on the ILS. Without the help of a homing beacon, intercepting such a narrow beam would be extremely difficult.

When, in the post-war years, many airports in Europe were fitted with ILS installations, the demand for the medium wave frequencies allocated to the outer and inner locators rose greatly and it was found necessary to assign the same frequencies to beacons that were separated by only several hundred miles. In order to prevent a chance of mutual interference, their transmission range was greatly reduced, in many cases to a nominal 5 nm distance. In heavy static their effective range could be even less. As a result of lower power, locators became much more susceptible to electrical and radio interference.

During instrument approaches at Basle Airport, the pilots relied on three short-range, crystal-controlled beacons: BN 306.5 kHz at the outer marker position, MN 335.5 kHz a holding beacon 10 nm north of the airport and BS 276 kHz, about half a mile to the south. BN and MN used A0/A1 transmission, which meant that during the coding cycle of the callsign – lasting several seconds – the ADF was not able to lock on and would give unstable indications. Only the BS beacon was up to the ICAO recommended standard of A0/A2 transmission. Whether the power output of the beacons was satisfactory at the time of the accident had never been properly established by the Investigating Commission.

The ILS installation, which was manufactured in the UK, was an older type; it was not transistorised and therefore required frequent calibrations. In the back course sector, it radiated a

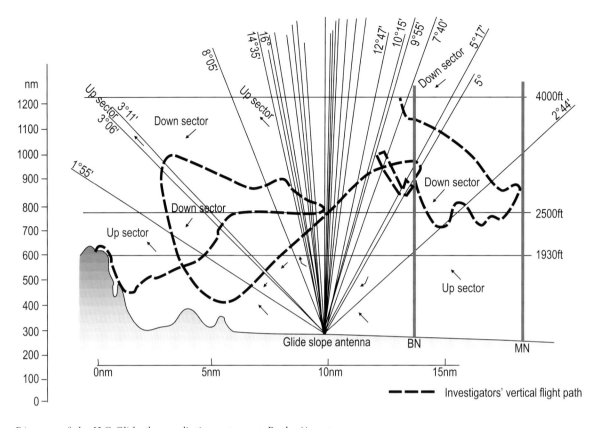

Diagram of the ILS Glide slope radiation pattern at Basle Airport.

localiser back-beam as well as a glide slope signal, both unusable for operational purposes. (See the diagram of radiation pattern at Basle Airport.)

A number of 'false' glide slopes in the front and the back sectors is a normal occurrence with the older types of ILS installations, as is outlined in a letter by an expert from the Royal Aircraft Establishment at Bedford:

'A conventional null-reference ILS glidepath would be expected to produce erroneous guidance at high glidepath angles. For example, for a nominal 3° glidepath installation, a false glidepath would be expected to be seen at an elevation angle of 9°, for which the guidance would be reversed. Thus, the elevation angle of the aircraft increases being full-scale on the pilot's instrument for all angles between about 4° and 8°, above which the fly-down deflection would decrease to zero at 9°, changing to a fly-up deflection above 9°.'

An examination of the ILS glide slope radiation pattern at Basle Airport, showed that above the glide slope angle of 2.44°, several 'ghost' signals were present and a similar pattern could be also observed in the back-beam sector. In the accident report it is stated that, during a flight test after the crash, a weak glide slope at 1.55° was clearly observed in the back-course sector.

Although there was an urgent requirement for a VOR, it could not be installed because of a problem with procuring land for a site.

The approach lights were 900 metres long with three cross-bars and these should have been fully visible before landing, had the aircraft broken cloud at the reported ceiling of 400 feet.

The Vanguard G-AXOP had a long history of problems with the ADF sets – manufactured in the USA by Collins. During service with Air Canada, No.1 ADF failed several times and had to be prematurely replaced. A year before the accident, when an Invicta crew complained about the No. 1 ADF, No. 2 ADF was changed instead, then repaired and installed back as No. 1 receiver.

Examination of the ADFs by Swiss radio experts after the crash revealed that the loop servo amplifier of the No. 1 set displayed signs of incompetent repairs, such as poorly soldered joints. The No. 1 ADF had been set to 335 kHz, although the frequency of the MN beacon was 336.5 kHz. Nevertheless, with an analogue way of tuning, 1.5 kHz would have hardly affected the reception. No faults were detected in No. 2 ADF, which was used to home on BN (306.5 kHz), the key beacon during instrument approaches.

Quite a few faults in the No. 1 (captain's) localiser receiver, as well as in the No. 2 (co-pilot's) glide slope receiver, were discovered by the Swiss technicians. Normally such faults should have been rectified during periodical maintenance. Adjustments on both sets were well outside normal tolerances. As a result, the alarm flag when an ILS signal became weak and unreliable would not come into view on the respective instrument. The sensitivity of both receivers was 50% too high.

PART X

The key evidence to the circumstances leading to the crash was two graphs, prepared by the Swiss investigating Commission from the FDR data, showing the horizontal and the vertical path of both approaches at Basle Airport. According to this evidence, the pilots had not properly adhered to the laid-down ILS procedure.

But do these graphs represent a correct picture of the events on the fateful day? My analysis, which took several weeks to complete, revealed startling inaccuracies. One basic error was to assume that the Vanguard passed overhead the BN beacon on the way from Héricourt. There is no evidence to that effect. Appendix 5b of the accident report gives the following entries concerning statements from the radar controllers at Basle Airport.

After Invicta IM 435 reported over Héricourt at 09.49 hrs:

'Identification of IM 435 over NDB HR with Basel [Basle] VHF direction finder. Basel (lady) aerodrome Controller observes IM 435 on radar from NDB HR to NDB BN.'

As beacons were not marked on the radar screen, the reported positions could not be verified

with any degree of certainty. Moreover, when six minutes later the pilots advised Tower about passing over BN, no entry exists of any attempt to check that position on radar. The only report from Aerodrome Control came after three more minutes (at 08:57.42), when the pilots called over MN:

'Basel Aerodrome Controller identifies IM 435 over NDB MN. Loss of radar contact shortly afterwards owing to clutter. Observes IM 435 again from BN heading for MN, then turn 0.5 nm beyond MN, for 2 nm on the localiser, echo vanishes again.'

This observation does not tally with the position obtained from the FDR data, corrected for wind. When the aircraft reported over MN, in fact it was four miles north-west of BN, as indicated on the investigators' graph (according to my analysis only 2 nm), while MN lies five miles to the north-east. Therefore it looks doubtful if it was the echo of the Invicta Vanguard. Even without video mapping showing the location of beacons, the difference in the aircraft's position was far too great for the controller not to recognise it.

The data obtained from the Vanguard's FDR gave details of four flight-parameters only, which was usual for the recording equipment of that era: altitude, vertical acceleration, pitch attitude and magnetic heading.

The read-out required specialised equipment, only available at Bournemouth. The way the plot of the Vanguard's ground track had been constructed was summarised in the accident report, as follows (an official translation):

'After the first rough analyses, an analysis was made in several refinement stages with the help of a computer which led to all parameters being determined with a very narrow margin of error. In order to define the main source of error in the wind, a read-out regarding this was undertaken from the flight data tape of an aircraft approaching Basel during the same period of time. The plot of the flight path thus obtained gives a quantitively good picture of the movements of the aircraft from the first time it passed the beacon BN until the crash. Owing to the fact that only an average value for the wind effect is known, the greatest inaccuracy must lie in the middle section of the reconstructed flight path where, compared with the witness reports, a lateral deviation of approx 800 m can be observed.'

In another section of the report, it is stated:

'FDR – The analysis took some time and it was a long time before the errors in the analysis were eliminated.'

An examination of the flight path graphs, constructed by the Swiss investigators, had shown that, contrary to the assurances in the report, errors were still present, accounting for substantial inaccuracies. Although it was already evident from the 800 m difference between the aircraft's ground positions on the graph and the observations by the witnesses that it was an unacceptable error, two reliable radar fixes, which could have improved the accuracy of the plot, had not been taken into consideration.

At 9:11.10 hrs Zurich Radar observed an unidentified echo at 3.5 nm south-west of Basle, heading in the direction of Hochwald VOR. After Basle ATC was questioned about the traffic, eventually thirty seconds later the controller spotted a target six miles from the airport, moving south. This gives an actual aircraft's position at 9:11.40 hrs.

The second fix comes from an entry in the log of Zurich ATC, which revealed that, at 9:12.00 hrs, the echo disappeared from the screen at a position 3.5 nm north-west of Hochwald VOR, (47° 28.1N 07° 40.0E), a check point on airway G4 from Schaffhausen to Héricourt. This was most likely a result of the Vanguard dropping below the line of sight from Zurich Radar when it had descended lower than the tops of the nearby Jura hills.

Once the investigators had acknowledged that, on the way from Héricourt, the aircraft passed over the BN beacon, a plot of the horizontal flight path was prepared to fit between BN and the point of impact. To comply with this assumption, a very high wind component of forty knots from the north was used. Although the investigators claimed that it was obtained from an FDR read-out of another aircraft that made an approach around the time of the accident, it was not specified at what altitude such a strong component was encountered.

According to other observations, wind in the Basle area was variable with height. The surface wind at the airport was reported as north-north-west at eight to ten knots and a competent met observer assessed its strength at the crash site (approx. 2,000 feet amsl) to be about fifteen knots. The two radar fixes taken shortly before impact indicate that, during the last part of the approach, the wind was not more than ten knots from a northerly or north-north-westerly direction. The

Vanguard mainly maintained about 1,500 feet above the ground.

From an operational point of view, forty knots of tail wind would have made the approach very tricky, calling for a rate of descent as much as 800 to 900 ft/min. Such a high rate is not evident from the FDR data.

PART XI

In view of the inconsistencies discovered in the investigators' graph, a revised plot was constructed with the help of a special computer program (the dotted line on the graphs on pages 215 and 216), and corresponding corrections were also applied to the graph of the vertical flight path. The figures for the magnetic headings and the indicated airspeed were obtained from the official graphs. However, instead of using a single, fixed, wind component, variable values were used: ten knots for altitudes up to 1,000 feet above the ground, fifteen knots between 1,000 and 1,500 feet and twenty knots above 1,500 feet.

In the revised plot, the aircraft's ground positions, with respect to time, concur with the two radar fixes and with the observations by several witnesses during the low pass over Basle and this represents a more realistic reconstruction of the events.

Even if the discrepancy between the aircraft's ground positions on the investigators' graph and on the revised plot is only about a mile when close to the point of impact and about two miles further away, the ILS indications in the cockpit at the time of reporting BN on final, would have been radically different. Whilst according to the investigators' graph, the pilots did not react rationally to the ILS readings and thus gave an impression of being disorientated, the revised plot reveals that they followed what must have looked to them the normal indications. This will be shown in the next paragraphs.

After leaving the tight holding pattern for the first approach, the aircraft began a descent to 2,500 feet in the direction of a spurious ADF signal emitted from a position 1.8 nm south-east of the airport. Before passing over the 'ghost' BN beacon, Dorman would have already intercepted the localiser with the help of the Flight Director (see the revised plot). However, as a result of a probable fault in the No.1 ILS receiver described earlier, the aircraft would have drifted to the left and begun to parallel the beam. But unlike during the approach at Luton, the discrepancy between

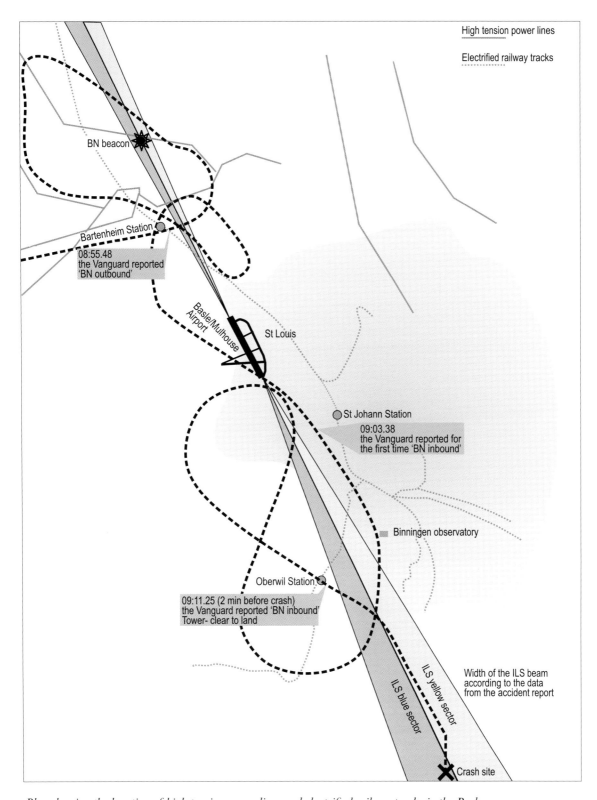

Plan showing the location of high tension power lines and electrified railway tracks in the Basle area.

the two ILS instruments could have been much smaller due to the greater width of the back-course beam and this could have looked to Terry, watching the co-pilot's instruments, as only a minor deviation from the centre line.

It is interesting to note that, after plotting the position of the 'ghost' BN on a topographical chart, the location turned to be at St Johann railway station, which serves a northern suburb of Basle. As there are no power lines in the vicinity, the spurious signal must have been generated by the electrified railway tracks.

It can be seen from the revised vertical flight path that, on passing the 'false' BN beacon, the cockpit instruments would have shown the Vanguard to be only slightly above 1,930 feet on QNH (the altitude of intercepting the glide slope at the outer marker). The progress would have appeared to be normal and the pilots would have expected to close on the glide slope shortly afterwards. A G/S null signal must have been received eventually, as denoted by the aircraft's steady rate of descent, which was remarked upon in the accident report. Therefore it must have come as an unexpected development when, upon breaking cloud, the pilots did not have the approach lights in sight but instead had just missed a tower at Binningen Observatory.

A quick glimpse of the ground through the snowfall would not have given them much of an idea as to their whereabouts. Had they at that moment suspected that, as a result of a faulty ILS receiver, they had drifted off to the left, they may have presumed that the built-up area was St Louis, a French town just north of Basle, rather than Binningen. So far, nothing could have alerted them to the fact that they were much further south than they expected.

In all probability, Terry took over handling of the aircraft shortly before Dorman advised Tower about the overshoot. From the approach chart it is evident that, with the highest obstacle in that area being 2,215 feet, it was prudent to continue climbing to at least 1,000 higher until the turn was completed. Only then was it safe to descend down to 2,500 feet, as cleared by Basle Tower. According to the FDR information, this is what Terry did and it indicates a careful evaluation of the situation rather than a lack of compliance with the laid-down procedure. He also increased the airspeed on that stretch to 178 knots, as he most probably intended to cut down the time on the way to the MN beacon. The higher speed had resulted in passing abeam the false BN (although

the pilots actually reported – 'over BN outbound') about three minutes after initiating the overshoot. This would have been close to the time required to return to the correct BN location, following an overshoot over the airport. Moreover, the ADF would have indicated the position of the MN beacon to lie to the north-east, as expected. So far everything pointed to Terry following a preconceived plan and, judging from the FDR data, his height keeping in the procedure turn was very accurate.

Due to a lack of realistic inferences, it is only possible to make certain presumptions as to why, on the outbound leg, the Vanguard took up a heading in the direction of St Louis. One source claimed that powerful electrical radiation had been traced to a factory there, emitting signals on 111 kHz. As the third harmonic is usually the strongest, and as the No. 1 ADF receiver was tuned to 333 kHz, it could have easily locked on the spurious signal. Another possibility that exists is that, due to an electronic fault in the loop circuit, the ADF had shown a wrong bearing. Although a scrupulous examination of the ADFs had been carried out by the Swiss radio experts, no practical tests were performed to determine the reliability of the indications.

After passing the false MN, the Vanguard made a normal procedure turn and ended up heading towards the same spurious BN beacon signal which had been encountered on the outbound leg. At that stage, no indication in the cockpit would have alerted the pilots that the aircraft was going to intercept the localiser in the back-beam sector.

When Dorman reported, 'BN inbound', the controller cleared the Vanguard to land without verifying its position on radar. At that moment, according to the revised vertical flight path, the aircraft was just about to intercept the glide slope at a correct height of 1,930 feet.

Plotting the position of the 'false' BN on the topographical chart revealed that the spurious signal came from a railway station at Oberwil, located on a secondary line from Basle. No power lines traverse that area.

Just after passing the 'ghost' outer locator, a null signal of the 'false' glide slope at 1.55° was likely received and to the pilots, who had made twenty-three instrument landings on that ILS, this must have appeared as no different from all previous occasions. Despite being queried by Tower – 'Are you sure you are over BN?' – Dorman's reply clearly indicated what they had observed: 'We are on the Lo... on the ILS now, Sir'. Evidently he corrected himself as soon as he noticed the glide slope pointer moving to the centre position. His first remark – 'I think we got spurious indication' – could have been a result of crossing shortly earlier on, a very narrow segment of 'up' and 'down' signals in quick succession (see the diagram of the G/S radiation pattern on page 216).

In spite of the false 1.55° G/S back beam sloping in the opposite direction to that of the descending aircraft, with the width of the beam between its upper and its lower edge, amounting to about 1,000 feet due to a considerable distance from the transmitter, the upper edge of the glide slope would have been intercepted at the 'ghost' BN and the aircraft would remain close to or on the null G/S signal for at least a minute. This was confirmed when fifty-three seconds before impact Terry had assured Tower: 'BN... established on localiser and glide path'.

The only warning that could have alerted the pilots to the G/S signal being unreliable was the 'G/S OFF' flag. According to the ILS experts, at that distance on the back-side of the transmitter antenna the flag should have normally appeared in view. However, the probable reason why it had failed to come on was the incorrectly adjusted G/S receiver.

According to my analysis, it is difficult to see against what indications the pilots were able to 'cross-check and double-check' their flight progress, as the investigators expected them to do. The instruments displayed all the signs of a normal approach, except for the absence of the 75 MHz marker signals. The only criticism which could be levelled at the execution of the procedures is that the pilots did not re-tune one ADF to the BS beacon according to the approach chart, to ensure that an overshoot was executed in a safe sector. But in view of problems with the ADF reception, it is doubtful if they would have received a reliable indication.

It is highly debatable whether the pilots were 'disorientated' when they commenced their approaches. The execution of procedures was based on what had turned out to be 'ghost' beacons or ILS indications that gave an impression of being on the right track. But it was the ill-fated crew's misfortune that the positions of false beacon signals happened to lie close to the points of interception of both the localiser and the glide slope.

A further point of interest emerged after plotting the revised horizontal fight path on a topographical chart. In addition to the two 'ghost beacons' at two different railway stations, another case of spurious signal was evident, emanating from a station at Bartenheim, situated on the main line from Basle to Mulhouse. This had likely made the pilots report 'BN' 1.8 nm south-south-east from where the beacon was actually situated. The radiation must have been particularly strong to override the transmission from the BN beacon, located only a short distance away. Although in that area the grid extensively criss-crosses the countryside, the reported BN position coincides exactly with the location of the railway station.

Why such powerful radiation was consecutively emitted in three different locations during the twenty-three minutes of the letdown, was impossible to establish after so many years. No doubt weather conditions helped in the leakage of electric currents and wet snow would have made the earth particularly conductive, leading to excessive sparking, a typical source of radio wave transmissions. It would have resulted in a particularly strong false BN signal, while static in clouds could have appreciably reduced the range of beacon reception.

A curious point emerged after measuring the distance between these three stations. They are approximately the same distance apart. Furthermore, the intervals at which radiation emulating the BN beacon had been transferred from one station to another appear to be more or less the same. Either it was pure coincidence or the result of a certain way that the testing of the electrified railway lines had been conducted.

The investigation by the Swiss Commission of Inquiry produced very few satisfactory answers to many pointed questions. It is evident from some of the conclusions in the report, that, although the members may have possessed high academic qualifications, their practical knowledge of flying was somewhat limited.

PART XII

The most tragic aspect of the Basle disaster is that it could have been easily averted. Evidence obtained during the investigation shows that Basle ATC received two warnings about the Vanguard's position to the south of the airport. As long as eight minutes before the aircraft struck the hill at Herrenmatt, several witnesses observed the ill-fated Vanguard flying low over the city and shortly afterwards disappearing into clouds. One of the witnesses was R. Beck, a retired Swissair captain who worked at the Binningen Observatory situated on the top of a small hill in a southern part of Basle.

At 09.05 hrs Beck heard a roar of engines and when he looked out of the windows, he spotted, through the heavy snowfall, a large turbo-prop aircraft flying so low that it had just missed the top of the Observatory. In spite of catching only a fleeting glimpse, he was able to observe red markings on the tail. It was undoubtedly the Invicta emblem of a white horse on a large red background, the horse being the symbol of Kent. To Beck, an old hand in operating to Basle, this spelt danger. With a range of hills in close vicinity, the aircraft was flying too low so far to the south of the airport. Beck immediately ran to the telephone and, according to the official record, three minutes later he had managed to get through to Basle Tower. The transcript of his call dismally reflects how little heed was paid to his crucial warning.

Beck: 'Good morning, Monsieur, this is Beck at the Basel–Binningen Observatory... there is an aircraft which has just passed two minutes ago heading south... probably a four-engine turbo-prop... and it is flying at 50 metres and then, it is snowing very heavily and I have the impression if it remain like this, it will crash in the mountains.'

Tower: 'Ah, hold on, you are really sure that is flying at 50 metres?'

Beck: 'Yes, certainly... listen... I was a pilot with Swissair... I have just retired and I work here... I am telephoning you as it was here at maximum 50 metres above the Observatory.'

Tower: 'Right, thank you.'

Beck: 'It had a red tail unit... I could not... I did not have time to see the markings.'

Tower: 'Yes but because you are being... [this part of the sentence is missing due to interference with another telephone conversation recorded on this tape]... there is an aircraft which has just overshot there which is going to return over... [again interference]'

Beck: 'It must be made to climb.'

Tower: 'Yes... agreed... thank you.'

Beck: 'It must be made to climb... it is going to crash in the mountains like this...'

Tower: 'Agreed... thank you.'

But the Vanguard pilots were never informed of Beck's observation. Three minutes later came a second warning, this time from another quarter.

Zurich Area Control Centre called Basle to check whether they had an aircraft flying outbound towards Hochwald, as they had just observed an unidentified echo approximately 3.5 nm southwest of the city. At first the Basle controller denied the presence of any traffic in that area. However, according to an entry in the appendix of the accident report, after he checked his radar he eventually noticed a clear echo on the extended centre line of the runway at 6 nm from the airport, moving south. But his reply to Zurich ATC's warning also sounded very much off-hand.

It is hard to believe that when fifteen seconds earlier Dorman reported leaving the BN beacon for final, the controller cleared the aircraft to land. But it took as long as forty-five seconds before he realised that something was wrong and only then did he begin to query the position report.

In spite of receiving two warnings, the controller took no action until it was too late for a safe overshoot. It is possible that the aircraft's echo may have disappeared for a while from the radar screen due to a blind spot overhead the antenna. Just the same, had the direction finding facility been used at that moment, it would have indicated at least the sector where the Vanguard was flying. It was a capital blunder that monitoring of the aircraft's movements had not been transferred to the Approach unit the moment there was suspicion that the Vanguard was descending on the wrong side of the airport. The delay in warning the pilots about their mistaken position cost many lives. The press later revealed that, at the critical time, a woman controller handling the Vanguard left her post to visit the toilet.

There is no doubt that, had the Basle controllers been more professional and alert, this tragedy could have been easily avoided. The report of the Swiss Investigating Commission does not sufficiently strongly condemn the inefficient way of keeping tabs on the aircraft's progress during the twenty-three minutes under Basle Tower control. With the weather conditions on landing-limits, this called for both radar and the direction finding facility on the Approach frequency to be used as effectively as possible, particularly in view of the radar's blind spot directly over the airport. The pilots were cleared to land twice, without the controller having made sure that the aircraft was actually over the outer marker.

On the other hand, it can be argued that the basic duty of ATC is traffic separation and passing landing information. In principle, alerting the pilots to an inadequate terrain clearance lies outside the controller's duties. There are no provisions in the ICAO procedures on Rules of the Air about warning the pilots that they are flying dangerously low. But failing to take steps to prevent a disaster, when in position to do so, would look to many to be culpable negligence.

In the history of aviation there are only isolated cases of a controller being held responsible for an accident or his actions being regarded as a contributory factor. But in other professions, negligence is not tolerated. Nowadays, doctors are frequently sued by patients for malpractices. Yet, this does not seem to apply to blunders committed by ATC services.

PART XIII

Five years after the Basle tragedy, the probable cause of the accident was given wide publicity in the UK by the Press and TV. Thames Television in

their programme *This Week*, *'The Ghost of Bravo November'*, claimed that the signals emitted by the power lines used for transmitting messages by Electricité de France on the same frequency as the BN beacon were the cause of the Invicta Vanguard crash.

In January 1978, the *Sunday Telegraph Magazine* published an article – 'THE PLANE THAT WAS LURED TO DESTRUCTION'. It dealt with cases of electricity companies having negligently used for their own convenience, a band of medium wave frequencies exclusively allocated to radio beacons and this had resulted in a potential danger to aircraft safety. The article gave a comprehensive insight into the efforts of various individuals to bring the consequences of harmful electrical interference to the attention of the respective authorities.

Unfortunately, the article is flawed by several incorrect statements as well as inaccuracies in the diagram of the Vanguard's flight path which showed that the power lines at Aschwil, in a

The wreckage of the Invicta Vanguard that crashed near Hochwald in Switzerland. (Associated Press)

western suburb of Basle, were the source of a spurious BN beacon signal. There are no power lines traversing the west side of Basle and certainly not at Aschwil.

PART XIV

It cannot be claimed that the Vanguard pilots had performed perfect approaches. Although minor blemishes were evident that could be expected in any flight, in general they conformed reasonably correctly to the laid-down procedures. But it was their unfortunate bad luck that the 'ghost' beacons positioned them on the back-course localiser and, contrary to expectations, the ILS instruments indicated relatively normal progress. Whether any blame for this tragic disaster should be placed on the shoulders of the two unfortunate pilots is left to the readers to decide.

A question could be raised as to why, prior to the Vanguard accident, there were so few reports on the confusing beacon signals encountered in general and in the Basle area in particular. Two factors would have to be simultaneously present for the power line radiation to affect ADF reception: precipitation or heavy moisture in the air and a transmission of messages taking place along the grid. At the same time, the aircraft would have to be flying over an area where, at that moment, spurious signals were strongly emitted.

As far as the case of Basle Airport, in view of a very low traffic density in the years when Electricité de France was using 306 kHz for the power lines transmissions, the chances of running into an adverse combination of the two contributory factors would have been extremely small.

Although reservations were expressed by some aviation circles as to whether 'ghost' beacons could have precipitated the Vanguard accident, my experience as another 'victim' of this freak phenomenon at Basle Airport had left me with no doubt. Fortunately in my case, the incident had ended without any serious consequences. Nevertheless, the lesson learnt made me particularly interested in the cause of the Basle disaster.

Although I had to check my flying logbook in order to refresh my memory about the date of the incident, every detail of the puzzling experience remains firmly imprinted in my mind. It happened three and a half years before the Vanguard crash, in October 1969.

I was flying a KLM South African service in a DC8 from Brazzaville to Amsterdam with an intermediate stop at Zurich. When I arrived at daybreak overhead the airport, visibility was down to 200 metres but the latest forecast indicated a chance of improvement. Luckily Basle, situated only forty-five miles away, was wide open with ten kilometres visibility, so I could safely hang on until the last possible moment.

Just as my holding reserves were coming to an end, I was advised that the visibility at Basle had suddenly dropped down to 1,800 metres. This cold douche meant getting down on the ground without the slightest delay, as I would have barely enough fuel to reach Stuttgart, the second-nearest alternative. Luckily, Zurich ATC displayed their usual efficiency by issuing diversion clearance the moment I requested it, while Zurich Radar took me directly to Basle Airport and kept informing me of the distance to go.

It was essential, as I had to lose height rapidly as a result of holding at FL250. Much to my dismay, visibility continued to decrease and when it dropped down to 800 metres I began to get a bit hot under the collar. This called for the shortest possible arrival procedure if I wanted to beat the rapidly thickening fog.

When Zurich Radar positioned me close to the downwind leg for runway 16, even from a distance I could see the approach lights shining through the fog, which meant that the layer was thin. Above, the conditions were perfect and I could rely partly on visual clues, so as to reach the runway threshold as quickly as possible.

After changing over to Basle Tower, I was advised that visibility had reduced further and that it was only 600 metres, which was my landing limits. Now, no second could be wasted on a time-consuming dogleg to the MN beacon. Instead I decided to proceed no further than sixty seconds past BN, relying on the ADF indication. From a correct downwind position as well as the correct altitude for final, after an 180° turn this distance should bring me on the localiser in ample time to intercept the glide slope. However, upon completing the turn, although the ADF needle pointed straight ahead, which meant that I should close onto the G/S beam after passing BN, to my dismay, both the G/S pointer and the view of the approach lights revealed that I was far above the correct approach angle. Thanks to clear conditions above the fog layer, a quick dive brought me on the glide slope in time to stabilise my approach, before I had to change over fully to the instruments. In the end, I got down on the ground in the nick of time, as shortly afterwards

Tower reported another drastic drop in the visibility.

Later, I kept asking myself time and again what could have gone wrong with the ADF, usually a most reliable aid to navigation, as after landing the needle began to point in the right direction. But finally I found the answer to the riddle that haunted me for years when I came across an article in *Tech Log, the Journal of the Association of Licensed Aircraft Engineers*, outlining the dangers of the power line interference, with a particular reference to the Basle crash.

After reconstructing the flight path of my precarious approach, I could see that the false BN signal had most likely originated from the area of the railway station at St Johann, the same spot which had subsequently raised its ugly head in the Vanguard crash. Although at the time of my incident, the existence of a 'ghost' beacon would have looked to me like an idea from a science fiction book, after extensive research and as a result of my painful lesson, I am convinced that spurious beacon signals sent the Invicta Vanguard to its doom.

10

1975 – 'I'll be Back Saturday Night'

PART I

'I'll be back on Saturday at 10.20 p.m.' – it was a message Graham Hill sent from France via the telex at Elstree Aerodrome to his wife Bette, who had arranged a dinner party for their friends that night. The message was relayed by phone to the Hills' country mansion in Hertfordshire by the obliging aerodrome staff. Graham left England in his private aircraft on Friday morning 28 November 1975, to supervise testing of his new racing car at the Paul Ricard circuit near Le Castelet in the South of France. At first he was going to fly back on Sunday but, as the tests had gone well, he decided to return a day earlier. The latest creation of the Embassy Hill Racing Team, the GH2 Formula One car, required only minor adjustments and appeared to be ready for its debut in the next Grand Prix race in January 1976. GH2 was the team's first car produced from scratch and much hope was pinned on its improved performance. The earlier model GH1, which the team was using during the 1975 season, was a derivative of a Lola.

With the capricious English weather, the South of France offered more reliable conditions for testing, particularly at the end of November. Another convenience was the close proximity of an airstrip at the Paul Ricard circuit, situated only a walking distance from the pits.

To Graham Hill, flying was his second passion and as strong as his first one, motor racing. He used his private plane on business as much as his car. But he also enjoyed a few hours in the air for the sheer exhilaration of it. He was happy to get off the ground, so that he could feel free from the pressure of constant business commitments and public engagements. He tried to pass his flying enthusiasm on to his family. He was teaching his fifteen-year-old son Damon the rudiments of

piloting an aircraft. Even his daughters, Bridget, aged sixteen, and Samantha, aged ten, had the taste of handling the plane in the air. The latest pupil was a promising new racing driver, Tony Brise.

Hill had learnt to fly in a Chipmunk at the Elstree Flying Club ten years earlier. He bought his first aircraft from the prize money of his Indianapolis 500 win in 1966. In 1970 he replaced it with the latest turbocharged version of the Piper PA 23-250 Aztec 'D'. Right from the start, he treated his second passion like a pro. He would never board his aircraft without inspecting it thoroughly. His technical background helped him to understand and respect all machinery. He was also known for his conservative approach to risks in the air. It was unlike another motor racing personality, also using Elstree as his home base, whose aviating antics were often a topic of conversation in Grand Prix circles. Those who knew Hill from Flying Club activities, such as local dentist Nigel Malcombe, held him in high esteem as a pilot. Although Hill was generally making relatively short flights, he made at least two per week, and as a result had managed to amass 1,600 hours in ten years, an impressive figure for a private pilot.

Lord Snowdon planned to join Hill on the flight to France. They had first met twenty years earlier at the London Rowing Club and had remained good friends ever since. Snowdon, then Anthony Armstrong-Jones, had served as a cox on the Cambridge University Team. However, shortly before Hill was going to leave for France, Snowdon changed his mind as he thought he had enough pictures of the GH2 taken during tests at Silverstone earlier on.

After arriving in the South of France, Hill spent the night at Le Castelet and next day he watched his new car undergoing rigorous tests at the Paul Ricard circuit. But he did not drive the

Graham Hill's aircraft, Piper PA 23-250 Aztec 'D', registered N6645 Y.

car himself. Rumours circulating after the accident that he overtaxed his stamina before flying back were unfounded. At midday, he had a sandwich lunch with his team and only a soft drink. He would never touch alcohol before a flight. Later the team members remarked that he appeared to be in good spirits.

In the afternoon, he phoned Nice Air Traffic Control in accordance with the prescribed rules and gave them the particulars of his flight to Marseille Marignane Airport, although it was only a twelve minute hop. Marseille was going to be an intermediate stop for customs and immigration clearance as well as for refuelling. He left the Paul Ricard airstrip at 3.30 p.m.

At Marignane, Hill filed an IFR (Instrument Flight Rules) flight plan along the designated airways to Elstree. He gave the estimated time *en route* as four hours, the expected time of arrival at 22.00 hours and an endurance of six hours. The extra two hours were more than ample in case of diverting, even to a distant North European airport. But he specified his alternative as Luton,

only twelve miles away. At Marseille, five team members boarded the Aztec, while the rest went back by road in a convoy consisting of a transporter and several private cars.

Hill elected to cruise at Flight Level 80 (8,000 feet on standard altimeter setting of 1013 millibars). Although a higher altitude would have been more fuel efficient for the Aztec's turbocharged engines and could have offered higher true airspeed thus shortening the flying time, he appears to have been conscious of a lesson he had learnt in the past. The incident, which reflects his attitude to safety, was recently recounted by the Hills' family friend, Keith Smith, an actor and a keen private pilot himself. When they were crossing the Pyrenees at 10,000 feet on a flight back from Barcelona, Hill turned back to talk to Smith and noticed that his friend was showing signs of anoxia. Although at that altitude only a very few people become affected by the shortage of oxygen, he immediately gave him an oxygen mask and, at the same time, decided to use one himself although he felt no ill-effects. But to him it was a sensible precaution. On subsequent flights he evidently made a point of avoiding flying at a critical height for oxygen when he carried passengers on board.

At Marseille the Aztec was refuelled to the maximum capacity, which was 140 gallons. With the long-range wingtip tanks fitted, the aircraft was capable of at least 1,200 miles range. According to a subsequent check by the accident investigators, Hill exceeded maximum take-off weight by 155 kilograms. However, this was only an estimated figure as no accurate weights of the occupants could be obtained after the crash.

The 155 kilograms excess represented 6% above the allowable limit. But this was only slightly more than a generally accepted 5% tolerance in respect of errors when calculating take-off weights.

The weather forecast, on display at the airport in the self-briefing meteorological unit, indicated that during the period from 13.00 to 22.00 hrs, with an approaching depression, visibility at Luton and at Stansted (19 nm away from Elstree), was expected to improve to 8 and 10 km respectively. London Heathrow would also go up to 9 km. Only Gatwick showed a pessimistic trend with the visibility dropping down to 1.5 km later

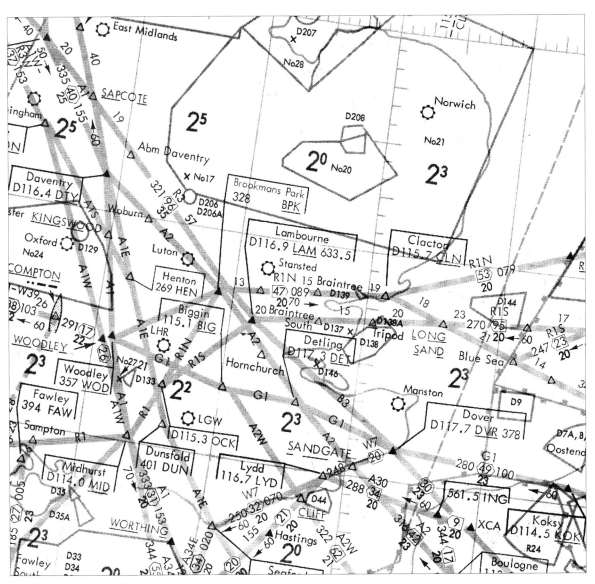

Low-level airway chart for 1975.

in the evening. However, a subsequent prognosis covering the period of 16.00 to 01.00 hrs, which was only available at the main Marignane Meteorological Office, gave an entirely different picture. Between 20.00 and 23.00 hrs a marked deterioration down to 800 metres was expected at Heathrow, Gatwick, Stansted and Southend. As Hill probably attended to his flight preparations as soon as he landed at Marignane, the later forecast was likely not yet on display at the time of his visit to the self-briefing unit.

He took off from Marseille at 17.47 hrs and, after an uneventful flight across France, made his first radio contact with London Air Traffic Control Centre three hour later. He was immediately informed that the 20.40 hrs weather conditions at Elstree were 2 km visibility and cloud base of 300 feet. He was subsequently given the usual clearance to Elstree via Detling and Lambourne VORs. When queried about his intention after passing Lambourne, he replied, 'I'll have a look at Elstree.'

Unfortunately, with flying at 8,000 feet, London Volmet South (area weather information broadcast on a VHF frequency) could not be received until the aircraft was close to the English coast. After Hill left Marseille, there had been a drastic weather deterioration in the whole London area. At 20.20 hrs Heathrow, Gatwick and Southend reported visibility of only 100 metres while Stansted was slightly higher at 400 metres. However, Luton still enjoyed reasonable conditions with 2.5 km visibility, but within half an hour this had changed to 800 metres.

After passing Dover VOR at 21.00 hrs, Hill was re-cleared directly to Lambourne VOR, although it was not an appreciably shorter route than via Detling. While on the stretch from Dover, London Air Traffic Control Centre tried to contact Hill several times between 21.08 and 21.18 hrs but without success. During these ten minutes he was most likely busy listening to the Volmet. So far the *en route* weather conditions had been without much concern.

When London Air Traffic Control Centre eventually managed to contact Hill, he reported his position as 'just coming up to Lambourne' and requested descent clearance. He was cleared down to 4,000 feet on London QNH 1002 millibars (QNH is an airport or an area altimeter setting with reference to sea level). When queried again about his plans, he confirmed his intention of having a look at Elstree and that Luton remained his alternative.

Shortly afterwards, Hill was picked-up by London Radar and informed that his position was eight nautical miles south-east of Lambourne. He was also warned that the visibility at Elstree had dropped down to 1 km. Upon acknowledging the message, he was told to contact London Heathrow Approach Control. The radar controller instructed him to turn onto magnetic heading of 290°, in order to take him directly to Elstree. At that moment the aircraft was passing overhead the A12 road between Hornchurch and Brentwood. Although the Aztec as a relatively small aircraft produced weak radar echoes, it was equipped with a transponder, so the ground controller would have a clearly defined target on his screen.

Three minutes after receiving his initial descent clearance, Hill reported reaching 4,000 feet. He was instructed to turn 10° to the left and maintain heading of 280°. He was also given a further descent clearance to 1,500 feet. The controller repeated London QNH – 1002 mb.

Once Hill informed control that he had reached 1,500 feet, he was advised that his range to Elstree was four nautical miles. He immediately requested further descent clearance and was told to continue at his own discretion. Shortly after, he was heard on the London Approach frequency calling out, 'Elstree... ', although he had not yet been instructed to leave that channel.

Omitting to switch over to a new frequency before inadvertently starting a call is a slip that pilots often make in pressing moments. Hill quickly corrected himself and reported to Elstree, '45 Yankee finals'. The '45 Yankee' was an abbreviation of the full callsign N6645Y. Although operated only out of England, the Aztec still bore United States registration markings.

In the meantime, London Approach Control unsuccessfully tried to pass on both the latest position as three miles to go to Elstree and Heathrow QFE (QFE – an altimeter setting to indicate zero feet upon touchdown). As Heathrow's elevation is about 100 feet and Elstree 334 feet, providing Hill with a London QFE served no useful purpose and could only lead to confusion. The ground speed at that stage was ninety-five knots. This is an indication that the aircraft was already prepared for a landing with the undercarriage down and the flaps extended.

When Graham Hill reported, '45 Yankee finals', Peter Wood, the Elstree Air Traffic Watch on duty, immediately recognised his voice and gave him the local QFE – which seemed rather late at that stage of the approach – and clearance to

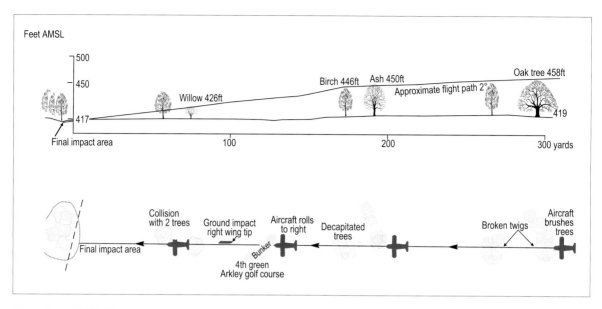

Piper Aztec N6645Y crash plan. (AIB investigation).

land. The reply from the aircraft was '45...' followed by a click as if the microphone button was suddenly released. From then on there was no further contact. At the same time, the London Approach controller observed that both the primary echo and the signal from the transponder suddenly disappeared from his screen at a distance of two and a half miles from the airfield.

At 21.31 hrs the London controller phoned Elstree to check up whether the Aztec had landed.

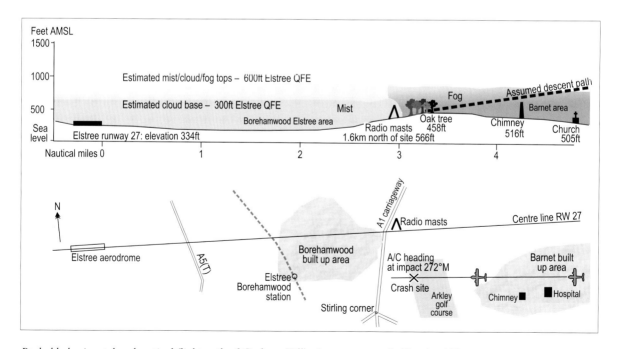

Probable horizontal and vertical flight path of Graham Hill's Aztec, as compiled by the AIB.

View of the crash site of Graham Hill's Piper Aztec, taken from a helicopter.
(F. Pringle, by permission of Chief Inspector of Accidents)

The crash site in 2000.

After Peter Wood advised him that he had also lost contact with the aircraft, the ALERT emergency phase was immediately initiated.

The Aztec initially brushed the top of a forty-five-foot-high oak situated just below the first brow on the eastern side of Arkley Golf Course. This was estimated to have taken place at 458 feet above sea level and was followed by clipping off upper branches of an ash, thirty metres further on. Upon striking the ash, the right fibreglass tip tank was torn off and the propellers left distinct marks on the tree. After subsequently running into a clump of young birches, the left wing came off and the fuselage was extensively damaged. This sent the Aztec into a 45° roll to the right and the starboard wing touched the ground. When the aircraft hit two willows 130 metres further on, it began to break up and fuel tanks ruptured. The fuselage became entangled in thick branches and it kept dragging them along. Finally, as the battered Aztec collided with a cluster of small trees at the boundary of the golf course, fuel exploded and the wreck became instantly engulfed in flames. The position of the crash was 3.1 nautical miles due east of the runway threshold at Elstree airfield.

Ted Dicken, the Arkley Golf Course steward, who was at the time in the clubhouse, thought that the explosion sounded like a wartime bomb and it felt as if the club house roof had come down. But when he realised that the loud bang had been caused by an aircraft which must have crashed somewhere on the golf course, he called 999. His message was at once relayed to the Metropolitan Police Station at High Barnet and four officers patrolling the area in cars were directed to the scene of the disaster. They arrived within ten minutes and saw that the Aztec was burning fiercely. It was immediately apparent that there were no survivors. The fire was so strong that it was not possible to get close to the wreckage. When the policemen contacted Elstree for information about aircraft that could have been making an approach to the airfield, they were told that Graham Hill was expected to land there but contact was lost.

The news of the accident was quickly broadcast by various television and radio stations. Suddenly the quiet road around Arkley Golf Course was full of cars. Some spectators stopped their vehicles, blocking the road. Rubbernecks were having a great time.

Next day the nation mourned the world's double motor racing champion with deep grief. The loss of an outstanding sportsman and a great personality was compared to the loss of Manchester United footballers at Munich. Many fans admired Graham Hill for his pluck and determination to get quickly back to motor racing after a horrendous crash in the US Grand Prix at Watkins Glen in 1969. His legs were so badly shattered that the doctors told him he might never walk again.

The funeral service was held in St Albans Abbey by the Bishop of St Albans, Dr Runcie, later the Archbishop of Canterbury.

PART II

On the night of the crash, PC Geoff Rowe was going to start his duty at 9.45 p.m. As he walked from his home to the Metropolitan Police Station at High Barnet, situated near the top of a hill, about two-thirds of the way up he ran into thick fog. But the fog layer looked to be shallow. With the misty conditions getting worse, a spate of traffic accidents could be expected and it meant a busy night. However, upon arrival at the station, he learnt that he was being given a special assignment, together with PC George Steffe, in the incident room. He was expected to help with the enquiries about an accident to a private aircraft that had crashed in the Barnet area. The officer in charge was Inspector Harry Hodgkinson.

The public are generally unaware of how much assistance is provided by the Police Force during an air crash. The manpower allocation is often as high as in a major road accident, although the investigating side is left to the aviation experts. On the fateful night, as soon as the policemen arrived on the scene of the disaster, they had to direct the emergency services by radio so no precious minutes would be lost on searching for the crash site because of poor visibility. The London Fire Brigade was first notified at 22.06 hrs and, in spite of the foggy conditions, the fire trucks arrived at the accident site twelve minutes later. Soon they were joined by the Hertfordshire fire service. Although as a result of exploding fuel, the blaze was at first extremely fierce, it had rapidly burnt itself out and the remaining small pockets of flames could be quickly extinguished with water. When the policemen managed to get closer to the wreckage, they could see that all bodies were burnt beyond recognition. They were careful not to touch any parts of the aircraft so as not to disturb vital clues. They knew that an inspector from the

Board of Trade Accident Investigation Branch was on his way. (At the time, it was called Accident Investigation Branch – AIB, and only later was the name changed to Air Accident Investigation Branch – AAIB.) One policeman remained at the crash site all night, guarding the wreck from souvenir hunters.

In the meantime, PC Rowe and PC Steffe tried to establish who were the occupants of the ill-fated plane. From the particulars provided by the Elstree Aerodrome staff, it looked certain that one of them was Graham Hill. A Sunday newspaper reporter immediately tried to contact Mrs Hill for comments. Weary of being frequently bothered by the media for all sorts of information about her husband, she put the phone down. But when the children saw the story on the television, they rushed with the news to their mother. For Bette Hill it was a devastating blow but she took it very bravely.

'Graham had taught us to be strong. He was a great example to many people, including the disabled,' she told a reporter next day, 'He had so much dedication and love for his fellow men. He was a great example to everybody. Thank God, because we all need the strength.'

It took several hours before the convoy returning from France could be contacted as they were all that time on the road. Eventually it was learnt that the other occupants of the Aztec were Andy Smallman, the designer of the GH2 car, Ray Brimble, the team manager, and twenty-three-year-old Tony Brise, a promising racing driver and Hill's protégé. On board were also two mechanics, Terry Richards and Tony Alcock. According to Chris Witty, a motor racing reporter, Brise, a former kart champion, was one of the greatest talents England had produced in the seventies. Supremely self-confident bordering on arrogance, he seemed a prototype of Michael Schumacher, the present-day German, Formula One ace.

It fell upon the shoulders of the officers in the incident room to break the news about the disaster to the families of the deceased. At the same time, they diplomatically tried to obtain information on special body marks or availability of the dental records. These were needed so an identification could be eventually performed. Later, Barnet Police Force received notes of thanks for the tactful manner in which these enquiries were conducted.

Many local policemen wondered why Hill did not try to use close-by Leavesden Airfield, as it

was equipped with an Instrument Landing System. As his Aztec was fitted with an ILS receiver, a landing could have been performed safely despite bad weather. Unfortunately, Leavesden was closed during weekends.

Five bodies were identified by B. Sims, senior lecturer in forensic odontology at the London Hospital, from dental records. The sixth body, that of Tony Alcock, could be only verified by exclusion. However, such a method was not accepted by the North London Coroner, Dr Paul, and he requested that a fingerprint check be subsequently performed.

PART III

It was the very early hours of a dark and foggy morning when the team from the Accident Investigation Branch assembled at Barnet Police office for a briefing before being taken to the scene of the accident at Arkley Golf Course. The team included an operational and a technical inspector, as well as an RAF pathologist. However, fieldwork could not be started until daylight broke and the weather conditions improved.

At the crash site, the team had split up to carry on with their respective tasks. While the operational inspector, a former KLM pilot with 15,000 flying hours to his credit, got busy looking for evidence of the flight path and surveying the surroundings, his technical counterpart began to examine the wreckage and the doctor attended to what was left of the bodies. The team would frequently meet to cross-reference their findings according to a checklist. Photographs of the crash site were taken from the ground as well as from a helicopter provided by the Metropolitan Police.

The team also received valuable assistance from Barnet Police Force, who secured the area of the accident with tapes to prevent pilfering by the souvenir-seeking public. Several officers carried out a detailed search for debris along the final path of the ill-fated Aztec.

As the aircraft first gently brushed the upper branches of an oak before colliding with a larger tree, from the measurement of the clipped treetops it was possible to determine the final part of the glide path. It looked surprisingly flat, only 2°, which represented a low rate of descent of 336 ft/min. While fieldwork was still in progress, Bill Tench, Chief Inspector of Accidents, paid a visit to Arkley to have a look at the scene of the disaster.

When the investigating team were satisfied that nothing more could be learnt at the crash site, what was left of the Aztec was removed from Arkley Golf Course and taken away for a detailed examination at Farnborough. A witness recently interviewed could recollect how, six days after the accident, an RAF transporter loaded with the wreckage went past her house. There appeared to be no large part of the ill-fated aircraft left intact.

During the technical examination at Farnborough it was found that the fire damage to the Aztec was so extensive that it was hardly possible to determine the position of the controls at the time of the impact, or what the last readings on the instruments were or the settings of radio and navigational equipment. But eventually certain facts have come to light. The aircraft must have been in an approach configuration, as both the undercarriage and the flaps were extended for landing. There was no sign of any engine failure prior to the final impact. The marks on the propeller blades indicated that a fair amount of power was still on when the propellers started to bite into the ground. Although the left-hand altimeter was badly damaged, it was possible to determine that it had been set to 1003 mb, which was very close to London QNH of 1002 mb. One millibar difference was an acceptable error in the conditions of a darkened cockpit. This represented only twenty-seven feet of the altitude difference.

The right-hand altimeter was found with a reading between 997 and 998 millibars and may have been set by Tony Brise for London Heathrow QFE of 999 mb, as he was probably sitting up in front with Hill. This information could have been obtained from a Volmet broadcast.

The radial of 312° selected on No. 1 VOR receiver, was most likely used to follow the airway from Dover to Lambourne VOR. An inspection of the No. 2 receiver revealed that it was set to 266°. Later, some amateur researchers claimed that Hill could have relied on this setting to establish on final with the help of a VOR, in view of the magnetic heading of runway 27 at Elstree being 266°. However, there was no VOR station within fifty miles that was in line with the runway.

A detailed examination of the accident site and the wreckage was only the beginning of the lengthy proceedings. In comparison with an investigation of a public transport airliner, the AIB team were at a disadvantage. The Aztec was not equipped either with a Flight Recorder or a Cockpit Voice Recorder. The only information about its final movements came from witnesses who had seen the aircraft's flashing lights as it passed very low over Barnet. Another major difference, as far as the investigating procedures were concerned, was that private flyers do not operate to the same standards as commercial or airline pilots. However, in spite of the limited evidence that it was possible to trace, a comprehensive history of the flight was compiled.

All aircraft documents and pilot's qualifications were checked. Unfortunately, some had shown irregularities. Although the Aztec carried US markings, in fact the US registration had been cancelled a year earlier, and it was not transferred to another country. An inquiry indicated that Hill believed his aircraft was still registered in the USA. But without a valid registration, the certificate of airworthiness was officially void. Nevertheless, the aircraft received meticulous maintenance by a reputable company.

According to the UK Air Navigation Regulations, Hill, as a holder of a UK Private Pilot's Licence but without an Instrument Rating, was not allowed to fly in weather conditions of less than three kilometres visibility and a cloud base lower than three thousand feet. However, he was entitled to fly at night as he had the appropriate rating. The situation during the ill-fated flight with regard to the respective rules was somewhat complicated. Except for the final part of the approach to Elstree, visibility was adequate to comply with the prescribed limitations. But because London Terminal Area was designated by the 1974 Air Traffic Control Regulations as a permanent IFR zone regardless of the weather conditions, by entering the Zone, Hill infringed the Air Navigation Regulations. On the other hand, he was also the holder of a US private pilot's licence with a FAA Instrument Rating. Unfortunately it had expired in 1971. But had he applied, it could have been easily re-validated. Nevertheless, the legal points had no bearing on the cause of the accident.

To get a better practical insight into operational circumstances surrounding the fatal approach, the AIB operational inspector checked the actual radar set in use at London Airport Approach Control Centre in order to observe its limitations for guiding private aircraft into Elstree. According to the UK Air Pilot, Heathrow Approach Control could provide advisory radar assistance. From the observations it was soon apparent that it was not precision guidance but only a general vectoring towards the airfield. The radar antenna was located eleven nautical miles away, and due to the built-in limitations of the system, the overall accuracy was not very high. The expected error was in the region of 1% in range and 2° in azimuth. Moreover, the accuracy also depended on the skill of the operator. As the radar was basically used for arrival and departures procedures at Heathrow, Elstree, being only a secondary airfield, was marked on the screen without any runway centre line and aligning an aircraft appeared to be a matter of guesswork.

The visit to Heathrow Approach Centre was followed by similar operational inquiries. At first, the AIB inspector closely examined Hill's final descent path from a helicopter. Later he chartered an Aztec from Elstree, to see for himself at dusk the various well-lit and dark areas that Hill passed over during the final seven miles from the direction of Lambourne. Flying the radar headings as issued on the night of the accident, resulted in revealing observations that the inspector believed could help to explain Hill's premature descent. The five-mile run before Elstree brought the aircraft over a large, well-lit suburban area of Barnet immediately followed by a dark patch which was Arkley Golf Course. On the other hand, when it was positioned on the centre line of the runway, hardly any lights were visible except when passing over Borehamwood. If Hill, flying in fog or cloud, mistook Barnet's lights for Borehamwood's lights, he could have assumed that he was clear of the 566 ft high masts (255 feet above the ground) located on the approach path 3 nm away from Elstree and that it was safe to make a further descent.

It took six weeks to complete the investigation and produce the report. Many operational aspects of the crash were covered and checked such as Elstree Aerodrome facilities, navigational and communications services, availability of weather forecasts and actual weather reports or diversion options.

Elstree had no electronic aids for landing in low visibility. Its bituminous runway 09/27, only 666 metres long, was equipped with standard lights. The approach lighting was limited – a red illuminated 'T' (four lights) located on each side of runway 27 and a low intensity two-colour approach-slope system, known as LITAS.

Of particular interest was a report on the actual weather conditions at Elstree four hours before Hill's crash. An experienced RAF pilot, who took a Piper PA 24 from Jersey to Elstree, made three unsuccessful approaches using radar positioning from Heathrow as Hill did. The Piper pilot recounted that he made his first attempt at 17.15 hrs when it was already dark. He contacted Elstree Aerodrome Control for landing information and used QFE throughout. On his first approach after he was positioned for final, he could not identify the runway at 500 feet and decided to try again. However, in spite of rather misty conditions, lights on the ground were clearly visible. Above the layer of fog, visibility was good. On the second attempt, he descended to 300 feet and, although he spotted the illuminated red 'T' on the left side of the runway, it was too late to make a successful landing. On his third go, he thought he saw the runway lights but as he was going to change to the Elstree frequency and report 'final', he realised that they were not runway lights but some other lights. He made an overshoot and diverted to Luton.

PART IV

The AIB accident report was published in 1976. It stated that, in the absence of evidence on any mechanical failure which could have affected the flight path of the ill-fated Aztec, the crash was most likely caused by purely operational factors. There was no question of fatigue or shortage of fuel that could have influenced Hill's decisions. Without any apparent indication on his intended course of action in the last minutes of the flight, it was difficult to come to clear-cut conclusions as to what might have induced him to descend so dangerously low. It would have been simple to blame it on pilot error for an attempt to land in bad weather with limited landing aids. But the investigating team tried to find a commonsense answer based on the available evidence as to what could have trapped a relatively experienced airman for a private pilot, and a cautious individual, into making such a fatal mistake. The team were aware that a landing in low visibility demanded a consistently high degree of skill and concentration, as well as adequate approach lighting and radio aids. By reputation, Hill had many skills but it seems that he may have expected too much of his abilities, in particular when a commercial charter operator, using a similar aircraft to the Aztec, would only have been allowed to make a landing at Elstree when the visibility was at least 1.5 km and the cloud base 500 feet.

The report analysis suggested three possibilities that could have accounted for striking the ground three miles from the airfield. They were: incorrect interpretation of the actual height, unexpectedly entering a layer of fog, or an error in estimating the distance from Elstree.

The first possibility was that Hill could have overlooked having set his altimeter to the London area QNH of 1002 millibars and thought that he was on Elstree QFE. As the altimeter was found to indicate one millibar higher than London QNH, the combined altitude difference would have amounted to 390 feet. As a result, believing that he was that much higher and well clear of the terrain, he continued his descent unaware that he was flying towards the highest point in that area. However, the report rightly stressed that Hill was given London QNH on two occasions. From his past experience, he must have been familiar with the procedure of changing the altimeter setting at certain stages of the approach. In view of this, such a possibility appeared to be very distant.

A similar theory was advanced by Tony Rudlan in his book *Mr Monaco* about Graham Hill. Rudlan, a former Lotus Team Manager, knew Hill well from the days when the double world champion drove for Colin Chapman. Rudlan also believed that Hill forgot to adjust his altimeter from 1013 millibars (QNE), which he used when flying on the airways. This could have accounted for even a bigger difference in the altitude indication. But as it was established that the No. 1 altimeter was set to the correct QNH, it was unlikely that Hill had been trapped by an erroneous altitude reading.

Rudlan took the trouble to retrace Hill's final route in a single engine Arrow, with Bette Hill as a passenger. He tried all possible combinations of the VOR bearings to see if the 266° radial would bring the aircraft over the crash site. Only Clacton VOR, situated fifty miles away, had positioned the Arrow within a mile. But it is unlikely that any pilot would elect to navigate on VORs when under radar surveillance. A departure from an instructed heading would soon be noticed and corrected with a warning.

The second possibility advanced in the AIB report, was that, during the descent from 1,500 feet, Hill had inadvertently run into a layer of fog. As he was flying at first in clear weather, he tried to re-establish visual contact with lights on the ground and, as a result, he went too low and struck the trees. The report, however, stressed that although no evidence had been found to support this presumption it cannot be

disregarded as a probable contributory factor to the accident.

The third possibility was that Hill, through simple disorientation about his position when flying in cloud or mist, mistook the lights of Barnet for those of Borehamwood and thus thought he was much closer to Elstree. As he believed there were no obstructions in his path, he commenced what he thought a safe descent at a slow rate of only 336 ft/min. Unfortunately, the unlit part of that area was not the final stretch to Elstree but led over a hill on which Arkley Golf Course was situated. Although this possibility could not be clearly substantiated, it appeared to be the most probable cause of the accident.

PART V

But were the three possibilities mentioned in the AIB report the only explanations that could have accounted for Graham Hill's tragic accident? In order to answer this question, it is necessary to re-examine the chain of events leading to the disaster, starting from the time Hill arrived over England. Until then, he was most likely unaware of the drastic weather deterioration, as at Marseille he received no warning.

Fog forecasting is an educated guess, often based on the meteorologist's past experience rather than on exact science. Minor differences in temperature or wind strength can greatly influence the speed with which fog forms.

Perhaps as a result of a different weather picture in his mind from the information he received earlier on, when Hill was queried about his intentions, he replied, 'I'll have a look at Elstree'. At that moment, the situation did not appear to be critical. However, when told by London Radar half an hour later that the visibility at Elstree had dropped to 1,000 metres, he still did not change his mind and confirmed his original intentions. Several factors could have affected his decision to consider an attempt to land at his home base, instead of straight away diverting to another airport. He could have been motivated by the fact that, from Dover to Lambourne, visibility varied greatly and he could have rightly wondered if the situation was the same in the Elstree surroundings. Manston in Kent, only twelve miles from Hill's track reported visibility from fifteen to twenty kilometres. On the other hand, Southend located further on but closer to his track, had already gone down to 100 metres.

A certain parallel can be seen in an accident that took place five years earlier. In January 1970, a Boeing 727 of Ariana Afghan Airlines crashed in similar weather conditions during an approach to Gatwick Airport with the loss of forty-nine lives. The captain, who survived, later told the investigators that when he sighted the English coast he could see that the fog was patchy. As he knew that patchy fog often shifts quickly, he decided to start the approach even if at that moment the visibility on the airport was reported to be only 100 metres. On final, the lights on the nearby roads were visible as well as the lights of London in the distance.

From the airmanship point of view, there is nothing wrong with attempting an approach in a critical visibility provided it is done cautiously. In respect of restrictions for private pilots, there is no rule in the Air Regulations which prevents them from trying to land in any conditions.

Due to the ground remaining still relatively warm in the early winter months, as fog begins to form, it is often shallow and usually becomes dense only a few feet above the ground. Such 'surface fog' can pose problems during a landing as a result of abrupt changes of visibility with altitude in the very last few feet of the approach. Even if it is possible to see some land features when flying above a layer of fog, as the pilot comes down and levels off over the runway, his field of vision may be drastically reduced, resulting in loss of orientation. The problem could be accentuated at night when electric lights are used as a reference for landing. Although in general lights can be spotted more easily in foggy conditions at night than land features in daytime, the contrast as they fade out or altogether disappear from a pilot's view, can cause far more dangerous disorientation.

The tricky aspect of surface fog is its depth. The shallower and denser the layer, a bigger difference between direct and slant visibility can be expected. If visibility on the ground is only 200 to 300 metres, slant visibility at a few hundred feet above the ground could be as much as 1,000 metres or even more. This could appear to a pilot of a small private aircraft as sufficient to make a successful landing relying solely on visual cues. In such circumstances, he may be lured into a false sense of security, thinking that what he sees ahead would continue all the way to the touchdown.

In that respect, the AIB report on the Ariana accident stated as follows: 'Experience in the UK has shown that surface fog on an otherwise clear night can lead the most careful pilots into disastrous errors of judgement when the anticipated visual references fail to appear or when such references suddenly become distorted or unexpectedly fade out.'

Fog density can also be influenced by local conditions, such as terrain, proximity of the sea, lakes or rivers. Pollution from smoke-producing fuels can accelerate the forming of fog patches in a particular locality.

In order to assess the odds with which Hill had been faced on the fateful night, establishing the picture of the actual weather during the entire approach, and not only in the final moments of the flight, was of paramount importance. As there were no reports available on the latter at the time, only corroborative evidence could be obtained in view of the twenty years' lapse.

The conditions on short final as reported by the Air Traffic Watch at Elstree Aerodrome, although not a qualified but an experienced meteorological observer, were as follows:

'20.43 hrs: wind calm, vis. 2 km, cloud 8/8 at 400 feet (estimated)
21.07 hrs: wind calm, vis. 1 km, cloud 8/8 at 400 feet (estimated)
21.15 hrs: wind calm, vis. 800 m, cloud 8/8 at 300 feet (estimated)'

The reported visibility appears to be relatively accurate, as determining it does not depend on specialised equipment. The usual procedure is to check with an object or a light that still remains discernible at a known distance. On the other hand, it is not possible to reliably assess the height of cloud base without a measuring apparatus. In view of this, the figures provided by the Air Traffic Watch appear to be only a rough estimate. Moreover, as there were no in-flight reports of any clouds in the area, it was more likely that the height of the top of the fog layer had been observed.

With the close proximity of two large water reservoirs to Elstree Aerodrome, one at Hilfield Park and the other at Alderham, it is possible that the short final was more affected by fog than the other parts of the approach. Heavy moisture and a light south-westerly wind could have accounted for the misty conditions that had formed already on the airfield in the afternoon. This was indicated by what the pilot of Piper PA 24 who made the three unsuccessful passes, later told the investigators.

During the day, the weather in the Arkley area was described by a recently interviewed witness who lives just across the road from the golf course, as murky but not particularly foggy. In fact, it was the general weather outlook rather than poor visibility that put her and her husband off flying from Elstree to Cornwall in their private plane that morning.

PC Rowe's recollection provides a good picture of the weather situation around the time of the crash. His observations indicate that thick fog had formed only on the hill at High Barnet and Arkley but the layer was very shallow. This was confirmed by three witnesses who were able to spot the flashing anti-collision lights of the ill-fated Aztec through fog as it passed overhead.

According to the weather analysis provided by the Meteorological Office at Bracknell, with a slack gradient over southern England the very light south-westerly wind at the surface would tend to produce upslope motions of air. As a result the hill would be completely covered by low stratus and a thick hill fog with visibility of less than 200 metres. The actual visibility at the crash site was assessed to have been between 50 to 100 metres.

An Elstree Air Traffic Watch, who was off duty on the night of the accident, recently described the conditions in the whole area as very patchy. As he drove from Edgware to Borehamwood, visibility varied from 100 metres to two kilometres. With his experience as a meteorological observer, such assessment is a good guide as to how the general situation looked that night.

This could have given Hill a confusing picture as he watched the pattern of lights on the ground from the aircraft. In the areas where fog was shallow, slant visibility was most likely relatively good and lights were probably shining through. On the other hand, where low stratus had formed with an appreciable thickness, not much could be observed of the ground below, and this could have appeared as a less densely populated area. The usual pattern of visual clues, such as town lighting, which local pilots used at night to establish their position in relation to the airfield, could have given a false impression in such patchy conditions.

There is no question of Hill's lack of experience in bad visibility landings. According to Peter Wood, 'an old-timer' as an Air Traffic Watch at Elstree Aerodrome, he had witnessed Hill landing in all sorts of weathers. (It was not possible to obtain any further recollections from Peter Wood as he was killed in an accident when a heavy excavating truck ran into the back of his car ten years, exactly to the day, after Graham Hill's crash.)

Keith Smith described him as a careful and an aware pilot. He was very confident of Hill's abilities from the numerous instances he had flown with his friend. On one occasion he was with Hill during a landing in heavy rain and with a slight crosswind. The touchdown was perfect and Hill showed hardly any signs of anxiety or emotion. But on another occasion when the visibility at Elstree was reported poor, and it looked equally uninviting from the air, Hill did not hesitate to divert straight away to Luton. His experiences with the local weather would have encouraged him to evaluate the situation by himself, and it could be the reason why he decided to have a look at Elstree.

The first indication of urgency in Hill's actions was that after he received descent clearance to 4,000 feet, he reported reaching the assigned altitude only three minutes later. Such a rapid descent could have been only achieved by a rate of 1,330 ft/min, which was rather high for a small aircraft. But by pushing the nose down, this must have helped Hill to keep the speed up, as is evident from the 160 knots that he maintained as soon as he was informed of the deteriorating visibility at Elstree. It is an indication that he intended to reach the airfield as soon as possible. In comparison, the stretch from Dover to Lambourne was covered at the ground speed of only 145 knots and the wind effect would have been negligible on both stretches.

At the time of receiving descent clearance from 4,000 to 1,500 feet, the aircraft was still seventeen miles from Elstree. The radar vector of 280° was taking Hill over Chingford and Southgate; a relatively well-lit suburban area and probably clear of fog. From the landmarks he must have been aware of the distance to the airfield, because from 4,000 feet he reduced his rate of descent to only 500 ft/min but still maintained high ground speed.

Unfortunately, London Radar's vectors were not bringing Hill close to the required direction of the approach path and it was an inexcusable mistake on the part of the radar operator. In such poor visibility greater care should have been taken to align the Aztec as accurately as possible with the centre line of the runway. The change from the original heading to maintain 280° appears to have been done prematurely.

At that stage there was no justification for any correction for drift. According to recent information obtained from the Meteorological Archives at Bracknell, on the night of the accident the wind between 4,000 and 8,000 feet, as interpolated from

Red lights at High Barnet Underground station. The top photo shows a close-up of the unshielded lights. The bottom photo shows the general layout of the tracks terminating at High Barnet.

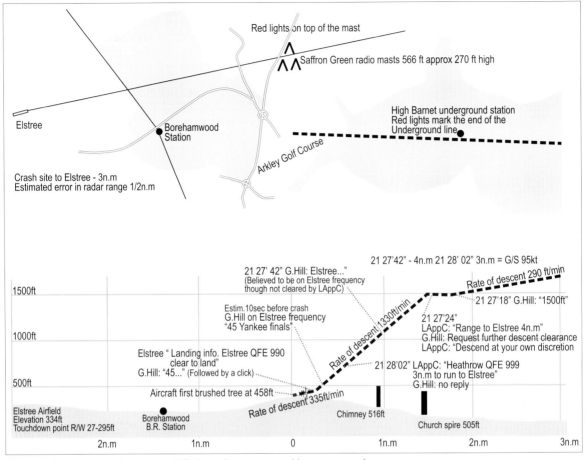

The probable horizontal and vertical flight path as computed by my research.

measurements at two weather stations close to Hill's route, was 260°/10 knots. This would have resulted in only 1° of drift.

The three earlier radar positionings given to the pilot of the Piper PA 24 appear to have been more accurate, as one of the attempts brought the aircraft very close to the illuminated red 'T' at Elstree.

Relying on radar as some sort of a 'magic wand' is a misconception often entertained even by experienced airline pilots. The Air Inter Airbus 320 crash near Strasbourg in January 1992, is an example of how a pilot expecting a radar operator to allow for terrain clearance can be trapped into believing that the man on the ground knows exactly what he is doing.

Unsatisfactory radar assistance appears to be one of the main contributory factors to the Arkley Golf Course disaster. Instead of being brought, as Hill expected, over Saffron Green, a

prominent landmark at night of radio masts with red lights on top, he ended up over Chipping Barnet, a mile to the south. With the closing angle to the runway centre line of 15°, applying final corrections in low visibility would not have been easy even in the case of a highly manoeuvrable aircraft such as the Aztec.

The pilots who use Elstree as their home base often rely on the red obstruction lights at Saffron Green as a 'homing beacon', in particular at night. It is like an 'Elstree Outer Marker' which, when crossed at 1,156 feet on QNH (or at 856 feet on QFE), puts the pilot on a 2° glide path, the angle generally used for approaches of light aircraft. If a rate of descent of 400 ft/min and a heading of 266° are maintained, the pilot finds himself in a perfect position for landing.

Hill's problems with orientation could have been further compounded when he was informed that his range to Elstree was four nautical miles while his actual range was four-and-a-half. This error could be determined from the fact that, when the aircraft struck the ground at three miles from Elstree, the radar operator observed that the echo had disappeared from his screen at two-and-a-half miles.

The radar vector of 280° and the actual range of 4 nm from Elstree would have put Hill just past High Barnet Underground Station. A recent search for red lights that could have given Hill an impression of passing the Saffron Green radio masts revealed that he could have mistaken the red lights that demarcate the end of the tracks at the Tube station. As the tracks are split into sidings, lamps are fitted on the top of stop barriers. Unlike the railway signal lights, they have no upper shields, and it would have been possible for Hill to spot them whilst passing overhead. In particular because, according to PC Rowe's recollections, fog on the night of the accident started only two-thirds up the hill at High Barnet and the Underground station lies somewhat lower.

Although what Hill's actual intentions were after leaving 1,500 feet will always remain a matter of conjecture, his certain actions suggest that he followed a preconceived plan. As in other similar kinds of accident, it is apparent that his decisions were influenced not by the actual picture of the features below, but by what, at that moment, certain landmarks such as red lights represented to him.

From the information in the AIB report, his horizontal and vertical flight path could be relatively accurately reconstructed. (*See* graph on page 244.) It is possible because, from the moment Hill reported leaving 1,500 feet, the recorded radio conversation between the ground and the aircraft was timed to the second, as against the minute until then.

He advised London Approach Control that he had reached 1,500 feet at 21.27 hrs and 18 seconds. At that time his position was over Chipping Barnet at a height of 1,100 feet above the ground, having had already left the red lights of the Underground Station behind. Six seconds later, when he was informed that his range from Elstree was 4 nm, he asked for further descent. He was told that he could do it at his own discretion. Assuming that the exchange of messages took two seconds, he must have left 1,500 feet at 21.27 hrs 26 sec. From the ground speed of ninety-five knots, determined from the two consecutive radar ranges of four and three miles, the time of brushing the first tree at 458 feet above sea level,

was calculated to be 21.28 hrs and 16 sec. (+/- 1 sec.). The resultant average rate of descent, between the start of final descent and coming into contact with the tree, amounts to 1,200 ft/min, which is rather high for that stage of the approach. This would have required the throttles to be fully closed and would have resulted in gaining speed. Indeed the ground speed did increase by eight knots to ninety-five knots. The Aztec's recommended approach speed was 100 mph or eighty-seven knots.

Such a high rate of descent must have been as a result of Hill presuming that after passing a line of red lights believed to be those on the Saffron Green radio masts, he was about 400 feet too high for a 2° approach path to Elstree airfield. The only solution was to push the nose down, in order to regain the required descent profile.

However, when the aircraft struck the trees, the rate of descent was only 336 ft/min. As at 650 metres east of the crash site, a witness heard the aircraft flying already very low, it means that by then, Hill must have flattened out his descent. From these two references it was possible to construct the vertical flight path, which shows that at first the rate of descent was as high as 1,350 ft/min, followed by a much lower rate of only 336 ft/min in the last six seconds before brushing the oak. To attempt such a drastic manoeuvre, flying conditions must have been relatively good and Hill must have been certain of his position in relation to Elstree.

Upon leaving the lights behind the presumed 'Elstree Outer Marker', Hill's attention would have been tunnelled on the next cluster of red lights expected to soon come into view, which was the illuminated 'T' on the airfield. In low visibility, these four lights would be more conspicuous than the weak, white runway lights. It is interesting to note that the Ariana pilots of the previously mentioned accident at Gatwick stated that the only light on the airport they spotted through shallow fog during the entire approach was a red light, which they thought to be the end-of-runway light. But it turned out to be a hazard beacon on Russ Hill, a bit further away.

Hill knew that the approach from Saffron Green led over an area below the airfield level of 334 feet, so it was safe to descend close to that height. In fact, the threshold of runway 27 (the current designation is 26 as a result of a change in the magnetic variation during last years) is only 295 feet high, in view of an appreciable down slope in the easterly direction. A landing from that direction resembles an aircraft carrier operation, as every Elstree pilot was bound to have quickly learnt.

Seventeen seconds after leaving 1,500 feet, Hill was heard to utter, 'Elstree...', on the London Approach frequency, a result of failing to change the radio channel. At that moment he would have been around 1,050 feet on QNH (or 650 feet above the ground). This instinctive call appears to be of special significance. Hill must have spotted something on the ground that gave him the impression of the red 'T' on the airfield and he urgently wanted to advise the airfield controller that he was on final. At that altitude slant visibility would have been still reasonable. What had probably helped him in getting a good view ahead was that during the descent the aircraft's attitude would have been nose-down.

Both the horizontal and the vertical flight path indicate that 'this special point' he was aiming for was not the 'T' on the airfield, but most likely red lights at Borehamwood and Elstree railway station. These lights would have been the same distance from High Barnet Underground Station as the illuminated 'T' was from the Saffron Green masts. However, an extensive search and local inquiries about the existence of unshielded red lights on the station or close to it, which Hill would have been able to spot from the air, were in vain.

Even if it may sound an 'if and but' supposition, a possibility cannot be ruled out that he could have been looking at red lights on the rear of a train that had just stopped. In view of the descent from 1,500 feet having taken less than a minute, this would have been long enough for the train to remain stationary at the station.

From the vertical flight path it is evident that Hill relied on his local knowledge to put himself relatively low on short final to be sure of spotting the runway lights sufficiently early. Believing that he was over terrain below the airfield level, a low approach at that stage would have been safe. Unfortunately he was positioned by radar over 'unknown' to him territory, a mile away to the south of his usual run, and he was descending towards one of the highest spots in the area.

Once he observed what he believed to be the red lights of the 'airfield T', it can only be expected that he would have immediately tried to report '45 Yankee finals'. At that moment he must have still been above the fog layer, to be so sure of his position. But only a fraction of second later the disaster struck. As PC Rowe recently remarked,

had Hill been only thirty to forty feet higher, he would have been in the clear as the ground falls away from the Arkley Golf Course and only slightly rises again at Elstree.

Hill, not a professional pilot, may not have been aware that an altimeter, as a pressure instrument, can be subject to a number of minor errors. On a rare occasion, their adverse combination could amount to the straw that breaks the camel's back, especially since during a low visibility approach every foot counts. Instrument error alone can be as high as forty feet before an altimeter is regarded as having exceeded the laid down tolerances. Temperature departure from the standard atmosphere conditions by which all altimeters are calibrated, can also add several feet. The most significant error can be the lag in an indication during descent or climb. In a dive, this would be particularly accentuated. Taking also into account the previously mentioned twenty-seven feet error in the QNH setting, the altimeter could have indicated 100 feet higher, or even more, when the aircraft first brushed the oak at 458 feet above sea level. At that moment Hill may have been under the impression that he had at least 200 feet clearance before touching down on runway 27.

Unfortunately, the majestically tall trees brought down the red-and-white Aztec, triggering off the disaster that followed. It took many years for shorn branches to grow back to their previous size. Some time after the accident, the members of the Golf Club planted a new tree surrounded by a flowerbed where the aircraft had finally come to rest. Bette Hill was invited for a round of golf so that she could get to the green where the tree had been planted and a short commemoration service was held on the spot.

The reason for Hill presuming to be on his customary approach run from Saffron Green was undoubtedly a badly misjudged positioning by the radar operator. Perhaps the initial high rate of descent after leaving 1,500 feet partly contributed to the subsequent tragic chain of events. It certainly had not helped that Hill flattened out his dive somewhat late. But behind it lies a recognised reason. A light that can be discerned through shallow fog appears to a pilot to be higher and nearer than it actually is, creating the illusion of the normal approach path being on the high side.

Although an attempt to land in poor visibility without adequate radio aids, moreover at night, may appear on the surface an act of imprudent airmanship, nevertheless using knowledge of local landmarks to locate the runway, while expecting to be over an area free of obstacles, was neither an act of foolishness nor flirting with danger. Shallow fog always appears to be more dramatic to observers on the ground than to those in the air.

Hill clearly realised what flying involved. In his autobiography, *Graham*, he claimed: 'There is always the problem of the weather – and that needs a lot of respect. Battling with the elements calls for a great deal of effort and concentration.'

He was not the only well-known personality who had the misfortune to run into the deceptive nature of shallow fog. Prince Bernhard of the Netherlands, an experienced pilot with 7,000 hours to his credit, had also encountered similar conditions on one occasion, but luckily without tragic consequences. In the late fifties he was flying his 'royal' DC3 PH-TPB from Holland to Northolt for a state visit. Unfortunately, just before his arrival, a layer of shallow fog had just crept in. In those days there were no radio aids at Northolt to guide the aircraft to the runway. But, as ground features were still visible from the air, the Prince made several passes to find suitable landmarks which could help him to align his DC3 on final. When he eventually managed to land, his bad luck was to run into a patch of dense fog at the end of the runway. It took twenty minutes for the 'FOLLOW ME' van to retrieve the royal Dakota. Dutch officials were horrified and the Prince was severely censured for taking unnecessary risks. Yet there appeared to be nothing unduly dangerous in attempting to land at Northolt under the pressure of the circumstances, which was the British government reception party waiting on the airfield. (Prince Bernhard recounted this incident to a group of airline pilots with the author present, at the IFALPA Annual Conference in Amsterdam in 1969.)

In flying, a certain amount of calculated risk is expected to be taken. I do not know of any pilot who has not tried once in his entire aviation career to stretch his luck in order to get back home on Saturday night. Fortunately thousands of airmen have managed to get away with it. Only a handful were unlucky.

11

1977 – The Worst Aviation Tragedy

PART I

On 27 March 1977, the world was shattered by the news of an air disaster reaching cataclysmic proportions. Many media interrupted their programmes to announce that 563 people had perished in a fire when two Boeing 747s collided on the runway at Tenerife Airport. There were seventy-two suvivors, six in extremely critical condition and many others on the danger list. By a stroke of luck, fifteen passengers and several crew members came out of the ordeal either with only minor injuries or with none. The final casualty figure varied from hour to hour as the airlines checked their passenger lists.

Regardless of the ultimate cause of this tragedy, the prime roots lay in a terrorist action by the local separatists. An organisation calling itself 'Movement for the Independence and Autonomy of the Canaries Archipelago', until then hardly known to the rest of the world, planted a small bomb at El Gando Airport near Las Palmas on Gran Canaria Island. It was hidden in a vase which had been deposited in a flower shop next to the check-in counters. The bomb exploded at 1.15 p.m. local time, causing extensive damage to the terminal building. Although, fifteen minutes earlier, the airport authorities were warned by a phone call and immediately arranged evacuation, eight people were injured, one seriously. Shortly afterwards, the separatists rang again, this time from Algiers, claiming responsibility for the terrorist act and hinting that another bomb was hidden somewhere in the building. As a result, the local police instructed the airport manager, Pedro Gonzales, to close the airport and to conduct a thorough search of the whole terminal.

As it was a Sunday, an armada of some sixty airliners bringing holidaymakers was already converging on the Canary Islands. The terrorists intended to create chaos at the airport and they were achieving their aim. The air traffic controllers watched their radar screen rapidly fill up with more and more echoes of aircraft which they could not accept. The only solution was to divert the approaching traffic to Tenerife. Unfortunately, the airport on the next-door island did not possess suitable facilities for handling more than just a handful of wide-body jets. Arranging re-clearances and diversion sequences put enormous strain on the Las Palmas controllers. With a limited staff to man the Approach unit, it was an amazing stroke of luck that there were no mid-air collisions.

Terrorist acts cannot be regarded as ordinary breaches of law. When a high toll of lives could be involved, such barbarities must be regarded as an offence against humanity, on a par with war crimes.

The rapid growth of airlines in many western countries into a mass transportation medium, made the aircraft and the airports particularly vulnerable to attacks from fanatical terrorist organisations. But the air transport industry could have done without that extra headache. At that stage of its progress, it was badly suffering from shortcomings of aeronautical facilities. At many airports approach and landing aids were still far below standard. Taxiway and runway markings were outdated. Air traffic control was based on a nineteenth century concept borrowed from the railways. Over the years, there was no improvement in communication systems and procedures. Above all, when, in addition to the weaknesses of the ground aids, weather suddenly turned sour, pilots were often faced with a nightmare. In such circumstances, a terrorist act would have been the last straw.

Planting a bomb at Las Palmas Airport does not appear to have resulted in any gains for the

Canary Islands independence movement. In fact, the reverse is probably true; it must have weakened its cause. Many years later the Islands are still a part of Spain and there are no signs of any change in future.

Although the bomb explosion injured only eight people, the other consequences of the terrorist act were far more reaching. The eventual loss of 583 lives speaks for itself and it must be recognised as a dastardly deed that stained the perpetrators' hands with the blood of innocent people. Even if later the separatists tried to absolve themselves by claiming that it was not their fault but that of air traffic control, planting the bomb was the first link in a tragic chain of events.

Nevertheless, the final findings by the Spanish Board of Inquiry placed the blame on the shoulders of the KLM Boeing pilots for having been predominantly responsible for one of the world's worst aviation catastrophes.

PART II

Among the armada of jets converging on Gran Canaria Island were two Boeing 747s. The PanAm aircraft – registration N736PA, bearing the name

Clipper Victor – was on a charter to Royal Cruise Lines. Flight PA 1736 left Los Angeles in the evening of 26 April with 364 passengers, predominantly retirees. Many were going to join MS *Golden Odyssey* at Las Palmas for a twelve-day 'Mediterranean Highlights' cruise.

After an intermediate landing at New York, where a further fourteen passengers, as well as a new crew, came on board, the aircraft left Kennedy Airport in the middle of the night. The new cockpit team consisted of Captain Victor Grubbs, First Officer Robert Bragg and Flight Engineer George Warns, and there were thirteen fresh cabin-attendants to look after the passengers.

The second Boeing – PH-BUF – belonged to KLM. It was a newer version of the 747, a series 206B, christened *River Rhine*. It left Amsterdam at 09.31 hrs (the times are in GMT, a standard practice at all accident investigations). The aircraft was carrying 234 passengers, mostly young holiday-makers and their children, for the Dutch tour operator Holland International. Flight KL 4805 was under command of fifty-one-year-old Captain Jacob 'Jaap' Veldhuijzen van Zanten (Veldhuijzen van Zanten being his full surname), chief instructor of the KLM Boeing 747 fleet. His first officer was nine-years-younger Klaas Meurs and the

Jaap Veldhuijzen van Zanten

Klaas Meurs

flight engineer, an 'old-timer', Willem 'Vim' Schreuder. There were eleven cabin attendants on board.

KLM Flight 4805 left Amsterdam at a convenient time of the day and, with the outbound stretch expected to take under four hours, it was expected to be a relatively easy assignment for the crew. On the other hand, although the PanAm flight was only two hours longer, the pilots had started their duties in the middle of the night, which was far more fatiguing.

After diverting from Las Palmas to Tenerife, Flight KL 4805 landed at Los Rodeos Airport at 13.38 hrs (local time – half an hour earlier). At the end of the rollout, the captain was advised by Tower that he was to park in the run-up position for runway 12. At first, he could not believe that the instruction was correct but it soon became apparent that apart from the apron in front of the terminal, this was the only hard stand available which was wide enough for a Boeing 747. Taxiways were too narrow and all other positions were occupied by the diverted aircraft.

Initially the KLM captain intended to keep his passengers on board. However, when twenty minutes later there was no sign of an imminent departure, he decided to give them a break by allowing them to stretch their legs in the airport terminal. But with the building situated more than half a mile away, they would have to be transported by bus. This was a risk, as bringing them back would take time and could preclude a quick departure if Las Palmas suddenly became open.

The PanAm Boeing landed at Tenerife at 15.15 hrs and was also assigned a parking position in the run-up area. It was the last available space in the far corner to the east, and at the end of a line of several diverted aircraft which included a SATA DC8, a Braathens SAFE Boeing 737, a Sterling Boeing 727 and finally the KLM 747. The hard stand in front of the terminal was already full, as well as most of the taxiways and the run-up area.

The arriving crews were never given any information by ATC as to why Las Palmas Airport had been closed and were told to stand by until the all-clear signal was sent from there.

At the time of the PanAm Boeing's landing at Tenerife – it was one of the last of the diverted aircraft to arrive – the weather conditions were good with visibility more than 10 km and a trace of clouds at 1,000 feet. But within fifteen minutes came a dramatic change. Suddenly low clouds appeared as if from nowhere. With Tenerife's Los Rodeos Airport situated on a 2,000-foot-high plateau in a valley between two steep mountain ranges, and with the proximity of a cool sea, weather conditions in that particular spot were known to fluctuate unpredictably. In the next hour visibility continued to deteriorate, and eventually dropped down to 1,500 metres. Then it alternated from 1 km to 500 metres, as patches of clouds drifted across the airport at ground level bringing intermittent drizzle.

Pilots watched the sudden weather change with anxiety. A further drop in visibility could ground them if it fell below their take-off limits.

The grim prospect soon became a subject of chat between the captains of the two Boeing 747s on their aircraft radios.

'The boys have forecasted some lousy weather for us,' quipped van Zanten.

'Forecast they can plenty,' replied Grubbs from PanAm, 'but the question remains, will the conditions improve?'

'Okay, then it looks that as always, we'll be dictated by the weather,' laughed van Zanten. 'Do you know if Gran Canaria has already given an all-clear?'

'No idea but the boys in the Tower sure take goddam long time.' Vic Grubbs sounded as if his patience had begun to wear thin.

He had a right to feel at the end of his tether. He had started his duty eleven hours earlier, but had been on the go for twelve hours from the time he left home. With every passing minute he became more and more impatient and kept calling the Tower for news about his departure. Every time the reply was the same – 'stand by'. There is nothing more frustrating for pilots than a lack of information on the expected time of departure or on the reasons for a protracted wait. During traffic hold-ups, it is a general practice for ATC to assign every aircraft a sequence number, which, although it may not denote the actual time of departure, at least gives the pilot a rough idea as to when he can expect to be given his clearance.

Eventually Grubbs had enough of being stuck in the cockpit and decided to take a stroll to the terminal. On the way back he noticed that the KLM 747 was being refuelled. His reaction was anger. 'Why in hell, didn't they decided to do it earlier?' he grumbled to himself.

Once in the aircraft, Grubbs again requested his start-up clearance. The controller explained that although there was no further traffic delay, the exit was blocked. One end of the taxiway was full of aircraft, and at the other, the KLM 747 was

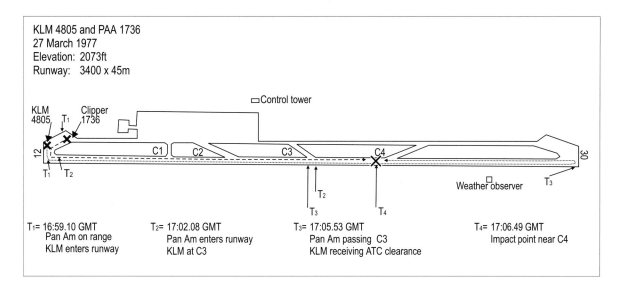

KLM 4805 and PAA 1736
27 March 1977
Elevation: 2073ft
Runway: 3400 x 45m

☐Control tower

KLM 4805   Clipper 1736   T₁

Weather observer

T₁= 16:59.10 GMT
   Pan Am on range
   KLM enters runway

T₂= 17:02.08 GMT
   Pan Am enters runway
   KLM at C3

T₃= 17:05.53 GMT
   Pan Am passing C3
   KLM receiving ATC clearance

T₄= 17:06.49 GMT
   Impact point near C4

full of aircraft, and at the other, the KLM 747 was in the way still being refuelled. For Grubbs this was a frustrating setback.

The PanAm co-pilot and flight engineer decided to check if it was possible to squeeze past the other Boeing. But after measuring the clearance between the wingtips, they could see that they were about four metres short. Their plane was hemmed in and they could do nothing about it except wait until KLM left its parking position.

Upon returning to the cockpit, the co-pilot immediately contacted van Zanten on the radio, only to be told that tanking was going to take another half an hour. Cursing the KLM captain's decision to bother with refuelling after such a long wait, Grubbs became resigned to the fact that there was no other way out but to endure the hold-up without losing his temper.

Unfortunately, KLM's departure was again delayed for another reason. Traffic from Europe was still streaming into Las Palmas, and this combined with the aircraft flying from Tenerife, was causing an acute shortage of handling facilities. There was simply no room for KLM to park at Las Palmas.

As it happened, when refuelling was about finished, van Zanten was advised that he could finally leave. He requested start-up clearance at 16.51 hrs. It was three hours and thirteen minutes after his landing at Tenerife and one hour and fifty-one minutes since Las Palmas Airport had become open to traffic.

At 16.58 hrs the KLM Boeing was cleared to enter runway 12 and backtrack to the take-off position at the other end. When the aircraft

reached about halfway, the PanAm 747 was instructed to follow KLM. It was not possible to use the parallel taxiway as there were still several aircraft parked there and following KLM would have been the only way to bypass them.

After experiencing difficulties in establishing his position while backtracking due to extremely poor visibility, when van Zanten reached the end of the runway, he lined up his Boeing for an immediate departure. After the checklist was completed, First Officer Meurs told the Tower that they were ready for take-off and were standing by for ATC clearance. The controller reeled off their clearance and as Meurs was in the middle of reading it back, van Zanten began to open the throttles and called out: 'We go... check thrust.'

Meurs hurriedly completed the read-back and at the end, uttered a sentence which later was difficult to transcribe, but which, in all probability, amounted to: 'We are now taking off.'

A second later, a squeal could be heard on the radio, preceded by just one word – 'Okay'. The squeal lasted four seconds and was followed by a message: 'Stand by for take-off... I will call you.'

The squeal was likely caused by PanAm and the Approach Controller transmitting at the same time. The next call came from the PanAm Boeing: 'Clipper one seven three six.'

The Approach Controller replied: 'Papa Alpha one seven three six report runway clear.'

This was acknowledged by: 'Okay... we'll report when clear.'

'Thank you,' the Tower controller added.

While the KLM Boeing was gathering speed, one of the crew members began to show signs the official transcript, a literal translation of the expression used by the Dutchman, would be: 'Is he not there off?')

Although the investigating team who transcribed the Cockpit Voice Recorder tape could not determine for sure who it was, the circumstances point to Flight Engineer Schreuder. At that stage of the take-off, the co-pilot would have been standing by to call out the decision and the rotation speed. This would have most likely precluded him from saying anything else except what the take-off procedure required.

However van Zanten appeared to have missed the foreboding expressed by someone in the cockpit and asked the remark to be repeated: 'What did you say?'

'Is he not clear that Pan American?' the same voice repeated the ominous query. (Again a literal translation would be: 'Is he not off that Pan American?')

'Oh yes,' van Zanten assured him.

At that moment, the PanAm captain became concerned about a possibility of a dangerous misunderstanding, reflected by him suddenly snapping out: 'Let's get the hell right here... get the hell out of here.' This was followed by a nervous chuckle.

The PanAm co-pilot felt critical about the KLM crew's attempt to get airborne in a great hurry: 'Yeah, he's anxious, isn't he?'

The flight engineer joined the chorus of uncomplimentary remarks: 'Yeah, after he held us up for an hour and a half, that ***'.

Although the actual expletive, as used by the flight engineer, appeared in several books and publications, it is omitted as it was not in the official transcript.

'Yeh, that ***,' the co-pilot echoed.

'Now he's in a rush,' the flight engineer jeered.

In the KLM Boeing, Meurs had just called out the speed 'V-One', which demarcated the aircraft's capability to stop within the remaining length of the runway if the take-off had to be abandoned. Suddenly Vic Grubbs spotted the KLM Boeing's landing lights in the distance. Diffused by fog, the lights at first looked to be stationary. Then as he realised that they were in fact rapidly converging upon him, he gasped out with horror: 'There is... look at him *** that ... that *** is coming.'

By now Bob Bragg was sure that the two aircraft were on a collision course and he frantically screamed out: 'Get off, get off, get off.'

As they were close to taxiway C4, which joined the runway at an angle of 45°, Grubbs desperately tried to move out of the way. The CVR later revealed that he advanced the throttles wide enough to pass the point at which the warning horn begins to sounds when the 'body-gear disarm' is still on. At the same time, the CVR also picked up the engine whine of the approaching aircraft. Horrified, Bragg could see that the KLM 747 bottom red anti-collision light was aiming directly at him.

With the PanAm Boeing's landing lights not having been switched on at the time, the KLM pilots probably spotted the fog-obscured silhouette only a split second before the collision. Once van Zanten was suddenly confronted with the sight of the other 747 still on the runway, he made a frantic effort to leapfrog the massive fuselage that was in his way. He rotated his Boeing so abruptly that the tailskid scorched the runway for twenty metres. Then as he realised that a crash was inevitable, he uttered one word he would have never dared to use normally.

What followed was the biggest carnage so far in the history of aviation. Although the KLM Boeing's nosewheel had just managed to clear the top of the other aircraft, which at that moment was already askew on the runway trying to make the taxiway, the right undercarriage struck the PanAm's left inboard engine and then ploughed through the first-class compartment, instantly killing many of the occupants. Surprisingly, the passengers who survived the collision had not found it particularly violent and claimed that it sounded like a blast of a small bomb. One of them recounted: 'It was just like a car crash at first. Then the left engine exploded and everything caught fire.'

Once the KLM 747's left wing had knocked off the PanAm's tail fin, the ill-fated PH-BUF went out of control and 200 metres further fell on the runway. It kept sliding for another 300 metres, while revolving ninety degrees around and shedding all its engines. Then it exploded and was instantly engulfed in an inferno of flames. There was not the slightest chance for anyone to survive.

The PanAm Boeing was so badly crippled that fuel began to leak from the tanks. But the undercarriage did not collapse and the two left-engines were still running. At first Bob Bragg tried to cut off fuel by the start levers but they would not budge. Then he reached for the handles of the emergency shut-off-valves, which were located overhead, but they were not there any more. The KLM 747's outboard engine had sliced the PanAm's cockpit roof completely off. It did not take long for the leaking fuel to be ignited by the running engines, and after several small explosions, the fire began to spread. At that moment, instant evacuation of the wreck which could blow up at any moment, became a matter of life and death.

Luckily, as a result of the impact several openings appeared on the left side of the front cabin, wide enough for some passengers to squeeze through and then scramble onto the top surface of the wing.

An American woman passenger who was sitting behind the first-class compartment, described her experience: 'The top of the plane in the front section was sheared right off and there was just a big open place. I immediately unfastened my seat belt, crawled through the debris, jumped down the side of the plane and ran.'

But the only way to get down in order to avoid being burnt or choked by fumes was to take a jump from the height of a two-storey building. Many ended up badly hurt. PanAm senior cabin attendant Dorothy Kelly broke her arm and fractured her skull. Nevertheless this had not stopped her from helping the more seriously injured passengers. Her prompt action saved her captain's life by pulling him away from the dangerous fumes.

A seventy-year-old American from Laguna Beach in California gave the following picture of what was happening at that moment: 'I heard a terrible crash and at first I thought it was a bomb. Then the ceiling began falling down and flames engulfed the plane. I crawled away and looked back and saw the other people in my group surrounded by flames, not moving and not saying anything.'

Due to the twisting of the fuselage, the doors and emergency exits in the rear cabin became jammed, trapping everyone inside. Once the wreck began to burn like a bale of hay they screamed and banged their fists on the windows, trying to attract the attention of the rescue party. None survived the fire. The eyewitnesses of the horrifying scene when the helpless victims were incinerated alive could not get over such a heartbreaking sight for weeks.

But there were some extremely lucky escapes. One passenger was blown out of the wreck by the explosion and fell on the runway. He suffered only minor injuries but his wife was not so lucky, as he recounted:

'She could not take the buckles off her seat belt and I helped her, but she was impossible to move. I tried to pull her up and there was another explosion. I fell the other way and she fell this way. Then, I tried to reach her again. Then there was another explosion. It was so fast that I was thrown out of the plane. I looked and the whole Boeing was on fire. "Oh God!", I thought, "My wife. That is the end of her." Then there was another explosion and she was thrown off. Unfortunately she suffered heavy injuries.'

The PanAm co-pilot, Bob Bragg, came out of the badly mangled cockpit completely unscathed. The captain, the flight engineer and the company representative who travelled in the cockpit suffered only concussions or slight injuries that did not require hospital treatment.

Others who had managed to get away from the wreck presented a tragic sight to a Danish travel agent, an eyewitness of the crash: 'They were walking singly, mechanically, without any sort of reaction, like puppets. Their skin and hair were more or less burnt and they were made to lie down on sofas and the doctors attended to them, while waiting for ambulances to take them to hospital.'

At first, the air traffic controllers did not realise what had happened. They thought that a fuel tank on the other side of the Tower had been blown up by a bomb and they rushed to the back windows to take a look in that direction. Only when the crew of an aircraft parked close to the scene of the crash advised the controllers over the radio that they could see a wall of flames through the fog, was the alarm sounded and the fire trucks rushed to the burning KLM Boeing. But it was soon evident that trying to beat the inferno was a losing battle.

Unfortunately due to poor visibility, the rescue party was not able to notice that another aircraft had been involved in the accident and was also on fire. Only after someone brought it to their attention did they hurry to the other Boeing trying to save those trapped inside the cabin.

Through a stroke of luck, seventy-two people came out of the heavily crumpled PanAm wreck alive; unfortunately a large proportion were badly injured or burnt.

Although they were quickly taken to the local hospitals, seven had soon succumbed to severe burns. To transport such a large number of casualties, every available ambulance on the island was called out to help. A state of emergency was declared and radio stations continuously broadcasted requests for blood donors. The response from the local population was overwhelming.

Remains of the KLM Jumbo jet that collided with PanAm Jumbo at Los Rodeos airport, Santa Cruz de Tenerife, 27 March 1977. More than 550 died in the world's worst air disaster when both planes exploded. (Associated Press)

As the three Tenerife hospitals were unable to cope with so many casualties, most of the badly injured survivors were flown out the same night to Brooks Burns Centre in San Antonio, Texas. A military C130 Hercules from an American base in Germany had managed to land on a section of the runway not littered by debris and brought the crash victims to Las Palmas. There they were transferred onto a C141 Liftmaster which took them directly to the United States.

Next morning a team of seventy investigators from Spain, the United States and Holland descended on the scene of the crash. The eleven-man-strong Dutch delegation made the last part of their journey from Las Palmas to Tenerife in a helicopter. The Dutch team consisted of the government investigators, air traffic control advisers and KLM personnel.

Despite strenuous efforts to extinguish the fire, the debris of ill-fated PH-BUF still continued to smoulder even the day after the accident.

PART III

From a number of the reports on major accidents in the past fifty years it is apparent that, no matter how investigations were supposed to be conducted without any influence from the government that had instituted the proceedings, the conclusions on the cause of the crash were often affected by national interests.

Although the guidelines in the ICAO Manual of Aircraft Accident Investigation specify that:

'...the nature of the inquiry should not be accusatory as the object is to take remedial

Picture of investigators examining the remains of two Boeing 747 airliners after they collided at the airport of Santa Cruz Tenerife Island in 1977. (Associated Press)

rather than punitive action. Nevertheless, it is unavoidable that acts or omissions by individual persons or organisations are sometimes clearly revealed and in such circumstances it is the duty of the inquiry to say so.'

Nevertheless on some occasions it was not the case.

It has happened during a number of inquiries that when governmental departments responsible for operating aviation services were implicated in the cause of an accident, legal or political means were used to prevent conclusions which could have been embarrassing to national prestige or could have involved financial liabilities.

One way of protecting national interests was to restrict the interviews with the personnel involved. This was to ensure that evidence which could have revealed a deficiency of a government service could not be later used in civil litigation for compensation.

In the case of the Tenerife disaster, the claims had amounted to £400 million, for which the Spanish authorities could have been held either partly or fully liable if the controllers were found to be negligent.

The accredited representatives from the state of the aircraft's registry, who in most cases represent the interests of the crew involved in the crash, can generally do little to prevent the investigating authority of the state of occurrence from restricting the scope of the proceedings.

Among the cases outlined in the book of restraining tactics pursued by the governmental departments, such as the French trying to protect their air traffic controllers at the Basle inquiry or the Taiwan authorities trying to cover up the deficiencies of landing aids at Taipei Airport, the Tenerife investigation was yet another example of the continuation of such practices, despite the ICAO guidelines clearly underlining that no stone should be left unturned.

When it appeared from the initial impressions

of the Tenerife disaster that either the pilots or the air traffic controllers could be responsible for the collision, the Spanish officials were quick to ensure that their men's reputation was protected.

Reports appeared in the European Press alleging that the tape of the Tower radio transmissions had been confiscated by the local authorities immediately after the accident.

Even before the Dutch and the US accredited representatives joined the investigating team, one of the interested parties, the Civil Governor of Tenerife, had already pre-judged the issue by making a public statement that the Spanish air traffic controllers were in no way to blame for the collision because they gave the pilots correct instructions. The grounds for such a statement could have only originated from learning ahead of the investigators the contents of the ATC tape impounded by the local authorities. The only person who was later granted the same right, before a copy of the tape had eventually been forwarded to the FAA office in Washington for analysing, was a member of the Dutch investigating team, a government lawyer.

As the inquiry continued, there was a succession of Spanish statements putting the blame for the accident on 'technical problems' or on the crews of the crashed aircraft. Such leaks of 'inquiry news' were unprecedented, but they indicated that the local officials were using all means to divert responsibility from the air traffic controllers. The Dutch investigating team objected in the strongest possible terms to the premature speculations, but in vain.

The final verdict of the Spanish Board of Inquiry placed the blame for the collision on the KLM captain's shoulders as a result of taking off without proper clearance.

When the report was published, the Dutch Civil Aviation authorities were not satisfied with some of the conclusions and compiled their own assessment of the probable contributory factors. Although the Dutch assessment concurred with the Spanish findings on many broad aspects, a strong disagreement was voiced on several important points. The Dutch claimed that serious errors committed by the controllers had made the crash inevitable. In the end, it was apparent that there were two strongly opposing views as to what had created a catastrophic situation.

Before I begin to analyse the relevant facts, it would be only fair to state that I cannot consider myself as an impartial judge of the two opposing views. As a former KLM pilot, it is only natural that my sympathies lie with my former employer. My thirty years of service left me with unshakeable conviction that KLM was, and still is, one of the most safety conscious airlines in the world.

But as an aviation historian, despite my divided loyalties, I have tried to remain impartial by presenting the facts as they really were. It will then be left to the readers to form their own opinion as to what had really precipitated this tragic disaster.

PART IV

After the Spanish refused to conduct inquiries into the human factors that could have affected the performance of duties by the Tenerife air traffic controllers, the investigation became one-sided. No amount of pressure from the Dutch accredited representatives, who believed that this was a relevant matter, could change the minds of the Spanish. A remark from a member of the Dutch delegation, a KLM pilot, was characteristic of the discriminatory proceedings: 'The Spanish were the boss.'

On the other hand, the actions of the controllers at the time of the accident could not be generally faulted and it appears that they had not committed any basic errors. Nevertheless, a combination of negligent practices, minor mistakes and failures to take precautions in the critical stage of the two Boeing departures had undoubtedly created a potentially dangerous situation.

The ATC procedures used during the back-tracking of the two Boeings on the runway in extremely poor visibility, and the frequency of the checks on their positions, do not appear to meet the demands dictated by such difficult circumstances.

The report of the Spanish Investigating Board stated that allowing two aircraft to enter the runway in the weather conditions that prevailed at the time of the accident was hazardous. Whether it was just hazardous or more likely very dangerous will remain a matter of opinion.

From the first days of all-weather operations, it became apparent that controlling surface movements on an airport in low visibility presented a major problem. On busy airports even surveillance radar was found to be insufficient and back-up systems had to be introduced in the form of 'GO' lights and red 'STOP' crossbars to ensure a fail-safe operation. It was possible for

R/T instructions to become blocked out when the time factor was critical.

Another problem was that while taxiing in thick fog, pilots often found it difficult to recognise even familiar landmarks. Moreover, the time required for the eye to react to visual cues was considerably longer. Tests indicated that in such conditions it took between six to twelve seconds to appraise a hazardous situation.

When wide-body jets were introduced into airline service, separation of surface traffic had to be increased, because such heavy aircraft, even at taxi speeds, require a relatively long distance to stop. In a patchy fog as on the day of the Tenerife accident, when it was possible to run into zero visibility that may have required a panic stop, this called for extra care in controlling the movements on the airport.

Although the official meteorological report stated that visibility at 17.00 hrs was 2.5 km, this could not have been correct. The hut of the weather observer was located 570 metres from the end of runway 30 and 75 metres to the left side, so the observation should have reflected the conditions along the runway.

From the time interval between the PanAm crew spotting the KLM 747's landing lights and the impact, the calculations using the speed of the KLM aircraft at that stage of take-off, indicate that the visibility in the first section of runway 30 was less than 500 metres. The transcript of the two Boeings' CVRs revealed that both pilots experienced great difficulties in identifying the exits of the adjoining taxiways, and showed concern about the sudden deterioration of visibility which could have prevented them from taking off.

At the time of the collision, the best indication as to how thick the fog was in the centre section of the runway was a radio message from the crew of an aircraft parked on a nearby taxiway. They reported observing a wall of flames no more than 200 metres away, which had eventually turned out to be the burning KLM Boeing. But from the Tower building, situated 150 metres further away, the controllers were unable to see what was happening on the runway.

In such low visibility, despite the Control Room in the Tower offering a commanding view of the airport, the two Boeings were so obscured by fog that they were out of sight even when they were taxiing past the Tower building. The only means of keeping a tag on their position was by radio contact. But as it was later revealed, communication with the pilots was far from satisfactory. Several messages had to be clarified as a result of the controllers' strong Spanish accents. Apart from the difficulties of making sense of every transmission from the Tower, this wasted time when every second was needed for frequent checks on the aircraft's progress along the runway, the only way to give the pilots an idea of the other plane's whereabouts.

One could appreciate the difficulties for ATC personnel who usually only handle surface movements in clear weather, but at Tenerife Airport, where clouds at ground level were frequent, the controllers should have had sufficient experience of directing aircraft in restricted visibility.

From a number of remarks recorded on the CVR, it is evident that the co-pilots of both Boeings had to assist their captains in taxiing because of extremely thick fog on some parts of the runway. An additional difficulty was the crews' lack of familiarity with the airport layout, as it was their first flight to Tenerife.

Wide-body jets, due to size, height of the cockpit above the runway and the cut-off view from the front windows, require a higher degree of concentration during taxiing than smaller aircraft. The only means of assessing how fast the aircraft is moving is by referring to the ground speed indication of the Inertial Navigation System. Problems are particularly accentuated when visibility falls below 500 metres. In such conditions, the pilots' attention may be fully absorbed by the task in hand, and they may not be able to pay undivided attention to ATC messages.

Allowing an active runway to be used for taxiing by two aircraft at once, even in clear weather, would have been regarded by many civil aviation authorities as a very questionable practice. But in low visibility, even if surface movements surveillance radar was available or other means of regulating the traffic flow such as stop-go lights, it is doubtful that many air traffic controllers would have accepted the responsibility of committing two wide-body jets to simultaneously backtrack on a runway. Above all, to allow one of them to line up for take-off while the other had not yet cleared the runway would be regarded as asking for trouble.

Insufficient vigilant supervision of the two Boeings' movements could have played a part in setting up the scenario for the disaster.

Indications emerged during the transcribing of the CVR and ATC recordings that, at the time of the two Boeings' departures, a sports programme was being played on a transistor radio in the Tower, with a commentary on an important football match between Spain and Hungary at Rico Perez Stadium in Alicante.

Through a chain of relay stations, the reception of mainland programmes on Tenerife island was excellent. It was a known fact that the controllers had brought a small transistor set to the Tower, as they had a particular interest in this match. The Spanish national goalkeeper Miguel Angel was a local hero. Although he played for Las Palmas Football Club, he actually came from Tenerife.

To what extent listening to the football match affected the controllers' concentration would not have been possible to determine. But the following facts speak for themselves. The match, captained by their star Pirri, was going badly for Spain. After Hungarian striker Pusztai scored a goal, the Spanish side was down 1–0. The match came to a climax at 17.04 hrs (KLM entered the runway at 16.59 hrs, PanAm at 17.02 hrs) when the referee allowed a free kick not far from the Spanish goal. The gripping development must have attracted the attention of the men in the Tower and they probably turned the radio on a bit louder, as about a minute later when the Approach controller confirmed the instruction for the PanAm 747 to turn off at the third taxiway, both aircraft's CVRs picked up a background conversation. This could have only emanated from a radio set in the Tower. At that moment, the Spanish supporters were loudly disapproving the referee's decision and their screams could be distinctly heard even on a relatively poor tape of the ATC recording. Despite a certain amount of background noise, which was masking the radio commentary picked by the ATC tape, the transcribing team in Washington were able to recognise quite a few words in Spanish, which revealed that the radio commentator was furious. One sentence was clear: 'I could see it even from here.' And it was possible to distinguish another word – 'cuero' – which means leather in Spanish.

The Spanish authorities claimed that what was on the ATC tape had not originated from the radio, but must have been spoken by a third person in the Tower. Nevertheless, the official information indicates that there were only two men on duty. The transcribing team were convinced that the sentences picked up by the ATC recorder came from the transistor radio which must have been played relatively loudly at that moment.

According to the CVR transcript, there were no Tower transmissions from 17:03.57 until 17:05.53 (one minute and fifty-eight seconds), that is around the time of the free kick. The only exception was a message on the Approach frequency at 17:04.58, hurriedly informing the pilots that the centre-line lighting was out of service. This message was barely readable and it sounded broken, as if someone was not using the microphone properly.

Another factor which could also have had a bearing on the vigilant execution of duties by the Tenerife controllers, had been reported by *The Times* the day after the accident, that is on 28 March 1977: 'To complicate the position further, the Spanish air traffic controllers were still working to rule in a labour dispute which began last summer.'

The same problem was echoed in an account of the Tenerife crash that appeared in the German weekly *Bunte*. The magazine alleged that, when many aircraft diverted to Tenerife, the controllers tried to use that opportunity to show their authorities what a detrimental effect a go-slow action would have on congested movements of air traffic.

It was generally known that discontent among Spanish controllers had been brewing for several years. In the days of the Franco regime, ATC was under military control and its personnel was treated with strict discipline, the same as all members of the armed forces. However, when a democratic government was elected and the Spanish ATC came under civil authority, working conditions remained unchanged. The controllers soon realised that by the standards of other European countries, they were grossly underpaid. But a strike was still out of question so the only alternate way to demonstrate their grievances was by applying go-slow methods. They were given an encouraging example as to how effective such a method could be by their German counterparts. The German controllers were able to paralyse many flights in and out of their country during their several months long 'work to rule' campaign.

A prolonged waiting for departure clearances from Tenerife, without the reason having been specified, was bound to increase mental pressure on the stranded pilots. In particular on the two crews involved in the accident whose long duty hours were being unnecessarily extended.

The Press brought up a third reason for the controllers to be half-hearted about arranging expeditious departures to Las Palmas. This subject appears to have been a particular taboo during the accident inquiry and the Spanish authorities flatly refused the investigating team permission to interrogate the controllers on this sensitive matter. But the facts remain as follows: the Secretary General of the Movement for the Canary Islands Independence, a far-left organisation based in Algiers, Antonio Cubillo, who was responsible for planting the bomb, came from a well-known family in Tenerife. He was about the same age as the controllers, who also came from Tenerife, and they all went to school together. Consequently, they were bound to know the terrorist well.

Cubillo, apart from being a radical separatist, was also strongly opposed to the Canary Islands' exploitation by tourism. The Islands have much to offer to the holidaymakers in the way of ideal climate. Being situated in a sub-tropical belt of high pressure, the skies are mostly blue. On the other hand, a cool Atlantic current passing by ensures that the temperature, helped by constant sea breeze, is never oppressive even at the height of the summer. Although the beaches are not particularly attractive, the Islands are relatively sparsely populated and there are many opportunities for exploring beautiful wild countryside. For the sun-starved North Europeans, the sub-tropical paradise became an ideal holiday destination throughout the whole year and this led to an explosion of package tours by air and with it a great expansion of hotel trade.

Even if the influx of tourists did bring prosperity to the Islands, frequent late night disturbances by drunken 'lager louts' were antagonising the local population. It was no secret that many people strongly resented the tourist invasion and sympathised with the Movement. In some cases, opposition was particularly strong. Although an airport had been built on Gomera Island, one of the most beautiful small islands in the archipelago, local residents banned its use for charter flights with package holidaymakers.

PART V

Tenerife Airport was equipped with three VHF frequencies: Ground Control – 121.7 MHz, Tower – 118.7 MHz and Approach – 119.7 MHz. As there were two men on duty, only two frequencies were used – Tower and Approach. At many airports, if instructions are passed on more than one channel, it is standard practice for a third man to coordinate the other two controllers' activities.

The division of the duties between Tower and Approach on the day of the accident does not appear to have been sensibly arranged. The Tower controller handled only the start-up clearances and the instructions to enter the runway. From then on the Approach controller took over, and he had to supervise the backtracking of the aircraft on the active runway, issue take-off and *en route* clearances as well as attend to other departing traffic. All this was bound to put a heavy strain on him, while the other controller had a relatively easy task.

It was a mistake of far reaching consequences to change the KLM Boeing's taxiing instructions from the original Tower controller's intention for the aircraft to leave the runway at taxiway C4 and then to proceed to the run-up area via the parallel taxiway. Instead, the pilots were instructed by Approach to backtrack to the end of the runway, which meant that the KLM aircraft ended up in a position for an immediate take-off.

The Approach controller's message was as follows: 'Okay... at the end of the runway make a one-eighty and report ready for ATC clearance (background conversation in the tower).' (Surprisingly the background conversation was only picked up by the PanAm CVR and not by the KLM CVR.)

The Approach controller's instruction was another example of non-standard practice. The controller omitted to emphasise that after making a turn at the end of the runway the aircraft should hold. This is a vital ATC directive.

The Spanish authorities tried to defend the fact that their controllers' messages lacked clarity, arguing that they had a long and busy day behind them and were constantly under pressure. Nevertheless, by the time of the two Boeings' departures, traffic had petered out and workload must have been considerably reduced.

Why the controllers suddenly decided to send out two aircraft so close after each other on the runway, was never queried during the investigation. From the operational point of view, there was no need for such a sudden hurry. After having been kept for several hours on the ground, a few more minutes for the sake of safety would not have made an appreciable difference to the duty time of the PanAm crew.

According to a remark recorded on the PanAm CVR, Captain Grubbs felt uneasy about entering the runway while the KLM Boeing was still backtracking. But he accepted the instruction, having most likely presumed that the controller must have had a valid operational reason for speeding up his departure.

PART VI

All incoming and outgoing R/T messages and the respective cockpit or Tower instructions were recorded on the CVRs of the two Boeings and the ATC recording system. When the KLM and the PanAm CVR tapes were replayed on high quality equipment during the transcribing in the FAA office at Washington, every slightest sound in the cockpit, such as a seat being moved, could be clearly heard. It was possible to synchronise the tapes to the highest possible degree of accuracy, which was one hundredth of a second.

On the other hand, the recording of the Tower transmissions, provided by the Spanish authorities, was of very poor quality. It was a copy of the official Tower tape, duplicated on a cheap audio recorder and it contained only what the Spanish authorities believed to be relevant. As a result, the tape was out of sequence with both CVRs and it was not possible to synchronise it with the aircrafts' recordings. When the transcribing team protested about the 'edited' tape and its poor quality, the Spanish ignored their objections.

Of all six crew members on board the two Boeings, KLM First Officer Meurs was the only one who was no stranger to the Spanish controllers' ways of pronouncing English words. For ten years he had often flown the West African route, with regular intermediate stops at Las Palmas. (He also made quite a number of flights as a co-pilot with me.) No doubt his past experiences made him familiar with the operational practices of the local ATC. This can be seen when van Zanten asked the Approach controller if the runway centre line lights were available and Meurs came up with a critical remark in the cockpit: 'Would he know?'

His sarcastic comment appeared to have been justified by the reply from Tower: 'Stand by, I don't think, so stand by ... I will check.'

A moment later, he said, 'They are working on them... anyway... ah... will check it.'

Normally the status of all airport lights should have been displayed on a console in the Tower. Take-off limits depend on the availability of the centre line lights.

PART VII

There is no doubt that van Zanten appeared anxious to get airborne as soon as the take-off checklist was completed. This is clearly indicated

when he began to advance throttles only to be stopped by Meurs: 'Wait a minute... we do not have an ATC clearance.'

He immediately corrected himself: 'No... I know... go ahead ask.'

At 17:05.43 came a crucial moment in the subsequent tragedy, when Meurs advised the controller: 'Ah...the KLM...four eight zero five is now ready for take-off...and we're waiting for our ATC clearance.'

The Tower transmission that followed could have easily left the KLM crew with an impression that they were cleared for take-off. A logical reply would have been to first issue a specific instruction to hold position, after Meurs indicated that they were ready to roll. Instead the controller came up with:

'KLM eight seven zero five... [an incorrect callsign which should have been – KL (without M) 4805 – and this hints that the traffic controller was not paying attention to his message and it was his second similar mistake] you are cleared to Papa beacon... climb and maintain flight level niner zero... right turn after take-off... proceed with heading zero four zero until intercepting the three two five radial from Las Palmas VOR.'

According to general practice, this should have been preceded by: 'Here is your ATC clearance,' – or simply – 'Your ATC clearance.'

In a situation where two aircraft were simultaneously using an active runway without the controller being able to keep visual track of them, it was of paramount importance that all instructions were clear and precise.

PART VIII

The interpretation of the sentence that Meurs uttered at the end of reading back the ATC clearance had also been a controversial subject among the investigators. Unfortunately, not all words could be clearly deciphered and as a result the message was subject to different interpretations.

The Spanish claimed that the actual wording was, '...and we're now at take-off.' Which was supposed to mean that the KLM Boeing was still at the take-off position. This does not appear to be a rational deduction. Meurs had already advised Tower earlier on that they were lined up for an immediate departure, so there was no reason for him to repeat it.

But what he most likely said was, '...and we're now...ah...taking off,' considering that he had a habit of slipping in 'ahs' in his messages.

Almost two minutes followed without any audible activity from the Approach controller and then he started his message with, 'You are cleared...', which could have easily left van Zanten with an impression, and probably the rest of the crew as well, that they were being given take-off clearance. It could have been a possible reason as to why no one in the cockpit had raised any objections when van Zanten started to open the throttles. Yet, thirty seconds earlier, Meurs stopped him from doing the same thing.

Only after the flight engineer heard the PanAm's message about still not having cleared the runway did he then began to question his captain's decision.

The Approach controller appeared to have taken no notice or, for some reason, did not hear Meurs's warning that they were on the roll. Even after having been informed that the PanAm Boeing was still on the runway, he made no attempt to stop the KLM plane. This was despite not receiving an acknowledgement from KLM of his message to stand by for take-off clearance.

Another danger signal was also ignored. The roar of the engines, delivering some 40,000 pounds of thrust each, would have reached the Tower from the take-off position of runway 30 situated 1,800 metres away in six seconds. The thundering sound should have penetrated the glass panels of the Tower Control Room, despite their noise deadening properties. This ought to have rung a warning bell for the controller. Yet, for thirty seconds, that is from the time when the engine roar should have been heard in the Tower until the KLM Boeing had rammed the PanAm plane, the controllers appeared to have been unaware that the two jets were on a collision course. Even when the disaster did occur, they presumed that the associated blast was a bomb explosion at the back of the building.

PART IX

On the one hand, the Spanish investigators were reluctant to consider any possibility of human failure on the part of their controllers, but on the other, they went deeply into the reasons why van Zanten tried to rush the take-off and why Meurs had made no attempts to stop him. It was alleged that, as the KLM crew were running into duty-hour limits, van Zanten was anxious to leave Tenerife as quickly as possible.

In KLM, the number of hours crew members could remain on duty was governed by two sets of rules. The provisions of the Collective Labour Agreement between the Dutch Air Line Pilots' Association – Vereniging van Nederlandse Verkeersvliegers – and the company were used to determine the maximum length of a scheduled flight. The Dutch Civil Aviation Authority – Rijks Luchtvaart Dienst – regulations, introduced in 1975 to replace the outdated directives of the piston engine era, were only applicable to delays *en route*. The RLD limits were longer and more involved as they depended on several factors such as the hour of departure and crew complement.

According to the new RLD regulations, offenders could face court proceedings for breaking the rules. Strict enforcement was found to be necessary as a result of past abuses. Although very isolated, there were some glaring examples of overstepping the maximum duty hours.

A further intention of the new rules was to stop ground personnel down-route from putting pressure on the captain to continue a flight, despite the crew having reached their duty limits, when obtaining accommodation for the stranded passengers was proving difficult. Nevertheless, provisions were incorporated to cater for extenuating circumstances, such as evacuating passengers from a war or a danger zone, or taking an aircraft out of an area where violent weather, such as a hurricane, was expected. In such cases, the captain was allowed to exceed the limits provided he reported his reasons in writing to RLD.

To ensure that a crew *en route* facing a delay did not interpret the rules erroneously, the deadline for departure to reach the next destination in time was usually worked out at Schiphol Airport by KLM Movement Control and was sent out to the respective crew either by radio or by telex.

Like many other airlines, KLM had their own channel in the H/F aeronautical band. The company frequency was linked to a large directional antenna, located near Amsterdam and principally used by the Dutch Post Office – PTT. With the help of this advanced installation, KLM aircraft could be contacted quickly and reliably in any part of the world. The crews could be alerted to a message from Schiphol by a 'Selcal' system, as long as the on-board H/F equipment remained switched on and the company frequency was selected. Generally, this was a far more effective way of communicating with the crews than by telex or by telephone, in particular when the aircraft was on the ground thousands of miles away.

As Flight KL 4805 departed in the morning, the crew, if delayed, could remain on duty for fourteen hours, the highest possible limit with two pilots and a flight engineer on board. With the flying time to and from Las Palmas expected to be eight hours, this allowed up to six hours on the ground.

After contacting KLM Movement Control at 15.00 hrs, van Zanten received the information on the deadline for departure of his return flight to Amsterdam, already one hour and twenty minutes after arriving at Tenerife. Although it was only a routine message, the Spanish investigators construed it as of particular significance and that the crew had taken it to heart. This was supposed to have been reflected by a discussion in the cockpit about the possible consequences of breaking the duty time regulations:

Flight engineer: 'What are the repercussions of exceeding flight limits?'

An unidentified crew member (either the captain or the co-pilot): 'You face the judge.'

The flight engineer commiserated: 'Then you are hanged from the highest tree.'

The captain: 'Suppose you get a flat tyre and you hit a couple of runway lights, then you are really hanging.'

The last remark throws doubt on whether the KLM crew were discussing the RLD duty limits in earnest or if it was just casual cockpit chitchat.

At the time of taking off from Tenerife, they would have one hour and fifty-four minutes left before reaching the deadline for the departure from Las Palmas. The expected flying time to Las Palmas, including taxiing, would have been only about twenty minutes, so there was ample time for a turnaround, especially as the aircraft did not need to be refuelled and the passenger load was only three-quarters of the maximum capacity.

With one-and-a-half hours in hand, it does not look likely that van Zanten would have been greatly concerned about a minute or so longer on the ground at Tenerife. So the fear of running out of duty hours does not appear to have been a compelling factor in his decision to get airborne in a particular rush. His more likely pressing worry was the rapidly decreasing visibility. Although it would not have been possible to appraise it accurately while the aircraft was on the move during backtracking, it must have appeared quite critical

because when van Zanten asked Meurs if they were expected to turn off at C4 intersection the co-pilot said no and then added: 'If you do not want to take-off, you will block it [the runway] for the others, would you not?'

Evidently, observing take-off limits was a point which had been previously discussed during take-off briefing, and this was reflected in van Zanten reply: 'Then I can still clear there at the end, otherwise if not...' (the end of the sentence was blocked out by a radio transmission from a departing aircraft).

In the absence of reports on Runway Visual Range, which are provided at many airports and on which take-off limits are based, a recommended procedure in KLM was to count the number of runway lights clearly visible ahead, once the aircraft was lined up for departure. On all airports these lights are a standard fifty metres apart, so it was a simple way of checking if the visibility was within the prescribed limits. van Zanten, as an instructor, was expected to operate the aircraft by the book and rigidly adhere to the laid down company directives.

Being stuck on the ground at Tenerife meant many complications for the crew. There were no KLM ground staff and the local handling agency, being small and already overworked, would not have been able to look after such a large group of passengers. Moreover, it would have been very difficult during a busy tourist season to find enough hotel rooms for the stranded passengers and the crew. Camping overnight on the airport appeared to have been a strong probability, a grim prospect facing a 'company-minded captain' such as van Zanten. This was the most likely reason why he was under pressure to get out of Tenerife at all costs.

In the middle section of the runway visibility was probably very critical, well below the 400 metres required for a take-off with only the centre line markings available. But after the Boeing had been lined up for take-off, van Zanten must have felt relieved when visibility on the first section of the runway appeared to be just within the limit and this was what counted. He must have been anxious to get off the ground, as the patch of thick cloud he had run into in the middle section of the runway could any second drift in his path.

Some validity must be given to the argument that at the back of van Zanten's mind could have been a worry about running out of duty hours. The un-orderly handling of traffic at Tenerife might have made him concerned about the same situation recurring at Las Palmas, which would not leave much leeway for the departure to Amsterdam. Nevertheless, with an hour and a half in hand, this does not appear to have been the most pressing factor for hurrying a take-off, as against the varying visibility where every second counted.

The reason for keeping the KLM Boeing so long at Tenerife had never been properly accounted for during the investigation. By the time van Zanten was issued with a start-up clearance, most stranded aircraft had already departed.

Nevertheless, the Spanish investigators regarded van Zanten's anxiety over exceeding the legal duty limit to be the prime factor behind trying to speed up his departure. The accident report stated: 'Uncertainty of the crew, who were not able to determine their limit exactly, must have contributed an important and psychological factor... a certain subconscious, though exteriorly repressed, irritation caused by the fact that the service was turning out so badly.'

But these pressing circumstances had been created through less than efficient handling of an emergency situation by the Canary Islands authorities. The stranded pilots were never informed of the reason for closing Las Palmas Airport. It is evident from the PanAm cockpit conversation that took place during backtracking on the runway.

Captain Grubbs: 'What really happened over there today?'

A local PanAm employee, who was given a lift to Las Palmas in the cockpit on the jump seat: 'They put a bomb in the terminal, Sir, right where the check-in are.'

Had the pilots been advised about the grounds for the emergency, they would have been bound to show more understanding of the local difficulties.

Another contributing factor was the refusal to allow the PanAm aircraft to hold overhead Las Palmas, as requested by the captain. He had sufficient fuel reserves and orbiting at high level would not have affected arriving or departing traffic, which was operating at lower altitudes. Grubbs was refused permission to hold and instructed to proceed to Tenerife. Yet twenty minutes later, as he was approaching Los Rodeos Airport at Tenerife, Las Palmas was declared open.

It was undoubtedly the lack of a proper plan to deal with an emergency and keeping the crews in the dark about the reasons for closing Las Palmas Airport that had mainly led to their frayed tempers.

PART X

An important factor that the Spanish investigators believed to have contributed to the unauthorised take-off was that the KLM first officer was too junior to contradict his captain's decisions. It was alleged that, although Meurs was aware that van Zanten had made a mistake in commencing take-off without clearance, he was not prepared to do anything about it in fear of rubbing the captain who had an influential position in the company, the wrong way.

The report of the Spanish Board of Inquiry pointed to a probability of the co-pilot feeling intimidated because he was flying with the chief 747 instructor, and this had resulted in a breakdown of teamwork.

The too-steep cross-cockpit authority had been strongly denied by the accredited representatives from Holland, in particular by a pilot on the KLM delegation, but in vain.

The image of the two KLM pilots representing very diverse statuses is far from the truth and it is not borne out by the facts. The difference in age and flying experience between van Zanten and Meurs was far less than normally expected with a captain and a co-pilot on most KLM 747 flights.

Van Zanten's seniority in the company was such that, although he was the chief of 747 training, he was only a reserve captain. When the 747 entered service in 1971 all instructors were senior captains and they were given a special course at the Boeing factory in Seattle. In later years, many older instructors were replaced by younger men of first officer rank. Van Zanten happened to be one of them. Although his seniority in the company was sufficiently high for a DC9 command, he opted for a co-pilot's position on the 747. He was keen to fly the flagship of the KLM fleet, a much newer and a more technically advanced aircraft, at the earliest opportunity.

When the chief of 747 training retired, van Zanten was appointed in his place and promoted to a captain. According to his position on the seniority list, this was done out of turn. Due to objections from the Dutch Pilots' Association, he was allowed to fly the line only when no other captain was available. As a result, his route experience was limited and this had led to the allegations by the Spanish investigators that he was out of touch with ATC procedures because he spent so much time on the simulator, where many take-offs were made without clearances.

On the one hand, such allegations may appear

to be justified. On the other hand, as an instructor he was required to cooperate very closely with ATC during his training flights at Schiphol Airport and be particularly vigilant in respect of line traffic.

Much had been made out of van Zanten having been the company's 'prestigious' pilot because his photograph appeared on KLM advertising pamphlets – copies of which were actually carried on board the ill-fated PH-BUF.

After so many years it was not possible to establish why his photo was used in the publicity material. It looks doubtful that it was due to him holding a 'prestigious' position within the Flight Division. The more likely explanation is that when the KLM Public Relations Department needed a picture of a captain, as an instructor he was the only one available, as most captains were either away flying or on flight leave.

As far as the allegations that co-pilots would not have the nerve to stand up to van Zanten during flight because of his senior position in the company, and that their career could be ruined by his adverse report, this was another example of completely false presumptions.

Van Zanten was a serious and introverted individual but with an open-hearted and friendly disposition. He was a studious type and was regarded as the company's pilot expert on the Boeing 747 systems.

Nevertheless, he would have been the last person on the flight deck not to accept his co-pilot's advice or warning. He believed in a partnership, to the extent that he insisted on his first officers addressing him during flight as 'Jaap' and not 'Captain van Zanten'. He had learnt much about cockpit management by representing KLM at an IATA Conference in Istanbul and was trying to put this into practice.

The allegations by the Spanish Board of Inquiry that van Zanten was a domineering captain and Meurs a submissive co-pilot, were echoed in the February 1978 issue of *Flight Safety Focus* under the title 'Is the captain always right?'

Many aviation journalists, who had subsequently analysed the Tenerife disaster, have accepted van Zanten's image of a 'macho' captain and Meurs's as a servile first officer at face value, without checking the facts.

In the book *The Naked Pilot*, David Beaty, author of many novels and books on air safety and a former BOAC captain, writes about van Zanten: 'But perhaps the most important factors were his egotism and his prestige.'

His critical view was also expressed about Meurs's actions: 'Whilst it was clear that the co-pilot knew they had no take-off clearance, he acceded to the captain's authority and impatience to be airborne.'

Two television programmes, recently broadcast, have portrayed these two men in the same light.

As they were my former KLM colleagues, I knew them for many years. Although I did not have the opportunity to meet van Zanten often as I was in the DC10 division, Klaas Meurs had made a quite number of flights with me as a co-pilot in my DC8 days. Moreover, he was a personal friend and I got to know him well outside flying duties.

Because of my past connection, I do not wish to appear to be whitewashing the alleged part of his blame for the collision and I have tried only to highlight the facts known to me, without any judgement. Nevertheless, my opinion about Meurs as a first class co-pilot was supported by several former KLM captains.

Meurs was not the type to have been easily intimidated by a superior rank and would not have easily given in under stress. Although new to the 747 (he had only ninety hours on that type), he was formerly a temporary DC8 captain. For personal reasons, he waived his seniority right for a DC9 command and opted to fly the 747 as a first officer. Meurs was an extrovert and liked to enjoy life, a contrasting disposition to van Zanten. Both complemented each other in personalities as well as in their operational background. What van Zanten lacked in route experience, particularly in the Canary Islands area, Meurs compensated for by his intimate knowledge of the local situation from his many past flights through Las Palmas. The reverse applied to the handling of the 747.

As for his proficiency as a co-pilot, I found Meurs cooperative, alert, and far from a meek and mild type. In fact, the opposite was more likely. He could be somewhat abrupt and direct in his manner, as was evident from the way he stopped van Zanten from opening the throttles.

'Wait a minute, we do not have an ATC clearance.'

Although it was his first line flight with his former 747 instructor, one would expect that their cooperation should have been good as they must have got to know each other well during a three-week-long simulator and flying course a few months earlier.

The Spanish investigators' allegations about a

lack of teamwork in the cockpit is not supported by what had been recorded on the KLM Boeing's CVR. It is apparent that van Zanten leaned on Meurs for advice during backtracking on the runway, when the visibility became very poor.

Van Zanten referring to a taxiway: 'What is this one here?'

Meurs: 'That according to me, is the one at an angle, Charlie 4.'

Van Zanten: 'Do we have to get off here?'

Meurs: 'No.'

As was previously mentioned, Meurs then pointed out to van Zanten that if he did not want to take-off, by backtracking to the end of the runway he would block it for the other aircraft.

Perhaps the most interesting reflection of the cockpit relations between the two pilots is Meurs's warning when van Zanten began to make a 180° turn on the runway: 'Don't you scrub the tyres.' (In the official transcript, the actual translation of that sentence from Dutch, reads as 'does not scrub the tyres'.)

What was revealed by the CVR is in total contrast to the Spanish investigators' allegation about inadequate teamwork. Surely, no co-pilot who feared his captain's authority and worried about his advice not being accepted in a constructive way would have come up with such a warning.

The Dutch investigating team were of the opinion that rather than too-steep cross-authority in the cockpit, it was more a case of two captains on the bridge. This appears to be a more likely probability.

PART XI

Another important aspect of the tragic collision cannot be ignored. Were the questionable standards of the Tenerife controllers on the day of the accident a result of a pressing situation, or were they a reflection of a deeper problem?

Although I was not familiar with the situation at Tenerife, my experiences of frequently flying through Las Palmas had left me with an impression that the local ATC practices, in comparison with North-west Europe, were not exactly confidence inspiring.

On two occasions I had to leave the aircraft during an intermediate stop and visit the Tower, in order to discuss the controllers' instructions, which either made no sense or were plain dangerous.

In the first case, I was refused a straight-in approach when arriving from the south. As a result, the procedure of landing from the other direction added ten minutes to my flying time as well as extra time on the ground due to long taxiing. When I queried the controller about the reason I received no satisfactory explanation. He claimed that according to the instruction he received from Madrid, all landings in no-wind conditions were to be made from the northerly direction. The only possible reason was noise abatement, but as there were no villages or holiday hotels at both ends of the runway, this could not have been the overriding factor. The controller refused to discuss the matter further.

The second incident, which could have resulted in serious consequences, was an instruction to carry out an overshoot while I was on short final, and at the same time, execute an immediate right turn. As the overshoot procedure on the DC8 was based on a climb-out without any bank until gear was raised and flaps were retracted to the take-off setting, and then speed increased by the prescribed safety margin, I could not commence the turn before these conditions were met.

Just prior to issuing the overshoot instruction and shortly afterwards, a lengthy chattering went on in Spanish on the Tower frequency. But what the controller had not reckoned with was that my Dutch co-pilot, who in the past had been seconded to ALM, a KLM subsidiary in Curaçao, learnt to use R/T in Spanish, as on many smaller airports in the Caribbean ATC personnel did not speak any English.

During the overshoot the co-pilot warned me that according to what he understood from the exchange of messages in Spanish, another aircraft was taking off right below us. I was forced to discontinue the climb, quickly increase speed and commence the turn as soon as possible, in order to keep away from the traffic taking off. At the first opportunity, my co-pilot explained what the rapid conversation between Tower and the departing aircraft was all about. The captain of an Iberia plane insisted on an immediate take-off clearance as he was behind schedule and his passengers could miss important connections in Madrid.

When I went to see Tower, I was not allowed to speak to the controller. Instead I was met by a supervisor, who made it apparent that as Las Palmas was on Spanish territory and Iberia was their national carrier, the interests of their airline had to be respected. The safety aspect of this incident was totally ignored.

PART XII

A series of accidents that took place on Spanish territory around the time of the Tenerife disaster, and in which a contributory factor could have been inexplicit ATC instructions, raises a question whether Spanish ATC systems had been brought up to proper ICAO standards after having been in the hands of military authorities.

On 3 July 1970, a Dan Air Comet 4, G-APND, on a charter flight from Manchester, crashed 35 nm east-north-east of Barcelona Airport, with a loss of 112 passengers and seven crew members.

Due to congestion over Paris, the Comet was re-routed over Toulouse and then as a result of a defect in its navigation equipment, entered Spanish airspace 13 nm to the east of the designated check point. At first the Barcelona Approach controller could not pinpoint the echo on his screen, although the aircraft by then was only 10 nm off track. Consequently he asked the pilot to make a 45° turn to the left for identification. But a minute later, after he was given the estimated time of arrival over Sabadell beacon (position: 19 nm north of the airport), which at that moment lay 47 nm away, he changed his mind. He then gave an instruction to proceed directly to the beacon and cleared the aircraft to level 60. Evidently he still was not sure of the Comet's position, because he asked the pilot if he had a DME on board but the reply was 'negative'. In spite of this, the controller told the pilot to steer heading 140° and asked him to confirm that the aircraft was just passing Sabadell beacon, although shortly earlier he had been informed that the Comet was due overhead in five minutes. What followed cannot be easily accounted for. The crew must have observed some spurious oscillation of the ADF pointer and they told the controller that they expected to pass the beacon in thirty seconds. Surprisingly, thirteen seconds later they reported they were over Sabadell. The false ADF indication of an overhead passage was most likely caused by the coding cycle of Sabadell beacon, which was an A0/A1 type (see chapter 9). The controller advised the pilot that he had radar contact and cleared the Comet to 2,800 feet while the aircraft was heading towards an area where the highest peak was 5,615 feet. Seven seconds after the pilot reported 4,000 feet, still descending in clouds, the Comet struck the slopes of a wooded hill.

The Spanish investigators claimed extenuating circumstances for an error of judgement on the part of the Approach controller. The Comet was off track. The pilot confused the controller about his actual position. Another aircraft happened to be passing Sabadell beacon and the controller mistook it for the Comet, as the speeds of the two aircraft were similar. Barcelona Airport was not equipped with secondary radar, which would have helped in positively pinpointing the target.

Nevertheless, it is evident that the accident had been caused by a careless identification procedure and a lack of effective monitoring of the Comet's progress.

The investigation of another disaster at Tenerife, which occurred on 25 April 1980, again ended up in a controversy between the Spanish investigators and the accredited representatives, this time from the UK.

The aircraft, a Dan Air Boeing 727, was on a charter flight from Manchester to Los Rodeos Airport at Tenerife. When descending towards Tenerife VOR, the Boeing 727 was cleared to the FP locator, situated 0.5 nm to the west of runway 12 threshold, for an ILS approach with no delay expected. When the aircraft was close to the VOR station, suddenly the Approach controller told the pilot to execute a standard holding pattern over the FP locator with an inbound heading of 150°, after making a left turn. As was evident from the CVR, the controller's instructions put the crew in a quandary. The holding was not officially promulgated and, moreover, it was not even in line with the ILS approach. But they realised that as its reason was likely to be for traffic separation, they were expected to comply as closely as possible with the ATC instructions, even if they had doubts about the safety of the holding pattern.

When the controller was advised by the crew, 'Level 60... taking up the hold', he cleared the aircraft to 5,000 feet. The cloud base was at that moment 3,000 feet (about 900 feet above the airport level). Shortly after commencing the left turn, the Ground Proximity Warning sounded and then it stopped. The captain, believing he was on the north side of a high ridge dividing the island, turned to the right where he expected the ground to be lower. However, without visual reference this proved to be the wrong decision and the aircraft struck a slope of a mountain at 5,450 feet, 6.5 nm south-west of the airport. In the crash, 138 passengers and eight crew perished.

The captain was blamed for the accident because of his imprecise navigation, in particular for not passing overhead but 2 nm south of the FP locator. He was also blamed for not checking with

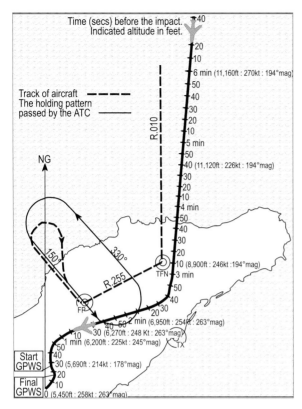

Time (secs) before the impact.
Indicated altitude in feet.

6 min (11,160ft : 270kt : 194°mag)

Track of aircraft — — — —
The holding pattern
passed by the ATC ————

R.010

NG

5 min

40 (11,120ft : 226kt : 194°mag)

4 min

330°

150

R.255

10 (8,900ft : 246kt :194°mag)

TFN 3 min

FP

20 30

40 50 2 min (6,950ft : 254kt : 263°mag)
10 30 (6,270ft : 248 Kt : 263°mag)
1 min (6,200ft : 225kt : 245°mag)
50
TX

Start
GPWS
40
30 (5,690ft : 214kt : 178°mag)
20

Final
GPWS
10
0 (5,450ft : 258kt : 263°mag)

Horizontal flight path of Dan Air Boeing 727 that crashed in Tenerife on 25 April 1980.

The captain was blamed for the accident because of his imprecise navigation, in particular for not passing overhead but 2 nm south of the FP locator. He was also blamed for not checking with ATC whether the turn he began to make was in accordance with the instructions.

The British Air Accident Investigation Branch objected to some of the conclusions. But unlike the case of the findings on the KLM/PAA crash, they insisted on including their own addendum in the official accident report. Such a supplementary assessment was allowed under the new provisions of ICAO Annex XIII – Accident Investigation. This was due to the indefatigable efforts of W. Tench, the AAIB Chief Inspector at the time, who at an ICAO meeting a year earlier, persuaded the other participants to accept this provision as an ICAO recommended practice.

The AAIB claimed that the pilots were confused by a non-standard hold and the way that the approach instructions were issued.

Several aspects of the Approach controller's

practices raise a particular concern. The sudden change of instructions after the aircraft had been cleared for approach, and which had not been accounted for during the investigation, seems to be a repetition of the reason for my overshoot at Las Palmas Airport.

The instruction to turn to the left on passing the FP locator is without comprehension. The Boeing 727 was sent into a sector where the safety height was 8,500 feet higher than its clearance to flight level 60. When the pilot reported, 'Level 60...Taking up the hold', he was further cleared to 5,000 feet without the controller having first ascertained the aircraft's position. A 4,947-foot-high peak lay only 4.9 nm from the airport, just ninety seconds flying at the speed the Boeing 727 was doing at that moment.

Similar unprofessional practices were brought to light during the investigation of the Avianca Boeing 747 crash at Madrid Airport on 27 November 1983.

Again the captain was blamed for the disaster in which 181 passengers and twenty-three crew members were killed. Eleven survivors were seriously injured. The Spanish investigators claimed that the captain descended below minimum safety height before intercepting the ILS due to an incorrect setting of his Inertial Navigation System, and also as a result of having been given the wrong altitude to cross the outer marker by his co-pilot.

But this time the Spanish investigators were more critical of their air traffic controllers and the report stated that deficient ATC practices could have contributed to the cause of the accident. Among them were the transfer of control between Centre and Approach, and the fact that the R/T language did not conform to the laid down ICAO standards. The Approach controller, after advising the pilot that he was closing in on the VOR, failed to inform him of the distance to go and that radar service had been terminated. Above all, he stopped monitoring his radar screen and thus he was no longer able to warn the pilot that the Boeing had deviated from the ILS beam and glide slope.

Despite many years having passed since the Tenerife disaster, the Spanish civil aviation authorities did not seem to have learnt a lesson from that tragic event. On 7 December 1982, only two weeks after the Avianca Boeing 747 crash, two aircraft collided on the ground at Madrid Airport. Due to thick fog, the pilot of an Aviaco DC9 mistook a runway for a taxiway and crossed the path of an Iberia B727, which was taking off. Because of the caught fire, all thirty-seven passengers and five crew members perished. The captain of the Boeing 727 tried to avert a disaster, but in the end he could not help ramming the other aircraft. The Boeing 727 fell back on the runway, and after turning around, skidded to a halt, ending up severely damaged. Fifty-one passengers and one crew member were killed but forty-two people survived, unfortunately some badly injured.

Why the DC9 had not been stopped from taxiing during that short period of time when the other aircraft was taking off is difficult to understand.

PART XIII

An impartial analysis of all the known contributory factors which could have led to the Tenerife disaster would not be complete without highlighting a minor but vital physical deficiency from which Captain van Zanten could have suffered. This could have been the reason for misinterpreting a certain R/T conversation.

The transcript of the KLM CVR revealed that, during the four minutes before the accident, on two occasions Captain van Zanten asked the co-pilot and the flight engineer to repeat what they had just said to him. In one instance take-off power was on, so it would have been easy to miss a remark. But the other incident happened during taxiing when the noise level in the cockpit was low, and at that moment there were no radio transmissions to interfere with the crew conversation.

There is no direct evidence that van Zanten's hearing was marginal. With the results of the pilots' medical examinations protected by the customary secrecy it would not have been possible to obtain any particulars of his hearing tests. Any detailed information of that kind is only provided for an investigation when there appears to be a direct connection with the cause of the crash – as, for example, a heart failure.

Van Zanten sounded convinced that the PanAm Boeing was off the runway when the flight engineer queried him about it. What had made him form such an impression, could have only derived from mishearing and thus misinterpreting certain communications.

The analysis of the CVR transcript pointed to only one possibility. During backtracking, the following exchange of messages took place about vacating the runway (an extract from the transcript of the CVR):

> Approach: '...er [most probably – Clipper] one seven three six report leaving the runway.'
> PanAm: 'Clipper one seven three six.'

It seems possible that van Zanten could have missed the word 'report' and assumed that the PanAm Boeing was leaving the runway and no longer in his way for take-off.

The hearing standards for the Air Line Transport Pilot's Licence are not finely defined and a certain amount of discretion is left in the hands of the medical examiners.

The Dutch Aviation and Aerospace Institute at Soesterberg, where all six-monthly medical examinations for KLM pilots are carried out, originally believed in flexibility according to the pilot's age and experience. The examiners claimed that modern radio and intercom installations compensated for a slight loss of hearing, and in the case of an older captain with many flying hours behind him this was a safer prospect than a much younger but far less experienced pilot with perfect ears.

This attitude drastically changed after the Tenerife accident. In the following months, all pilots, including myself, were given a strict practical hearing test, in addition to the usual audiograph check. As a result, two older captains had their pilot's licences withdrawn.

PART XIV

Tenerife Island appears to be the most notorious graveyard of aircraft in the world. In five air accidents, either at Los Rodeos airport or in its close vicinity, 917 people have perished. Apart from the two Boeings and the Dan Air 727, another three tragedies had added to this extremely high toll of lives.

In 1965 an Iberia L049 Constellation crashed during a second attempt to land. Thirty-two lives were lost.

In September 1966 a Spantax DC3 sank just off the coast. One passenger was drowned.

On 3 December 1972 a Spantax Convair 900A Coronado plunged down from 300 feet, striking the ground several hundred metres past the end of the runway. An abnormal manoeuvre after the pilot had run into zero visibility just after lift-off was believed to have been the cause of the accident. All 155 occupants were instantly killed.

In the end, Los Rodeos Airport outran its usefulness. It was unsuitably located as far as weather conditions were concerned, and too close to Santa Cruz, the principal town on the island, in respect of noise abatement. It was eventually replaced by a new airport built on the southern tip of the island.

Nowadays Los Rodeos is hardly used. It is left forlorn and neglected. But the grass on both sides of the runway is still littered with small metal fragments, the mementoes of the world's worst aircraft disaster.

1989 – A TRIAL WITHOUT JUDGE, JURY OR DEFENCE

PART I

'The Guildford Four' were reprieved. 'The Birmingham Six' followed. Nowadays, appeals are frequently heard and, in quite a few cases, juries' decisions are reversed. But with what corresponds to a court verdict in the aviation sphere, namely the findings of an accident investigation, challenging an adverse ruling generally ends up in a blind alley. Once the conclusions as to who is liable for the disaster are finalised, there appears to be no chance of redress. Although the purpose of a crash inquiry is to determine the cause and not to apportion the blame, a judgement that implicates a party involved in an aircraft accident may result in serious consequences. In modern society where legal decisions play a pivotal role, conclusions reached by investigators can be used in civil proceedings to claim financial compensation. Moreover, aviation authorities can take the 'guilty party' to court. If the party happens to be a pilot, his licence could be revoked and this would mean the end of his flying career.

Even if the airman does not have to face legal proceedings, the adverse publicity in connection with an accident may influence the airline to dispense with his services. By shifting the blame entirely on the cockpit, such a mercenary measure can be a 'convenient' way of defending the airline's reputation by claiming that, as a safety conscious operator, they cannot keep a black sheep in their pilots' workforce.

Assessing evidence obtained from investigation, in principle, resembles court proceedings. Certain parties are entitled to representation. Such parties include the country of the aircraft's registration if the accident happened to take place on foreign soil, the airframe, the engine and the airborne equipment manufacturers as well

as the operator. But only a handful of civil aviation authorities permit an ill-fated pilot to be represented. In the majority of cases 'the airman in the dock' is not provided with a defence counsel. When he is no longer alive there is no one to see that an adequate defence on his behalf is put across while his responsibility for the crash is being assessed.

Aviation history is blemished with quite a few cases of airlines using an incriminating judgement of an accident investigation to pick out a scapegoat for a disaster. In that respect, pilots feel that some of their colleagues are often given an unjustified raw deal. The most glaring example is that of Jim Thain, the captain of the British European Airways Airspeed Ambassador, which crashed at Munich. As a result of the Manchester United football team having been decimated and three top sport reporters losing their lives, the accident received widespread publicity. But as the echoes over the Munich tragedy continued to linger, Thain was in the end, dismissed by his airline. The reason was not because he failed to inspect the wings of his aircraft for snow deposit, which the German investigators blamed him for, and which in their opinion, was the cause of the poor take-off performance and the subsequent crash. It was the public's outcry over losing England's favourite footballers that had motivated the airline management to fire Thain. After two and a half years of endless inquiries, the grounds for his dismissal had been eventually found. But these were totally unconnected with the probable cause of the crash. BEA had dispensed with his services due to his allowing a more senior captain, acting on that flight as a co-pilot, to make the fateful take-off from the left hand seat. According to the company rules, a first officer could only perform take-offs and landings from the right hand seat. Nevertheless the operational directives gave no guidance in the case of two pilots of an equal status rostered to fly together, as happened on the flight with the Manchester United team on board. Since all BEA captains were used to handling aircraft from the left-hand seat only, a take-off from an unaccustomed position would not have been safe practice, and sharing take-offs and landings was an accepted routine to maintain flying proficiency. But a contravention of this rule was used to deprive Thain of his livelihood. Adding to his tribulations was the death of the other captain, his good friend Ken Rayment. A week after the accident, Rayment had died in a Munich hospital from the injuries sustained from the collapsing cockpit.

After Thain was fired by his airline, he became a marked man. Finding another flying job proved difficult, and it meant that as a result of the dismissal on purely arbitrary grounds, he was hounded out of the profession he loved. Yet, ten years later, the British civil aviation authorities exonerated him when it became apparent that slush on the runway was the most likely cause of the Munich tragedy. Unfortunately for Thain, little was known about the effect of slush on the take-off performance at the time of the accident. In the end, unable to bear the stigma, he died from a heart attack at the early age of fifty-four.

The statistics compiled by the International Civil Aviation Organisation attribute as much as 70% of all accidents to human failure. Although on the surface it may hold true, nevertheless, with the complexity of flying operations, pilot error is seldom the sole reason for a disaster. Even if the final assessment may classify it in that category, other factors such as inadequate operational indoctrination, deficient airborne equipment or below standard navigational and landing facilities, can also contribute to the crash.

In spite of vast improvements in training methods through introduction of sophisticated simulators, it is still possible to come across a baffling emergency in flight that is not covered by the training curriculum. In the absence of evident clues, a pilot may not be able to diagnose the root of the mechanical problem and may be at loss as to what remedial action to take. The Boeing 737 crash at Kegworth is an illustration of such a misfortune.

PART II

British Midland Airways Flight BD 092 left London Airport on a miserable night, on 8 January 1989. Although the reported visibility of 6 km was not that critical, with the cloud base of only 500 feet and occasional light rain, the sensation of the pitch-black darkness was greatly accentuated. The two pilots on board the Boeing 737-400, G-OBME, were Captain Kevin Hunt and First Officer David McLellan, flying a double shuttle between London and Belfast. They took off from Heathrow at 7.52 p.m. for the third sector of their day's work just after an hour-long stop on the ground. On this stretch the co-pilot was given the opportunity to fly the aircraft from the right-hand seat.

As it subsequently emerged from the analysis of the Cockpit Voice Recorder, they acted as a well-knit team in spite of a considerable difference in their flying experiences. Kevin Hunt, with over 13,000 hours to his credit, had four times as many hours, and also years, in civil aviation as the co-pilot had. But what probably helped in their harmonious relationship was the fact that they were both mature men. Hunt was forty-three and McLellan thirty-nine. They addressed each other by their first names, although this is not an unusual custom among pilots even on their first flight together. As they had just completed one shuttle from London to Belfast and became familiar with their flying habits, this should have made the cockpit cooperation more efficient and their mutual trust stronger.

After take-off, the flight progressed as would have been expected from the usual situation in a crowded Terminal Control Area. At first the aircraft was cleared to 6,000 feet, which brought it over the murky layer of low clouds. After two minutes it was further cleared to Flight Level 120 and shortly later to Flight Level 350, while being vectored by London Radar directly to the VOR station at Trent.

The climb was uneventful until passing 28,300 feet thirteen minutes after take-off, when the crew were alerted to a rattling sound emanating from behind them. A split-second later, loud bangs were heard and the aircraft began to shudder violently. The cockpit was quickly filled with smoke, which bore a distinct smell of burning. However, none of the visual or aural warnings indicated an outbreak of fire. For a while the Boeing convulsed so intensely that as one of the flight attendant described it later, the walls in the front galley shook visibly. Even if at that moment the source of a serious mechanical breakdown still remained a puzzle to the crew, their airmen's instinct warned them that the alarming development had most likely to do with dire trouble afflicting one of the engines.

Seven seconds after the rattling noise could be heard and the burning smell filled the cockpit, the co-pilot said: 'We've got a fire.'

Hunt's reaction was to take over the controls and disconnect the autopilot. He did not have to advise the right-hand seat colleague as, under the circumstances, such action was an accepted practice.

After a further four seconds had ticked away, smoke in the cockpit was getting denser and the smell of burning stronger, and McLellan observed: 'It's a fire, Kevin, coming through.'

The coherent manner of appraising their predicament indicated that he was far from panicky. For the next five seconds both pilots peered intensely at the engine instruments and the engine fire warning lights for a possible clue. Nevertheless, the puzzle as to whether it was the left or right engine still remained unsolved. As Hunt could not spot any telltale signs of a malfunction from the engine instruments, this prompted him to query McLellan: 'Which one is it though?'

But, even nineteen seconds from the moment the trouble had erupted, the dials were still not betraying any apparent fault. To a layman it might sound surprising that the pilots were unable to determine from which side vibrations or signs of fire were emanating. But, sitting thirty feet (ten metres) ahead of the engines, the only way to pinpoint the actual location of the severe vibrations was by the cockpit instruments and by various warning signals. Moreover, with the nose curvature obstructing the view to the rear, the engines were out of sight.

The minds of both pilots must have frantically whirled to determine whether the right or the left engine had gone haywire. With the instruments not revealing any apparent disparity between the engine parameters, any other hint, no matter how insignificant, could have perhaps thrown light on the growing enigma.

During the previous month a minor defect on the right engine had been entered in the aircraft's Technical Log. McLellan must have come across it during the aircraft's inspection prior to departure, as it was the usual practice for the co-pilot to check the list of past snags. On two occasions the right engine showed a high level of vibrations when the throttles were closed for descent. These entries were bound to have been at the back of McLellan's mind. Could these vibrations have something to do with the present emergency?

On the other hand, from his knowledge of the air-conditioning system Hunt tried to work out how it was possible for the smoke to enter the cockpit. He recollected from the ground course that the air supply came from the right engine.

As the violent shuddering could end up in a catastrophe, both pilots realised that the decision on a corrective action could not be indefinitely delayed. Eventually McLellan offered an explanation: 'It's the le... it's the right one.'

Hunt, evidently of the same opinion, responded by instructing his co-pilot: 'Okay, throttle it back.'

McLellan disconnected the autothrottle and pulled the right-engine power lever to idle. This action seemed to have cured the problem. The vibrations appreciably dropped and the smoke as well as the burning smell began to abate. It looked as if they had pinpointed the erratic engine. Both men in the cockpit must have sighed with relief.

But the emergency was far from over. Grave danger still existed. They were aware that if there was fire somewhere in the engine it would be unlikely to have died down on its own. Without any indication from the warning lights about its exact location, it was not certain that the fire extinguishers would be effective, as they mainly covered the engine nacelles, the only zone that was monitored by the fire detecting system.

In those circumstances, the pilots would have to shut down the ailing engine by cutting off the fuel supply and land as soon as possible, hoping that the fire would not spread. From now on, no second could be wasted. Both pilots wished that they had an extra pair of eyes and hands.

Immediately after throttling back the troublesome engine, McLellan warned London Air Traffic Control Centre that they had an emergency on board, which at the moment looked like an engine fire. After the message was passed, Hunt instructed McLellan to shut down the right engine. However, as the instruments appeared to indicate a normal operation and Hunt began to wonder where the trouble really lay, he decided to wait a few seconds longer, which was reflected by his remark: 'Seems to be running all right now. Lets just see if it comes in.'

At that moment, the cockpit activities were interrupted by a radio call. London Radar gave them their position and inquired where they intend to divert. The co-pilot specified Castle Donington, East Midlands Airport, but he added that he would confirm it later. When about to start on the engine failure and shut-down checklist, he made an observation:

'Seems to have stabilised...We've still got the smoke.'

By now Hunt decided to inform his company at Castle Donington of their predicament and this delayed the execution of the checklist. Eventually, two minutes after the severe shuddering broke out, the engine was finally shut down and the Auxiliary Power Unit started. Soon smoke disappeared from the flight deck and this convinced Hunt that he had taken the correct remedial action because the left engine appeared to be operating normally.

As the aircraft was only ten nautical miles north-west of East Midlands Airport, London Radar immediately gave clearance for a right turn

and descent to Flight Level 100. Hunt closed the left engine throttle and started to go down. Shortly afterwards Manchester Air Traffic Control Unit took over and began to issue a series of radar vectors to bring the Boeing in for an ILS approach to runway 27.

Even during the descent, the workload in the cockpit was still high. Hunt had to listen out to radar vectors and fly the aircraft by hand, although he had the help of the autopilot for stabilisation and auto trim by using the mode known as Control Wheel Steering. At the same time, McLellan urgently tried to obtain the latest weather information from Castle Donington. As the minutes rapidly ticked away, he also made

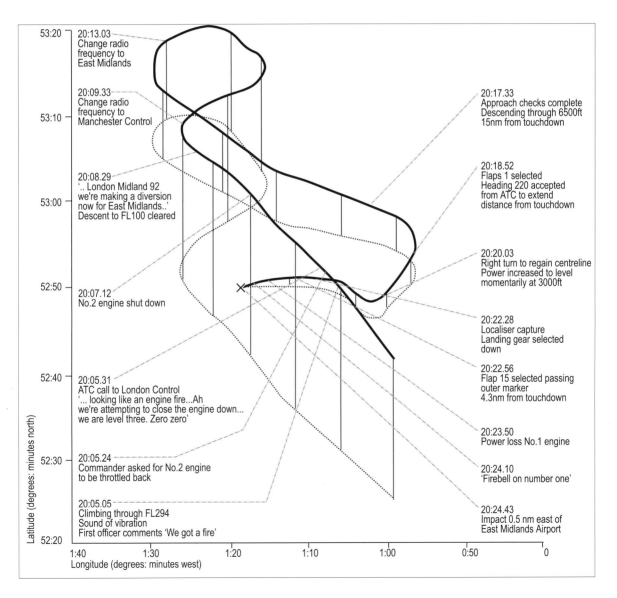

several attempts to re-program the Flight Management System, in order to get a display of the landing chart of East Midlands Airport. However, he was unable to do it in the available time. Anyway, the electronically displayed landing chart was not essential as they were very familiar with Castle Donington, the BMA home base, and they were monitored by radar.

In the cabin an extremely tense atmosphere reigned. Loud bangs, later described by one of the passengers as if a car badly backfired, violent vibrations, light-coloured smoke and evident signs of fire on the left engine in the form of flying sparks and flickers of flames, sent blood-chilling shivers through all passengers and the flight attendants. They did not have to be told that there was something radically amiss with one of the engines. The telltales of fire could be easily observed through the windows because it was dark outside.

Once the checklist for shutting down the engine had been completed, Hunt called the flight attendant-in-charge – known in British Midland Airways as the Flight Service Manager – to the cockpit. After he was asked if there was smoke in the cabin and he had replied, 'Yes', Hunt told him to prepare the aircraft for an emergency landing. This involved stowing all loose equipment and instructing passengers how to bend down in the seats with their heads between the knees after they were warned about crash landing.

Soon the Flight Service Manager was back, uttering: 'Sorry to trouble you... the passengers are very, very panicky.'

Hunt immediately informed the passengers via the cabin address system about the problem with the right engine, resulting in the spreading smoke, and the necessity of shutting the engine down, as well as about diverting to Castle Donington. Surprisingly, with 117 passengers on board, not one of them had brought to the attention of the cabin staff that they had observed signs of fire on the left engine. Nor had anyone sitting in the area close to the left engine pointed out that the shuddering came from that side. Yet there was no question of not being certain that the captain mentioned the right engine on the cabin address system, because some passengers later confirmed it in a television interview.

In spite of his preoccupation with flying the aircraft by hand, briefing the Flight Service Manager and giving information to the passengers, Hunt still found a few moments for trying to review the events with his co-pilot. He started with: 'Now, what indications did we actually get?

Just rapid vibrations in the aeroplane... smoke...'

This was unfortunately interrupted by a radio message from Manchester ATC with a radar heading, descent clearance to Flight Level 40 and an instruction to change over to the Castle Donington Approach frequency. What added to the pressure on the crew, were other aircraft using the same channel. This could have ensued in dangerous consequences if a vital message from the Boeing in distress was blocked out.

Even the last words from the Manchester controller, no matter how well intended, seemed superfluous when he passed on his sympathy to the crew: 'I hope you make it.'

To which Hunt replied: 'So do I.'

On the new channel Hunt was asked to make a test call to the airport fire service but could not get through. Although a frequent changeover from one air traffic control unit to another is normal procedure during final descent and landing, in these circumstance it seemed poor practice. An emergency situation called for imposing radio silence on the frequency in use and not for burdening the crew with non-essential requests.

Later the investigators blamed the captain for failing to ask for a discrete channel. But it was clearly the air traffic controller's duty to make arrangements for a special frequency. He was the only one aware of the channel allocation to the area under his control.

Hunt continued to descend and at 3,000 feet the aircraft was eventually positioned on the ILS localiser for final approach. After flaps and gear were extended, power was applied to maintain the glide path and the engine responded to the throttle movements without any protest. So far everything was going according plan. The tragedy of Flight BD 092 began when, on passing 900 feet above the ground, the left engine suddenly lost power. At that point only sixty seconds separated the ill-fated Boeing 737 from reaching the runway safely.

McLellan frantically advised East Midlands Tower: 'And we're having trouble with our second engine as well.'

Hunt immediately ordered the co-pilot to restart the starboard engine. 'Try lighting the other one up... there's nothing else you can do.'

However, all efforts were in vain. The engine rotation was far too slow for a windmilling start. The other method using a starter-assisted procedure would not have been effective, due to low bleed-air pressure on the ailing engine. In any case, the Quick Reference Handbook only listed a procedure for starting the left engine. An attempt on the other engine would have required some improvisation and time was running out.

In desperation, Hunt again asked the co-pilot to have a go at the shut-down engine but it did not respond. From now on, the aircraft was doomed to disaster and the only possibility of averting striking the ground before the runway was to stretch the glide as much as possible.

Adding to the avalanche of tribulations, at 500 feet the fire alarm on the left engine activated. McLellan asked if he should perform the fire drill but Hunt stopped him. Every remaining fraction of thrust on the sick powerplant was at this stage, a matter of life or death. The runway was close but unfortunately not close enough. At the same time, the Ground Proximity Warning System began to sound, indicating that they were rapidly dropping below the glide path. Eventually Hunt could see that they would not reach the runway and a few seconds before impact, he warned the passengers on the cabin address system: 'Prepare for crash landing... prepare for crash landing.'

He still tried to get as close as possible to the runway by lifting the nose high until the Stick Shaker began to make itself felt, protesting at the speed having been allowed to drop too close to the stall.

The aircraft struck the ground just east of the M1 motorway. It cut through a line of trees, slid down the embankment, then across the motorway and ended up hitting the slope on the other side. Upon final impact, the fuselage disintegrated into three parts. The Boeing was only 900 metres short of the runway threshold, its safe goal.

After the accident, both handles that control fuel supply to the engines were found in the closed position. The right-engine lever would have been pulled back in flight during the checklist. But as it was subsequently established, none of the BMA ground engineers who entered the cockpit after the crash had touched either of the levers. This leaves only one possibility. It must have been the alertness displayed by one of the pilots that made him move the left-engine handle to the off position just before hitting the M1 embankment. This was to prevent a fire outbreak from a likely fuel spillage if the wings broke off.

Thirty-nine passengers perished in the crash. A further seven died later in hospital. Seven crew members, sixty-six passengers and an infant sustained serious injuries. Only one crew member and four passengers escaped relatively unscathed. Among the dead were three sisters from County Monaghan, on the way to their father's funeral.

PART III

Hardly a day after the inspection of the wreckage had begun, the Kegworth disaster received unprecedented publicity from information given to reporters by Ed Trimble, the investigator-in-charge and the technical expert. He ruled out an unlikely chance of a double-engine failure, claiming that only the left engine showed sign of fire damage while the right one appeared to be fully serviceable prior to impact. It was the first case in the several-decades-long history of the Air Accidents Investigation Branch where the details of an early discovery were so hastily released to the Press.

Although the wreck was not yet removed from the busy M1 motorway, Paul Channon, the Transport Secretary, had already made a statement to the House of Commons saying that while the pilot reported a problem on the right engine, the investigators had only found evidence of fire on the left engine, which had been relied upon for landing.

In an interview on Channel 4 News, when specifically asked if it was possible for the pilot to have made an error by switching off the wrong engine, the Transport Secretary replied: 'I don't rule it out, but it is unwise for me to speculate on that until we have got more information.'

It looked as if the politicians had already pre-judged the verdict of the crash inquiry, even though the pilots had not yet been interrogated. Both Kevin Hunt and David McLellan were still in hospital under sedation, unfit to recount their harrowing experiences. Drawing inferences before every scrap of evidence was at hand seemed an unprecedented departure from the most cardinal principle of accident investigations.

The AAIB findings were published nineteen months later, in August 1990. In September 1989 *Flight International*, the UK's leading aviation magazine, reported that the proceedings should be completed by mid-December. In October, conclusions would be submitted to the interested parties for comments and, if there were no requests for a review before the usual twenty-eight-day deadline, the final version would be then presented to the Minister of Transport. *Flight* also reported that the proceedings were prolonged to incorporate the findings on two more serious incidents with the Boeing 737-400 engine, the CFM56-3C,

Aerial view of the wreckage of the British Midland Airways Boeing 737 lies on the embankment of the M1 Motorway, just a few hundred yards short of the runway at East Midlands airport after the crash which left more than 40 dead. (Press Association)

which were similar to the Kegworth case. These incidents revealed that the fan blades were affected by metal fatigue, which caused their disintegration leading to the engine failure, and not by ingestion of foreign objects, as was at first suspected.

The proposed cure was to derate the CMF56-3Cs to the level of thrust used on the early version of that engine. What *Flight* magazine had not at the time mentioned, was that, from the very few Boeing 737-400s operated in the UK, three cases of engine failure was an alarming proportion.

The final paragraph in the *Flight* article is of particular interest: 'The human factors section of the report is likely to provoke further debate, but the AAIB is heartened by the success of the crews in dealing with the later two incidents.'

The 'success' was due, no doubt, to the new procedure that was quickly introduced. It stipulated that the vibration indicators should be primarily relied upon to determine which engine was suffering from out-of-balance conditions. The indicators fitted to the earlier models of jets had shown poor reliability and often produced confusing signals. As a result they were disconnected on some types of aircraft. A pointed question must be raised. Why were these procedures not in use before the Kegworth disaster?

PART IV

The 152-page-long report is an example of the most thorough technical investigation. No efforts had been spared to examine every piece of collected evidence with the help of the latest scientific methods. Credit must be given to the technical inspectors for establishing explicitly which damage to the right engine was sustained through impact and which through the in-flight failures.

The cause of the disaster was summarised as being a consequence of the crew shutting down the right engine although the left engine had been damaged by a fan blade failure, and had subsequently suffered a major loss of power when power was applied on final approach.

The report specified five factors that contributed to the erroneous response of the crew:
1. The conditions of heavy vibrations, disturbing noise and smoke to which the crew were exposed, were outside their training and experience.
2. The crew's reaction to the initial symptoms of the engine failure was too hasty and contrary to their training.

3. The crew did not check all engine instruments before throttling back the wrong engine.
4. When, after retarding the power lever of the right engine, the vibrations and noise dropped, the crew incorrectly assumed that they had identified the malfunctioning engine.
5. The crew were not provided with information about the signs of fire on the left engine as observed either by the passengers or by the three flight attendants working in the rear cabin.

The investigators evidently believed that the pilots were at fault by incompetently handling the emergency in spite of some extenuating circumstances. After an event and from the comfort of one's desk, it is easy to take a critical view of those who had the misfortune to have been confronted with a perplexing emergency through a design fault on the engine. It was a case of a mechanical enigma to which a remedial action could be only speculated upon.

These five points will be examined in detail. The analysis is not intended to whitewash Kevin Hunt or David McLellan. Nevertheless, there are usually two sides to every issue and many airline pilots were not happy with some of the conclusions reached by the accident investigators. The judgement appeared to have been based on how the crew were expected to perform in ideal circumstances, such as a simulator session. However a number of contributory factors, normally not encountered during training, had escalated the difficulties in determining which engine had failed.

The report stated that the combination of heavy vibrations, noise, shuddering and the smell of fire was outside the crew's training and experience. As far as experience was concerned, this would have been expected. With the high reliability of jet engines, failures are extremely rare and many pilots may never be exposed to any kind of malfunction during their entire flying career. Even Hunt, with a relatively high number of flying hours for his age, could not have been expected to have much experience in dealing with this kind of engine trouble.

Although the report comprehensively discussed every aspect of the crew's actions and reactions during the emergency, one factor does not appear to have been taken into consideration. It is the element of surprise. Only those who have been exposed to a 'baptism of fire' on board an aircraft are able to appreciate how a bombshell development can affect the crew's ability to absorb every telltale sign pointing to the root of the mechanical problem.

During a simulator session, pilots know that they can expect a failure of some sort and they are able to concentrate ahead on the required actions. The hectic atmosphere associated with an emergency on board can never be reproduced in training. Cockpit workload, depending on the stage of the flight, can vary appreciably. It is usually at its highest during departures and arrivals, when the pilots may have to attend to more than one function at the same time. Should a baffling emergency suddenly occur while they are preoccupied, the element of surprise could make them miss a vital clue, which could have otherwise pointed immediately to the cause of the mechanical trouble.

The accident investigation report claimed that the circumstances were outside the ill-fated crew's normal training. This casts doubt on whether the prescribed programme for maintaining pilots' proficiency was adequate. Although the aircraft manufacturer is entrusted with setting up procedures for dealing with normal, abnormal and emergency situations on board, the regulatory bodies such as the Federal Aviation Administration in the US or the Civil Aviation Authority in the UK (a department of the Ministry of Transport), have the final say on the composition of the training curriculum.

Many current simulator programmes are a legacy from the days of the older types of jets, sometimes going as far back as the first generation. It is evident from the Kegworth crash investigation that no fresh ideas, based on an analysis of the most frequent causes of aircraft emergencies in recent years, had been incorporated in the UK version of the Boeing 737 Operations Manual. Unfortunately, this was not the only example of safety directives which the aviation regulatory bodies were expected to enforce that lagged behind developments in the air transport industry.

By tradition, engine fire is the most practised emergency during periodical re-training, even though the new fire detecting systems have reached a high degree of sophistication in unambiguously displaying which powerplant is affected. The fire drill is performed at every simulator session and pilots are expected to memorise all appropriate actions and perform them without referring to the checklist.

Perhaps as a result of concentrating on training for engine fire drill, little attention was paid to other kinds of engine failures, which could

be equally catastrophic. After by-pass turbines were introduced into service, new problems were encountered with the large fan assembly. The relatively long titanium-alloy blades, which rotate at extremely high rpm, have been shown to be very prone to damage from strikes by foreign objects or from fatigue. A blade break-up invariably leads to severe out-of-balance conditions, and in unfortunate cases, the ingested pieces can play havoc with compressors, turbines and combustion chambers.

Percentage figures must have been available to the CAA in respect of past incidents with ingestions of birds or stones, resulting in crucial damages to the fan blades. These figures would have indicated this to be a more frequent cause of engine failures than fire. Just the same, the CAA appear to have taken no notice of the operational experiences and never requested Boeing to amend the Operations Manuals to include emergency procedures specifically dealing with out-of-balance engine conditions.

In the Kegworth crash report thirty-one safety recommendations were listed, most of them directed at the CAA. It reflects badly on the UK aviation regulatory body, which appears to have been perfunctory in prescribing and supervising the execution of important safety measures. The most significant deficiency was the lack of reviewing the curriculum for pilots' periodic re-training, which was evidently inadequate in several areas. It seems therefore, a questionable procedure for Captain Vivian of the CAA Flight Operations Department to have been co-opted by the AAIB during the investigation, in order to assist with the final assessment on the operational aspects of the crash. His participation would have given the CAA a chance to negate any criticism arising out of the inquiry, while the two pilots were never given an equal opportunity due to lack of provisions to be represented by their pilots' association.

Although responsibility to oversee the training curriculum lies with the CAA, it is the operator's duty to put it effectively into practice. Unfortunately, as maintaining pilots' proficiency is a costly undertaking, many airlines were forced to cut down periodic re-training to a minimum in the lean years of passenger traffic.

From the report it is evident that the BMA curriculum did not include practising procedures to deal with out-of-balance engine conditions, nor had the attention of the pilots been clearly drawn to the fact that the vibration indicators fitted to the Boeing 737-300/400, were extensively redesigned and capable of reliable information.

Perhaps the next generation of simulators will include true-to-life symptoms of fan blade failure and its associated consequences. In the meantime, one of the ways to keep pilots up to date with the findings on problems in connection with the fan blade failures could be through the company safety bulletins. It is not mentioned in the Kegworth report whether this had been a practice in BMA.

With regard to puzzling symptoms of a malfunction in flight, the report stressed the need for pilots to be trained in the flexibility of decision making, in order to enable them to cope with novel situations. However, the report does not indicate how any training could achieve that goal. Perhaps one way to broaden the pilots' perception of unforeseen emergencies would be through highlighting every accident and dangerous incident by frequent safety digests. The CAA should have been expected to give a lead in that respect but it appears to have been so far sadly deficient.

The second point in the summary of contributory factors to the disaster, blamed the crew for hasty action which was contrary to their training.

Whether it was a premature step, as the report claimed, or whether the crew, through being at a loss to find a correct solution from the lack of positive clues, were eventually forced to apply measures which on the spur of the moment, appeared to them to be appropriate, must be examined at length.

Having been twice exposed during my aviation career to a dire emergency, both extremely baffling cases in the initial stages, I can assure readers that a 'bolt out of the blue', particularly one which does not conform to anything described in the Operations Manual, puts an airman's composure and abilities to a severe test.

Nothing in the report indicated that the crew were affected by the stress of events on board. On the contrary, the transcript of the Cockpit Voice Recorder revealed that they acted calmly and rationally. Therefore there could be no question of having been pushed into a hasty move of throttling back the wrong engine. On the other hand it must be appreciated that a relatively prompt remedial action was dictated by the concern over violent shuddering, which could have led to serious consequences, such as engine separation, should there have been undue delay.

In my opinion, two factors primarily contributed to the crew's inability to pinpoint the ailing engine. One, which the investigators also regarded as very probable, was the new type of engine instruments. The novel high-technology idea could have looked perfect on the factory test bench; in operational practice it had shown minor, nevertheless crucial, drawbacks.

The other factor that could have affected the ability to determine which engine was at fault was the cockpit manpower available to cope with the emergency. This subject can be summarised by a question. Had there been one more crew member such as a flight engineer on board, could the tragedy have been averted? It may be a highly debatable point but it cannot be dismissed as irrelevant to the Kegworth crash. With the two pilots preoccupied with multiple tasks, and moreover, strapped in their seats, only a flight engineer would have time to concentrate entirely on the engine instruments or to make a quick visit to the cabin to inspect the engines through passenger windows.

Over the years, the three-man versus two-man crew complement had been a controversial issue between manufacturers, licensing authorities, and operators on the one hand and pilots' organisations on the other. In the piston-engine era, the requirement for the flight engineer was determined by the weight of the aircraft. When jets were introduced, they were flown at first with three crew members. But eventually, through pressure to reduce the operating costs, airlines began to scale down the crew complement to two men on twin-engine jets. This was met with strong objections from pilots' organisations. On a number of occasions the disputes had risen to such a pitch that they had culminated in industrial action. But the pilots were not concerned about the flight engineer's job. They feared that some cockpits were not designed for two-man operation. With these cockpits lacking a centralised means of indicating technical defects, and in view of the fact that jets operated at a much closer margin between normal cruising speed and maximum permissible speed, this called for adequate manpower to cope effectively with every emergency, regardless of the aircraft's size or the number of engines.

After the Kegworth disaster, a similar opinion on the cockpit manpower requirements was expressed in a letter to the editor of *Flight* magazine, which appeared just after the accident report was published.

'Perhaps the much maligned flight engineer is not cost-effective for a regional airline. He could however, be of assistance at time of stress.'

PART V

The issue of whether the engine instruments provided sufficiently self-evident indications to diagnose out-of-balance conditions of the fan must be deeply looked into. Such indications could come from two separate sources: either from the primary engine instruments or from the secondary engine instruments.

On the Boeing 737, the primary engine instrument panels, a separate one for each engine, are mounted above the central pedestal. As on most jets, four correlated parameters denote the level of power or thrust, as it is generally referred to in aviation jargon. Starting from the top, vertically placed circular dials, 3½ cm in diameter, indicate N1 – low-pressure compressor rpm, EGT – exhaust gas temperature, N2 – high-pressure turbine rpm, and finally FF – fuel flow. Neither N1, nor N2 are calibrated in revolutions per minute but in percentages, the 100% figure not necessarily representing the maximum power output. Placed in-between the arrays of the primary engine instruments, two panels only 20 cm by 7 cm in size contain secondary engine instruments with even smaller circular dials, about 2 cm, indicating engine oil pressure, oil temperature, the level of vibrations and hydraulic pressure.

The engine instruments on the Boeing 737-400, unlike the 300 version, are not mechanical gauges controlled by electrical impulses but solid-state devices relying for the presentation of dials and pointers on a complex set of tiny Light Emitting Diodes. In comparison with the needles on the electro-mechanical indicators, the pointers are much slimmer and shorter, and consequently, far less conspicuous. On some dials there is also a digital display in the middle, but this is generally used for fine adjustments.

According to an informal survey of UK Boeing 737 pilots, which had been undertaken by the AAIB, the solid-state engine instruments were not regarded in normal operating conditions as particularly inferior to the electro-mechanical gauges. Nevertheless, unfavourable comments were received about the ability of the LED displays to convey rapid changes in the engine parameters. This probably stems from electronic processing which injects hysteresis into the signals generated by the engine instrument sensors in order to stabilise the display. As a result the peaks of any rapid fluctuations are, to a certain extent, flattened out. On the other hand, the inertia of the needles on the electro-mechanical gauges would tend to accentuate their oscillating movements.

Another important aspect of the solid-state displays is the way by which their brightness is controlled by sensors according to the ambient light on the flight deck. The brighter the light, the stronger the LEDs shine. At night, the sensors respond to the edge lighting of the instrument panel, which is controlled by a switch in the cockpit. It is surprising that no tests had been performed to check the readability of symbols at night when the sensors are affected by smoke.

Moreover, it is known that LEDs are capable of a much faster response to the electronic impulses than corresponding electro-mechanical gauges to the electrical signals. Only tests could have established if the reaction of the retina is quick enough to follow rapid changes of the LED's pattern under various conditions.

Whether the indications from the primary instruments could have warned the pilots about the out-of-balance engine conditions will be first analysed. The Flight Recorder read-outs revealed there were three short dips in the level of N1, from 98% to 75%, as a result of the compressor stall. To clarify what caused the temporary loss of thrust associated with the violent shuddering, and why N1 was basically the only parameter on the primary engine panel capable of indicating to the pilots which engine was defective, a short description of jet engine operation may be of help.

On the CMF56 engine, the fan and the low-pressure booster as well as the four-stage low-pressure turbine are attached to a common inner shaft. The function of the fan is to duct cold air around the engine casing, in order to mix it with extremely hot and fast exhaust gases expelled from the turbines. Propulsive efficiency of such types of jet engines, known as high bypass-ratio turbofans, is thus greatly enhanced with a substantial improvement in fuel consumption. On the CMF56 with a bypass ratio of 5:1, the fan produces about 80% of total thrust. Its speed – N1 – is therefore the most representative indication of the applied power and an engine parameter on which pilots constantly keep an eye.

The high-pressure compressor and the high-pressure turbine are interconnected through an outer concentric shaft. Although they run independently of the fan and the low-pressure booster, their speeds are correlated through the flow of air from the fan and the exhaust gases generated by the combustion chambers. The exhaust gases propel both the low- and the high-pressure turbines. Thrust depends on the amount of fuel

ELECTRO-MECHANICAL ENGINE
INSTRUMENTS OF BOEING 737-300

LED ENGINE INSTRUMENTS
OF BOEING 737-400

The engine instruments on Boeing 737-300 and Boeing 737-400. The photographs show that the LED instruments on the Boeing 737-400 are far less conspicuous than the electro-mechanical instruments on the earlier version of Boeing 737. (AAIB report of the B737 Kegworth accident) injected into the combustion chambers, and this can be controlled by levers on the throttle pedestal. The levers can be coupled to an autothrottle system capable of setting various modes such as take-off power, climb power or constant airspeed, by pressing the required mode button. In many airlines, it is mandatory to keep the autothrottles engaged throughout the flight, including take-off and landing.

Even if the two rotating assemblies run independently, any disruption in the flow of air ducted by the fan will induce a compressor stall. The stall can be best described as a powerful engine 'hiccup' which invariably brings on a temporary loss of thrust with its prime indication shown by a drop in N1. At high thrust, the 'hiccup', an interaction of gases between compressors and turbines, can occur with such intensity that the engine is often shaken to the limits of its mounting. Surprisingly, even a small reduction of thrust can stop compressor stall and stabilise the engine.

The variation in N1 and severe vibrations were not the only signs of problem with the malfunctioning engine. Smoke and the burning smell filtering into the cockpit had unfortunately diverted the pilots' attention from the engine instruments to the engine fire warning indicators. But smoke and a burning smell, as it was later established, were not reflections of any serious defect but a result of the blades tips rubbing the nacelle liner, made from abradable material, once the fan assembly had been thrown out of balance.

It may appear on the surface that the three 'dips' in N1 indications, each lasting about two seconds, and which occurred within twenty seconds prior to the right engine having been throttled back, should have been sufficiently apparent to attract the crew's attention. But the displacement of the N1 pointer, which denoted the 'dips', was only about one centimetre in travel, not exactly a significant amount, in particular when viewed from eighty centimetres, the approximate position of the pilot's head in relation to the instrument panel. Moreover, the severe vibrations affecting the eyeball muscles, could have impaired the ability of the crew to focus their eyes. Taking all these factors into consideration, including the distraction by smoke and the burning smell, it looks as though there was little chance for the pilots to observe the changes in N1. According to the Flight Recorder, no other engine parameters had shown an appreciable departure from the normal indications.

In spite of tests carried out to prove that the engine instruments were fully serviceable at the time of the emergency showing that the AAIB inspectors and the personnel from the manufacturer were able to notice the 'dips' in N1, no checks were undertaken to determine if such observations would have been equally effective in a smoke-filled cockpit.

Many arguments on the inferior presentation by the primary engine instruments equally apply to the secondary instruments, which include the vibration indicators. In respect of the clarity of presentation, the report underlined a likely problem of determining at a glance whether the pointer of the vibration indicators is at maximum or at minimum. The two extreme ends of the circular scale are too close together, one at the two o'clock and the other one at the four o'clock position. Should the pointer happen to swing rapidly to the maximum position whilst the pilots' attention was drawn to other instruments, it is likely that they would have not noticed the movement. Moreover, the pointer would have remained at the maximum reading for only three minutes when high thrust was maintained on the left engine prior to commencing the descent. As soon as the throttle was retarded, it would have returned to the low indication.

The questionable characteristics of the solid-state instruments appear to have been the prime reason for the pilots' inability to evaluate which engine had sustained critical damage. In addition, the element of surprise had most likely magnified the difficulty of noticing the three rapid variations of N1, the only clue provided by the primary engine instruments. The investigators admitted in their report that, if the pilots did gain the impression from these instruments that the right engine rather than the left engine was failing, then a possibility existed that the way information was displayed could have contributed to their error.

The captain of the second BMA Boeing 737-400 on which disintegration of a fan blade had also occurred, told the investigators that when the engine failed, all indications on the primary engines' instruments looked alike and it took him time to be certain that he had identified the correct engine, as the only warning came from the vibration meter.

In view of lack of confidence in the earlier vibration monitors, the pilots of the ill-fated G-OBME cannot be blamed for not having relied on information provided by the new type of monitors. Until attention of Boeing 737-400 crews was clearly drawn to the fact that they were reliable, to

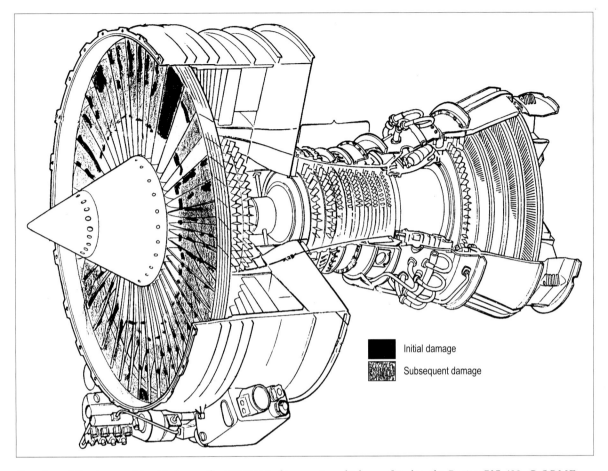

Initial damage
Subsequent damage

Drawing of the damaged fan blades on the CFM56 turbine engine which was fitted to the Boeing 737-400, G-OBME.

determine which engine had suffered from a broken fan blade would have been like tossing a coin.

If the vibration indications were of such crucial importance, why had a warning light not been fitted to these instruments, so as to alert the pilots to a potential hazard? An extract from a reader's letter to *Flight International*, which appeared in November 1990, points the finger at the responsible quarters.

'Perhaps the Civil Aviation Authority should share the blame for not learning from the past and insisting that a latched warning on EVM system (Engine Vibration Monitor) should be mandatory.'

After the Kegworth crash, the AAIB recommended that such a light should be a CAA laid-down requirement for all public transport aircraft.

According to the accident report, although the solid-state instruments were certified for the operational use by both the FAA and the CAA, they were introduced into service without any evaluation of their presentation efficiency. As to any advantages over previous engine instruments, the accident investigators considered the LED displays to be a retrograde step. A recommendation was put forward that all future methods of displaying engine parameters should be subject to specified evaluations and that 'average' line pilots, and not FAA test pilots, should be used in the trials.

The reason for replacing the electro-mechanical engine instruments with the solid-state units, was to reduce maintenance costs. When designing the new display, the instrument manufacturer was requested by Boeing, no doubt as a result of demands from the prospective buyers, to conform to the old pattern of dials as on the 737-300, in order to avoid a need for familiarisation.

Surprisingly, two vital changes had been made in the new layout, and this fact was not highlighted in the report. The location of the vibration indicators was interchanged with the hydraulic pressure gauges, that is from the bottom of the panel to one place higher up. Furthermore, the solid-state vibration indicators differed in the position of the null and the maximum level markings. On the old scale they were at eight o'clock and at three o'clock respectively, while on the new scale they were transferred to the two and four o'clock positions. These changes would certainly not help to make a reading easier in moments of stress, poor light and smoke in the cockpit.

Several pages of the report were devoted to the discussion on a layout of engine instrumentation that would be more suitable in two-man crew operation. It was suggested that placing the primary and the secondary instruments together on one panel for the left engine and on another panel for the right engine might be a better answer to the problem of determining on which side a fault had developed.

Whether such an arrangement would be more effective is highly debatable. In any case, it could only serve as a stopgap solution. No mention was made in the report on other engine-instrument displays such as vertical scale indicators, also known as tape instruments, or, in layman's language, the thermometer type. On the tape displays, the level of engine parameters is denoted by a bar moving up and down. In the case of thrust it is the most logical way of indicating the actual amount, as pilots are not interested how many rpm the fan produces but how much power has been applied.

Circular scales are a legacy from early aeroplanes, and over the years, no progress has been made in more self-evident methods of engine data presentation. The introduction of tape displays to military aircraft came as a result of limited cockpit space and proved so effective that some civil aircraft, such as the DC10-30 serving with KLM, SAS and Swissair, were also fitted with this type of instrument. From my several thousand hours of experience with the tape displays, the reader can be assured that their indications are unambiguous and far more positive than those provided by the circular dials and needles. With the engine parameters such as N1 or Fuel Flow positioned close together, side by side, no scanning from instrument to instrument is necessary, and any disparity in a reading is instantly apparent. For a

pilot to convert from the dial to the tape displays takes little adjustment. The only drawback of such instruments is their high cost due to a much more complex construction. For a DC10 unit it was five times as much as an equivalent circular dial gauge, and of course, with the additional mechanical complications, the maintenance costs would also be higher. But incorporating solid-state techniques in manufacturing the tape displays could make the cost comparable to the old electro-mechanical units with circular dials.

However, the ultimate solution lies in a central, computerised warning system. Such systems are fitted to the newest generation of jet and cathode-ray tube displays are used to draw the crew's attention to a mechanical fault. Many pilots are of the opinion that only aircraft so equipped are safe to be flown by a two-man crew.

The introduction into operational service of instruments lacking self-evident data presentation is a consequence of inadequate dialogue between the manufacturer and the ultimate users, the line pilots. It is disappointing that Smith's Industries Ltd, pioneer of the LED displays, had not consulted pilots' organisations about their members' preferences when designing the new instruments. Perhaps the Kegworth disaster could have been avoided. In the development of all-weather landing systems, Smith's extensively cooperated with IFALPA to determine the most 'flyable' solutions.

Since the early days of their safety activities, IFALPA and pilots' associations endeavoured to provide the aircraft industry with an as broad as possible cross-section of opinions on a variety of subjects, predominantly on the cockpit layouts, cockpit ergonomics and flight instrumentation. The advice was not only limited to the end products but was extended to the design philosophy, so as to avoid costly or dangerous mistakes at an early stage. The Federation held many technical symposia and the fruits of discussions with the manufacturers were evident in a number of significant changes to the proposed designs. One such example is the cockpit windows on the Concorde. Originally, the cruise at Mach 2 was going to be performed without a forward view. However, under pressure from the pilots, who argued that from the safety standpoint there is no substitute for a pair of eyes, a heatproof, quartz shield was eventually developed that in supersonic flight would slide over the normal cockpit windows.

Another example was the aircraft symbol on the artificial horizon of the new integrated flight instruments destined for low-limit operations.

Originally, the manufacturer intended to dispense with this traditional reference marking. In their opinion it was superfluous and would only clutter the display. The manufacturer argued that relying on an aircraft symbol was a past habit and even the old hands would eventually find its absence preferable. There was no need for a fixed reference symbol, as it was never used in visual flying conditions. But as a result of objections from IFALPA that the new concept was unflyable, simulator trials were conducted that proved the pilots' concern to be well founded and the aircraft symbol was in the end, retained.

Such examples were the writing on the wall. Only a close cooperation between the aircraft industry and the pilots' organisations in planning and designing new concepts can prevent inferior tools, such as the solid-state engine instruments on the Boeing 737-400, finding their way into the cockpit, and through their ineffective presentation, becoming a source of confusion and contributory factors to an accident.

PART VI

As for Hunt and McLellan's execution of emergency actions, there are no indications that they did not do their best in the baffling circumstances. Smoke and a burning smell must have aggravated the difficulty of determining the actual cause of engine malfunction. Unfortunately, such symptoms could not have been demonstrated on the present types of simulator. No one can blame the crew for trying to use whatever knowledge they possessed of the aircraft systems, even if it had resulted in erroneous conclusions. As for the ensuing tragedy, a case of really bad luck must be fully recognised.

Had the left engine continued to display signs of out-of-balance conditions after the right engine was closed, it would have immediately alerted the pilots to an incorrect diagnosis. Unfortunately, the rapid engine stabilisation after the autothrottle was disconnected, sent them on a wrong track. The accompanying slight drop of thrust had been sufficient to stop further compressor stalls, the cause of heavy vibrations. A similar misfortune played a crucial role in the last moments of the flight. Fifteen more seconds of power available on the left engine would have allowed a safe landing. Only four seconds more were needed to reach the flat stretch of land and avoid fatally striking the bank of the M1 motorway. This could have

perhaps prevented the fuselage breaking up into three pieces, the cause of most casualties.

The third point in the report on the contributory factors that had led to shutting down a wrong engine specifies an ineffective liaison between the cockpit and the cabin as one of the reasons for the fatal decision. The investigators considered that the failure to pass the information to the pilots about signs of fire emerging from the left engine, observed by the passengers and by the flight attendants working in the aft cabin, had deprived the cockpit crew of a vital tip-off.

But an understanding as to what has to be reported in such circumstances can only come from firmly laid-down company policy. Neither the BMA pilots nor the cabin staff can be blamed for unsatisfactory communication in such pressing moments. A close cooperation in a dire situation can only derive from specific directives, and this is the basis of all survival preparations. When the chips are down, there is no time for improvisation.

In KLM, a long established policy dating back to the early post-war years, had led to the development of well-knit teamwork on board. According to company instructions, flight attendants were expected to report at once anything abnormal noticed in the cabin or outside, no matter how trivial. The cockpit crews had to promptly investigate all cabin crews' observations even if these may have appeared to be ludicrous on the surface. The cabin staff should never be shown that their observations could have been a folly. Their duty was to visit the cockpit at least once every forty-five minutes, in particular during long intercontinental flights.

Training or company directives are not the only means of improving collaboration on board in a pressing situation. A personal contact when the whole crew meet for the flight can make it more effective. A few words exchanged at the start to break the ice could make a considerable difference in moments of stress. Many airlines insist on the captain giving a short safety briefing to the flight attendants before departure.

The subject of deficiencies in the training of cabin staff only comes to the surface when shortcomings are uncovered during an accident investigation, otherwise it is conveniently swept under the carpet and is seldom given proper highlighting by the media. Yet its importance cannot be underestimated. The standards vary greatly not only from country to country but from airline to airline. The differences stem from the ways by which the training is conducted. How realistically

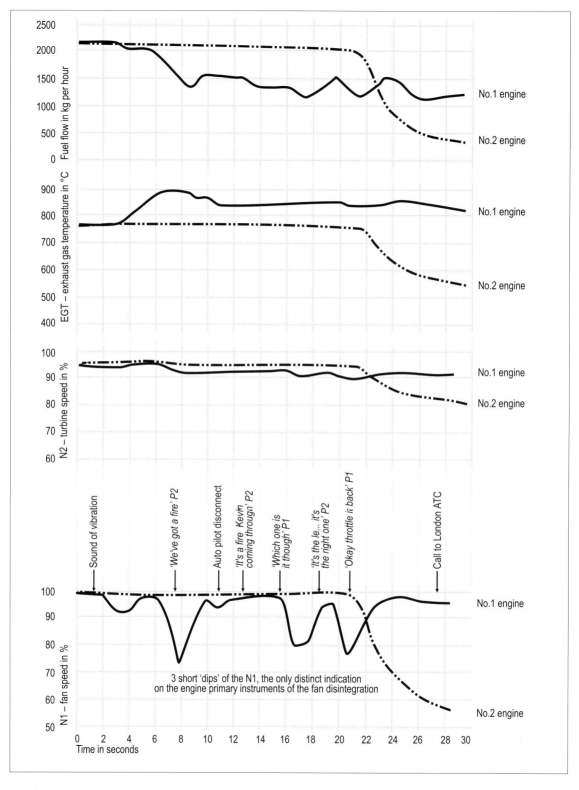

Graphical representation of the FDR read-out of the failed engine parameters of the Boeing 737-400, G-OBME.

it can be performed depends on the facilities available to the airline. Some operators use a trainer, a replica of an aircraft cabin fitted with all safety features, such as the emergency chutes, which can be used several times during the same training session. Moreover, some trainers are capable of turning over on one side, in order to emulate a crash situation.

But the airlines cannot be singled out for failing to recognise the importance of such preparations. Criticism must be also extended to the regulatory bodies whose main interest appears to be predominantly orientated towards the cockpit requirements. As a result, the machinery to check the cabin crew's proficiency on safety procedures is often non-existent.

A share of responsibility must be also placed on the shoulders of the travelling public for their complacency over safety matters. A passenger who is only interested in the cabin service can blame himself for the consequences of his wishy-washy concern as to whether his flight attendants were given proper training on emergency procedures. Unfortunately, most of the passengers prefer to close their eyes to the possibility of a crisis in flight. This shows itself in how little attention is paid to the demonstrations of safety instructions before take-off. Instead of devoting a few moments to familiarise themselves with the various directives, which can differ from one type of aircraft to another, and as a result, can be a matter of life or death in a dire situation, the public on board adopt the attitude, 'I've heard this before', and either read a newspaper, are busy with their drink or are engrossed in a conversation. But, should a deficiency in the performance of the flight attendants come to light from a subsequent inquiry into a crash, a loud public outcry would likely follow. Equally irresponsible is the derogatory attitude of many businessmen to 'grandmother' stewardesses, which, as a result, forces the airlines to employ glamorous but immature youth at the expense of adult wisdom.

The quality of emergency training cannot be traded for tantalising frills in flights. Pilots believe that the primary duty of a flight attendant is to assist passengers in surviving an accident and that the service on board is secondary to it. Unfortunately, the policies of many airlines are generally more orientated towards attracting prospective customers with exotic dishes, drinks, extra leg-room or even air miles rather than by assuring their passengers that the flight attendants were given the best possible training on safety procedures.

A lack of a clearly laid-down policy in British Midland Airways on the cooperation between cockpit and cabin during an emergency played in my opinion, a crucial role in the last chance of averting the Kegworth disaster. But the fault for the ineffective liaison does not lie with the BMA personnel but with the airline management and supervisory staff. Cabin crews must be clearly instructed as to when and how to communicate with the cockpit in cases where they believe they have something vital to report. They must also be taught how to do it with a minimum of interference while emergency procedures are being performed.

What had undoubtedly added to the communication problems on ill-fated flight BD 092 was the fact that the majority of flight attendants were very inexperienced. Even the Flight Service Manager, with just two and a half years of service with BMA, would have been considered by many major airlines as relatively unseasoned. The senior stewardess was only with the company for twenty months; another stewardess only nine months, and two male and one female flight attendant joined the airline just three weeks before the accident. Their actual line service amounted to only two weeks. Some of the businessmen on board, who frequently commuted between London and Belfast, could have had more hours in the air. It is inconceivable that BMA, the former Derby Airways and now the second largest airline in the UK, allowed so many inexperienced flight attendants to be rostered together. Furthermore, it was unfair to the cabin staff who could eventually suffer the consequences. Should a senior cabin-crew member become incapacitated as a result of a crash, the less experienced flight attendants, left without a guiding hand, could be at loss as to what to do next. No amount of training is a substitute for the exposure to hours onboard an aircraft.

In the case of the cockpit crews, the regulatory authorities lay down specific requirements for a minimum of flying hours to be allowed to act as a co-pilot on jets. Yet in the case of the cabin personnel, there appear to be no similar directives and the airlines evidently do not bother to check if there are too many inexperienced flight attendants in one crew. If only from the service on board point of view, one would expect it to be looked upon as being of some significance.

Surprisingly, the AAIB report does not make any issue of the unsatisfactory cabin staff complement on flight BD 092. On the other hand, it would be difficult to assess whether the lack of hours in the air could have had any direct bearing on failing to report the signs of fire. Nevertheless, the first weeks of flying are a novel experience, and a young steward or stewardess could not be blamed for having been overwhelmed by the frightening developments on board.

Another possibility of avoiding the Kegworth disaster had been missed by the CAA in their failing to implement the safety recommendation issued by the AAIB after the crash to the British Airways Boeing 737 at Manchester Airport in 1985. The findings of the accident inquiry called for fitting electronic spy-eyes to provide the pilots with an external view of the aircraft and also with the capability of monitoring the wheel bays or the cargo compartments that are inaccessible in flight. In addition, a video recording of the cockpit instruments by similar means had been strongly recommended.

Nevertheless, in the intervening years the CAA made hardly any progress towards putting the AAIB recommendation into practice. Finally the idea seemed to have got bogged down through bureaucracy. Although several manufacturers displayed interest in this project, 'the CAA,' as quoted from the AAIB report, 'found it necessary to go to competitive tendering for the proof of concept trial.' As a result, by 1989 the airborne closed-circuit monitoring had not moved past the experimental stage. On the other hand, the spy-eyes found their way into many other uses. Nowadays every railway or bus station, public concourse, block of offices or even flats is fitted with video monitoring equipment, which police often find invaluable in catching criminals. It is greatly disappointing to find that multimillion-dollar aircraft have not been fitted with such an important safety tool, so commonplace in other areas. In contrast, on many of the newer jets each row of seats is provided with separate video monitors for watching films. It appears that the pendulum between attracting air travellers with frills and providing the crew with improved tools has swung in favour of the 'champagne' on board at the expense of safety.

PART VII

Equally, the Kegworth tragedy need not have happened if the certification trials for the increased thrust on the C1 version of the CMF56-3 engines, which were fitted to Boeing's 737-400,

had been properly carried out.

The CMF56 turbofan was a product of cooperation between US manufacturer General Electric and French manufacturer SNECMA, under the auspices of a parent company, CMF International. The new engine, developed to meet the demand for a ten-tonne range of thrust, was a scaled-down version of the highly reliable and sturdy CF6, originally produced by GE. The CF6s were fitted to a variety of transport aircraft such as the DC10 and the Airbus, as well as some Boeing 747s. The area of responsibility for the design and production of CMF56 had been divided between GE, concerned with the compressor and turbines assemblies, and SNECMA, which was allotted the fan assembly as well as some ancillaries.

The CMF56 family of engines were at first fitted to military aircraft, then later to some civil planes, and have proved to be reliable. The C version of the CMF56 was specifically designed for the Boeing 737/300 and 400 series. The fan was scaled down from 173 cm (68.3 inches) to 152 cm (60 inches) resulting in a lower bypass ratio of 5:1 in cruise flight as against 6:1 on the earlier models. The fan blades were also extensively re-designed but no flight tests were carried out to check whether the new blades were susceptible to undesirable excitations or harmonic vibrations. This would have been particularly significant in the cases when higher take-off and climb thrust ratings were used, such as in the C 1 version of the CMF56, especially evolved for the Boeing 400 series.

It was assumed that as the original blade design was well proven, a ground test to run the engine fitted with the new blades at power up to 103% of the allowable limit, would be sufficient. Unfortunately this had turned out to be wrong. Subsequent flight tests using strain gauges revealed that at altitudes above 10,000 feet, the fan blades were showing over-limit vibrations that could induce metal fatigue in a short period of time.

The airworthiness specifications further required that tests should be performed to prove that a failure of a single blade would not result in a catastrophic damage to the whole engine. Even if some damage had occurred, it should be possible to use maximum thrust for a certain period. Nevertheless, the Kegworth inquiry had shown that the fan had not withstood even four minutes of this requirement. The critical power failure on short final at 900 feet was due to the disintegration of the remaining fan blades. Little damage was found in the core of the engine, including the compressor and the turbine assemblies.

What had activated the fire warning system on short final has not been clearly established. The investigators found no signs of fire inside the engine nacelle that could have triggered the fire warning system. However, it was suspected that it could have been due to heat generated by the failing fan assembly.

The fire on the left engine, although clearly observed by the passers-by on the M1 motorway, did not contribute to the accident. It became very intense only a few seconds before impact. What the passers-by saw was a minor fire from a leakage of the fuel lines, which sprayed fuel onto a hot part of the engine. The joints in the lines were found to be loose from the severe shuddering. Although it was standard practice on many other parts of the engine to wire-lock the joints, this had not been done here, although it would have been expected because it was in the fire-hazard zone of the engine nacelle.

PART VIII

Like aircraft, engines must also be approved for operational use according to the airworthiness standards of the country in which they are manufactured. However, the CMF56 was a Franco–US product and was supposed to comply with the joint requirements of the FAA and the French Directorate of Civil Aviation. Although these rules were more stringent in specifying methods of engine testing than the FAA regulations, the least elaborate way was selected. As it was a standard practice among US manufacturers to test for excessive vibrations only on the ground, this method was used. The FAA, the CAA when the CMF56 C was accepted in England, and the French DCA never queried whether this was satisfactory.

The manufacturer CMFI must take the blame, not only for the faulty design of the fan blades which became weakened through metal fatigue from undetected vibrations in an alarming short time, but also for sidestepping crucial tests which could have revealed an unacceptable level of blade excitation in flight. Both these shortcomings led to a catastrophic engine failure after only 550 hours of operational service on the Boeing 737 that crashed at Kegworth.

Following the accident, a review of the past records indicated that during ground test, signs of excitation problems were already noted but they were considered insignificant in view of the past reliability of the blades. However, from the subsequent flight tests it became evident that, when a higher climb-thrust was applied, the so-called 3C-1 rating, the fan blades suffered from destructive vibration forces, which were as high as 80% of the blades' endurance limit, at altitudes between 25,000 and 30,000 feet.

The procedures invoked to approve the airworthiness certificates issued by an aircraft's state of registry, or an engine's state of origin leave very much to be desired. This appears to be a matter of rubber-stamping the certificates, and is particularly evident in the case of jet engines. Three countries, the US, the UK and France, have virtually a monopoly in the manufacturing of turbofans on a large scale. As a result, they automatically accept each other's airworthiness certificates without questioning the testing methods. With three sets of rules in existence, the US Federal Airworthiness Regulations, the Joint Airworthiness Requirements and the British Civil Airworthiness Requirements, although the rules do not differ appreciably in substance, loopholes could be found in the least stringent regulations to reduce the extent of testing.

PART IX

After reading the AAIB accident report one cannot help being left with an impression that the pilots were singled out as predominantly responsible for the Kegworth disaster. All other factors appear to have been regarded as purely secondary, and in the chain of involved parties, no individual or organisation were apportioned as much blame as the pilots.

How was it possible for the regulatory bodies to allow perfunctory testing on a section of the engine which was extensively re-designed, as in the case of the fan assembly on the CMF56-3? Why was a higher thrust allowed to be used on the C1 version of that engine without any trials in the air, even though the increase, from 20,000 pounds of thrust to 23,500 pounds, was quite significant?

Although it is generally accepted in the aviation world that the captain is ultimately responsible for all events on board his aircraft, he can only perform his task safely if his tools are of unquestionable standards. Instruments that did not reveal any signs of engine malfunction when distressing symptoms indicated otherwise should not have been certified as airworthy.

As numerous events in aviation history have shown, the man in the cockpit is the individual most vulnerable to being labelled as the prime accessory to a disaster. But his ultimate responsibility cannot be used as a cover for the blunders committed by other parties.

Perhaps the most distressing finale of the Kegworth tragedy was when the Managing Director of British Midland Airways elected to appear on television to announce the dismissal of the two unfortunate pilots, one of whom will never walk again. This news item was repeated on all European TV stations. The grounds were that, according to the conclusions of the Kegworth report, the pilots were to blame for the premature action of shutting down the serviceable engine, which was contrary to their training. But no one pointed the finger at the BMA management for the lack of an effective company policy on cockpit/cabin cooperation, for which the company executives were ultimately responsible, and which

appears to have been a missing ingredient in the BMA safety procedures that could have perhaps averted the disaster.

An extract from a letter to the editor of *Flight* magazine, which was published after the accident report was released, summarises many pilots' sentiments about the one-sided judgement of the ill-fated Boeing 737 crew: 'Can the Board of Inquiry understand the feelings in the cockpit from the time of alert to the knowledge that a crash was imminent? Can it imagine the workload and the stress placed on these two men? I believe that the "scapegoat" sign should be taken away from Captain Hunt and F/O McLellan. They were not to blame.'

In February 1996, the press reported that Captain Hunt received £100,000 from the British Midland Airways insurers in compensation for his injury. The court ruling was that he had not been given simulator training that would have enabled him to cope with the emergency situation when the Boeing 737 developed an engine fault which had eventually led to the crash.

INDEX